EXERCISE SCIENCE

An Introduction to Health and Physical Education

DEVELOPMENT TEAM FOR EXERCISE SCIENCE

Textbook

Ted Temertzoglou, *Toronto District School Board*

Paul Challen, *Hamilton Author*

Workbook / Lab Manual

Ted Temertzoglou, *Toronto District School Board*

Paul Challen, *Hamilton Author*

Jamie Nunn, *Hamilton-Wentworth District School Board*

Kim Parkes, *Hamilton-Wentworth District School Board*

Carolyn Temertzoglou, *Conference of Independent Schools*

This textbook represents a long-term commitment to the PSE4U course. To this end, we have provided a Student Workbook, a Teacher's Manual, and PowerPoint slides. We have made every effort to ensure that these support materials integrate with the textbook, making the course an enjoyable one for both the teacher and the student. We would also welcome suggestions as to how to make this course even better.

Ontario Physical and Health Education Association

The writing and publishing team would like to thank the management and staff at Ophea (the Ontario Physical and Health Education Association) for their support at every stage of this project – from our early discussions about developing a textbook to match the PSE4U curriculum, to their input during the writing and reviewing process, to their endorsement and widespread promotion of the text. Without Ophea's support and assistance, the completion of this textbook and its supporting materials would not have been possible.

EXERCISE SCIENCE

An Introduction to Health and Physical Education

Ted Temertzoglou

Paul Challen

THOMPSON EDUCATIONAL PUBLISHING, INC.

Toronto, Ontario

Information on how to obtain copies of this book may be obtained from:

Website: www.thompsonbooks.com
E-mail: hpe@thompsonbooks.com
Telephone: (416) 766-2763   Fax: (416) 766-0398

National Library of Canada Cataloguing in Publication Data

Temertzoglou, Ted, 1964-
    Exercise science: an introduction to health and physical
education/Ted Temertzoglou, Paul Challen.

Includes index.

ISBN 1-55077-132-9
    1. Physical education and training – Textbooks. I. Challen, Paul, 1967-
II. Title.

GV341.T35 2003 613.7'1   C2003-903214-0

Cover design, graphs, and charts: Elan Designs, Toronto. *Cover Photos:* Canadian sprinter Donovan Bailey of Canada blasts out of the starting blocks in 100-metre heats at the Olympics in Sydney, Australia, September 22, 2000 (CP PHOTO/Kevin Frayer). Shot putter, unknown, (TEP archives, Toronto).

Occupation charts: The occupation charts on pages x-xi are adapted for this text, courtesy of the Canadian Association for Health, Physical Education, Recreation and Dance (Ottawa).

Anatomical illustrations: Illustrations not otherwise acknowledged in the text have been provided by Bart Vallecoccia, B.Sc. AAM, Medical Illustrator (Toronto) and are copyrighted by him. Illustrations of bones, muscles, and joints have been redrawn specifically for this text from illustrations provided courtesy of Bartleby, Inc. from Henry Gray's *Anatomy of the Human Body.* Philadelphia: Lea & Febiger, 1918; © 2000 copyright Bartleby.com, Inc.

Credits: All text and photo references and credits are provided on the appropriate page in the text with the exception of the following, which could not appear in the text owing to reasons of space:

Pages 14, 15, 44, 45: reprinted by permission of Lippincott Williams & Wilkins (*Anatomy and Physiology Made Incredibly Easy,* Springhouse Corporation, 2001).

Page 86: (1) photo used on cover (see above); (2) Catriona Le May Doan of Saskatoon, Saskatchewan, powers round a turn in the women's 1,000-metre speed-skating final at the Salt Lake City 2002 Olympic Games, February 2002 (CP PHOTO/Frank Gunn); (3) Alison Sydor of Vancouver, British Columbia, at the Atlanta Olympic Games in 1996 (CP PHOTO/(STF-Frank Gunn).

Pages 195, 211, 213, 214, 215: courtesy of Ted Temertzoglou with thanks to the following students: Kalani King (mCAFT step-test); Stephanie Lovering (curl ups and skinfold measurements); Richard Dunlop (subject for the skinfold measurements); Crispin Duenas (trunk forward flexion test); Branden Sinclair (squats to demonstrate the overload principle).

Page 231: (1) Kelvin Anderson is tackled by Troy Asbell and Clinton Wayne during CFL action in Calgary, September 2002 (CP PHOTO/Adrian Wyld); (2) Maryse Turcotte, from Montreal, at the 2000 Summer Olympics in Sydney, Australia, September 2000 (CP PHOTO/Ryan Remiorz).

Page 232: (1) Colorado Rockies' Larry Walker, of Maple Ridge, British Columbia, watches the flight of his two-run home run, June 2001 (AP Photo/David Zalubowski); (2) The starting blocks at the Canada Summer Games in London, Ontario, August 2001: (front to back) Kelly Watson of Winnipeg, Manitoba; Hannah Moffatt of St. John's, Newfoundland; Elaine Hua of Edmonton, Alberta; Yvonne Mensah of Surrey, British Columbia; Ashley Purnell of Metcalfe, Ontario; and Laurelie Harvey of Lac Beauport, Quebec (CP PHOTO/*London Free Press*-Dave Chidley).

Page 233: Toronto Argonauts' Mike Clemons is grabbed by B.C. Lions' linebacker David Maeva during CFL action in Vancouver in 1996 (CP PHOTO/STF-Chuck Stoody).

Page 234: (1) Sandy Newsham from Winnipeg, Manitoba, pitches in the women's World Softball Championship in Fujinomiya, Japan, July 1998 (AP Photo/Itsuo Inouye); (2) Alexandre Despatie in a diving event at the 2000 Olympic Games (CP PHOTO/COA).

Every reasonable effort has been made to acquire permission for copyrighted materials used in this book and to acknowledge such permissions accurately. Any errors or omissions called to the publisher's attention will be corrected in future printings.

We acknowledge the support of the Government of Canada through the Book Publishing Industry Development Program for our publishing activities. We acknowledge the support of the Government of Ontario through the Ontario Media Development Corporation Book Initiative.

Printed in Canada by Transcontinental Printing Inc., Ontario.
1 2 3 4 5   08 07 06 05 04 03

Table of Contents

About the Authors

Ted Temertzoglou is co-director of the Birchmount Exceptional Athlete Program (BEAP) for the Toronto District School Board at Birchmount Park Collegiate Institute. He also teaches Anatomy and Physiology for Fitness at Seneca College in Scarborough. He was a member of the writing team for the course profile and support documents for Exercise Science (PSE4U), the new Grade 12 health and physical education curriculum in Ontario. He was also a contributing writer for the book *Serious Strength Training: Periodization for Building Muscle Power and Mass* by T. Bompa and L. Cornacchia (Human Kinetics, 1998). He is a fitness consultant, certified by the Ontario Association of Sport and Exercise Sciences, and has appeared on CBC's *Marketplace* and CityTV's *Breakfast Television*. He conducts workshops and conferences across Ontario promoting health and physical education and was the recipient of the CAHPERD's *Young Professional Award* (2001). In 2000, Temertzoglou was inducted to the University of Toronto's Varsity Blues Football All-Century Team. Temertzoglou holds a B.P.H.E and a B.Ed. from the University of Toronto. He lives with his family in Toronto.

Paul Challen has written several non-fiction books on popular culture and sport, including *The Book of Isiah* (1996), a biography of basketball legend Isiah Thomas, and *Gardens of Shame* (2002), an account of the Maple Leaf Gardens sexual abuse case. His writing on sport has also appeared in the *Toronto Star*, the *National Post*, the *Hamilton Spectator*, and *Toronto Life* and *SLAM* magazines. In 2003, his series of athlete profiles was part of a special edition of *Toronto Life* that won a Silver Award at the National Magazine Awards. He has also written and narrated sport documentaries for the CBC Radio One program *The Inside Track*. As an athlete, he represented Canada by competing in the 1985 IAAF World Junior cross-country running championship event in Lisbon, Portugal, and is a three-time Ontario age-group champion in indoor and outdoor track and cross-country running. He earned his B.A. in 1989 from Dartmouth College in New Hampshire, where he was a member of four consecutive Ivy League cross-country championship teams, and his M.A. from Queen's University in Kingston, Ontario, in 1992. He lives with his family in Hamilton, where he coaches youth soccer and chess.

Acknowledgements

This book was truly a collaborative effort, and the authors wish to thank, first of all, Keith Thompson of Thompson Educational Publishing, for his unending support and belief in this project, and Elizabeth Phinney, for her tireless editorial work and support.

A special thank you is due to the staff of Ophea (Ontario Physical and Health Education Association), in particular, to Myra Stephen, Provincial Curriculum Consultant; Carolyn Murdoch, Projects Leader; and Craig Wellington, Manager of Marketing and Development.

We also wish to thank the following individuals for their important contributions to the text: John Griffin of George Brown College, Craig McKie of Carlton University; Susan Morton-Stewart and Sandra Braun of Colborne Communications (Toronto), and Dr. Brian Roy of Brock University. Thanks also to Faye Thompson for her support and encouragement throughout.

Original illustrations for the text were created by Bart Vallecoccia, to whom we express our sincere thanks. As well we would like to thank Steven van Leeuwen, President of Bartleby Inc., for providing many original drawings of the skeleton, muscles, and joints from which new illustrations were re-created specifically for this book.

Content Reviewers

The following reviewers provided invaluable substantive reviews and comments that aided us greatly in finalizing the content of the text: Dr. Mark Babcock and Dr. Peter Tiidus, Wilfrid Laurier University; Dr. Dee Ballyk, Course Director of Anatomy for Physical and Health Education in the Faculty of Medicine, University of Toronto; Dr. Digby Elliot, McMaster University; Dr. Kelly Gammage, Brock University; Dr. Pierre Gervais, University of Alberta; Dr. David Hood, York University; Jason Krell, University of Waterloo; Dr. Kathleen Martin-Ginis, McMaster University; Dr. Stuart Phillips, McMaster University; Dr. Stephen Prentice, University of Waterloo; Dr. Ian Ritchie, Brock University; Dr. Danny Rosenberg, Brock University; Dr. Digby Sale and Dr. Martin Gibala, McMaster University; Dr. David Sanderson, University of British Columbia; Dr. Douglas W. Stoddard, Sports and Exercise Medicine Institute (Toronto); Dr. Phillip Sullivan, Brock University; and Dr. Phillip White, McMaster University.

Teacher Reviewers

Our acknowledgements would not be complete without an expression of our gratitude towards the many teachers who reviewed draft material and provided valuable feedback. More than two hundred and fifty teachers were involved in this process. We cannot thank them all individually here, but we do wish especially to thank Kim Parkes and Jamie Nunn, Westdale Secondary School (Hamilton); Pat and Angeline Lacasse, Colonel By Secondary School (Gloucester); Carolyn Temertzoglou, Havergal College (Toronto); Debra Courville, Consultant with the Halton District School Board; Nancy Schad and Sophie O'Brien, Toronto District School Board; Michele Van Bargen, Strathroy District Collegiate Institute; and Jennifer Powles, Trinity College School (Port Hope).

Colleagues

Thanks as well to colleagues who, directly and indirectly, gave us support and encouragement during this project: Lorna Bradley, Bell High School (Ottawa), Margaret Chaput, Ottawa-Carleton Catholic District School Board; Dave Clipper, Cameron Heights Collegiate Institute; Ron Lopez, District School Board of Niagara; Joan Millard, Ancaster High School; Susan Orchard, Halton District School Board; Principal Kathy Owen and Head Secretary Ronda Sinclair of Birchmount Park Collegiate Institute (Toronto); Rob Pacas and Joe Rumolo, Birchmount Exceptional Athlete Program; Kelly Pace, St. Clement's School (Toronto); Anthony Petitti, Toronto Catholic District School Board; Gary Reilly, retired teacher; Nick Rowe, Earl Haig Secondary School (Toronto); Principal Randy Ruttan, Gananoque Secondary School; Heather Sears-Hochfellner, York Region District School Board; Richard Ward, Toronto District School Board; and Martha Wenn, Waterloo Region District School Board.

Simon Whitfield jumps across the finish line to win the gold medal in the men's triathlon at the 2000 Summer Olympic Games in Sydney, Australia, September 17, 2000 (AP Photo/David Guttenfelder).

Preface

"It is exercise alone that supports the spirits and keeps the mind in vigour."
— Cicero (106-43 B.C.), Roman orator and statesman

In writing this book, the authors faced a unique challenge – to put together a comprehensive text that would cover topics ranging from physiology and anatomy to social issues in sport, from biomechanics and human performance to the history and business of sport, from motor learning and skills development to ethical questions – and to present all this material in a way that would be entertaining and informative, and a pleasure to teach.

Exercise Science: An Introduction to Health and Physical Education represents the result of this challenge. This text will appeal to students seeking a solid grounding in the basics of exercise science in preparation for more advanced courses in college or university. As well, the book may prove useful to instructors and students just beginning post-secondary courses in kinesiology or physical education. The authors hope that students will take many of the concepts covered in this text and apply them to their daily lives and thereby maintain a healthier, more active lifestyle.

In a world in which many important facets of life seem beyond our influence, our bodies, what we put into them, and how we train them are items over which we have control. Unlike many other academic subjects, exercise science is a field that encourages personal application of the things learned inside the classroom. Students can take what they will learn in this text and use it to make positive changes in their own lives and in the lives of others in areas such as diet, exercise, sport participation, and coaching.

As well, this text will allow readers to become more informed consumers and to make wiser decisions regarding the claims made by marketers. Is a new diet plan safe, and will it really lead to the long-term weight loss its promoters say it will? Is a "revolutionary" pair of running shoes really going to help you run faster? Should an older relative take up exercising – and to what extent – after experiencing heart problems? Do highly paid professional athletes really deserve their huge salaries? Should girls be given the same access to community sport as boys? After working through this book, the student will be much better equipped to answer these and similar questions.

Although every effort has been made to provide advice and information that complies with "best practices" in the medical and physiological professions, everyone should be aware of their own unique health concerns before attempting any type of exercise. In many instances, the authors have attempted to detail certain worst-case scenarios that could result from exercising or sports participation, such as injury, dehydration, or athletic burnout. These are not intended to deter anyone from adopting an active, healthy lifestyle, but rather to make the reader aware of what can occur if safe practices are not followed and physiological principles are not observed. A visit to a family physician is almost always the best first step for anyone who is looking to engage in an exercise program.

We have attempted to make the material presented in *Exercise Science* relevant to current trends in physical activity, health, and sport. As well, the text contains profiles and photographs of both well-known and not-so-well-known athletes, coaches, and events. Although the emphasis is on Canadian figures, exercise science is a international field, and one filled with inspiring people and events from around the globe.

The Student Workbook that accompanies this text has been designed to reinforce the book's central concepts through a range of practical exercises. These tests and exercises require the student to utilize the knowledge they have gained in a number of interactive ways with a view to enhancing their understanding of the material in the text.

As is befitting a book on physical activity and health, *Exercise Science* is the result of a team effort by writers, editors, and reviewers. In that spirit, we are always seeking to expand this team and to improve the material. We welcome suggestions, improvements, and corrections from teachers, students, coaches, and parents on how to continue our mission of delivering the best possible learning experience on this topic to a wide range of classrooms.

Ted Temertzoglou
Paul Challen
July 2003

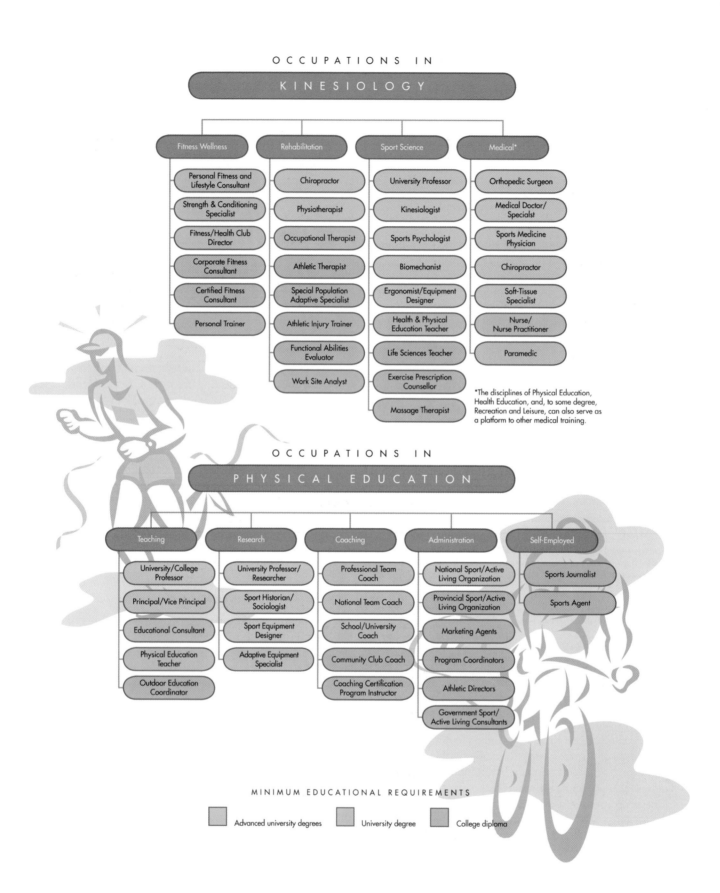

OCCUPATIONS IN

KINESIOLOGY

Fitness Wellness
- Personal Fitness and Lifestyle Consultant
- Strength & Conditioning Specialist
- Fitness/Health Club Director
- Corporate Fitness Consultant
- Certified Fitness Consultant
- Personal Trainer

Rehabilitation
- Chiropractor
- Physiotherapist
- Occupational Therapist
- Athletic Therapist
- Special Population Adaptive Specialist
- Athletic Injury Trainer
- Functional Abilities Evaluator
- Work Site Analyst

Sport Science
- University Professor
- Kinesiologist
- Sports Psychologist
- Biomechanist
- Ergonomist/Equipment Designer
- Health & Physical Education Teacher
- Life Sciences Teacher
- Exercise Prescription Counsellor
- Massage Therapist

Medical*
- Orthopedic Surgeon
- Medical Doctor/ Specialst
- Sports Medicine Physician
- Chiropractor
- Soft-Tissue Specialist
- Nurse/ Nurse Practitioner
- Paramedic

*The disciplines of Physical Education, Health Education, and, to some degree, Recreation and Leisure, can also serve as a platform to other medical training.

OCCUPATIONS IN

PHYSICAL EDUCATION

Teaching
- University/College Professor
- Principal/Vice Principal
- Educational Consultant
- Physical Education Teacher
- Outdoor Education Coordinator

Research
- University Professor/ Researcher
- Sport Historian/ Sociologist
- Sport Equipment Designer
- Adaptive Equipment Specialist

Coaching
- Professional Team Coach
- National Team Coach
- School/University Coach
- Community Club Coach
- Coaching Certification Program Instructor

Administration
- National Sport/Active Living Organization
- Provincial Sport/Active Living Organization
- Marketing Agents
- Program Coordinators
- Athletic Directors
- Government Sport/ Active Living Consultants

Self-Employed
- Sports Journalist
- Sports Agent

MINIMUM EDUCATIONAL REQUIREMENTS

Advanced university degrees   University degree   College diploma

OCCUPATIONS IN
RECREATION AND LEISURE

Municipal Parks and Recreation
- Community Sports Administration Director
- Sport and Fitness Program Coordinator
- Programs for Individuals with Disabilities
- Seniors' Programs Coordinator
- Day Camps for Children Coordinator
- Swimming Pool, Rink, or Other Facility Manager
- Community Development Facilitator
- Special Event Coordinator

Provincial and Federal Governments
- Director
- Sport and Program Consultant
- Fitness/Wellness Consultant
- Facility Design Manager
- Tourism Promotion Coordinator
- National/Provincial Park Employee

Youth Service Agencies (Not-for-Profit Sector)
- YMCA/YWCA Youth Program Manager
- Recreation Manager with Correction Agencies
- After-School Program Coordinator
- Scouts/Guides/Cadets Recreation Programmer
- Church-Sponsored Programs Coordinator
- Education-Sponsored Programs Coordinator

Institutional Employment
- University/College Instructor/Researcher
- Senior Citizen Homes Recreation Manager
- Hospitals Therapeutic Recreation Manager
- Prisons Recreation Programs Worker
- Rehabilitation Centres Worker

Commercial Recreation
- Workplace Recreation Programs Manager
- Fitness Centre Management
- Sport Club Manager (e.g., golf, racquetball)
- Hotel Recreation Manager
- Cruise Ship Recreation

Camping and Outdoor Education
- Camp Facility Administrator/Director
- Outward Bound Schools Manager
- Ecotourism Manager
- Sports Instructor
- Adventure Tourism Manager
- Water Safety Instructor

OCCUPATIONS IN
HEALTH EDUCATION
(NON-MEDICAL)

Teaching
- University Professor/Researcher
- College Instructor
- Junior High and High-School Teacher

Volunteer/Community
- Specialist with Disease-Specific Agencies
- Wellness Programs with Special Populations
- Smoking/AIDS, etc., Organizations Coordinator
- Fund-raising Organizations Coordinator
- Special Projects Coordinator
- Rehabilitation Programs
- YMCA/YWCA
- Advocate/Activist
- Dietician/Nutritionist
- Wellness Coordinator

Government Agencies
- Director
- Manager in Public Health Agencies
- Manager in Hospital Health Centre
- School Boards – Manager Level
- Workers' Compensation – Manager Level
- Social Outreach Worker

Self-Employed
- Health Behaviour Consultant/Researcher
- Writer of Health-Related Books and Articles
- Health Workshop Presenter
- Software Developer

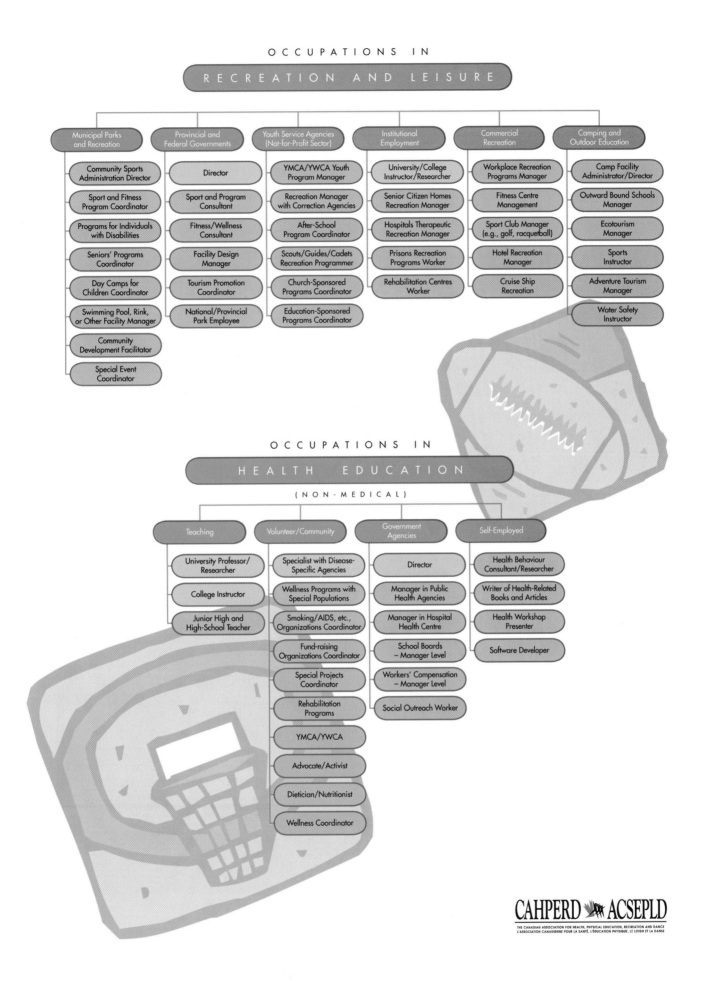

Anson Carter holds a Canadian flag as he celebrates with teammates after winning the gold medal at the Ice Hockey World Championship in Helsinki, Finland, May 2003. Canada beat Sweden 3-2 in overtime on a goal by Carter (AP Photo/Martin Meissner).

UNIT 1

INTRODUCTION TO ANATOMY AND PHYSIOLOGY

Jayna Hefford of Kingston and Danielle Goyette of St-Nazaire hug as teammates celebrate Canada's 3-2 victory against the U.S. for the Olympic gold medal in women's hockey at the Olympic Winter Games in Salt Lake City, Utah, February 2002 (CP PHOTO/Tom Hanson).

1

Principles & Terminology

"Those who think they have no time for bodily exercise will sooner or later have to find time for illness."
— Edward Stanley (1826-1893) from *The Conduct of Life*

KEY CONCEPTS

- Anatomy
- Physiology
- Exercise physiology
- Anatomical position
- Anatomical planes/axes

- Flexion/extension
- Abduction/adduction
- Internal/external rotation
- Circumduction
- Supination/pronation

- Protraction/retraction
- Dorsiflexion/plantar flexion
- Eversion/inversion
- Elevation/depression
- Opposition/reposition

The material presented in this first Unit serves as a foundation for what follows in the rest of the book, but anatomy and physiology are vast fields and we can only touch the surface here. The biological systems introduced are those that directly affect human movement (the skeletal system, the muscular system, human energy production, the nervous system, and the cardiorespiratory system).

As you go through this Unit, try to gain familiarity with the key terms highlighted in the text. These terms are also listed in the glossary. Many of these terms will arise in a different context later on.

BASIC TERMINOLOGY

The field of **anatomy** is a branch of science that deals with the *structural* organization of living things – how they are "built" and what they consist of. The word itself comes from the Greek root *anatome,* meaning "dissection." Anatomy is one of the "life sciences" and is closely related to medicine and to various branches of biology. The major subdivisions of anatomy are "plant anatomy" and "animal anatomy." The latter is further subdivided into human anatomy and comparative anatomy (a field that looks at similarities and differences among various animal types).

Anatomy is usually studied in conjunction with another key area of scientific enquiry: physiology. **Physiology** is concerned with basic processes such as reproduction, growth, and metabolism as they occur within the various systems of the body. The divisions within the field of physiology are similar to those within anatomy.

Structure and Function

In other words, anatomy is concerned with the *structure* of the body and its various organs, and physiology is the study of how all these parts *function.* Indeed, physiology is often referred to as "functional anatomy." This distinction between structure and function is a useful one that you will encounter often.

Both anatomy and physiology have distinguished histories. Today, our knowledge of the human body, its various organs and parts, and how they all function together is highly advanced due largely to the pursuits of scientists in these important fields.

Exercise Physiology

Exercise physiology is a branch of physiology, with the important distinction that exercise physiologists concentrate their research specifically on how the body responds and adapts to the stresses placed on it by exercise. In the remainder of this text, we will look at bodily systems and functions largely from the exercise physiologist's viewpoint; that is, how the body's various components work together within the context of exercise.

One major branch of exercise physiology is concerned with the maximization of athletic performance and exercise in general, and research is conducted to find out how people can run faster, throw farther, and jump higher. But this is not the only area where exercise physiology comes into play. Exercise physiologists also play an important role in working with patients, for example, those with lung or heart ailments, by implementing testing, exercise programs, nutrition, and rehabilitation, using the same basic physiological principles that apply to athletes.

THE ANATOMICAL POSITION

In the same way that maps of the world are universally oriented in the North-South/East-West position, anatomists and physiologists look at the human body from a standard starting point. This standard starting point is known as the anatomical position.

Diagrams of the anatomical position portray the body in an upright, standing position, face and feet pointing forward, with the arms at the side, and the forearms fully supinated (with palms facing forward). See the figures below. This anatomical position is accepted as an unambiguous starting point from which to begin to describe anatomical features and positions.

Sagittal, Frontal, and Transverse Planes

The anatomical position is further standardized by dividing the body into three anatomical planes or sections. Anatomical planes relate to positions in space and are at right angles to one another.

The **frontal (coronal) plane** is vertical and extends from one side of the body to the other side. The **transverse (horizontal) plane** is horizontal and divides the body into upper and lower segments. The **sagittal (median) plane** is vertical and extends from the front of the body to the back. (The coronal and sagittal planes derive their names from the direction of sutures in the cranium.) In standard diagrams, each of these three planes is depicted by a single line, but there can be any number of these imaginary divisions, depending on which part or parts of the body are being studied.

Planes can be used to describe directional cuts (sections) through parts of the body. For example, a "frontal section" of the heart exposes the various parts of the heart from the front. A "sagittal section" exposes the parts of the heart from the side. If the heart is sectioned on the "transverse plane," the heart can be viewed from the top or bottom.

Horizontal, Longitudinal, and Antero-Posterior Axes

The human body is also divided into anatomical axes – again, a series of imaginary lines. Anatomical axes are used to describe the direction of movement at joints.

The **horizontal axis** extends from one side of the body to the other. The **longitudinal axis** is vertical, running from head to toe. The **antero-posterior axis** extends from the front of the body to the back.

A body movement can be described in terms of the anatomical plane through which it occurs and the anatomical axis around which it rotates. The general rule is that the axis of rotation is always perpendicular to the plane of movement.

Later, in Unit 2, we will examine several key principles of biomechanics that rely on these anatomical planes and axes for the study of human movement (beginning on page 225). Using these imaginary planes and axes, biomechanists apply some of the key principles of physics to exercise and thereby gain greater insights into the the basics of human movement.

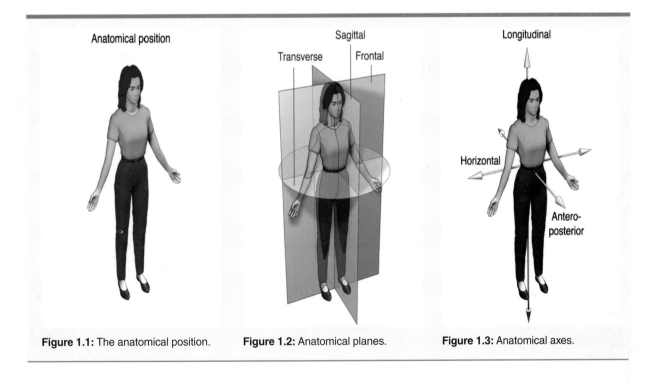

Figure 1.1: The anatomical position.　**Figure 1.2:** Anatomical planes.　**Figure 1.3:** Anatomical axes.

Table 1.1: Basic movements involving a joint

Term	Meaning of term	Example of this movement
Flexion	Flexion is bending the joint to reduce the angle between two or more bones. It occurs in the sagittal plane. Flexion is motion in the anterior (forward) direction at the joints of the neck, trunk, upper extremities, and hips. For the knee, ankle, foot, and toes, flexion occurs in the posterior (backward) direction.	If you touch your right shoulder with your right hand, then your elbow is in flexion (flexed).
Extension	Extension is straightening a joint to increase the angle. It also occurs in the sagittal plane.	If you straighten your legs, the knees have undergone extension (extended).
Abduction	Abduction is movement away from the median plane. This movement occurs in the frontal (coronal) plane.	If you stand with your feet apart, your legs are abducted.
Adduction	Adduction is the opposite of abduction. It is movement towards the median plane.	If you squeeze your knees together, then you are adducting your legs.
Internal Rotation	Internal rotation of a limb moves its anterior surface medially.	Internal rotation of the hip turns the knee and foot towards the midline.
External Rotation	External rotation is the opposite of internal rotation.	You externally rotate your hip when you point your feet out to the side.
Circumduction	Circumduction is a circular motion combining flexion, extension, abduction, and adduction.	Making circles in the air with your arms is an example of circumduction.
Supination	Supination is the lateral rotation of the hand and forearm such that the palm faces forward as in the anatomical position.	When putting a screw into the floor using your right hand, you have to supinate your forearm.
Pronation	Pronation is the medial rotation the hand and forearm such that the palm faces backward from the anatomical position.	When unscrewing a screw from the floor with your right hand, you must pronate your forearm.
Protraction	Protraction is moving in an anterior (forward) direction.	Sticking your chin out is an example of protraction.
Retraction	Retraction is moving in a posterior (backward) direction.	Pushing your shoulders back to squeeze your shoulder blades is an example of retraction.
Dorsiflexion	Dorsiflexion is movement of the ankle in the sagittal plane that decreases the angle between the foot and the lower leg.	When you point your foot towards your head, your ankle is dorsiflexed.
Plantar Flexion	Plantar flexion is movement of the ankle in the sagittal plane that increases the angle between the foot and the lower leg.	When you stand on "tip-toes," your ankles are plantar flexed.
Inversion	Inversion occurs when the medial border of the foot is raised such that the sole of the foot is turned inward.	When you stand on the outer edge of your foot, your foot is inverted.
Eversion	Eversion occurs when the lateral border of the foot is raised such that the sole of the foot is turned outward.	When you stand on the inner edge of your foot, your foot is everted.
Elevation	Elevation involves the raising up to a more superior position.	When you hunch your shoulders, your shoulders are elevated.
Depression	The opposite action to elevation, depression, involves the pulling down to a more inferior position.	When you slouch your shoulders, your shoulders are depressed.
Opposition	Opposition occurs when the thumb comes into contact with one of the other fingers.	Bring your thumb over to touch any one of the other fingers.
Reposition	Reposition occurs when the thumb is returned back to the anatomical position.	When you move your thumb from your finger and return it to the anatomical position, the thumb is repositioned.

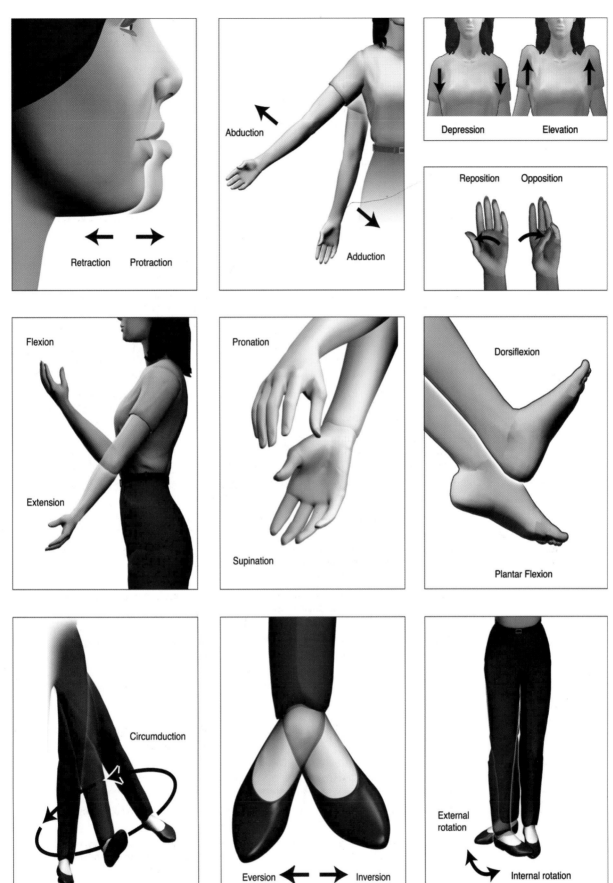

Figure 1.4: Basic types of body movement.

DESCRIBING POSITION AND MOVEMENT

Planes and axes are often referred to by the same name (e.g., the coronal plane and the coronal axis; the sagittal plane and the sagittal axis). We have opted for different names in each case (e.g., frontal plane, but horizontal axis; sagittal plane, but antero-posterior axis). With practice, the principles will become clear and one can use either set of terminology.

Here are some examples of how to use the idea of planes and axes to describe basic human movements (see Table 1.2):

- **Flexion** (bending a joint to reduce the angle between two bones) occurs around the horizontal axis and through the sagittal plane. (**Extension** is the opposite motion of flexion.)

- **Rotation** of extremities and axial rotation of the spine (twisting) occurs around the longitudinal axis and through the transverse plane.

- Movements of **abduction** (raising one's arms upward to the side) and **adduction** (the opposite) occur around the antero-posterior axis and along the frontal plane.

Terminology

The following terms pertain to body position and movement:

- **Anterior** refers to the front surfaces of the body, whereas **posterior** refers to the back surfaces. These terms are also used to describe the relationship of structures within the body. For example, the sternum is anterior to the heart (so anterior also means "in front of"). The heart will also have an anterior surface. (*Dorsal* means towards the back, whereas *ventral* means towards the front – posterior and anterior are more commonly used terms.)

- **Superior** refers to upward surfaces, whereas **inferior** refers to downward surfaces.

- **Medial** means towards the midline or towards the median plane, whereas **lateral** means away from the midline or away from the median plane.

- **Proximal** means towards the point of attachment of the limb to the body, whereas **distal** means farther away from the point of attachment.

- **Plantar** means on or towards the sole of the foot, whereas **dorsum** refers to the uppermost surface of the foot.

- **Superficial** means on, or close to, the surface of the body, whereas **deep** means farther away from the surface of the body.

Table 1.2: Relationship between axes and planes of movement		
Axis of rotation	**Plane of motion**	**Example**
Horizontal	Sagittal	Flexion, extension
Longitudinal	Transverse	Rotation of extremities, axial rotation
Antero-posterior	Frontal	Abduction, adduction

WHERE DO WE GO FROM HERE?

The remainder of this unit is devoted to looking at some of the body's major biological systems. The ten major systems are described briefly on the adjacent page. In the following sections, we will focus on those systems (and subsystems) that pertain more directly to physical activity and health. These systems are: the skeletal system, the muscular system, joint mechanics, the energy system, the nervous system, and the cardiorespiratory system. It is important to keep in mind as you work through the rest of this text that, although physiologists do study these key systems as distinct groups, they are all part of a much bigger picture when it comes to the study of physical activity and human movement.

For example, this text devotes much space to the study of muscles, their location, name, and functions. But simply knowing this information alone will not take us very far. If we wish to know more about how exercise is performed, we also need to know how individual muscles work in conjunction with other muscles, as well as with bones, joints, and the body's systems of delivering energy to them. As you read ahead, keep in mind the integrated nature of these biological systems.

This book aims to take a comprehensive look at all areas of sport and physical activity, with anatomy and physiology as just one (albeit important) part of the larger picture. While the current Unit will provide a solid introduction to anatomy and physiology, the subject matter is vast, and the Unit can really only touch the surface. Fortunately, there are many resources available – including many websites, several of which are listed on page 135. Any student interested in following up with a much more thorough examination of the concepts of anatomy and physiology should have no problem doing so.

The Ten Biological Systems of the Human Body
A quick overview

While this book focuses on physical movement and exercise, it is useful to keep in mind that the human body consists of ten major biological or physiological "systems." Together, these groups of tissues and organs carry out the various functions necessary to sustain human life. Needless to say, a breakdown in one or another system, or even a small part of a system, can be disastrous.

The following is a quick overview of these ten basic biological systems. In the remainder of this Unit, we will look at a few of these systems at greater length insofar as they pertain directly to human movement.

1. The Skeletal System

The human skeleton consists of some 206 bones, and is divided into the *axial skeleton* (mainly the skull, spine, and rib cage) and *appendicular skeleton* (the limbs and supporting girdles). The skeleton supports the body, protects vital organs, and works in conjunction with the muscles to cause movement. Bones also produce the blood cells and store many of the minerals that the body needs. The bones of the skeletal system range from the flat rib bones, to the long bones of the arms and legs, to fused skull bones, to the minute and delicate bones in the hands and feet, and to the irregular-shaped bones of the vertebral column protecting the spinal cord.

2. The Muscular System

The muscular system consists of three types of tissue: skeletal, smooth, and cardiac. *Skeletal muscles* connect bones and are responsible for voluntary movements. *Smooth muscles* are found within organs and are involved with processes that occur automatically, such as digestion. *Cardiac muscles* are found in the heart, pumping blood to other parts of the body. Muscles work by contraction. Skeletal muscles make up a substantial proportion of human body weight and are directly involved in locomotion.

3. The Respiratory System

The respiratory system consists of the lungs and the airway leading to them. This system allows air to enter the lungs through the mouth and nose, where oxygen is extracted and diffuses into the bloodstream for distribution throughout the body. Carbon dioxide (a waste product) is returned to the lungs and is exhaled into the atmosphere.

4. The Circulatory System

The circulatory system serves to deliver oxygen and nutrients to the body and remove waste products from it. The circulatory system includes the heart, the blood, and various blood vessels that transport blood throughout the body. The system is sometimes linked to the respiratory system and is then referred to as the cardiorespiratory system.

5. The Nervous System

The nervous system oversees all the other systems and acts as a kind of command centre. It includes the *central nervous system* (which consists of the brain and spinal cord) and the *peripheral nervous system* (consisting of the network of nerves connecting the brain and spinal cord to the rest of the body).

6. The Digestive System

The digestive system allows the body to break down food into simpler substances so they can enter the bloodstream. It also serves to filter and remove waste from the body. The major organs of the digestive system include the mouth, throat, esophagus, stomach, the large and small intestines, and the liver.

7. The Reproductive System

This system consists of specialized organs that allow males and females to reproduce. In the case of males, its primary role is to form sperm (male reproductive cells) and deliver them to the female. For females, it involves not only producing the sex cells (ova or eggs), but also protecting and nurturing the fetus and nursing the newborn baby.

8. The Immune System

The immune system helps to defend the body against infection and disease. The *innate immune system* responds directly to invaders, whereas the *adaptive immune system* involves specialized white blood cells (lymphocytes) that remember and respond to specific types of invaders.

9. The Endocrine System

The endocrine system consists of glands that secrete hormones that, in turn, regulate various activities, including metabolism, growth, and development. The major glands are the pituitary, the thyroid, the adrenals, the pancreas, and the sex glands.

10. The Urinary System

The urinary system allows the body to eliminate waste products and regulate its water and chemical balance. It consists of two kidneys, the bladder and connecting tissue, and the urethra, which allows waste to leave the body.

In the context of physical activity, it is easy to see how some of these "systems" are closely linked to human performance in sport and other forms of exercise. We will concentrate on these in this text. That being said, however, it should be emphasized that there are important connections between all the main biological systems, and each has a bearing on sport and exercise. For example, the endocrine system, which regulates human growth and metabolism, comes into play when athletes look to enhance their performance by means of steroids and other performance-enhancing substances. And the urinary system comes into play when athletes such as marathon runners or long-distance cyclists are required to take in large amounts of liquids in hot conditions while eliminating, as efficiently as possible, waste products after these liquids have been processed.

Markham, Ontario, native Tammy Sutton-Brown, playing for the Charlotte Stings, is surrounded under the basket by the Washington Mystics' Helen Luz and Murriel Page, June 2002 (AP Photo/Rick Havner).

2
The Skeletal System

"Humankind is designed for exercise and not rest — hence the legs are located below the torso. If designed for rest, we would at best have castors."
— Arthur Stewart, Scotland (from Stephen Seiler, The Institute for Sport, Kristiansand, Norway)

KEY CONCEPTS		
• Skeleton	• Compact bone	• Bone remodelling
• Axial skeleton	• Diaphysis/epiphysis	• Epiphyseal plates/lines
• Appendicular skeleton	• Cancellous bone	• Simple, compound, and comminuted fractures
• Articulating cartilage	• Cortex	• Stress fracture
• Periosteum	• Trabeculae	• Osteoporosis
• Medullary cavity	• Ossification	

The word "skeletal" is derived from the Greek word *skeletos*, which means "dried up." In truth, bones only appear that way. They are actually composed of living tissue – bone cells, fat cells, and blood vessels – as well as non-living material such as water and minerals.

In this section, we will take a look at how the bones are situated within the skeleton, how each of the major bones performs its own unique function and, in turn, complements the work of the other bones and the muscles attached to them.

THE HUMAN SKELETON

The adult human skeleton is made up of 206 bones, accounting for about 14 percent of total body weight. Humans start life with more bones than that – above 300 at birth. However, over time, several bones fuse as growth takes place (such as in the skull and lower part of the vertebral column).

The bones of the human skeleton come in many different sizes. The longest is the femur, or thigh bone, and the smallest is the tiny stirrup bone found inside the ear. Many parts of the body are made up of several bones joined together (see Figures 2.4 and 2.5 on pages 14 and 15). For example, each hand has twenty-seven bones and the pelvic girdle consists of three paired bones (ilium, ischium, and pubis).

Among humans, males and females have skeletons that, on average, have slight differences. For example, males have slightly thicker and longer legs and arms; females have a wider pelvis and a larger space within the pelvis to facilitate the birth process.

Compared to other body systems, the skeletal system is extremely hard and durable. As bones are composed primarily of calcium, people whose diet is low in this mineral may find their bones becoming increasingly brittle and breakable. This is a particular concern for older people.

As anyone who has ever experienced a fracture knows, bones are able to repair themselves, although casts, splints, pins, or other aids are often required to make sure that they heal correctly.

Role of the Skeleton

While the skeleton supports the body, and works in conjunction with the muscles to cause movement, it also protects vital organs. For example, the skull protects the brain and various sense organs, the rib cage protects the lungs and heart, and the vertebral column protects the spinal cord. Blood cells are produced in the marrow of bones, and bones also serve as a reservoir to regulate calcium and phosphate levels in the body. The main functions of the skeletal system are listed in Table 2.1.

One distinctive characteristic of humans in comparison to other mammals is that we have an erect posture. Maintaining and utilizing an upright posture places unusual stresses on the lower part of the skeleton, and on affected joints and muscles. In addition, the skeleton is subject to a number of pathological conditions, most important of which are fractures, bone loss with aging, and a deficiency disease known as rickets – a disease of infancy and childhood characterized by defective bone growth, and caused by a deficiency of vitamin D.

Table 2.1: Main functions of the skeletal system	
Structural support	Structural support for soft tissue, including muscles and viscera.
Protection	Protective cage for more delicate parts of the body (e.g., the brain is protected by the skull; the rib cage protects the heart and lungs).
Growth centre for cells	Red blood cells and platelets are made in bones.
Reservoir of minerals	A reservoir that the body can call upon in order to regulate the level of calcium and phosphorus in the body.
Movement	Muscles attach to bones by tendons. Muscles contract and move bones to facilitate movement.

THE STRUCTURE OF THE SKELETON

As illustrated in Figure 2.1, the skeletal system is generally divided into two main parts: the axial skeleton and the appendicular skeleton. (Sometimes a third division, the visceral, is distinguished, comprising the lower jaw, some elements of the upper jaw, and the branchial arches – bar-like ridges, the bones, and cartilage on either side of the throat.)

The Axial Skeleton — 80 Bones

The axial skeleton is comprised mainly of the vertebral column (the spine), much of the skull, and the rib cage. Of these, the small, stacked vertebrae of the spine protect the spinal cord, the cranium protects the brain, and the twelve pairs of ribs protect the lungs and heart. The muscles associated with this part of the skeleton include those of the face, tongue, and neck, muscles for chewing (mastication) and drinking, as well as the muscles around the vertebrae of the spine.

Most of the body's muscles originate from the axial skeleton, since it is medially located with respect to the appendicular skeleton. Most muscles anchor or originate here and insert on the appendicular skeleton. These muscles are often referred to as "core muscles" as they are centrally located and provide the body with stability and support. Examples of axial core muscles include rectus and transversus abdominis, and the erector spinae group. These muscles help stabilize and support the axial skeleton, thus providing proper posture and alignment.

The Appendicular Skeleton — 126 Bones

The appendicular skeleton includes the movable limbs and the supporting structures (girdles). As such, the appendicular skeleton plays a key role in allowing us to move about.

The upper limbs are attached to the pectoral girdle (shoulder girdle) and the lower limbs are attached to the pelvic girdle (hip girdle). The pectoral girdle consists of two scapulae (shoulder blades) and two clavicles (collar bones). The humerus attaches to the pectoral girdle at the glenoid cavity, the socket at the shoulder. The pelvic girdle consists of two sturdy hip bones. The two hip bones and the sacrum form the complete ring of the pelvis. On the outer side, where the fused bones meet, there is a socket (the acetabulum cavity) into which the head of the femur fits.

The muscles associated with the appendicular skeleton include those muscles of the pectoral girdle, and those of the upper limbs (muscles around the humerus, the forearm, the wrist, hand, and fingers). The muscles of the appendicular skeleton also include those of the pelvic girdle, and those of the lower limbs (muscles around the thigh, leg, ankle, foot, and toes).

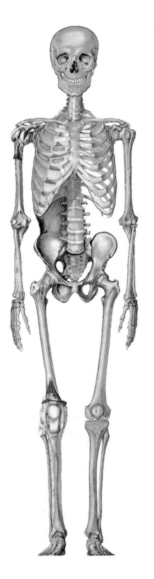

2.1: The axial (in blue) and appendicular skeletons.

FIVE TYPES OF BONES

Bones are normally classified according to their shape – long, short, flat, irregular, and a fifth type (sesamoid) that is found within tendons (for an example of each type, see Figure 2.2).

- **Long bones** are found in the arms and legs. The femur is the best example of a long bone.

- **Short bones** are most common in the wrists, such as the carpal bone, and ankles.

- **Flat bones**, as the name implies, are flat and thin and, as in the case of the parietal bone from the roof of the skull, often protect vital organs of the body from injury.

- **Irregular bones** include such odd-looking bones as the sphenoid bone or vertebrae.

- **Sesamoid bones** are unusual bones in that they are small, flat bones wrapped within tendons that move over bony surfaces (e.g., the patella).

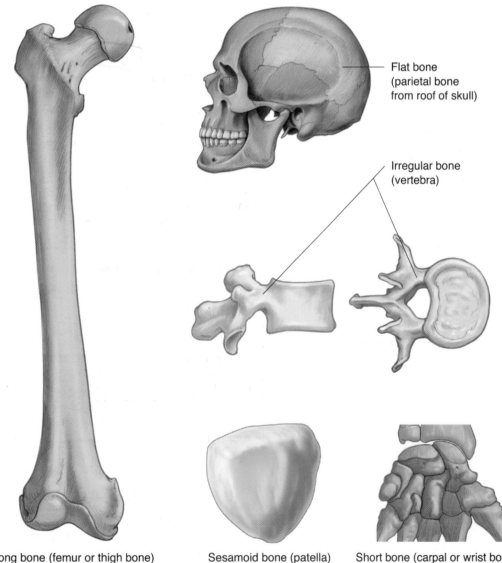

Flat bone
(parietal bone
from roof of skull)

Irregular bone
(vertebra)

Long bone (femur or thigh bone)   Sesamoid bone (patella)   Short bone (carpal or wrist bone)

Figure 2.2: Five types of bones.

ANATOMY OF A LONG BONE

Starting at cartilage and working our way counter-clockwise, let us examine the key features of a long bone. These features are illustrated in Figure 2.3.

Cartilage is located on both ends of long bone and is referred to as **articulating cartilage**. It allows smooth movement (articulation) within joints while protecting the ends of bones. Cartilage does not have a blood supply or nerve endings.

Periosteum is the name given to the outer connective tissue that covers the entire length of the bone. This tissue does not unite with the articulating cartilage. Periosteum fibres and those of ligaments and tendons unite to connect bone to bone or muscle to bone.

The **medullary cavity** is found inside the shaft of the bone (diaphysis, see below) and is filled with red and yellow bone marrow. Red marrow is where blood-cell formation (hematopoiesis) occurs, and yellow marrow is made up mostly of adipose (fat) cells and connective tissue that has no role in blood-cell formation. Generally, children have a higher concentration of red marrow in their long bones, and as they grow into adulthood, it changes to yellow marrow. In adults, red marrow is present mostly in the bones of the axial skeleton, with the exception of the skull.

Compact bone is the more dense part of the bone, and it is responsible for the bone's structural integrity. It is thickest along the **diaphysis**, or shaft of the bone. **Cancellous** or **spongy bone**, on the other hand, is filled with marrow in its matrix or small cavity-like spaces. Compact and cancellous bone will strengthen with exercise, specifically exercise that increases the loads that the bones are accustomed to. This is an important point, since it explains the benefits of following a resistance-training program. At the very ends of long bone is a region known as the **epiphysis**. The outer surface of the epiphysis is made up of compact bone, and the part that articulates with another bone is covered with cartilage.

The exterior layer of bones, known as the **cortex**, is dense and smooth and of varying thickness, depending on the type of bone. The interior core consists of networks of fibres (trabeculae) that mesh with blood vessels and the bone marrow. The **trabeculae** consist of continuous units of bony fibres arranged in a strut-like system running throughout the cancellous tissue. The density of the trabeculae varies with the type of bone and the amount of stress it bears. Vertebrae, for example, which are subject mainly to compressive forces, consist of thin cortices, with their rigidity provided through the trabeculae. Long bones (such as the humerus or femur), which are subject to bending forces, are tube-like, with thick cortices, and a cavity running through the centres (medullary cavity).

Two other important features, which may or may not be present depending on the stage of development, are the epiphyseal plate and epiphyseal line; they will be discussed on page 29 under the heading "Epiphyseal Plates and Lines."

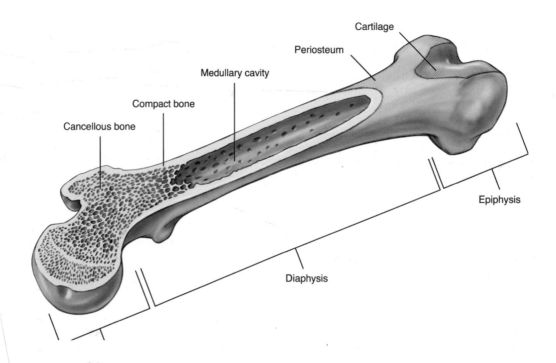

2.3: The composition of a long bone.

The Body's Key Bones
An Overview

CRANIUM AND FACE BONES (Skull and face bones)

The skull protects the brain as well as many of our sense organs. The cranium is the unit that contains and protects the brain. At the base of the cranium is the occipital bone (which admits the spinal cord). The parietal and temporal bones comprise the sides and uppermost portion of the cranium, the frontal bone forms the forehead. The facial area includes: the zygomatic bones; the mandible; the palatine bones (the hard palate and the floor of the nose); and the maxillary (or upper jaw) bones. The skull is supported by the top vertebra (the "atlas," which permits nodding) and turns on the next vertebra (the "axis," which allows one to shake one's head "no").

VERTEBRAL COLUMN (Backbone or spine)

We are born with thirty-three vertebrae but those at the bottom of the spine fuse to form two bones, the sacrum and the coccyx. The remaining twenty-four make up the rest of the spine. The adult backbone consists of twenty-six separate vertebrae that support the back of the body and extend from the brain down to the tailbone. Each of the vertebrae is separated by cartilage to prevent the bones from grinding against one another. Excluding the sacrum and coccyx, the backbone can be divided into three areas. Seven vertebrae at the top form the neck and are known as the "cervical vertebrae." The next twelve connect to the ribcage and are called the "thoracic vertebrae." The five vertebrae making up the lower back (the "lumbar vertebrae") are the largest in the spine.

COCCYX (Tailbone)

The coccyx, or tailbone, is found at the base of the spinal column and articulates with the sacrum (part of the vertebral column that also forms a part of the pelvis). The coccyx usually consists of four fused vertebrae.

CLAVICLE (Collar bone)

The clavicle attaches to the upper arm at the shoulder. It makes up the front part of the shoulder. A bone of the pectoral girdle, the clavicle serves to link the upper limb to the axial skeleton.

SCAPULA (Shoulder blade)

The scapula is the second bone of the pectoral girdle. Movement of the scapula against the thoracic cage contributes significantly to the overall movement of the upper limb.

THORACIC CAGE (Thoracic vertebrae, ribs, and sternum)

The thoracic cage consists of the twelve thoracic vertebrae, the twelve ribs, and the sternum. The thoracic vertebrae provide attachment for the twelve ribs. The first seven ribs – the "true" ribs – attach directly to the sternum anteriorly. Ribs 8, 9 and 10 – the "false" ribs – attach anteriorly to the seventh rib, and thus indirectly to the sternum. Ribs 11 and 12 – the "floating" ribs – have no bony attachment anteriorly and end in the musculature of the lateral body wall.

HUMERUS (Upper arm bone)

The humerus connects the shoulder and the lower arm. At the lower end of the humerus is the elbow, the point at which it joins with the lower arm.

RADIUS AND ULNA (Lower arm bones)

The lower arm is made up of two separate bones – the radius and the ulna. These join the upper arm, or humerus, with the wrist. The radius and the ulna are parallel to each other, but when you twist your arm so that your palm is facing backward, the radius crosses over the front of the ulna.

METACARPALS, PHALANGES, AND CARPALS (Hand and wrist bones)

Muscles and tendons join the twenty-seven separate bones of the hand. The hand bones themselves are called the metacarpals, while the bones of the finger are called the phalanges. Each finger has three phalanges, while the thumb has two. In the wrist are eight carpal bones that support the muscles that move the fingers and thumb.

PELVIC GIRDLE (Hip bone)

The pelvic girdle connects the trunk and legs. It also supports the trunk and internal organs (intestines, bladder, and sex organs). It consists of two pelvic bones connected in the front at the pubic symphysis and behind by the sacrum and coccyx. Each pelvic bone is made up of three bones – the ilium (above and to either side), the ischium (behind and below), and the pubis (in front). The pelvic ring is formed in early childhood.

FEMUR (Thigh bone)

The femur is the longest bone in the body, and the upper leg's only bone. It connects the hip bone to the knee.

PATELLA (Kneecap)

The patella protects the largest joint, the knee. It is located where the femur and the tibia join together.

TIBIA AND FIBULA (Lower leg bones)

The lower leg bones consist of two separate bones, the tibia (or shin bone) at the front of the leg and the fibula at the back of the leg. The tibia is larger and is another important bone in supporting the body's weight. At the back of the leg, the fibula is crucial in allowing movement at the ankle.

TARSALS, METATARSALS, AND PHALANGES (Foot bones)

Each foot is made up of twenty-six bones that in turn comprise the ankle, heel, body of the foot, and the toes. The ankle is made up of seven bones called the tarsals, while the bones in the main part of the foot are called the metatarsals. The toes each have fourteen bones, called, as in the case of the fingers, the phalanges.

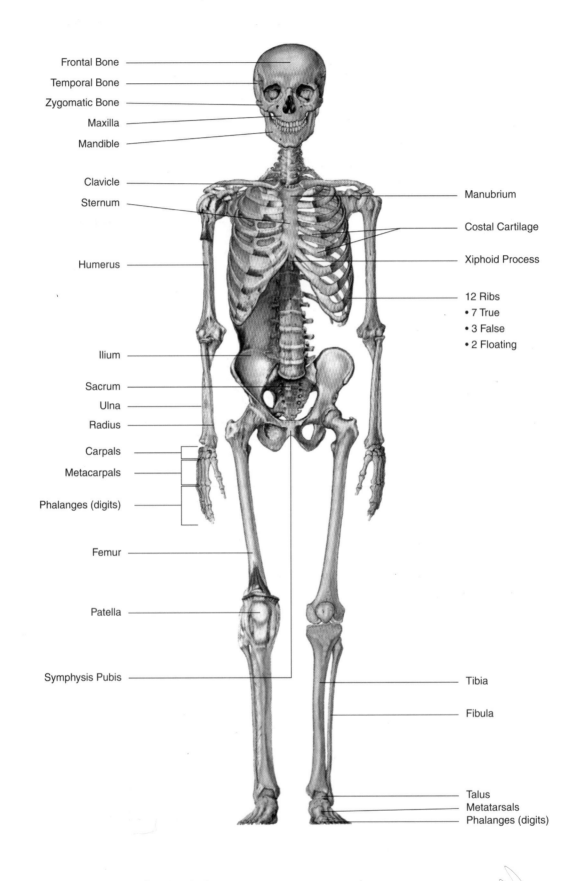

Frontal Bone

Temporal Bone

Zygomatic Bone

Maxilla

Mandible

Clavicle

Sternum

Manubrium

Costal Cartilage

Xiphoid Process

Humerus

12 Ribs
• 7 True
• 3 False
• 2 Floating

Ilium

Sacrum

Ulna

Radius

Carpals

Metacarpals

Phalanges (digits)

Femur

Patella

Symphysis Pubis

Tibia

Fibula

Talus
Metatarsals
Phalanges (digits)

Figure 2.4: The human skeleton (anterior view).

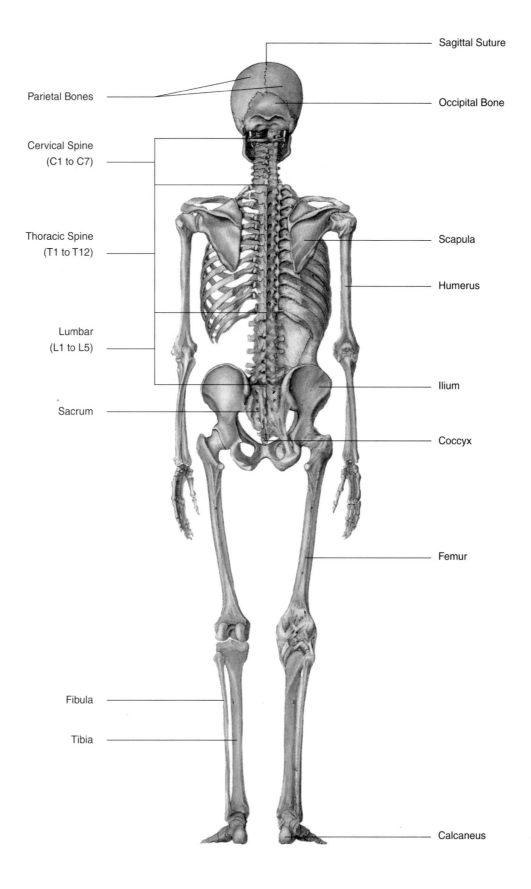

Sagittal Suture

Parietal Bones

Occipital Bone

Cervical Spine
(C1 to C7)

Thoracic Spine
(T1 to T12)

Scapula

Humerus

Lumbar
(L1 to L5)

Ilium

Sacrum

Coccyx

Femur

Fibula

Tibia

Calcaneus

Figure 2.5: The human skeleton (posterior view).

Table 2.2: Major bone landmarks and muscle origins and insertions

Bone	Important landmarks	Muscles that originate	Muscles that insert
Skull	mastoid process		sternocleidomastoid, longissimus
	nuchal line	trapezius	splenius, semispinalis capitis
Vertebral column	cervical	levator scapulae, rhomboid minor, spinalis, longissimus, splenius, scalenus anterior and medius	splenius, spinalis
	thoracic	latissimus dorsi, rhomboid minor and major, spinalis, splenius, semispinalis capitis, longissimus	spinalis
	lumbar	diaphragm, latissimus dorsi, psoas major and minor, spinalis, longissimus	
Sternum	manubrium	pectoralis major, sternocleidomastoid	
	body	pectoralis major, diaphragm	
	xiphoid process	transverse thoracis	external oblique, rectus abdominis
Clavicle	body	pectoralis major, deltoid, sternocleidomastoid	trapezius
Rib cage	ribs 1–12	external oblique, pectoralis major and minor, all intercostals, serratus anterior, scalenus (anterior and medius)	scalenus (anterior and medius), rectus abdominis, quadratus lumborum, transverse thoracis, all intercostals, iliocostalis
Scapula	coracoid process	biceps brachii (short head), coracobrachialis	pectoralis minor
	acromion	deltoid	trapezius
	supraglenoid tubercle	biceps brachii (long head)	
	infraglenoid tubercle	triceps brachii (long head)	
	spine of scapula	deltoid	trapezius
	lateral border	teres minor, teres major	
	inferior angle		serratus anterior
	superior angle		levator scapulae
	medial border		serratus anterior, rhomboid major and minor, levator scapulae
	supraspinous fossa	supraspinatus	
	infraspinous fossa	infraspinatus	
	subscapular fossa	subscapularis	
Humerus	greater tubercle		supraspinatus, infraspinatus, teres minor
	lesser tubercle		subscapularis
	intertubercular groove		latissimus dorsi, pectoralis major, teres major
	deltoid tuberosity		deltoid
	surface	(post.) triceps brachii (medial and lateral head), (ant.) brachialis	(med.) coracobrachialis
	medial epicondyle	pronator teres, wrist and finger flexors	
	lateral epicondyle	(upper) brachioradialis, anconeus, wrist and finger extensors, supinator	

Bone	Important landmarks	Muscles that originate	Muscles that insert
Radius	radial tuberosity		biceps brachii, (lat.) pronator teres
	styloid process		(above) brachioradialis
	surface		(ant.) pronator quadratus, (lat.) pronator teres, (ant. lat.) supinator
Wrist and hand	surface	thenar and hypothenar eminences	wrist and finger flexors and extensors, thenar and hypothenar eminences
	metacarpals		wrist and finger extensors
Ulna	surface	pronator quadratus, extensor carpi ulnaris	
	olecranon	flexor carpi ulnaris	anconeus, triceps brachii
	coronoid process	pronator teres	brachialis
Pelvic girdle	iliac crest	gluteus maximus, quadratus lumborum, tensor fasciae latae	external oblique, transversus abdominis
	sacrum	iliocostalis, latissimus dorsi, gluteus maximus, iliopsoas	
	anterior superior iliac spine	sartorius	
	anterior inferior iliac spine	rectus femoris	
	pubic crest	pectineus; adductor longus, brevis, and magnus; rectus abdominus	
	pubis	gracilis	
	ilium	iliacus, gluteus medius and minimus	
	ischial tuberosity	biceps femoris, adductor magnus, semitendinosus, semimembranosus	
Iliotibial tract (band)			gluteus maximus (to gluteal tuberosity), tensor fasciae latae
Femur	surface	(ant.) vastus intermedius	
	greater trochanter	vastus lateralis	gluteus maximus, medius, and minimus
	lesser trochanter		psoas major, iliopsoas, pectineus
	medial condyle	gastrocnemius	
	lateral condyle	gastrocnemius, popliteus	semimembranosus
	adductor tubercle		adductor magnus
	linea aspera	vastus lateralis and medialis, biceps femoris	adductor longus, brevis, magnus
Tibia	surface	flexor digitorum longus, extensor hallucis longus, tibialis anterior and posterior, soleus	(upper) semitendinosus, (med.) gracilis, (med.) sartorius, (post.) popliteus
	medial condyle		semitendinosus, semimembranosus
	lateral condyle	extensor digitorum longus	
	tibial tuberosity		rectus femoris, vastus medialis, lateralis, intermedius
Fibula	body	fibularis brevis, flexor hallucis longus, soleus	
	head	fibularis longus	biceps femoris
Calcaneus/tarsals	posterior side	flexor digitorum brevis, quadratus plantae	gastrocnemius, soleus (via tendon)
Metatarsals/ Phalanges (Digits)		extensors and flexors of toes	fibularis brevis and longus, tibialis anterior, flexor digitorum brevis

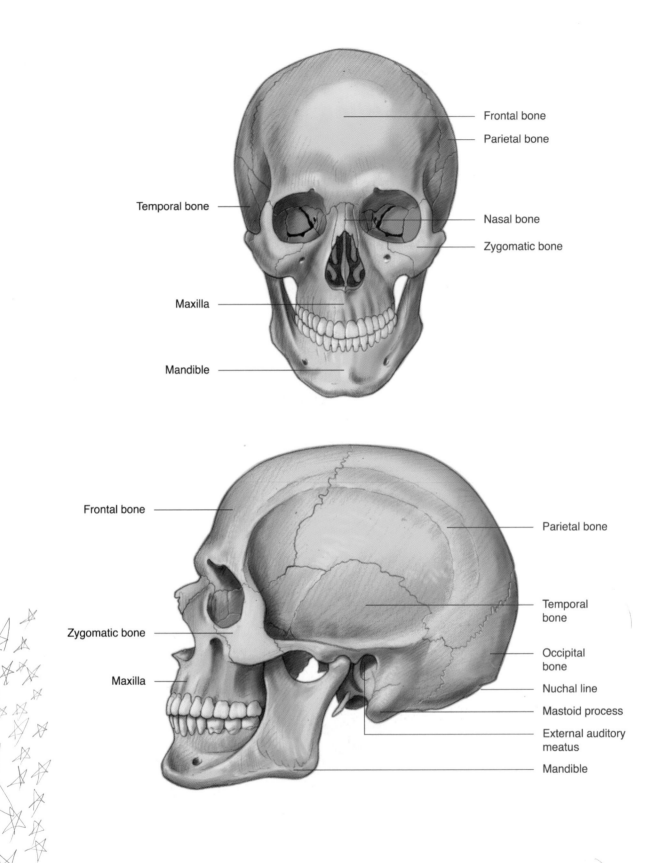

Figure 2.6: Bones of the skull, anterior and lateral views.

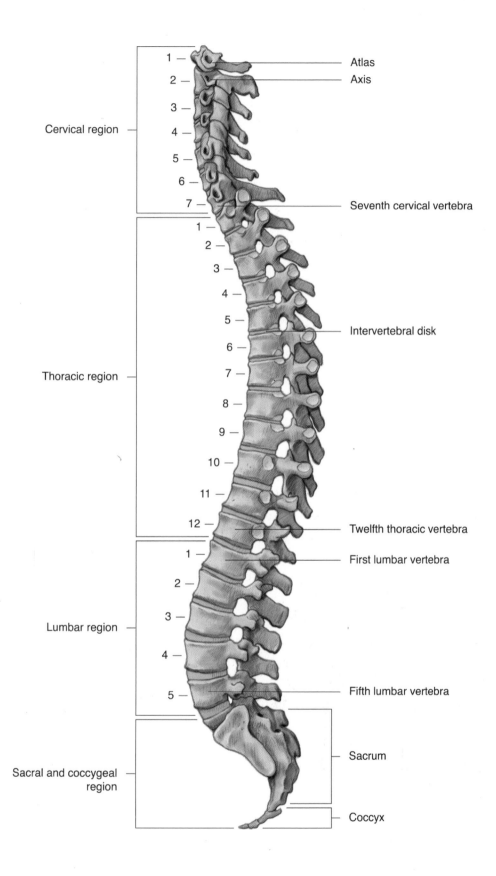

Cervical region

1 — Atlas
2 — Axis
3 —
4 —
5 —
6 —
7 — Seventh cervical vertebra

Thoracic region

1 —
2 —
3 —
4 —
5 — Intervertebral disk
6 —
7 —
8 —
9 —
10 —
11 —
12 — Twelfth thoracic vertebra

Lumbar region

1 — First lumbar vertebra
2 —
3 —
4 —
5 — Fifth lumbar vertebra

Sacral and coccygeal region

Sacrum

Coccyx

Figure 2.7: The vertebral column, lateral view.

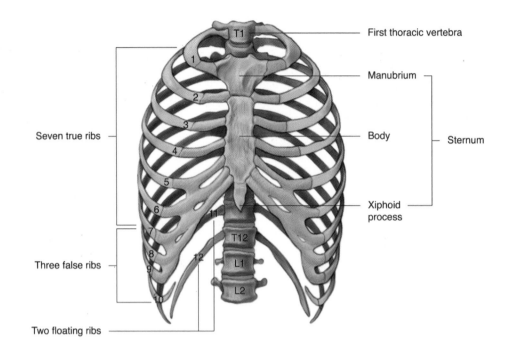

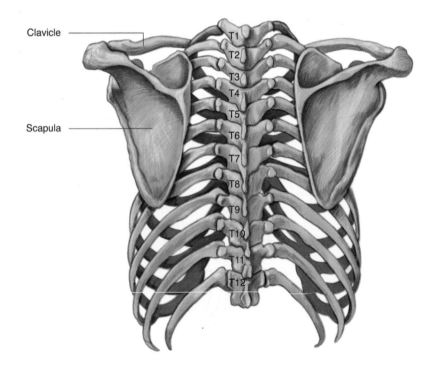

Figures 2.8 and 2.9: Thoracic cage, anterior and posterior views.

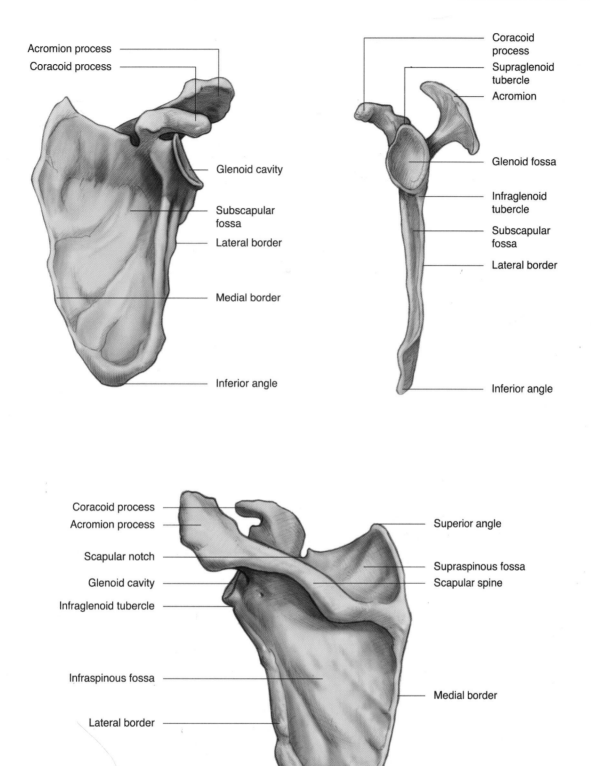

Figure 2.10: Left scapula (top left), anterior view.
Figure 2.11: Left scapula (top right), lateral view.
Figure 2.12: Left scapula (bottom), posterior view.

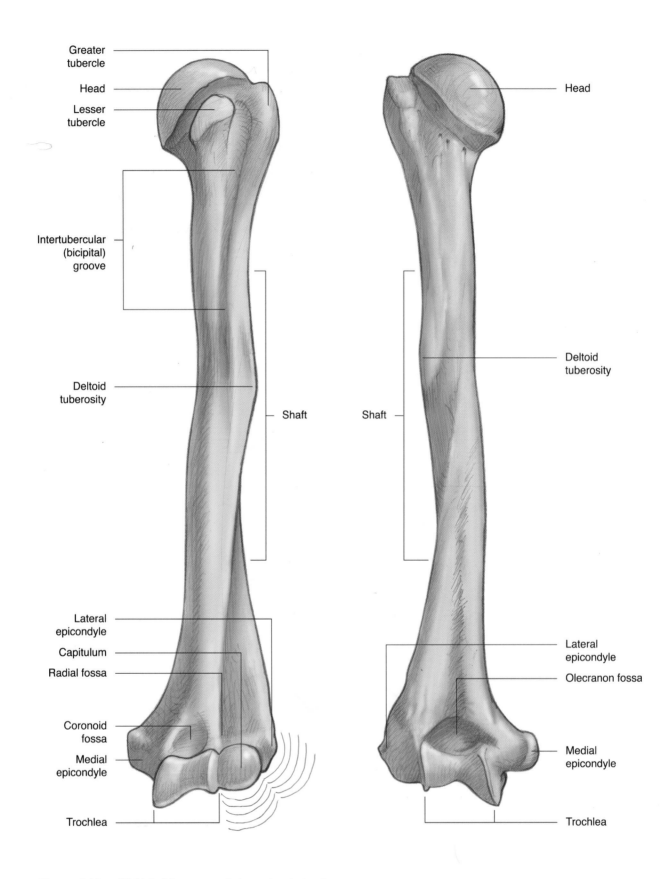

Greater
tubercle

Head

Lesser
tubercle

Intertubercular
(bicipital)
groove

Deltoid
tuberosity

Lateral
epicondyle

Capitulum

Radial fossa

Coronoid
fossa

Medial
epicondyle

Trochlea

Shaft

Head

Shaft

Deltoid
tuberosity

Shaft

Lateral
epicondyle

Olecranon fossa

Medial
epicondyle

Trochlea

Figures 2.13 and 2.14: Left humerus, anterior and posterior views.

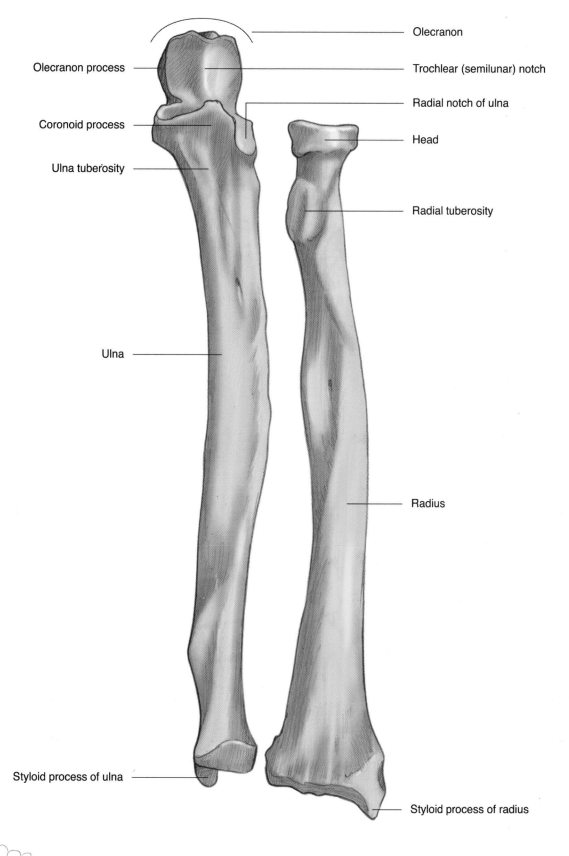

Olecranon

Olecranon process

Trochlear (semilunar) notch

Radial notch of ulna

Coronoid process

Head

Ulna tuberosity

Radial tuberosity

Ulna

Radius

Styloid process of ulna

Styloid process of radius

Figure 2.15: Left ulna and radius, anterior view.

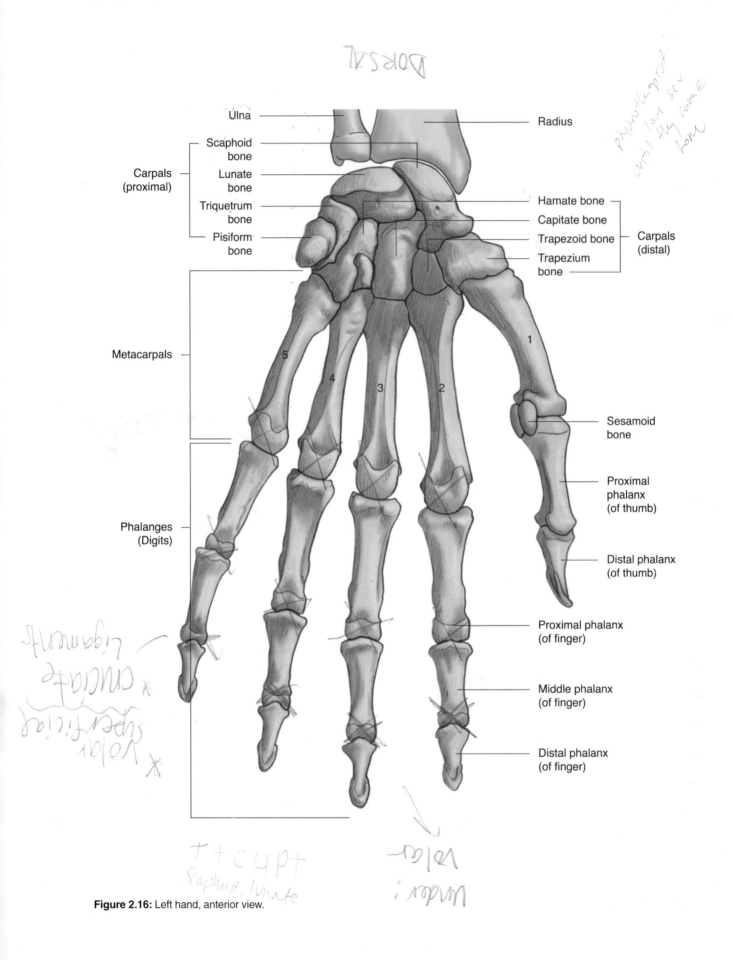

Figure 2.16: Left hand, anterior view.

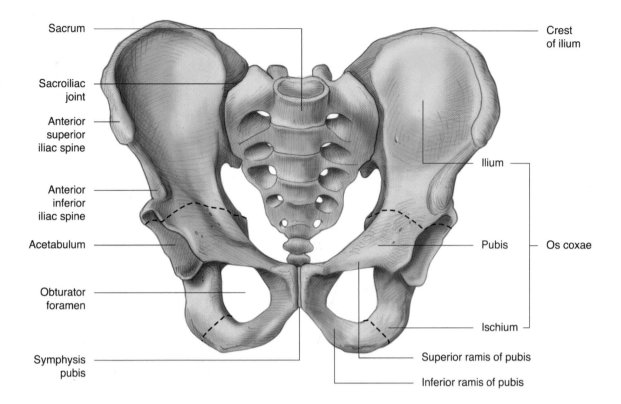

Sacrum

Sacroiliac joint

Anterior superior iliac spine

Anterior inferior iliac spine

Acetabulum

Obturator foramen

Symphysis pubis

Crest of ilium

Ilium

Pubis

Ischium

Os coxae

Superior ramis of pubis

Inferior ramis of pubis

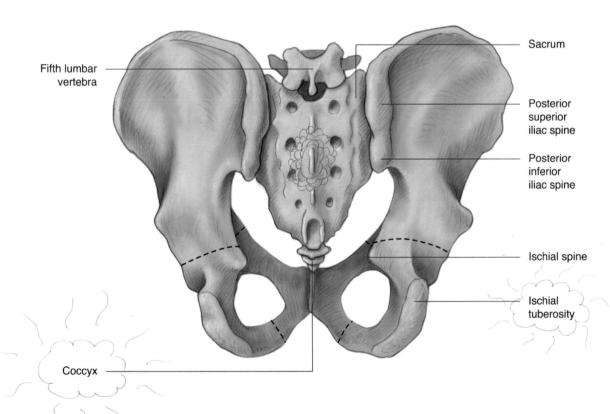

Fifth lumbar vertebra

Coccyx

Sacrum

Posterior superior iliac spine

Posterior inferior iliac spine

Ischial spine

Ischial tuberosity

Figures 2.17 and 2.18: Pelvis (male), anterior and posterior views.

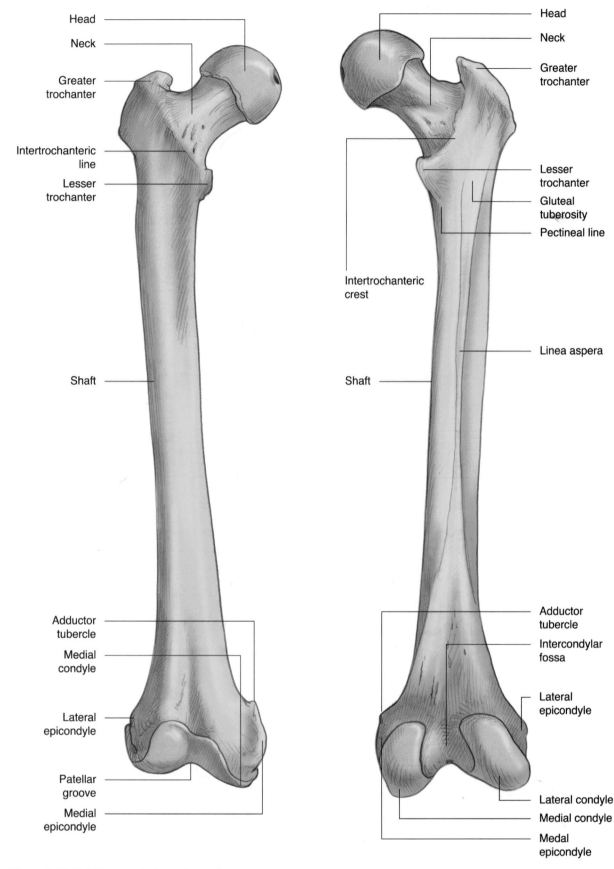

Head

Neck

Greater
trochanter

Intertrochanteric
line

Lesser
trochanter

Shaft

Adductor
tubercle

Medial
condyle

Lateral
epicondyle

Patellar
groove

Medial
epicondyle

Head

Neck

Greater
trochanter

Lesser
trochanter

Gluteal
tuberosity

Pectineal line

Intertrochanteric
crest

Linea aspera

Shaft

Adductor
tubercle

Intercondylar
fossa

Lateral
epicondyle

Lateral condyle

Medial condyle

Medal
epicondyle

Figure 2.19: Right femur, anterior and posterior.

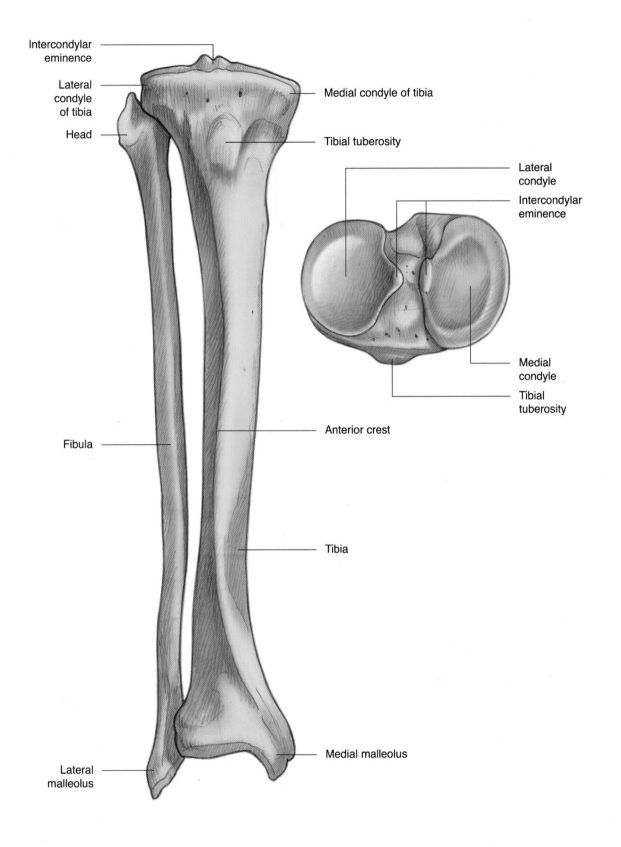

Figure 2.20: Right fibula and tibia, anterior view; and tibial plateau, superior view.

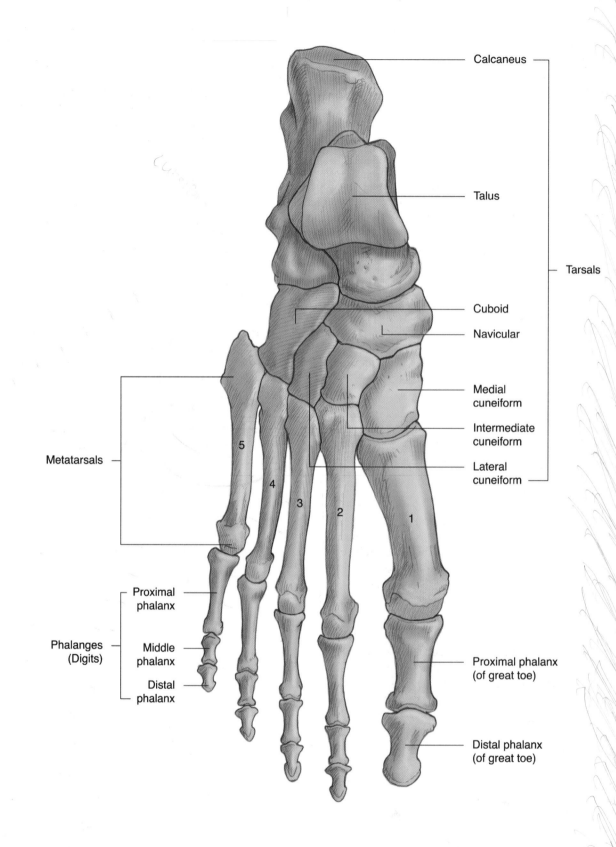

Calcaneus

Talus

Tarsals

Cuboid

Navicular

Medial
cuneiform

Intermediate
cuneiform

Lateral
cuneiform

Metatarsals

5

4

3

2

1

Phalanges
(Digits)

Proximal
phalanx

Middle
phalanx

Distal
phalanx

Proximal phalanx
(of great toe)

Distal phalanx
(of great toe)

Figure 2.21: Right foot, superior view.

BONE FORMATION AND REMODELLING

The general process by which new bone is produced is referred to as ossification (or osteogenesis). Further development occurs through a process known as remodelling, a continuous process whereby bone is created and destroyed.

Bone Formation

The ossification of bone tissue takes two forms. Compact bone begins as cartilage. Bone-forming cells (**osteoblasts**) within the cartilage discharge a gelatin-like substance (osteoid) into which inorganic salts (minerals) are deposited to form the hardened material recognized as bone. Most short bones have a single ossification centre near the middle; the long bones of the arms and legs typically have three, one at the centre of the bone and one at each end (see Figure 2.22).

Cancellous bones, on the other hand, such as the flat bones of the skull, begin as fibrous membranes. Osteoblasts release osteoid into this membrane, which forms a sponge-like bundle of fibres. The new cancellous bone formation then develops outward from these centres in the membrane. In the skull, for example, there are several such ossification centres at birth, and since bone formation is still incomplete, "soft spots" can be felt between them. (The lines where the bone from the adjacent centres meet form the cranial sutures on the surface of an adult skull.)

Bone Remodelling

Bones cannot grow by cell division as do other tissues. Rather, the process is similar to the remodelling of an office or home. Bone remodelling has two main phases: bone-resorbing cells called **osteoclasts** remove old bone by releasing acids and enzymes; following this, protein-secreting cells (the osteoblasts, mentioned above) deposit new tissue.

This remodelling process is most active during the early years of human growth, when new deposits prevail over removal of the old. Thereafter, remodelling gradually declines until about age thirty-five. From the fourth decade onward, the process reverses and resorption begins to exceed bone reformation. This results in a 5-10 percent loss in bone mass per subsequent decade.

Since bone contains about 99 percent of the body's calcium, it is particularly necessary as one gets older to ensure one has an adequate intake of calcium. If not, the overall calcium levels in the body become affected through the loss of bone tissue with aging. With calcium supplements, this problem can be minimized. Vitamin D plays a useful role in such cases by helping the body to utilize calcium supplements taken to boost one's natural levels.

EPIPHYSEAL PLATES AND LINES

For years, people believed that resistance training stunted growth. Fortunately, through research conducted on young children and resistance training, we have discovered that this is not the case. In fact, when done properly, resistance training can actually facilitate growth. This does not mean that growth cannot be stunted; it simply means that one must learn the proper techniques and follow training guidelines.

From an X-ray a doctor can tell whether or not linear growth (growth in height) continues. The presence of either an epiphyseal plate or epiphyseal line will be the determining factor. Epiphyseal plates, also known as growth plates, occur at various locations at the epiphyses of long bones as illustrated in Figure 2.22. If we were to take an X-ray of the femur illustrated, we would discover spaces at various locations throughout the epiphyses. X-rays pass through cartilage, and they appear as black spaces between the diaphysis and epiphyses. If this is the case, then linear growth is still possible. If, however, the X-ray shows a solid epiphysis, (no black spaces on the X-ray), then linear growth is not possible since the epiphyseal plates have fused or come together. They are referred to as epiphyseal lines.

Generally, children or adolescents who are still growing should avoid maximal lifts. Maximal lifts could, over time, damage the epiphyseal plates.

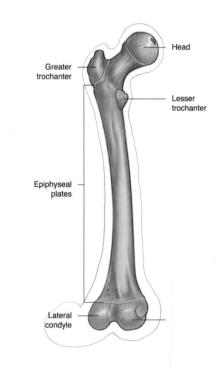

Head

Greater trochanter

Lesser trochanter

Epiphyseal plates

Lateral condyle

Figure 2.22: The primary ossification sites (left femur).

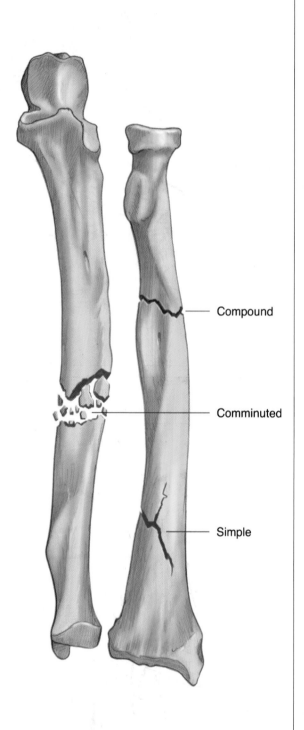

Compound

Comminuted

Simple

Figure 2.23: Fractures are distinguished by the severity of the break.

FRACTURES

Problems of the skeletal system can be associated with many factors, including nutrition, infection, and physical accidents. Many are serious and can greatly impair movement. Young children generally have weaker bones since calcification is still incomplete, whereas older people can suffer from weak bones because of the loss of calcium associated with aging.

Fractures are bone "breaks," and are normally divided into two types: simple fractures and compound fractures. With simple fractures, the bone is not exposed to the air through the skin; with compound fractures the bone is exposed. If the bone breaks through the skin, there may also be more serious complications such as muscle and ligament damage. As illustrated in Figure 2.23, fractures are also distinguished according to the type or severity of the break.

- A simple fracture occurs when there is no separation of the bone into parts, but a break or crack is detectable. This is also referred to as a "hairline fracture" or "greenstick fracture."

- A compound fracture occurs when the bone breaks into separate pieces (sometimes referred to as a "transverse fracture"). This would be the result of a major blow.

- A comminuted fracture occurs when the broken ends of the bone have been shattered into many pieces, as might occur in the case of a major automobile accident.

The symptoms of a bone fracture are sharp pain and tenderness, swelling, discolouration of the skin, and a grating or grinding movement. In serious cases, there will be an inability to use the body part supported by the bone.

Healing

Bones heal from breaks by rebuilding themselves in the same way as they grow. If the break is attended to properly, the process will go smoothly. Complications arise when there is infection at the site or if the bone repairs itself but is misaligned (and needs to be broken again and realigned). Where there is extensive damage, bone chips from another part of the body may be added to facilitate the healing process.

Serious problems arise with breaks that occur at or near joints, since these kinds of fractures will impede motion unless they are properly treated and unless they heal in alignment. Even though they may have occurred many years earlier, such breaks can be particularly troublesome as one grows older due to normal bone loss and to osteoarthritis (inflammation of joints that also involves a degeneration of the cartilage and bone).

BONE DISEASE

Physical activity has a profound effect on bone tissue, and is even believed to stimulate bone formation. The capacity of bone to replenish itself is retained even in older people.

Bone diseases range from problems related to abnormal stress on bones (for example, a dislocation due to misaligned healing or a congenital dislocation involving a defective joint at birth), to problems of metabolism and growth (for example, deficient mineralization, a condition called rickets in children and osteomalacia in adults), infectious organisms (osteomyelitis), and tumours. Bone disease can also be inherited, such as osteogenesis imperfecta (a hereditary disease affecting connective tissue) and hypophosphatasia (an inherited enzyme deficiency).

Stress Fractures

Bones are also the locations for one of the most common injuries in sports: the stress fracture. When muscles become too fatigued to absorb the shock placed on them – for example, through the continual pounding of long-distance running – the overstressed muscle transfers the impact to the bone. This causes the bone to develop a tiny crack, or stress fracture.

Stress fractures can be caused by a rapid increase in activity when an athlete switches to a new surface for training – such as a soccer player who is used to playing on grass and then moves to a harder gym floor for indoor training and competition – or poor footwear with improper cushioning capability. Experts recommend, first and foremost, that those who suffer a stress fracture take six to eight weeks of rest from the activity that caused the injury, and all related activities. If the activity that caused the stress fracture is resumed too quickly, larger stress fractures can develop that take much longer to heal. (Stress fractures are discussed further in the context of sport injuries, which begins on page 72.)

Effects of Aging on the Skeletal System

By far, the most widespread serious medical problem associated with bones is osteoporosis. Osteoporosis (or porous bone) is a degenerative condition that involves low bone mass as well as a deterioration of the bone tissue. It leads to bone fragility and, therefore, an increased susceptibility to bone fractures, especially of the hip, spine, and wrist. Whereas a certain amount of bone mass is lost naturally during aging, this process can be slowed down by good nutrition and moderate exercise throughout one's life.

Osteoporosis is sometimes called the "silent disease" because people may not know that they have osteoporosis until their bones become so weak that a sudden bump or fall causes a fracture or a vertebra to collapse. Collapsed vertebrae may initially be felt as severe back pain and may involve loss of height or spinal deformities such as kyphosis (stooped posture). According to the National Osteoporosis Foundation, women can lose up to 20 percent of their bone mass in the five to seven years following menopause, making them more susceptible to osteoporosis.

Building strong bones during childhood and adolescence is the best defense against developing osteoporosis later. There are four recommended steps that will help to prevent osteoporosis:

- a balanced diet rich in calcium and vitamin D;
- weight-bearing exercise;
- a healthy lifestyle (no smoking or excessive alcohol); and
- bone density testing and medication when appropriate.

Although there is still no cure for osteoporosis, these precautions will aid in preventing its onset.

While osteoporosis is a bone disease that has traditionally been associated with older women who have undergone menopause, it also has an unfortunate link to exercise. In many young women, this condition is part of the so-called "**female triad**" (see page 326 for more on this phenomenon) and occurs when excessive exercise, poor diet, and weight loss combine to cause damage to bones. A lack of calcium in the diet is the main reason for this condition. Most experts recommend consulting a nutritionist to develop a diet that is appropriate to one's exercise needs and includes sufficient amounts of calcium for healthy bone development and maintenance.

WHERE DO WE GO FROM HERE?

In this section we have examined the basic structure of the human skeleton, and its function in supporting the body. Although it is an analogy that has been used many times, it is nevertheless apt to consider the skeletal system to be the body's "frame." It provides a crucial supporting role for the muscles, as well as protecting organs such as the brain, heart, and lungs. Knowledge of the skeletal system also provides a "frame" upon which to hang information about the body's key functions.

In the following section, we will look at the muscular system, which operates in closest harmony with the human skeleton to produce movement. We will examine a wide range of muscular concepts related to exercise and physical activity, including the composition of muscle, and its function and location throughout the body.

Daniel Igali waves the Canadian flag after winning the gold medal in wrestling at the 2000 Sydney Olympic Games (CP PHOTO/COA).

3

The Muscular System

"Muscles come and go; flab lasts."
— American social commentator Bill Vaughan

KEY CONCEPTS

- Muscle tissue
- Tendons
- Skeletal muscles
- Cardiac muscles
- Smooth muscles
- Neuromuscular system
- Muscle twitch
- Motor unit
- Neuromuscular junctions
- All-or-none principle
- Perimysium
- Epimysium

- Endomysium
- Sarcolemma
- Sarcoplasm
- Myofibrils
- Sarcomere
- Adductor muscles
- Abductor muscles
- Extensor muscles
- Flexor muscles
- Agonist muscle
- Antagonist muscle
- Origin and insertion

- Isotonic exercise
- Isometric exercise
- Isokinetic exercise
- Sliding filament theory
- Myosin crossbridges
- Adenosine triphosphate
- Transient/chronic hypertrophy
- Muscle atrophy
- Hyperplasia
- Excitation-contraction coupling
- Transverse tubulae system
- Troponin and tropomyosin

Anyone who has ever felt soreness after a workout, bike ride, or a session of moving heavy items knows that we use muscles in all kinds of ways, and place demands on them to perform a wide range of tasks. Indeed, there are many muscles in the human body that we cannot see but which perform a huge number of crucial tasks that help to keep us alive, such as providing support for the skeleton and our many organs.

There are more than 600 muscles in the human body. Muscles are responsible for our breathing and eating – even the beating of our heart involves, in large part, muscle activity. See Figures 3.8 and 3.9 on pages 44 and 45 for the major muscles and muscle groups.

THREE TYPES OF MUSCLES

When classifying anatomical parts, scientists define *tissue* as masses of cells that are similar in function and form (along with the intercellular substances they produce). Muscle tissue refers to a collection of cells that shorten during contraction and, in doing so, create tension that results in movement of one kind or another. For the purposes of skeletal movement, this action is usually achieved by means of tendons, tough bands of connective tissue that join muscles with bones and transmit the force that the muscle exerts.

In humans (and other mammals) muscle tissue can be classified into three main groups, based on the tissue's structure and function: skeletal muscles, cardiac muscles, and smooth muscles.

Skeletal Muscles

Skeletal muscles are those muscles that are attached to the bones (by tendons and other tissue) and are the most prevalent in the human body. They comprise 30-40 percent of human body weight. Skeletal muscles are *voluntary* – humans have conscious control over their skeletal muscles; that is, the brain can tell them what to do. Skeletal muscle tissue is also referred to as "striated" (or striped) because of its appearance under a microscope as a series of alternating light and dark stripes.

Cardiac Muscles

Cardiac muscles are, as the name suggests, found in only one place in the body – the heart. They are responsible for creating the action that pumps blood from the heart to the rest of the body and form the heart's thick wall. Cardiac muscles are *involuntary muscles* because they are not controlled consciously, and are instead directed to act by the autonomic nervous system. Like skeletal muscle tissue, cardiac tissue is also striated.

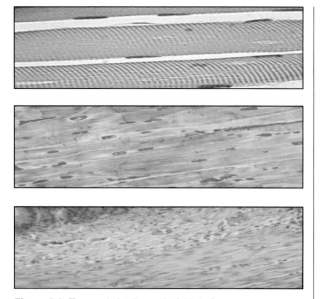

Figure 3.1: Top — skeletal muscle (striated);
Middle — cardiac muscle (striated);
Lower — smooth muscle (dense sheets).

Smooth Muscles

Surrounding the body's internal organs, including the blood vessels, hair follicles, and the urinary, genital, and digestive tracts, are smooth muscles. This type of muscle tissue contracts more slowly than skeletal muscles, but can remain contracted for longer periods of time. Smooth muscles are also involuntary, and their spindle-shaped fibres are usually arranged in dense sheets.

The properties of muscle fibre are listed in Table 3.1, below.

Table 3.1: Properties of muscle fibre	
Irritability	This refers to the ability of a muscle to respond to a stimulus.
Contractibility	This refers to the muscle's ability to shorten in length.
Elasticity	This refers to a muscle's ability to stretch and return to its normal position.
Extensibility	This refers to a muscle's ability to extend in length.
Conductivity	This refers to a muscle's ability to transmit nerve impulses.

THE NEUROMUSCULAR SYSTEM

The neuromuscular system is a general term referring to these complex linkages between the muscular system (the various groups of muscles in the human body) and the nervous system (the system of nervous impulses originating in the brain and spinal cord). This involves two sophisticated bodily systems "linking up" and working together in a complex interface. The actual steps in this process are discussed a little later in this section.

When you prepare to kick a soccer ball, to take a simple example, the messages needed to execute this action are sent from the brain or spinal cord and ultimately cause a chemical reaction in the leg muscle area. All of this happens in an instant, and many nerves and muscles are affected, yet kicking the soccer ball is seemingly effortless.

Constant use and regular practice will improve the quality and efficiency of these two systems, and their ability to work together. In Unit 2, you will build on the knowledge you have gained here and see how to incorporate strength-training programs that will further develop your athletic performance levels. Figure 3.2 below shows the junction point between the nervous and muscular systems (the **neuromuscular junction**) along with some key components and structures.

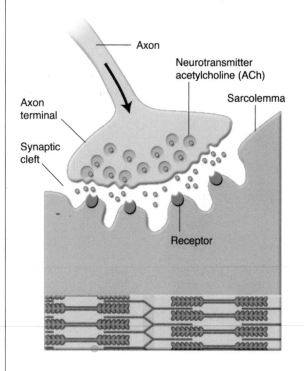

Figure 3.2: The neuromuscular junction.

THE MOTOR UNIT

Nerves transmit impulses in "waves" that ensure smooth movements. A single nervous impulse and the resulting contraction is called a **muscle twitch**. (Muscle twitch is discussed more extensively later in this Unit.) One neuron or nerve (called the "motor neuron") may be responsible for stimulating a number of muscle fibres. As illustrated in Figure 3.3, the motor neuron, its axon (pathway), and the muscle fibres it stimulates are together referred to as the **motor unit**.

The nerves that transmit the message directing the muscle to move come into contact with the muscles at points called **neuromuscular junctions** (see Figure 3.2). The electrical impulse travels along nerve pathways to the contact point between the nerve and a muscle (the junction). There, a chemical "neurotransmitter" is then released (the chemical acetylcholine). This chemical is detected by receptors on the surface of the muscle fibre, and the process ultimately results in muscle contraction. (A discussion of the sliding filament theory and excitation-contraction coupling begins on page 40.) The entire process is an excellent example of the principle of energy transfer – electrical energy ultimately reaches the surface of the muscle fibre, is converted to chemical energy, and is eventually transformed into mechanical work.

The All-or-None Principle

Motor units can be categorized into small or large units. Simply stated, this means that a small motor unit can have a few muscle fibres that it stimulates, which produce fine motor (muscle) movement (such as the motor units of the eye). Other motor units, such as the ones found within the quadriceps group, are larger and produce gross (large) motor movements.

A single motor unit within the quadriceps may stimulate 300 to 800 muscle fibres. In order for maximal muscle force to be produced, all motor units within that muscle or muscle group must be recruited (such as in a maximal squat lift in the case of the quadriceps). Each motor unit must fire and contract at the same time. This could include thousands of motor units contracting to their fullest. Generally, slow-twitch muscle motor units are smaller because they have fewer muscle fibres than fast-twitch motor units.

Motor units also comply to a rule known as the **all-or-none principle** (or law). This principle stipulates that, when a motor unit is stimulated to contract, it will do so to its fullest potential. In other words, if a motor unit consists of 10 muscle fibres (or 800) and they are "turned on," either all fibres will contract or none will contract.

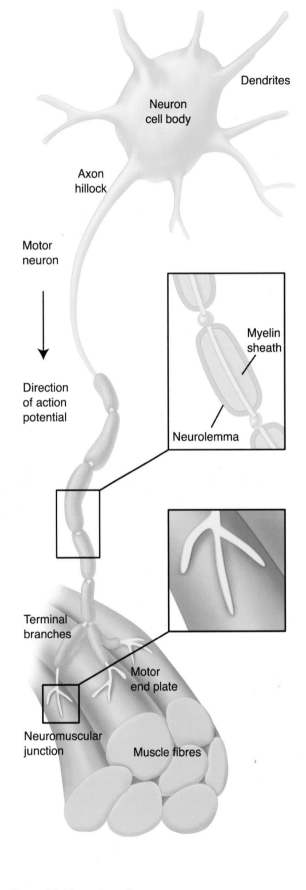

Figure 3.3: The motor unit.

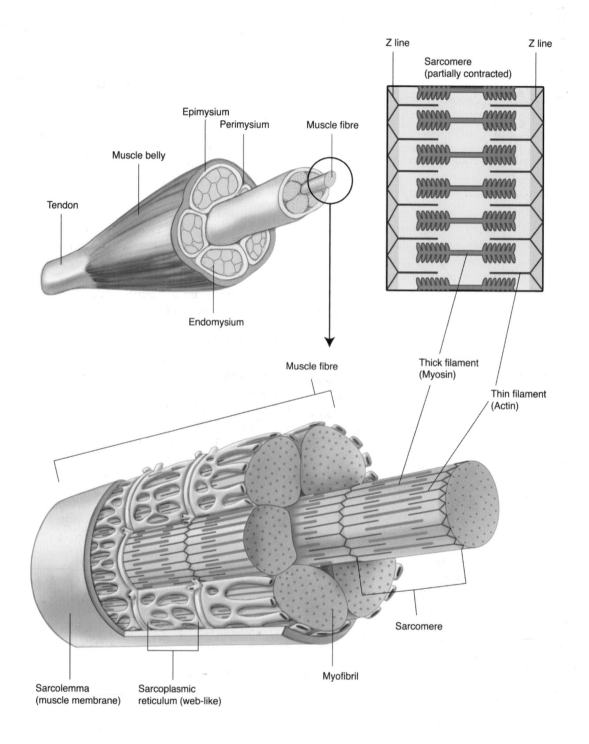

Figure 3.4: Myosin and actin filaments interact at the molecular level. This action is synchronized across the muscle fibre and contraction of the entire fibre occurs.

THE ANATOMY OF SKELETAL MUSCLE

As a substantial portion of human body weight is made up of skeletal muscles, and these muscles are directly involved in movement and locomotion, we will now look more closely at this type.

The basic unit of skeletal muscle is the individual muscle fibre. If we look outward and inward from this basic unit, we can better see how skeletal muscle as a whole is constructed (see Figure 3.4).

Looking Outward

Looking outward, a sheath of connective tissue (the perimysium) binds groups of muscle fibres together. These bundles (fasciculi) in turn are bound together by a larger and stronger sheath (the epimysium) that envelopes the entire muscle.

The epimysium then extends beyond the muscle and changes its properties as it becomes one with the tendon. This tendon will now extend itself and becomes one with the bone's periosteum. This happens at both ends of the attachment sites (that is, both at the muscle's origin and at its insertion).

Looking Inward

Looking inward, a sheath of connective tissue (the endomysium) also surrounds the muscle fibre. Beneath the endomysium lies a plasma membrane (the sarcolemma), which contains the muscle cell's cytoplasm (the sarcoplasm).

Running along the muscle fibre's length are thread-like structures (myofibrils). Within these are finer "thick" and "thin" filaments (the cellular proteins myosin and actin). Myosin and actin themselves are contained within compartments (sarcomeres). Myosin is comprised of a "head" and "tail" and looks similar to a golf club. The myosin head has an attachment site for actin, and actin has a binding site for the myosin head. Actin has two other proteins: troponin, which has a binding site for calcium, and tropomyosin, which is the "stringy looking" cord-like structure that covers the binding site on actin (see Figure 3.6). Together, these two proteins behave like a swivel-locking mechanism – they will not allow the myosin head to attach until calcium is released by the sarcoplasmic reticulum. This sequence is discussed in detail on page 42 under "Excitation-Contraction Coupling."

During contraction, these protein filaments interact at the molecular level causing them to slide across one another (i.e., the sarcomere shortens). This sliding action is synchronized across the muscle, and what we see and know as muscle contraction occurs. This mechanism is discussed further below under the heading "Sliding Filament Theory" (see page 40).

NAMING MUSCLES

The name given to a muscle often reveals the main kind of functional movement that the muscle permits. Some examples will illustrate this.

Adductor muscles squeeze limbs in towards the median line of the body. For example, the three muscles of the thigh – the adductor longus, adductor brevis, and adductor magnus – are attached along the femur and their main role is squeezing the thighs together. Abductor muscles, on the other hand, "push out" from the median line of body. In the hand, the abductor digiti minimi manus acts upon the little finger, and both the abductor pollicis longus and abductor pollicis brevis act upon the thumb.

Extensor muscles extend the limbs and increase the angle between two limbs. Extensor movement is usually directed backward (with the exception of the knee joint). For example, the extensor carpi radialis brevis, extensor carpi radialis longus, and extensor carpi ulnaris run from the humerus along the back of the forearm to the metacarpal bones at the back of the hand and wrist and are named for this function. Flexor muscles, on the other hand, withdraw the limbs and thereby decrease the angle between bones on two sides of a joint. The flexor carpi radialis and flexor carpi ulnaris stretch from the humerus along the inside of the forearm to the metacarpal bones of the hand, and flex the wrist.

Table 3.2 below indicates other reasons why muscles are named the way they are.

Table 3.2: How muscles are named	
Action of the muscle	Flexion, extension (flexor carpi ulnaris, extensor carpi ulnaris)
Direction of the fibres	Rectus, transversus (rectus abdominus, transversus abdominus)
Location of the muscle	Anterior, posterior (tibialis anterior, tibialis posterior)
Number of divisions/heads	Number of heads (2 or 3) (biceps brachii, triceps brachii)
Shape of the muscle	Deltoid (resembling the Greek letter, *delta*), trapezius (resembling a trapezoid)
Muscle's points of attachment	Sternum, clavicle, mastoid process (sternocleidomastoid)

HOW MUSCLES ATTACH TO BONE

Skeletal muscle is attached to the bone either indirectly or directly. The most common of the two forms of attachment is the indirect method.

- **Indirect attachment.** When attached indirectly, the epimysium (the sheath of connective tissue that surrounds the exterior of the muscle fibre) extends past the muscle as a tendon and then attaches to the periosteum of bone.

- **Direct attachment.** When attached directly, the epimysium adheres to and fuses with the periosteum (the outer membrane that covers the bone).

Antagonistic Pairs

Whether attached directly or indirectly, skeletal muscles are arranged as opposing pairs (see Table 3.3 for examples). Since a muscle cannot expand, another muscle (e.g., the extensor) is required to move the bone in the opposite direction and stretch the first muscle (known as the flexor). The flexor and extensor in this case are described as antagonistic muscles.

The muscle primarily responsible for movement of a body part is referred to as the agonist muscle. The muscle that counteracts the agonist, lengthening when the agonist muscle contracts, is the antagonist muscle.

This antagonistic pairing of muscles can be illustrated by the example of the human ankle. The tibialis anterior muscle (which originates at the upper half of the tibia) dorsiflexes the ankle (i.e., raising the toes) and the soleus muscle (whose origin is the posterior surface of the fibula) extends the ankle. These two muscles comprise an antagonistic muscle pair. (In this case, the gastrocnemius muscle helps the soleus.) The same ankle joint also exhibits inversion (where the sole of the foot faces the other leg) and eversion (the opposite movement). These movements are controlled by the tibialis posterior, which inverts the ankle, and the fibularis (peroneal) muscles, which are antagonistic and evert the ankle.

Origin and Insertion

When skeletal muscle contracts, it causes movement of the attached bones. The point where the muscle attaches to the more stationary of the bones of the axial skeleton is known as the origin. The other end, the point where the muscle attaches to the bone that is moved most, is known as the insertion.

For example, the short head of biceps brachii originates from the "coracoid process" of the scapula. When you contract your biceps, you pull your forearm towards your shoulder, so you are pulling towards the origin, while the origin stays relatively fixed in its position. The insertion is on one of the bones of the forearm (the radius), called the radial tuberosity, and it is the forearm that moves during contraction.

Major Muscles: Origin, Insertion, and Function

The series of muscle illustrations beginning with Figure 3.10 (along with tables on the opposing pages) show some of the major muscles and muscle groups, as well as their origin, insertion, and function. The bone and landmark where specific muscles attach are highlighted in bold type for easier identification.

When studying these tables, try to remember the muscle's function, as one can usually determine the bones they attach to once function is determined. Also remember that the origin usually stays fixed and the insertion moves closer to it.

Table 3.3: Examples of opposing muscles and muscle groups		
	AGONIST (Prime Mover)	**ANTAGONIST**
Elbow flexion	Biceps brachii	Triceps brachii
Shoulder abduction	Deltoid	Latissimus dorsi
Medial shoulder rotation	Pectoralis major	Infraspinatus
Knee extension	Quadriceps	Hamstrings
Wrist flexion	Flexor carpi radialis	Extensor carpi radialis
Dorsi flexion	Tibialis anterior	Gastrocnemius
Trunk flexion	Rectus abdominis	Erector spinae group
Hip flexion	Iliopsoas	Gluteus maximus

TYPES OF MUSCLE CONTRACTION

The contraction of a muscle does not necessarily mean that the muscle shortens but merely that tension has been generated. There are three types of muscle contraction, as illustrated in Figure 3.5.

1. **Concentric** (shortening). This occurs when muscle fibres shorten – for example, the biceps shorten when lifting an object.
2. **Eccentric** (lengthening). This occurs when the muscle fibres lengthen – for example, the biceps lengthens as the same weight is placed back on the ground.
3. **Isometric** (static). This occurs when the muscle fibres do not change in length – for example, when you try to lift an immovable object.

Muscle Contraction during Exercise

Below is a description of isotonic, isometric, and isokinetic exercise, and their relationship to muscle contraction.

Isotonic exercise involves a controlled shortening (concentric contraction) and lengthening of the muscle. A classic example is weight training with dumbbells and barbells. As the weight is lifted throughout the range of motion, the muscle shortens. Free body weight exercises are also a good example of isotonic exercise. These kinds of exercise include chin-ups, push-ups, and sit-ups, all of which use body weight as the resistance force.

With isometric exercise, on the other hand, the muscle fibres maintain a constant length throughout the entire contraction and there is no motion. These exercises are usually performed against an immovable surface or object (such as pressing one's arms against a wall). This kind of training is especially effective for developing particular muscles or groups and is used in rehabilitation exercise programs for just this reason. Isometric training provides a relatively quick and convenient method for strengthening muscles without special equipment and with little chance of injury.

Isokinetic exercise involves using machines to control the speed of contractions within the range of a muscle's motion and thereby seeks to combine the best features of both isometric and isotonic training. Such devices allow for force to be exerted at a constant and pre-set speed through the full range of motion. For example, with an isokinetic knee-extension machine, no matter how hard and fast the individual works, the apparatus will only allow him or her to exert a force equal to the selected speed or weight. Such advanced machines are used by high-performance training centres and professional teams and are not readily available to the public.

Table 3.4: Advantages and disadvantages of different types of exercise

	ADVANTAGES	DISADVANTAGES
Isotonic Training	Relatively cheap	Uneven force throughout each exercise
	Ability to exercise all major muscle groups	Exercises may not fully strengthen each muscle group
Isometric Training	Very cheap and convenient	Will increase strength at one joint angle at a time
	Specific muscles can be isolated	Can be only part of a strength training program

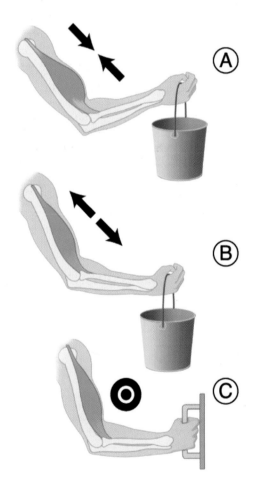

Figure 3.5: Types of contraction: (A) concentric, (B) eccentric, and (C) isometric.

Sliding Filament Theory
Brushing your teeth

When you decide to brush your teeth, one of the most important motions is the voluntary action of lifting the toothbrush to your teeth. A closer physiological look shows how this is accomplished.

Just before the biceps brachii is activated, the following occurs, leading to activation:

1. A message originates and is released from the central nervous system, specifically at the elbow flexor control centre of the brain.

2. The message travels down the spinal cord and branches off at shoulder level and travels to the peripheral nervous system.

3. The message then travels from the axon branch to the axon terminal of the elbow flexors. Since the weight of the toothbrush is minimal, only a few muscle fibres (a small motor unit) will be recruited.

4. The message is carried through the axon terminal via acetylcholine (ACh) to the sarcolemma of each muscle fibre involved.

5. ACh causes the sarcoplasmic reticulum to release calcium ions from the terminal cisterna.

6. The calcium ions then find their way to attachment sites on troponin, which are located on the actin's tropomyosin.

7. The tropomyosin swivels, causing the binding sites for myosin on the actin filament to be exposed.

8. The myosin heads attach themselves to the binding sites on actin.

9. ATP is broken down by ATPase, causing the power stroke and the sliding of actin along the myosin filament.

10. Contraction of the filaments will continue until you decide to stop the activation of the biceps brachii muscle. As long as calcium is present, contraction will continue.

11. Once you decide to stop the activation, calcium will be removed into the sarcoplasmic reticulum. Troponin and tropomyosin will once again cover the binding sites for myosin on the actin filament, and the muscle will return to a resting state.

This process occurs each and every time we decide to use our muscles, whether during exercise or in common daily activities.

"SLIDING FILAMENT THEORY" OF MUSCLE CONTRACTION

Muscles "pull"; they never "push" (a limb may push but it is the result of a muscle pulling on the bones). A muscle will shorten (contract) and move the object if the load is light; it will remain the same length if the load equals the muscle strength. But the basic mechanism is one of contraction so as to move limbs or maintain a certain position or posture.

Myosin Crossbridges

However, whereas the muscle as a whole contracts, the mechanism by which this is achieved is not through a shortening but rather an overlapping of the actin and myosin filaments, relative to one another. This causes the sarcomere (and thus the whole muscle fibre) to contract (i.e., to shorten). This is known as the sliding filament theory of muscle contraction and is accepted as a description of the process of muscular contraction. (See Figure 3.6.) The discovery of sliding filaments dates back to the 1950s and accurately describes what happens during contraction, but it does not explain why it happens. What causes the filaments to slide in the first place, and what is the energy source and mechanism enabling this to happen?

The explanation for the sliding of the filaments is that a special set of conditions are created that causes the thick and thin filaments to interact at the molecular level. In fact, at very high levels of magnification, it is possible to detect small bridges on the thick filaments that extend to the thin filaments. Over and over, these myosin crossbridges, as they are referred to, attach, rotate, detach, and reattach in rapid succession (in a ratchet-like fashion). This process results in the sliding or overlap of the filaments, a shortening of the sarcomere, and what we see and know as "muscle contraction."

The Role of Adenosine Triphosphate (ATP)

At the molecular level, the "trigger mechanism" for the sliding filament process is the release of calcium ions when the nerve impulse is transmitted through the muscle fibre. The release of calcium (in the presence of the proteins troponin and tropomyosin) facilitates (or removes the obstacles to) the interaction of myosin and actin molecules. The energy source behind the release of calcium is adenosine triphosphate (ATP), the energy-carrying molecule that results from food metabolism. ATP is also used to detach myosin from the actin molecule. As the work of the muscle increases, more and more ATP is used up and must be replaced through food metabolism for the process to continue.

A discussion of the role of ATP is provided in the section on "Energy Systems" (beginning on page 81).

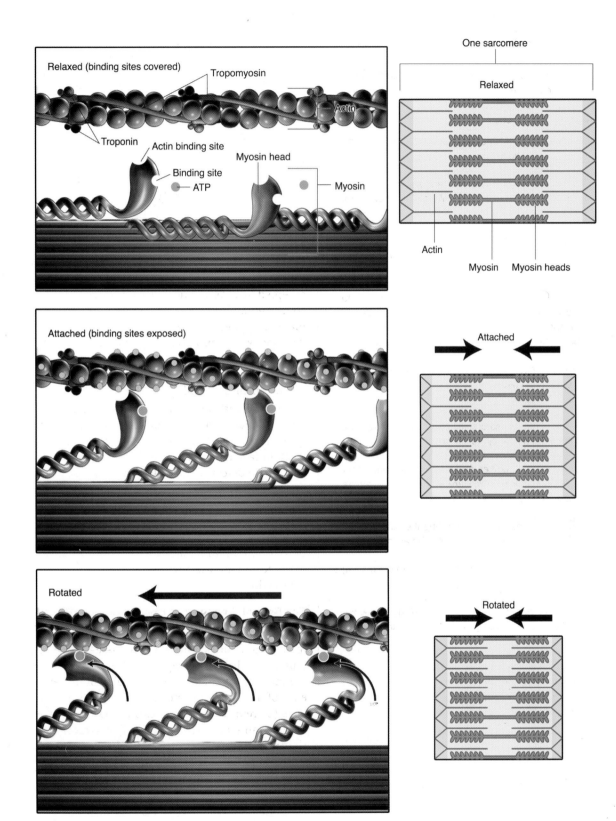

Figure 3.6: The mechanism of the sliding filament theory.

Muscle Fibre
Responses to training

When a muscle is exercised, its fibres react in two basic ways, both of which contribute to a muscle's size and strength.

Hypertrophy is defined simply as muscle growth in response to overload training. Hypertrophy occurs primarily as enlargement of the individual fibres – in other words, as the muscle fibres grow, so do the muscles themselves.

There are two types of hypertrophy: transient and chronic. Transient hypertrophy is commonly called "the pump." It is associated with an increase in fluid accumulation (edema) to the specific muscle or muscles exercised. After finishing a few sets of biceps curls, bench presses, or any other exercise, a sudden rush of blood to the muscles make them look bigger instantly. This type of hypertrophy does not last. Shortly after the completion of the exercise, the blood leaves the area and seeks newly worked muscles to nourish. Chronic hypertrophy is what most of us seek. It sticks around for days, months, or years, depending on the level of intensity and the frequency of your workouts. It is a result of long-term resistance training. Generally, the increase in muscle size is thought to be a result of

- increased capillary density;
- increased muscle proteins, actin and myosin; and
- increased storage capacity for glucose, glycogen, ATP, and CP.

Physiologists often speak of preferential hypertrophy, that is, the tendency of certain fibre types to respond to certain types of stress. To study the effects of hypertrophy, researchers take cross-sections of fibres before and after a period of exercise to see how they have grown. For example, one landmark study showed that an 11 percent increase in arm circumference took place after a five-month weight-training program, and another showed a 9.3 percent increase in the cross-section area of the quadriceps muscles of a group of men after twelve weeks of training.

The opposite process, known as muscle atrophy, occurs when a muscle is not exercised, and results in a shrinking of muscle size and strength. Atrophy can also occur following malnutrition and disease or after a long-term resistance program has been abandoned.

One of the more controversial theories in muscle gain is that of hyperplasia, a phenomenon that has yet to be proven to occur in humans. Hyperplasia is literally defined as "fibre splitting." The idea is that, once a fibre has reached its maximal hypertrophy, any further size and strength gains will come only through the formation of two "daughter cells," created by fibre splitting. To date, this has only been proven to occur in animals.

EXCITATION-CONTRACTION COUPLING

As described above, muscles work essentially by converting chemical energy (ATP) into mechanical energy. The process as a whole is often referred to as excitation-contraction coupling.

The electrical signal that begins the process originates in the spinal cord and moves along the nerve axon to the neuromuscular junction, the contact point of the motor nerve with the muscle fibre. Once there, the signal is then transmitted by chemical means across the synapse to the muscle fibre through the release of acetylcholine at the nerve terminal.

The Transverse Tubulae

The signal is then transmitted down into the muscle fibre through tubular membranes. The transverse tubulae system is a network of interconnecting rings, each of which surrounds a myofibril, and serves as a link between the outside of the muscle fibre and the actin and myosin deeper inside (see Figure 3.7).

By a process that is yet not fully understood, a change takes place in the electrical properties of the tubulae. This change causes a rapid release of calcium ions (the energy for which is provided by ATP), which in turn sets off a series of other chemical reactions, leading to contraction of the muscle fibre. The signal for the contraction to begin is synchronized over the entire muscle fibre such that all of the myofibrils (which together make up the sarcomere) shorten simultaneously.

The Role of Calcium

The release of calcium ions is the critical "trigger mechanism" in this complex process. Calcium ions are released into the sarcoplasm (the complex of substances external to the nuclear membrane of a muscle cell) by the **terminal cisternae**. These cisternae sacs form part of the **sarcoplasmic reticulum** (a network of membranes surrounding the myofibrils).

On the actin filament, there is one troponin and one tropomyosin molecule for every seven actin units. These troponin and tropomyosin proteins serve to "inhibit" or regulate the interaction of actin and myosin. If calcium is not present, the actin and myosin proteins do not interact.

The interaction of calcium with troponin and tropomyosin removes this obstacle to actin-myosin interaction (although the exact process by which this interaction is brought about at the molecular level is not fully agreed upon). The "coupling" effect is then allowed to unfold, and muscle contraction occurs.

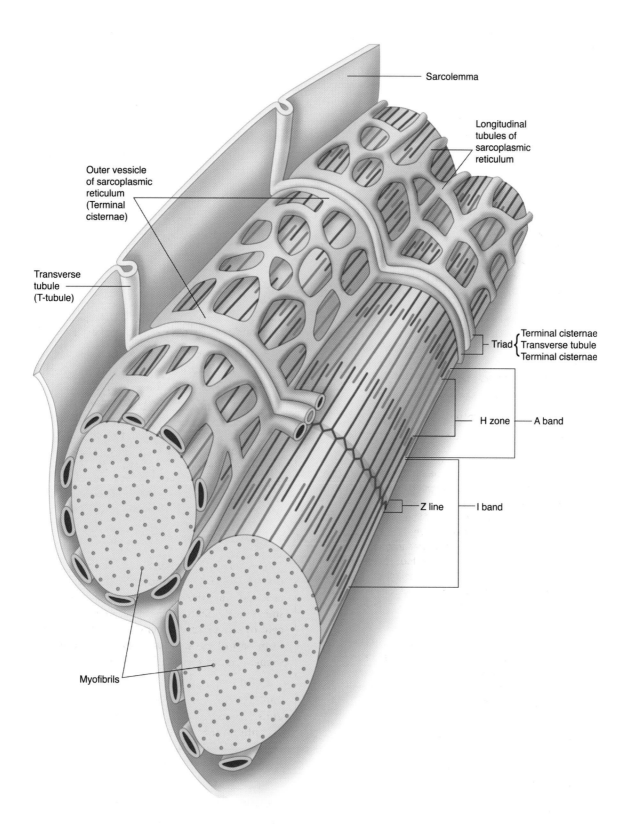

Figure 3.7: The structure of muscle fibre, illustrating the sarcoplasmic reticulum and the transverse tubulae system.

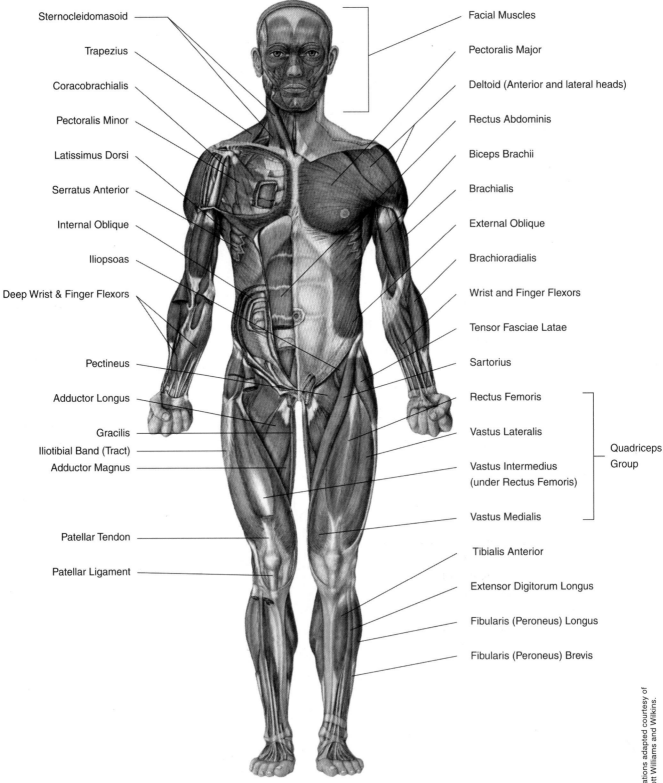

Sternocleidomasoid

Trapezius

Coracobrachialis

Pectoralis Minor

Latissimus Dorsi

Serratus Anterior

Internal Oblique

Iliopsoas

Deep Wrist & Finger Flexors

Pectineus

Adductor Longus

Gracilis

Iliotibial Band (Tract)

Adductor Magnus

Patellar Tendon

Patellar Ligament

Facial Muscles

Pectoralis Major

Deltoid (Anterior and lateral heads)

Rectus Abdominis

Biceps Brachii

Brachialis

External Oblique

Brachioradialis

Wrist and Finger Flexors

Tensor Fasciae Latae

Sartorius

Rectus Femoris

Vastus Lateralis

Vastus Intermedius
(under Rectus Femoris)

Vastus Medialis

Quadriceps
Group

Tibialis Anterior

Extensor Digitorum Longus

Fibularis (Peroneus) Longus

Fibularis (Peroneus) Brevis

Figure 3.8: Major muscles and muscle groups (anterior view).

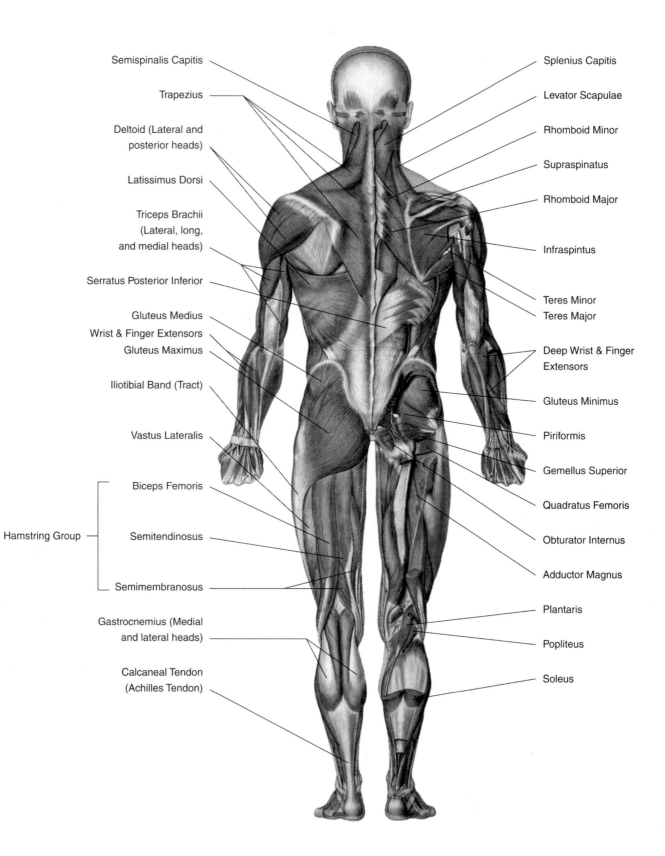

Semispinalis Capitis

Trapezius

Deltoid (Lateral and posterior heads)

Latissimus Dorsi

Triceps Brachii (Lateral, long, and medial heads)

Serratus Posterior Inferior

Gluteus Medius

Wrist & Finger Extensors

Gluteus Maximus

Iliotibial Band (Tract)

Vastus Lateralis

Biceps Femoris

Hamstring Group

Semitendinosus

Semimembranosus

Gastrocnemius (Medial and lateral heads)

Calcaneal Tendon (Achilles Tendon)

Splenius Capitis

Levator Scapulae

Rhomboid Minor

Supraspinatus

Rhomboid Major

Infraspintus

Teres Minor

Teres Major

Deep Wrist & Finger Extensors

Gluteus Minimus

Piriformis

Gemellus Superior

Quadratus Femoris

Obturator Internus

Adductor Magnus

Plantaris

Popliteus

Soleus

Figure 3.9: Major muscles and muscle groups (posterior view).

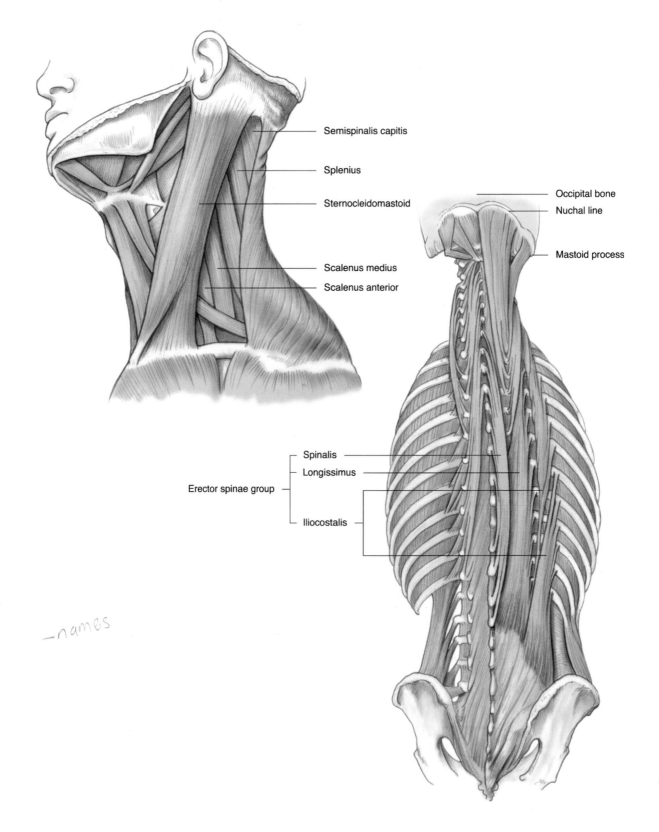

Semispinalis capitis

Splenius

Sternocleidomastoid

Scalenus medius
Scalenus anterior

Occipital bone
Nuchal line

Mastoid process

Spinalis
Longissimus

Erector spinae group

Iliocostalis

_names

Figure 3.10: Muscles of the neck, lateral view.

Figure 3.11: Deep muscles of the back, posterior view.

TABLE 3.5: MUSCLES OF THE NECK AND VERTEBRAL COLUMN

For convenience of presentation, this section combines two separate muscle groups, those of the neck and those of the back.

MUSCLES OF THE NECK (FIGURE 3.10)

The neck supports the most valuable anatomical entity of all, the brain, and the supporting organs that go with it, as well as muscles required for mastication and facial expression. Not unexpectedly, the musculature is complex, largely to facilitate the function of vision. To simplify, these muscles can be divided into the posterior, anterior, and lateral compartments.

Anterior, posterior, and lateral neck muscles. On the anterior, lateral, and posterior are the three major muscles, sternocleidomastoid, splenius, and semispinalis capitis. The lateral muscles of the neck are scalenus anterior and scalenus medius.

Sternocleidomastoid is the broad, superficial muscle running upward at each side of the neck.	It has two origins (the **sternum** and **clavicle**).	It inserts at the **mastoid process** (**temporal bone**, behind the ear).	It flexes the head from side to side and rotates it.
Splenius runs along the posterior side of the neck and joins the skull with the spine.	Its origin is the last four **cervical vertebrae** and the **upper thoracic vertebrae**.	Splenius inserts onto the **temporal and occipital bones (nuchal line)** and the **upper cervical vertebrae**.	It rotates the head and neck.
Scalenus anterior	It originates on the third to sixth **cervical vertebrae**.	It inserts on the crest of the **first rib**.	Scalenus anterior and medius elevate the first rib and rotate the neck. They also help during forced breathing.
Scalenus medius	It originates on the second to seventh **cervical vertebrae**.	It inserts on the surface of the **first rib**.	
Semispinalis capitis	It originates on the **first six thoracic vertebrae** and the **fourth to seventh cervical vertebrae**.	It inserts on the **occipital bone (nuchal line)**.	It extends the neck.

DEEP MUSCLES OF THE VERTEBRAL COLUMN (FIGURE 3.11)

The muscles of the back can conveniently be divided into the superficial and the deep muscles. The main superficial muscles of the back are the trapezius and latissimus dorsi, which will be discussed later under "Muscles of the Scapula."

The deep muscles are quadratus lumborum (discussed under "Abdominals,") and the erector spinae group. The erector spinae group consists of several muscles that together form a long, thick mass that runs from the neck to the lower back. They consists of (a) spinalis, (b) longissimus, and (c) iliocostalis. The erector spinae group is chiefly concerned with keeping the body in an upright position – and, since we spend most of our day standing and walking, they are frequently in use.

Spinalis is the most medial of the erector spinae group and is comprised of capitis, cervicis, and thoracis parts that attach to the head, cervical and thoracic vertebrae respectively.	They originate from the **cervical** and **thoracic vertebrae**.	They insert on the **cervical** and **thoracic vertebrae** above.	They extend and laterally flex the spine.
Longissimus is lateral to spinalis, and it also has capitis, cervicis, and thoracis attachments.	They originate on the **cervical, thoracic,** and **lumbar vertebrae**.	They insert on the **mastoid process** and the **cervical** and **thoracic vertebrae**.	They extend and laterally flex the spine and head.
Iliocostalis is the most lateral of the erector spinae group.	It originates from the **sacrum, lumbar vertebrae,** and the **ribs**.	It inserts on the **ribs** and the **cervical vertebrae**.	They extend and laterally flex the spine.

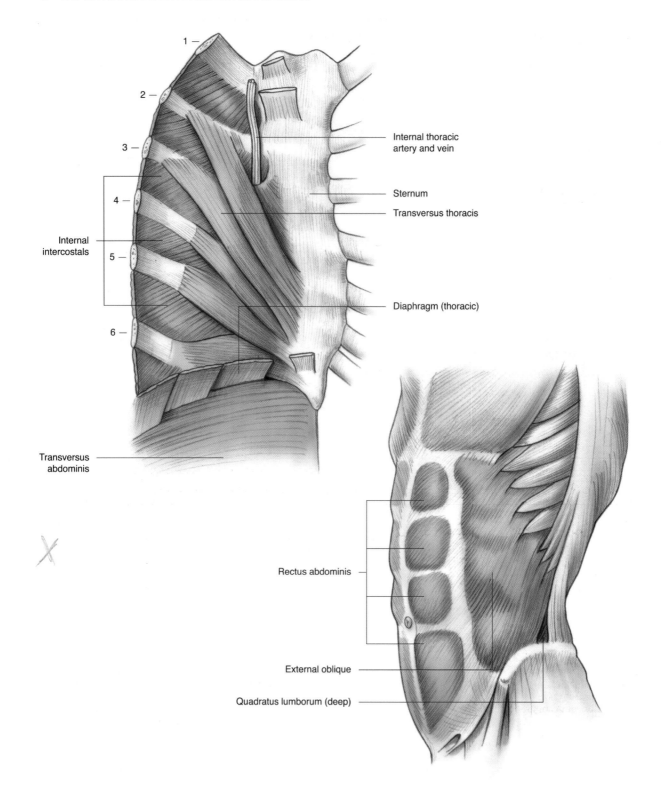

Figure 3.12: Muscles of the anterior thoracic wall, posterior view.

Figure 3.13: Muscles of the abdominal wall, lateral view (superficial).

TABLE 3.6: MUSCLES OF RESPIRATION AND THE ABDOMEN

The muscles of the thoracic cage are mainly involved with breathing; those of the abdominal wall, with flexion and rotation of the vertebral column. When included with the back muscles, these groups represent the major muscles of the trunk.

MUSCLES OF THE THORACIC CAGE (FIGURE 3.12)

There are three main groups of muscles affecting the rib cage and regulating the process of breathing.

The **diaphragm** acts as an anatomical border, separating the thoracic and abdominal cavities. Think of it as a plate, in the middle of the thorax held together by a central tendon.	The diaphragm originates from the **sternum** and the cartilage of the **ribs** and the **lumbar vertebrae**.	It inserts on the **central tendon** (not illustrated).	The thoracic cavity is an enclosed space. Therefore, an increase in the volume of this space with the contraction of respiratory muscles decreases the pressure in the thoracic cavity, drawing air in.
The **intercostal muscles** (external, internal, and the innermost intercostals) are arranged in layers. They are located between each rib, and are often referred to as the breathing muscles.	All originate on the inferior aspect of all the **ribs**.	All insert on the superior aspect of all the **ribs**.	The role of each varies, but all three layers essentially serve to keep the ribs elevating and depressing during expiration and inspiration, especially during heavy exercise.
Transversus thoracis is a triangular muscle acting on the abdominal wall.	It originates from the **xiphoid process** and the **sternum**.	It inserts in the cartilage of the **second** through to the **sixth ribs**.	It pulls the abdominal wall inwards.

MUSCLES OF THE ABDOMEN (FIGURE 3.13)

The muscles of the abdomen can be separated into those of the anterior and those of the posterior abdominal wall.

Anterior Abdominal Wall. The muscles of the anterior abdominal wall include the traditional muscle of the "abs" (rectus abdominus) and three separate layers of muscle on each side – external abdominal oblique, internal abdominal oblique (not illustrated), and transversus abdominis.

Rectus abdominis is located on each side of a tendinous line (the linea alba) extending from the xiphoid process of the sternum to the pubis. It is also transected horizontally by three "tendinous intersections," giving the abs the classic "washboard" appearance.	Rectus abdominus originates at the **pubic crest** and **symphysis pubis**.	It inserts at the **xiphoid process** and the **inferior ribs**.	Rectus abdominus serves not only to flex the trunk but also aids in such functions as expiration, defecation, and childbirth.
External oblique (the most external of the abdominal oblique muscles), and **transversus abdominis**	These originate on the **lower eight ribs**.	They insert on the **iliac crest** and **linea alba** and **pubis**.	These muscles (shown superficial to deep) generally serve to flex and rotate the vertebral column and compress the abdomen during forced expiration.

Posterior Abdominal Wall. The main muscle of the posterior abdominal wall is quadratus lumborum, already mentioned as one of the deep muscles of the back.

Quadratus lumborum, as its name suggests, has a quadrilateral shape and it has an attachment site on the lumbar region of the body.	Quadratus lumborum has its origin at the **iliac crest** and lower **lumbar vertebrae**.	It inserts at the **twelfth rib** and **upper lumbar vertebrae**.	This muscle serves to extend and laterally bend the vertebral column and to depress and stabilize the twelfth rib (thereby helping with breathing).

N,F,I

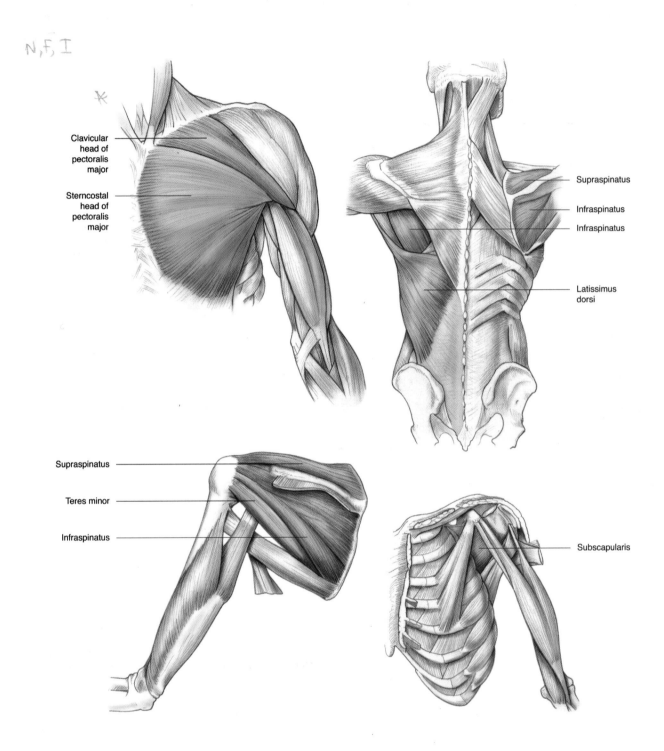

Clavicular
head of
pectoralis
major

Sterncostal
head of
pectoralis
major

Supraspinatus

Infraspinatus

Infraspinatus

Latissimus
dorsi

Supraspinatus

Teres minor

Infraspinatus

Subscapularis

Figure 3.14: Muscles acting on the upper limb, (1) anterior view, (2) posterior view.

Figure 3.15: Muscles of the rotator cuff, (1) posterior view, (2) anterior view.

TABLE 3.7: MUSCLES OF THE SHOULDER

The muscles that affect the shoulder joint can be grouped into four categories. Two large muscles serve mainly to act on the upper limb to the axial skeleton, and four rotator cuff muscles act directly to stabilize and rotate the joint itself. The other two sets of shoulder muscles (those more directly associated with the scapula) are considered in the following section.

MUSCLES ACTING ON THE UPPER LIMB (FIGURE 3.14)

These superficial muscles act on the upper limb.

Pectoralis major is the thick muscle covering most of the front of the chest. It is comprised of two sub-regions – the clavicular and sternocostal heads.	The upper part originates from the **clavicle**, the lower portion from the **sternum** and the costal cartilage of the **first to sixth ribs**, and the abdominal portion from the **external oblique muscle**.	The two heads unite within a common tendon and insert on the lateral lip of the **intertubercular groove.**	It allows internal rotation, adduction, and flexion of the arm.
Latissimus dorsi makes up about a quarter of the back area and is commonly referred to as "lats" or "wings."	It originates along the **lumbar** and lower half of the **thoracic vertebrae** and the **iliac crest** and **sacrum** below.	Its tendon inserts on the **humerus** on the floor of the **intertubercular groove** under pectoralis major's muscle tendon.	Latissimus dorsi functions as an adductor, extensor, and internal rotator of the arm.

MUSCLES OF THE ROTATOR CUFF (FIGURE 3.15)

The **rotator cuff** (musculotendinous cuff) consists of four muscles that extend from the scapula to the humerus and wrap around the the shoulder joint, essentially holding it in place. The group is commonly referred to as the S.I.T.S. or S.S.I.T. muscles (an acronym of the muscle names) because they "sit" on the shoulder girdle. In addition to stabilizing the shoulder joint, the rotator cuff helps to decelerate arm movements (e.g., during a throwing action).

If any of the rotator cuff muscles is damaged, due to strain or bad mechanics, the consequences are serious for actions that involve the shoulder and arm.

Supraspinatus is located above (hence, "supra") the spine of the scapula.	Supraspinatus originates and rests on the posterior surface of the **scapula** above its spine in the **supraspinous fossa**.	All three of these muscles come together to form a common tendon that inserts on the **greater tubercle** of the **humerus**.	All three of these muscles help to stabilize the shoulder joint. Supraspinatus abducts the shoulder. Infraspinatus and teres minor laterally rotate the shoulder.
Infraspinatus is located below (hence, "infra") the spine of the scapula.	Infraspinatus originates on the posterior of the **scapula** below its spine in the **infraspinous fossa**.		
Teres minor	Teres minor is a small muscle that originates on the the **lateral border** of the **scapula**.		
Subscapularis is a large triangular muscle, and the only S.I.T.S. muscle located on the anterior surface of the scapula**.**	Subscapularis originates on the anterior surface of the **scapula** on the **subscapular fossa**.	Subscapularis is the only rotator cuff muscle that inserts on the **lesser tubercle** of the **humerus**.	It rotates the humerus medially, and stabilizes the shoulder.

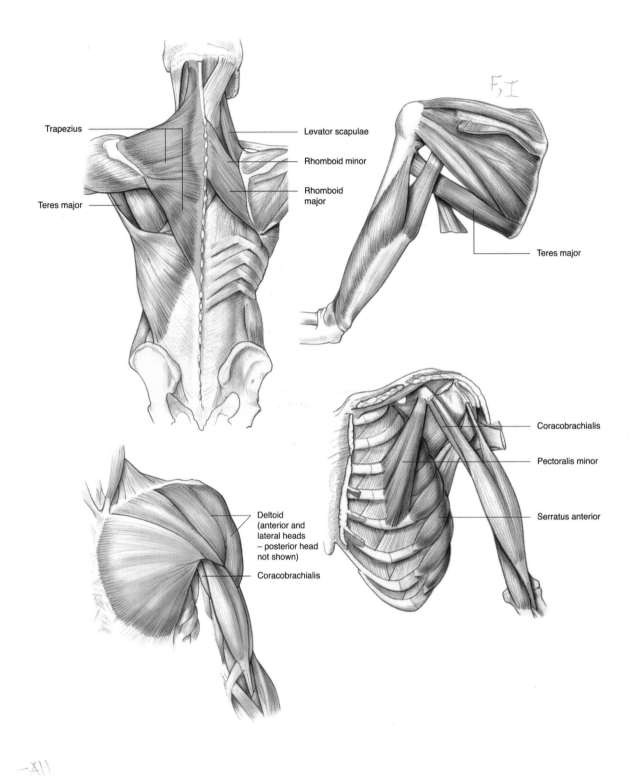

Figure 3.16: Muscles of the scapula (1) posterior view, (2) posterior deep view, (3) anterior superficial view, (4) anterior deep view.

TABLE 3.8: MUSCLES THAT ACT ON THE SCAPULA

The scapula facilitates a wide range of movement at the shoulder. Apart from the rotator cuff muscles, the scapular muscles can be grouped into two categories: (1) those anchoring it to the axial skeleton, and (2) those muscles directly acting on the humerus.

MUSCLES THAT POSITION THE SCAPULA (FIGURE 3.16)

The scapula is linked to the axial skeleton by six muscles.

Trapezius is the large muscle of the upper back that gets name from its trapezoid-like shape.	It originates at the base of the **occipital bone (nuchal line)** and all **cervical** and **thoracic vertebrae.**	It inserts on the **spine of the scapula**, the **acromion**, and **clavicle**.	Its functions are scapular elevation, adduction/ retraction, upward rotation, and depression. It also extends the neck.
Rhomboid major and **minor** lie underneath trapezius. Rhomboid minor is superior to rhomboid major.	Rhomboid major originates from **T2-T5**, whereas rhomboid minor originates from **C1-T1**.	Rhomboid major inserts on the **lower medial border** of the **scapula**. Rhomboid minor inserts on the **medial border** of the **scapula** at the level of the scapular spine.	They assist the trapezius in downward rotation of the scapula and also in adduction or retraction of the scapula.
Levator scapulae lies along the back and side of the neck and, as its name suggests, raises the scapula.	It originates from the **four upper cervical vertebrae** near the base of the **skull**.	Levator scapulae inserts on the **upper medial border** of the **scapula**.	This muscle elevates the scapula (with the help of the trapezius) and, along with rhomboid, rotates the scapula downward.
Serratus anterior is a large muscle that runs along the rib cage, also known as the "boxer's muscle."	It originates from the **first eight to nine ribs**.	It inserts on the **anterior surface** of the **medial border** of the **scapula**.	Serratus anterior helps in upward rotation and abduction or protraction of the scapula.
Pectoralis minor is generally classified as a muscle of respiration during sub-maximal and maximal work.	It originates from the **third, fourth, and fifth ribs**.	It inserts into the tip of the **corocoid process** of the **scapula**.	Pectoralis minor elevates the ribs and depresses and protracts the scapula.

SCAPULAR MUSCLES THAT MOVE THE HUMERUS (FIGURE 3.16)

Three of the muscles that move the humerus have their origin on the scapula.

The **deltoid** gets its name from its resemblance to the Greek letter *delta* (hence, it is referred to as the "Delts"). It has three heads — anterior, lateral, and posterior.	The muscle originates from the **clavicle**, the **acromion**, and **spine** of the **scapula**.	The anterior, lateral, and posterior heads meet at a common insertion on the **humerus**, called appropriately the **deltoid tuberosity**.	The anterior head flexes and medially rotates the shoulder joint. The lateral head abducts the arm. The posterior head extends and laterally rotates the arm.
Coracobrachialis is a small muscle that gets its name from its attachments sites.	It originates from the **coracoid process** of the **scapula** and runs medially to the short head of the biceps brachii.	It inserts on the **medial aspect** of the **humerus**.	It chiefly acts as a flexor and adductor of the arm.
Teres major is often confused as one of the rotator cuff muscles.	It originates from the **inferior lateral border** of the **scapula**.	Along with pectoralis major and latissimus dorsi, teres major inserts at the medial lip of the **intertubercular groove** of the **humerus**.	Teres major functions as a medial rotator, adductor, and, along with the posterior head of the deltoid and latissimus dorsi, extends the humerus at the arm.

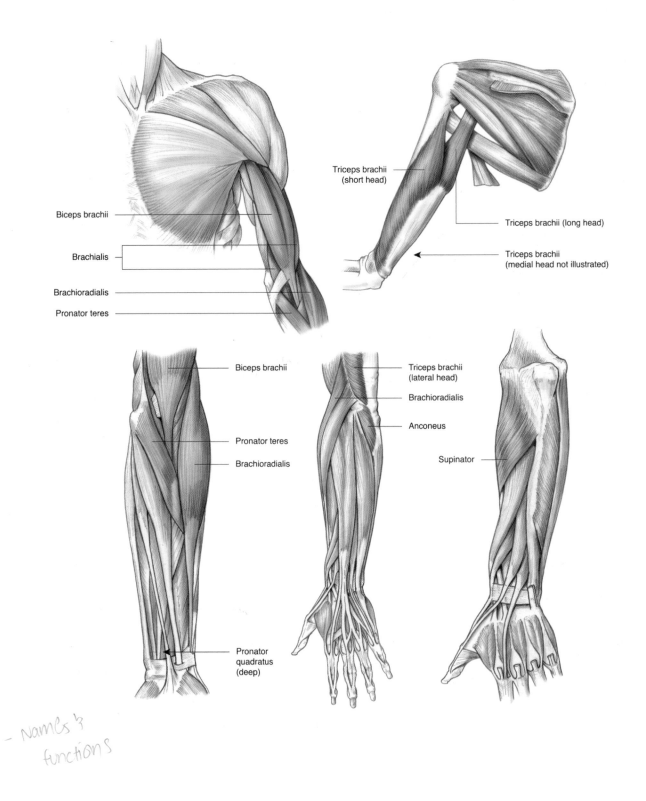

Figure 3.17: Elbow flexors and extensors, (1) anterior view, (2) posterior view.

Figure 3.18: Muscles of the forearm, (1) anterior view, (2) posterior view, (3) posterior deep view.

TABLE 3.9: MUSCLES OF THE ARM

The muscles of the arm control the movement of the forearm. Two major groups can be distinguished – those muscles that flex and extend the elbow (the elbow flexors and extensors) and those responsible for pronation and supination of the forearm.

ELBOW FLEXORS AND EXTENSORS (FIGURE 3.17)

Elbow flexion occurs mainly through the action of the biceps brachii, the brachioradialis, brachialis, and pronator teres.

Biceps brachii (the "biceps") is the prominent muscle on the front side of the upper arm. Its long head tendon passes within the intertubercular groove.	It originates in two places on the **scapula**: (1) the short head originates at the tip of the **coracoid process**; (2) the long head originates at the **supraglenoid tubercle**.	Its tendon attaches on the radius on a landmark known as the **radial tuberosity**.	Biceps brachii is a powerful supinator of the forearm, and once the forearm is in the supine position. the biceps brachii acts to flex the elbow.
Brachialis is sometimes referred to as the lower biceps.	It originates on the **lower anterior surface** of the **humerus**.	It inserts at the **coronoid process** of the **ulna**.	Along with biceps brachii, brachioradialis and pronator teres, brachialis acts as an elbow flexor.
Triceps brachii has three heads – short, long, and medial. As with the term "biceps" (two heads), "triceps" describes any muscle with three heads or points of origin.	Its lateral head originates on the **posterior aspect** of the **humerus**. The long head originates on the **infraglenoid tubercle** of the **scapula**. The medial head originates on the **posterior aspect** of the **humerus**, distal to the origin of the lateral head.	It inserts on the upper part of the **ulna** called the **olecranon**.	Triceps brachii works antagonistically with the biceps brachii and is the main extensor of the arm.
Brachioradialis gets its name from its attachment to the upper arm (brachium) and the radius (radialis).	The brachioradialis has its origin above the **lateral epicondyle** of the **humerus**.	It inserts at the **styloid process** on the **radius**.	Brachioradialis is a powerful elbow flexor when the radioulnar joint is midway between supination and pronation. If the forearm is pronated, the brachioradialis plays a bigger role than biceps brachii.
Anconeus is a triangular muscle.	Anconeus originates at the **lateral epicondyle** of the **humerus**.	It inserts on the **lateral surface** of the **olecranon** on the posterior surface of the **ulna**.	It assists the triceps in extending the forearm.

SUPINATION AND PRONATION OF THE FOREARM (FIGURE 3.18)

Supination of the forearm is brought about by the **biceps brachii** (above) and the supinator. Pronation of the forearm is brought about by pronator quadratus and pronator teres.

Pronator quadratus gets its name from its function and shape.	Pronator quadratus originates on the **anterior surface** of the **distal ulna**.	It inserts on the **anterior surface** of the **distal radius**.	Along with pronator teres, it pronates the forearm.
Pronator teres gets its name from its function.	Pronator teres originates on the **medial epicondyle** of **humerus** and the **coronoid process** of the **ulna**.	It inserts on the **lateral surface** of the **midshaft** of the **radius**.	Pronator teres pronates the forearm and also helps flex the elbow along with biceps brachii, brachialis, and brachioradialis.
Supinator derives it name from its function.	It originates at the **lateral epicondyle** of the **humerus**.	It inserts on the **anterior** and **lateral aspect** of the **radius**.	Supinator assists biceps brachii in supinating the forearm.

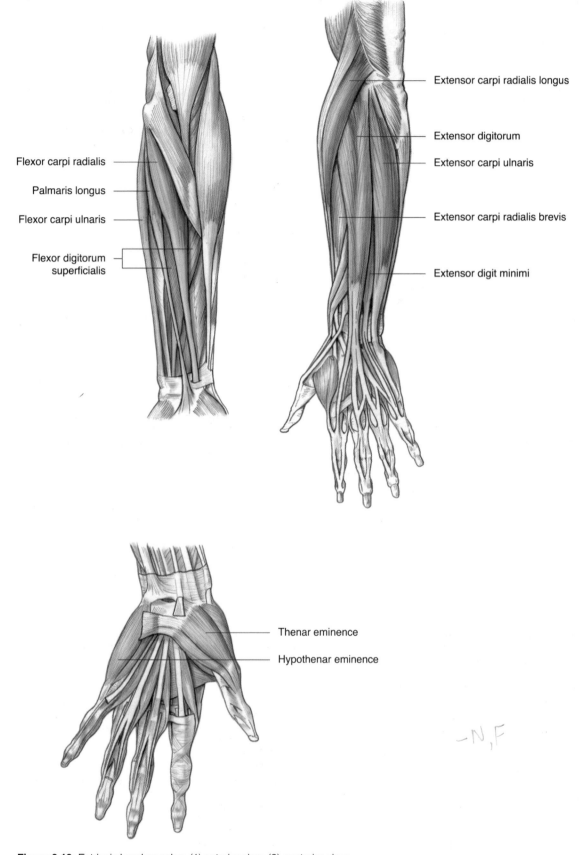

Flexor carpi radialis

Palmaris longus

Flexor carpi ulnaris

Flexor digitorum
superficialis

Extensor carpi radialis longus

Extensor digitorum

Extensor carpi ulnaris

Extensor carpi radialis brevis

Extensor digit minimi

Thenar eminence

Hypothenar eminence

Figure 3.19: Extrinsic hand muscles, (1) anterior view, (2) posterior view.

Figure 3.20: Intrinsic hand muscles, anterior view.

TABLE 3.10: MUSCLES OF THE FOREARM AND HAND

The muscles of the forearm (extrinsic hand muscles) are responsible for flexion, extension, abduction, and adduction of the wrist. The intrinsic hand muscles are those contained within the hand itself.

EXTRINSIC HAND MUSCLES (FIGURE 3.19)

The major anterior muscles of the forearm are the wrist flexors. The major posterior muscles of the forearm are wrist extensors. These muscles are often named after their attachment sites, their location, and their function (e.g., "flexor," meaning flexing; "carpi," meaning carpals; "radialis," meaning along the radius; and "ulnaris," meaning along the ulna).

Flexor carpi radialis Lateral to the distal end of this muscle's tendon, you can find your radial pulse.	As with all the wrist flexors, it originates at the **medial epicondyle** of the **humerus**.	It inserts at the **second metacarpal bone** (that of the index finger).	It flexes and abducts the hand at the wrist.
Palmaris longus	It originates on the **medial epicondyle** of the **humerus**.	It inserts in a dense connective tissue structure called "**Palmaris aponeurosis**" (not illustrated).	It is a weak flexor of the wrist and is often absent.
Flexor carpi ulnaris	Located on the ulnar side of the forearm, this muscle has two heads – the **medial epicondyle** of the **humerus** and the **olecranon**.	These heads combine and insert via the **pisiform bone** into the base of the **fifth metacarpal** at the wrist.	It flexes and adducts the wrist.
Flexor digitorum superficialis	It originates on the **medial epicondyle** of the **humerus**, **coronoid process** of the **ulna**, and the **anterior midshaft** of the **radius**.	It inserts at the **second phalanges** of **fingers 2 to 5**.	It flexes the interphalangeal joints of digits 2 to 5.
Extensor carpi radialis longus	It originates above the **lateral epicondyle** of the **humerus**.	It inserts at the base of the **second metacarpal**.	It mainly helps to extend and abduct the wrist.
Extensor carpi radialis brevis	It originates from the **lateral epicondyle** of the **humerus**.	It inserts at the base of the **third metacarpal**.	It extends and abducts the hand at the wrist.
Extensor carpi ulnaris	The most superficial muscle on the ulnar side, it has two origins, the **lateral epicondyle** of the **humerus** and the **ulna**.	The tendon inserts at the base of the **fifth metacarpal bone**.	It extends and adducts the hand at the wrist.
Extensor digitorum	It originates on the **lateral epicondyle** of the **humerus**.	It inserts on all the **digits** except the **thumb**.	The name is also its function: it extends interphalangeal joints.
Extensor digit minimi	Like all the wrist and finger extensors, it originates from the **lateral epicondyle** of the **humerus**.	It inserts on the **fifth digit**.	It serves to extend the interphalangeal joints of the little finger (digit 5).

INTRINSIC HAND MUSCLES (FIGURE 3.20)

The intrinsic hand muscles are those contained within the hand itself; i.e., both the origin and the insertion of these muscles are distal to the wrist. The thumb and little finger are largely controlled by the thenar and hypothenar muscles – the bulky muscle groups (referred to as "eminences") at the base of the thumb and the side of the hand respectively.
Abduction of the fingers is brought about mainly by the dorsal interossei and abductor digiti minimi (neither is illustrated).
Adduction of the fingers is a function of the palmer interossei (not illustrated).

Thenar eminence • **Flexor pollicis brevis** • **Abductor polliicis brevis** • **Opponens pollicis**	These originate at the strong fascia known as "**flexor retinaculum**" and the **trapezium bone** of the wrist at the base of the thumb.	Flexor pollicis brevis and abductor pollicis brevis insert at the **proximal phalanx** of the **thumb**. Opponens policis inserts at the **first metacarpal**.	As their names suggest, they serve to flex, abduct, and oppose the thumb.
Hypothenar eminence • **Abductor digiti minimi** • **Flexor digiti minimi brevis** • **Opponens digiti minimi**	Abductor digiti minimi originates at the **pisiform bone** of the wrist. Flexor digiti minimi brevis and opponens digiti minimi originate at the **hamate bone** of the wrist.	Abductor digiti minimi and flexor digiti minimi brevis insert at the **proximal phalanx** of the **fifth digit** (little finger). Opponens digiti minimi inserts at the **medial border** of the **fifth metacarpal**.	As with the thenar eminence group, their names tell their functions: abduction, flexion, and opposition of the little finger.

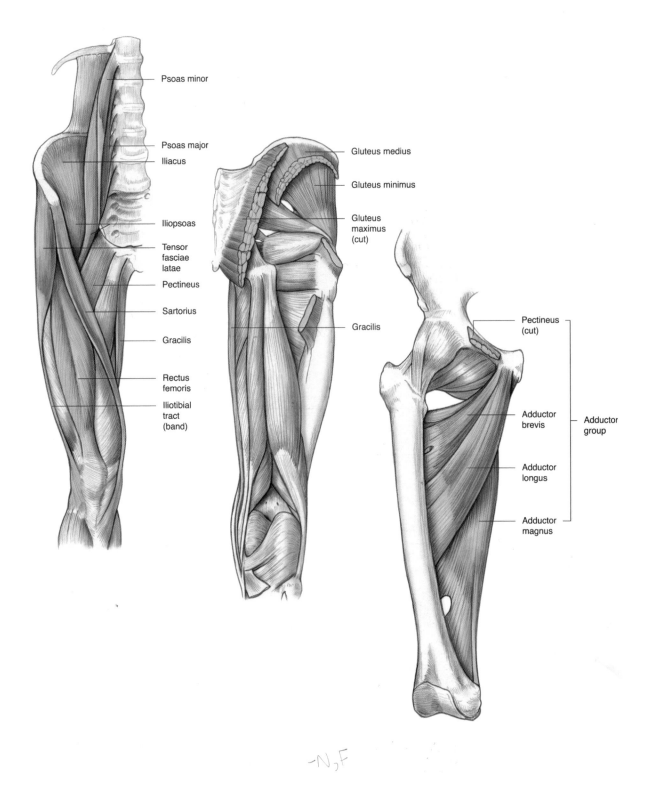

Figure 3.21: Muscles of the hip, (1) anterior view, deep; (2) posterior view, deep; (3) anterior adductors, deep view.

TABLE 3.11: MUSCLES OF THE HIP

HIP FLEXORS AND EXTENSORS (FIGURE 3.21)

POSTERIOR HIP MUSCLES

Gluteus maximus is the largest, strongest, and most superficial muscle of this group.	Gluteus maximus originates along the **crest** of the **ilium**, the **sacrum** and **coccyx**.	It attaches to the **posterior aspect** of the **greater trochanter** of the **femur** and the **iliotibial tract**.	It is responsible for hip extension and external rotation.
Gluteus medius lies on top of gluteus minimus.	Gluteus medius and gluteus minimus originate on the **lateral surface** of the **ilium**.	Gluteus medius attaches to the **posterior surface** of the **greater trochanter**.	Gluteus medius and gluteus minimus are responsible for abduction and internal rotation of the hip.
Gluteus minimus is the deepest of this group.		Gluteus minimus attaches to the **anterior surface** of the **greater trochanter**.	
Tensor fasciae latae	Tensor fasciae latae originates at the **anterior iliac crest**.	It inserts at the **iliotibial tract**.	Tensor fasciae latae serves to flex, abduct, and medially rotate the thigh.
Sartorius is a superficial anterior muscle of the thigh. It derives its name from the Latin word *sartor* meaning "to mend."	It originates at the **anterior superior iliac spine**.	It inserts on the **medial surface** of the **tibia**.	Sartorius acts across two joints. It is responsible for flexion and outward rotation of the hip and it helps to flex the knee.

Not included in the list is **rectus femoris**. Rectus femoris, one of the quadriceps group (discussed in Table 3.12), acts as a hip flexor as well as a knee extensor.

ANTERIOR HIP MUSCLES

Iliopsoas is a coming together of iliacus and psoas major. • **Iliacus**	It originates on the inner surface of the **ilium**.	It inserts on the **lesser trochanter** of the **femur**.	It is responsible for hip flexion.
• **Psoas major**	It originates from the **first 5 lumbar vertebrae**.	It inserts on the **lesser trochanter** of the **femur**.	It is responsible for hip and/or trunk flexion.
Psoas minor is present in approximately 40 percent of the human population and is relatively unimportant as it does not aid in hip flexion.	It originates from the **twelfth thoracic** and **first lumbar vertebrae**.	It inserts at the top of the **pubic bone**.	It is a weak trunk flexor (if present).

HIP ADDUCTORS (FIGURE 3.21)

Adductor longus	It originates at the **body** of **pubis**.	It inserts at the **linea aspera**.	It is responsible for hip adduction.
Adductor magnus	It originates at the **inferior ramus** of **pubis** and **ischial tuberosity**.	It inserts at the **linea aspera** and **adductor tubercle**.	It is responsible for hip adduction and extension.
Adductor brevis	It originates at the body of the **inferior ramus** of **pubis**.	It inserts at the **pectineal line** and **linea aspera**.	It is responsible for hip adduction and flexion.
Pectineus	It originates at the **superior ramus** of **pubis**.	It inserts at the **lesser trochanter** to **linea aspera**.	It is responsible for hip adduction and flexion.
Gracilis	It originates at the **inferior ramus** of **pubis**.	It inserts below the **medial tibial condyle**.	It adducts the hip and flexes the knee.

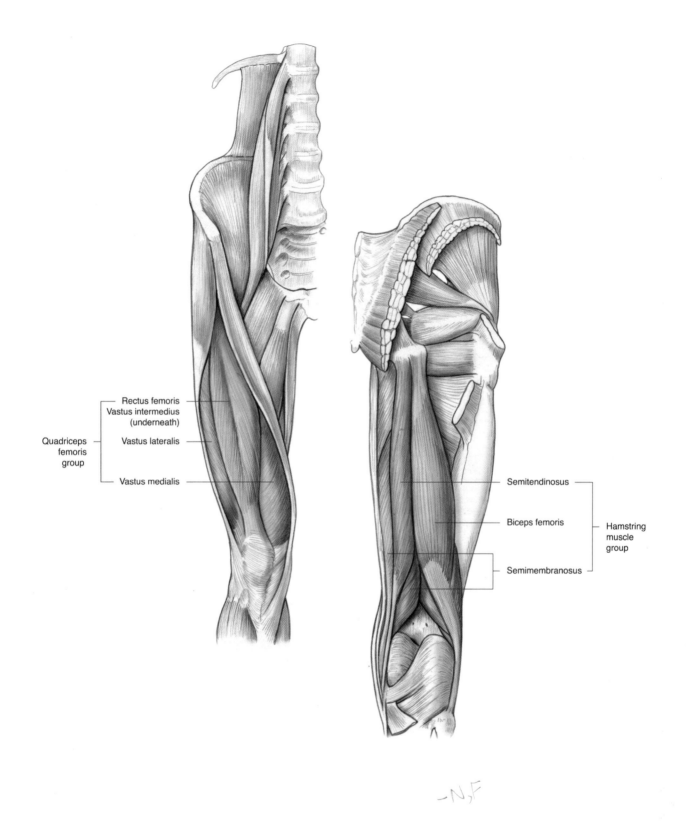

Figure 3.22: Quadriceps and hamstring muscle groups, (1) anterior view, (2) posterior view.

TABLE 3.12: MUSCLES OF THE THIGH

ANTERIOR THIGH — QUADRICEPS GROUP (FIGURE 3.22)

The muscles of the anterior thigh include the quadriceps femoris group. Quadriceps femoris is the large muscle group that covers the front and sides of the thigh. In this group, there are four separate muscles (hence the "quad"): rectus femoris, vastus lateralis, vastus medialis, and vastus intermedius.

Rectus femoris As mentioned earlier, this is also a hip flexor, but it is shown here as part of the quadriceps group.	This muscle originates at the **anterior inferior iliac spine**.		This muscle is responsible for knee extension and hip flexion.
Vastus lateralis	Vastus lateralis originates on the lateral side of the **linea aspera** and **greater trochanter.**	All the quadriceps muscles join at a common tendon (the **patellar tendon**), which wraps around the patella to a ligament (the **patellar ligament**) and finally inserts on the **tibial tuberosity** of the **tibia**.	These three muscles are responsible for knee extension.
Vastus intermedius	Vastus intermedius originates on the **anterior shaft** of the **femur**.		
Vastus medialis	Vastus medialis originates on the **medial aspect** of the **linea aspera**.		

POSTERIOR THIGH — HAMSTRING GROUP (FIGURE 3.22)

There are three muscles of the posterior thigh. They are referred to collectively as "the hamstrings." They are: the biceps femoris, the semimembranosus, and semitendinosus.

Biceps femoris is the largest of the "hamstring" muscles.	It originates in two places (two heads), the **ischial tuberosity** and the **linea aspera**.	Its fibres join and then insert into the **head** of the **fibula**.	It is an extensor of the hip and a flexor of the knee; furthermore, it acts to externally rotate the flexed knee.
Semimembranosus This muscle gets its name from its appearance (it looks like a membrane).	Semimembranosus originates from the **ischial tuberosity.**	Its fibres insert in the **posterior aspect** of the **medial tibial condyle**.	This muscle flexes the knee and rotates it inward. It also extends the hip.
Semitendinosus lies in a groove formed by the semimembranosus muscle at the inner back of the thigh. It gets its name from its appearance (it looks like a tendon).	Like semimembranosus and biceps femoris, semitendinosus originates at the **ischial tuberosity**.	Its "belly" ends two-thirds of the way down the thigh at its tendon, which continues on to insert at the **proximal part** of the **tibia** below the **medial condyle**.	It flexes and internally rotates the knee and extends the hip.

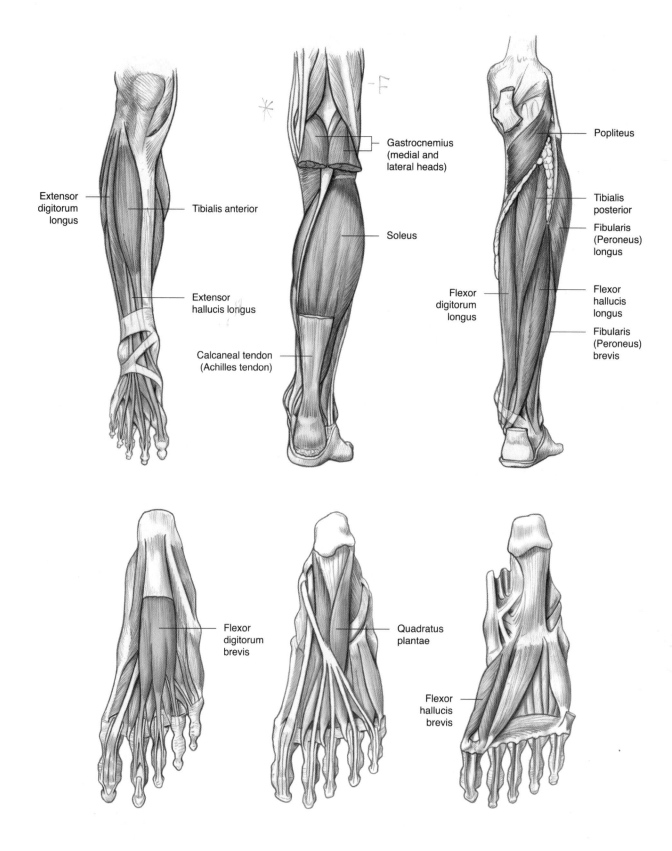

Figure 3.23: Extrinsic foot muscles, (1) anterior view, (2) posterior view, deep, (3) posterior deeper view.

Figure 3.24: Intrinsic foot muscles, plantar views, (1) superficial, (2) intermediate, (3) deep.

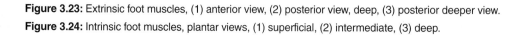

TABLE 3.13: MUSCLES OF THE LEG AND FOOT

Anatomically speaking, the "leg" refers to the lower limb below the knee. The muscles of the leg can be categorized into two broad groups, the extrinsic foot muscles and the intrinsic foot muscles.

THE EXTRINSIC FOOT MUSCLES (FIGURE 3.23)

The extrinsic foot muscles are those located between the knee and ankle that act on the ankle and foot.

ANTERIOR COMPARTMENT

Extensor digitorum longus	It originates on the **lateral condyle** of the **tibia**.	It inserts on the **phalanges** of the **second to fifth digits**.	It extends the toes.
Extensor hallucis longus	It originates on the **anterior middle region** of the **fibula**.	It inserts on the **distal phalanx** of the **first (great) toe**.	It extends the big toe.
Tibialis anterior	It originates on the **anterior shaft** of the **tibia**.	It inserts on the **medial cuneiform** and base of the **first metatarsal**.	It dorsiflexes the ankle and inverts the foot.

POSTERIOR COMPARTMENT

Gastrocnemius (cut away in the illustration so as to reveal soleus)	Gastrocnemius consists of a lateral head and a medial head (originating from the **lateral** and **medial condyles** of the **femur**) that come together to form the bulky "calf."	The heads attach to a common tendon, which fuses with the tendon of the soleus (the muscles just beneath it) to form the **calcaneal tendon** (Achilles tendon), which inserts at the **calcaneus**.	Gastrocnemius plantar flexes the ankle and flexes the knee.
Soleus This muscle is named because it looks like the fish (sole).	It originates from the upper part of the **fibula** and the arch connecting the fibula to the **tibia**.	Its tendon combines with that of the gastrocnemius as the **calcaneal tendon** (Achilles tendon), which inserts at the **calcaneus**.	Along with gastrocnemius, the soleus muscle plantar flexes the ankle.
Flexor digitorum longus	It originates on the **posterior middle region** of the **tibia**.	It inserts on the **phalanges** of the **second to fifth digits**.	It flexes the toes.
Flexor hallucis longus	It originates on the **posterior aspect** of the **fibula**.	It inserts on the **distal phalanx** of the **big toe**.	It flexes the big toe.
Tibialis posterior	It originates on the **posterior surface** of the **tibia** and **fibula**.	It inserts on the **tuberosity** of the **navicular bone**.	It plantar flexes the ankle and inverts the foot.
Popliteus	It originates on the **lateral condyle** of the **femur**.	It inserts on the **proximal shaft** of the **tibia** on the posterior side below the **medial condyle**.	It medially rotates the leg to "unlock" the knee and initiate flexion.

LATERAL COMPARTMENT

Fibularis brevis and **fibularis longus** (peroneus brevis and peroneus longus)	These originate on the **fibula**.	They insert at the **fifth** and **first metatarsal** respectively.	They allow plantar flexion of the ankle and eversion of the foot.

THE INTRINSIC FOOT MUSCLES (FIGURE 3.24)

The intrinsic foot muscles are located entirely within the foot itself and act on the toes.

Flexor digitorum brevis	It originates from the **calcaneus bone**.	It divides into four tendons, and extends to the **phalanges** of each **toe** (except the big toe).	Flexor digitorum brevis, in the middle of the sole of the foot, helps to flex the toes.
Quadratus plantae	It originates from the **calcaneus bone**.	It inserts on the **tendons** of the **flexor digitorum longus**.	Also on the sole of the foot, it assists flexor digitorum longus in flexing the toes for push-off in walking/running.
Flexor hallucis brevis	It originates from the **cuboid bone** and the **middle** and **lateral cuneiform bones** (metatarsals).	It inserts at the **base** of the **first phalanx**.	Flexor hallucis brevis flexes the big toe.

Table 3.14: Exercising major muscle groups

Muscle group	Free weights	Cable machines (universal)	Tubing and medicine ball	Body weight (for beginners)
UPPER BODY				
Neck flexors, extensors, and rotators	• Neck harness for all neck movements attached to plate	• Neck harness attached to machine for extension and flexion	• Tubing with harness	• Hand on anterior, lateral, or posterior side of head providing resistance with self or partner
Trunk extensors	• Holding plate tight to chest on back extension roman chair	• Back extension machine	• Standing up with tubing held in hands, with feet anchored, bending forward	• Lying on stomach and extending trunk upward
Trunk rotators	• Barbell lateral twists • Dumbbell side bends	• Trunk rotation machine	• Medicine ball twists • Tubing side bends • Hanging medicine ball twists	• Twisting crunches • Roman chair side bends • Hanging leg twists
Trunk flexors	• Weighted plate on chest crunches • Weighted vest crunches	• Abdominal machine crunches • High pulley crunches	• Various medicine ball crunches	• Crunches • Lying leg thrusts • Towel crunches
Medial shoulder rotators	• Bench press, flat, incline, and decline using barbells or dumbbells • Dumbbell flys	• Bench press • Incline pec-deck flys • Flat cross-cable flys • Decline cable flys • Pec-deck	• Lying down on back pass medicine ball to self • Unbalanced medicine ball push-ups	• Various push-ups using benches, stability ball, and different grips and hand positioning • Medial bent arm shoulder rotation in shallow end of pool
Lateral shoulder rotators	• Bent over dumbbell or barbell raises • Bent arm lying on side lateral rotations with dumbbell	• Cross-cable machine lateral shoulder rotation	• Various tubing lateral rotations using a door or pole to attach tubing	• Lying on side straight or bent arm lateral rotations • Lateral bent arm shoulder rotation in shallow end of pool
Shoulder elevators	• Shrugs using dumbbells or barbells and various grips	• Overhead press • Shrugs using universal machine	• Medicine ball shrugs	• Partner-assisted shoulder shrugs
Shoulder adductors	• T-bar rows • One-arm dumbbell rows • Bent over rows	• Wide grip lat pull downs • Seated rows	• Various tubing pull downs	• Partner-assisted straight arm push downs • Shoulder adduction in shallow end of pool
Shoulder abductors	• Lateral raises using dumbbells	• Cross-cable lateral raise • Incline bench press machine	• Medicine ball or lateral tubing raises	• Partner-assisted lateral raises • Shoulder abduction in shallow end of pool
Shoulder flexors	• Dumbbells or barbell front raises using various arm positions	• Cross-cable front raise • Flat bench press	• Tubing frontal raises • Two handed medicine ball frontal raises	• Partner-assisted frontal raises • Shoulder flexion in shallow end of pool
Shoulder extensors	• Bent over rows with dumbbells or barbell • Standing straight arm extensions with dumbbells	• Low pulley standing or bent over shoulder extensions	• Tubing shoulder extensions	• Shoulder extension with partner
Elbow flexors	• Various arm curls using dumbbells or barbell with varying grips • Preacher curls	• Seated arm flexion machine • Seated preacher curl machine	• Tubing concentration curls • Medicine ball curls • Tubing reverse curls	• Chin-ups with partner assisting • Towel curls with partner resisting

Muscle group	Free weights	Cable machines (universal)	Tubing and medicine ball	Body weight (for beginners)
Elbow extensors	• Various triceps extensions • Lying down on back triceps extensions	• Seated triceps extension machine • Triceps pull down with rope	• Tubing kickback triceps extensions	• Triceps dips using benches and or dip bar
Wrist and finger flexors	• Wrist and finger rolls	• Wrist and finger flexion machine	• Tubing wrist curls	• Self-assisted wrist curls with towel and partner
Wrist and finger extensors	• Reverse wrist and finger rolls	• Wrist and finger extension machine	• Tubing wrist extensors	• Self-assisted wrist extensions with towel and partner
Hand muscles	• Various bar grips • Finger curls	• Finger curls with universal machine	• Medicine ball volley	• Squeezing sponge ball

LOWER BODY

Muscle group	Free weights	Cable machines (universal)	Tubing and medicine ball	Body weight (for beginners)
Hip flexors	• Weighted shoes or ankle weights • Step-ups with ankle weights	• Standing hip flexion machine • Hip flexion on leg extension machine	• Hanging medicine ball knee tucks • Partner-assisted tubing step-ups	• Hanging knee tucks • Stability ball knee balance thrusts • Hip flexion in shallow end of pool
Hip extensors	• Squats using barbells or dumbbells • Reverse hack squats • Step-ups with dumbbells or barbell	• Hip extension machine • Cable hip extensions	• Tubing hip extensions	• Lying down with feet on bench or straight leg extensions • Stability ball hip extensions
Hip abductors	• Lateral lunges using dumbbells or barbell • Floor hip abduction using ankle weights	• Standing or seated straight or bent leg hip abductor machine • Cable hip abductor cross-overs	• Standing or seated tubing straight leg abduction	• Lying on side, straight leg raises • Hip abduction in shallow end of pool
Hip adductors	• Lying on side with ankle weights, straight leg adduction	• Standing or seated straight or bent leg hip adductor machine • Cable hip adduction cross-overs	• Tubing straight leg hip adduction	• Lying on side, lower leg raises • Hip adduction in shallow end of pool
Knee flexors	• Standing knee flexion with ankle weights	• Standing leg flexion machine • Lying knee flexion machine	• Lying on stomach, medicine ball between ankles, flex knees	• Stability ball knee flexion • Heel kicks in shallow end of pool
Knee extensors	• Step-ups • Squats using dumbbells or barbell • Lunges with dumbbells or barbell	• Various squat machines • Reverse hack squats • Leg press machine	• Lying on back, medicine ball knee extension • Various tubing knee extensions	• Lying down knee extensions from floor • Running in shallow end of pool
Dorsi flexors	• Dorsiflexion free weight machine	• Seated dorsiflexor machine	• Tubing dorsi raises	• Stability ball dorsi-flexor rolls from push-up position
Plantar flexors	• Calf raises using single leg and both legs with dumbbells or barbell	• Seated or standing calf machine • Donkey calf machine	• Medicine ball/tubing standing calf raises (single or double leg)	• Standing calf raises

Pool training provides an excellent medium for both agonist and antagonist muscle groups as the water provides resistance in each direction – in essence, working both pairs alternately at the same time. Pool training is also an excellent modality for injury rehabilitation. All pool training can be done in either the shallow or deep end of a pool with proper floatation devices and training equipment such as flutter boards, noodles, pull-buoys, pool dumbbells, resistance tubing, and medicine balls. Some movements may require stabilization, as in hanging on to the pool's edge or dynamic movement such as running or bounding, using the entire length or width of the pool.

Important note: A trained lifeguard should always be on duty when performing pool workouts.

Table 3.15: Effects of resistance training

Effects	Adaptations
Increased muscularity (hypertrophy)	• Increased size and efficiency of fast- and slow-twitch muscle fibres depending on program design • Improvement in body composition from increase in fat-free weight • Increase in resting metabolic rate • Increased muscular strength, power, and endurance depending on resistance program • Increased mitochondrion density • Increased capillary density • Increased muscle protein levels such as myosin and actin • Improved body posture and muscular imbalances
Increased motor unit recruitment	• Increased strength, power, and endurance throughout entire joint range • Increased neuromuscular efficiency and coordination • Increased neuromuscular junction efficiency
Increased strength of connective and support tissues	• Increased bone density • Increased ligament strength • Increased tendon strength • Increased joint stability • Decreased susceptibility of joint injuries
Increased fuel storage capacity of muscle fibres	• Local muscle can store more ATP and PC • Increased glucose storage capacity • Increased local muscle anaerobic threshold • Muscles become more efficient in fuel utilization
Specific adaptation to exercised muscles	• Local improvement on joint, power, speed, and endurance of the muscles exercised
Increased blood supply to muscles	• Increased capillary density • Increased O_2 delivery • Increased CO_2 removal • increased delivery of nutrients and removal of waste from muscle • Increased tolerance to lactic acid and lactic acid removal
Improvement in the energy pathways	• Increased ATP-PC, glycolysis, and aerobic energy pathway efficiency depending on exercise design
Depending on program design and individual needs	• Enhanced metabolic needs for athlete • Reduced risk of developing cardiorespiratory illnesses such as strokes and heart attacks • Reduced risk of joint ailments and diseases such as osteoporosis • Slows down the aging process • Enhanced performance in sports skills • Leads to improvements in self-esteem • Leads to a better quality of life

Benefits of Resistance Training for Females

Make resistance training a priority — the rewards will be numerous

The first documented weightlifter, Milo of Crotona, was a famous Greek athlete in 684 B.C. He was rumoured to be the strongest in the world. He captured six Olympic Games wrestling victories as well as triumphing at other sacred festivals. He also won six championships at the "Pythian Games." Milo's secret training program consisted of lifting a growing calf daily. As the calf grew in size, Milo grew in strength.

Since then, scientists have been conducting studies to find out exactly how this form of training can enhance and prolong human life. The benefits of weight training are well documented for all individuals, but let us explore in more detail how it is particularly beneficial to women.

Increased Muscle Hypertrophy

Some women, particularly younger ones, still think that lifting weights will make them "bulky" and muscular. The truth is that women have only one-tenth the circulating testosterone that men have. Testosterone is the natural male steroid that is responsible for most of the male secondary sex characteristics, including muscle gain.

Although some women naturally have higher levels of testosterone than others, these levels are not near that of men. In order for women to achieve "bulky" muscularity, they must take in, using injections or pills, real testosterone, human growth hormone, or any type of anabolic steroid, be it water or oil based. This is not a practice that is recommended by the medical community as the side effects can be extremely dangerous.

Increased Strength in Support and Connective Tissue

One of the best preventative measures in battling osteoporosis is a steady regime of resistance training, which forces the body to adapt by strengthening cartilage, ligaments, and tendons. Resistance training, especially when using loads that are ten times the

Helen Vanderburg at her fitness club in Calgary, 2001. In the 1970s, she put Canada on the world championship map in synchronized swimming (CP PHOTO/Adrian Wyld).

typical loads that females bear in daily activities, will also help strengthen bone.

The remodelling of bone is directly related to the intensity of the overload, which is the amount of weight applied above the normal load the body is accustomed to. Therefore, greater loads elicit a greater amount of bone remodelling. All types of resistance training are beneficial, especially before puberty – greater gains in bone mass are experienced by premenarchal women than by those who have already started menstruating.

Strong connective tissue is essential for joint integrity, stability, and injury prevention. This is thought to be especially the case for women, since their Q-angle is usually greater than that of men, tending to make them more susceptible to injuries involving the knee. (For a discussion of the Q-angle, see page 77.)

Lean Body Mass and Fat Loss

Males tend to have a higher metabolic rate than females. One of the key

reasons for this is that males tend to have a greater lean body mass, or more muscle weight, than females. The best way to lose excess body fat is to do aerobic exercise and incorporate a resistance training program, including a balanced diet with a slightly reduced caloric intake (see page 150 on assessing daily caloric needs). Strength training develops lean muscle, which is more metabolically active than fat tissue. This results in greater amounts of calories being burned.

The more efficient and "toned" your muscles become, the more fuel your body will need to sustain them. Your total body weight will surely increase, but your body fat will decrease. You will notice this most in your clothing size or belt notches.

Remember that muscle weighs more than fat. It is for this reason that we should not rely solely on weigh scales found in fitness facilities and homes. These scales measure total body weight; they do not separate fat weight from muscle weight.

Self-Esteem and Performance

In the context of relentless media bombardment about how women "should" look, resistance training can provide women with an opportunity to have control over their own bodies. Whether the desire is to "lean out" a bit or to seek athletic prowess, resistance training can get them there.

A stronger body helps us both in the athletic arena and in our daily lives. It helps us to feel better about ourselves and our lives, and enhances the lives of those around us.

Whether you use free weights, body weight, resistance machines, medicine balls, stability balls, or tubing to increase your load, the benefits will be the same. The key component is to design an exercise program that progressively increases the load, or the weight lifted, and includes a variety of resistance training equipment to prevent boredom.

Montreal Express' Tracey Kelusky gets by Calgary Roughnecks' Chris Prat during National Lacrosse League action in Montreal, Quebec, November 2001(CP PHOTO/Ryan Remiorz).

4
Joint Mechanics and Joint Injuries

"The human body is a machine which winds its own springs."
— English novelist Thomas Hardy

As the term implies, joints are the points of contact (or **articulations**) between two connected bones. Joints hold bones together, and many of them also allow for flexibility and movement.

A quick look at our own bodies reveals a number of easy-to-recognize joints at the elbows, knuckles, shoulders, ankles, and so on. Joints are part of the musculoskeletal system taken as a whole.

THE DIFFERENT TYPES OF JOINTS

Joints are classified according to their structure (what they are made of) or their function (the type and extent of movement they permit). Again, recall the distinction between structure and function, discussed on page 2. The structural classification generally recognizes three main types of joints: fibrous joints, cartilaginous joints, and synovial joints. Fortunately, these correspond more or less to a functional classification based on the range of motion the joint permits: an immovable joint (synarthrosis), a slightly movable joint (amphiarthrosis) and a freely movable joint (diarthrosis).

Fibrous joints are bound tightly together by connective tissue and allow no movement. These are the joints between the interlocking bones of the skull, known as *sutures*. After birth, all sutures joints become immobile.

With **cartilaginous joints** (or fibrocartilaginous joints), the body of one bone connects to the body of another by means of cartilage, and slight movement is possible. The intervertebral "discs" of the spinal column (of which there are twenty-three) are of this type. These have a hard, elastic outer ring with a soft core, permitting some movement while at the same time providing protection against severe jolts, such as landing hard on one's feet.

However, it is the **synovial joints** – the joints that allow the most movement – that usually come to mind when we think of joints. In this type of joint, the bony surfaces are separated by a lubricating fluid (the **synovia**) and by cartilage. They are also joined by ligaments, tough bands of elastic tissue that enclose the ends of articulating bones and form the capsule containing the synovial membrane. Typical synovial joints are the knee, the shoulder, and the ankle. Because synovial joints play such an important role in human movement, we will concentrate on these.

CHARACTERISTICS OF SYNOVIAL JOINTS

Synovial joints permit movement between two or more bones and can be distinguished by the following characteristics, as illustrated in Figure 4.1 below:

- **Articulating cartilage** is located on the ends of bones that come in contact with one another. This hyaline cartilage protects the ends of the bone and allows for a smooth contact surface for the bone to move about while also acting as a shock absorber.

- The **joint capsule** is a fibrous structure that consists of the synovial membrane and fibrous capsule. The **synovial membrane** allows certain nutrients to pass through while the **fibrous capsule** keeps synovial fluid from leaking.

- The **joint cavity** is located between the two bony articulating surfaces. It is filled with synovial fluid, which acts as a lubricant for the joint. This lubricant is essential in reducing friction and providing nutrients for the articulating cartilage.

- The **bursae** are the small, flattened fluid sacs found at the friction points between tendons, ligaments, and bones (bursa is the singular).

- **Intrinsic ligaments** are thick bands of fibrous connective tissue that help thicken and reinforce the joint capsule.

- **Extrinsic ligaments** are separate from the joint capsule and help to reinforce the joint by attaching the bones together (not illustrated).

TYPES OF SYNOVIAL JOINTS

Synovial joints are often distinguished by the kind of movement the joint permits. There are six types (illustrated in Figure 4.2 on the adjacent page).

- Gliding (or plane or arthrodial) joints. This group connects flat or slightly curved bone surfaces. Examples include joints in the foot between the tarsals and in the hand among the carpals.

- Hinge (ginglymus) joints. Hinge joints have a convex portion of one bone fitting into a concave portion of another, and allow movement in one plane. The joints between the bones of the fingers (phalanges) and between the ulna ("inner" bone of the forearm) and the humerus are examples.

- Pivot (or trochoid) joints. This joint allows rotation in one plane (uni-axial) – a rounded point of one bone fits into a groove of another. An example is the atlantoaxial articular joint between the

first two vertebrae in the neck, which allows the rotation of the head (as when signifying "no").

- Ellipsoid joints. These joints allow movement in two planes. An example is found between the second metacarpal and the first phalanx of the second finger. The wrist is also an example of an ellipsoidal joint.

- Saddle joints. Saddle joints, like ellipsoidal joints, allow movement in two planes (for example, flexion-extension and abduction-adduction), but do not allow for rotation like a ball-and-socket joint. A key saddle joint is found at the carpo-metacarpal articulation of the thumb.

- Ball-and-socket (spheroidal) joints. In this type, the "ball" at one bone fits into the "socket" of another, allowing movement around three axes. The most familiar joints of this type are at the hip (the femur rests in the acetabulum of the pelvis) and the shoulder (the humerus rests in the glenoid cavity).

A joint that moves mainly in one plane (such as the elbow or knee) is uni-axial; a joint that moves in two planes is bi-axial; and one that moves in three is tri-axial. There are often slight movements in other planes (e.g., knee rotation after flexing).

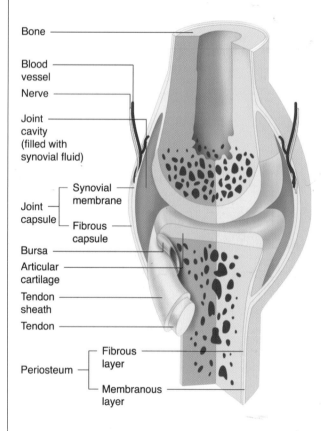

Bone
Blood vessel
Nerve
Joint cavity (filled with synovial fluid)
Joint capsule — Synovial membrane / Fibrous capsule
Bursa
Articular cartilage
Tendon sheath
Tendon
Periosteum — Fibrous layer / Membranous layer

Figure 4.1: Synovial joint.

Ball and socket (hip)

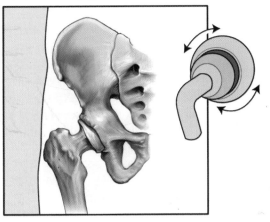

Gliding (foot)

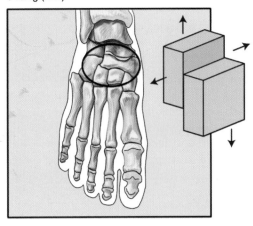

Hinge (elbow)

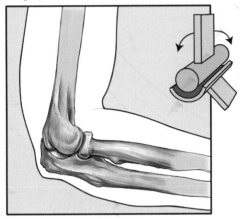

Pivot (neck)

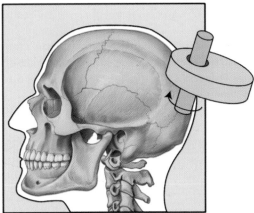

Saddle (thumb)

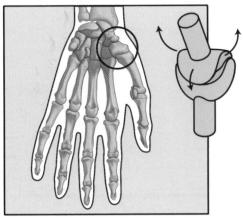

Ellipsoid (wrist)

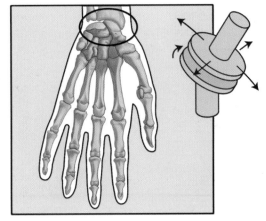

Figure 4.2: Six types of synovial joint.

COMMON SPORT INJURY TERMS

Given the universality of sports injuries, it is important to build a basic knowledge of the common joint injuries that occur in structures within a joint. Before we examine the specific types of joint injuries, let us first look at the properties of these tissues and the similarities of injuries in general.

Tissue Properties

Each tissue is unique in its design and role, and, as a result, each one will have a tolerance or a breakpoint. If exceeded, it will tear, sprain or pull, depending on its threshold to stretch. Let us work our way through joint properties and the tissues that surround them, from the most to least rigid. The more rigid tissues are, the more resistant they are to injury. Bones are examples of rigid tissues; in the adult skeleton they will break before they bend.

The tissue that attaches one or more bones together is called a ligament. Ligaments are significantly less rigid than bones. They are made up of tough bands of white, fibrous tissues that allow a certain amount of stretch, but they do not have the same stretching ability as tendons. Because of these properties, ligaments are generally referred to as static stabilizers of joints, while tendons and muscles are called dynamic stabilizers. The stronger these tissues become as a result of a proper strength and conditioning program, the stronger the joint itself becomes, and the more resistant it is to injury. When ligaments reach their threshold, they will stretch minimally but usually will tear.

Tendons, which attach muscle to bone, are composed of large bundles of white, fibrous protein known as collagen. They possess a greater stretching range than ligaments. However, if the force is great enough, they also will tear.

These tissues also have vascular properties. Vascularity refers to the amount of supplied blood a tissue has or requires. Ligaments and cartilage are said to be *avascular* – in other words, their nutritional needs are not met through blood; hence the prefix "a," meaning without, and "vascular," meaning blood supply. These tissues receive their nutritional needs through compression.

Bone and muscles, on the other hand, are vascular; their nutritional needs are met through blood. It should also be mentioned that the more vascular a tissue, the less time it takes to recover from an injury. Muscle, for example, is a very vascular type of tissue, and behaves in a similar fashion to a bungee cord or elastic with their ability to stretch and recoil.

Yet muscle too will pull and tear if its limits are exceeded. The factors that govern the muscles' ability and potential to stretch is reflected in the individual's joint range of motion (ROM); the physical condition of the individual, including proper hydration and nutrition; and how much effort they place on improving their muscular strength and flexibility.

First- to Third-Degree Tears, Sprains, and Pulls

The terms **strains, pulls, and tears** are usually used to describe injuries to all joint tissue types. Sprains are associated with ligaments and tendons while pulls and strains are associated with muscles. Tears, sprains, and pulls basically fall into three categories of severity: first, second, and third degree (sometimes known as grade). **First-degree injuries** are mild and are considered the least severe. They usually take a relatively short time (a day or a few days) to heal if proper care is taken the moment an injury happens. (Treatment of injures will be discussed on page 73). **Second-degree injuries** are said to be moderate and are more severe. They require treatment from a physiotherapist once diagnosed by a doctor. **Third-degree injuries** are the most severe and may require surgery and rehabilitation. They may take from six to twelve months to fully repair.

Tendinitis

Tendinitis is an inflammation of a tendon caused by irritation due to prolonged or abnormal use. In fact, any condition ending with the suffix "itis" means an inflammation to that particular organ or tissue. For example, bursitis refers to inflammation of the bursa, tonsillitis means the inflammation of the tonsils, and arthritis means inflammation of the joint.

Treatment involves rest and cold and heat therapy, and may also include cast, splints, or, in severe cases, injections of corticosteroids (a group of anti-inflammatory agents). Your doctor may also prescribe oral medication for inflamation and pain.

Dislocations and Separations

A dislocation occurs when a bone is displaced from its original location. The most common form of dislocation occurs at the finger joints. This usually involves damage to the joint capsule and the ligaments that hold the two bones together. Depending on the severity of the dislocation, muscle and tendons may also be torn. The following are general symptoms of dislocations:

- the joint looks awkward or deformed
- the joint is painful when it is touched or moved
- the joint is not usable

One should seek medical attention after sustaining a dislocation – do not have a friend, or fellow player try to put the bone back into place as this may cause further damage to the joints, ligaments, tendons, muscles, blood supply, and nerves.

Separations occur when bones held together by fibrous ligaments, such as the acromioclavicular and sternoclavicular joints, tear and separate from each other. These joints are located on the anterior thorax – the sternoclavicular joint is located where the clavicle meets the sternum (medial end of the clavicle), and the acromioclavicular joint is the union of the clavicle and acromion on the scapula (lateral end of the clavicle; see Figure 4.3 on page 74). When these ligaments tear, depending on the severity, one is said to have sustained a separation. Acromioclavicular separations are commonly called shoulder separations and they vary in degree depending on how extensively the ligaments are torn.

Cartilage Damage

There are three main types of cartilage. **Hyaline cartilage** is the most widespread and is found at the ends of bones and free-moving joints; at the ends of the ribs; and in the nose, larynx, trachea, and bronchi. **Fibrocartilage** is the tough, very strong tissue that is found mainly between the vertebrae of the spine. **Elastic cartilage** or "yellow cartilage" makes up the external ear, the auditory tube of the middle ear, and the epiglottis. Cartilage surface is covered by a membrane known as the *perichondrium*. Cartilage is avascular (has no blood supply), and injuries take time to heal.

Cartilage damage or injuries (known in popular sports language as "torn cartilage") in the knee is common among football and basketball players and athletes in many other sports in which vigorous lateral movement and contact is common. Arthroscopy – a surgical procedure in which a few small incisions are made so that small fibre optic camera devices can assess the damage – is commonly used to diagnose and treat such injuries.

Shin Splints

Although the most common type of bone fracture is a stress fracture (see discussion on page 31), shin splints are also a result of overuse without adequate time for recovery. The term shin splints refers to a painful condition occurring on the medial or lateral side of the tibia, on its shaft. This is caused by the tearing of the interosseous membrane (located between the tibia and fibula) or the periosteum (the lining of the bone). The risk factors for shin splints are similar to that of stress fractures, and include training surface and regimen; a sudden change in frequency, duration, or intensity of training; training in athletic shoes that are older than six months; and training on uneven surfaces or on hard surfaces such as cement.

Some athletes can endure enormous pain before seeking medical attention. This is not wise when it comes to shin splints. If shin splints are left untreated, they can develop into serious problems such as stress fractures. If athletes seek medical attention early, they can avoid much pain and suffering and also be able to return to their normal activity levels sooner.

PROPER TREATMENT OF AN INJURY

Injuries are a common occurrence in all levels of sport, and, as such, it is important to know the signs of an injury and to take immediate action in order to stop further damage. Whenever an injury occurs, one or more of the following signs will appear, as noted by the simple acronym **S.H.A.R.P**:

- **Swelling**, instantly or over time,
- **Heat,** or increased temperature of the area,
- **Altered**, the tissue will not function properly, the injured area may turn
- **Red** in colour, and the area might be
- **Painful** to touch or move.

The P.I.E.R. Principle

When you or one of your fellow players sustains an injury, you should immediately follow the P.I.E.R. principle, an acronym for pressure, ice, elevation, and restriction.

Pressure and ice are used at the same time. Once the injured area has been identified, the area should be covered with a paper towel, or something similar, to avoid direct contact of the ice on the skin. Ice should be left on for no more than 10-20 minutes at a time, with a 10-20 minute break between repeated icings. While the injured area is being iced, it should also be elevated; this along with the ice will stop and reduce future swelling, which will help the doctor make a better diagnosis as to the extent of the injury. Lastly, the injured limb or muscle should be restricted, and the area must be rested, using tensors or slings.

Even though heat may feel good, it must be avoided during the initial days of an injury. Heat will promote swelling and make diagnosis difficult. When an injury does happen, make sure it diagnosed and treated by a sports medicine doctor or a chiropractor who has a sports injury background.

Below, we examine the more common injuries that occur to the shoulder, knee, and ankle joint. Some are a result of muscle imbalances. To help avoid such injuries, generally a 1-1 ratio should be followed during resistance training – when you work on the knee extensor muscles (quadriceps), you should also work the antagonistic muscle group (hamstrings) in order to minimize any imbalance.

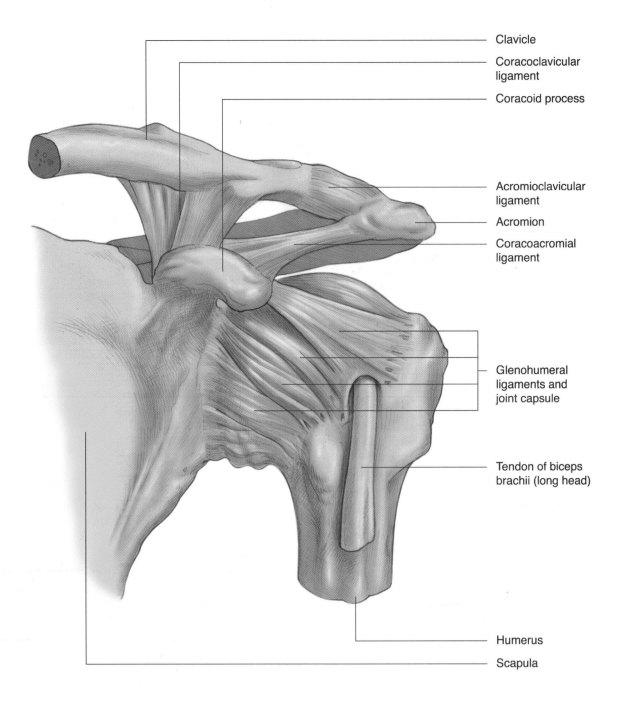

Clavicle

Coracoclavicular
ligament

Coracoid process

Acromioclavicular
ligament

Acromion

Coracoacromial
ligament

Glenohumeral
ligaments and
joint capsule

Tendon of biceps
brachii (long head)

Humerus

Scapula

Figure 4.3: Left shoulder joint, anterior view.

THE SHOULDER JOINT

The shoulder, or glenohumeral joint, is a very intricate joint that, for the most part, is unstable. It is this unstableness that gives the shoulder such versatility and permits us to perform all sorts of movements, including abduction, adduction, flexion, extension, elevation, depression, circumduction, protraction, retraction, and medial and lateral rotation.

This synovial ball-and-socket joint is made up of two bones directly, the scapula and the humerus, and indirectly with the clavicle. The humeral head articulates within the glenoid fossa of the scapula, and it is held in place by the ligaments of the shoulder, some of which are illustrated in Figure 4.3. The long head tendon of the biceps brachii also helps to support the shoulder joint anteriorly.

Athletes involved in sports that involve overhead actions such as throwing, swimming, and lifting are susceptible to shoulder injuries as a result of overuse. Athletes involved in sports that involve heavy physical contact, such as football, hockey, lacrosse, and rugby are susceptible to more severe injuries to the joint that could even require surgery. Let us take a look at the causes, symptoms, and treatment of common shoulder injuries.

Biceps Tendinitis

Biceps tendinitis is generally an overuse injury and happens when adequate rest is not given to the biceps brachii muscle when it has been worked or overloaded. The symptoms include pain on the proximal end (top end) of the biceps, making flexion of the shoulder and elbow painful.

As you can see from Figure 4.3, the long head of the biceps tendon passes within the intertubercular groove of the humerus, and when exposed to overuse or improper exercise technique, it will become inflamed and irritated.

Shoulder Separation

A shoulder separation is a tearing of the acromioclavicular ligament, which holds together the acromioclavicular joint (AC joint, the union of the clavicle to the acromion). The severity of the tear is usually determined after an X-ray has been taken, which will show to what extent the clavicle has separated from the acromion.

Injuries of this nature are a result of falls directly on the shoulder, usually as a result of contact from another player or a tumble on the shoulder. Surgery may be required if severity of the tear is third degree. Recovery can be accelerated after surgery with the help of physiotherapy, which will allow the athlete to return to activity sooner.

Shoulder Dislocations

A shoulder dislocation occurs when the humerus "pops out" of the glenoid fossa. This is usually a result of a hit or fall resulting in a tear to the glenohumeral ligaments and joint capsule (see Figure 4.3 for the location of these ligaments). There are numerous vital nerves known as the brachial plexus, and blood vessels that supply the shoulder and arm. Attempts to relocate the shoulder should only be performed by qualified personnel in a medical environment. If not, permanent damage to those structures may result. Surgery may be required to repair the shoulder in third-degree dislocations.

Rotator Cuff Tears

Rotator cuff tears usually involve one or all four muscles that make up the rotator cuff: supraspinatus, infraspinatus, teres minor, and subscapularis. Supraspinatus, infraspinatus, and teres minor share a common tendinous insertion on the greater tubercle of the humerus. Thus, when a part of the tendon is torn, all three muscles are affected in one way or another. Recall the functions of these muscles. Athletes who have sustained a rotator cuff injury find it hard to abduct and laterally or medially rotate the shoulder. Again, the severity of a tear must be diagnosed by a doctor, and, if severe enough, surgery many be required. When one sustains this type of injury, the P.I.E.R principle (see page 73) should be followed to help speed up diagnosis and healing.

THE KNEE JOINT

The knee joint is made up of the articulation of the femur and the tibia. The femur does not come in contact with the fibula; the fibula, however, does articulate with the tibia. The knee joint has been classified as a modified hinge joint because it was, at one time, believed to be responsible only for flexion and extension. However, the knee has the ability to slightly rotate the leg medially and laterally, classifying it, more precisely, as a modified ellipsoid joint.

The distal end of the femur is covered with articulating cartilage that rests on the proximal end of the tibia, which has two thick fibrocartilage articular discs known as menisci (meniscus, singular). They sit on the tibial condyles that are located on either side of the intercondylar eminence. Two ligaments that cross each other, called the cruciate ligaments, also cross over the intercondylar eminence and extend into the intercondylar fossa of the femur. The anterior cruciate ligament (ACL) helps stop anterior movement of the tibia with respect to the femur, and the posterior

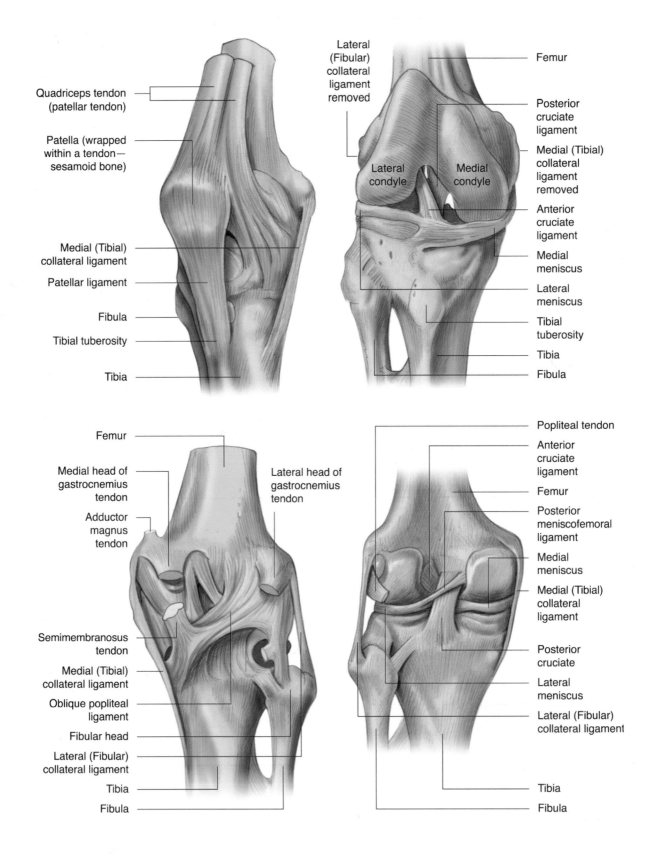

Quadriceps tendon (patellar tendon)

Patella (wrapped within a tendon — sesamoid bone)

Medial (Tibial) collateral ligament

Patellar ligament

Fibula

Tibial tuberosity

Tibia

Lateral (Fibular) collateral ligament removed

Lateral condyle

Medial condyle

Femur

Posterior cruciate ligament

Medial (Tibial) collateral ligament removed

Anterior cruciate ligament

Medial meniscus

Lateral meniscus

Tibial tuberosity

Tibia

Fibula

Femur

Medial head of gastrocnemius tendon

Adductor magnus tendon

Semimembranosus tendon

Medial (Tibial) collateral ligament

Oblique popliteal ligament

Fibular head

Lateral (Fibular) collateral ligament

Tibia

Fibula

Lateral head of gastrocnemius tendon

Popliteal tendon

Anterior cruciate ligament

Femur

Posterior meniscofemoral ligament

Medial meniscus

Medial (Tibial) collateral ligament

Posterior cruciate

Lateral meniscus

Lateral (Fibular) collateral ligament

Tibia

Fibula

Figure 4.4: Top — right knee, anterior and anterior deep views.
Bottom left — right knee, posterior view.
Bottom right — left knee joint, posterior deep view.

cruciate ligament (PCL) prevents posterior movement of the tibia with respect to the femur.

The knee joint is also held together by the fibrous capsule and medially by the tibial collateral ligament, commonly called the **medial collateral ligament (MCL)**, and laterally by the fibular collateral ligament, commonly called the **lateral collateral ligament (LCL)**. Respectively, these ligaments provide medial and lateral stability of the knee. The muscles that help stabilize the knee on the anterior side are the quadriceps muscle that inserts on the tibial tuberosity, and posteriorly by the gastrocnemius and hamstring group (see Figure 4.4). Much like any muscle around a joint, the more they are strengthened, the greater the integrity of the joint and injury resistant they become.

Let us now take a look at some common injuries of the knee joint.

Knee Ligament Tears

The most common knee ligament tears involve "blows" to the lateral side of the knee. When this happens, the severity of the blow determines the degree of the tear and the amount of tissue damage. As with all ligaments, the amount of tear is the determining factor in rehabilitation and in surgical intervention.

Generally, when one sustains a blow to the lateral side of the knee, as perhaps during a field hockey game when one player's knee strikes the lateral side of another player's lower leg, knee damage will result to the medial side. The first tissue to tear is the joint capsule, if the blow is of the severe variety, then damage to the medial collateral ligament, the medial meniscus, and anterior cruciate ligament (ACL).

If all three are torn, then the knee must be reconstructed through surgery. In the past, this would have been a career-ending injury, but with the advancement in modern diagnostic equipment and surgical procedures, most athletes return to play within a year. Steve Yzerman of the Detroit Red Wings, Terrel Davis, formerly with the Denver Broncos of the National Football League, and Sean Elliot of the NBA's San Antonio Spurs are such examples.

It should be mentioned that some individuals are more predisposed to ACL tears and other knee injuries because of their wider Q-angle. The Q-angle (quadriceps angle) is formed in the frontal plane by a line drawn from the centre of the patella to the anterior superior iliac spine, and another from the centre of the tibial tuberosity to the centre of the patella extending up the thigh. If the angle created by the intersection of these two lines above the patella is greater than twenty degrees, this puts the individual at greater risk of experiencing a knee injury. The width of the pelvis determines the size of the Q angle. Since women generally have a wider pelvis than men, their Q angle tends to be greater. At this greater angle, forces are concentrated on the ligament each time the knee twists, increasing the risk for an ACL tear. Proper stretching and strengthening will decrease the chance of injury.

Osgood-Schlatter Syndrome

Doctor Robert Osgood, a U.S. orthopedist, and Doctor Carl Schlatter, a Switzerland physician, discovered this syndrome, which in many textbooks is also referred to as a disease. It is a result of a condition known as osteochondritis, a disease of the ossification centres in the bones of young children. Specifically, Osgood-Schlatter syndrome affects the epiphyseal plate of the tibial tuberosity.

The standard explanation for this syndrome is growing pains for the child. Osgood-Schlatter syndrome is more prevalent in males than females. In the growing child, the epiphyseal plates or growth plates allow the bones to lengthen and increase in size. The tibial tuberosity has such a growth plate, and, if overloaded or overused, can become irritated and inflamed. Running and jumping stresses the patellar tendon and ligament, thus causing inflammation of the cartilage layer in that growth plate. Like tendinitis, this can cause much swelling and discomfort. This does not effect the growth of the child, in that it does not damage the epiphyseal plate. Once again this must be diagnosed by a sports physician and the principles of P.I.E.R (see page 73) should be followed until a doctor has completed an examination.

Patellofemoral Syndrome (PFS)

The major symptom of patellofemoral syndrome (PFS), is the gradual onset of anterior knee pain or pain around the patella. PFS usually affects adolescents or young adults, and women are often affected more than men. Similar to Osgood-Schlatter disease, the pain is aggravated by sports such as running, volleyball, and basketball.

Patellofemoral syndrome is characterized by a group of symptoms that are easily diagnosed and often respond to simple rehabilitation. Unlike Osgood-Schlatter disease, the pain is a result of increased or misdirected forces between the kneecap and the femur. There are many theories as to what causes PFS, yet the medical community lacks consensus on the fundamental factors associated with PFS. Thus, the exact physiology of PFS is a matter of debate.

Overuse, overloading, and misuse of the patellofemoral joint seem to be the factors upon which most researchers agree. Any pain on the knee as a result of overuse or trauma should be treated with the P.I.E.R principle (see page 73), and if pain persists, professional medical care should be sought.

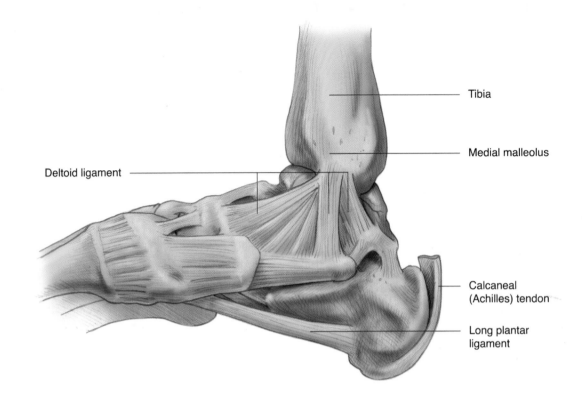

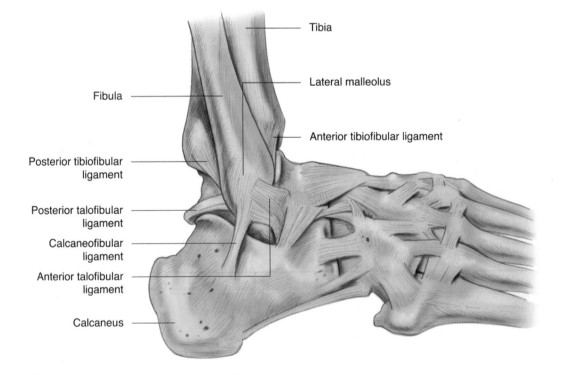

Figures 4.5 and 4.6: Right ankle joint, medial and lateral views.

THE ANKLE JOINT

The ankle joint is a modified hinge joint that comprises the distal ends of the tibia and fibula resting on the talus to form the ankle joint. This joint is responsible for plantar flexion and dorsiflexion. Inversion and eversion are usually discussed as ankle joint movements, yet, in fact, they occur at the transverse tarsal joint of the foot (not illustrated). The lateral border of the ankle joint, on the fibula side, is called the lateral malleolus, and the medial border, from the tibia side, is called the medial malleolus. Similar to all the synovial joints we have discussed in this section, the ankle joint is also wrapped within a thick fibrous capsule.

Some of the important ligaments include the **anterior** and **posterior tibiofibular ligaments**, which are superior to the **anterior** and **posterior talofibular ligaments**, and the **calcaneofibular ligament**. Of all the ligaments in the ankle joint, these are the weakest. Strengthening exercises for the ankle should be included in the exercise program of anyone involved with sports or activities that require jumping and rapid changes of direction. Surgical tubing exercises are an excellent training tool to help strengthen the muscles around the ankle that invert and evert the ankle. These ligaments are clearly illustrated in Figure 4.6 in the lateral view of the ankle. On the medial side of the ankle is a "delta"-shaped and very strong ligament called the **deltoid ligament**. This can be seen in Figure 4.5.

Let us now take a closer look at inversion and eversion ankle sprains and how they are caused.

Inversion Sprains

The ankle is at its weakest when it is plantar flexed, a movement that is essential to most athletic events. In sports that involve jumping and quick changes of direction, such as basketball, volleyball, soccer, and football, inversion sprains are a common occurrence.

Inversion sprains are commonly called "rolling over on your ankle" or "twisted ankle." Since the ankle is most unstable during plantar flexion, when you jump up in the air, or plant hard to change your direction, the ankle plantar flexes with great force coming up and does not return back to neutral position as the body comes down, causing the ankle to be inverted past the joint's normal range of movement and resulting in a sprained ankle (hence "rolling over"). This type of injury can affect one or all of the lateral ligaments of the ankle, specifically the anterior and posterior talofibular and calcaneofibular ligaments. Once again, the severity of the sprain will dictate the amount of time needed for healing to take place.

Surgery is extremely rare even in third-degree inversion ankle sprains. You may recently have heard of ankle sprains being described as low, as in the above case, or high. High ankle sprains involve damage to one or both of the anterior and posterior tibiofibular ligaments. The P.I.E.R principle (page 73) should be adhered to when an ankle injury of any type has been sustained, with extra attention taken to elevate the ankle to help reduce the amount of swelling in the area and thus leading to early diagnosis and quick recovery.

Eversion Sprains

Eversion sprains are rare because of the strength of the deltoid ligament. This ligament attaches the medial malleolus to three bones of the foot. This ligament is so strong that, instead of tearing completely, it tears off the tip of the medial malleolus. The most severe eversion injury is known as a Pott's Fracture, which is a break of the tip of the medial malleolus and a break of the fibula. This is a result of a force on the medial side of the ankle, causing the deltoid ligament to rip off the tip of the medial malleolus and a break of the fibula.

A Pott's Fracture is treated much like any other fracture in that the patient is placed in a cast for eight to twelve weeks, followed by intense physiotherapy to increase the strength of the surrounding musculature and the ROM of the joint. This is not a career-ending injury. When bone heals, it never breaks at the same spot again. However, care and rehabilitation should be adhered to in order to prevent any future weakness in that area.

WHERE DO WE GO FROM HERE?

Prior to this section, we examined all of the body parts and functions that play a key role in exercise and sport. In this section, we examined what happens when many of these parts cease functioning as they should because of some structural damage – in other words, an injury. Consequently, when you think about the functions of joints, muscles, tendons, ligaments, and so forth, and the role they play in allowing the human body to work through the wide range of movement required for exercise, you should consider both their "ideal" functions, their less-than-ideal functions (i.e., through injury), and the ways in which the latter can be improved through treatment.

In the following section, we will add another piece to the puzzle of exercise and the role of the anatomical and physiological systems in examining the role of the energy systems and the various types of muscle fibre they supply. Knowing how muscles function on a structural level is a beginning, but we must also understand how they are "fuelled" by the three ways in which the body creates energy for them.

Cyclists start the men's Criterium event at the Canada Summer Games in London, Ontario, August 14, 2001. Quebec's Martin Gilbert went on to win the event (CP PHOTO/Jonathan Hayward).

5
Energy Systems and Muscle Fibre Types

"Some call it 'hitting the wall.' Others have names for it we can't print here."
— Marathon runner Dave Keuhls on what happens when the body's glycogen stores
become depleted in the last 10 km of a 42-km race

KEY CONCEPTS

- Bioenergetic conversion
- Carbohydrates
- Glycogen
- Metabolism
- Adenosine triphosphate (ATP)
- Anaerobic system
- Aerobic system
- ATP-PC (Anaerobic alactic)
- Glycolysis (Anaerobic lactic)

- Lactic acid
- Cellular respiration (Aerobic)
- Krebs cycle
- Electron Transport Chain
- Blood lactate threshold/anaerobic threshold
- Cori cycle
- Fatty acids
- Beta oxidization

- Amino acids
- Myoglobin
- Type I fibre (SO)
- Type IIA fibre (FOG)
- Type IIB fibre (FG)
- Tonic muscles
- Phasic muscles

Our bodies have complex ways of generating the energy they need. And people who make extraordinary demands on their bodies – athletes being a prime example – need great amounts of energy. In this section, we will take a look at how the human body generates energy, and how the body makes use of this energy for working muscles.

THREE KEY ENERGY NUTRIENTS

The food we take in is broken down into three energy nutrients in the course of digestion: (1) proteins, (2) fats, and (3) carbohydrates. It is through the bioenergetic conversion of these nutrients that our bodies are able to function and we are able to carry out physical activity. (These essential nutrients are discussed further in the section on "Nutrition," beginning on page 141.) Carbohydrates yield 4.1 Calories per gram, proteins yield 4.3 Calories per gram, and fats yield 9.3 Calories per gram. Of these three, however, carbohydrates are our most important source of energy. While they do not contain as much energy as fat on a weight basis, carbohydrates are plentiful throughout the body and are easily accessible as an energy source.

Because of the central role carbohydrates play, the first part this section focuses on how our bodies harness energy from these sources. Fats and proteins enter the energy system through a somewhat different route and are dealt with later in the section.

The Role of Carbohydrates

Carbohydrates are the most abundant organic substances in nature, and they are essential for human and animal life. They come to us almost entirely from foods that originate from plants, such as vegetables, fruits, and grain-based foods, such as bread and pasta.

Carbohydrates are formed by green plants from carbon dioxide and water in the course of photosynthesis. During photosynthesis, carbon dioxide from the air combines with water in the presence of sunlight to yield carbohydrates; oxygen is released as a by-product of this reaction. We humans, along with others in the animal kingdom, reverse this process – we extract energy from these organic compounds and release carbon dioxide.

Glucose (a derivative of the Greek word *glykys* meaning "sweet") is the usual form in which carbohydrates are assimilated by humans. It is stored within skeletal muscle and within the liver as glycogen. Glucose that is stored in this way can be be broken down under conditions of stress or the demands of muscular activity, carried through the body by the blood, and brought into action as an energy source.

This highly complex process by which energy is supplied throughout the body and energy-rich material (fats and proteins as well as carbohydrates) are assimilated by the body for the purposes of energy renewal is referred to as metabolism.

ATP — THE COMMON ENERGY CURRENCY

As noted above, the energy we use comes directly from the nutrients in the food we eat, particularly from carbohydrate sources. But, to be usable, these nutrients need to be reconstituted into a universal form of energy – a "free energy" that can then be used for muscle contraction and many other physiological processes that go on in our bodies.

The final form this free energy takes is adenosine triphosphate (ATP), the common energy molecule for all living things. In effect, ATP captures the chemical energy resulting from the breakdown of food and can be used, conveniently, to fuel the various cellular processes. (Fritz Albert Lipmann and Herman Kalckar discovered the importance of ATP in 1941.)

At the molecular level, adenosine triphosphate consists of three phosphates attached by high-energy bonds to adenosine. Energy is released when a trailing phosphate (P_i) is broken from the ATP molecule (see Figure 5.1). This results in ADP (adenosine diphosphate) plus energy, as shown below:

$$ATP \Rightarrow ADP + P + \text{ENERGY}$$

Of course, being in high demand, ATP energy supplies are used up very quickly, and the problem then becomes how to re-create new supplies of ATP so as to ensure that bodily functions, including physical movement, continue. The means by which the body addresses this "reconstruction" problem is the main subject of this section.

Two Energy Systems

There are two methods for resynthesizing ATP – anaerobic (without oxygen) and aerobic (with oxygen). The anaerobic system occurs relatively quickly in the muscle fibre, utilizing chemicals and enzymes readily at hand for powerful but relatively short-lived physical actions.

The aerobic system is a much more complicated process and takes place in the **mitochondria** (the cell's power station). The aerobic process, which involves many enzymes and several complex sub-pathways, leads to the complete breakdown of glucose. Fats and protein also enter the cycle at this stage.

The anaerobic and aerobic energy systems are sometimes presented, incorrectly, as if they were two completely opposing systems. In fact, as we will see, the two systems coexist, overlap, and interact in various combinations. If one tracks the contribution of each system over time, it is clear that the anaerobic system is more important in short-run, high-intensity activity, whereas the aerobic system is the key to endurance events. Nevertheless, all sporting events

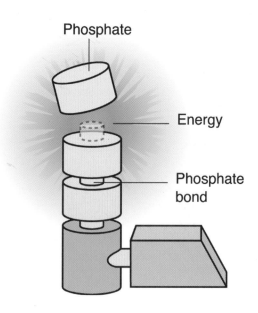

Phosphate

Energy

Phosphate bond

Figure 5.1: ATP molecule.

and all physical activity relies on some combination of aerobic and anaerobic systems. The precise way these systems are utilized for ATP energy production depends on the individual athlete, the sport, and the intensity and duration of physical activity.

Three Metabolic Pathways

Within these two "systems" (anaerobic and aerobic), there are three main "metabolic pathways" by which ATP energy reserves are restored:

- the ATP-PC pathway (anaerobic alactic);
- the glycolysis pathway (anaerobic lactic); and
- cellular respiration (aerobic).

Let us now examine the role each of these chemical pathways plays in helping our bodies create sufficient energy reserves to carry out not only physical activity and movement of all kinds, but all our vital processes (neural activity, organ function, breathing, and so on) as well. These three pathways are compared in Table 5.1 that follows this discussion (page 86).

PATHWAY 1: ATP-PC (ANAEROBIC ALACTIC)

The enormous burst of ATP energy required for a speed skater such as Catriona LeMay Doan to begin her journey down the track is produced anaerobically (without the aid of oxygen). This system is known as the ATP-PC system. This is the first and simplest of the two anaerobic energy pathways. It yields enough ATP for about 10-15 seconds of work.

The ATP-PC System

The **ATP-PC system** (also referred to as the phosphagen system), relies on the action of phosphocreatine, a compound that is normally stored in muscle and readily accessible. Like ATP, phosphocreatine (PC) is a high-energy molecule where the phosphate can be broken off easily and can be used to convert ADP back to ATP (see Figure 5.2). This small reservoir of creatine phosphate within the muscle can sustain the level of ATP required during this initial phase of short but intense activity.

The chemical formula that represents this process is

$$PC + ADP \Rightarrow ATP + CREATINE$$

In sports, the ATP-PC system plays an important role in such power events as the 50- and 100-metre dash, the high jump, and Olympic weightlifting. These events last only a few seconds and require a large burst of energy. ATP-PC is important in these events as it provides the highest rate of ATP synthesis that cannot be matched by other, more complex, energy systems.

However, muscles do not have large supplies of phosphocreatine. After about 10-15 seconds, when the ATP produced by this method is largely depleted, the athlete needs to rely increasingly on a second system to resynthesize still more ATP in order to satisfy the energy demand. The full replenishment of phosphocreatine itself requires ATP and occurs during the recovery period. It occurs rapidly and is achieved mainly as a result of supplies of ATP being created during aerobic processes. This ATP is utilized to recombine phosphate and creatine, and takes 2-5 minutes of recovery time.

The ATP-PC system is commonly known as the "anaerobic alactic system" (the prefix "a," means without), since it does not yield lactic acid as a by-product. This system relies solely on readily available phosphocreatine stores in the muscle fibre and does not involve the metabolism of glucose as an energy source.

The bioenergetic reaction that occurs during this process is relatively simple, yet it is very effective in producing sufficient ATP energy to enable short, powerful bursts of effort.

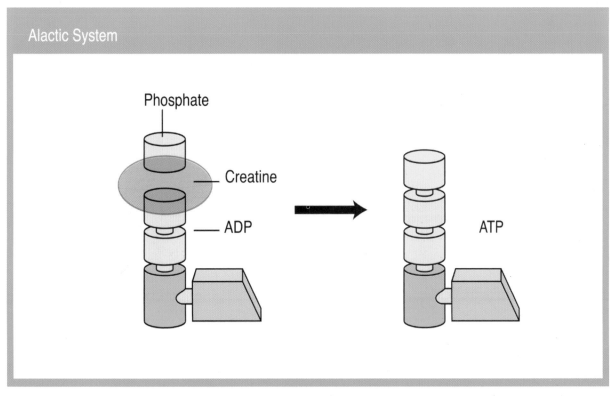

Figure 5.2: Energy pathway 1: The ATP-PC system (anaerobic alactic). This system relies on the action of phosphocreatine, a compound that is normally stored in muscle and is readily accessible. It yields one molecule of ATP.

PATHWAY 2: GLYCOLYSIS (ANAEROBIC LACTIC)

Glycolysis is the name given to the second energy pathway. The ATP energy produced during this process will allow an athlete to engage in a high level of performance for about an additional 1-3 minutes. Since glucose is normally plentiful throughout the body, glycolysis is an ideal backup to the ATP-PC system for medium-term physical activities – such as 400-metre and 800-metre track events or, say, a typical shift in a hockey game.

Glycolysis can be thought of as the first sequence of reactions in the full metabolism of glucose. During this process, glucose is partially broken down to provide usable energy in the form of ATP as illustrated in Figure 5.3 below. Considerably more complex than the ATP-PC system, glycolysis involves eleven separate biochemical reactions and yields twice as much ATP.

Like ATP-PC, this second metabolic pathway is also capable of producing ATP rapidly and without the need for oxygen. Through a series of chemical reactions, glycolysis transfers energy from glucose and rejoins phosphate to ADP (adenosine diphosphate).

The chemical representation of glycolysis is

$$C_6H_{12}O_6 + 2ADP + 2P_i \Rightarrow 2C_3H_6O_3 + 2ATP + 2H_2O$$
(Glucose)   (Lactate)

Pyruvate and Lactic Acid

The main product of glycolysis is pyruvate (pyruvic acid). Under aerobic conditions (when oxygen is readily available to the muscles), pyruvate is the beginning of the third (aerobic) system that eventually leads to the complete breakdown of glucose and to very large quantities of ATP. In the absence of adequate oxygen (say, in intense exercise or exercise in high-altitude conditions), the process is halted at the glycolysis stage. Pyruvic acid is converted to **lactic acid** and exhaustion or painful muscle agony begins to set in. This gives the system its secondary name, the "anaerobic lactic system."

The buildup of lactic acid eventually hampers the breakdown of glucose and decreases the ability of the muscle fibres to contract. In strength and power sports, such as short-distance track events and weightlifting, which rely heavily on the aerobic lactic system, the buildup of lactic acid is associated with the intense burning sensation felt in muscles during an intense workout (although there is some debate as to whether it directly causes it).

For intermediate types of activities that involve the production of lactate, it is generally recommended that exercise recovery methods be adopted. These involve light aerobic activity combined with rest intervals. Lactic acid removal requires 30-60 minutes of exercise recovery or 1-2 hours of rest recovery.

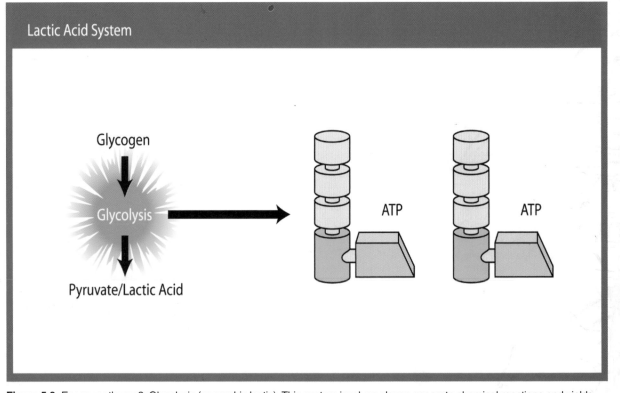

Figure 5.3: Energy pathway 2: Glycolysis (anaerobic lactic). This system involves eleven separate chemical reactions and yields twice as much ATP as the ATP-PC system (two molecules for every molecule of glucose).

PATHWAY 3: THE AEROBIC SYSTEM

For any athlete to sustain intense activity longer than 90 seconds or so, a third energy system must come into prominence. This involves molecular activity in the mitochondria of the cells, and is referred to as **cellular respiration**. Fats and protein can be used as energy sources at this stage. Fats are the predominant source of energy in exercise lasting longer than 20 minutes; proteins are used in chronic situations such as that of starvation.

This is the energy pathway that our bodies depend most heavily upon to sustain endurance-type events, such as a marathon run or swim or an entire soccer match. The aerobic pathway results in the complete breakdown of glucose.

Cellular Respiration

The chemical equation for cellular respiration of glucose is

$$C_6H_{12}O_6 + 6O_2 + 36ADP + 36P_i \Rightarrow 6CO_2 + 36\ ATP + 6H_2O$$

The ATP produced by the aerobic method far exceeds the other two pathways (see Figure 5.4). In the end, thirty-six molecules of ATP are produced (or a few more, depending on the fuel source) for every molecule of glucose – nearly twenty times the anaerobic system. In the presence of oxygen, the aerobic system can, in theory, sustain activity for a very long time, or until other physiological limits are reached.

Cellular respiration actually involves three separate sub-pathways:

- **Glycolysis.** The first stage or sub-pathway is the same as in the anaerobic lactic system except that, in the presence of oxygen, pyruvic acid is converted to acetyl CoA (rather than lactic acid). Acetyl CoA then enters a more complicated pathway known as the Krebs cycle (or citric acid cycle), which is a central pathway for the metabolism of fats and proteins as well (named for Sir Hans Krebs, 1900-81, the German-born, British biochemist who first described the pathway).

- **Krebs cycle**. Through a series of eight reactions, two ATP molecules are produced at this stage, along with new compounds capable of storing "high-energy" electrons. From here, the high-energy electrons produced during the Krebs cycle are sent to a process within the mitochondria, known as the electron transport chain.

- **Electron transport chain**. During the final stage of aerobic respiration, large amounts of ATP are produced, with carbon dioxide and water as the only by-products. Some research suggests that, as electrons pass down the chain, highly reactive molecules (known as free radicals) are by-products and these molecules may be a contributor to long-term muscle fatigue.

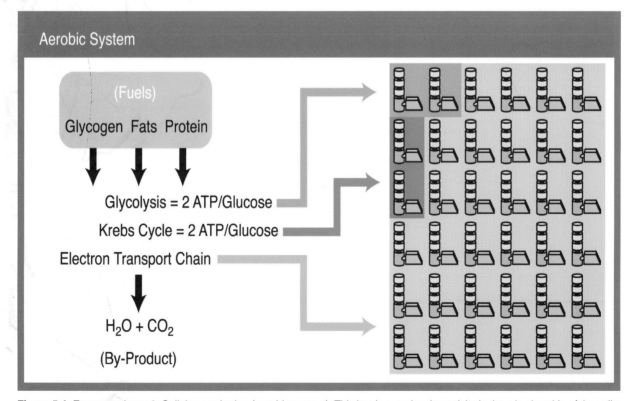

Figure 5.4: Energy pathway 3: Cellular respiration (aerobic system). This involves molecular activity in the mitochondria of the cells and yields nearly twenty times more than the anaerobic system.

Table 5.1: Three energy pathways compared

Name	ATP-PC (Anaerobic alactic system)	Glycolysis (Anaerobic lactic system)	Cellular respiration (Aerobic system)
Location of activity	Cytoplasm	Cytoplasm	Mitochondria
Energy source	Creatine phosphate	Glucose (glycogen)	Glycogen, fats, proteins
Uses oxygen or not	Anaerobic (without oxygen)	Anaerobic (without oxygen)	Aerobic (with oxygen)
ATP	1 molecule	2 molecules per molecule of glucose	36 molecules per molecule of glucose
Duration	10-15 seconds	15 seconds to 3 minutes	120 seconds and beyond
Number of chemical reactions	1-2	11	Glycolysis, Krebs cycle, and the electron transport chain
By-products	None	Lactic acid	Water and carbon dioxide
Basic formula	$PC + ADP \Rightarrow$ $ATP + Creatine$	$C_6H_{12}O_6 + 2ADP + 2P_i \Rightarrow$ $2C_3H_6O_3 + 2ATP + 2H_2O$	$C_6H_{12}O_6 + 6O_2 + 36ADP +$ $36P_i \Rightarrow 6CO_2 + 36 ATP +$ $6H_2O$
Type of activities	Power surges, speed events	Intermediate activities/sprint finish	Prolonged activities
Types of exercise that rely on this system	Sprints, jumping, weightlifting	200-800-metre runs; a shift in hockey	Marathons
Advantages	Very quick surge of power	Quick surge of power	Long duration; complete breakdown of glucose
Limitation of energy system	Short duration; muscles store small amounts of ATP and creatine phosphate	Buildup of lactic acid causes pain and fatigue	Slow; requires large amount of oxygen
Muscle fibre type recruited	Type IIB (fast-twitch)	Type IIA (fast-twitch)	Type I (slow-twitch)

Energy pathways	Anaerobic pathways				Aerobic pathway			
	Alactic	Lactic						
Primary energy source	ATP produced without the presence of O₂				ATP produced in the presence of O₂			
Fuel	Phosphate system ATP/CP stored in muscle	Lactic acid (LA) system glycogen→LA by-products			Glycogen completely burned in the presence of O₂		Fats	Protein
Duration	0 s 10 s	40 s 70 s			2 min 8 min		25 min 1 hr 2 hr 3 hr	
Sports events	Sprinting 100 m dash Throws Jumps Weightlifting Ski jumping Diving Vaulting in gymnastics	200-400 m sprint 500 m speed skating Most gym events Cycling, track 50 m swimming	100 m swimming 800 m track 500 m canoeing 1,000 m speed skating Floor exercise gymnastics Alpine skiing Cycling, track, 1,000 m and pursuit		Middle-distance track, swimming, speed skating 1,000 m canoeing Boxing Wrestling Martial arts Figure skating Synchronized swimming		Long-distance track, swimming, speed skating, canoeing Cross-country skiing Rowing Cycling, road racing Triathlon	
		Most team sports/racquet sports/sailing						
Skills	Mostly acyclic	Acyclic and cyclic					Cyclic	

Figure 5.5: The overlapping energy systems and energy sources during intense exercise.

Adapted, by permission, from Bompa, T.O. (1999). *Periodization: Theory and methodology of training* (4th ed., p. 23). Champaign, Il: Human Kinetics.

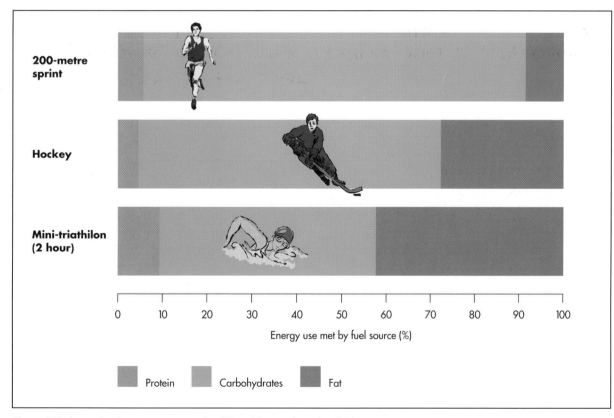

Figure 5.6: Approximate energy sources for different types of sport activities.

LACTIC ACID

In the context of continued physical activity, lactic acid presents a serious problem. The point at which lactate levels in the blood increase abruptly beyond resting values is known as the blood lactate threshold or the anaerobic threshold. (The term onset of blood lactate accumulation (OBLA), refers to the point at which blood lactate levels begin to accumulate very rapidly – OBLA is discussed in greater detail on page 130.) The anaerobic threshold varies from person to person, but if the threshold is reached at lower intensities of exercise, this suggests that the oxidative energy systems in the muscles are not working well or are being overtaxed.

Generally, untrained individuals have a low anaerobic threshold, whereas elite endurance athletes have a high threshold. Untrained individuals typically may reach their lactate threshold at about 50-60 percent of their VO_2 max, whereas trained athletes may not reach their threshold until 70-80 percent of their VO_2max. This topic is discussed further towards the end of the Cardiorespiratory section (beginning on page 128).

Raising the Lactic Acid Threshold

Raising the lactate threshold is an important objective of physical training. This involves anaerobic (power) training to extend the point at which lactate buildup occurs as well as aerobic-style (endurance) training to improve cardiorespiratory capacity, increase the concentration of mitochondria and the oxygen-carrying molecule myoglobin in muscle fibres, and improve the efficiency of oxygen transfers at the cellular level.

The recovery stage is also important in limiting the effects of lactic acid. Many sporting events involve relatively short bursts of intense exercise followed by a rest interval, followed by more bursts – hockey, basketball, soccer, and tennis, for example. Research on blood lactate levels during intermittent exercise indicates that monitoring and adjusting these rest intervals can lead to significant improvements in individual and, therefore, team performance. (Oxygen deficit and oxygen recovery are dealt with more fully in Section 7, "The Cardiorespiratory System.")

The Cori Cycle

Because it hampers continued activity, the buildup of lactic acid is usually thought of in a negative light by sports enthusiasts. Nevertheless, lactic acid should be seen as a by-product of a process rather than simply an end-product. Lactate is transported by the blood to the liver where most of it is converted back to glucose, from which glycogen is formed in a process known as gluconeogensis. About one-sixth of the lactate is oxidized to carbon dioxide.

The Cori cycle (named after Carl Ferdinand Cori, Czech-born American biochemist, 1896-1984) is the name given to the process by which lactic acid is converted to pyruvate for future conversion to glucose and glycogen (see Figure 5.7 below). In effect, expended from the cycle in the first round, lactate re-enters the cycle as an energy source in its own right.

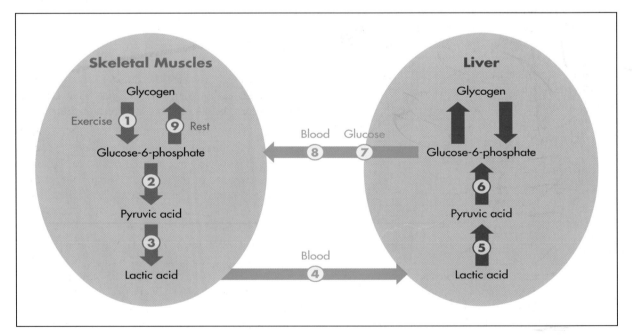

Figure 5.7: The Cori cycle, showing the sequence of steps by which lactic acid is converted to pyruvate and subsequently to glucose and glycogen.

ENERGY FROM FATS AND PROTEINS

Thus far we have focused mainly on how ATP energy is produced from carbohydrates/glucose sources – anaerobically (through glycolysis), and aerobically (through cellular respiration). But the body uses fats and proteins as energy sources as well. During physical exercise, the primary sources are carbohydrates and fats. Protein, because it is less accessible, normally contributes a relatively small percentage of the total energy used.

Fats

Fats are, of course, an ideal fuel source in that they contain large quantities of stored energy – as we have noted above, they contain more than twice as much, on a unit mass basis, as either carbohydrates or protein. The primary types of fats found in muscle cells and adipose tissue, and subsequently converted for use as energy, are known as fatty acids. These fatty acids are stored in the body as triglycerides. Through a process known as **lipolysis** (the release of lipids or fats), triglycerides are broken down and the resulting fatty acids become available as an energy source.

The point at which fatty acids enter the energy system is the Krebs cycle (the citric acid cycle), mentioned earlier. Because of the Krebs cycle's strategic importance for the energy system as a whole, this rather complex chemical sequence has gained the reputation, deservedly, as a kind of "metabolic mill" for the human body.

Before entering the energy supply chain, fatty acids need first to be converted to acetyl-CoA. This is achieved through a process known as beta oxidation. Beta oxidation of fats occurs within the mitochondria of cells and involves four chemical reactions, ultimately yielding acetyl-CoA. Acetyl-CoA then enters the Krebs cycle and becomes a primary energy source for the production of ATP within the electron transport chain (in the same manner as the acetyl-CoA that results from the final stage of glycolysis).

While fats are an important energy source, as in the case of the other other essential nutrients, the key seems to be maintaining a balanced intake. Less than the necessary amount will mean that energy reserves will be depleted quickly; more will result in unhealthy fat accumulation on the body.

Proteins

As a fuel source, protein contains about as much potential energy as carbohydrate (and half as much as fat). However, unlike carbohydrates and fats, there are no "protein reserves" in the body. All proteins are part of existing body tissue or are actively engaged as component parts of the metabolic system.

Protein in the body is comprised of about twenty different amino acids, which are used by the body to form the various body tissues. Nine of these (called essential amino acids) cannot be synthesized by the body and must be consumed as food. To be utilized as an energy source, protein must first be broken down into these separate amino acids. The amino acid alanine, for example, is the main contributor. It is converted in the liver to glycogen, which is then transported as glucose through the bloodstream to working muscles. Other amino acids participate in various ways in the bioenergetic process.

Protein, as a source of energy, plays an important role in endurance-type activities and more generally in chronic conditions when glycogen reserves are significantly diminished. This would suggest that, in the absence of adequate levels of other energy sources, the body may draw upon protein as a kind of energy backup. (In this respect, the use of protein in endurance events has been said to mimic the conditions created during short-term starvation.)

Protein Supplementation

Contrary to popular belief, eating large amounts of high-protein foods (e.g., lean meats), or taking protein supplements, does not automatically result in an increase of muscle mass, a lean body, or an increased ability to perform better at sports. Indeed, excessive intake or the use of protein supplements may lead to serious bodily harm by putting excessive strain on the liver and kidneys. Protein powders, for example, have become promoted and popularized as a way athletes can increasing their protein intake, yet there is no scientific evidence that they are useful at all, nor are there long-term studies of their effects on heath. Even if protein supplements were shown to be effective under certain conditions, it is still unclear as to how much additional protein an athlete might need in order to improve his or her performance, and what might be the long-term health effects of such supplements.

At this point, nutritionists and exercise physiologists generally maintain that protein supplementation is unnecessary and unwise in light of the possible health damage that could result. The general consensus among experts is that, at best, protein supplements are given too much publicity and, at worst, they may be harmful to the individuals who take them. The best way to ensure that one's body has the energy reserves it needs, when it needs them, is to maintain a diet that contains appropriate and balanced amounts of all three energy nutrients – carbohydrates, fats, and proteins. For most people, including serious athletes, supplementation should never replace sensible eating habits and one should always be aware of the potential dangers of dietary supplements of any kind.

MUSCLE FIBRE TYPES

As noted above, the body utilizes two (or three) different systems for producing energy. It should not be surprising, therefore, that certain muscles and groups of muscles are more adapted to one energy production system than another.

Slow-Twitch and Fast-Twitch Muscles

A distinction commonly drawn is between slow-twitch and fast-twitch muscle fibres. While "twitch" may not do full justice to the complex bioenergetic processes involved, the distinction is a useful one.

In general, there are two kinds of muscle fibres – slow-twitch and fast-twitch.

- **Slow-twitch muscle fibres** are red or dark in colour, and generate and relax tension relatively slowly. The trade-off, however, is that they are able to maintain a lower level of tension for long durations. Slow-twitch fibres have low levels of an enzyme called myosin ATPase, which the body uses to provide instant energy for muscle contraction. Also, these fibres contain low levels of what are known as glycolytic enzymes, which permit the release of glycogen within muscles and contain high levels of oxidative enzymes. Slow-twitch fibres can produce lower tension and/or contraction levels over a longer period of time. This makes them the ones that are most active during activities such as long-distance swimming, cycling, and running.

- **Fast-twitch muscle fibres** are more pale in colour, have the ability to tense and relax quickly, and can generate large amounts of tension with relatively low endurance levels. Fast-twitch fibres have a high level of myosin ATPase and contain high levels of glycolytic enzymes. Fast-twitch fibres can activate at a rate of two to three times faster than slow-twitch fibres, making them ideal for the fast, powerful muscle contractions needed for activities such as short sprints, powerlifting, and explosive jumping.

The Importance of Myoglobin

The differences in muscle fibre types are mainly due to the extent to which a particular muscle relies on oxygen in the production of energy. The protein myoglobin is the oxygen storage unit that delivers oxygen to working muscles, thereby enabling energy-producing biochemical reactions to be sustained over a long period.

The more a muscle utilizes aerobic processes for energy production, the more it is able to sustain longer-term activity. Slow-twitch, red muscle fibres are high in myoglobin and are ideal for endurance activities. Fast-twitch fibres (with low myoglobin concentrations) are more adapted for shorter bursts of effort.

From the discussion on muscle structure, you will recall that contraction involves: (1) the transmission of an impulse (action potential) through the transverse tubulae system; (2) the release of calcium into the sarcoplasm; and (3) the attachment and detachment of myosin and actin filaments. Fast-twitch and slow-twitch muscle fibres can be distinguished on these criteria as well, with fast-twitch muscles performing each of these tasks more efficiently and more quickly.

Table 5.2: Approximate distribution of muscle fibre types for different sports

	Slow-twitch	Fast-twitch
Cyclist	61%	39%
Canoeist	61%	39%
Middle-distance runner	59%	41%
Swimmer	58%	42%
Weightlifter	46%	54%
Orienteer	69%	31%
Sprinter	26%	74%
Soccer player	53%	47%
Untrained person	42%	58%

From research based on the vastus lateralis muscle (the muscle that is used to extend the knee). From Bergue, U., et al. (1978). Maximal oxygen uptake and muscle fibre types in trained and untrained humans. *Medicine & Science in Sports & Exercise, 10*, 151. Reprinted by permission from Lippincott Williams & Wilkins.

Kenya's Famous Long-Distance Runners
The greatest concentration of achievement in the annals of sport

Athletes from Kenya (with roughly the same population as Canada) have dominated the world of long-distance running for more than thirty years. In Olympic events of between 800 and 10,000 metres, Kenyan men have won thirty-eight medals since they first started competing in the Games in 1968, far more than any other nation. In the 3,000-metre steeplechase, a Kenyan has won every gold medal since 1968 (except in 1976 and 1980, when Kenya was part of the Olympic boycotts). And in women's competition, a Kenyan runner, Catherine Ndereba, holds the world record in the marathon with a time thought unthinkable even five years ago. She and her teammates have been dominant over the past few years.

Remarkably, most of these runners come from a single tribe, the Kalenjins, and, even more specifically, the Nandi subgroup, who live along the country's Great Rift Valley. Such has been the success of this relatively small group of people that sports sociologist John Manners has called the Kalenjin dominance "the greatest geographic concentration of achievement in the annals of sport."

Muscle Fibre Type

Recently, Danish scientists compared twelve top Kalenjin runners with their own elite athletes. (Ironically, while the top Danish middle-distance runner, 800-metre runner Wilson Kipketer, lives in Denmark, he was born and raised in Kenya.) The study found that, in addition to favourable body characteristics (such as long, thin legs and low heart rates and low overall body fat percentages), the Kenyans' muscle fibres are capable of converting oxygen more efficiently than their Danish counterparts.

One amazed American runner once likened this combination of a perfect frame for running and a high capacity to utilize oxygen to "a V8 engine in a Volkswagen."

Kenyan Jackson Omweri wins the 2001 Canadian International Marathon in Toronto (CP PHOTO/Frank Gunn).

Of course, muscle fibre is only a small part of a bigger picture, and many other theories for their collective success have been advanced. For example, the fact that the Kalenjin/Nandi have lived for generations at relatively high altitudes has meant that their bodies have developed the ability to take in and use air that is relatively thin in oxygen content (compared to that at sea level) – which means that once they drop down to sea level to compete, they have an advantage.

Others have cited the traditional Kenyan diet, which is high in both protein and starch, as ideal "fuel" for running. And still others have cited the typical rural Kenyan lifestyle, which places a premium on transport by foot and not car. Most top Kenyan runners, for example, tell of getting to school from a very young age by running there – sometimes more than 10 kilometres each way.

Social Factors

It is important to consider social factors as well. Often, a role model will inspire younger runners for generations. In Kenya, Kipoghe Keino emerged,

seemingly out of nowhere, to win the prestigious 1,500-metre race at the 1968 Mexico Olympics. His success in the years that followed inspired countless young Kenyans to take up the sport.

There was a powerful economic incentive, too, as many young Kenyan men discovered that success in running was a way both to escape rigorous farm life at home and to support large families with the prizes they won in international competition.

For many of these athletes, there was also a powerful educational motivation to succeed at running. Starting in the 1970s, many Kenyan runners travelled to the United States to compete in intercollegiate races on full athletic scholarships. Far from being campus "jocks," many used the opportunity to pursue degrees that were not available to them at home. They then returned to Kenya to take up careers in medicine, engineering, and other professions.

Kenyan Women Runners

In Kalenjin society, women have traditionally been expected to bear responsibilities for agricultural work, child bearing and raising, and many other tasks, with very little time for leisure interests outside the home. This is beginning to change, slowly.

In much the same way as Kip Keino inspired Kenyan men in the late 1960s, Lornah Kiplagat did the same for Kenyan women. She defied social conventions by training and competing in distance races, first in Kenya, and then abroad. Kiplagat returned home in the late 1980s and, with her winnings from a number of European races, built a running camp for women that attracted the best young talent in the country.

From then on, it was just a matter of time before Kenya started to produce champion women runners – and national sporting heroes – changing the way much of that country's men viewed "women's" roles in society.

THREE FIBRE TYPES

Nowadays, exercise scientists normally distinguish not simply two but three different types of muscle fibre, using a combination of the tension-generating features and the metabolic properties of the fibre. These types are:

- **Type I or Slow-Oxidative (SO).** These fibres generate energy slowly, are more fatigue-resistant, and primarily depend on aerobic processes.

- **Type IIA or Fast-Oxidative Glycolytic (FOG).** These intermediate-type muscle fibres allow for high-speed energy release as well as glycolytic capacity.

- **Type IIB or Fast-Glycolytic (FG).** These fibres store lots of glycogen and sufficiently high levels of enzymes necessary for quick contraction without requiring oxygen.

The main reason for the subdivision within the Type II fibres is that there is strong research evidence suggesting that Type IIB fibres can, as a consequence of aerobic endurance training, become Type IIA fibres (whereas Type IIA fibers do not make the transition to Type I fibres). Researchers are seeking to determine whether it is possible to distinguish further meaningful subdivisions. This information is hard to gather and maintain because of the complexity and care that must be administered when extracting and examining human muscle tissue samples. See Table 5.3 for a listing of the main characteristics of each fibre type.

The Distribution of Muscle Fibre Types

A muscle's fibre makeup generally determines its function, and vice versa – what a muscle does is usually a pretty good indication of what it is made of. As a way of describing their basic functions, physiologists often speak of tonic muscles and phasic muscles.

- **Tonic muscles** are ones that assist the body with maintaining posture or stability during activities such as standing, walking, and throwing. Tonic muscles are also characterized by a high percentage of Type I fibre; that is, slow-twitch fibres with little ability to function explosively, but with considerable endurance capacity. For example, the soleus muscle (the broad, flat muscle in the calf of the leg, beneath the gastrocnemius muscle) that dorsiflexes the foot and is a key muscle in ensuring body posture, has been found to contain a high percentage of Type I fibres.

- **Phasic muscles** are characterized by a higher percentage of Type IIA and Type IIB. The biceps, for example – a key muscle for lifting and power in the arm – has a lower percentage of Type I fibres.

The only way of knowing what percentage of muscle fibre types are found in either tonic of phasic muscles is to conduct a biopsy. This involves acquiring a tissue sample using a needle, and snipping out a portion of muscle and placing it under a microscope in order to determine the ratio of fast- to slow-twitch muscle fibres.

Table 5.3: Characteristics of different muscle fibre types

	Type I Slow oxidative (SO)	Type IIA Fast oxidative glycolysis (FOG)	Type IIB Fast glycolysis (FG)
Colour	Red	Red/white	White
Fibre diameter	Small	Medium	Large
Contraction speed	Slow (110 ms)	Fast	Very fast (50 ms)
Force production	Low	Intermediate	High
Energy efficiency	High	Low	Low
Myoglobin content	High	Moderately high	Low
Myosin ATPase	Low	High	High
Fatigue resistance	High	Moderate	Low
Aerobic capacity	High	Moderate	Low
Anaerobic capacity	Low	High	High

Source: From Fox, E.L., Bowers, W., & Ross, M.L. (1988). *The physiological basis of physical education and athletics* (4th ed., p. 110). Dubuque, IA: Wm. C. Brown Publishers. Reproduced with permission of The McGraw-Hill Companies.

FIBRE TYPE AND ATHLETIC PERFORMANCE

For elite athletes in various sports, differences in muscle fibre types is often very pronounced. Olympic sprinters, such as Donovan Bailey, for example, may possess as much as 70-80 percent fast-twitch fibres, whereas those who excel in marathon-style events (e.g., Simon Whitfield) may possess an equivalent in slow-twitch fibres.

While every sport (indeed, all physical activity) involves a mix of power and endurance, most sports can be located on a continuum as involving predominantly one or the other. Some will emphasize rapid bursts of energy while others will need to be fatigue resistant over the long haul. Still other sporting events will fall in between. Table 5.2 (page 90) shows the approximate involvement of each muscle fibre type for various sports.

Knowing that the body has different energy systems has important implications for training. To maximize performance, an athlete should match training methods to energy needs. In training for strength, the goal is to increase the load-bearing capacity or explosiveness of the muscles. During training, athletes such as football linemen, shot putters, or sprinters seek to increase the power of the actions they must duplicate in competition. Short powerful training exercises lasting a few seconds will result in increased creatine phosphate in muscle fibres. Intense exercise lasting for up to 90 seconds or so will increase glycogen stores and enhance the ability of enzymes to convert glucose quickly. Both will delay the point at which lactic acid buildup begins to impede physical performance.

Endurance training, on the other hand, is less concerned with building large, powerful muscles than with developing muscles that can hold up over the long run (or ride or swim). Training involves working to improve the oxygen-processing capacity of the lungs and blood. Aerobic training will enhance endurance activities by increasing the number of mitochondria in muscle cells, increasing the amount of the oxygen-storing myoglobin molecules, and enhancing the ability of enzymes within the muscle cells to utilize this oxygen in the complete breakdown of glucose. This is achieved, typically, by engaging in exercise that raises the heart rate to well above normal for long periods of time.

Because of the demands it places on the heart and lungs, aerobic exercise is usually recommended for reducing the risk of heart disease and increasing endurance. Aerobic exercise, being generally of long duration, will also help in weight reduction.

If improving muscle strength is a concern, an anaerobic routine involving weights, sprints, or plyometrics (hopping and jumping) may be more useful. Providing their health is otherwise good, even older people can benefit from moderate weight training. Muscle atrophy (i.e., muscle loss) is prevented, and strength as well as coordination is improved.

Individual Differences

Undoubtedly, some individuals are better suited for certain kinds of sports for purely physical or physiological reasons, whether it be slow-twitch muscle fibre (distance running), height (basketball), build (football players), or speed (sprinters). Such differences are to be welcomed and even applauded.

It should be emphasized, however, that these are individual-level differences. While there is much debate, there is as yet no sound scientific evidence that individuals belonging to different ethnic groups or cultures are, on average, better suited to one type of physical activity than another. (For the complexity of this discussion, see the information on page 91 pertaining to muscle fibre types and Kenyan distance runners.)

Furthermore, while muscle fibre composition provides important clues to understanding and improving human performance, it is but only one element in a very complex equation. Like most other things, physical performance is multi-faceted and a great many things, apart from fibre type (or even height and strength), are involved in enabling an athlete to perform well. Among these are psychological and sociological factors, in addition to purely biological and physiological mechanisms.

The point that needs to be made here is that different physical activities emphasize different physiological processes and that no one activity is necessarily better than the other. First, one should choose an activity that one enjoys, then train hard to get better at it, and finally enjoy the lifelong benefits, including friendships, that accrue from participating in the activity.

WHERE DO WE GO FROM HERE?

In this Unit, we have looked at how the human body derives energy from the nutrients we take in, and how it uses this energy to fulfil human needs. In addition, we have examined the ways in which different muscle fibre types work to produce the forces necessary to generate human movement.

As we have noted many times, the various biological systems identified here are ultimately interconnected and interdependent. To a large extent, it is not possible to discuss one without the other. With this in mind, we will now step back to look at the critical role played by the nervous system in coordinating and refining our movements.

Myriam Bedard competing in the biathlon event at the 1992 Albertville Olympic Winter Games (CP PHOTO/COA/Ted Grant).

The Nervous System and the Control of Movement

"He's got what you might call a control problem. The guy has a million-dollar arm,
but only a ten-cent brain."
— line from the baseball movie *Bull Durham* (1988)

The body systems that we have looked at to this point are all ones that "work" in some mechanical way to promote the motion of the body. We now understand how the muscles, bones, and joints work with one another to allow, say, the fingers to move, or the knee to bend. But that movement is only part of the story. Where and how, for example, do these parts get the "commands" that tell them to move in the first place?

The nervous system is the body's way of gathering information, storing it, and responding to it. Its main role is to assemble information about conditions external and internal to the body, to analyze this information, and to initiate responses that may be necessary to satisfy certain needs. The nervous system comprises not one system, but several interrelated subsystems.

Two Components of the Nervous System

There are two major components to the human nervous system. Each division plays a distinctive role, but they are interconnected and work together. For an overview of the structure of the nervous system, see Figure 6.1 on the following page.

The brain and spinal cord make up what is known as the central nervous system. The peripheral nervous system, on the other hand, is responsible for other bodily functions. These include the beating of the heart and the digestive system, muscular control, and

all other voluntary and involuntary neuromuscular controls.

Let us briefly look at these two components.

THE CENTRAL NERVOUS SYSTEM

As noted above, the central nervous system (CNS) is divided into two parts: the brain and the spinal cord.

The Brain

The brain, of course, is the main control centre for movement, sleep, hunger, thirst, and virtually every type of activity necessary for human survival. Although it is an often-used analogy, the brain functions like the body's "computer." Incapable of performing any physical task itself, it sends out commands to other parts of the body to perform them. All human emotions are also controlled by the brain.

The brain receives and interprets endless signals that are sent to it from other parts of the body and from the outside world. The brain has six main parts.

- **The cerebrum.** This is the largest part of the brain, containing the nerve centres that control sensory and motor activities as well as intelligence. The cerebrum can be divided lengthwise down the middle into two halves called the cerebral hemispheres, which have nerve fibres

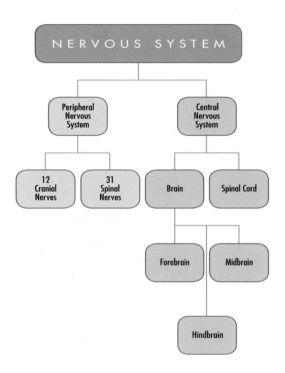

Figure 6.1: The structure of the nervous system.

communicating between them. Each hemisphere is divided into four lobes, named after the cranial bones that lie over and protect them: the frontal lobe, the temporal lobe, the parietal lobe, and the occipital lobe.

- **The cerebellum**. The second largest region, the cerebellum, lies behind and below the cerebrum. Its main function is to coordinate muscle movement and control balance.

- **The brain stem.** Lying below the cerebrum and in front of the cerebellum, the brain stem links the cerebrum with the spinal cord just below. As well, it houses the brain centres that are responsible for autonomic functions, postural control, muscle tone, and eye movement, to name a few.

- **The diencephalon.** The diencephalon, consisting of the thalamus and the hypothalamus, is located between the cerebrum and the brain stem. The thalamus relays most sensory stimuli to the cerebral cortex and controls primitive awareness of pain, screening of incoming signals, and focusing attention. The hypothalamus controls such things as body temperature, appetite, emotions, and various automatic functions.

- **The limbic system.** The limbic system is composed of a collection of structures within the cerebral hemispheres that regulate basic drives (such as hunger, aggression, and emotional drives) and screens information going to the cerebral cortex.

- **The reticular activating system.** This is a network of neurons that fans out through the cerebral cortex and directs information to appropriate centres for interpretation. Its functioning is crucial for maintaining consciousness.

The Vertebral Column and the Spinal Cord

The spinal cord, the second major component of the central nervous system, is the main pathway for information connecting the brain and peripheral nervous system. The spinal cord runs through a column of irregularly shaped bones, called vertebrae. This is the vertebral column. Each of these vertebrae is separated from the other by cartilage that prevents the bones from grinding against one another.

The spinal cord starts from the base of the brain stem and travels all the way down to the second lumbar vertebra. In adults, the spinal cord averages in length from 42 to 45 centimetres. It is thicker on both the superior and inferior ends than it is in the middle to accommodate the upper and lower limbs. As the spinal cord travels down the vertebral column, spinal nerves branch off between each vertebra, allowing nerves to travel to various organs and tissues. Spinal nerves carry sensory information towards the CNS and motor commands away from the CNS, and are named according to the vertebral level at which they exit. For instance, if you need to abduct your shoulder joint by activating the deltoid muscle, the message exits at cervical vertebra six (C6). If the message needs to get to your rectus femoris in order for you to extend your knee, the message must exit at lumbar vertebrae three and four (L3, 4).

PERIPHERAL NERVOUS SYSTEM

The peripheral nervous system (PNS) consists of those parts of the nervous system that lie outside the central nervous system (that is., outside the brain and spinal cord). The PNS can be thought of as a kind of massive road network (or computer network) carrying traffic (information) in and out of the CNS.

The PNS includes the twelve pairs of cranial nerves that emerge from the brain as well as the thirty-one pairs of spinal nerves that leave the spinal cord for various parts of the body. Each of these spinal pairs has two roots (an anterior root, carrying motor nerve fibres, and a posterior root, carrying sensory fibres). Motor nerves (or efferent nerves) carry information from the CNS to the body's organs. Sensory nerves (or afferent nerves) carry information from sensory receptors to the CNS.

The peripheral nervous system contains both autonomic and somatic components.

The Autonomic Nervous System

The involuntary contraction of our cardiac muscles and the smooth muscles of our internal organs is regulated by the **autonomic nervous system** (ANS). This subsystem is comprised of two branches, which frequently act as opposing systems.

- The **sympathetic system** causes localized bodily adjustments to occur (e.g., sweating or cardiovascular changes), and it prepares the body for emergencies. This involves the release of adrenaline from the adrenal gland, an increase in heart rate, a widening of the blood vessels, and similar "fight or flight" responses to deal with imminent danger.

- The **parasympathetic system** helps to return the body to normal after it has been altered by the sympathetic system. For example, whereas the sympathetic system increases the heart rate, the parasympathetic system has the opposite effect.

On a daily basis, these two systems work in unison to prepare the body for emergencies or a return to normalcy. This unification exemplifies the complexity of the human body, and it is comforting to know that we do not have to worry about controlling our heart rate as we do our muscles.

Somatic Nervous System

Our awareness of the external environment – and the corresponding motor activity allowing us to cope with it – operates through the **somatic nervous system**. The somatic division contains both afferent and efferent nerve fibres. Afferent nerves send information to the central nervous system and efferent nerves send instructions to skeletal muscle. Through this system, the PNS receives and processes information from receptors in the skin, in voluntary muscles, tendons, and joints, and gives us the sensations of touch, pain, heat, cold, balance, body position, and muscle action.

The somatic nervous system handles the muscles in our extremities, and it is through this system that we are able us to move our arms and legs and therefore move about. Another difference between the autonomic and the somatic nervous system is that, while the central cell bodies of somatic neurons extend all the way out to the peripheral target organs. Autonomic output consists of a two-neuron chain between the CNS and the effector organ.

Using the example of the sound of a starter's pistol and the reaction of the athlete, the relationship between the autonomic and somatic nervous systems can be clearly seen in Figure 6.2.

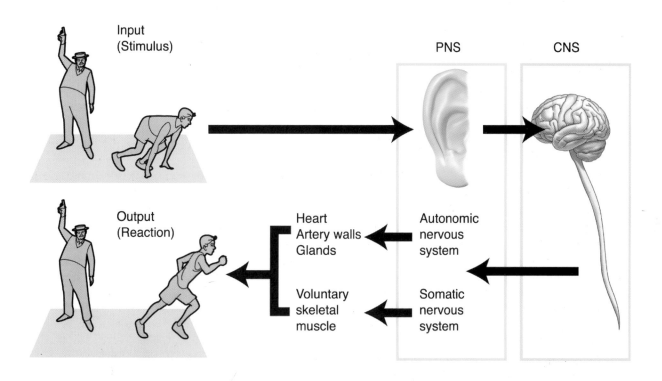

Figure 6.2: Relationship between the autonomic and somatic nervous systems.

Rick Hansen: Man in Motion
"Anything is possible"

Although spinal injuries have extremely serious consequences for those who suffer them, there are many stories of people who have overcome quadriplegia and paraplegia and gone on to successful careers in sport. One of them is the Canadian wheelchair athlete Rick Hansen.

As a kid, Hansen (b. 1957) lived a typical teenager's life in Williams Lake, British Columbia. He had a keen interest in sports and outdoor activities. But in 1973, he and a friend were returning from a fishing trip when they were involved in a motor-vehicle accident. For Hansen, the result of the accident was that he became a paraplegic – doctors told him he would never walk again.

But Hansen's love of sport did not diminish with the accident – nor did his determination not to let his injuries diminish his enjoyment of life. After extensive rehabilitation, he was able to return home and complete high school, and begin competing in wheelchair sports.

A few years later, he became the first person with a physical disability to graduate in physical education from the University of British Columbia in the history of the school.

His progress in wheelchair athletics was rapid, and to date, he is one of the most internationally accomplished Canadian athletes in history. He competed at the 1984 Olympic Games in Los Angeles. During his competitive career, Hansen won nineteen international marathon races over the official 42.195 km distance, including the prestigious Boston, Honolulu, and Ottawa Marathons, and he has captured three world championships in track events as well.

During his competitive days, Hansen was also successful against the clock. He set five world records and one Pan Am Games record on the outdoor track, and has won an amazing twelve gold medals in track at the B.C. Games.

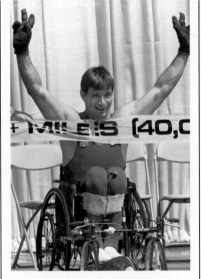

Rick Hansen marks the end of his two-year Man in Motion Tour, May 1987 (CP PHOTO/STR-Jon Murray).

Not content with his own sporting achievements, however, Hansen decided, in 1985, to raise awareness of persons with disabilities and sport competition for the disabled. That year, he embarked on the "Man in Motion World Tour," covering more than 40,000 kilometres around the world from 1985-87 and passing through thirty-four countries. He provided an inspirational example for people who may not have been aware of the potential for physical activity on the part of people with spinal injuries. Hansen has also competed internationally for Canada in wheelchair basketball.

He has also led his team to three national championships in wheelchair volleyball and is an accomplished wheelchair tennis player, having won the B.C. provincial singles title in 1981-82.

To date, Hansen has co-written two books, including his 1987 autobiography, written with the well-known sportswriter Jim Taylor, called *Man in Motion*. He also runs the Rick Hansen Institute (see www.rickhansen.com, for more information) and the Rick Hansen Man in Motion Foundation, two organizations that have raised an estimated $137 million to aid spinal-cord injury research and to further awareness of these injuries and their rehabilitation.

With this tremendous level of financial support, Hansen and his team maintain that accelerating the pace of spinal cord research – and associated rehabilitation practices – will ultimately lead to a cure for the kind of injury he suffered. Experts point out that, with the support of organizations such as Hansen's, 90 percent of the currently accumulated information on how to treat these injuries has been developed in the last ten years – leading to the belief by many researchers and survivors alike that the knowledge needed to "walk away" from these injuries will be available in the very near future.

Hansen and his organization are also active in working with schools to raise awareness of the athletic possibilities available for people with disabilities. One initiative, the Rick Hansen Awards Program, has been implemented in more than 145 schools in B.C. and Ontario. The goals of the program are to recognize "outstanding student leadership and student activities that demonstrate social responsibility, goal accomplishment, determination and perseverance to overcome obstacles and/or disabilities."

Students who are judged to have made significant contributions to the lives of others in their school and/or community receive award certificates. Far from being simply a figurehead, Hansen himself figures prominently in inspiring those students who are competing for awards within this program. Schools that participate in the program receive information on his career and two short videos that include a personal message from Rick and footage from the Man In Motion World Tour. (Additional information on the Rick Hansen Awards Program are available by sending an e-mail to: nearly@rickhansen.com.)

THE REFLEX ARC

Reflexes are an important part of all physical movement. They are an automatic and rapid response to a particular stimulation. If the command centre for the reflex is located in the brain, it is commonly referred to as a cerebral reflex; if the control is located in the spinal cord, it is called a spinal reflex.

Autonomic reflexes are mediated by the autonomic division of the nervous system and usually involve the activation of smooth muscle, cardiac muscle, and glands. They regulate such bodily functions as digestion, elimination, blood pressure, salivation, and sweating.

Somatic reflexes involve stimulation of skeletal muscles by the somatic division of the nervous system, and include such reflexes as the stretch reflex and the withdrawal reflex (discussed below). Reflex contraction of skeletal muscle is not dependent on conscious intervention by higher centres of the brain but are a way that the body responds to an unexpected stimulus. More than one contraction may result, as when the opposing muscle is stimulated in a complex reflex action.

The Reflex Arc

The **reflex arc** is the name given to the pathway (or circuit) along which the initial stimulus and the corresponding response message travel. The basic arrangement of the reflex arc involves a receptor, an adjustor (usually), and an effector (see Figure 6.3 below). The afferent (incoming) impulse from the receptor is passed along the sensory nerve axon to the adjustor, which then interprets the message and sends an efferent (outgoing) impulse along the motor nerve axon to the effector organ or muscle.

There are five parts to a reflex arc:

1. the **receptor**, which receives the initial stimulus (say, a pinprick to the skin or a loud noise);

2. the **sensory (or afferent) nerve**, which carries the impulse to the spinal column or brain (e.g., the afferent neuron of the muscle spindle or tendon organ);

3. the **intermediate nerve fibre** (the adjustor or interneuron), which interprets the signal and issues an appropriate response;

4. the **motor (or efferent) nerve**, which then carries the response message from the spinal cord to the muscle or organ; and

5. the **effector organ** itself (e.g., a skeletal muscle), which carries out the response (such as removing the hand or leg away from danger).

Reflex actions are generally the way the body responds rapidly to painful situations or the threat of painful situations. The reflex arc is the mechanism by which the response occurs.

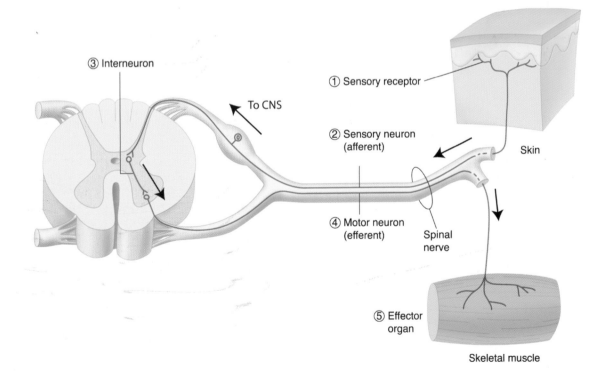

Figure 6.3: The reflex arc.

PROPRIOCEPTORS AND THE CONTROL OF MOVEMENT

The process (excitation-contraction coupling) and mechanism (sliding filaments) by which a single nerve impulse or series of such impulses is translated into muscle contraction was outlined in an earlier section (see Section 3, "The Muscular System"). But how exactly does a muscle fibre know how much to contract, when to relax, and how to coordinate with other muscles and with other muscle groups in the area?

It does so by means of specialized receptors located within tendons, muscles, and joints. These receptors are called **proprioceptors**, and they provide sensory information about the state of muscle contraction, the position of body limbs, and body posture and balance. This all-important feedback and control over muscles is provided primarily by the afferent (sensory) input from two sensory receptors: tendon organs and muscle spindles.

The proprioceptor system plays an indispensable role in physical movement. Tendon organs and muscle spindles continuously monitor muscle actions and are essential components of the neuromuscular system. They "tell" the nervous system about the state of muscle contraction, act as a kind of safety device, and allow the nervous system to respond accordingly. Let us examine these two in greater detail, by looking first at their general anatomy, then at their function.

Golgi Tendon Organs (Tension Reflex)

Golgi tendon organs (GTOs; named after the discoverer, Italian scientist Camillo Golgi, 1844-1926) are sensory receptors that terminate where tendons join to muscle fibre. Aligned in series with the muscle, such that any muscle stretching also stretches the GTO receptor, tendon organs are ideally positioned to detect increased tension exerted on the tendon.

The tendon organ, illustrated in Figure 6.4 below, projects to the motor neurons located within the spinal cord. When the change in tension is detected, an impulse is sent along afferent neurons to the central nervous system, where they synapse with motor neurons of that same muscle. The efferent neurons instantly transmit an impulse, causing the muscle to relax, thereby preventing injury. The sequence of steps is the same as in the muscle spindle (stretch reflex) described on page 102.

Essentially, GTOs serve as a kind of tension detection device for the muscle system. They help protect the muscle from excessive tension that would otherwise result in damage to the muscle or the joint or both. GTOs provide feedback to the central nervous system regardless of magnitude. For this reason, it is likely that they play a central role in the development of strength and power, since, in order to be able to exert greater force, it is necessary to overcome obstacles presented by the tendon organ itself.

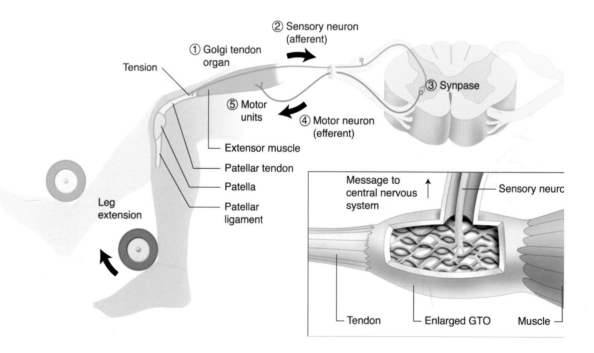

Figure 6.4: Golgi tendon organ (tension detector).

The Muscle Spindle

Muscle spindles are more complex than tendon organs. They lie parallel to the main muscle fibre and send constant signals to the spinal cord. The spindle (so-called because it resembles the spindle of a spinning wheel) consists of specialized muscle fibres, known as intrafusal muscle fibres, that run the length of the muscle (see Figure 6.5, below).

The spindle itself is several millimetres long, and about five intrafusal muscle fibres run through it. The spindle fibres are thinner and shorter than the ordinary skeletal muscle fibres, though they behave much the same way and look more or less the same. The swelling of the spindle is produced by fluid contained in a capsule surrounding the central area of the intrafusal fibres.

Muscle spindles help to maintain muscle tension, but, unlike the Golgi tendon organs, they are sensitive to changes in muscle length (rather than tension). The muscle spindle contains two afferent and one efferent nerve fibres. The spindle detects changes in the muscle fibre length and responds to it by sending a message to the spinal cord, leading to the appropriate motor responses. The resulting contraction allows the muscle to maintain proper muscle tension or tone (e.g., an erect posture). The fact that there are two sensory nerves explains not only the high level of sensitivity of muscle spindles but also the critical role they play in regulating muscle contraction and in maintaining posture and balance.

Muscle spindles are involved in the reflex contraction of muscles (the so-called stretch reflex). The stretch reflex action is present in all muscles and plays an especially important role in the major extensor muscles of the limbs. The usual example is the knee-jerk reflex (the patella reflex) but it is also responsible for overcompensation responses when additional weight is suddenly placed on a weight-bearing muscle.

Muscle spindles play an important role in all physical movement. They are the means by which muscles constantly and automatically adjust to the changing demands placed on them by providing a kind of constant negative feedback.

Table 6.1: GTOs and muscle spindles		
	Golgi tendon organs	**Muscle spindles**
Location	Where tendon meets muscle fibre	In belly of muscle fibre
Position	In series with muscle fibre	Parallel to muscle fibre
Respond to	Changes in muscle/tendon tension	Changes in muscle length
Sensory neurons	1	2

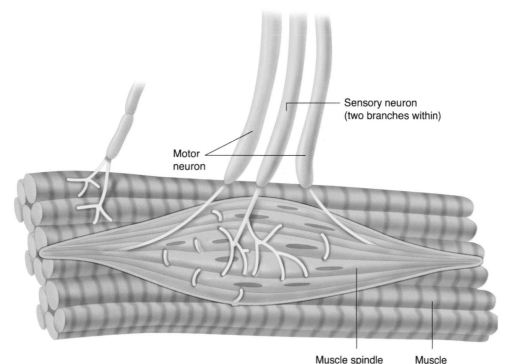

Figure 6.5: Muscle spindle (stretch detector).

MUSCLE SPINDLES AT WORK (THE STRETCH REFLEX)

The **stretch reflex** is the simplest spinal reflex. Whereas most reflexes have several synapses in the reflex arc, the stretch reflex depends only on the single connection between primary afferent fibres and motor neurons of the same muscle. (For this reason, it is referred to as a monosynaptic reflex.) The knee-jerk is often used to demonstrate this reflex.

Tapping the patella ligament below the kneecap pulls on the tendon of quadriceps femoris, the extensor muscle that serves to extend the lower leg. As the muscle is stretched, information is sent to the spinal cord. These signals act directly on motor neurons that then quickly proceed to contract the quadriceps (see Figure 6.6 below).

A more general case of the stretch reflex might be when a weight that a person is carrying is suddenly increased. This causes the the weight-bearing muscle to lengthen, which in turn increases the activity of the muscle spindle and leads to a stimulation of the motor neurons. The result is an increase in muscle contraction, and the individual is then better able to deal with the increased weight.

The sequence of nerve impulses and motions involved in the stretch reflex would be as follows:

1. The receptor muscle senses the action of the hammer against the patella ligament (or, say, an additional weight) through the muscle spindle's sensory neuron;

2. The message is transmitted along the afferent (sensory) nerve axon to the spinal cord;

3. The afferent neuron synapses with the efferent pathway (motor neuron) of the same muscle;

4. An impulse is transmitted along the efferent pathway (motor neuron) to the muscle; and

5. The motor units contract, which brings about a knee-jerk action to accommodate the additional stretch.

Reciprocal Inhibition

While tapping on the ligament causes the muscle to contract, it is now widely accepted that the opposing muscle group is also simultaneously inhibited in a process is known as **reciprocal inhibition**. Thus, as the quadriceps femoris (the extensor) contracts, the hamstring group (the flexor) is inhibited in a slightly delayed response. This action provides for a constant adjustment between the two muscle groups.

Unlike the stretch reflex, which is monosynaptic, reciprocal inhibition occurs through intermediary neurons (interneurons) in the spinal cord. Some of these slightly delayed inhibitory-type responses may not be pure spinal reflexes but result from the afferent impulse being transmitted at high speed to the motor areas of the cerebral cortex.

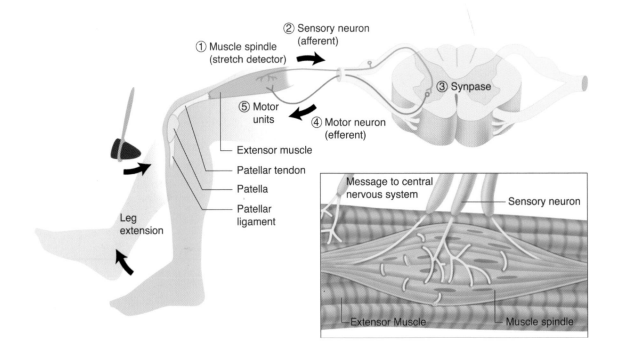

Figure 6.6: The stretch reflex.

POLYSYNAPTIC REFLEXES

With other spinal reflexes, one or more interneurons lie between the primary sensory fibres and the motor neurons. (Such reflexes are referred to as polysynaptic.) Generally, the more interactions involved, the more complex (and slow) the reflex behaviour.

The Withdrawal Reflex

A common example of a polysynaptic reflex is the withdrawal reflex, which involves the withdrawal of a body part from a painful stimulus (such as a sharp or hot object). Here, the reflex action involves transferring the impulse from a sensory neuron to a motor neuron through a connecting interneuron (or interneurons) in the spinal cord. The process, again, is extremely rapid and occurs even before the brain itself has time to interpret the information.

Crossed-Extensor Reflex

A more complex example is the so-called crossed-extensor reflex. This is observed when one leg or arm automatically compensates for a reflex action in the opposing leg or arm. Here the reflex involves multiple synapses and muscle groups. See Figure 6.7 below.

The sequence of nerve impulses and stages activated in this complex reflex action would be follows:

1. The stimulus is detected by receptors (say, on the skin), as shown below in Figure 6.7;

2. The receptors initiate nerve impulses in the sensory neurons leading from the receptors;

3. The impulses travel into the spinal cord where the sensory nerve terminals synapse with interneurons;

4. Some of these interneurons synapse with motor neurons that travel out from the spinal cord to the effector organ;

5. The knee flexors withdraw the foot from the danger zone; and

6. Still other sensory neurons synapse with interneurons that affect motor neurons in the opposing leg and cause these muscles to come into action.

In adults, this complex coordination of the nervous and muscular systems has evolved greatly from infancy. The reflexes of infants become more coordinated as they increase in strength and as they become familiar with their surroundings. They quickly learn to avoid pain and seek pleasure.

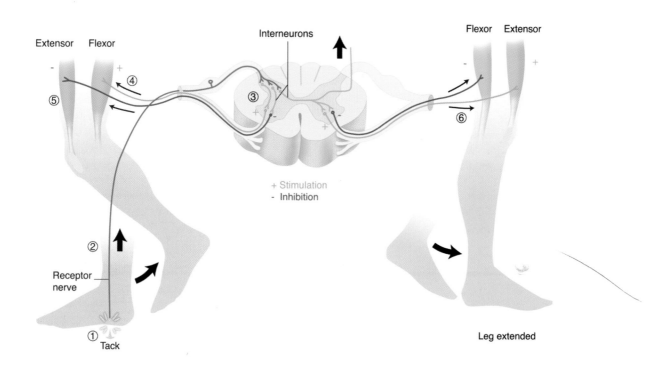

Figure 6.7: The withdrawal reflex and the crossed-extensor reflex.

Medical Technology in Action
MRIs and CAT Scan

Over the past several decades, our ability to discover – and diagnose – various health-related afflictions has improved tremendously. Much of this has come about as the result of advances in technology that allow medical practitioners to look inside the body in a non-invasive way.

Let us take a look at the two most common of these non-invasive exploratory techniques.

MRI Technology

MRI, or magnetic resonance imaging, uses a device called a nuclear magnetic resonance spectrometer. The spectrometer produces electronic cross-sectional images of the human cells, organs, and tissues that have been targeted for inspection.

A patient undergoing an MRI procedure lies inside a long hollow cylinder, filled with a strong electromagnetic current. This current causes the nuclei of certain atoms in the body (especially those of hydrogen) to align magnetically. The cylinder is then filled with radio waves, which cause the aligned nuclei to "flip," returning to their original positions when the radio waves are withdrawn. This back-and-forth movement of the nuclei causes them to emit radio waves that are detected by the MRI receiver and then turned into a two-dimensional computer picture.

The MRI procedure has an advantage in that the image is not obstructed by bones that are inevitably "in the way" with conventional X-rays. Doctors use it to diagnose tumours and disorders of the brain, spinal disorders, multiple sclerosis, and cardiovascular disease.

Generally, MRI examinations are without major health risks, but can cause problems for people with mechanical aids such as pacemakers or hearing aids.

CAT Scans

The acronym CAT stands for computerized axial tomography. This is a technique that doctors use to obtain a

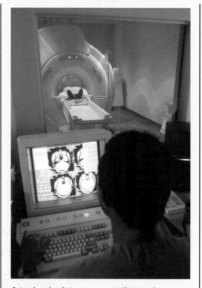

A technologist scans a patient using new MRI technology (CP PHOTO/Jeff McIntosh).

relatively safe, quick, and painless diagnosis in various areas of the body, including the spine and brain.

Unlike MRI scanning, CAT scans use X-ray technology. A rotating X-ray tube disperses a set amount of X radiation around the tissue. When the area has been subjected to the radiation, the scanner takes pictures of the tissue from different angles. (Some scanners have eliminated the rotating-tube design and instead use a stationary tube that deflects the X-ray beam to the desired body part.)

When these pictures are taken, the scanner then uses a computer program to form a composite image from all the angles captured by the camera. Doctors can then analyze these to look for irregularities.

Most medical practitioners, and especially those who study and treat brain and spinal cord disorders, see CAT scan technology as a major medical advance because of the way it has improved our ability to examine brain and spinal cord disorders, cancer, and many other conditions.

The Sports Connection

The influence of MRI and CAT scan technology on the sporting world has also been considerable. They provide readily accessible, non-invasive ways of assessing the damage that an athlete may have suffered in a sports injury to the head or spinal cord.

Recent history is filled with stories of several professional players in contact sports such as hockey and football who have declared themselves "ready to play" despite having suffered what appeared to be fairly serious blows to the head in action on the field or rink Given the "tough-guy" attitude that often prevails in these sports, athletes often dismiss the ringing sensation in their ears or headaches they feel after contact to the head as something they should "shake off" in an effort to avoid missing playing time. But in many instances, insisting on continuing to play after suffering even a mild concussion can lead to far more serious problems (see the sidebar on hockey stars Eric and Brett Lindros on page 106 for more on this issue).

With CAT Scans and MRIs, however, doctors can make quick diagnoses on head injuries and associated damage to the spine. They can then tell team officials and players just how serious that persistent headache, brought on by contact to the head, really is.

Of course, the results yielded by this diagnostic technology can only go so far. Test results might indicate that a player should stop competing, perhaps forever, or at the very least, wear more protective gear. One example of such gear is the ProCap, a device that can be worn under a helmet and is estimated to reduce the force of blows to the head by up to 30 percent.

But, as in the Lindros case, at this point it is still the individual athlete who who decides whether to risk further injury. Many commentators are beginning to question whether there should not be rules or regulations in this regard.

SPINAL CORD INJURIES

Reflex testing is an important medical diagnostic tool. Weak, exaggerated, or absent reflex responses may indicate problems with portions of the nervous system. If the spinal cord is damaged, then reflex testing can help to determine the exact area of spinal injury. Similarly, in the case of a serious head injury, reflex testing can provide useful information. (For example, the oculomotor nerve stimulates eye muscles; if pressure increases in the brain due to bleeding, then there is likely to be variations in eye reflex response.)

Since even minor injuries to the nervous system can be debilitating and very serious, extra caution is well advised in these matters. The remainder of this section is devoted to some of the problems that may arise with the nervous system in connection with physical activity.

Paraplegia and Quadriplegia

There are thirty-one pairs of spinal nerves flowing from the spinal cord (each has an anterior and a posterior root). Through these, the spinal cord sends messages to and from the brain and to and from all parts of your body – for example, your lungs (to control breathing) and your bladder and bowels (to control their emptying). When the spinal cord receives a severe impact – car and diving accidents are two of the most common instances – damage to the spine can profoundly affect its ability to send impulses to body parts.

When there is a serious injury to the spinal cord, the nerves above the injury keep working, whereas those below the injury may or may not still function. If the injury prevents the use of the legs but not the arms, the injury is known as paraplegia (the individual becomes a "paraplegic"). If the injury prevents movement of both arms and legs, the injury is quadriplegia (the individual is said to be "quadriplegic").

Specialists in spinal cord injuries have developed a system whereby such injuries are categorized based on where on the spine they occur. For example, a "C4" injury means the damage is at the level of the fourth cervical spinal cord segment, and a "T6" injury is one that occurs at the thoracic (upper back) level's sixth spinal cord segment.

There is a further classification based on the level of functional loss – that is, the injury can result in absolute loss of function in a limb or set of body parts (complete) or partial levels of such loss (incomplete). Furthermore, diagnoses are not always accurate in the first instance – a complete injury may turn out to be an incomplete one.

Facts and Causes

There are an estimated 900 Canadians who sustain a spinal cord injury each year – or 35 per year per million of population (not including non-deficit or fatal injuries).

On average, of the newly injured clients referred to the Canadian Paraplegic Association each year, 80 percent are male, 50 percent are paraplegic, and 50 percent are quadriplegic.

The following are common causes of spinal cord injury:

- Car accidents: 35%
- Falls: 16.5%
- Medical: 10.8%
- Sports: 6.7%
- Other motor vehicle accidents: 6.2%
- Diving: 5.3%
- Industrial accidents: 5.3%
- Other: 14.2%

Source: Canadian Paraplegic Association, 2002.
www.canparaplegic.org

Rehabilitation

The physical trauma of spinal cord injuries is made still worse by the psychological impact. Rehabilitation usually involves extensive physiotherapy (and perhaps surgery), as well as counselling to help the person and his or her family deal with this difficult new situation. Regardless of the severity of the injury, it is crucial to work with physicians and therapists to enhance the function that remains in limbs affected by the spinal cord injury. As an example of how this approach can pay off, consider Rick Hansen, a Canadian who persevered through rehabilitation to develop a successful athletic career despite his injuries.

For many people who have undergone rehabilitation therapy, the act of regaining mobility in damaged limbs has been as draining – physically and psychologically – as any sport or physical activity they once engaged in. Because humans, and especially athletes, have come to expect a high degree of response from limbs, back muscles, and so forth, the process of "relearning" how to walk or lift an object can be extremely frustrating. For this reason, people undergoing the rehabilitation process often add a psychologist to their "rehab team" of doctors and therapists.

Those involved in sports where there is the possibility of spinal injury (diving, surfing, and football, for example) can minimize the risk by being conscious of the danger, strengthening neck and back muscles, and wearing protective gear where possible.

Brett and Eric Lindros

Just what constitutes "serious" when it comes to brain injuries?

Anyone who follows professional hockey is familiar with the name Lindros. Eric's father, Carl, is also well known to hockey fans as Eric's agent and manager. And fans will also recall the name of Brett Lindros, Eric's brother, who was forced into retirement in 1996 at age twenty, after only fifty-one NHL games.

The reason for Brett Lindros' early departure from pro hockey? A series of concussions that he and his doctors deemed serious enough to warrant quitting the game in the face of possible long-term brain injury.

After leaving the game, Brett joined forces with his brother, father, and the Ontario Brain Injury Association to promote awareness of the possibility of this type of lasting injury among hockey players. Speaking at a 1997 press conference, Eric said: "It's time to understand that we have a problem. We just don't want anyone to go through this again." Added Carl: "We're trying to promote a message.... We want young athletes to know that concussions aren't something you should try to play through. Every time you have a concussion, neurons are killed. The remaining neurons have to reconnect. You have to give it time – if you're not careful, even a very light subsequent blow can cause serious injury, or death."

Absolutely Stunned

That is why many fans were absolutely stunned when, almost three years later, Eric lay crumpled on the ice during Game seven of the NHL's Eastern Conference Finals, after a vicious – but legal – check by Scott Stevens of the New Jersey Devils.

The horror was heightened by the fact that, far from being Eric's first experience with being knocked out cold, this was actually the sixth such blow he had suffered in twenty-seven months, and the fourth in a five-month period! So while good sense seemed to indicate that the elder Lindros should consider hanging up his skates in order to

Team Canada player Eric Lindros during team practice at the XIX Olympic Winter Games in Salt Lake City, February 2002 (CP PHOTO/Tom Hanson).

prevent an extremely serious injury, he appeared unwilling to do so.

Medical Opinion

There is reason to believe that concussions can have very serious and lasting effects. A study at Simon Fraser University (SFU) in British Columbia tested more than two hundred and fifty young hockey players in B.C. who reported concussions.

"We found that functional brain responses looked significantly different in players with concussions," said SFU researcher Mike Gaetz. "The more complex the tasks [in the test], the more the chances of showing the effects of concussion increased.... It's not just NHL players who are being hurt. Players as young as twelve or thirteen are sustaining these injuries."

The *Journal of the American Medical Association* reported an "increased likelihood of long-term neurological damage and learning disability among athletes who have had multiple concussions," and noted that well-known football players such as Steve Young and Al

Toon and hockey stars such as Pat Lafontaine and Geoff Courtnall decided to retire after multiple concussions, instead of facing permanent brain damage.

But what about Lindros? After his fourth concussion – the Stevens hit was his sixth – in March of 2000, Dr. Donald Leslie, medical director of the brain injury unit at the Shepherd Center in Atlanta, told *Sports Illustrated* that "one more injury and he may not be on the team. He may not even be able to take care of his own daily activities.... I would recommend that someone with four consecutive concussions not put himself at further risk for a fifth."

Yet Lindros did play on, suffering a fifth, and then sixth concussion (which sidelined him for a full fifteen months). Unbelievably, he returned for the 2001-02 season, having been traded by the Flyers to the New York Rangers. Why?

Greed or Passion

Some argue that money has a lot to do with it. It was easier for Brett Lindros – an up-and-coming player, but not a superstar at that point – to hang up his skates. The decision for Eric Lindros may not be so clear-cut. Another view, however, emphasizes just how competitive pro athletes can be, in spite of obvious medical reasons for them not to continue in their chosen sport.

Harry Carson, a retired NFL football player who consults with athletes on the advisability of playing after brain injury put it this way: "It doesn't matter what the public says or what the newspapers report. Until he has the sport out of his system and tells himself it's best to move on, he will continue to play. Eric Lindros still loves to play the game. He loves the sport, loves the camaraderie."

Whether it is greed or sheer love of the game, the question still remains: Is it worth risking serious brain injury after the warning signs have been clearly registered? In the case of Eric Lindros, only time will tell.

HEAD INJURIES — CONCUSSIONS

Whereas severe spinal cord injury is rare, head injuries are all too common in "contact sports" (boxing, hockey, football) as well as in many non-contact sports (soccer, skateboarding, baseball). Any head injury, such as a fractured skull, torn blood vessels, or brain damage, is serious and possibly life-threatening.

A common head injury is a concussion, usually caused by an accidental or intentional blow to the head. A concussion results from the blow, literally shaking the brain within the skull, and often involves injury to nerve fibres. Concussions can be mild or severe and, unfortunately, it is often difficult to tell the difference. And you do not necessarily need to hit your head to suffer a concussion. A quickly moving player that hits another player and causes a sudden change in direction may produce a rapid back and forth movement of the head and neck. Those forces not absorbed are transmitted to the brain.

With a concussion injury, brain cells become abnormal and do not function properly. Sometimes the player may get knocked out, but most of the time the main problems are headaches, dizziness, fatigue, and memory problems. These are called post-concussion symptoms. A second direct or indirect impact to the injured brain (when post-concussion symptoms are still present) can cause a dangerous change in the brain's blood supply. This leads to a rapid brain swelling that can cause coma and death.

There is great pressure – financial and otherwise – on athletes to continue to play after sustaining successive concussions. Sometimes the decisions that must be made are difficult ones to make, and professional medical advice is key. NHL hockey player Eric Lindros, for example, continued to play, whereas his brother, Brett, decided to end his promising hockey career early as a result of head injuries he had sustained.

WHERE DO WE GO FROM HERE?

To this point, we have examined most of the key anatomical and physiological systems that are involved directly with human movement. But while the skeleton, muscles, and nervous systems all play a crucial role, their functions would be for naught if not for the two interconnected systems we will examine next: the cardiovascular and respiratory systems.

The precise ways in which these two systems take up and use oxygen from the air we breathe is the subject of the following section. As you read ahead, keep in mind that, as with other biological systems, the cardiovascular and respiratory systems exhibit special characteristics during intense exercise.

Concussed?

You don't need to be knocked out to have a concussion

Which changes will you or someone else notice in your behaviour?

- Inappropriate playing behaviour (skating in the wrong direction, shooting on own net)
- Significantly decreased playing ability from earlier in the game
- Slowness in answering questions or following directions
- Inability to focus (easily distracted)
- Inability to do normal activities
- Display of unusual emotions (crying/laughing)
- Changes in personality
- Irritability and low frustration tolerance
- Anxiety and depressed mood
- Sleep disturbance

What will tell you that you or someone else is unaware?

- Unawareness of time
- Unawareness of date
- Unawareness of place
- Unawareness of the period or score in the game
- General confusion

How will you feel?

- Dazed, dinged, or stunned
- Like you have had your bell rung
- Blank
- Dizzy
- Like you are seeing stars or flashing lights
- Ringing in the ears
- Like you have a headache
- Sick or nauseous
- Aware of blurred vision
- Not seeing well
- Poorly coordinated or unbalanced
- Aware of slurred speech

The presence of any of these symptoms can be a sign that you have suffered a concussion. You should sit down right away, talk to your coach, and be evaluated by a doctor.

Source: The Pashby Sports Safety Fund Concussion website at www.concussionsafety.com.

Charmaine Crooks (centre) competes in an athletics event at the 1996 Olympic Games in Atlanta, Georgia (CP PHOTO/COA/Claus Andersen).

7

The Cardiovascular and Respiratory Systems

"Trust no thought arrived at while sitting down."
— Long-distance running expert Dr. George Sheehan

All tissues in the body depend on a constant supply of oxygen (O_2). Some tissues and organs, like the brain, are also dependent on a constant supply of energy supplied by the blood (blood glucose). Skeletal muscles are also dependent on a constant supply of O_2 and other nutrients, especially during exercise.

The cardiovascular and respiratory systems are responsible for providing a constant supply of O_2 to the body. These two systems are often considered to work in parallel, because they share this common mission. In this section, however, the anatomical structure of the cardiovascular and respiratory systems are dealt with separately, followed by an outline of how these systems work together. The organization of this section is as follows.

This section begins with a description of the cardiovascular system. In this context, we examine cardiac muscle, the excitation of the heart, coronary circulation, the vascular system, cardiovascular dynamics/exercise response, the effects of training on this system, and cardiovascular disease.

We then turn to the respiratory system and its structure. We examine the conductive zone and respiratory zone, the mechanisms involved in breathing, oxygen transport, respiratory dynamics, and finally respiratory disease.

The section concludes by exploring the integration of the cardiovascular and respiratory systems, beginning with oxygen consumption (limiting factors for VO_2max); the rest to exercise transition; oxygen deficit; and excess post-exercise oxygen consumption.

THE CARDIOVASCULAR SYSTEM

The cardiovascular system is composed of the heart, blood vessels, and blood. It has many important functions, but the main ones are: (1) the delivery of O_2, fuel and other nutrients to the tissues of the body, and the removal of carbon dioxide (CO_2) and waste products from the tissues; (2) maintenance of a constant body temperature (thermoregulation); and (3) prevention of infection (immune function).

The three parts of this system – the heart, the vessels, and blood – work together. The heart acts as the "pump" of the system, pushing blood through the vessels. The blood carries O_2 and nutrients to the tissues, and also carries CO_2 and waste products away from the tissues.

THE HEART

The heart is a hollow organ found in the middle of the chest formed from specialized muscle tissue called cardiac muscle or **myocardium**. It is about the size of a closed fist and weighs approximately 250-350 grams. The heart is considered a "double-pump" and is divided into the right and left heart. The two sides of the heart are separated by the interventricular septum. The right heart is one-half of the double pump, and the left heart is the other half. The main function of the right heart is to pump deoxygenated blood, which has just returned from the body, to the lungs (pulmonary circulation), while the role of the left heart is to pump oxygenated blood, which has just returned from the lungs, to the rest of the body (systemic circulation). Oxygenated blood is bright red in colour, while deoxygenated blood is much darker and is often depicted as being blue in colour. In reality, deoxygenated blood is not blue, but a very dark red.

Within the chest, a tough protective sac, the **pericardium**, surrounds the heart. The pericardium fits loosely over the heart, since it must allow the heart to expand and contract. The outer layer of the heart that lies against the pericardium is called the **epicardium**. Directly under the epicardium is the myocardium. Finally, the layer of tissue that lines the inside of the heart is the **endocardium**.

The heart is made up of four separate chambers. The upper chambers are called **atria**, and the lower chambers are called **ventricles**. The atria are separated from the ventricles by specialized valves that allow blood to flow only from the atria into the ventricles. These valves are called **atrioventricular (AV) valves**. On the right side of the heart, the atrioventricular valve is called the **tricuspid valve**, because it is composed of three special flaps, while on the left side of the heart, the valve is called the **bicuspid (or mitral) valve**, because it is composed of two special flaps. These valves are attached to special muscular extensions of the ventricle walls (**papillary muscles**) by strands of strong specialized tissue (**chordae tendinae**). The papillary muscles and chordae tendinae help to prevent the AV valves from being turned inside out. If they were not present, the valves could be pushed up into the atria much like an umbrella being blown inside out by the wind.

Valves are also found in the heart where the blood leaves the ventricles. On the right side of the heart, the valve is called the **pulmonary semilunar valve**. This valve prevents blood from flowing back from the pulmonary arteries into the right ventricle. On the left side of the heart, the valve that separates the aorta from the left ventricle is called the **aortic semilunar valve** (see Figure 7.1 on page 111).

Path of Blood through the Heart

It is important to understand the circulation of blood through the heart. Blood is delivered to the **right atrium** from the superior and inferior **vena cava**. The vena cava is formed from the coming together of the inferior and superior vena cava. The superior vena cava returns blood to the heart from the upper body, while the inferior vena cava returns blood from the lower body. Once the blood is in the right atrium, it passes through the tricuspid valve and enters the **right ventricle**. From there, the blood is pumped through the pulmonary semilunar valve and out the **pulmonary arteries** to the **lungs** (pulmonary circulation). During the contraction of the right ventricle, the chordae tendinae and papillary muscles help to anchor the tricuspid valve in place and prevent it from being pushed back into the right atrium.

The blood returns from the lungs through the **pulmonary veins** to the **left atrium**. From the left atrium, the blood then passes through the bicuspid (mitral) valve and enters into the **left ventricle**. The bicuspid (mitral) valve is also anchored in place by the chordae tendinae and the papillary muscles, just like the tricuspid valve. The blood is then pumped out through the aortic semilunar valve into the **aorta** and throughout the systemic circulation, eventually returning to the heart through the **inferior** and **superior vena cava**.

Arteries, by definition, are vessels that carry blood away from the heart, while veins are defined as vessels that carry blood toward the heart. In the systemic circulation, which includes the vast majority of the body's blood vessels, arteries carry oxygenated blood

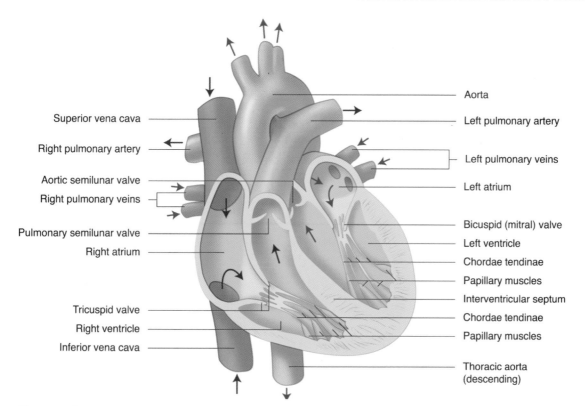

Figure 7.1: Internal anatomy of the heart (red arrows indicate O_2-rich blood; blue arrows, CO_2-rich blood).

from the heart toward body tissues, while veins carry deoxygenated blood back to the heart. In contrast, the pulmonary circulation has a critical difference: pulmonary arteries carry deoxygenated (blue) blood from the heart to the lungs, and pulmonary veins carry oxygenated (red) blood from the lungs back to the heart.

Cardiac Muscle

The muscle tissue that makes up the heart, the myocardium, is similar in structure to the muscle tissue that is used to move the skeleton (skeletal muscle). However, the cardiac muscle cells are interconnected and allow the passage of electrical signals from cell to cell. The ability of these cells to pass electrical signals allows all of the cardiac muscle cells that make up the myocardium to contract as a single unit. Therefore, when a single cell is stimulated to contract, it causes all of the other cardiac muscle cells to contract as well. The term **syncytium** is used to describe this ability, and myocardium or cardiac muscle cells are said to act as a syncytium.

Excitation of the Heart

The cardiac muscle cells that make up the myocardium are excitable, meaning that with electrical stimulation they will contract, leading to the contraction of the heart. The contraction of the heart leads to the pumping of blood. Within the heart there is a number of areas of specialized tissue that are

important in the regulation and coordination of this electrical activity. These regions help spread the electrical signal rapidly through the heart, and aid in coordinating the contraction (see Figure 7.2 on page 112).

One specialized region of tissue is found in the wall of the right atrium and is called the sinoatrial node (SA node). The SA node is also called the "pacemaker" because it is the location where electrical signals are initiated that lead to the contraction of the heart. The basic rate of contraction of the heart, as set by the SA node, is modulated by the autonomic nervous system. The electrical signal spreads through both atria via the **internodal pathways**, causing the atria to contract from the top down and forcing blood into the ventricles.

The electrical signal then moves to the bottom of the atria and passes into another specialized region of tissue called the atrioventricular node (AV node). The AV node passes the electrical signal from the atria into the ventricles. It also passes the signal along into another region of specialized tissue that runs down the ventricular septum, the tissue that separates the two ventricles. This specialized tissue within the ventricular septum is called the **bundle of His** (which is also sometimes called the atrioventricular bundle), and splits to form the right and left bundle branches. The bundle branches pass the signal on to the Purkinje fibres, which in turn pass the electrical signal to the myocardium that forms the ventricles.

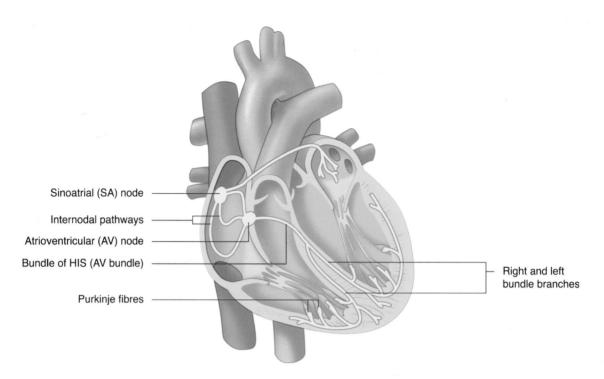

Sinoatrial (SA) node

Internodal pathways

Atrioventricular (AV) node

Bundle of HIS (AV bundle)

Purkinje fibres

Right and left
bundle branches

Figure 7.2: The electrical conduction system of the heart.

This arrangement of specialized tissue allows the contraction of the heart to be initiated in the atria from the top downward, pushing blood into the ventricles. The ventricles then contract from the bottom up, forcing blood into the aorta and pulmonary arteries.

As stated previously, the heart has the ability to stimulate itself and cause contraction, whereas most other types of muscle within the body require stimulation from the nervous system. The SA node, without any input from the nervous system, will cause the heart to contract at approximately 70–80 beats per minute. In situations where the SA node is damaged, the AV node takes control and becomes the pacemaker of the heart.

As we have seen, the SA node acts as the pacemaker of the heart, setting its basic rate of contraction, but the SA node is influenced by the autonomic nervous system. Stimulation from the nervous system can result in either an increase or decrease in heart rate and the force of contraction of the heart.

The electrical activity of the heart can be measured using an **electrocardiogram** (ECG). The ECG provides a graphical representation of the electrical sequence of events that occurs with each contraction of the heart (Figure 7.3). Each of the electrical waves generated during contraction has been named.

The first wave is called the **P wave**, and it represents the depolarization, or the spreading of the electrical signal to contract, through the atria.

Immediately after the depolarization of the atria, it resets itself and readies for another contraction. This process of resetting is called repolarization. However, no indication of atrial repolarization is visible on the ECG. Once the P wave has completed, the electrical wave has reached the AV node. The next major occurrence on the ECG trace is what is called the **QRS complex**, and is usually a slight dip, followed by a steep peak, and then a quick return back to near baseline levels. The QRS complex represents depolarization of the ventricle. Finally, the last wave that is observed is called the **T wave**. The T wave is very similar in size and in shape to the P wave, but the T wave represents the repolarization of the ventricle.

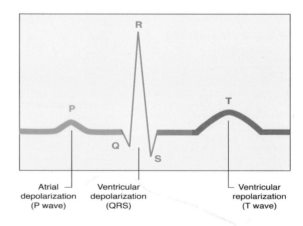

Atrial
depolarization
(P wave)

Ventricular
depolarization
(QRS)

Ventricular
repolarization
(T wave)

Figure 7.3: An illustration of the electrical activity of the cardiac cycle at rest as seen on an electrocardiogram.

CORONARY CIRCULATION

We must remember that the heart is a working muscle that needs not only a constant supply of O_2, but also fuel and nutrients to maintain proper function. When blood supply to a region of the myocardium is reduced or cut off for a prolonged period, that part of the myocardium will be damaged or die, a phenomenon known as a **myocardial infarction**, or more commonly as a heart attack. The system of vessels that supply blood to the heart is called the coronary circulation (see Figure 7.4). Blood is supplied to the heart through two main arteries, the right and left coronary arteries. These arteries branch off of the aorta just above where the aorta leaves the heart. These two arteries divide multiple times, supplying all regions of the myocardium with O_2-rich blood. As the arteries divide and branch, each new branch decreases in size, and eventually these smaller vessels are called arterioles. The coronary arterioles continue to branch and divide, and become even smaller in diameter. Eventually the vessels are so small that a red blood cell can barely get through, and the walls of the vessels are one cell thick.

These microscopic vessels are called capillaries. It is here in the capillaries that O_2, CO_2, and nutrients are exchanged between the blood and the myocardium. Within the myocardium there are millions of capillaries. If we were to look at one square millimetre of myocardium under a microscope, we would be able to see 3,000-4,000 capillaries. Once through the capillaries the vessels become larger, and many smaller vessels come together to form larger vessels. These larger vessels that are collecting blood from the capillaries are called coronary venules. As the blood moves through the venules, the coronary venules come together and form larger vessels called coronary veins. Eventually, all of the coronary veins come together to form the **coronary sinus**, which drains into the right atrium of the heart, completing the path of blood through the coronary circulation.

Cardiac Cycle

The cardiac cycle is defined as the series of events that occurs through one heart beat. During this cycle there is both a phase of relaxation (**diastole**), where the heart is filling with blood, and a phase of contraction (**systole**), where the heart contracts and ejects the blood. During this cycle there are dramatic changes in pressure, which propel the blood through the circulation. These changes in pressure in the heart create pressure waves that are measured in the arteries and are referred to as systolic and diastolic blood pressure.

Systolic blood pressure refers to the pressure observed in the arteries during the contraction phase (i.e., 120 mmHg), whereas the diastolic blood pressure is the pressure observed in the arteries during the relaxation phase of the heart (i.e., 80 mmHg). When blood pressure is reported or measured, it is often stated as being the systolic pressure over the diastolic pressure (i.e., 120/80 mmHg).

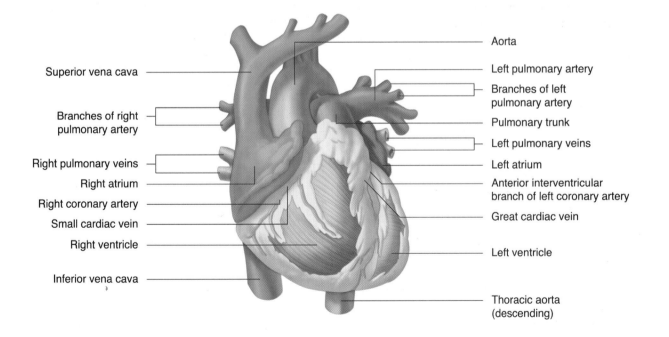

Figure 7.4: Anterior view of the coronary vessels, including other major heart structures.

THE VASCULAR SYSTEM AND BLOOD

The **vascular system** is formed by a network of vessels that transport blood throughout the body (see Figure 7.5). As you follow the path of the blood away from the heart, in either the systemic or pulmonary circuit, the structure of the vessels begins to branch out and get smaller. The different vessels are divided into four main categories: arteries, arterioles, capillaries, venules, and veins. All of these different types of vessels share one common feature – a thin layer of cells that lines the inside of the vessels, a layer known as the **endothelium**.

Arteries

The arteries are vessels with very thick muscular walls, which carry blood away from the heart to the different organs. Even though the walls of arteries are very thick, they are still very elastic and can stretch and then recoil back to their original diameter. This ability to stretch and recoil is important in assisting the movement of blood during diastole (relaxation phase of the heart). As stated previously, blood pressure is measured in the arteries. Systolic blood pressure is the pressure caused by the contraction of the heart, while the recoil of the arteries causes diastolic blood pressure during diastole.

Arterioles

The arterioles are smaller than the arteries and are important in the regulation of blood distribution to the various tissues of the body. Arterioles are surrounded by rings of smooth muscle, and these can contract, constricting the arteriole and reducing the amount of blood flow, or relax, opening the arteriole and increasing the amount of blood flow. These rings of smooth muscle are controlled by two factors: the nervous system, and local chemical factors released by the tissues that are supplied by the arterioles. Nerves interact directly with the arterioles, and can be signaled by the central nervous system to contract or relax the layers of smooth muscle, depending on the needs of the body. For example, during exercise, the arterioles that supply the muscles that are involved in the exercise would be opened by local chemical changes and by the nervous system, increasing blood flow to the muscles. At the same time, the arterioles that supply the intestine would be constricted, reducing blood flow to this organ. Therefore, the nervous system can control the distribution of blood flow to different organs using the arterioles.

Blood flow is also influenced by a process called **autoregulation**. The process of autoregulation refers to the effects of locally produced chemical compounds

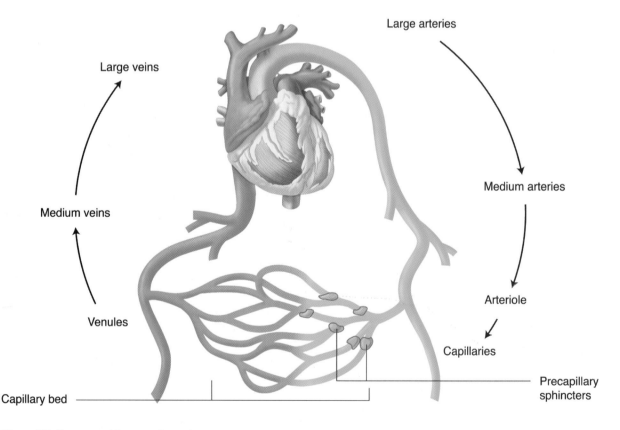

Figure 7.5: Summary of the vascular system.

on blood flow. For example, many local chemical factors are produced in skeletal muscle during exercise. These factors are released by the muscle and will diffuse to the arterioles. These factors cause the arterioles to relax, increasing the delivery of blood to the working muscle. This is a very interesting system, in that it attempts to deliver blood directly to where it is needed. Many different chemical factors that are produced in skeletal muscle during contraction have been thought to influence blood flow. Probably the most potent stimulator of blood flow produced in skeletal muscle is nitric oxide. This compound has been the focus of much research and has been implicated in the local control of many factors, one of which is blood flow. It should also be noted that most of the time the arteries carry oxygen-rich blood, with the only exception being the pulmonary arteries that carry deoxygenated blood to the lungs.

Capillaries

The capillaries are the smallest vessels within the body and have the most important function of all the vessels. Capillaries are so small that the red blood cells can barely fit through, and the walls of the capillaries are very thin (one cell thick). Despite being so small, there are millions of capillaries within the body. All body tissues have an extensive supply of capillaries. If you were to line up all of the capillaries from one person, they would form a line more than 40,000 kilometres long.

It is in the capillaries where the main function of the cardiovascular system occurs, as well as the exchange of gases and nutrients with the tissues. The transfer of gases and nutrients from the blood to the tissues depends on diffusion. For example, the concentration of O_2 is high in the blood when it arrives in the capillaries, but in the tissues there is less O_2. So, the O_2 leaves the blood by diffusion and goes into the tissues where it is needed, moving from a higher concentration to a lower concentration. The diffusion pathway of O_2 will be discussed in more detail in the section dealing with ventilation/respiration.

Veins

Veins return blood to the heart, and become larger as they move away from the capillaries. Many smaller veins, called venules, come together to form larger veins, until they all come together to form either the superior or inferior vena cava. The superior and inferior vena cavae drain the venous blood into the right atrium of the heart. The walls of the veins also contain smooth muscle, which allows the veins to dilate and contract, similar to the arterioles. Veins have the ability to dilate and contract to make sure that enough blood is returned to the heart, so that the heart can

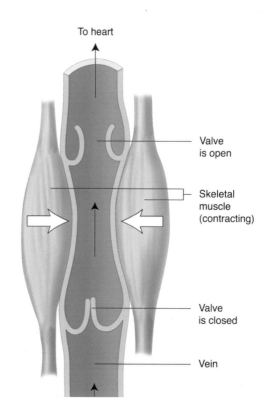

Figure 7.6: The skeletal muscle pump as it aids in venous return.

meet the needs of the body. Veins usually carry deoxygenated blood, with the only exception being the pulmonary veins that carry oxygen-rich blood. Veins are different from all of the other vessels in that they have one-way valves. These valves ensure that the blood can only go back to the heart. The blood pressure in the veins is very low, and if there were no valves, the blood could travel in the wrong direction, back towards the tissues.

The low pressure within the veins creates a problem for the cardiovascular system – how to get all of the blood in the veins back to the heart. There are three main tools that the body uses to assist in the return of blood in the veins to the heart. The first is called the skeletal muscle pump. The **skeletal muscle pump** is a general term used to describe a phenomenon where, with each contraction of a skeletal muscle, blood is pushed or massaged back to the heart. This occurs because of the one-way valves found within the veins. Each contraction of a muscle compresses the veins within or around that muscle, increasing the pressure within that vein. The increase in pressure moves the blood along, and because of the one-way valves, the only direction the blood can travel is back towards to the heart (see Figure 7.6 above).

The second system that the body uses to assist in the return of blood in the veins to the heart is called the thoracic pump. The thoracic pump is related to breathing. With each breath taken by the respiratory system, pressure in the chest cavity is very low for a few short seconds, while the pressure in the abdominal cavity increases. The pressure within the veins that are found in the chest also drops, while the pressure in the veins within the abdominal cavity increases. This creates a difference in pressure between the veins in these two body cavities, and this pushes blood from the veins in the abdominal cavity into the veins in the thoracic cavity, again because of the one-way valves found in the veins.

The final system that the body can use to assist in the return of blood from the veins is the nervous system. During times when cardiac output needs to be increased, such as during exercise, the nervous system sends a signal to the veins, causing them to slightly constrict (venoconstriction). This slight constriction helps to return more blood back to the heart.

Blood

Blood is the specialized fluid that is found in the heart and all of the vessels. Its main role is to act as a transport medium for O_2, CO_2, and nutrients. Blood is made up of two main components: plasma and blood cells. Plasma is the fluid component of blood. It is composed mostly of water and makes up about 55 percent of blood. Within the plasma you will find many different dissolved substances, such as nutrients, proteins, ions, and gases.

The blood cells make up the other 45 percent of blood, with the most abundant blood cells being the red blood cells or erythrocytes. The erythrocytes are the specialized cells that transport O_2 and CO_2 in the blood. Erythrocytes contain a specialized protein called hemoglobin, which can bind O_2 and CO_2. It is this protein in erythrocytes that gives blood the ability to transport and deliver O_2 to the tissues, and remove CO_2 to the lungs.

Another type of cell found in blood is white blood cells, or leukocytes. Leukocytes make up less than 1 percent of the blood and are an important part of the body's immune system. They play an important role in protecting the body from disease. Platelets are also found in blood. They are not complete cells, but fragments of cells, and they are important in the regulation of blood clotting.

To collect a sample of blood, a needle is inserted into a vein or an artery and the blood is withdrawn into a syringe or blood collection tube. The blood is opaque and red in colour due to the large number of erythrocytes. To separate blood into its component parts, the blood is put into a centrifuge and spun at very high speeds for a few minutes. The centrifugation results with the heaviest components of the blood being at the bottom of the tube (erythrocytes) and the lightest at the top (plasma), as illustrated in Figure 7.7 below.

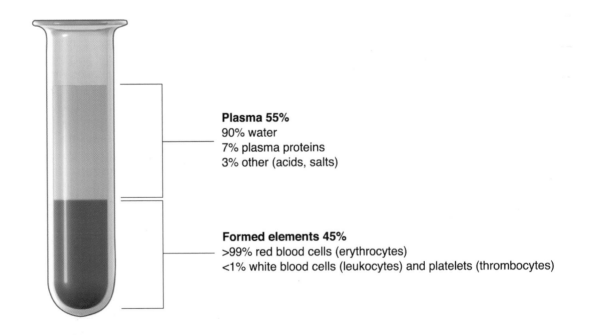

Plasma 55%
90% water
7% plasma proteins
3% other (acids, salts)

Formed elements 45%
>99% red blood cells (erythrocytes)
<1% white blood cells (leukocytes) and platelets (thrombocytes)

Figure 7.7: The composition of centrifuged whole blood.

CARDIOVASCULAR DYNAMICS (EXERCISE RESPONSES)

Cardiovascular dynamics deals with the functioning of the cardiovascular system and how it adapts to meet the demands that are placed on it. Essentially, the heart and the vessels must constantly adapt to accommodate the ever-changing requirements of the body. For example, during exercise, dramatic changes in cardiovascular dynamics occur. Some of the factors that are considered when discussing cardiovascular dynamics are cardiac output, blood pressure, distribution of blood flow, and O_2 consumption.

Cardiac Output

The volume of blood that is pumped out of the left ventricle in 1 minute is called **cardiac output (Q)**, and is measured in litres per minute (L/min). At rest, a typical person's cardiac output will be approximately 5-6 L/min, but during heavy exercise, cardiac output can increase up to greater than 30 L/min.

The two other factors that contribute to cardiac output are stroke volume and heart rate. **Stroke volume (SV)** is the amount of blood that is ejected from the left ventricle in a single beat, and is measured in millilitres (mL). SV is calculated by subtracting the left ventricular end-systolic volume (LVESV) from the left ventricular end-diastolic volume (LVEDV). LVESV is the amount of blood remaining in the left ventricle after the contraction of the ventricle, while LVEDV is the amount of blood in the left ventricle after the contraction of the left atrium. Therefore, SV can be represented by the following formula:

$$SV(mL) = LVEDV(mL) - LVESV(mL)$$

Stroke volume is regulated by three main factors, both at rest and during exercise: (1) LVEDV, (2) aortic blood pressure, and (3) the strength of the ventricular contraction. Alterations to any of these three factors will result in changes in stroke volume.

LVEDV is the amount of blood that is returned to the ventricle before it contracts. The ventricle has the capacity to stretch to accommodate increases in LVEDV, and this stretching of the ventricle results in a more forceful contraction of the cardiac muscle and an increase in the amount of blood that is ejected. This ability of the heart to stretch and increase the force of contraction is called the **Frank-Starling Law**. Therefore, the most important factor that regulates SV would be the amount of blood that is returned to the heart (venous return).

During exercise, venous return increases as the result of four main factors: (1) constriction of the veins (venoconstriction); (2) the skeletal muscle pump; (3) the thoracic pump; and (4) nervous stimulation of the heart. The walls of the veins contain some smooth muscle, and during exercise, the smooth muscle is stimulated to contract, slightly reducing the diameter of the veins and reducing the volume of blood in the veins, directing it towards the heart. The skeletal muscle pump and the thoracic pump also contribute to increases in venous return (discussed previously). Finally, nervous stimulation of the heart leads not only to an increase in heart rate, but also results in an increase in the force of contraction of the heart, further contributing to the increases in SV that are observed during exercise.

The efficiency of SV is measured through the calculation of ejection fraction. **Ejection fraction (EF)** is the proportion of blood that is ejected from the left ventricle during a single heartbeat. Ejection fraction is calculated using the following formula:

$$EF(\%) = \frac{SV(mL)}{LVEDV(mL)} \times 100$$

On average EF at rest is ~50-60 percent, and increases during exercise as the intensity of exercise increases. During maximal exercise, EF can increase to ~85 percent.

Heart rate (HR) is the number of times the heart contracts in a minute (beats per minute; beats/min). Cardiac output can be calculated as the product of stroke volume and heart rate:

$$Q(L/\min) = SV(mL) \times HR(beats/\min)$$

For example, an average HR at rest would be ~72 beats/min, and an average SV at rest would be ~71 mL. Therefore, using the equation for Q, resting Q would be calculated as 5040 mL/min, or 5.04 L/min.

During exercise, Q can increase to 15-25 L/min, depending on the intensity of the exercise. The increase in Q occurs very early in the exercise and then becomes constant at the new higher level. These increases are mediated by both an increase in SV and HR. The increase in SV also occurs very early in exercise and then maintains a plateau. The increase in HR is very similar to those observed in SV and Q. If the exercise is very prolonged, there might be a slight decline in SV late in the exercise. Such declines result from excessive fluid loss from the body due to sweating. Despite the slight decline in SV, Q is maintained with a gradual increase in HR. Generally, the increase in Q with exercise is related to the intensity of the exercise, with increases in Q observed with increases in exercise intensity.

During prolonged exercise, Q is maintained, but significant changes are observed with HR and SV. This phenomenon is called **cardiovascular drift**, and is characterized by a slow and steady rise in HR and a corresponding decline in SV. Cardiovascular drift results from the physiological changes associated with the increase in body temperature that occurs during the exercise. Some of these changes include decreases in plasma volume, redistribution of blood flow to the skin, and dehydration. All of these changes result in a decrease in venous return of blood to the heart, resulting in a decrease in SV. Despite the decline in SV, the body compensates through increases in HR, and Q is maintained.

Blood Pressure

As stated previously, blood pressure is the force exerted by the blood against the walls of the arteries. During exercise, profound changes in blood pressure can occur depending on the type, duration, and intensity of the exercise. For example, acute aerobic or endurance exercise generally leads to a sustained increase in systolic blood pressure, but no change in diastolic blood pressure during the activity. The increase in systolic blood pressure is often proportional to the exercise intensity – meaning the greater the exercise intensity, the greater the rise in systolic blood pressure. Resistance exercise, such as weightlifting, can result in very short, but very large increases in both systolic and diastolic blood pressure. As with endurance exercise, the increase in blood pressure with resistance-type exercise is also proportional to the intensity of the exercise, with greater increases in blood pressure observed with higher exercise intensities.

Following exercise, both endurance and resistance, there is a prolonged period where blood pressure drops below normal resting values. This phenomenon is called post-exercise hypotension, and occurs even with low-intensity exercise.

Blood Pressure Health and Exercise

Blood pressure is a commonly used indicator or measure of cardiovascular health. Persistently elevated blood pressure, also called hypertension (blood pressure consistently greater than 140/90 mmHg), is a major risk factor for cardiovascular disease. This is considered a modifiable risk factor, because through modifications to lifestyle, blood pressure can be returned back to near normal levels. It is well established that aerobic exercise training leads to improvements in resting blood pressure in people with moderate to high blood pressure within three weeks to three months of starting to exercise.

Further improvements are also observed when modifications are also made to other health behaviors, such as diet. For example, it is recommended that individuals with elevated blood pressure consume a diet low in saturated fats and cholesterol and high in fibre and complex carbohydrates. When modifications in diet are combined with increases in aerobic exercise, improvements in blood pressure are common. However, in some extreme cases, additional medical intervention is required, and no person with elevated blood pressure should start exercising without clearance from their doctor.

Blood Flow Distribution

During exercise, the working skeletal muscle has an increased need for O_2, and the cardiovascular system attempts to match the delivery of O_2 to meet this need by altering the blood flow distribution. The increase in the delivery of O_2 is achieved in two ways: an increase in Q, and a redistribution of blood flow. The system increases the amount of blood flow that is directed to the working muscle while blood flow to less active organs, such as the stomach, intestine, and kidneys, is decreased (see Table 7.1 below).

The redistribution of blood flow is dependent on the intensity of the exercise, with a greater amount of blood shunted towards the working skeletal muscle with increasing exercise intensities. Interestingly, one of the only organ systems where blood flow distribution remains unaltered during exercise is the brain. The absolute amount of blood delivered to the brain is maintained both at rest and during exercise.

Table 7.1: Distribution of cardiac output to various vascular regions during progressive exercise to maximum aerobic power (mL/min.)

Vascular region	At rest (6%)	Light exercise (30%)	Heavy exercise (75%)	Maximal Exercise (100%)
Cerebral	720 mL (12%)	720 mL (6%)	720 mL (3%)	720 mL (2%)
Myocardial	240 mL (4%)	480 mL (4%)	960 mL (4%)	1,200 mL (4%)
Muscle	1,260 mL (21%)	5,760 mL (48%)	17,280 mL (72%)	26,400 mL (88%)
Renal	1,320 mL (22%)	1,200 mL (10%)	720 mL (3%)	300 mL (1%)
Digestive	1,560 mL (26%)	1,440 mL (12%)	960 mL (4%)	300 mL (1%)
Skin	540 mL (9%)	1,920 mL (16%)	2,640 mL (11%)	900 mL (3%)
Other	360 mL (6%)	480 mL (4%)	720 mL (3%)	180 mL (1%)
TOTAL	**6,000 mL**	**12,000 mL**	**24,000 mL**	**30,000 mL**

Modified from Vander, A.J., Sherman, W.J., & Luciano, E.S. (1985). *Human physiology: Mechanisms of body function* (4th ed.). New York: McGraw-Hill. Reprinted by permission of The McGraw-Hill Companies.

THE EFFECTS OF TRAINING ON THE CARDIOVASCULAR SYSTEM

Regular aerobic exercise leads to a number of alterations, not only to the functioning of the cardiovascular system, but also the structure of some of its components. These changes result in improvements in efficiency at rest and during sub-maximal exercise, and also during maximal exercise (see Table 7.2).

The most influential changes observed with aerobic training are alterations in the structure of the heart. With prolonged training, increases in the mass and dimensions of the heart are observed. Specifically, increases in ventricular volume and thickness of the ventricles walls are observed. These changes likely occur due to the persistent increases in venous return that occur during exercise. The increase in ventricular volume would lead to an increase in SV, while the increase in ventricular wall thickness would contribute to an increased force of contraction of the ventricle. Both of these factors would contribute to an increase in SV and therefore Q during exercise.

Other structural changes that are observed in the heart include an increase in the number of capillaries that deliver blood to the myocardium. This adaptation likely occurs in response to the increase in O_2 demand because of the increase in work being performed by the heart. There has been some evidence to suggest that training may also lead to an increase in the diameter of the coronary arteries. Such an increase would also increase the delivery of blood to the myocardium.

Another important and very rapid adaptation that occurs with training is an increase in blood volume. Within the first few days of initiating training, measurable increases in plasma volume can be observed. Increases upward of 15 percent have been observed within two days of starting training. Such increases contribute to an increase in venous return, and therefore SV and Q. Eventually, as the training continues, there is also an increase in erythrocytes. If training is stopped, blood volume returns back to pre-training levels within a week or two.

Many of the previously discussed training adaptations contribute to changes in Q during exercise. Despite the alterations in Q during exercise, it remains unchanged at rest. However, the factors that contribute to Q, SV, and HR are altered at rest, with an increase in SV and a decrease in HR. These alterations are persistent during exercise, with an increase in SV being observed during both sub-maximal and maximal exercise. HR is decreased at rest and during sub-maximal exercise. This decrease in HR is often referred to as bradycardia.

Bradycardia is one of the most classic and easily observed adaptations to the cardiovascular system that occurs with training. Despite the alterations in HR at rest and during sub-maximal exercise, HR is unchanged at maximal exercise. These alterations together contribute to the increases in maximal exercise capacity that is observed following training. Bradycardia is characterized by a heart rate of 60 beats per minute or less at rest while **tachycardia** is a heart rate of 100 beats per minute at rest. Generally, a lower heart rate is an indication of an athletic or strong heart.

Cardiovascular Disease

The term cardiovascular disease encompasses any disease associated with the cardiovascular system. More often people use this term to refer to coronary artery disease or coronary heart disease. This disease (**atherosclerosis**) is associated with a gradual narrowing of the coronary arteries resulting from the accumulation of hard deposits of cholesterol, called plaque, on the lining of the vessels. If allowed to progress, partial or complete closing of the artery could occur, resulting in a myocardial infarction or heart attack. A myocardial infarction results in death of some of the cardiac muscle. The severity of the disease is determined by where in the coronary artery and how many coronary arteries are involved.

There are many risk factors associated with coronary artery disease, including smoking, elevated blood lipids, hypertension, family history, and physical inactivity. Each of these factors individually increase the risk of development of coronary artery disease, but when combined, the risk is magnified.

Table 7.2: Effects of training				
	Q	=	SV (mL)	x	HR (beats/ min)
Untrained					
Rest	5.00	=	70	x	72
Exercise					
Light	9.35	=	85	x	110
Moderate	14.25	=	95	x	150
Maximal	22.00	=	110	x	200
Trained					
Rest	5.00	=	100	x	50
Exercise					
Light	9.40	=	125	x	75
Moderate	14.85	=	135	x	110
Maximal	34.2	=	180	x	190

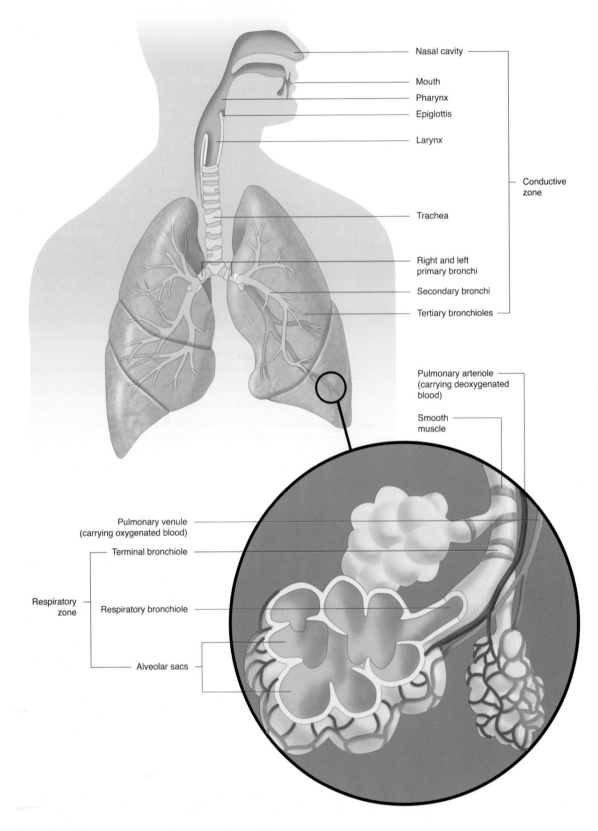

Nasal cavity

Mouth
Pharynx
Epiglottis
Larynx

Conductive zone

Trachea

Right and left primary bronchi
Secondary bronchi
Tertiary bronchioles

Pulmonary arteriole (carrying deoxygenated blood)

Smooth muscle

Pulmonary venule (carrying oxygenated blood)

Terminal bronchiole

Respiratory zone

Respiratory bronchiole

Alveolar sacs

Figure 7.8: The main structures of the respiratory system.

THE RESPIRATORY SYSTEM

The respiratory system is composed of structures that allow the passage of air from outside the body to the lungs, as well as the structures therein that allow gas exchange to occur. (Figure 7.8 on page 120). The three main functions of the respiratory system are to:

- supply O_2 to the blood;
- remove CO_2 from the blood; and
- regulate blood pH (acid-base balance).

Respiration is a term used to describe a number of different processes related, not only to the respiratory system, but also involving the movement of gases throughout the body. External respiration refers to the processes that occur within the lung involving the exchange of O_2 and CO_2. Internal respiration refers to the exchange of gases at the tissue level, where O_2 is delivered and CO_2 removed. Finally, cellular respiration is the process where the cells use O_2 to generate energy through the different metabolic pathways found in the mitochondria.

RESPIRATORY SYSTEM STRUCTURE

The actual structure of the respiratory system can be divided into two main zones. These zones include the conductive zone and the respiratory zone. The conductive zone transports air to the lungs, while the respiratory zone is where gas exchange occurs (see Figure 7.8).

The Conductive Zone

The conductive zone is composed of all of the structures that convey air from the outside of the body through to the lungs. This zone includes the **mouth and nose**; **pharynx**; **larynx**; **trachea**; **primary and secondary bronchi**; and **tertiary bronchioles** and **terminal bronchioles**. As stated previously, the main role of these components is the transport of air to the lungs. Another function of this zone is to warm and humidify air before it enters the respiratory zone. By the time air reaches the respiratory zone, it is at body temperature (37°C) and is almost completely saturated with moisture. This helps to maintain body temperature and protect the sensitive tissues that make up the respiratory zone.

Another role of the conductive zone is to filter air that is taken in with each breath. The nasal cavity is lined with hairs to trap larger foreign bodies and prevent them from being inspired (breathed in). Additionally, structures of the conductive zone are lined with mucous membranes that act to trap smaller substances that are inspired with each breath.

The Respiratory Zone

The respiratory zone is composed of the **respiratory bronchioles**, **alveolar ducts**, and the **alveolar sacs**. All of these structures are involved with the exchange of gases between inspired air and the blood. The alveolar sacs (alveoli) are grape-like structures found within the lungs. The alveolar sacs provide a large surface area for the diffusion of gases into and out of the blood. The average person has about 300 million alveolar sacs. If all of these alveolar sacs were stretched out, they would cover an area as large as a tennis court. Each of these structures is surrounded by a web of capillaries as well as a network of delicate elastic fibres. Both the wall of the alveolar sacs and the wall of each capillary surrounding these sacs are one cell thick, which provides a very short distance for gases to diffuse. Therefore, the structure of the lungs provides a large surface area and a minimal distance for the diffusion of gases to occur, maximizing the rate of gas exchange (see Figure 7.8).

MECHANISMS OF BREATHING

The movement of air from the outside of the body to the inside of the body and into the lungs is dependent on differences in air pressure. Air moves from regions of higher pressure to regions of lower pressure, and the body uses this principal to mediate breathing. The lungs are found within the chest cavity, which is separated from the abdominal cavity by a large flat specialized muscle called the diaphragm. With stimulation from the brain, the diaphragm contracts and moves downward towards the abdominal cavity, creating more space in the chest cavity. This results in a decline in air pressure within the chest and lungs. With the contraction of the diaphragm, the air pressure within the chest and lungs is lower than the air pressure outside the body in the atmosphere. The lower air pressure in the chest causes air to rush into the lungs, and results in an inspiration, equalizing this pressure differential, as illustrated in Figure 7.9 on page 122.

As described, inspiration is an active process, requiring the contraction of various respiratory muscles, including the diaphragm. Expiration, on the other hand, may be passive as in quiet breathing or active as in forced breathing. In **quiet breathing**, the delicate elastic fibres lining the alveolar sacs recoil passively as the diaphragm relaxes and air is expelled. Thus, during quiet breathing, expiration is similar to the release of air from an inflated balloon. In **forced breathing**, as occurs in vigorous exercise, the passive recoil of the lungs is not fast enough to keep up with

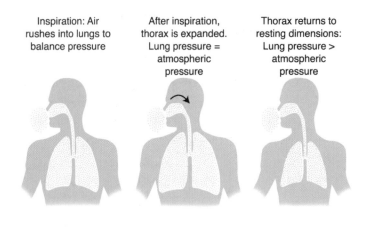

Figure 7.9: The movement of the ribs and diaphragm alter the size of the thoracic cage, enabling inspiration and expiration.

the required rate of respiration. Thus, muscles in the thoracic and abdominal wall contract, actively decreasing the volume of the thoracic cavity and increasing the air pressure within the lungs. This process forces air out of the lungs rapidly, as when one attempts to blow out birthday candles.

Ventilation

The combination of inspiration and expiration together is known as **ventilation** (V_E). More specifically, V_E is the volume of air that is moved by the lungs in 1 minute. V_E is influenced by two factors: the volume of air in each breath, and the number of breaths taken per minute. The volume of air in each breath is also known as the **tidal volume** (V_T). At rest, a typical V_T is about 0.5 L/breath, while during exercise, V_T can increase up to 3 to 4 L/breath. The number of breaths taken per minute is also known as the **respiratory frequency** (*f*). Under resting conditions, a typical frequency of respiration is about 12 breaths/min, while during exercise, frequency can increase up to 30 to 40 breaths/min. Therefore, we can calculate ventilation using the following mathematical relationship:

$$V_E(L/\min) = V_T(L) \times f(breaths/\min)$$

During very intense exercise, rates of ventilation can increase up to 100 to 200 L of air per minute.

Control of Ventilation

Breathing results from the contraction and relaxation of the inspiratory muscles and expiratory muscles. The contraction of muscles is dependent on stimulation from the central nervous system, and in the case of the muscles involved in breathing or ventilation, there are highly specialized regions within the brain that initiate the stimulation of the muscles involved in ventilation. All aspects of breathing are closely associated with the overall need of O_2, metabolic processes, muscle activity, and the production of CO_2. Control of breathing is very complex and involves many different forms of feedback from specialized sensory systems to the neural control centres within the brain.

The **respiratory control centres** are found within the brain stem. The brain stem is the region of the brain found just above the spinal cord and is involved in many body processes that are not under conscious control (autonomic). The areas of the brain stem that are important in the regulation of ventilation are the **medulla oblongata** and the **pons**.

Within the medulla oblongata is the inspiratory centre and the expiratory centre. The specialized nerves that are found in the inspiratory centre spontaneously generate a rhythmical signal(on-off pattern) that is sent to the respiratory muscles, the diaphragm, and the external intercostals. At rest, without any other influences, the inspiratory centre will stimulate a frequency of breathing of ~ 12-15 breaths/min. During periods of increased need, such as exercise, additional information or feedback is provided to the respiratory centre and a fast rate of signalling is achieved. The expiratory centre appears to have two main functions, with the first being to ensure that the inspiratory muscles never completely relax. The second function is to stimulate forceful expiration when required, such as during exercise.

There are also two specialized respiratory centres that are found in the pons, and they are called the **Pneumotaxic** and **Apneustic centres**. These centres act to ensure that the transition of inhalation to exhalation is smooth. They also act to fine-tune the breathing pattern.

In addition to the respiratory control centres in the brain stem, other areas of the brain can also influence ventilation. For example, the stimulation of skeletal muscles also leads to stimulation of the breathing control centres of the brain, in an attempt to "turn-on" respiration with the initiation of movement. There are also specialized sensory systems in place to provide feedback to respiratory control centres to ensure that an adequate rate of respiration has been achieved. Some of these sensory systems provide information on chemical and pH changes in the blood. All of these systems work together to ensure that ventilation requirements are met.

Lung Volumes

Lung volumes are divided into two different categories: static volumes and dynamic volumes. **Static lung volumes** are those that are determined by the actual structure of the lung and are not determined or influenced by breathing or the flow of air. In contrast, **dynamic lung volumes** are those that are dependent, not only on volume, but also on the movement or flow of air.

There are three important static lung volumes: (1) total lung capacity, (2) vital capacity, and (3) residual volume. Total lung capacity (TLC) is the maximum volume of air that the lungs can hold. TLC is the sum of the vital capacity (VC) and the residual volume (RV). VC is the maximum amount of air that can be exhaled following a maximal inhalation, while RV is the air that remains in the lungs following a maximal exhalation. Therefore the relationship between TLC, VC, and RV is expressed by the following formula:

$$TLC = VC + RV$$

VC is measured using a test called a forced vital capacity (FVC), during which the individual takes in as deep a breath as possible and then forcefully exhales as much of the air as possible.

Tests that involve the measurement of the movement of air by breathing are called dynamic lung volumes. The two most common tests include force expiratory volume (FEV) and maximal voluntary ventilation (MVV). The measurement of FEV is done over a set period of time, either 1 or 3 seconds (FEV1 or FEV3), and is a measurement of how much air is moved during 1 or 3 seconds of an FVC. In contrast, the MVV is a measure of how much air an individual can move over a period of 15 seconds. The value that is obtained during the MVV is then multiplied by 4 to give a value per minute. These tests are used to investigate lung function and are often used to screen for respiratory diseases, such as asthma and chronic obstructive pulmonary disease (COPD).

Gas Exchange

The primary factor that mediates **gas exchange** both at the lung (where the blood becomes oxygenated and CO_2 removed) and at the tissue (where O_2 is delivered for metabolism and CO_2 is removed) is diffusion. **Diffusion** is defined as the movement of a gas, liquid, or solid from a region of high concentration to a region of low concentration through random movement. Diffusion can only occur if a difference in concentration exists, and such a difference is called a concentration gradient.

The concentrations of specific gases involved in respiration are measured using a system called **partial pressures**. Recall that air is made up of a number of different gases, including nitrogen, O_2, and CO_2. The relative percentage of each of these gases stays the same in air, but the partial pressure of each gas can change depending on the air pressure (barometric pressure) and barometric pressure changes depending on the weather. For example, higher levels of barometric pressure are observed during clear weather, while lower measures are observed during bad weather. To calculate the partial pressure of a gas, multiply the barometric pressure by the fraction of the gas. For example, the average barometric pressure is 760 mmHg, and the fraction percentage of O_2 in the air is 20.93 percent. Therefore, the partial pressure of O_2, or PO_2, is 760 mmHg x 0.2093 = 159.1 mmHg.

Table 7.3: Fractional concentrations and partial pressures of main gases found in air

Gas	Barometric Pressure*		Fractional Concentration		Partial Pressure
Nitrogen (N_2)	760 mmHg	X	79.04%	=	600.7 mmHg
Oxygen (O_2)	760 mmHg	X	20.93%	=	159.1 mmHg
Carbon Dioxide (CO_2)	760 mmHg	X	0.03%	=	0.23 mmHg

*Assuming dry atmospheric air at sea level.

When it comes to the respiratory system, we are interested in the **diffusion pathway** for gases moving from the lungs into the blood and from the blood into the tissue, and back. The rates of diffusion of a gas between two different areas, such as from the lungs into the blood, depend on a number of different factors. The first factor that must be considered is the size of the concentration gradient. As the concentration gradient increases, greater rates of diffusion are observed. The diffusion of a gas into a liquid is

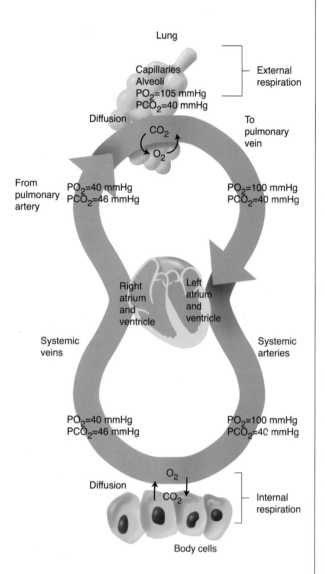

Lung

Capillaries
Alveoli
PO_2=105 mmHg
PCO_2=40 mmHg

External respiration

Diffusion

CO_2
O_2

To pulmonary vein

From pulmonary artery

PO_2=40 mmHg
PCO_2=46 mmHg

PO_2=100 mmHg
PCO_2=40 mmHg

Right atrium and ventricle

Left atrium and ventricle

Systemic veins

Systemic arteries

PO_2=40 mmHg
PCO_2=46 mmHg

PO_2=100 mmHg
PCO_2=40 mmHg

Diffusion

O_2
CO_2

Internal respiration

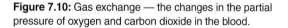

Body cells

Figure 7.10: Gas exchange — the changes in the partial pressure of oxygen and carbon dioxide in the blood.

governed by **Henry's Law,** which states that the amount of gas that will dissolve and/or diffuse into a liquid is proportional to the partial pressure and the solubility of the gas. Furthermore, Henry's Law also states that the gas will continue to dissolve and/or diffuse into the liquid until an equilibrium has been achieved, meaning that the partial pressures within the liquid and the air are the same. Using O_2 as an example, the PO_2 within the alveoli is 105 mmHg, while the PO_2 within the deoxygenated blood as it enters the lungs is only 40 mmHg. This creates a diffusion gradient, which mediates the diffusion of O_2 into the blood (see Figure 7.10).

The second factor that must be considered is the thickness of the barrier between the two areas. Thinner barriers mediate faster rates of diffusion as compared to thicker barriers. Within the lung, the distance between the alveoli and the capillaries that surround each alveoli is extremely small, essentially only two cells thick, optimizing the diffusion distance.

The third factor that must be considered is the surface area between the two areas. If a larger surface area exists between the two areas, faster rates of diffusion are observed. The anatomy of the lung provides a huge surface area for diffusion. As mentioned, if you were to stretch out all of the alveoli from the lungs, it would provide a surface area for diffusion about the size of a tennis court. Therefore, the respiratory system takes advantage of all of these factors to maximize the rate of diffusion of O_2 from the air inhaled in the lungs into the blood, and the movement of CO_2 out of the blood.

OXYGEN (O_2) TRANSPORT

Oxygen transport within the blood is achieved in two ways. First, a small amount of O_2 is actually dissolved within the plasma, or the fluid component of the blood. This only represents about 2 percent of the O_2 found in the blood. The other way in which O_2 is transported is by binding to a specialized protein found in erythrocytes, called **hemoglobin**. Each gram of hemoglobin in the blood has the capacity to bind 1.34 mL of O_2 and the average concentration of hemoglobin is ~16 mg/100 mL of blood. Therefore, the average O_2 carrying capacity for blood is ~21.4 mL O_2/100 mL of blood (O_2 carrying capacity = [Hgb] x 1.34). The majority of the O_2 transported in the blood is bound to hemoglobin. However, remember that a very small amount of O_2 is also transported in the plasma (~0.5 mL O_2/100 mL of blood).

Under different conditions the amount of O_2 bound to hemoglobin can vary. The relative amount of the O_2 carrying capacity that is used is termed the percent saturation of hemoglobin (SbO_2%). However, the main factor that affects SbO_2% is the PO_2 within the blood. The relationship that describes the influence of PO_2 on SBO_2% is called the oxyhemoglobin dissociation curve. This curve has an "S" shape, and essentially, the lower the PO_2, the less O_2 will bind to hemoglobin. This relationship ensures that O_2 will be delivered to where it is needed. For example, in the arterial blood PO_2 is ~ 100mmHg and SBO_2% is ~95-100%. In the capillaries of skeletal muscle, PO_2 would decline to ~40 mmHg, and SBO_2% declines to ~75%.

Carbon Dioxide (CO₂) Transport

Carbon dioxide must be moved from body tissues, where it is produced, back to the lung where it can be moved into the alveoli and then exhaled and removed from the body. There are three ways in which CO_2 is carried within the blood. A small amount of CO_2 is found dissolved in the plasma, much like O_2. Only about 5-10 percent of CO_2 is transported dissolved in the plasma. The remaining 90-95 percent of CO_2 diffuses into the erythrocytes.

Carbon dioxide (~20%) can also bind to the hemoglobin, forming what is called carbaminohemoglobin, when there are low concentrations of O_2. Having arrived in the lung, the elevated concentrations of O_2 stimulate the hemoglobin to release the CO_2, which then diffuses out into the alveoli and is exhaled.

The third way in which CO_2 is transported is through what is called the bicarbonate system. The remaining CO_2 (~70-75%) diffuses into the erythrocytes, but undergoes a chemical reaction with water, forming a weak acid called carbonic acid. This chemical reaction occurs because of a specialized enzyme found in the erythrocytes called carbonic anhydrase. The newly formed carbonic acid then dissociates, forming a hydrogen ion and a bicarbonate ion. The resulting H+ ion binds to the hemoglobin, while the bicarbonate ion diffuses into the plasma. At the lungs, the partial pressure of CO_2 is low, and this process is reversed. Furthermore, the higher partial pressure of O_2 mediates the release of the H+ ion from the CO_2. Once the CO_2 is returned back to its original form, it is free to diffuse out of the blood and into the alveoli, and is then exhaled. It is important to remember that the respiratory system is so efficient that these processes occur very rapidly and do not limit exercise performance in any way.

Ventilation and the Regulation of Blood pH

Ventilation plays an important role in the regulation of the pH of the blood. Blood pH is a measure of how acidic or how basic the blood is. Generally, blood pH is maintained very close to a pH of 7.4. However, situations where large amounts of acid are released into the blood, such as during exercise (lactic acid), result in a decline in blood pH. A decrease in pH (an increase in acidity) means that there is an increase in the accumulation of H+ ions in the blood.

Ventilation plays an important role in the regulation of the amount of H+ ions in the blood because of the transport of CO_2 through the bicarbonate system. Recall the carbonic anhydrase reaction that was discussed previously. Essentially, if ventilation is increased, expelling extra amounts of CO_2, this causes more H+ to combine with bicarbonate to form carbonic acid and eventually CO_2 and H_2O. At the same time, this lowers the concentration of H+ ions, increasing pH back to normal levels. Therefore, increases in ventilation can assist in returning blood pH back to near-normal levels.

RESPIRATORY DYNAMICS

During exercise, the body responds to the increased need of oxygen at the working muscle through a series of responses that attempt to match oxygen delivery with oxygen demand. With respect to the respiratory system, changes occur in pulmonary ventilation (V_E), external respiration, and internal respiration. Exercise results in increases in pulmonary ventilation, external and internal respiration, and cellular respiration.

Pulmonary Ventilation (V_E)

Pulmonary ventilation (V_E) is closely matched to the rate and/or intensity of the work being done. The increases in V_E that occur with sub-maximal exercise can be divided into three phases. The first phase is termed the rapid on phase. During this phase V_E is increased at a very rapid rate, almost immediately upon the onset of the activity. The second phase is characterized by a slower exponential increase from the rapid increase observed in phase one. Phase three of the response is characterized by a leveling off of V_E at a new steady-state level. The new steady-state level is predominately determined by the intensity of the exercise and the level of fitness of the individual. The increases in V_E are due initially to a rise in V_T, and then, as the exercise continues, a rise in f. With more intense exercise, f will increase to a greater extent to accommodate the increased demands for V_E.

External Respiration

Total gas exchange at the lungs is increased as the result of two main factors: the increase in V_E, and the increase in blood flow to the lungs. The increase in gas exchange is closely matched to the increase in requirements of the working skeletal muscle. The increase in V_E serves to maintain the necessary gradients in the partial pressures of both O_2 and CO_2, to maintain gas exchange.

The increase in Q, discussed previously, also results in an increase in blood flow to the lungs. Generally, V_E is closely matched to the delivery of blood to the lungs, thereby maintaining the partial pressures in the alveoli and in the blood, and the normal diffusion gradients. The maintenance of the diffusion gradients ensures proper oxygenation of the blood and removal of CO_2 (see Figure 7.11).

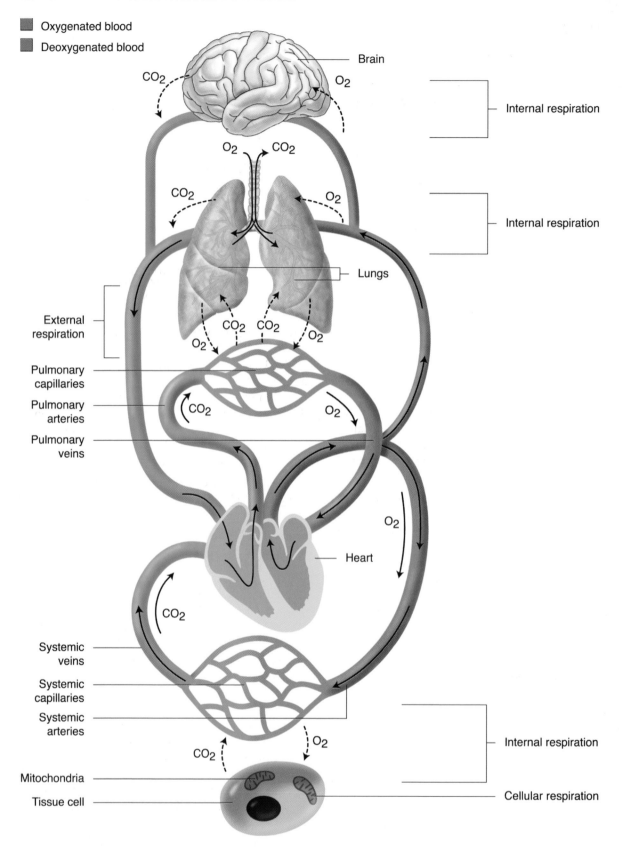

Figure 7.11: Flow diagram of external and internal respiration.

Internal Respiration

Internal respiration involves the exchange of gases at the level of the tissues. Essentially, the extraction of O_2 at the tissues is increased. This occurs as the result of four main factors: (1) an increase in the PO_2 gradient, (2) an increase in PCO_2, (3) a decrease in pH, and (4) an increase in temperature. During exercise, the skeletal muscle increases cellular respiration, and O_2 is used to generate ATP. This increase in the use of O_2 results in a decline in the PO_2 within the skeletal muscle, and increases the gradient between the PO_2 within the blood and the muscle. The increase in the gradient further enhances the diffusion of O_2 out of the blood into the working muscle.

The increase in muscle activity results in an increase in CO_2 production, a decline in pH (resulting from increases in CO_2 and lactic acid), and an increase in temperature. These three factors influence the binding of O_2 with hemoglobin and result in an increase in the unloading of O_2. Essentially, the alteration in CO_2, pH, and temperature contribute to what is called the Bohr shift. This shift is in reference to the oxyhemoglobin dissociation curve, in that the curve is shifted to the left. This means that, for a given PO_2, more O_2 will be unloaded. This results in an enhanced unloading of O_2 at the working muscle, contributing to the increase in internal respiration that occurs during exercise.

One way to determine how much oxygen has been delivered to skeletal muscle is to measure the amount of oxygen in the arterial blood before it arrives at the muscle, and then measure the venous blood that drains from the same muscle. The difference between the amount of O_2 in the artery and vein reflects the amount of O_2 delivered to the muscle. This is termed the a-vO_2 difference (a-vO_2 diff), as shown in Figure 7.12.

Adaptations to Training

Regular aerobic training leads to very few adaptations in the respiratory system. Essentially, the only observable changes to respiratory function with training are in V_E. Generally, training results in an increase in V_T and a decrease in f, with no observed changes in V_E at rest.

During sub-maximal exercise, similar responses are observed, but in some cases slight declines in V_E are also observed. However, training does result in increases in V_E during maximal exercise. These changes have been suggested to be the result of increases in both the strength and endurance of the respiratory muscles.

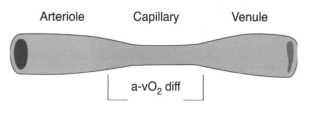

Arteriole   Capillary   Venule

a-vO_2 diff

Figure 7.12: The a-vO_2 difference. From *Exercise Physiology: Theory and Application to Fitness and Performance*, by S.K. Powers and E.T. Howley, 4th ed., 2001, Toronto: McGraw-Hill.

	O_2 Content in Arteriole	O_2 Content in Venule	a-vO_2 Diff
At Rest	20 mL O_2 per 100 mL of blood	15-16 mL O_2 per 100 mL of blood	4-5 mL O_2 per 100 mL of blood
Maximal Exercise	20 mL O_2 per 100 mL of blood	5 mL O_2 per 100 mL of blood	15 mL O_2 per 100 mL of blood

RESPIRATORY DISEASE

The lungs and the respiratory system generally are not considered to limit exercise performance in healthy individuals. However, there are a couple of disease states where respiratory system function is impaired, resulting in poor physical functioning. The two most common respiratory diseases are asthma and chronic obstructive respiratory disease.

Asthma is a disease characterized by spasm of the smooth muscle that line the respiratory system, an oversecretion of mucous, and swelling of the cells lining the respiratory tract. Together, these changes results in shortness of breath, also called dyspnea, and wheezing sounds during breathing. These events can be acute or chronic in nature. Many factors can lead to the stimulation of an attack, including exercise, allergic reaction, contaminates, and stress. Fortunately, most cases of asthma can be controlled through the use of different medications, and many very successful Olympic level athletes have been diagnosed with asthma and yet are able to compete internationally.

Chronic obstructive pulmonary disease (COPD) is a general term that describes a family of diseases that lead to a dramatic reduction in airflow through the respiratory system. These diseases are different and unique from asthma in that the conditions persist and cannot be relieved as quickly or as effectively through the use of medications. Individuals with COPD cannot perform normal everyday activities without experiencing dyspnea.

Treatment of these conditions will include not only medications, but also supplemental oxygen therapy for severe cases, and respiratory muscle training. Tragically, COPD is chronic and can often be fatal in severe cases.

VO$_2$max and Sport Performance
Bjorn Daehlie: Putting the "Max" in VO$_2$max

VO$_2$max is the maximum volume (V) of oxygen (O$_2$) in millilitres that the human body can use in 1 minute, per kilogram of body weight, while breathing air at sea level. In a sports setting, VO$_2$max measures how efficiently the cardiovascular system can process oxygen for use by the athlete. One would expect that athletes involved in endurance and/or aerobic sports would have higher scores than those in non-endurance events – and data compiled by the Coaching Association of Canada on the VO$_2$max scores of athletes in certain sports bears this out.

A high VO$_2$max score measured in a laboratory, though, does not guarantee sports success. Even though an endurance athlete might have a great "engine" (heart and lungs) behind his or her efforts, there are a number of factors that go into competitive success that cannot be measured. These include high motivation levels and proper training and diet – a complete athletic package that achieves its peak when it is time to compete. There have been many examples of athletes who have attained very high VO$_2$max scores on a treadmill who have been unable to defeat lower-scoring athletes in an actual skiing, running, cycling, or running event.

However, the history of sport does hold one important instance in which an athlete with a superior VO$_2$max score achieved tremendous, repeated success on the race course. That athlete is Norwegian skier Bjorn Daehlie, regarded by many to be the greatest athlete in any sport to have ever competed in the Winter Olympics.

Daehlie competed in three Olympic Games, winning eight gold medals (twelve in total), the most won by any Winter Olympic athlete. At the 1992 Winter Games in Albertville, he earned three golds and one silver; in 1994, in front of his home crowd in Lillehammer, Norway, he won two golds and two silvers; and finally, in his final Games, he skied to three more golds and one silver

at the 1998 Nagano Winter Olympics. As well, Daehlie won several World Championship medals during his long career.

Although official world records are not kept for VO$_2$max totals, Daehlie's score of 94 is usually given as the best-ever result. Other top marks include Miguel Indurain of Spain and Lance Armstrong of the United States, both multiple Tour de France-winning cyclists (VO$_2$max of 88 and 84, respectively); Grete Waitz of Norway, the former women's world-record holder in the marathon (VO$_2$max of 73); and Frank Shorter of the United States, an Olympic gold medallist in the men's marathon (VO$_2$max of 71). Interestingly, the highest-scoring long-distance runner of all time, the American Steve Prefontaine, who recorded a VO$_2$max of 84 during his peak years in the 1970s, never won an Olympic gold or world championship-level race.

Table 7.4: Comparison of average VO$_2$max scores in various sports

	Male	Female
Untrained	40-50	30-45
Nordic (cross-country) skiing	70-95	55-75
Middle-distance running	70-85	-
Distance running	65-80	55-70
Rowing	55-75	45-70
Cycling	55-75	-
Swimming	55-70	45-70
Soccer	50-70	-
Figure skating	-	40-55
Wrestling	50-70	-
Gymnastics	45-75	35-45
Ice hockey	45-65	-
Field hockey	40-50	-
Basketball	45-65	40-55
Football	40-60	-
Baseball	40-60	-

Adapted, by permission, from Wilmore, J.H., & Costill, D.L. (1999). *Physiology of sport and exercise* (2nd ed., p. 300). Champaign, Il.: Human Kinetics.

In his autobiography *Bjorn Daehlie: The Hunt for Gold*, the skier maintains that it was no accident he was able to race as successfully as he did. Daehlie estimates that, in a ten-year span when he was at the top of his sport, he covered approximately 150,000 kilometres while training – roller skiing, skiing, running, and biking for about 8,000 hours to maintain top fitness.

Although genetics might have played a part in Daehlie's ability to take up and use oxygen at such a prodigious rate, he was certainly willing to put in the training necessary to achieve success. In fact, it could be argued that it was his tremendous training effort that enabled him to score highly on the VO$_2$max test.

As the old adage goes, "Nobody gives you prizes for your performance in training." So it is not surprising that Daehlie credits a large amount of his success to his mental preparation, which led him to seek what he calls "the perfect race that every top athletes dream about, strives for, year after year, but which you only rarely experience, and then with years in between." In *The Hunt for Gold*, he describes the mental state he was trying to achieve:

You can feel that every part of your body is functioning at an optimal level, the technique is perfect. You feel so strong that you are impatient, yes, almost desperate....You are thinking that all the spectators that always crowd the side of the hills are going to see you at your best. I'm going to ski so fast that I will scare both the competitors and the spectators.... And regardless of how fast you are skiing it's like you can't use up all your energy. You feel unbeatable. (Reproduced from www.fasterskier.com/daehlie.php.)

Clearly, Bjorn Daehlie combined superb conditioning with a top-notch attitude towards competing and training. A world's-best VO$_2$max score formed the physiological basis for his success – but it was only when that measurement was combined with other factors that he was able to become one of the most successful athletes of all time.

THE INTEGRATION OF CARDIOVASCULAR AND RESPIRATORY FUNCTION

OXYGEN CONSUMPTION (VO₂)

The amount of O_2 taken up and consumed by the body for metabolic process is called oxygen consumption (VO_2). It is equal to the amount of O_2 inspired minus the amount of O_2 expired. VO_2 is proportional to workload, meaning that the greater the workload, the greater the VO_2 or the greater the amount of O_2 used by the body. In the laboratory, VO_2 can be determined using a computerized metabolic cart system, which is also called indirect calorimetry. These metabolic cart systems measure the amount of air expired over a period of time and the concentration of O_2 in the expired air. A computer then interprets this information, and VO_2 is calculated using mathematical formulae. The formula that is most commonly used is as follows:

$$VO_2 (L/\min) = \left[\text{volume of air inspired} \, (L/\min) \times \%O_2 \text{ inspired}\right]$$
$$- \left[\text{volume of air expired} \, (L/\min) \times \%O_2 \text{ expired}\right]$$

or

$$VO_2 (L/\min) = \left[V_I (L/\min) \times \%O_2 \text{ inspired}\right]$$
$$- \left[V_E (L/\min) \times \%O_2 \text{ expired}\right]$$

Theoretically, VO_2 is a function of both O_2 delivery to and O_2 uptake by the working muscle and other tissues. Another way to describe or represent O_2 delivery is Q (cardiac output). Q can be thought of as the total blood flow distributed throughout the body. Another way to describe O_2 uptake is a-vO_2diff, which represents the average amount of O_2 found in the arteries minus the average amount of O_2 found in the vena cava. This relationship is described mathematically by a derivation of the Fick equation, and is represented by the following:

$$VO_2 (L/\min) = Q \, (l/\min) \times \left[a - vO_2 diff \, (mlO_2 / 100mL \, of \, blood)\right]$$

or

$$VO_2 (L/\min) = (SV \times HR) \times \left[a - vO_2 diff \, (mlO_2 / 100mL \, of \, blood)\right]$$

Therefore, the maximal rate of oxygen consumption (VO_2max) would theoretically occur at maximum SV, HR, and a-vO_2 diff. VO_2max is more properly defined as the maximal amount of O_2 that can be taken in and used for the metabolic production of ATP during exercise.

To determine VO_2max in the laboratory, VO_2 is measured using a metabolic cart and computer system, as previously described, while the participant performs incremental exercise to exhaustion. Incremental exercise means that the exercise workload progressively becomes more difficult every minute or two, much like climbing a steeper and steeper hill. Such exercise can be performed using either a cycle ergometer, or a treadmill. VO_2max is used as a measure of aerobic fitness, and is indicative of aerobic exercise performance.

Another factor that can be measured at the same time as VO_2 is the production of CO_2 (VCO_2). VCO_2 is calculated by measuring the difference between the amount of CO_2 expired and the amount of CO_2 inspired. Both VO_2 and VCO_2 provide a considerable amount of information individually in relation to exercise, but together they provide even more information. The ratio between VCO_2 and VO_2 is used to calculate the respiratory exchange ratio (RER). RER is indicative of what metabolic systems are being used within the working muscle.

The amount of CO_2 produced and O_2 consumed varies, depending on what fuels are being used by the working muscle. When fat is being oxidized and used to produce ATP, more O_2 is consumed as compared to the amount of CO_2 produced. In contrast, when carbohydrate is the major fuel being used to produce ATP, not as much O_2 is consumed relative to the amount of CO_2 produced. When only carbohydrate is being used, the ratio of VCO_2 to VO_2 is equal to 1. RER is close to 0.7 when the main fuel being used is fat. Therefore, RER allows a way to estimate the relative contribution of the different fuels used in skeletal muscle during exercise.

Limiting Factors for VO₂max

Limitation of VO_2max has been a much debated topic in the field of exercise physiology. Theoretically, any of the components of the different systems involved could potentially be limiting. However, research has focused on the three main systems involved: the respiratory system, the cardiovascular system, and the metabolic system within the working muscle that uses the O_2.

The respiratory system could potentially limit VO_2max through a couple of different ways, including inadequate ventilation and oxygen diffusion limitations. In contrast, the cardiovascular system could limit VO_2max because of inadequate blood flow and/or cardiac output, or inadequate oxygen-carrying capacity (hemoglobin concentration). Finally, within the working muscle, a lack of mitochondria and the metabolic systems involved with the use of O_2 could also potentially limit VO_2max.

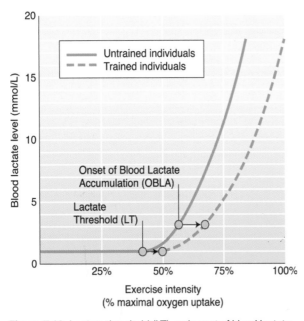

Figure 7.13: Lactate threshold (LT) and onset of blood lactate accumulation (OBLA) for untrained and trained individuals. With proper training, LT and OBLA shift to the right.

There is evidence and theory to support each of these possible limitations, but recently most exercise physiologists are supporting the notion that it is the cardiovascular system that limits VO_2max in healthy people. More specifically, it appears that the cardiovascular system is unable to meet the demands of the working muscle and deliver adequate amount of O_2. The limitation to VO_2max within the cardiovascular system appears to be related to cardiac output (Q). It should be noted that not all exercise physiologists support this view, and it is likely that this topic will continue to be debated over the next few years.

THE REST TO EXERCISE TRANSITION

During incremental exercise, such as that done during a VO_2max test, pulmonary ventilation initially increases at a rate proportional to the increase in workload. However, eventually a point is reached where ventilation increases much more rapidly than workload. This point is called the **ventilatory threshold**, and it normally occurs at an exercise intensity that corresponds to 65-85 percent of VO_2max, depending on the individual's level of fitness.

This increase in ventilation is thought to occur because of an increase in the accumulation of lactic acid within the blood. **Lactic acid** is a by-product of the anaerobic metabolic processes in the working skeletal muscle. The energy demands of the exercise can no longer be met by only the aerobic metabolic

systems. Hence, the anaerobic systems are also used to meet the increasing energy requirements of the exercise. The body increases ventilation to deal with the accumulation of the lactic acid in the blood and the corresponding drop in pH. Therefore, the ventilatory threshold is often used as a marker of an increased reliance on anaerobic metabolic systems during exercise.

It is also possible to measure blood lactate repeatedly during incremental exercise. Blood lactate remains low (~1.0 mmol/L) initially and as the exercise progresses. Eventually, a point is reached where blood lactate concentrations rise exponentially, resulting in very high concentrations. This point is referred to as the **lactate threshold** (see Figure 7.13). Interestingly, the lactate threshold is usually closely associated with the ventilatory threshold. When blood lactate levels begin to accumulate rapidly (shortly after the lactic acid threshold is reached), this is referred to as the **onset of blood lactate accumulation (OBLA)** (see Figure 7.13). With proper aerobic training, the OBLA curve can be shifted to the right such that OBLA occurs later and during higher levels of intense exercise.

The specific cause of the increased accumulation of lactate in the blood is unclear, but there have been many hypothesized causes. The potential causes include increased reliance on anaerobic metabolism, decreased delivery of oxygen to the working muscle, and/or a decrease in muscle blood flow. No single specific cause has been established to explain lactate threshold. Much like the respiratory threshold, the exercise intensity where it occurs can range from ~65% of VO_2max to ~85% of VO_2max, depending on the type of exercise and the fitness of the individual.

As stated previously, the coordination of the delivery of O_2 to the working skeletal muscle is achieved through a combination of physiological mechanisms. Ultimately, the delivery of O_2 is matched to the demand of O_2. However, the physiological mechanisms that have been discussed are not instantaneous – there is a "lag" between the initiation of exercise and the achievement of a new steady state. Eventually all systems will have been turned on and O_2 delivery will be matched again with O_2 demand. However, during this "lag" a phenomenon called O_2 deficit occurs. During this period, the working muscle must partially rely on metabolic systems that do not require O_2 (anaerobic metabolic systems). These anaerobic systems make up the difference and compensate for the "lag" in VO_2, allowing the exercise to continue at the new workload. (Figure 7.14).

Oxygen Deficit

Generally, when we breathe heavily during very intense exercise, it is to meet the demand for oxygen in

(a) Light exercise

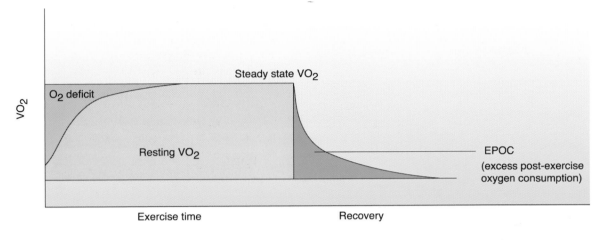

(b) Heavy exercise

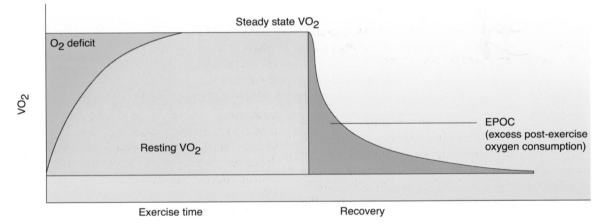

Figure 7.14: Oxygen requirements during light and heavy exercise and recovery, showing the oxygen deficit and EPOC.

the working muscles. A major function of the cardiorespiratory system is to allow the body to address this shortfall (or deficit).

Oxygen deficit represents the difference between the oxygen required to perform a task and the oxygen actually consumed prior to reaching a new steady state (see Figure 7.14). By "steady state" we mean sub-maximal exercise levels, where oxygen uptake and heart rate level off, where energy demands and energy production are evenly balanced, and where the body maintains a steady level of exertion for a fairly extended period of time.

The trained individual will reach this steady-state plateau quicker than an untrained individual and therefore will have a smaller oxygen deficit for an exercise of a given duration. This difference is due to more developed aerobic capacity in the trained individual. Regardless of current physical condition, individuals can increase their aerobic capacity through proper aerobic training.

Excess Post-Exercise Oxygen Consumption (EPOC)

When intense physical activity terminates, a period of time elapses before the body returns to a resting state. The additional oxygen taken in during this recovery period in order to restore the balance is referred to as **recovery oxygen uptake** or excess post-exercise oxygen consumption (EPOC). The term EPOC replaces a narrower interpretation of the processes involved, referred to as "oxygen debt" or the "lactic acid theory of oxygen debt," which is now generally out of favour.

The additional oxygen requirements during this period are due to the demands from the body to replenish oxygen to the various body systems that were taxed during the exercise. This includes refilling phosphocreatine reserves in muscles, replenishing oxygen in blood and tissue, lowering elevated heart rate and breathing, lowering body temperature, and increasing blood lactate removal.

The Healing Power of Oxygen?
The controversy over hyperbaric oxygen therapy

One of the newest trends in helping athletes overcome the aches and pains incurred in their sporting exploits has caused considerable controversy.

Proponents of **hyperbaric oxygen therapy** (HBO_2) – a process in which a person is placed inside a HBO_2 chamber for a set amount of time – say that it can help the healing process for a number of sports injuries and other ailments, including crush injuries, compartment syndrome, anemia, soft-tissue injuries, muscle soreness, and even thermal burns. Long used by the military and to treat deep-sea divers for decompression sickness, some professional sports teams have even invested in on-site HBO_2 chambers to minimize the time it takes for an injured athlete to receive treatment.

Inside the hyperbaric chamber, the subject breathes air that is 95-100 percent oxygen at atmospheric pressures greater than that which exists at sea level. The combination of increased barometric pressure and greater oxygen concentration leads to much higher levels of oxygen in the blood plasma and significantly increases oxygen delivery to the tissues.

The use of hyperbaric chambers to treat injuries, however, is not the main source of controversy in the sports world. That comes from another of their main uses among athletes. As well as providing a solution to many sports injuries, there are many athletes and coaches who advocate their use as tools for boosting an athlete's capacity to process oxygen into energy at a high rate of efficiency – an essential ingredient for success in endurance events. By spending non-training time in a chamber and continuing to train at sea level, athletes are in effect getting the "best of both worlds." Many who have tried to both live and train at higher altitudes have found that it is simply too difficult to run fast enough in the rarified air to get the desired physiological effect.

One runner, the American marathoner Khalid Khannouchi, touched off

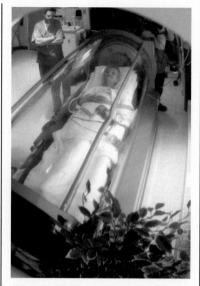

Juliette Holstein receives oxygen therapy in a hyperbaric chamber under guidance of a respiratory therapist in Moose Jaw, Saskatchewan, 2003 (CP PHOTO/*Moose Jaw Times Herald*-Geoff Howe).

considerable debate in 2002 when he announced that he would be installing one of the chambers in his house. Critics immediately questioned the ethics of this device, based on the fact that the chamber and the banned drug erythropoietin (EPO) both essentially increase one's oxygen-processing capacity.

Whatever the ethical pros and cons of using the chamber, the results certainly seem to bear out the suggestion that spending time in an atmosphere designed to simulate living at altitude pays off in endurance events. The 2:06 barrier has been broken only four times in the history of the 42.2-kilometre marathon race. Three of those times have been recorded by Khannouchi.

The jury is still out among the medical community as to whether or not use of the chamber really does increase performance in endurance sports. The main reason that many physiologists believe that it does not lies in the fact that, after exposure to hyperbaric treatment, most muscle tissues seem to return to normal states of oxygenation

in a very short time, which means that the long-term effects of hyperbaric exposure would be limited.

Oxygen Bars

In our society, bars that serve alcohol are often considered to be places where people can go for an evening's activity that will very likely not have many benefits to their health. But an increasingly popular form of bar is emerging that proponents say will provide a considerable boost to one's well-being. They are called "oxygen bars," and after a period of great popularity in Japan and Korea, they are catching on in North America as well.

Oxygen bars are places where patrons inhale high-purity oxygen in regulated amounts. The scientific basis for this is simple: the air around us is actually comprised of about 21 percent oxygen, but at an oxygen bar, people inhale a much higher concentration. The theory is that air that is more "pure" in terms of its oxygen content will actually enhance the body's ability to process that oxygen – a process that is, after all, the basis of most of human physiology. (Some have likened the practice to putting gasoline with higher octane levels into a high-performance car.)

Supporters of oxygen bars have argued that this inhalation of clean air can reduce stress, increase energy, and reduce the effects of aging. But many medical experts hold that there is no scientific basis for any of these claims. If people do feel better, it is simply due to the so-called "placebo effect;" that is, the benefits are purely psychological.

What experts on both sides of the debate do agree upon is that breathing in too much oxygen can have very harmful effects. Breathing in air that consists of more than 60 percent oxygen for longer than 10 hours is generally considered to have fatal consequences. To counter that argument, oxygen bar supporters maintain that the oxygen they breathe in at the bars is inhaled in relatively small doses.

Table 7.5: Physiological adaptations due to endurance training

	Sedentary normal male		World-class endurance runner
	Pre-training	Post-training	
Cardiovascular			
HR at rest (beats per minute)	71	59	36
HRmax (beats per minute)	185	183	174
SV at rest (mL)	65	80	125
SVmax (mL)	120	140	200
Q at rest (L * min^{-1})	4.6	4.7	4.5
Qmax (L * min^{-1})	22	25.6	34.8
Heart volume (mL)	750	820	1,200
Blood volume (L)	4.7	5.1	6.0
Systolic BP at rest (mmHg)	135	130	120
Systolic BP max (mmHg)	210	205	210
Diastolic BP at rest (mmHg)	78	76	65
Diastolic BP max (mmHg)	82	80	65
Respiratory			
V_E at rest (L * min^{-1})	7	6	6
$V_E$max (L * min^{-1})	110	135	195
Metabolic			
a-VO$_2$ diff at rest (mL * 100mL^{-1})	6.0	6.0	6.0
a-VO$_2$ diff max (mL * 100mL^{-1})	14.5	15.0	16.0
VO$_2$ diff at rest (mL * kg^{-1} * min^{-1})	3.5	3.5	3.5
VO$_2$ diff max (mL * kg^{-1} * min^{-1})	40.5	49.8	76.7
Blood lactate at rest (mmol * L^{-1})	1.0	1.0	1.0
Blood lactate max (mmol * L^{-1})	7.5	8.5	9.0

Adapted, by permission, from Wilmore, J.H., & Costill, D.L. (1999). *Physiology of sport and exercise* (2nd ed., p. 296). Champaign, Il.: Human Kinetics.

Understanding the dynamics of the recovery period is critical so as to minimize the negative physiological effects of training, particularly lactic acid buildup. Procedures to facilitate the recovery period normally distinguish between passive recovery and active recovery techniques – the former being, essentially, total rest, and the latter involving moderate aerobic activity (i.e., a cooling down period of moderate aerobic exercise).

Since blood lactate does not accumulate as a result of the ATP-PC system or aerobic system, passive procedures (complete rest) are recommended on the grounds that additional activity will raise overall metabolism levels and thereby slow recovery. On the other hand, for intermediate types of physical activities that involve the production of lactate, it is generally recommended that more active recovery methods should be adopted. These involve moderate aerobic activity combined with rest intervals as part of a wider interval training program.

WHERE DO WE GO FROM HERE?

This section introduced the structure and function of the cardiovascular and respiratory systems, two systems that work together to ensure a constant supply of O_2 to all body organs and tissues. The response of these systems to increased energy demands (exercise) was also presented. Although these systems work in one way when the body is at rest, their functions change and adapt to the increased demands of the muscles and other body parts during exercise.

When the body is exercising, these systems have the ability to cope with the increased O_2 demands of the working skeletal muscle through many different adaptive processes. In previous sections of this Unit, we saw how the various body systems function to allow the body to exercise. With the final piece of the puzzle now in place – the cardiorespiratory system – we have a complete picture of the fundamental building blocks of how the body performs.

8
Careers and Websites

"The human body experiences a powerful gravitational pull in the direction of hope."
— peace activist Norman Cousins

Below is a guide to the many career choices that are available to those who are interested in specializing in one or more of the areas covered in this unit. On the following page are website links that you will find useful in connection with the many topics touched on in the unit.

CAREER OPPORTUNITIES

- **Sports Medicine Physician**
  Doctors of this distinction have an excellent understanding of the skeletal and muscular systems, as well as a solid background in exercise physiology and injury treatment and prevention.

- **Orthopedic Surgeon**
  This type of doctor is a joint specialist who operates on people that have various joint problems; that is, attaching torn tendons, repairing torn ligaments, and inserting artificial hips and knees.

- **Chiropractor**
  Chiropractors are doctors that specialize in joint manipulations in order to promote healing. There are only two chiropractic colleges in Canada. They are Canadian Memorial Chiropractic College in Toronto and Université du Québec à Trois-Rivières. Because of the competition for places, Canadians wishing to study in this area often must consider chiropractic colleges in the United States with much higher registration fees.

- **Soft-Tissue Specialists**
  This relatively new field of medicine involves the mild manipulation of joints and soft tissue to promote healing. Some chiropractors and doctors are soft-tissue specialists, and many of them work with the various professional sports teams in Canada.

- **Exercise Physiologist**
  Exercise physiology is both a research area and an applied field of work. Some scientists are interested in how activity affect diseases, such as heart disease, cancer, hypertension, and so on; others focus more on ways of improving athletic performance. In the area of applied exercise physiology, careers in cardiac and pulmonary rehabilitation and wellness are popular. Researchers are to be found mainly at universities and in the private sector. Training includes a four-year degree with a strong emphasis in the biological sciences.

- **Nurse**
  In the nursing profession there are numerous levels of specialization and disciplines that can be attained through university or college courses. Nurses, like doctors, can specialize in one particular field; for example, operating nurse, emergency nurse, or orthopedic nurse.

- **Massage Therapist**
  Registered massage therapists are trained to help relieve various physical conditions, such as repetitive strain injury (e.g., carpal tunnel syndrome); headaches and migraines; or post-injury and post-surgical rehabilitation.

- **Athletic Trainer**
  Athletic trainers work with injured athletes at all levels, throughout the rehabilitation process, from the time of initial injury to the athlete's unrestricted return to practice or competition. In many cases, an athletic trainer is directly responsible for all phases of health care in a sporting environment.

- **Athletic Therapist**
  A certified athletic therapist usually deals with an injured athlete from the point of assessment, aiding the athlete with prevention, immediate care, and reconditioning of musculoskeletal injuries. Prevention includes musculoskeletal and postural evaluation, equipment selection, fitting and repair, warm-up, conditioning programs, prophylactic or supportive taping, and adaptation to the activity environment and facilities.

- **Physiotherapist**
  A physiotherapist plans, organizes, and directs a wide range of programs for athletes, coaches, and teams, including pre-season screening, first aid, rehabilitation, education, and counselling. He or she may work directly with athletes or may serve in a consulting role for sports organizations.

USEFUL WEB LINKS

The URLs for these websites were active at the time this book went to press. For an up-to-date listing check the supporting student workbook or the website for this textbook: www.thompsonbooks.com/hpe.

- **Anatomy of the Human Body by Henry Gray**
  www.bartleby.com
  This online version of the classic 1918 text by Henry Gray contains more than 1,200 illustrations and a searchable index of more than 13,000 anatomical entries.

- **Human Anatomy Online**
  www.innerbody.com htm/body.html
  A comprehensive description of the human body, with major body parts and systems illustrated with hundreds of diagrams and thorough descriptions.

- **MEDtropolis**
  www. medtropolis.com/VBody.asp
  A vast educational site that covers all aspects of health and healthy living. Particularly informative for students of anatomy and physiology is the "virtual body" component.

- **Internet Subject Guide for Human Anatomy**
  http://library.mtroyal.ab.ca/subguides/anatphysiol.htm
  A site with a comprehensive list of topics and journals for the entire body.

- **Loyola University Medical Center - Structure of the Human Body**
  www.meddean.luc.edu/lumen/MedEd/GrossAnatomy/learnem/learnit.htm
  Provides muscle tables for easy access to the origin, insertion, and function of every muscle in the human body. It also provides information on other systems of the body.

- **An Online Examination of Human Anatomy & Physiology**
  www.getbodysmart.com
  This site provides picture of real human bones and important landmarks. It also provides quizzes on all the landmarks of each bone.

- **Web Anatomy**
  www.gen.umn.edu/faculty_staff/jensen/1135/webanatomy
  From Murray Jensen General College, University of Minnesota, this site offers quizzes on all systems of the human body.

- **Hypermuscles: Muscles in Action**
  www.med.umich.edu/lrc/Hypermuscle
  A comprehensive look at joints; includes animations of all anatomical joint movements.

- **The Hosford Muscle Tables: Skeletal Muscles of the Human Body**
  www.ptcentral.com/muscles
  This site contains detailed information about the muscles of the human body, including a description of each muscle's origin, insertion, action, blood supply, and innervation (nerve control).

- **Muscles Tutorial**
  www.gwc.maricopa.edu/class/bio201/muscle/mustut.htm
  This site's coverage of the human muscular system is enhanced by tutorials that cover the names, location, and functions of the major superficial muscles.

- **Canadian Society for Exercise Physiology (CSEP)**
  www.csep.ca
  A useful site for information on fitness and all areas of exercise physiology, with links to many practical applications and organizations across Canada.

- **Rotator Cuff Injuries Tutorial**
  http://www.nlm.nih.gov/medlineplus/tutorials/rotatorcuffinjuries/op159101.html
  This interactive site gives a detailed explanation, using Flash software, on the anatomy, diagnosis, symptoms and causes, and treatment and prevention of rotator cuff injuries.

- **CyberAnatomy Tutorials**
  http://anatome.ncl.ac.uk/tutorials/index.html
  Posted by the School of Medical Education Development in the Faculty of Medical Sciences at the University of Newcastle upon Tyne in England, this site contains interactive tutorials and self-tests on various topics in anatomy.

- **California State University/Chico Athletics Injuries site**
  www.csuchico.edu/~sbarker/injury
  This site has a list of all joints and the injuries that may occur. Some of the information is interactive and requires Shockwave software to run.

- **Heart Tutorial**
  www.gwc.maricopa.edu/class/bio202/cyberheart/hartint0.htm
  This site depicts the detailed anatomy of the heart and all of its structures, including an interactive testing site and tutorials on the anatomy of the heart.

- **Virtual Sports Injury Clinic**
  www.sportsinjuryclinic.net
  This site has a list of sports-related injuries, and a self-assessment option. Keep in mind that this diagnosis is only an estimation based on the information entered by the user, and should not be taken seriously until a physician has been consulted.

Emilie Heymans and Anne Montminy perform a well-timed synchronized dive at the 2000 Olympic Games in Sydney, Australia (CP PHOTO/ COA).

UNIT 2

HUMAN PERFORMANCE AND BIOMECHANICS

Kwaku Boateng from Montreal clears the bar during men's high jump qualifying at the Commonwealth Games in Manchester, England, on July 28, 2002 (CP PHOTO/Andrew Vaughan).

9
Principles & Terminology

"Citius, altius, fortius."
— The credo of the Olympic Games, which, translated from Latin, means "faster, higher, stronger"

People have long been interested in figuring out ways to run faster, lift heavier and heavier weights, and generally expand the limits of human speed, endurance, and strength. The study of how the body's basic functions perform in the real world is a logical extension of the study of anatomy and physiology.

The study of human performance is concerned with every aspect of physiology and anatomy as it applies to exercise and activity; that is, how humans "perform" a wide range of tasks and activities. Such activities may take place in a sport context, at work, or simply in the course of everyday life, and also within a number of research contexts, such as among aging persons, children, and athletes.

After completing this Unit, you will be ready to move on to a more in-depth look (Unit 3, "Motor Learning and Skills Development") at how humans learn and develop a whole range of complicated skills used in sport and exercise.

IMPORTANT TERMINOLOGY

Before examining the various key terms and concepts we will be working with in this Unit, it is important to establish a central working principle for the information that follows; that is, the difference between the theoretical concepts of human performance and their practical application. It is one thing to scientifically study the "correct" way to jump over a high-jump bar or punt a football or maintain a diet appropriate to a regular exercise regimen, and quite another to perform these activities correctly on a consistent basis.

For example, thousands of golfers around the world follow the advice given on numerous instructional videotapes. This instruction is based on sound, thoroughly researched biomechanical principles. But, for the most part, these videos offer advice for the "ideal" golfer – a highly trained professional who is in peak physical condition for his or her sport. While the advice given for top-flight golfers might be presented in an appealing fashion, it would be nearly impossible for players who are not at their physical peak to follow.

What is clear is the importance of being aware of the gap between theory and practice, and of the need to adapt "ideal" advice to an individual's particular circumstances and fitness and skill levels.

The following are a number of key terms found throughout this Unit:

Exercise

Exercise can be defined as any activity that improves the body's basic functions, such as one's ability to take up and use oxygen, metabolic processes such as blood flow, muscular strength and endurance, or one's range of motion in the joints and muscles. Throughout this Unit, we will examine exercise in this context – that is, as a way of contributing to an individual's overall health. It is important to keep in mind that exercise should not be viewed as the domain of those who participate in sport alone. With a thorough understanding of the principles outlined in this Unit, a program of regular exercise can become a reality for everyone.

Fitness

Although definitions of this term vary, most people agree that fitness comprises two main areas: cardiovascular capacity, and muscular strength and endurance. Just how one arrives at improvements in these areas, however, has been the subject of much research. As well, how much of one's focus should be on improving the cardiovascular system versus building muscle strength is a matter of debate. For athletes, the needs of a particular sport dictate how this should be resolved. But in general, any activity that contributes to either of these areas can be said to contribute to a person's fitness.

There are two other important components associated with fitness. These are:

- **External factors.** Since exercise cannot be performed effectively without considering other aspects of life, overall fitness demands attention to one's diet, sleep and rest, one's ability to handle stress, one's psychological well-being, and many other factors.

-138-

- **Fitness for life.** A key component of human performance is not only maximizing it at peak points in life, but throughout one's lifespan. Science accounts for a natural deterioration in bodily function as we age. However, recent evidence suggests that, with the adoption of many of the basic principles we will discuss in this Unit – including exercise and proper nutrition – the aging process can be slowed down at least a little.

Training

As we will see in Section 13, the simplest definition of training is a combination of exercises that serve to make the human body more efficient.

Historically, science has helped athletes and their coaches understand more about how performance can be enhanced, and, over time, a number of key principles and methods by which to do this have been developed. The two key areas of athletic training, enhancing endurance and enhancing strength, require two very different physiological approaches. An understanding of both is essential.

It is important to mention here that, contrary to an often-held belief, training is not something that only elite athletes can engage in – any person, regardless of ability, age, or previous experience, can adapt the basic principles of training into a schedule that is right for their needs. Exactly how this can be accomplished is the subject of Section 14 ("Personal Fitness and Training").

Biomechanics

Essentially, the field of biomechanics takes the principles of physics and applies them to the workings of the body, specifically to how the body moves, how the muscles flex, how the joints interact, and how the skeleton is propelled by the muscular system. In the context of sport and physical activity, we can come to an even more focused definition of what biomechanics means: the use of physics to explain how the body is affected by physical forces – both those generated by the athlete and those derived from his or her environment – in sport.

Biomechanics is also used to describe the mechanics of a specific part or function of the body, such as the heart or movement. Scientists who study in this field perform a wide range of experiments to help us understand more about human movement and exercise. These can include having an athlete run on a treadmill so as to better understand the mechanics of his or her running stride (i.e., internal forces), or videotaping a soccer player while he or she kicks a ball into the wind to analyze the exact forces at play. Biomechanical concepts can often appear complicated, especially when they are presented within a framework of formulae and specialized terms. But within these lie the fundamentals of sports as they are played at the most basic level. As you become familiar with the elements of biomechanics in this section, it is important to remember that, while the equations and numbers may appear daunting, the ability to understand the basic principles – for example, the shoulder rotation needed to throw a curving pitch in baseball or to hit a backhand shot in tennis – is critical.

Kinesiology and Related Fields

Closely related to biomechanics is another field of study, called kinesiology. A look at the word's Greek roots explains what this field is all about: it is a combination of *kinen* (to move) and *logos* (or, discourse). In other words, kinesiology is discourse about – or, the study of – movement. It is also defined as a combination of anatomy, the study of the body's structure, with physiology, the study of the body's functions. Today, researchers have developed kinesiology into an accepted academic discipline, and many universities in North America have schools or faculties in which kinesiology is the sole focus of teaching and research.

Closely related to kinesiology are two other areas of focus within mechanics and biomechanics: kinematics and kinetics. Kinematics centres on the space and time aspects of movement – that is, measuring how far and how fast things travel. Here the emphasis is on the measurement and calculation of changes in space and time (displacement, velocity, and acceleration) rather than on explaining how and why.

Kinetics, on the other hand, focuses on the forces that may be involved in a particular situation to make that movement happen in the first place. A sound knowledge of kinetics is important for coaches and athletes who want to find ways to help improve performances and performance times.

WHERE DO WE GO FROM HERE?

Since our bodies need to take in outside substances – food, drink, vitamins, and so forth – to enable human performance, we will begin with the subject of nutrition as it relates to the needs of athletes and others who exercise regularly.

Many of the nutritional concepts in this section are closely tied to the body's energy systems and other specific aspects of physiology. For this reason, it may be a good idea to review some of the information contained in Unit 1 – in particular, Section 5 on "Energy Systems and Muscle Fibre Types" – before moving ahead with the information on nutrition that follows.

Lisa Faust and Amy MacFarlane help teammate Karen Macneill (centre) celebrate her second goal of the game on the team's way to a 5-0 win over Trinidad and Tobago in Pan Am Games field hockey action in Winnipeg, Manitoba, August 1999 (CP PHOTO/Frank Gunn).

10
Nutrition for Performance

"As for butter versus margarine, I trust cows more than chemists."
— Joan Gussow, assistant professor of Nutrition and Education, Columbia University

A range of important bodily functions depend on diet. In addition to pure health concerns, however, nutrition also affects physical performance. Athletes need to ensure that they take in sufficient nutrients for their bodies to produce the energy they need for their particular activity level.

In this section, we will explore the basic nutrients that are important in maintaining a healthy diet. We will then examine the notion of energy balance and how this is determined, as well as body composition, and then move on into the nutrient needs of athletes.

FOOD CATEGORIES

The foods we eat for energy can be divided into two categories: macronutrients and micronutrients.

- Macronutrients are our direct sources of energy. These are carbohydrates, proteins, and fats. These, in effect, supply the energy for daily life and for physical exercise and work.

- Micronutrients, consisting of vitamins and minerals, act as co-agents in this bioenergetic process – they do not provide energy themselves but rather play an indispensable role in helping the process along. Without them, the normal processes of life, digestion, and food metabolism would not happen (see Table 10.1 on page 143).

The Macronutrients

Protein. Proteins are directly involved in the fundamental chemical processes of life. They are species-specific and organ-specific (that is, within a single organism, muscle proteins differ from that of the brain or liver). When proteins are ingested, the body breaks them down into amino acids. Each gram of protein when used as fuel yields 4 Calories of energy. Human proteins are composed of at least twenty different amino acids, nine of which must be supplied by the foods we eat. Because we must ingest them, these nine are called essential amino acids. Our bodies, through synthetic processes performed in our cells, produce the other amino acids. Foods that contain all twenty of the amino acids, and are consequently known as complete proteins, include animal products such as meat, eggs, cheese, and milk. Vegetable proteins often contain one or more amino acids in limited amounts and are sometimes called incomplete proteins.

All body tissues contain protein, and it is necessary for their growth and repair. Protein is also a critical component of hormones, enzymes, the immune system, and the body's fluid balance. The body can also use proteins as a source of energy when its supply of preferred sources (fat and carbohydrates) runs low. Whenever the growth process is at its peak – such as in a young child or in an adult following an illness – the body needs a diet that is proportionally higher in proteins. In general, the average adult needs a daily diet that contains .8 grams of protein for every kilogram of body weight, and it is recommended that from 10 to 15 percent of our daily caloric intake consist of protein. For children, this can be up to two to three times higher. The recommended intake for adult athletes varies from 1.2 to 1.7 grams per kilogram of body weight depending on the sport and training intensity.

Carbohydrates. Carbohydrates are the most accessible energy source for the body, and in fact our bodies need more carbohydrates than any other nutrient except water. Each gram yields 4 Calories of energy when used as fuel. It is generally recommended that from 55 to 60 percent of our daily caloric intake come from carbohydrates, and that most – around 80 percent – should come from what are known as **complex carbohydrates**, such as cereals, fruits, vegetables, legumes, and pasta. Complex carbohydrates, in the form of starches, take longer to absorb than **simple carbohydrates**, or sugar. As an added benefit, foods containing complex carbohydrates often contain many of the vitamins, minerals, proteins, and fibre that our bodies need.

The **glycemic index** indicates the rate of carbohydrate digestion and its effects on blood glucose levels. Foods such as sugar and honey have a high glycemic index. Their digestion leads to a quick rise in blood sugar accompanied by a rise in the hormone insulin, which is responsible for the uptake of glucose by body tissues and hence the lowering of blood glucose. Whole-grained breads, rice, bran, and peas have a moderate glycemic index. Fruits, beans, and lentils have a low glycemic index.

Fats. A diet that is heavy in fats is obviously not a desirable one. **Saturated fats** come to us from animal sources and tend to have higher concentrations of low-density lipoprotein (LDL). **Polyunsaturated fats** come from plant sources and have higher concentrations of high-density lipoprotein (HDL). An excess of saturated fats – the so-called "bad fat" – raises cholesterol or lipid levels in the blood. It tends to build up in artery walls, which will in time lead to heart disease (see the discussion on page 145).

Nutritionally, however, there is a place for fats in the diet. Fats (and oils, which are similar in chemical makeup) are important sources of energy. They are less oxygen-rich than other nutrients and consequently release more energy, more quickly. Dietary fat provides the body with a concentrated source of energy – 1 gram of fat yields about 9 Calories, compared with 4 Calories per gram of carbohydrates or protein, and it is recommended that from 25 to 30 percent of our daily caloric intake consist of fats. When they are stored in the body, fats not only supply us with energy, but they also insulate and protect vital parts of the body. Key sources of fats include milk, butter, meat, and oils, such as vegetable (i.e., sunflower or canola) and nut oils.

The Micronutrients

Vitamins. **Vitamins** assist the body in performing several important processes, and most come from the foods we ingest (with the exception of vitamin D, which the body produces from sunlight and which is added to milk and margarine in Canada and the United States). They vary in chemical makeup, and include the vitamin groupings A, B, C, D, E, and K, as well as thiamine and riboflavin. Vitamins regulate reactions that occur in metabolism, in contrast to other dietary components (e.g., fats, carbohydrates, proteins), which are utilized in the reactions. Absence of a vitamin blocks one or more specific metabolic reactions in a cell and eventually may disrupt the metabolic balance within a cell and in the entire body. They facilitate energy release and are important in the synthesis of bone and tissue. Fat or lipid soluble vitamins include A, D, E, and K and an excess of these may be toxic as they can accumulate in body tissue. Water soluble vitamins include C and the B-complex vitamin, and an excess of these is thought to be non-toxic so long as they are not consumed in excessive doses, as they are eventually secreted through urine.

Minerals. In natural form, **minerals** come from the Earth's waters and topsoil and are absorbed by plants that we eat. The seven key minerals are calcium, phosphorous, magnesium, sodium, potassium, chloride, and sulfur. Important "trace minerals," of which we require less than 100 milligrams per day, include iron, manganese, and zinc. If an athlete's individual requirements of vitamins and minerals is deficient, there may be a decrease in physical performance. Heavy training may also alter their concentration in bodily tissue. An iron deficiency is common among sports participants (especially females, who must replace the loss of iron caused by menstruation) and those who do not include red meat in their diet. Iron is necessary for the transport and use of oxygen, and this deficiency must be addressed as it can seriously affect performance. With the exception of calcium derived during fetal development, all calcium in our bodies comes from external sources. Low calcium intake can result in low bone mineral density. Athletes whose diets contain inadequate calcium are at risk of osteoporosis, a serious deterioration of bone tissue that leads to bone fragility and increased risk of fractures.

Water. Dietary experts also recommend that a sufficient amount of **water** be consumed – up to 2 litres per day for adults – to assist with a range of functions, including aiding in digestion and carrying nutrients to (and eliminating waste products from) cells.

Table 10.4: The fat finder

0-5 GRAMS OF FAT/SERVING	6-10 GRAMS OF FAT/SERVING	11-20 GRAMS OF FAT/SERVING	MORE THAN 20 GRAMS OF FAT/SERVING
GRAIN PRODUCTS:	1 serving = 1 slice bread or 125 mL (1/2 c) cooked cereal/pasta/rice or 175 mL (3/4 c) ready-to-eat cereal or equivalent as indicated		
• All types bread/rolls, English muffin, cereals, except granola • Pasta/rice • 1 pancake, small waffle • 4 crackers, 1 small muffin • 250 mL (1 c) plain popcorn		• Granola • 1 croissant	
FRUIT & VEGETABLES:	1 serving = 125 mL (1/2 c) or equivalent as indicated		
• All fruits and vegetables (except for those listed)	• Mashed potatoes • Scalloped potatoes • 10 french fries	• Potato salad • Hash brown potatoes • 5 onion rings, ½ avocado	
MEAT & ALTERNATIVES:	1 serving = 90 g (3 oz) cooked lean meat, fish, poultry (visible fat and/or skin removed) or 250 mL/1 c cooked dried peas, beans, lentils or equivalent as indicated		
• Cooked sliced deli ham or beef • Pastrami • Beef top round steak • Pork tenderloin • Lobster/scallops/shrimp/ water-packed tuna, sole/clams/crab/halibut/ haddock/chicken/turkey breast/beans/peas/lentils	• Beef rump/sirloin tip/round, beef rib/sirloin/loin/flank • Lamb roast/chop • Pork leg/picnic shoulder, pork loin, centre cut/tenderloin end • Back bacon, Montreal smoked meat • Chicken/turkey dark meat, roast chicken • Salmon/oil packed tuna, fish sticks • Veal, 2 eggs	• Salami/corned beef/ground beef, beef blade/cross rib • Pork loin/rib end • 4 slices side bacon, 3 sausages • Herring, mackerel, canned salmon • 30 mL (2 tbsp) peanut butter	• 125 mL (1/2 c) nuts or seeds
MILK PRODUCTS:	1 serving = 250 mL (1 c) or 50 g (1½ oz) cheese or equivalent as indicated		
• All milk except whole • 2% or dry cottage cheese • Skim processed cheddar • Part skim ricotta cheese • 125 mL (1/2 c) ice milk/frozen yogurt	• Whole milk, milkshake • Mozzarella/feta/ricotta cheese • Creamed cottage cheese • 125 mL (1/2 c) regular ice cream	• Cheese (except those listed) • Eggnog, goats milk • 125 mL (1/2 c) premium ice cream	
COMBINATIONS/OTHER:	1 serving = 250 mL (1 c) or equivalent as indicated		
• Water-based soups • Fettuccine marinara	• Stew • 90 g (3 oz) meat loaf • 1 slice cheese pizza	• Cream soups, chop suey • 1 regular hamburger • 1 taco • Beans & wieners/chili con carne • Fettuccine Alfredo	• Chicken à la king • Fish sandwich (fast food) • Macaroni & cheese • 1 large cheeseburger • Quiche • 1/3 meat pie
EXTRAS: I SERVING:	1 serving = 15 mL (1 tbsp) or equivalent as indicated		
• Sour cream/table cream • Reduced-calorie salad dressing • Cream cheese, 5 olives • 5 mL (1 tbsp) butter/margarine • 2 cookies (except those listed) • 6 hard candies	• Regular salad dressing • 2 shortbread/sugar/peanut butter cookies • 1 cake doughnut • 1 piece fruit/pound cake • Coffee cake/cake with icing • 10 potato chips	• Mayonnaise • Lard/shortening/oil • 1 piece pie/carrot cake, cheese cake • 1 Danish, 1 yeast doughnut • 1 chocolate bar	

Source: Sport Nutrition for the Athletes of Canada. Reproduced by permission of the Coaching Association of Canada..

BASAL AND RESTING METABOLIC RATE

There are two factors that can influence our ability to balance the energy equation: the rate at which we burn energy (**metabolism**) and our ability to manage heat produced in this process (**thermal regulation**).

Metabolic rate (MR) measures the energy that needs to be consumed in order to sustain essential bodily functions such as heartbeat, breathing, nervous activity, active transport, and secretion. Think of metabolic rate as the energy you would expend even if you were doing nothing at all. Additional calories would be used to meet supplemental energy needs, depending on the amount of physical activity.

Age, sex, weight, lean muscle mass, and general level of physical fitness affect one's metabolic rate – for example, it increases with the amount of muscle tissue that a person has and reduces with age. Two measures of metabolic rate are distinguished:

- **Basal metabolic rate (BMR)** measures metabolic rate under rigorous (laboratory) conditions – 12-14 hours after the last meal, with the individual completely at rest (but not asleep) and a background temperature of 26-30°C.

- **Resting metabolic rate (RMR)** measures metabolic rate under less rigorous conditions.

Laboratory conditions are normally difficult to achieve, so RMR is the more common measurement in practice. However, the two terms (BMR and RMR) are used interchangeably, with RMR the more common term. For those individuals with a relatively low level of physical activity, resting metabolic rate accounts for about 60-70 percent of total energy expenditure.

Harris-Benedict Equation

The following equation, known as the **Harris-Benedict Equation**, will allow you to determine your RMR. Note that there are separate RMR calculations for males and females. Note also that someone with more muscle mass will have a higher RMR than someone with less muscle mass. Keep in mind that this is just an estimation of one's resting metabolic rate.

Males: RMR $= 66.5 + (5 \times H) + (13.7 \times W) - (6.8 \times A)$

Females: RMR $= 665 + (1.9 \times H) + (9.5 \times W) - (4.7 \times A)$

Where, *W* equals actual weight in kilograms; *H* equals height in centimetres; and *A* equals age in years.

For example, Bob weighs 68 kilograms, is 168 centimetres tall, and is twenty-two years old.

$$RMR = 66.5 + (5 \times 168) + (13.7 \times 68) - (6.8 \times 22)$$
$$= 66.5 + 804 + 931.6 - 149.6$$
$$= 1,653 \text{ Calories/day}$$

Other RMR Calculations

Here is a quick formula for estimating your RMR using a simple conversion. *For adult males:* convert your weight from kilograms to pounds (multiply your kg weight by 2.2) and then multiply your weight in pounds by 11. *For adult females:* follow the same conversion from kilograms to pounds and than multiply the weight in pounds by 10.

Here is an example of how this works for both sexes: Mark weighs 68 kg (150 lbs.); Wendy weighs 54.5 kg (120 lbs.).

Mark's RMR $= 150 \times 11 = 1,650$ Calories/day

Wendy's RMR $= 120 \times 10 = 1,200$ Calories/day

Another method of estimating RMR is by based on one's **body surface area (BSA)**. This process involves the use of specialized tables that utilize one's height and weight and correlate it to a number that estimates one's BSA. This number is then taken and multiplied by a set number for males and females.

Whichever method you choose, remember that these are only estimations and should not be taken as absolute values. Another factor to consider is that, after the age of twenty, RMR declines by 2 percent per decade. One way of combating this natural decline in RMR is by participating in a resistance training program to build, maintain, and tone lean muscle.

ESTIMATING DAILY CALORIC NEED FROM RMR

The BMR/RMR calculation establishes an important baseline for a weight control program using diet and exercise. Having determined RMR, it is possible to gain a general guide to the daily caloric need in sustaining (or raising or lowering) one's current body weight.

For a person who is relatively sedentary, for example, with no regular exercise routine, RMR could be multiplied by 1.4. For a person who is relatively active and who exercises moderately at least three days per week, multiply RMR by 1.6.

For those who are highly active and who exercise in moderate to high activity at least four days per week, multiply RMR by 1.8.

THE EFFECT OF EXERCISE ON FAT LOSS AND MUSCLE GAIN

Now that we can estimate our daily caloric need, we can proceed with either increasing muscle gain or decreasing body fat. Despite the long-held belief that the most effective way of losing fat was to eliminate it from our diets, this is not entirely the case.

Let us take the example of an individual who needs 2,000 Calories to sustain their daily caloric need. If the individual decides to fulfil that requirement with 2,000 Calories of fat or carbohydrate, the balance at the end of the day would be zero; that is, the Calories consumed would equal the Calories expended, resulting in no weight gain or loss. The diet mentioned above is not recommended, since all the daily nutrient requirements of the body are not met, but it serves to illustrate that, as far as weight gain is concerned, the total amount of Calories consumed will determine whether or not most individuals gain or lose weight.

If the same individual exceeded their daily caloric need by 500 Calories for seven consecutive days, his or her caloric gain for the week would be 3,500 Calories (500 Calories x 7 days = 3,500 Calories). Thirty-five hundred Calories is equal to .45 kilograms (1 pound) of fat. If the individual continued with this behaviour for 4 weeks, he or she would gain 1.8 kilograms (4 pounds) of fat. Regardless of food intake, be it fat, protein, or carbohydrate, the body will take the excess and convert it and store it as fat. Twenty-five percent of excess Calories from carbohydrate sources are lost in their conversion to fat. Therefore, if one consumes an extra 1,000 Calories of carbohydrate, 750 of those Calories will be stored as fat.

The general rule regarding losing body fat without hindering one's RMR is: to decrease the number of calories consumed and increase one's exercise level by 500 Calories a day, eat breakfast and smaller more regular meals throughout the day, do not skip meals, and incorporate a resistance program to build and maintain lean muscle. Reducing calorie consumption and increasing exercise levels by 500 Calories a day would mean a weight loss of 3,500 Calories per week (about .45 kg of fat). While one may also lose weight from other body compartments (i.e., muscle), this can be minimized through exercise, particularly resistance exercise, which would allow one to maintain one's most metabolically active tissue – muscle.

Body Mass Index (BMI)

One measure widely used by medical practitioners to assess the extent to which individuals are balancing the energy equation (i.e., are underweight or overweight relative to their height) is Body Mass Index (BMI). BMI is the ratio of a person's weight in kilograms to the square of his or her height in metres:

$$BMI = \frac{weight}{height^2}$$

In most cases, BMI correlates well with increased risks of disease, particularly cardiovascular, pancreatic, and kidney disease (see Figure 10.2 below). Generally, those with a BMI of 27 or more are considered to be overweight; those with a BMI of 30 or more are considered obese. Those with a BMI of 18.5 or lower are considered to be underweight.

While BMI is well established, the index has limitations. The most important is that it does not distinguish between fat and excess muscle. For this reason, athletes such as wrestlers, weightlifters, and football players would record high BMIs, but this may have no relation to their overall risk for mortality.

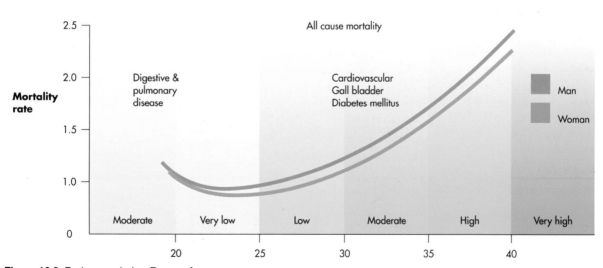

Figure 10.2: Body mass index: Range of responses.

Source: Adapted from Bray, G.A. (1992). Pathophysiology of obesity. *American Journal of Clinical Nutrition, 55* (suppl.), 488s-498s. Adapted with permission by the *American Journal of Clinical Nutrition.* © AM J CLIN NUTR American Society for Clinical Nutrition.

READING FOOD LABELS

If you wish to keep closer tabs on your nutritional intake, a good place to start is the nutritional values posted on food labels. Most pre-packaged foods we purchase from the store provide nutritional labelling. However the information is often difficult to find, is inconsistent in its presentation, and is sometimes very hard to read. For ordinary folk, this presents a serious obstacle to eating right; for those with special needs, it is a positive health hazard.

Health Canada has recently introduced proposals to require nutrition information on food labels with respect to nutrient content claims, and diet-related health claims. Once they come into effect across Canada, the regulations will provide more and better information to help us make informed choices.

Fat Free Does Not Mean Calorie Free

High fibre, low sodium, fat free – these nutrient content claims are often found on the front of a food package. The new regulations seek to ensure that such claims are based on sound science, and are consistent and accurate. The regulations will define the exact conditions required for a food to qualify for a claim.

The move to improved nutrition labelling includes: (1) a new title (Nutrition Facts); (2) a more consistent serving size on which the nutrient information is based; (3) more clearly identified nutrient information; and (4) an expanded list of nutrients. The Daily Value category on the label gives a context to the actual amount by indicating if there is a lot or a little of the nutrient in a serving of food. In addition, the look will be consistent from product to product and the information will be in a standardized format that is bold, clear, and easy to read.

Low-Fat Food and Transfats

In the past twenty years or so, low-fat foods have become a veritable growth industry, and in principle, waistlines should have decreased. But the low-fat food diets did not work as well as one might have expected. The main reason is because low-fat foods often contain a high simple sugar content to make them appealing. The result is that people are not actually consuming less energy, which is what determines weight gain and loss. The food industry does not always alert people to this problem – high sugar content is not mentioned as often or as prominently as low-fat content.

Chemically, transfats are close in composition to saturated fats, and studies have found that they are equally harmful to people's health – they appear to increase concentrations of LDLs ("bad cholesterol") while reducing concentrations of HDLs ("good cholesterol"). Of course, some food manufacturers have disputed much of the research, arguing that the impact of transfats on heart conditions has not been proven.

Apart from these concerns, however, what is inarguable is that, from a nutritional standpoint, transfats have no benefit at all. For these reasons, consumers should likely reduce their intake of both saturated fats and transfats if they wish to maintain a healthy diet. As a general rule, this means avoiding hydrogenated or partially hydrogenated fats, and, when eating fast food, avoiding fried foods.

The nutrient information is based on a specified quantity of food

This number is the actual amount of the nutrient in the specified quantity of food

The Nutrition Facts box would always include this list of Calories and 13 nutrients even if the amount is zero

Nutrition Facts
Per 1 cup (264g)

Amount	% Daily Value
Calories 260	
Fat 13g	20%
Cholesterol 30mg	25%
Sodium 660mg	28%
Carbohydrate 31g	10%
Fibre 0g	0%
Sugars 5g	
Protein 5g	
Vitamin A 4%	**Vitamin C** 2%
Calcium 15%	**Iron** 4%

The % Daily Value gives a context to the actual amount. It indicates if there is a lot or a little of the nutrient in the specified quantity of food

Figure 10.3: Sample of Canada's new nutritional label.

The Controversial "Zone Diet"
Fad diets often fall short of nutrition standards for active people

One of the benefits of developing a familiarity with the principles of human physiology and performance is that this knowledge will help you to evaluate information about exercise and health.

In this context, a key area of interest is the widespread promotion of diets and so-called "revolutionary" diets. One such popular diet is the so-called "Zone Diet," which was introduced by author Barry Sears in his 1995 book *The Zone* (actually, *The Zone* was an elaboration of Sears' earlier work on something he called the "Eicotect" diet). Since Sears published his first book on the Zone, the diet has spawned nothing less than its own sub-industry in the health and fitness world, with a wide range of books, tapes, and even "energy bars" branded with the Zone name.

According to Sears, this diet regimen was designed to change common perceptions about how people and athletes should eat by revising popular thinking about the relationship of carbohydrates to athletic performance, especially that of endurance athletes. For many decades, prevailing wisdom held that these athletes should obtain most of their calories – and therefore, their energy – from carbohydrates. But Sears maintains that "carbs" should be balanced in a "40-30-30" plan, with only 40 percent of the body's daily energy coming from carbohydrates, 30 percent from fat, and 30 percent from protein.

Sears based this 40-30-30 formulation on his research into a variety of the body's metabolic regulators, called eicosanoids, which help our immune and cardiovascular systems to regulate a number of processes. In the same way that researchers have divided lipoproteins (HDLs and LDLs) into "good" and "bad," Sears identified two kinds of eicosanoids. "Bad" ones, he claims, are released during the increase of insulin production that takes place when an athlete consumes a high-carbohydrate diet. The result, claims Sears, is a diminished capacity for the body to break down fats. (It is this

It is important to seek medical advice before embracing any particular diet program. In most cases, sensible eating habits and regular exercise will achieve the desired results (PHOTO/TEP Archives)

claim that opponents of the Zone Diet have criticized the most, since there appears to be no hard evidence that insulin affects the buildup of eicosanoids in the body.)

By diminishing the relative overemphasis on carbohydrates and lessening the production of insulin, Sears maintains that the body can break down fats more effectively, leading to weight loss, enhanced athletic performance, and even anti-aging effects.

Sears' claims ran so contrary to the accepted wisdom about dieting that they led to considerable debate among those who study the ways in which the body's intake of certain kinds of foods reflects athletic performance, weight loss, and overall health.

Two American researchers, Melinda Manore and Janice Thompson, in their 2000 book, *Sport Nutrition for Health and Performance*, did a thorough analysis of the Zone Diet. They have identified four main areas where it falls short of generally agreed-upon standards of nutrition for athletes and physically active people.

1. The Zone's recommendation that endurance athletes take in only 40 percent of calories from carbohydrates is simply too low a percentage.

2. The Zone's recommendation that 30 percent of daily calories come from protein is too high for most athletes. Extra protein can be converted by the body into an energy source, but not as efficiently as carbohydrates, and the extra nitrogen that the body does not use is eliminated in the urine.

3. The Zone's recommendation that 30 percent of calories come from fat may be too high. In order to reduce the risk of heart disease, most people – athletes and non-athletes alike – are advised to consume no more than 25-30 percent of their daily calories in the form of fats.

4. In general, the recommendations of the Zone are too low in calories. Most people are counselled to take in between 1,200-1,300 Calories per day, which is simply not enough for most active people. In general, most experts recommend a caloric intake for athletes consisting of 55-60 percent carbohydrates, 15 percent protein, and the remainder from fats.

Some very recent research findings point in the other direction and suggest that top athletes – as Sears has written – may benefit from following the Zone Diet, and that indeed many do. However, since it is difficult to obtain candid responses from top athletes, one must be cautious. The area is fraught with research difficulties, and conflicting opinions are widespread. Until more is known, its is wise to avoid fad diets of all kinds.

In general, Manore and Thompson (and many other experts) advise staying away from fad diets, especially if you are an athlete. They also warn that no single mass-recommended diet can work for everyone.

OBESITY IN CANADA

A recent study in the *International Journal of Obesity* reveals that Canadians on average are becoming more overweight and that obesity is becoming a serious health problem. Moreover, there is concern that weight increase is even more dramatic for children. Contributing factors are many and include activity levels; diet; genetic factors; rates of metabolism; and environmental, social, and psychological factors. However, the two primary contributors to excessive weight gain are simply poor diet and inactivity.

Life Expectancy

The findings of a study on the individual mortality of those who are obese were recently published in the *Journal of the American Medical Association* and indicate that it is even more important to prevent and treat obesity in childhood. A man's life expectancy is reduced by up to twenty years if he is obese at twenty; a woman's life expectancy is cut by eight years. Another study published in *The Annals of Internal Medicine* found that obesity reduces life expectancy at the same rate as smoking.

Weight loss is more difficult once we reach adulthood. Therefore, preventing children from becoming obese in the first place is especially important. There are various programs running in schools throughout Canada such as Activ8 and Active Schools in Ontario (Ophea); EverActive Schools and the PE Curriculum in Alberta; and Quality Daily Physical Education (Canadian Association for Health, Physical Education, Recreation and Dance). The goal of these programs is to have children and the school community become more active through physical activities.

The Canadian government, in anticipation of an epidemic of heart attacks, strokes, arthritis, and diabetes, has begun to take action. The federal health minister recently issued a physical education guide to public schools and parents, recommending that daily exercise for children be increased by half an hour. Many schools are now reversing cutbacks caused by budget constraints in sports activities and physical education classes.

Aging and Obesity

Hormonal changes due to age and stress also affect how much and what type of food or "fuel" we require in a day. As we age, growth hormone (responsible for the building of bone, muscle, and tissue) levels start to decrease. Near thirty-five years of age, we move from a building to a sustaining mode.

During their thirties, many baby boomers ate a healthy high-fibre, low-fat diet consisting of salads, pasta, high-fibre grains, and very little meat. Despite exercising and keeping their weight stable, by their mid-forties and fifties, many noticed a sudden weight gain. Many individuals fail to realize that our eating habits must be adapted to meet activity levels and body composition as well as changing hormone levels – all of which can be balanced with appropriate (i.e., healthy) dietary change and regular exercise.

Obesity Facts

- In 1998, 47.9 percent of Canadians were considered overweight.

- Only 2 percent of boys aged from seven to thirteen were considered obese in 1981, but by 1996, the rate was 10 percent. The number of obese girls of the same age group rose from 2 percent in 1981 to 9 percent in 1996.

- The estimated total direct cost of obesity in Canada in 1997 was more than $1.8 billion. The three contributors were hypertension, Type 2 diabetes mellitus, and coronary artery disease.

- Thirty-three percent of Canadian boys aged from seven to thirteen in 1996 were considered likely to be overweight when they reached the age of eighteen, up from 11 percent in 1981. For girls, 27 percent were likely to be overweight when they reached adulthood, compared to 13 percent in 1981.

- The National Institute on Nutrition (Canada) reports that there is an 80 percent chance that a child will become obese if both parents are also obese, likely due to a combination of lifestyle and genetic factors.

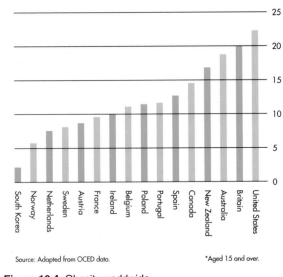

OBESITY
% of population* with Body Mass Index over 30, latest year available

Source: Adapted from OCED data.   *Aged 15 and over.

Figure 10.4: Obesity worldwide.

WEIGHT MANAGEMENT FOR ATHLETIC PERFORMANCE

All athletes are conscious of their weight and a successful management program is essential to their competitive success. A weight-management program should be initiated well before the onset of the competitive season so that the athlete has reached his or her optimal performance weight before the season begins.

In order to develop a successful weight-management program, an athlete should first determine his or her body fat level and set realistic weight goals. For most athletes, excess body weight impairs performance, contributes to the possibility of heat exhaustion, and impairs oxygen utilization. However, rapid and extreme weight loss can have many detrimental consequences. A gradual weight loss ensures maximum fat loss and the preservation of lean tissue.

Small decreases in caloric intake are best. A diet high in nutrients and low in calories is recommended, but it must be nutritionally balanced and varied. In general, an athlete should try to reduce his or her caloric intake, reduce fat intake, increase regular physical activity, and change eating behaviours to promote weight loss.

Athletes involved in sports such as track and field, swimming, and cross-country skiing seek a lean build for successful performances; for those involved in activities such as gymnastics and bodybuilding, a successful score is dependent on their lean appearance. This stress on maintaining a lean build can lead to poor eating habits, a greater risk of eating disorders, and an increased risk of injury due to lack of rest. Many athletes are concerned with weight gain, including those in such sports as wrestling, boxing, and judo, in which weight requirements determine one's competitive category. Although overthin athletes may wish to gain some weight in fat, football and hockey players and bodybuilders often want to gain lean muscle weight. Extra muscle mass increases an athlete's stability, increases strength, and serves as added protection in contact sports. A successful formula to increase lean muscle mass is to combine intense workouts with adequate energy and protein intake.

In order not to gain extra weight in body fat, an athlete should generally maintain a diet that is high in carbohydrates and low in fat. Realistic weight-gain goals should be set along with adequate time to reach these goals. Required energy and nutrient levels for weight maintenance need to be assessed, along with daily energy expenditure, before appropriate increases for weight gain can be established. It is also useful for the athlete to introduce a progressive strength training program into his or her exercise regimen.

Being Underweight
One in ten Canadians

Being underweight (officially designated as a BMI of less than 18.5) is a major health concern. Indeed, about one in ten Canadians (2.2 million) was underweight in 1998-99, according to a recent Statistics Canada survey. There is strong evidence that being underweight is linked to chronic conditions and a shortened lifespan.

As with obesity, the causal factors associated with being underweight are complex. Prominent among them, however, seems to be the relentless urge to conform to our society's ideal of an impossibly lean physique. Indeed, the high value we place on thinness may explain why being underweight is not thought of as a serious health concern despite the known health risks.

According to the survey, the odds of a woman being underweight are nearly three times that of a man, and these differences remain even when other factors are removed. While large muscle and bone mass may account for some of the gender disparity, other research suggests that women are more likely to try to lose weight and that gender differences in body shape and weight aspirations may start as early as nine years of age.

Eating disorders are not uncommon among athletes involved in appearance sports, such as gymnastics, ballet, figure skating, and diving. They also occur in other sports in which appearance should not figure so strongly, such as tennis, swimming, and running.

A high level of physical activity is taxing enough on the body. When rewards are attached to a lean appearance as well, the mix can be positively unhealthy and dangerous. The following are signs suggestive of disordered eating:

- Preoccupation with food and weight
- Repeatedly expressed concerns about being fat
- Increasing criticism of one's body
- Frequent eating alone
- Use of laxatives
- Trips to the bathroom during or following meals
- Continuous drinking of diet soda or water
- Compulsive, excessive exercise
- Complaints of always being cold

There is another issue that many athletes must confront. Those in endurance events such as cycling and running must deal with the fact that a relatively lean BMI actually appears to increase performance. The key consideration, however, is that most of these athletes are able to maintain low BMIs without experiencing associated health problems. Far from developing unhealthy attitudes about calorie consumption and eating, many top marathon runners and cyclists consume staggering amounts of calories on a daily basis, but burn this intake off quickly.

NUTRITION AND ATHLETIC PERFORMANCE

Athletes at every level need to ensure that their diet is one that provides optimum nutrition in order to benefit from their training. As well, an athlete must consider other factors, such as availability, cost of food, time of preparation, and taste. In general, all sports participants should modify the basic requirements of Canada's Food Guide to ensure that their diet is high in carbohydrate, low in fat, and varied. This means eating from five to twelve servings daily of grain products, from five to twelve servings of vegetables and fruit, from two to six servings of milk products, and from two to four servings of meat or meat alternatives, such as soy products and legumes. Nutrition experts recommend that an athlete's diet consist of from 55 to, at most, 65 percent carbohydrates, from 10 to 15 percent protein, and from 25 to 30 percent fats (see Table 10.5 below).

Protein

Although only a small percentage (2-5 percent) of daily protein intake is used to fuel activity (the remainder restores and repairs tissue), the amino acids that comprise protein are an important source of energy for certain types of exercise. Intense forms of activity draw significantly on protein, and if insufficient amounts of carbohydrates and fats are consumed to maintain muscle energy stores, the muscle tissue itself becomes an energy source. As some protein from muscle tissue is inevitably consumed with an increase in training or exercise intensity, it is necessary to maintain adequate daily protein intake (see Table 10.3 on page 147).

Carbohydrates

One of the most utilized sources of fuel for both anaerobic and aerobic activity is carbohydrate. Simple and complex carbohydrates are broken down, most commonly into glucose molecules, which are stored primarily in the liver and skeletal muscle as glycogen. The glycogen stored in the liver is released into the bloodstream following exercise to restore blood glucose levels to normal. Muscle glycogen, however, is not released into the bloodstream but is a preferred source of energy for the muscle. Maintaining a diet that contains a sufficient amount of carbohydrate to restore muscle glycogen is essential for optimal performance (see Table 10.2 on page 146).

Fats

Fats contribute significantly as an energy source for activities that are of low- to moderate-aerobic intensity; the greater the intensity, the less fat is used (short-burst activities derive energy through glycolysis and carbohydrate consumption). As an athlete adapts to endurance events, such as cross-country skiing or marathon running, there is an increase in the amount of fat used as a fuel source (see Table 10.4 on page 149).

Table 10.5: Recommended servings for athletic performance			
FOOD GROUP	**ATHLETE 1**	**ATHLETE 2**	**ATHLETE 3**
	For athletes such as gymnasts, divers, synchronized swimmers. *No athlete should eat less than this to maintain good nutritional status.*	For most athletes.	For the endurance athlete, e.g., a cyclist competing in road racing, a cross-country runner or triathlete.
Grain Products	minimum 5 servings	8 servings or more	10-12 servings or more
Vegetables and Fruit	minimum 5 servings	8 servings or more	8-10 servings or more
Meat and Alternatives	minimum 2 servings	2 servings	2-4 servings
Milk Products	adults minimum 2 servings; teens 3-4	adults 2 servings; teens 3-4	adults 2-6 servings; teens 3-6 servings
Extra Foods	Minimize extra choices. There just is not room for extra energy coming from foods without many nutrients.This action plan provides maximum nutrition with a minimum of calories.	Choose in moderation after you have had enough servings from the other food groups.	If you are finding it difficult to eat a large enough volume of food to meet your energy needs then extra sweets and fat can be added.

Source: Sport Nutrition for the Athletes of Canada. Reproduced by permission of the Coaching Association of Canada.

Competitive Meals

Pre-exercise meals. Meals consumed prior to competition are eaten to minimize fatigue during performance, to ensure the body has an adequate supply of glucose, and to promote glycogen synthesis. This meal should be eaten from 2 to 6 hours pre-competition and should be familiar to the athlete. (Note that the timing and composition are very personal and each athlete should find their optimum balance.) Ideally, it will be high in carbohydrates, low in both fat and fibre, and contain a moderate percentage of protein.

During exercise. Rehydration is the main focus of an athlete during competition; liquids that contain carbohydrates will also prevent a drop in blood glucose and thereby forestall fatigue (although this is not generally a concern unless intense exercise is more than one and a half hours in length). During events that last for more than 4 hours, an athlete may benefit from a small meal that is high in carbohydrate.

Post-exercise meals. As with during exercise, the main focus of the athlete is on fluid replacement (see "Dehydration and Fluid Replacement" opposite) and the intake of carbohydrates. Eating an easily digestible high-carbohydrate meal immediately after exercise restores glycogen to the muscles and ensures quick recovery.

Vegetarian athletes have special needs: they must ensure that their diet contains sufficient nutrients. Semi-vegetarians, who exclude red meat and milk products from their diet, should be concerned with their intake of vitamin D, zinc, protein, iron, calcium, and riboflavin. Lacto-vegetarians, who eat eggs and milk products but exclude meat, poultry, and fish, need to monitor their intake of iron and zinc. Vegans, who do not eat any animal products, need to ensure that their diet contains all the vitamins and minerals of other vegetarians as it is challenging to eat plant food in sufficient quantities to supply all these nutrients.

One key area to keep in mind when considering pre-competition meals is digestion. In most sports, large amounts of blood fuels the legs, arms, and other large muscle groups. This means that the stomach is often "ignored," making it hard to digest certain foods. Here again, carbohydrates are ideal as pre-competition food, since they are easily digested. Just a few decades ago, heavy protein meals such as steak and eggs were recommended for athletes at even the highest levels because these large amounts of protein were thought to give an athlete "strength." But the extreme difficulty in digesting these foods prior to the game soon made athletes, such as professional hockey and football players, realize that they did not make for good pre-game meals.

DEHYDRATION AND FLUID REPLACEMENT

Using energy for physical exercise creates heat. If the body did not release this heat, the body's temperature would rise — in other words, it would overheat very quickly. Extreme environmental conditions can make this situation potentially worse, since such things as hot and humid weather will compound the problems.

The solution here is, of course, water. Water makes up 50-60 percent of the human body's overall weight and as much as 90 percent of the blood plasma by weight. The role of water is to transport nutrients to cells and to carry away waste products. It also distributes heat throughout the body and enables heat to be released from the body.

A heat-regulating centre that is located in the hypothalamus of the brain functions much like a heat thermostat for the human body. Two neurological reflexes facilitate the cooling process. A constancy of body temperature is achieved by these two mechanisms.

- **Reflex dilation of skin.** The first reflex is the dilation of the blood cells in the skin, which forces blood to flow and transfers heat to the surface of the skin.

- **Sweating reflex.** The second reflex activates the sweat glands and thereby sends excess fluid to the surface where it can evaporate.

The overall effect is to cool the body, but the cost is dehydration. The body also loses water through urination, through the feces, and through breathing (water vapour). For this reason, especially under physically active conditions, a constant replacement of fluids is required for the system to continue to operate at peak performance.

Fluid Replacement

Since the assimilation of water by the body under active conditions cannot keep up with its use, it is important that replenishment take place before, during, and after the physical activity. The rule of thumb is that one should not wait to become thirsty, since at that point it is impossible to catch up with one's fluid requirements.

The precise content of the fluids is also important. The level of carbohydrates in undiluted fruit juices, high-sugar drinks, and carbonated beverages is too high and ingestion may cause cramping and diarrhea. Tea, coffee, and cola drinks act as diuretics and will dehydrate the body further. Plain water may be best.

- **Before Exercise.** Athletes should begin training or a competitive event well hydrated. This can be accomplished by consuming two to three cups of

"Carbo-Loading"
Can we simply store up energy?

Endurance athletes usually maintain a diet that is high in carbohydrates so they can last over the "long haul." There has been much debate among athletes and exercise physiologists, however, as to how much energy the body can store up ahead of time in the form of glycogen.

Those who advocate the process of carbohydrate-loading (known among athletes as carbo-loading) believe that this kind of saturation is possible, and that muscles with extra glycogen will perform better in long events such as marathon runs, cycling races, and swimming. It is generally agreed that, since it takes the body, on average, 90 minutes to 2 hours to fully deplete its normal glycogen stores through exercise, carbo-loading can only take effect at this point. In other words, advocates of this practice maintain it can only help an athlete in events of these durations.

Carbo-loading was originally conceived by physiologists in Sweden as a way of allowing factory workers to perform more effectively at their jobs over the span of 8-hour shifts. Sports scientists soon questioned whether the technique could help endurance athletes as well.

In its early stages, the process went like this: During the normal course of training in preparation for a big event, an athlete would suddenly cut out all carbohydrates from his or her diet while maintaining training loads (a process known as the "carbohydrate-depletion" phase). This would, in effect, "starve" the muscles of all their glycogen. Then, as the competition drew nearer, the athlete would simultaneously begin to reduce training – in an effort to begin recovering from training and resting for the competition – and re-introduce carbohydrates into the diet in large quantities. The muscles would, at least in theory, respond by being "stuffed," or saturated, by the glycogen that the body would produce. By race time, they would be packed with extra stores of glycogen that would "kick in" as the body required.

Over time, the theory of carbo-loading evolved to eliminate the depletion phase. Athletes found it far too difficult to train through this period, and often succumbed to injuries or "burnout" during depletion. Also, when the depletion phase ended, and the loading phase began – along with the accompanying decrease in training – many athletes found that weight gain could occur, hampering performance. Consequently, the practice changed to include only the loading phase.

Most endurance athletes today, however, generally frown upon stuffing themselves with carbohydrates prior to a big race and favour a more balanced pre-competition diet that does contain a relatively high percentage of "carbos."

Some world-class performers actually seem to maintain a fairly unsophisticated eating regimen. In the 1970s and 1980s, American runner Bill Rodgers repeatedly won many of the world's top marathon races and shocked the running world by publishing a few sample weeks of his training diet, which featured regular doses of chocolate, mayonnaise, pizza, and beer.

WHAT THEY EAT

Daniel Igali, wrestler, world and Olympic champion

"[I eat] big breakfasts with large quantities of tea, four pieces of bread, four boiled eggs, Cheerios, oat cereal, apples, several cups of water. Very light afternoon meal, usually yogurt. Heavy evening meal with rice, chicken, or beef and lots of vegetables. [I] alternate this North American fare with a dish from [my] native Nigeria called *fufu*, which consists of mashed yams or potatoes and a soup containing lots of fish and vegetables."

Claire Carver-Dias, synchronized swimming, Olympic bronze

"I tend to eat a lot more protein in training than in competition weeks, to build muscle, recuperate, and recover from eight-hour training days. During breaks I'll have yogurt, a piece of cheese, some fruit and almonds. I take in lots of water, at least a cup for every hour of exercise. Water is the most important nutritional habit. Dinner at home is the big meal and that will include red meat or lots of fish and veggies."

Shane Niemi, 400-metre runner, six-time Canadian champion

"I eat a full range of foods, but heaviest on fruits and veggies and pasta. I try not to take really heavy (greasy) stuff. My coach told me to go easy on red meats, but I need some to survive. I try not to change anything in my diet from training to competition weeks, because if you change, your body will react differently and you want to function as normally as possible."

Original quotations from Christie, J. (2002, July 5). Athletes thrive on real foods without fads, experts say. *Globe and Mail*, p. A4.

fluid containing carbohydrates 2-3 hours prior to exercising and one cup 10-20 minutes prior. Ingesting drinks that contain carbohydrates 2 to 3 hours before exercise will aid in maximizing the athlete's glycogen stores.

- **During Exercise.** A sports beverage containing carbohydrates should be consumed if the activity is longer than 50 minutes in duration. The ideal carbohydrate concentration is from 6 to 8 percent, as it is better absorbed than at higher concentrations. Thirst is increased as is voluntary fluid intake if the beverage contains salt (sodium chloride), which replenishes that lost through perspiration. For optimal fluid replacement, the beverage will contain a 6 percent electrolyte-carbohydrate solution. Generally, an athlete should drink at least one-half cup of cool fluid (10-15°C) after each 10 minutes of exercise.

- **After Exercise.** Fluid losses during exercise should be regained within 2 hours by drinking fluids containing carbohydrates to rebuild glycogen stores and electrolytes (sodium and potassium) to speed rehydration. Bodily fluids can also be replaced by foods high in water content, such as watermelon, oranges, grapes, and tomatoes.

HEAT CRAMPS, HEAT STROKE, AND HEAT EXHAUSTION

One sure sign that a person has become dehydrated is when he or she is exercising strenuously but not sweating. Contrary to the myth that highly trained athletes do not "break a sweat" where others might, sweating is usually a sign that their efficient bodies are able to cool themselves off, particularly in hot conditions, by perspiring freely.

The eventual outcome of dehydration can be heat cramps, heat stroke, or heat exhaustion.

- **Heat cramps** occur when muscles spasm or tighten due to excessive loss of fluid and electrolytes through sweating. The symptoms include short painful muscle twitches, followed by total muscle cramp.

- **Heat exhaustion** is a severe condition requiring medical attention and is associated with a cumulative loss of water and a weakening of the body's ability to regulate its internal temperature. Symptoms include a high body temperature; pale, cool, and clammy skin; light-headedness; and possibly loss of consciousness.

- **Heatstroke** (sunstroke) is a very serious condition when there is a complete failure of the body's heat-regulatory system, and should be treated as an absolute medical emergency. Symptoms include a very high body temperature, headache, confusion or behavioural change, and very possibly a loss of consciousness.

WHERE DO WE GO FROM HERE?

We now have a basic understanding of how the human fuel system operates and the basic nutritional principles.

Let us now move on to examine how human performance can be affected by performance-enhancing substances and techniques.

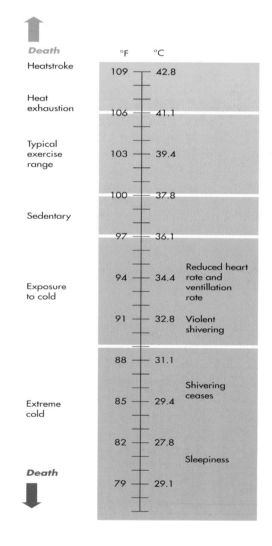

Figure 10.5: Consequences at various internal body temperatures.

Source: Adapted from Kamen, G. (2001). *Foundations of exercise science* (p. 92). Baltimore, MD: Lippincott Williams & Wilkins. Adapted with permission from Lippincott Williams & Wilkins.

Ben Johnson raises his hand in victory as American Carl Lewis comes in second in the 100-metre final race on September 24, 1988, at the Seoul Olympics. Johnson subsequently tested positive for the banned steroid stanozolol and was stripped of his gold medal. Questions have since been raised as to whether Carl Lewis had been taking performance-enhancers as well (CP PHOTO/STF-Fred Chartrand).

11

Performance-Enhancing Substances and Techniques

"An era of chemical McCarthyism is at hand, and 'guilty until proven innocent' is the new slogan."
— George Lundberg, editor, *American Medical Association Journal*

KEY CONCEPTS

- Nutritional supplements
- Protein and amino acid supplements
- Carnitine
- Creatine
- Caffeine
- Deceptive advertising
- Doping

- Pain-masking agents
- World Anti-Doping Agency
- Anabolic steroids
- Prohormones
- Human growth hormone (HGH)
- Canadian Centre for Ethics in Sport (CCES)
- Erythropoietin (EPO)

- Restricted pharmacological substances
- Drug policies
- Blood doping
- Drug masking
- Dubin Inquiry
- Drug testing

The practice of using a wide variety of substances and methods in an attempt to increase human performance is centuries old. Today, in the demanding reality of competitive sports, athletes are increasingly pressured to improve their performance in order to achieve not only victory but the sizeable economic and social rewards of success.

In this section, we will examine three types of performance-enhancing substances and techniques (referred to generally as "ergogenic aids") used by athletes: (1) **nutritional aids** (vitamins and minerals, protein and amino acid supplements, carnitine, creatine, caffeine); (2) **pharmacological aids** (pain-masking drugs, anabolic steroids, prohormones, human growth hormone, erythropoietin); and (3) **physiological aids** (blood doping, drug masking). We will explore the effectiveness, availability, short- and long-term health risks of these aids, and the testing procedures that are in place to detect their use. Finally, we will address the ethical issues raised by the use of such aids and techniques.

NUTRITIONAL AIDS

Many athletes have turned to readily available natural products and nutritional supplements in order to enhance their performance. These products include vitamins, minerals, protein and amino acid supplements, so-called releasers of growth hormone, carnitine, creatine, caffeine, and various extracts from plant sources.

Although these supplements are promoted for their ergogenic properties, it remains unproven as to whether these items are truly effective (or merely the cleverly crafted products of slick marketing campaigns). This area is not well regulated and some "natural" products contain hidden amounts of steroids and other banned substances, so caution is well advised. Athletes should be aware of the toxic effects of large doses of micronutrients, the poor quality control of supplemental aids, and the false labelling of such products.

Vitamins and Minerals

Athletes undergoing heavy training may believe they need to supplement a healthy diet with vitamin and mineral supplements. In general, however, the taking of such vitamin and mineral supplements has not been shown to produce improved performance or training potential. Despite their promotion in magazines and fitness journals, high levels of vitamins and minerals are not required to help with the stress of competition, to meet the nutrient demands of heavy exercise, or to boost energy levels. Rather, athletes are advised to increase their dietary intake of varied and healthy foods.

Many studies show that those who exercise tend to take supplemental vitamins and minerals well in excess of recommended levels. In fact, athletes who ingest megavitamins regularly (in doses up to 1,000 times the Dietary Reference Intakes) may be doing themselves harm. The practice of taking vitamins at

Table 11.1: Classes of substances and methods prohibited by the International Olympic Committee, including substances subject to certain restrictions

Following are various ergogenic aids prohibited for Olympic athletes during competition.

1. Stimulants
2. Narcotics
3. Anabolic agents
4. Diuretics
5. Peptide and glycoprotein hormones and analogues (e.g., growth hormone)

Prohibited Methods

1. Narcotics
2. Anabolic agents
3. Diuretics
4. Peptide and glycoprotein hormones and analogues (e.g., growth hormone)

Classes of Drugs Subject to Restrictions

1. Alcohol (restricted in the modern pentathlon)
2. Marijuana
3. Local anesthetics
4. Corticosteroids
5. Beta-blockers

Source: From Catlin, D.H., & Murray, T.H. (1996). Performance-enhancing drugs, fair competition and Olympic sport. *JAMA*, *275*, 231-237.

these dosage levels can cause illness and tissue damage. When taken in excess, fat-soluable vitamins in particular are toxic as they accumulate in the body. Toxic effects can even be caused by water-soluable vitamins, such as C and B, when ingested in excess quantities.

Vitamin and mineral supplements can be of benefit only where a clear deficiency is indicated. For example, endurance runners may benefit from the use of carbohydrate drinks and energy bars, and athletes with low-energy intakes may also benefit from vitamin and mineral supplements.

Protein and Amino Acid Supplements

Athletes who are concerned with increased muscle mass, strength, and endurance may frequently use protein and amino acid supplements. Protein is an essential component of any balanced diet, but should athletes use protein supplements and/or individual amino acid supplements or should they focus on increasing high-protein foods in their diets?

Studies have shown that some amino acids may enhance muscle development by stimulating the release of growth hormone, insulin, and/or glucocorticoids (adrenal cortical hormones, active in protecting against stress and in influencing protein and glucose metabolism). These studies, however, involved intravenous infusions and the findings could not be replicated with oral amino acid and protein supplements. More evidence is needed before the effectiveness of protein and amino acid supplementation is definitive.

Some studies report that ingesting excessive amounts of protein can produce toxic effects due to the overproduction of urea, which leads to loss of water. This can result in dehydration and cause muscle cramps and impairment of thermoregulatory function. However, athletes such as distance runners and gymnasts may ingest too little dietary protein, in which case they may need to monitor their regular food intake more closely.

This area is fraught with conflicting research findings and conflicting evidence. For example, the ingestion of oral amino acids is sometimes promoted to increase the release of growth hormones but this claim has been disputed. It is also uncertain as to whether body composition or performance enhancement in healthy athletes is affected by a rise in growth hormone. For example, the intravenous infusion of the amino acid arginine produces an increase in growth hormone secretion, and is the basis for the marketing claims of "growth hormone releasers," but there is no evidence that the oral ingestion of arginine replicates a similar rise or has any performance-enhancing effect.

Similarly, a more potent amino acid, ornithine, produced a rise in circulating ornithine levels in bodybuilders, but the increase was less than that observed during sleep in normal people. As well, the rate of ornithine required to produce this rise also caused intestinal cramping and diarrhea, and it remains unclear as to whether the ornithine or these symptoms caused the rise in growth hormone levels.

Carnitine

Carnitine is widely advertised as a "fat burner" – it is claimed that it decreases lactate production, increases VO$_2$max, delays fatigue, spares glycogen, and induces loss of body fat. Because of these claims, valid or not, athletes have used this supplement in their diets to promote fat loss and to enhance aerobic and anaerobic capacity. Carnitine, which is stored primarily in skeletal and cardiac muscle, is a short-chain carboxylic acid containing nitrogen that serves to transport long-chain fatty acids into the mitochondria for energy and also transports excess coenzymes out of the mitochondria. As fatty acids are essential sources of energy during resting metabolism and low- and moderate-intensity exercise, and the biochemical pathways that take part in the production of energy from fatty acids are located inside the mitochondria (see discussion on page 89), theories suggest that carnitine supplementation will enhance fat metabolism and increase body fat loss. Given the role of carnitine in preventing the buildup of excess coenzymes in the mitochondria during abnormal metabolism caused by exercise, it is theorized that carnitine supplements could spare glycogen and reduce the production of lactate, thus delaying fatigue and increasing anaerobic power. Once again, however, experimental data, however, has failed to support these theories.

Despite popular claims of its properties, carnitine deficiency is not a concern for active athletes as adequate levels of carnitine remain in muscle tissue during exercise. Carnitine is synthesized in the kidneys, and liver, meat, poultry, fish, and milk products are excellent dietary sources.

Creatine

Athletes whose sport involves short-term, high-intensity exercise commonly use the ergogenic aid of creatine. This amino acid is readily present in normal skeletal muscle and facilitates the rapid production of ATP, providing an immediate source of energy during short periods of muscular exertion.

As muscle phosphocreatine stores deplete during exercise, muscle fatigue develops. Athletes therefore take creatine supplements (creatine monohydrate) to increase its content in skeletal muscle, and it appears to benefit performance by the subsequent increase in creatine phosphate in fast-twitch muscle fibres. The saturation point is quickly reached, however, as there is a limit to the amount of creatine that can be stored by muscle tissue, and the dietary excess is simply excreted. Although creatine may improve an athlete's ability to maintain performance close to maximum as exercise continues, it will not increase the maximal force that an individual can produce.

The findings of current research on the effectiveness of the oral supplementation are still unclear. Although creatine increases muscle phosphocreatine content, it appears not do so in every individual, and increases in performance are manifested only during specific exercise conditions, such as repeated sprint performance in swimming, running, and cycling. Oral supplementation does appear to be well tolerated by most healthy individuals. It is found in high concentration in meat, and the intake of carbohydrate can increase creatine uptake by more than 50 percent. However, some researchers believe that adverse effects of this oral supplementation may surface in the near future in light of its current popularity and widespread use.

Table 11.2: Principal anabolic steroids used by athletes

Generic name or category	Example trade names
Orally active steroids	
Methandrostenolone	Dianabol
Oxandrolone	Anavar
Stanozolol	Winstrol
Oxymetholone	Anadrol
Fluoxymesterone	Halotestin
Methyltestosterone	Oreton-M
Mesterolone	Proviron
Injectable steroids	
Testosterone esters*	Delatestryl, Sustanon
Nandrolone esters*	Deca-Durabolin
Stanozolol	Strombaject
Methenolone enanthate	Primobolan Depot
Boldenone undecylenate	Parenabol
Trenbolone acetate	Parabolan

*These are general categories of substance; many different preparations of each are available.

Reprinted, by permission, from Friedl, K.E. (2000). Performance-enhancing substances. In Baechle, T.R., & Earle, R.W. (Eds.), *Essentials of strength training and conditioning*, NSCA (p. 214). Champaign, Il.: Human Kinetics.

Caffeine

Caffeine is an alkaloid, found in such foods as coffee, tea, and chocolate. The rate of its metabolism by the liver, its storage, and its clearance varies greatly depending on frequency of use. Evidence is mounting to suggest that ingesting caffeine increases performance during prolonged endurance exercise and short-term intense exercise. The ingestion of caffeine increases alertness and reduces fatigue, effects that may be mediated through adenosine receptors.

Caffeine has a potential diuretic effect, which could theoretically produce dehydration, and also causes nervousness and irritability. Coffee and other stimulants, by creating euphoric effects and delaying fatigue, present other risks to an athlete's performance and health, as he or she may go beyond safe physiological limits. There is also the additional risk of drug dependency.

An athlete would have to drink more than three cups of coffee prior to competition to exceed the upper urinary caffeine limit set by the International Olympic Committee.

Buyer, Beware
Deceitful advertising practices

Companies that manufacture ergogenic aids often resort to deceptive advertising tactics in order to convince consumers to purchase them. Unfortunately, many athletes fall prey to such tactics and fail to consider the underlying science or truth of claims made of a particular product.

Mass-media marketing videos and infomercials are popular tools of such companies, as are editorial comments, stories planted in the press, and talk show interviews where what is being communicated is not recognizable as advertising.

Be a smart consumer:

- Watch for ads that are supported only by anecdotes or testimonials, as testimonials can be embellished, purchased, or outright faked.

- Realize that a synthetic supplement is no less effective than a "natural" one in many cases, and that "natural" products often contain drugs and compounds that are banned as well as unidentified substances.

- Know that if a product promises miraculous results in a short period, the claim is probably false. With the use of most aids, success is not achieved overnight – long-term use yields the best results. If it sounds too good to be true, it likely is.

- Be wary of any sports manufacturing company that claims that its product will compensate for poor eating habits.

- Watch for ads for products that claim to reduce body fat without mentioning the importance of exercise and proper nutrition.

- Ask yourself if the claim made by a supplement manufacturer is one you can measure; for example, it is difficult to analyze the claim that using a product will make you feel more energetic.

- Question ads that are supported by only one scientific study. Data collected from several studies prove that manufacturer's results can be

Wendy Mesley and Erica Johnson co-host the CBC's weekly *Marketplace* program, which takes a critical look at advertising claims (Photo courtesy of the Canadian Broadcasting Corporation).

reproduced. The ad may also be missing adequate information to enable you to locate the study.

- Watch for genuine research that may be presented out of context or used in an unproven manner. If the company claims that the product has been university tested, a specific professor may be named. However, the company may have directly controlled the study, the study may have been conducted by only a single researcher, or the research may never have been done at all.

- Realize that patents merely indicate differences among products rather than their effectiveness and that they can be obtained based merely on a model of a product.

- If the company claims the product has been endorsed by an organization, it may mean that a member of a professional team actually uses the product but it is not endorsed by the whole organization.

Helping Hand

Luckily, consumers are not alone in assessing whether advertisers goods and services are telling the truth. In the 1960s, the American consumer-affairs advocate Ralph Nader began pointing out unsafe practices in the American automotive industry. His 1965 book, *Unsafe at Any Speed*, a harsh criticism of the U.S. auto industry for producing unsafe vehicles, had worldwide appeal and also touched off an international consumer-awareness movement.

In Canada, the well-known CBC Television program *Marketplace*, which takes a weekly critical look at the questionable claims made by some advertisers, was a pioneer in consumer journalism. Now in its thirty-second season, the *Marketplace* team is a group of passionate, persistent diggers, not easily intimidated, who get the goods and tell compelling stories using their own original testing and hidden cameras where warranted. *Marketplace* gets beyond the smoke and mirrors of companies and institutions to inform Canadians about the way they spend their money, and about issues of health and safety.

Over its history, *Markeplace* has developed a reputation for tough investigative consumer reports, and has earned a high level of trust among its viewers. Its team of seasoned investigators continues to test and blow the lid off assumptions in consumer products and behaviours. It continues its tradition of award-winning investigative journalism with hosts Wendy Mesley and Erica Johnson and offers one of the most comprehensive websites for consumers (www.cbc.ca/consumers/market/).

Straight Goods, another Canadian organization, also acts as a "watchdog" for consumers. It offers articles that expose shady practices in advertising and commerce (as well as in politics and the financial and/or business world). Its website offers a forum where people can share their experiences (www.straightgoods.com).

PHARMACOLOGICAL AIDS

Some athletes use drugs to mask pain. Some use them to increase their muscle mass, and thereby boost their speed and strength. Other athletes use them to help them recover more quickly from intense training or to increase their oxygen-processing capacity. Still other athletes use drugs to assist in maintaining a certain body weight, crucial in such sports as boxing and wrestling where weight limits apply.

Such practices are referred to as doping. It is defined by the World Anti-Doping Agency as "the use of an artifice, whether substance or method, potentially dangerous to athletes' health and/or capable of enhancing their performances." The more popular pharmacological aids used by athletes to enhance performance include:

- pain-masking drugs;
- anabolic steroids;
- prohormones;
- human growth hormone; and
- erythropoietin.

Because the worldwide legislative bodies that govern sports have determined that the use of many of these drugs not only gives athletes a competitive edge, but that they are harmful to both the short-term and long-term health of athletes, their use has been almost universally banned. Consequently, all of the world's major sporting events – such as the Winter and Summer Olympic Games, and competitions at world championship levels – conduct regular testing of competing athletes to insure that they are not taking any banned substances. If such drugs are detected in an athlete's urine, the penalty may be high. The athlete is usually banned from competing for a long period of time and must forfeit any medal or prize money won.

Of course, there are also a number of legal drugs that are taken regularly by serious athletes that contain traces of banned substances. These include a wide range of over-the-counter and prescription anti-inflammatory drugs for the treatment of injuries as well as various remedies for ailments, such as the flu or the common cold, that can make training and competition difficult or even impossible.

Pain-Masking Drugs

A category of performance-enhancing drugs, known as narcotic analgesics, are used by athletes, not to build up muscle or increase its ability to perform, but to allow them to ignore the tremendous pain that can result from injury. These pain-masking agents include morphine, heroin, pethidine, and dextropropoxyphene. They work by interfering with the

Sport	U	A	T	I
Alpine Ski	18	0	18	
Archery	1	16	17	
Athletics	59	107	166	2
Baseball	20	8	28	
Basketball	25	2	27	
Biathlon	0	4	4	1
Bobsleigh	42	8	50	1
Boxing	16	13	29	
Canoeing	28	30	58	
CIS: Basketball	36	0	36	1
CIS: Field Hockey	6	0	6	1
CIS: Football	139	12	151	1
CIS: Ice Hockey	64	4	68	1
CIS: Rugby	20	0	20	
CIS: Soccer	26	0	26	
CIS: Track & Field	12	6	18	
Colleges: Football	42	4	46	
Cross Country Ski	6	5	11	
Curling	4	12	16	
Cycling	28	50	78	
Diving	6	2	8	
Equestrian	8	12	20	
Field Hockey	21	4	25	
Figure Skating	7	10	17	
Freestyle Ski	8	0	8	
Gymnastics	20	13	33	
Hockey	50	0	50	
Judo	40	19	59	
Junior Football	94	16	110	1
Luge	6	13	19	
Pentathlon	0	8	8	
Rowing	22	23	45	
Rugby	17	4	21	
Shooting	0	13	13	
Snowboarding	19	8	27	
Soccer	37	2	39	
Speed Skating	40	36	76	
Squash	0	5	5	
Swimming	58	25	83	
Table Tennis	9	0	9	
Tae kwon do	6	10	16	1
Tennis	0	2	2	
Triathlon	7	10	17	
Volleyball	30	2	32	
Water Polo	18	6	24	
Water Ski	0	15	15	
Weightlifting	21	23	44	3
Wrestling	12	18	30	
Other Sports	140	52	192	
Total	**1288**	**632**	**1920**	**13**

Table 11.3: Doping control statistics on Canadian athletes for 2001 under the domestic program (U = Unannounced; A = Announced; T = Total; I = Infractions)

Source: Adapted from the Canadian Centre for Ethics in Sport 2000, March 15). Media release. Reprinted with permission.

The World Anti-Doping Agency
The facts about doping

The **World Anti-Doping Agency** (WADA) promotes and coordinates at the international level the fight against doping in all its forms. Through this autonomous agency, the Olympic Movement and the world's public authorities have intensified their efforts to keep drugs out of sport.

These questions and answers are provided by permission of the World Anti-Doping Agency based in Montreal:

1. What is doping?

Doping is defined as the use of an artifice, whether substance or method, potentially dangerous to athletes' health and/or capable of enhancing their performances, or the presence in the athlete's body of a substance, or the ascertainment of the use of a method on the list annexed to the Olympic Movement Anti-Doping Code.

2. Why is doping prohibited?

Doping is fundamentally against the ethos of the spirit of Olympic Games: the fair game. Many of the prohibited substances and methods are harmful to athletes' health and can cause short and long-term damage.

3. Where do we draw the line between doping and normal medication?

Many common medicines, such as painkillers and asthma medicines, can contain prohibited substances. That is why athletes must be very cautious of any medication they are taking.

If a competitor wants to use a prohibited substance for therapeutic use, he/she must obtain the prior written approval of the IOC Medical Commission and/or relevant sporting federation. Any application for approval must be made before the Games.

4. Are all athletes tested during the Olympics?

At the Olympic Games, in each event, the first four competitors plus two other randomly selected athletes are tested against doping.

Canada's Dick Pound, Chairman of the World Anti-Doping Agency, at the Sports Media Canada awards in 2001 (Photo courtesy of WADA).

5. Is it possible to cheat in a doping test?

To prevent cheating athletes are accompanied by a chaperone – who is always the same gender as the athlete – who must stay with the athlete during the whole testing process. Because of this surveillance, and the very carefully selected handling procedure of the samples, fraudulently manipulating a test is very unlikely.

6. What are the sanctions if an athlete tests positive in the Olympics?

The minimum required sanction for major doping substances or prohibited methods is a suspension of the athlete from all competition for a period of two years, for a first offence.

In specific, exceptional circumstances there may be a provision for a possible modification of the two-year sanction.

Any records or medals achieved by the athlete at the time of, or after the sample was taken, are removed. The suspension will start from the time the positive sample was discovered.

In addition, other organizations (such as the International Federation) may choose to impose additional sanctions on the competitor.

7. What substances are banned?

Each sport has banned those substances it considers would result in an unfair advantage to the athlete using them.

Anabolic steroids help build muscle and are thus being used in sports that require strength and speed, for example, shot put and sprints.

Beta blockers lower blood pressure and help keeping the hands of the athlete's steadier, and are thus used in archery and pistol shooting.

Diuretics remove the excess water from the body. Diuretics are used in sports where the athletes are categorized by their body weight, such as rowing and boxing. Use of diuretics can lead to severe dehydration.

8. What is blood doping?

Blood doping involves the intravenous administration of blood, red blood cells, and related blood products to raise the blood's oxygen carrying capacity, thus enhancing aerobic athletic performance. Athletes may use their own blood or someone else's blood. Blood doping is banned by the IOC.

9. Is caffeine banned?

Caffeine is banned by the IOC. Taken in certain specific doses, caffeine can raise an athlete's metabolic level, body temperature, blood pressure, and blood sugar level.

10. How long has doping existed?

Unfortunately, using artificial substances has always played part of sport history. The first evidence of doping can be traced back to the third century B.C., at the ancient Olympic Games. There is evidence that competitors were willing to take performance enhancing substances, such as mushroom and plant extracts.

Reproduced by permission of the World Anti-Doping Agency (www.wada-ama.org).

body's ability to sense pain, blocking the impulses that normally travel to the brain.

There are two major drawbacks to this type of drug. Being able to detect pain is a natural human response that prevents an athlete, if possible, from suffering serious injury. When that response is turned off, an athlete may injure a previously damaged muscle or tendon, for example, so badly that it cannot heal again.

The other side effect is equally serious: pain-masking drugs can be highly addictive. Regular use may produce a physical or psychological dependence on the substance long after the injury has healed. It is not uncommon to read of an athlete becoming addicted to painkillers after a serious injury.

Anabolic Steroids

Anabolic steroids, the most highly publicized of performance-enhancing drugs, are referred to interchangeably as androgens, androgenic steroids, or anabolic steroids. Anabolic steroids are synthetic derivatives of the male hormone testosterone. They produce retention of phosphate, potassium, and nitrogen, decrease amino acid breakdown, and increase protein synthesis. Because anabolic steroids increase lean body mass, they are frequently abused by athletes in strength sports, such as bodybuilding (see Table 11.2 on page 163 for a list of anabolic steroids).

While athletes take anabolic steroids to increase their muscle mass and strength, decrease body fat, and for quicker recovery from training, no enhancement of athletic performance has been truly demonstrated, other than an increase in lean body mass (i.e., muscle mass). No studies have determined their effect on anaerobic power or on whether they aid aerobic endurance athletes even though many claims have been made for the overcoming of performance-limiting responses.

Anabolic steroids also have many harmful side effects, including liver damage and increased aggressiveness. In women, anabolic steroid use may lead to masculinization, including the growth of excessive facial hair, a deepening of the voice, and irregularities in the menstrual cycle.

Prohormones

Prohormones are a type of androgenic steroid. They either convert to testosterone or simulate it by forming derivatives similar to androgen.

One of the most popular of these prohormones is androstenedione, particularly so after Mark McGwire admitted using it while breaking home run records in 1998. In theory, the anabolic effects of androstenedione supplements are created by its conversion in the liver to testosterone. It is often combined with

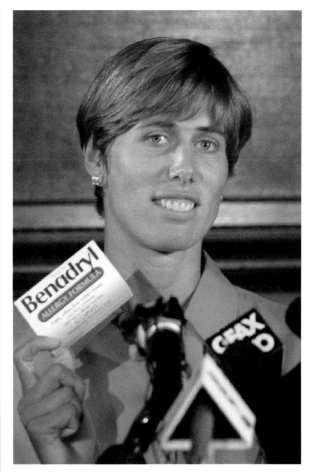

Anti-doping advocate Silken Laumann (rower) mistakenly purchased a wrong brand name and subsequently tested positive for a banned stimulant in 1995 (CP PHOTO/Chuck Stoody).

the herb tribulus terestris, and together these two substances are claimed to increase testosterone production and thereby increase the synthesis of protein. It is touted to increase physical power and decrease body fat by lessening the catabolic effects on muscle resulting from weight training, and bodybuilders use it to increase muscle mass.

Although one study has shown that large doses of androstenedione convert to testosterone, most research shows that it does not do so. There is no support for androstenedione stimulating an increase in protein synthesis, strength, or muscle mass. Harmful effects include acne, baldness, breast enlargement in males, stunted growth in adolescents, and an increase in aggressive and violent behaviour. Although such agents are banned by most sport-governing bodies, they seem to be freely available for purchase through retail outlets.

Human Growth Hormone

Human growth hormone (HGH) is abused by athletes much less frequently than steroids. Although the

Canadian Centre for Ethics in Sport
Towards a more ethical sports environment

Almost every time you turn to the sports page in your newspaper or check out the sporting news on television or radio, there are reports of some kind of dubious practice among athletes, coaches, fans, or officials. From fighting among parents at a youth hockey game, to steroid scandals, to violence among players, it seems as though unethical practices are rampant.

In many cases, ethical decisions in sport have to be made by coaches, athletes, and organizers as situations arise. Based on their experience with such issues and their personal philosophies about moral matters, sport participants must often decide how to act without outside guidance or advice. And while many leagues and other sport organizations often have well-developed policies in place to address ethical issues, others are continually looking for guidance in putting such ethical guidelines in place.

Luckily, there are organizations whose business it is to assist people at all levels of sport in becoming more aware of the process of both developing and implementing policies on ethics, and of the field of ethics in sport in general. In Canada, an organization that is committed to a more ethical sports environment is the Canadian Centre for Ethics in Sport (CCES).

Some History

The CCES was formed when two like-minded organizations – the Canadian Centre for Drug-Free Sport and Fair Play Canada – joined forces in 1995. Its board of directors is composed of a number of prominent Canadians, including Charles Dubin, who led the famous Dubin Inquiry into steroid use in Canadian sports following Ben Johnson's disqualification at the 1988 Seoul Olympics.

Its board of directors also includes Charmaine Crooks, five-time Olympic sprinter and silver medallist, and Dr. Andrew Pipe, a leading expert on doping.

Dr. Andrew Pipe, chair of the Canadian Centre for Ethics in Sport (CP PHOTO/ Joe Bryska).

There are many Canadians who agree with the Centre's contention that the sporting world needs a full-scale ethical clean up, especially in the area of performance-enhancing drugs and other illegal medical aids – commonly known to athletes as "doping." In a recent online poll, more than three-quarters of those who answered said that they believed that governing bodies of sports around the world meted out penalties in uneven fashion to athletes from different countries.

Fair Play

While an opposition to drugs in sport is clearly a leading mandate of the CCES, another of the organization's concerns is the promotion of Fair Play. "The notion of Fair Play is a universally understood concept, which underpins all of sport," states the CCES on its website. "Without fairness, sport is devoid of any meaning or purpose."

With these philosophical underpinnings in mind, in 1986 the Canadian federal government established a Commission for Fair Play to address a number of ethical issues in sport, particularly those centred around violence, and to promote Fair Play in schools and other educational outlets.

The commission evolved into Fair Play Canada, which, as mentioned above, merged with the Canadian Centre for Drug-Free Sport to become the Canadian Centre for Ethics in Sport.

For more information on Fair Play and its programs and resources, go to the Spirit of Sport Foundation's website at www.spiritofsport.ca.

International Impact

A significant example of how the CCES plays a major role in world sport policy making occurred in the spring of 2003, as the Canadian organization contributed to the establishment of the Norway-based Association of National Anti-Doping Organizations (ANADO), a group comprising the anti-doping bodies of twenty countries around the world. Most importantly, from a Canadian perspective, Paul Melia, head of the CCES, was chosen to be the ANADO president.

The development of this international organization is important. Many anti-doping advocates have observed, during the past decade, that it is often hard to catch users of performance-enhancing substances in sport as policies that one country might have regarding banning or suspension can vary widely from others.

"The establishment of ANADO is another important piece in the worldwide fight against doping in sport," said Melia in a press release. "Building strong, independent NADOs around the world will help ensure the effective implementation of the World Anti-Doping Code and build athlete and public confidence that sport is practiced fairly and without the use of performance-enhancing substances."

For more information on the Canadian Centre for Ethics in Sport and its programs and resources, go to its website at: www.cces.ca.

body produces human growth hormone naturally through the pituitary, some athletes may seek to raise its level in their bodies by injecting synthetic preparations. Extra amounts are believed to increase muscle mass, strengthen bones, limit weight gain, and improve aerobic endurance.

Growth hormone is critical in energy metabolism, and its use is beneficial for adults with growth hormone deficiencies. However, its effectiveness in helping to improve recovery from intensive exercise, increasing muscle strength, or improving athletic performance remains unproven when compared with results that come from sound training practices. High use of HGH can also lead to heart problems, excessive growth of the hands and feet, and dangerous enlargement of key internal organs such as the heart, kidneys, and liver. Irreversible side effects include skeletal abnormalities.

The use of human growth hormone is banned for athletes by the IOC and other major sport-governing bodies, but there is as yet no approved means of detection.

Erythropoietin

Some athletes who compete in endurance sports such as cycling, cross-country skiing, or long-distance running may take erythropoietin (EPO), a natural protein hormone that is produced primarily in the kidneys. Synthetic erythropoietin has been shown to cause an increase in levels of hemoglobin, which increases the oxygen-carrying capacity of red blood cells. More oxygen, therefore, is carried to the tissues that need it. The drawback is that a higher red-cell causes the heart to work harder, which in turn increases the risk of cardiac fatigue and heart failure.

Because EPO is a naturally occurring hormone, testing for this banned substance is very difficult. In an effort to reduce the practice in bike racing, the officials of the international cycling at Union Cycliste Internationale (UCI) rely on a test that measures the density of cells in the blood. A study from the 1980s, before synthetic EPO was in use, showed that the blood of bike racers had on average a red-blood cell content of 43 percent. The UCI decreed that any racer with a level above 50 percent would be disqualified for taking EPO.

In fact, EPO was at the heart of one of the highest-profile drug cases in cycling in recent years, and led to the demise of a hugely successful athlete. In June 1999, the Italian rider Marco Pantani, one of the few riders to have won both the Tour de France and the Giro d'Italia races in the same year (1998), failed a test because traces of EPO were detected in his blood. Pantani was in a position to win the Italian tour again that year, but was expelled from the race and

sentenced to jail for sporting fraud, a sentence that was later overturned. The resulting disgrace led to Pantani losing his status as Italy's most popular athlete. In the summer of 2001, when Pantani was again found with traces of a banned substance in his blood during the Giro, he was suspended from cycling by the Italian Cycling Federation, and he ultimately retired.

Restricted Pharmacological Substances

In addition to the performance-enhancing substances and methods listed above, there is another class of substances established by the International Olympic Committee (see Table 11.1 for a breakdown of prohibited and restricted substances). These are known as restricted pharmacological substances and include alcohol, marijuana, local anaesthetics, corticosteroids, and beta blockers.

- **Alcohol.** The use of alcohol is detrimental to most sport performances, which is why this substance is subject to restriction. Low doses have some sedative effects, but increased doses cause confusion, lessened reaction time, and poor coordination. The use of alcohol is prohibited and may be detected by blood or breath testing.

- **Marijuana.** Derived from the hemp plant, marijuana can adversely affect psychomotor function for up to 24 hours. Although it is unlikely to be used to enhance sporting performance, its use is controlled and regulated in a number of sports.

- **Local anaesthetics.** Although use of local anaesthetics is permitted, the IOC Commission or sports federation must be informed in writing and their use must be medically justified. If they are used to block pain, their use will mask the body's natural pain threshold and injury may result.

- **Corticosteroids.** Synthetically produced versions of these anti-inflammatory and analgesic drugs are used legitimately in the treatment of asthma. Athletes may misuse them to open up airways, increase training ability, or mask injury, and prolonged use can be toxic. Their use is now restricted to topical use, inhalation therapy, or injections, and written notification must be given to the IOC Commission or sports federation.

- **Beta blockers.** The nervous system's response to stress and arousal is moderated by the use of beta blockers, which moderate the cardiac output and muscle blood flow. Athletes whose sport requires steady action may find their performance enhanced by their use. Side effects produced by misuse include low blood pressure and sleep disturbances.

Drug Policies in Pro Sports
A comparison of drug testing in five major-league sports

The five major North American pro sports leagues each have their own drug policies when it comes to dealing with players and drug use. In each case, these policies have a direct relationship to the league's players through their collective labour organizations.

What follows is a brief examination of each league's policy.

The National Hockey League (NHL)

The NHL has banned the use of all illegal substances – including steroids – but, based on an agreement with the NHL Player's Association (the organization that represents the league's players in matters such as contract negotiations and pensions benefits), does not test for them. This means that, while the possession of steroids and other performance-enhancing drugs, as well as "recreational" substances such as cocaine and marijuana can be grounds for league-enforced suspensions and fines, the league cannot actually test one of its players to prove these substances are in his system.

The National Football League (NFL)

Because of the strength requirements of pro football, there is also a tremendous temptation for NFL players to use steroids. Consequently, the NFL is very clear about its position on steroids, according to a statement released by the National Football League Players Association (NFLPA): "The National Football League prohibits the use by NFL players of anabolic/androgenic steroids (including exogenous testosterone), human or animal growth hormones, whether natural or synthetic, and related or similar substances as well as masking agents or diuretics used to hide their presence."

This means that NFL players can potentially be tested at any time during the year – in the pre-season, during the regular season, the playoffs, and even in the off-season – in random fashion, or they can be tested if there is "reasonable cause" to suspect that they are

St. Louis Cardinals' Mark McGwire admitted to using androstenedione, a testosterone-producing pill that is perfectly legal in baseball but banned in the NFL, Olympics, and the NCAA (AP Photo/Mary Butkus).

using banned substances. Only when a player notifies the league in writing will he be excused from these tests.

The Canadian Football League (CFL)

The CFL does not test its players for drug use, primarily for financial reasons. According to a December 2002 report by the Canadian Press, the cost of conducting a single test was in the order of $2,500. "While that doesn't sound like much," the report stated, "consider that each week the nine CFL teams carry 40 players each on their active rosters alone. And then there's the matter of five practice-roster players and others on injured reserve."

The news that a CFL player had been charged following a huge police "bust" of a steroid-production lab in Milton, Ontario, however, forced CFL officials to begin reconsidering their drug policies. But any decision on the matter will have to wait – the league cannot implement any testing without first obtaining consent from the CFL Players Association, since drug tests are prohibited

under the collective bargaining agreement reached in 2002 between the league and its players.

The National Basketball Association (NBA)

The NBA is the one professional league whose players have received the most publicity for drug infractions, usually based on testing positive for, or being charged with possession of, so-called recreational drugs such as cocaine and marijuana. (Oddly enough, based on negotiations with the NBA Players Association, the league cannot test for the presence of marijuana in a player's system, but can suspend a player for being found in possession of it.)

All NBA players are tested at least once during the four-week pre-season. First-year players are tested without prior notice three more times each season, while veterans are tested once during the pre-season. If a veteran tests positive, he is tested again during the season, but only if league officials have "reasonable cause" to suspect that he is using recreational or performance-enhancing drugs. Suspensions occur if players test positive.

Major League Baseball (MLB)

During the 2002 season, a major negotiating point in the labour talks between baseball's owners and players revolved around the issue of drug testing and use, especially since there had been countless rumours that the recent increase in home-run hitting was the result of many players using steroids to boost their strength.

When the league's collective bargaining agreement was ratified in September 2002, it included the plan that pro baseball players would be tested on the basis of "just cause" until a predetermined number (widely reported at 5 percent) of all the MLB players who are tested have recorded positive tests. Following that, the agreement, in effect until 2006, calls for random mandatory testing of all players.

PHYSIOLOGICAL AIDS

Physiological methods and techniques used by athletes include blood doping and drug masking. Both practices are of course banned by the IOC and other sport-governing bodies.

Blood Doping

As defined by the World Anti-Doping Agency, blood doping involves the intravenous administration of blood, red blood cells, and related blood products to raise the blood's oxygen carrying capacity, thus enhancing aerobic athletic performance. Athletes may be using their own blood or someone else's blood.

About two units of blood are removed from an athlete, which are then stored for six to eight weeks. It is then reinfused into the athlete (or infused into another) from one to seven days before athletic competition. Following the reinfusion, cardiorespiratory endurance performance is improved – the blood can carry more oxygen, cardiac output is increased, lactate levels are decreased, and sweating responses are improved.

In the past, it was not uncommon for bike racers, for example, to increase the number of red blood cells at race time by withdrawing their own blood beforehand, storing it, and then injecting it just before the race. Nowadays, blood doping has been replaced by injecting EPO (see above), which causes the body to create new red blood cells.

Blood doping is, of course, banned by the International Olympic Committee, but because hemoglobin levels rise only slightly following blood doping, this technique is difficult to detect. In fact, the sport of track and field has long been fraught with rumours that many top long-distance runners use blood doping to enhance their performance, although the practice is allegedly far less popular than it was in the 1970s and 1980s.

One champion runner – Finland's Lasse Viren, the only man to win the 5,000-metre and 10,000-metre races in successive Olympic Games (1972 and 1976) – was often accused of blood doping by fellow competitors and the press. One reason Viren was widely suspected was that his performances in non-Olympic years were decidedly unspectacular, leading some to conclude that he used this practice to enhance his performance when the Games rolled around. Viren argued that he took periodization training (see page 195 for an explanation of this term) to its logical extreme, and attempted to peak every four years when Olympic medals were at stake. The question, said Viren, is not how he was able to perform so well in Olympic competition, but why others were not. Further adding to the controversy, at the 1984 Olympics in Los Angeles, several Finnish runners claimed that

Show jumper Eric Lamaze during the Capital Classic Horse Show in Nepean, Ontario, in 1997. Lamaze had just returned to competition after being banned for four years for drug use (CP PHOTO/Tom Hanson).

their national team had been promoting blood doping for many years.

Drug Masking

Technological means of escaping detection have long been in place in the drug-testing realm. Over the last two decades, methods of avoiding detection have expanded from the substitution of urine samples to include drug masking, whereby certain drugs are used to mask or reduce the presence of banned substances.

These include agents that dilute the concentration of banned drugs in the bloodstream, and diuretics, which increase the amount of urine produced and therefore can dilute the concentration of banned substances in the urine tested. For example, probenecid is a weak diuretic that reduces excretion of androgenic steroids. In major sporting competition, rumours abound about the substitution of a clean person's urine for that of an athlete using banned substances and the use of catheterization. Any technique used by an athlete to escape detection is banned.

Ben Johnson and the Dubin Inquiry
Canada's drug scandal at the 1988 Summer Olympics in Seoul

There are likely very few Canadians who do not know the story of Ben Johnson. Even those who do not regularly follow sports were aware of the rise and subsequent fall of the Toronto-area sprinter at the 1988 Summer Olympic Games in Seoul, Korea, and the implications this had on the controversial issue of performance-enhancing drugs and sport.

Johnson capped a brilliant career as a sprinter by winning the 100-metre final in Seoul. He defeated his bitter rival, the American Carl Lewis, and, in the process, set a new world record for the event. But our celebration at having a Canadian become the "world's fastest man" quickly turned sour as a post-race drug test found that the twenty-six-year-old runner had traces of steroids in his urine.

The Seoul disqualification marked the beginning of the end of Johnson's sporting career. Not only did he lose the Olympic gold medal he had won, but the record he had set the year before in winning the 100-metre World Championship was revoked because of his admitted steroid use.

Johnson returned to the sport in 1991, after being banned by track and field's governing body, the International Amateur Athletic Federation (IAAF). His comeback, however, was a lacklustre one, and in 1993, he was kicked out of the sport for life by the IAAF for testing positive for steroid use after a meet in Montreal.

The Dubin Inquiry

Johnson's disqualification in Seoul prompted a full-scale Canadian investigation, starting in 1989, into steroid use in track and field. The so-called Dubin Inquiry, lead by Chief Justice Charles Dubin, sought to ascertain just how widespread the use of illegal performance-enhancing drugs was in this country. The inquiry forced those involved with track and field to question whether Johnson was the only high-profile athlete using steroids – or

Carol Anne Letheren was Chef de Mission during the 1988 Olympics drug scandal (CP PHOTO/COA/T. O'lett).

just the only one who had been caught. Certainly Johnson's coach, Charlie Francis, himself a one-time high-calibre sprinter, suggested that Johnson's use was not isolated.

One woman, the American Florence Griffith Joyner, for example, broke world records by huge margins in both the 100-metre and 200-metre races in Seoul after increasing her muscle mass noticeably from years past. She then promptly retired after the Games. (When Griffith Joyner died at a relatively young age a few years later, rumours of her alleged steroid use resurfaced.)

Even though the Johnson disqualification in 1988 was a real blow to Canadians' pride, the subsequent investigation into drugs in Canadian sports forced more prominent individuals in sport and sports associations around the world to take the issue seriously. The Dubin Inquiry also exposed associated issues, such as the potential for tampering with an athlete's urine samples during testing.

Unfortunately, drug-related bans and disqualifications continue to occur at

many major international sporting competitions, including the recent 2002 Winter Olympic Games, held in Salt Lake City. It is apparent that some athletes' use of banned substances continues to be a problem.

Fifteen Years Later

Strangely, Johnson's ex-coach Charlie Francis, whom the Dubin Inquiry found had advised the athlete to take the steroids, resurfaced fifteen years after the Seoul scandal, this time as an adviser to the American multiple gold-medal winner, Marion Jones. According to Jones, it was a move designed to help her make her sprinting style more efficient. Although Francis had been banned from working with Canadian athletes, the exclusion does not cover athletes from other countries.

The relationship was short-lived, however. By early 2003, Jones and her training partner (and boyfriend), world 100-metre record-holder Tim Montgomery (who had also begun working with Francis), had decided to split with the Canadian coach.

The IAAF – which was previously unstinting in its condemnation of Francis – said in a press release that it was pleased that Jones had acted "not just in her own best interests but for the good of the sport. Although there is nothing in our rules to prevent selecting the coach of their choice, the special status of Marion means that her choice and actions also have a major impact on the image and reputation of the sport."

In breaking with Francis, Jones – who won three gold medals and two bronze medals at the 2000 Sydney Olympics – said she had been concerned about rumours that her sole purpose in working with Francis was to get his advice on performance-enhancing substances. "I'm a proponent of a drug-free sport and I always will be.... I've never tested positive and I never will, but everybody is putting guilt by association into this, which is so ridiculous."

DRUG TESTING

Drug testing is performed to ensure an even playing field for all athletes. Because new methods are continually being developed and current ones, improved, athletes who use banned substances in a competition run a high risk of detection. A successful drug testing program involves random, year-round, and unannounced testing.

The testing procedure usually involves the athlete in question supplying one or several urine samples, usually after the competition, but in some cases before it as well. These samples are then sent to a laboratory and are tested for the presence of banned substances. The mere detection of such a substance in an athlete's urine is not always enough for him or her to be found guilty and subsequently banned from competition. Each sports-governing body has pre-set limits for each banned substance, and an athlete must exceed these levels to, in the parlance of sport, "test positive."

Problems can occur in the detection of particular substances. Although efficient chemical identification of previously ignored substances is now possible, some substances, such as human growth hormone, synthetic testosterone, and erythropoietin, are more difficult to detect as they cannot be distinguished from the natural hormones produced by the body. Currently the only available test for the use of growth hormone or erythropoietin is to measure for higher than normal levels in the blood. A threshold value has been established for naturally occurring substances such as caffeine so that an athlete is not banned merely for using the substance.

As mentioned above, substances used to mask banned substances are themselves banned and can be detected in drug screens.

ETHICAL ISSUES

Even though increased strength and endurance can be achieved through exercise and diet alone, many athletes consider ergogenic substances to be a necessary part of successful training and competition. If these athletes then set records, other athletes feel the need to use to them in order to "level the playing field."

Athletes need to ask themselves on which basis they are making an ethical decision to use or not to use an ergogenic substance or aid. Athletes may seek to follow the Olympic ideal, in which each athlete succeeds through his or her own efforts. A particular sport association may put forth rules of conduct for athletes to follow. Or, an individual athlete may be guided by his or her own moral principles, which may be contrary to those stipulated by any sports-governing body.

Although the use of ergogenic aids is highly unlikely to cease, reliance on such substances can distract an athlete from attending to proper and proven training techniques and thereby seeking the ethical ideal.

Of course, a large part of any ethical decision involves knowing the consequences of a given action. In the case of using ergogenic aids to enhance sports performance, these outcomes can involve serious health risks. Athletes – especially those competing at sport's highest levels – want to succeed at what they do. But perhaps the largest ethical question is this: Should a person use performance-enhancing drugs when the adverse, long-term health effects have been shown, without question, to be seriously harmful? Attempting to assess the ethical implications of such actions, without taking into account the physical consequences, simply does not make sense.

WHERE DO WE GO FROM HERE?

The "performance improvement" versus "negative side-effects" dilemma introduced in this section in connection with performance-enhancing drugs and methods is a good starting point for examining the impact of science and technology on other areas of sport performance. In the next section, we will continue to look at how recent advances in science and technology have allowed athletes to achieve results unheard-of in decades past.

Before continuing, it is useful to consider exactly what constitutes an "advantage" in sport. For example, there are some (albeit a small minority) who argue that there is no real difference between using a new high-tech kayak that slices through the water more efficiently or a fine-tuned golf ball that flies further off the tee, and using performance-enhancing drugs to run faster or to lift heavier weights. When confronted with the argument that using a new kayak or golf ball does not adversely affect a person's health, while drug use almost certainly does, these people insist that an athlete should have the absolute right to determine what is best for his or her body, regardless of what officials or governments tell them.

This is an extreme position, to be sure, but it does make one think more deeply about certain aspects of the role of both technology and ethics in sport. At what point are technological advances – in both equipment and drugs – permissible? Should athletes be forced to compete in a "technology-free" environment, or is it better to open sport up to a technological "free for all" in which questions of health and well-being are left up to the individual? These are just a sample of the intriguing issues raised in the following section on the influence of technology on human performance.

Women's skeleton rider Lindsay Alcock of Calgary jumps onto her sled as she heads down the track at the 2002 Olympic Winter Games in Salt Lake City, Utah (CP PHOTO/COA/Andre Forget).

12

Technological Influences on Human Performance

"If a horse can't eat it, I don't want to play on it!"
— Baseball star Dick Allen, speaking in 1970 as artificial turf was being introduced

KEY CONCEPTS

- Ergonomics
- Repetitive stress injury
- Personal protective equipment
- Equipment revolution
- Wicking properties

- Clap skate
- Full-body swimsuits
- Lifting shirt
- Artificial turf
- Motion analysis

- Virtual reality technologies

Science and technology have provided a wide range of means for enhancing performance – from major advances in athletic equipment, to improved sports playing surfaces, to advanced training techniques.

In this section we will look at the field of ergonomics and its influence on sports performance, ranging from training techniques to safety equipment. We will then explore the effect of technology on sporting equipment by examining improvements in a select number of sports. Finally, we will discuss how computer technology is revolutionizing the sport industry, from timing to training.

ERGONOMICS

Those who study a field known as ergonomics – sometimes called "human-factors engineering" – are interested in finding out how the relationship between humans and machines can be made as efficient as possible. In the interest of maximizing our performance, ergonomists look at ways of improving our use of mechanical objects. To do so, they consider a wide range of factors, including a person's physical structure, strength, and visual acuity, as well as the physiological stresses that machines place on their users. Ergonomics promotes a holistic approach in which considerations of physical, cognitive, social, organizational, environmental, and other relevant factors are taken into account.

Most technological equipment that people use today – whether it be a kitchen utensil at home, a computer in the workplace, or the vehicles we drive – is of a fairly "fixed" nature. That is, someone designed and manufactured it in mass quantities, and there is little we can do to modify it to change its basic structure and function. So, while ergonomists do often work to implement design changes to the machines or tools we use, they are also heavily concerned with the physical characteristics of people. These include our physical and cognitive abilities and limits, including height, weight, and so on; our ability to handle information and make decisions; our ability to see and hear; and our ability to work under extreme stresses, such as high temperature or fatigue.

An ergonomist studies the variations in these characteristics in a group of people. With this data in hand, the ergonomist is able to determine whether systems, products, places, and processes can be used comfortably, efficiently, and safely. Recommended changes in design make the human-machine interface smoother.

Ergonomics and Sport

The same ergonomic principles that apply in the workplace also apply to enhancing human performance and achieving physical efficiency. Any endeavour that involves physical exertion and repetition is a form of "work," be it for pleasure or exercise. And just as we can modify our ergonomic environment in the workplace, athletic performance can be enhanced and stress on the body can be reduced by

Tennis Technology
Back to wood?

Every sport has been revolutionized in recent years by advances in basic technology. New-style golf clubs, hockey sticks, and improvements in protective equipment and training techniques come readily to mind. Even the common soccer ball was significantly redesigned, using advanced materials, in time for the 2002 World Cup.

In the case of tennis, just to take one example, the change from wooden racquets to larger racquets made of graphite and other synthetic materials has changed the game in a big way. Many argue that, if top-level tennis has improved over the last few decades, this improvement is a result of better equipment and not enhanced technique, training, and athletic ability. Others maintain that the advances in equipment actually allow superior athletes to perform on the court as never before – and that, in the same way that advances in transportation, communications, and so on are a "natural" part of human existence, progress in sport equipment such as tennis racquets should be allowed to go on unimpeded.

Back to the Old-Style Tennis Racquets?

The point on the face of the racquet that produces the least amount of vibration and maximum rebound velocity is technically known as "the point of percussion." New over-sized racquets are made of composite graphite and other materials and are designed to increase this area, more commonly known as the "sweet spot."

The mechanical effect of making the sweet spot larger is to increase the "moment of inertia" around the racquet's main axis. (For more on this concept, see the discussion on biomechanics, page 229.) With these racquets, there is less of a rotating effect when the ball is hit off-centre. The player has better control and power.

Safety First, Always

One positive effect of reducing unwanted racquet rotation and vibration is to reduce the likelihood of "tennis elbow" and shoulder-related injuries. Another is to give players more control and allow them to improve their game more quickly, especially in the case of junior players.

However, another consequence is that the new-style racquets increase the "power" element of the game, and this can lead to problems when players overexert themselves just to keep up.

There is no reason (or even, way) to return to the slower game using the smaller wooden racquets, but there is a general lesson to be learned from the tennis example.

The lesson applies to all sport and all physical activity, and it is this: while technology can change the nature of a sport, sometimes significantly, it is still human beings who play, and there are physiological limitations to what the body's bones, muscles, and joints can endure.

using support aids and equipment and training technologies. Athletes must condition themselves to achieve accuracy, strength, and endurance for specific muscle groups. As a result, one of the roles of the ergonomist in sport is in the development of training techniques that isolate and improve specific muscle movements.

Another role that ergonomists play in athletic performance is in the design of bracing and supports that aid an injured athlete in avoiding downtime for recovery, which can mean the loss of an athlete's conditioning and skill and possibly an entire competitive season. Supports have been used for some time to treat persistent non-union fractures.

Amateur athletes as well as those at the elite level are at risk of injury, mainly due to their lack of conditioning and use of incorrect technique. Injuries tend to be sport specific and repetitive stress injuries or motion injuries (RSIs), otherwise known as cumulative trauma disorders (CTDs), are as common among athletes as they are for those who continually use high-tech keyboards, computer mice, and trackballs every working day. Simply defined, a repetitive stress injury is damage caused by repetitive movement to tendons, nerves, muscles, and other soft body tissues. As in the workplace, ergonomists can suggest aids that protect the body while enhancing performance. By applying efficient technologies, higher levels of performance are incrementally achieved without injury.

PERSONAL PROTECTIVE EQUIPMENT

It is difficult to perform well when an injury – or even the threat of one – makes striving to maximize one's efforts physically or psychologically difficult. Technology has been responsible for all kinds of improvements designed to protect people as they seek to enhance their performance.

Personal protective equipment protects players against injury and should be used wherever possible. This equipment includes padding, bracing and taping, mouthguards, and headgear. We are all familiar with advances in personal protective equipment in the sports world, such as hockey goaltenders' masks, football shoulder pads, cycling helmets, baseball catchers' masks, and the fireproof suits of racing-car drivers, all of which have evolved considerably over the past decades. Today, the use of protective equipment is mandatory in most sports. For example, NHL hockey players must wear helmets (as opposed to a generation ago, when the decision to use such gear was left up to the individual player), and in youth soccer leagues, the wearing of shin guards is mandatory, as are batting helmets in all levels of baseball, from minor to professional.

Hockey

For example, it is tough to imagine an NHL hockey goalie facing lightning-fast pucks without protective equipment. Goalies' pads, formerly made of water- and sweat-absorbent leather, gained weight during the course of the game. Today, they are made of synthetic materials that are much stronger, lighter, and less absorbent. Most goalies' masks are made with fibreglass and/or Kevlar, which is the same material used to fabricate bulletproof vests. Goalies' sticks, although made out of wood, are curved to allow them to "play" the puck and not simply stop it.

Football

Football players exposed to the high temperatures of the football field in summer, which can reach 130°F, formerly wore heavy and heat-retaining foam-filled helmets and polyurethane shoulder pads. These players can now receive protection from the same materials developed by NASA for the space shuttle. As the U.S. Center for Catastrophic Sports Injuries reports over one hundred deaths among football players from heatstroke since 1960, this new technology could help alleviate heat-related injuries. The Radiant Heat Deflection System, for example, developed by Creative Football Concepts, uses aluminized polyester that can be inserted into helmets, shoulder pads, and other protective equipment, and the manufacturer claims that it reflects over 90 percent of heat generated by the sun. As well, the technology utilizes a layer of air within the material, reducing the skin's conduction of heat from the material.

To maximize the technology's effectiveness and to aid in fighting internal heat buildup, its creators suggest that players wear undergarments made of Hydroweave. This fabric is a water-absorbing fibre that is fitted between two layers of micro-porous material. Once soaked in cold water and then wrung dry, the trace amounts of water in the middle layer act as a coolant and also draw heat away from the skin. Several NFL teams have tried out the new inexpensive space-age gear with favourable results, and its creators believe that equipment managers and coaches need to find out more regarding such cutting-edge technologies that can alleviate the effects of the oppressive heat on the field.

Cycling

Although the health and environmental benefits of cycling are well recognized, each year there are from 100 to 130 bicycle deaths in Canada and about 50,000

injuries that require medical attention. The bicycle death rate rises rapidly from about five years of age to the mid-teens, and about 40 percent of the deaths from cycling occur in this age group. Cyclists are exposed to motor vehicles and a hard road surface, and bicycles themselves are rather unstable. This means that bicycle riders are at great risk of significant head injury; not wearing a helmet increases the risk of sustaining a head injury by as much as seven times.

At speeds of 15 kilometres per hour (a common cycling speed), helmets meeting approved safety standards can reduce the energy absorbed by the skull by over 90 percent, and cyclists who wear helmets also experience fewer facial injuries. A helmet that bears a certification label from the Canadian Standards Association (CSA), Snell, The American Society for Testing Materials (ASTM), or the Consumer Product Safety Commission (CPSC) has been tested to withstand certain levels of impact and will give the best protection possible. Despite these proven safety statistics and safety legislation, there is still reluctance among some riders to wearing a helmet.

Baseball

When professional baseball began in the late 1800s, catchers wore equipment much different from that of today. Chest protectors, protective pads, shields, masks, and gloves were far thinner and offered far less protection. No helmets were worn. Today, innovations in plastics have revolutionized safety in baseball and softball. Catchers' masks are made from a solid vinyl-coated metal frame. Simulated leather pads, which help protect the catcher's eyes, nose, and mouth from injury, are made of soft plastic. The catcher's rib cage, heart, and lungs are protected from base runners, bats, and fast-moving balls by chest protectors covered in nylon and made from polyethylene plastic sternum inserts. Leg guards, padded with durable plastic foam, protect the knees and lower legs.

Batters wearing plastic batting helmets are no longer vulnerable when on the receiving end of fastballs travelling at speeds of over 152 kilometres (95 miles) per hour. Once made of leather or wood, today's helmets are composed of hard, injection-moulded plastic, such as ABS (Acrylonitrile-Butadiene-Styrene). In order to protect the ears, the interior contains plastic foam pads made of EVA (Ethylene Vinyl Acetate) or polypropylene. Plastic batting helmets with one earflap are required for all batters and runners who play in the major leagues, and the International Olympic Committee requires helmets with two earflaps for both softball and baseball. Plastic cleats protect infielders from injury if they collide with a sliding base runner and provide for maximum traction on both natural and artificial surfaces. Both infielders and outfielders wear gloves lined with a polyurethane surface film to provide comfort, flexibility, and protection.

Base sliding is a major cause of recreational softball accidents, which occur when runners risk broken or strained ankles by sliding into a stationary, hard base. Safety-release or "breakaway" bases prevent common leg and foot injuries for Little League baseball and amateur softball players, although they are not used in international competition or the major baseball leagues. The soft plastic safety-release bases are dislodged by sliding runners and no hard parts emanate from the ground.

Car Racing

The racing-car driver's suit, often covered with patches of the racing team's sponsors, is perhaps the most recognizable piece of racing gear and is the driver's main defence against injury from burns. These suits are made out of either Proban or a material trademarked as Nomex. Nomex is a fire-retardant material that offers protection for 12 seconds in a blaze as hot as 704°C – all threading and advertising patches must meet the same standards. Both the crew and the driver are protected from a fire resulting from a crash or a fire in the pits.

The Nomex is woven into a material that is used to line the inside of the driver's helmet, and to make the shoes, gloves, and socks as well as the suit worn by the driver. The flame resistance of Nomex, unlike other materials, will not wash out or wear away. These suits are rated based on how long they will protect drivers from second-degree burns in a gasoline fire, which can reach temperatures from 982°C to 1,149°C. Ratings range from 3 to 40 seconds of protection. New suits have been designed using a combination of Nomex, Kevlar, and Indura material and offer excellent protection without multi-layering.

THE EQUIPMENT REVOLUTION

The evolution of the equipment that athletes use to push themselves to greater and greater achievements is instructive when investigating the relationship between technology and human performance. The equipment revolution in recent years has even led some experts to speculate that advances in sporting records over the years may be as much the result of technological improvements as they are the product of superior training.

At the Summer Olympic Games, for example, literally every sport provides evidence of improved equipment. Divers perform more advanced manoeuvres on fibreglass boards of a design and makeup unheard of twenty years ago. Rowers, canoeists, and kayakers race in fibreglass boats designed to cut valuable time with their lightweight construction and aerodynamic shape. Cyclists sprint around the track on featherweight bicycles wearing space-age racing helmets, and vaulters launch themselves skywards with poles made of the most flexible and durable material possible. In the pool, high-tech wet suits may be revolutionizing a sport where every millisecond counts. And at the Winter Olympic Games, speed skaters speed faster than ever over the ice on clap skates and skiers race on parabolic skis in high-tech racing suits.

Compared to Olympic competitions of the past, recent Games have not only provided an example of how technology is changing the appearance of competition, but of how it is empirically improving it as well. These athletes are truly stronger and going higher and faster than ever before.

What follows is a more detailed description of several technological advances in a select number of sports, beginning with an overview of the changes in materials used in sportswear.

Fabrics

The invention of elastic was probably the most critical in the evolution of sportswear. First used to hold up pants and shorts, now entire garments are fabricated from elasticated materials such as Lycra. Elastic also plays an important role in compression bandages in the treatment of injuries. Clothes that keep the body at a constant temperature regardless of external conditions are being designed and used in protective clothing such as hats, boots, and gloves. The wicking properties of fabrics describes their ability to draw moisture away from an athlete's skin and new innovation in sportswear design has much improved this property. For example, "Phase Change" materials for sportswear contain a chemical that changes from a liquid to a gel when it reaches body temperature, and thereby alters its insulation properties.

Athletic socks are now high wicking, complete with anti-odour finishes. Athlete's foot can now be guarded against by the addition of an anti-microbial layer. The latest design is fractionally fitted anti-friction socks. The friction is absorbed by two layers of the sock rather than by the skin. The inner layer grips the foot, and the outer layer grips the shoe.

Athletics: On the Track

In 1954, the first 4-minute mile was run by Roger Bannister on a cinder track. In 1965, Australian athlete Ron Clarke set the world record in the men's 10,000-metre run, also on a cinder track. Many experts believe that if Clarke had run on a modern all-weather track, 25 seconds would have been cut from his time of 27 minutes and 39 seconds. Soon after, a synthetic track surface consisting of asphalt covered with polyurethane (liquid rubber) was introduced. In 1992, at the Barcelona Olympics, sheets of neoprene were laid for the track surface, and these have become the international standard.

Running shoes. The modern sneaker dates back to 1836 and made use of vulcanized rubber, patented by U.S. inventor Charles Goodyear. In 1917, the first high-performance athletic shoe was launched by the Converse Rubber Company for basketball players who favoured high-tops for ankle support. Since then, and particularly in the last decade, manufacturers have been racing to develop high-performance athletic footwear both for sprinters, whose shoes need to be light and rigid, and for distance runners, who require more flexible footwear.

A new type of track shoe, developed at the University of Calgary, is claimed to dampen the muscle vibration that occurs during running and thereby reduces loss of energy. Conventional sole materials have been altered to change stiffness, elasticity, and viscosity, and because each individual's muscles vibrate at different frequencies, the blend of materials can be varied to suit each individual. It is believed that the shoe can boost performance by about 4 percent. The rights to the shoe were purchased by Adidas who named the product Sightless. After analysis revealed that traditional spikes waste energy by inserting and extracting from the track, Adidas equipped the shoe with a Z-shaped implement made of an alloy. This implement grips the track and is lighter than conventional spikes.

Bodysuits. Track athletes have been wearing bodysuits since the Seoul Olympics in 1988. Current versions claim to reduce leg muscle vibration in the track events and reduce wind resistance. Nike, the maker of Swiftsuit, claims that the mesh earholes in the suit's hood will reduce drag. All seams are at the back, the front zipper is covered, and the suit extends over the hands. Different colours of material are used to control the temperature of different parts of the body – leg and arm muscles are kept warm, while the rest of the body is cooler. The Full Body Suit made by Adidas is inspired by NASA's research on blood circulation in space. Adidas claims that when muscles are compressed, blood is forced to flow through them more quickly, thereby reducing vibration.

Hockey: On the Ice

In 2001, Calgary sportswriter Bruce Dowbiggin not only chronicled the iconic importance of hockey sticks to Canadian hockey fans of all ages – a stick autographed by an NHL player has always been a cherished artefact – but looked at how the hockey stick has gone from a rough wooden tool carved out of tree roots by the Mi'kmaqs of Nova Scotia, to the two- and three-piece models made in small-town Ontario and Quebec, to the scientifically precise graphite sticks now produced. This change to a lighter implement with a more precisely curved blade means that shooting and passing can now be achieved, albeit by better players, with a high degree of accuracy.

Speed Skating: On the Ice Track

With the traditional speed skate, skaters were giving up power: the old speed skate prevented the skater from using the full potential of their leg muscles and limited the work of some knee extensors and the plantar flexors. Enter the clap skate, which allows the skater to raise the heel off of the ice as the blade of the skate rotates on a hinge. Invented by a team of Dutch scientists, the inclusion of a spring-loaded hinge on the toe of the skate is what allows the skater's heel to lift away from the blade at the end of a longer stride than a traditional skate would accommodate. Thus, the blade is in contact with the ice longer and delivers more power per stride. It is also, however, the end of the swooshing particular to this sport; the blade creates a loud clap as it reconnects at the heel of the boot.

If there was any doubt as to the effectiveness of the clap skate, the tremendous performances by speed skaters at the 1998 Winter Olympic Games using this innovative piece of equipment certainly silenced the sceptics. In the speed-skating competition at Nagano, all ten Olympic records were broken by athletes using the clap skate – as well as five world records. Of course, this huge, across-the-board performance improvement caused considerable controversy, since many people felt that the bevy of records were being broken because of technological – and not athletic, or "human" – advances. But, as often happens in sport, the clap skate, and the new skating techniques needed to use it, soon became an accepted part of the sport. By the 2002 Olympic Games, the controversy had dissipated. As one international coach indicated at the latter competition, once everyone had become used to the advantage offered by the clap skate, there simply was no more controversy.

Swimming: In the Pool

It used to be commonly believed that the less hair and less material with which swimmers entered the pool, the faster they could go. Now, most swimming competitors wear a version of a new full-body swimsuit. Fastskin, a suit developed by Speedo, has been designed to reduce drag in the water. Made of super-stretch fabric with built-in edges similar to a shark's

Race Car Technology

Leading-edge technologies make for a faster, safer car and driver

Open-wheel racing cars are sometimes dismissed as computers on wheels – flashy, garishly painted vehicles that control themselves, leaving little for the celebrity drivers to do. While there is some truth to this, drivers such as Michael Schumacher, who drives for Ferrari, and Canada's Jacques Villeneuve and Paul Tracy still make a huge contribution, in no small part due to their skill at controlling the computers that in turn control their cars.

From the ground up, contemporary race cars represent the best in available technology, from the rubber compounds in the tires, to the carbon fibre composite structural members, to the high-revving engines that are designed to last only for the duration of the race. Here are some of the ways leading-edge technologies make for a faster, better-controlled and safer car and driver.

Canadian F1 driver and defending world champion Jacques Villeneuve in 1998 (AP Photo/Jerome Delay).

- **Launch and traction control.** Software on the race car's computer takes over the entire task of getting Formula 1 cars up to speed from their traditional standing start. The computer controls the firing of each of twelve engine cylinders, producing just enough power for smooth acceleration but not enough to cause wheel spin and collisions produced by uneven acceleration. The driver need only steer and keep the accelerator down to produce a smooth, spin-free acceleration. If the computer senses the beginnings of wheel spin, it causes some cylinders not to fire, slowing the engine just enough to retain traction. This software also acts as a speed limiter in the garage area to avoid accidents with technicians. Traction control works like launch control to allow the onboard computer to take power from the drive wheels selectively to retain traction. It is especially effective under wet or oily road conditions.

- **Shifting gears.** Control of the race car's transmission is now typically carried out by computer as well. The driver has paddles on the steering wheel that signal the computer to shift gears up or down without the need for a foot clutch mechanism.

- **Carbon fibre in brakes, suspension parts, and the skin and structural parts.** Having lightweight structural parts on a race car has the effect of both stiffening the chassis and lowering the centre of mass, making it more stable and crash survivable. Carbon fibre parts are as strong as or stronger than comparable steel parts but are much lighter. Massive carbon brake discs that glow red hot during the race slow cars down and are almost used up by the end of the race.

- **Computer-assisted design and manufacturing.** The exterior shells of race cars reflect the aerodynamic conditions expected in each race. The shells are designed with specialized computer software. Subtle adjustments of wing shape and airflow can make the difference between winning and finishing well back in the field or even crashing out if downforce created by the shell design is too little or too great.

- **Driver information systems.** Race-car drivers now have a complete set of performance information available to them on an LCD display panel that is situated in the middle of the steering wheel. Factors such as track temperature and wind conditions can be relayed to the car by radio telemetry, and the car in turn continuously reports readings from its performance sensors back to the garage. In some cases, technicians in the paddock area can carry out adjustments remotely while the car is moving.

- **Tire and fuel technology.** Manufacturers supply racing teams with several sets of tires for each race. These come in various tread patterns and compositions so that the best tires can be chosen for race conditions. Likewise, oil companies sponsor specially formulated fuel for each team and race to reflect conditions as well as safety. Fuel fires, which once caused serious racing accidents, have now largely ceased because of advanced fuel storage technology.

- **Driver safety.** Additional driver protection is provided by advanced restraint systems, crumple zones, helmets with voice communications, and layers of rip-off clear plastic strips on the visor that the driver removes one at time to get rid of dirt and oil from the visor.

For the future, one thing is fairly certain: the sheer amount of information coming to the driver from onboard computers will increase.

However, since it is highly doubtful that fans would ever pay to see driverless cars race, there should always be a place for those skilled operators who can drive and absorb all this information while moving at 250 km/h towards a hairpin turn.

skin, the pattern of the suit causes the seams to emulate tendons and provide tension while its fabric panels stretch and return to their original shape, mimicking muscles. As the fabric also compresses muscles, it limits vibration in the tissue and reduces the buildup of lactic acid. Although this suit can take up to 15 minutes to put on, the company claims that, by reducing drag and increasing lift in the water, a swimmer's performance can be improved by 3 percent. Adidas has also made a full-body suit for swimmers, the Equipment Bodysuit, which can be used in conjunction with an hydrodynamically styled swimming cap. It too is claimed to reduce drag.

Powerlifting: In the Gym

Weightlifters in the gym can now enjoy the protection provided by the new bench press shirt designed by John Inzer, originally created to improve his own performance. The stretch-type material used in the shirt provides support through the middle to the top of the lift and provides a spring off the chest. Teenage lifters, whose connective tissue is more delicate, are helped with their lifting and better prevented from injury by wearing the shirt. The shirt also provides protection during incline and decline bench presses.

Inzer Advance Designs offers custom-fit shirts tailored to every body type and size – the lifting shirt acts as a spring, aiding in control as the bar is lowered and also as the bar is pressed up. A too-tight shirt will lose its spring; a too-loose shirt is simply not as effective. The downside is that helpers are required in donning the shirt, and they may need to protect their knuckles to avoid injury. A shaved chest on the part of the lifter can also aid in pulling the shirt into proper position. The use of these lifting suits has been banned in most international competitions.

Bicycles: On the Road

The faster cyclists go, the more wind resistance they encounter. In order to overcome this, they must use more energy, which eventually leads to a decrease in speed. The dynamics of moving an object through air creates two problems: that of drag (pulling the cyclist backwards), and that of friction (caused by wind contact with bicycle and the cyclist). The cyclist can become more streamlined by wearing a skin-tight suit, but designers and aerodynamic engineers are constantly trying to improve the modern bicycle as a racing machine. They have eliminated crossbars and tapered the lightweight carbon fibre frame, thereby reducing friction. The spokes of the front wheel are designed to cut through the air like blades and the rear wheel is enclosed, thereby reducing drag. The modern bicycle is thin and strong as designers and engineers ever seek to increase its maximum speed.

Soccer: On the Field

At the 2002 World Cup of soccer, held in Japan and Korea, the Adidas company introduced, with some controversy, what it called "the most accurate soccer ball ever" as the official ball of the tournament. Known as the Fevernova, the new ball used a syntactic polyurethane foam base composed of highly elastic, exceptionally resistant gas-filled microcells of equal size, encased in three layers of polyurethane applied to a woven fabric. These cells, according to the manufacturer, gave the ball the "ability to convert energy evenly at any point," resulting in "more effective play and more precise and calculable flight of the ball." In other words, the new ball would, in theory, be easier to control when passing it, shooting it, or trapping it. It would respond better than older balls when the players attempted to "swerve" their shots on goal by intentionally kicking the ball off-centre in an attempt to fool opposing goaltenders. However, during the World Cup, reaction to the new ball among players seemed to be mixed. Many complained that it was "dead" in comparison – that is, when struck with equal force, it would not fly as fast or as accurately, making it harder to score goals or to pass it long distances.

Soccer, Football, Baseball: On the Turf

Sport played on artificial turf has long been reputed to be less safe than when played on natural grass. In a contact sport such as football, the turf often offers less cushioning than grass – when a player is hit and falls down, the impact can be much greater. Artificial turf is also harder to maintain and often consists of several pieces of playing surface joined together, which can cause players to trip over the raised seams between pieces. And, as a harder playing surface, artificial turf has been known to lead to impact-type injuries to the ligaments, joints, and tendons – including the notorious foot injury known as "turf toe."

The manufacturers claim that the conditions of playing on real grass, without its drawbacks, have been duplicated in the creation of FieldTurf, a synthetic fibre attached to a porous backing. Developed by FieldTurf International Incorporated, each fibre is designed to emulate real grass and is surrounded by a mixture of silica sand and ground rubber, providing a resilient, natural feel. Part of the rubber mix is a recycled material from Nike Grind (Nike's Reuse-A-Shoe program). The turf allows for maximum drainage and therefore optimum conditions regardless of the weather. It is also UV protected and extremely durable.

The new synthetic surface has been chosen for Giants Stadium in New Jersey. It has also been approved by FIFA for World Cup play.

The Outer Limits
How much technology is too much?

While designers and athletes become excited about the performance-enhancing possibilities of new equipment, not all sport-governing bodies welcome them. Several design innovations have presented problems for particular sports, challenging the "integrity" of the game itself.

For example, the Polara golf ball was asymmetrically dimpled to reduce hooks and slices, with shallower dimples on the poles than on its circumference. The ball was banned by the U.S. Golf Association who claimed that it reduced the skills necessary to participate in golf.

In tennis, rules and regulations were first imposed on tennis racquets following the 1977 ingenious design of a new stringing system. It consisted of three planes of non-intersecting, plastic-coated planes that held the ball longer, and allowed the player to impart greater top-spin than with a normal stroke. This created a huge upset in professional tennis, and regulations were introduced to limit the innovations that provide the ball with more rotations per second.

In baseball, a recurring controversy involves the so-called "juiced" baseball. Although it has never been proven, it has widely been rumoured that, in an effort to increase fan interest, Major League Baseball officials have, from time to time, allowed the use of baseballs that will fly further when hit. The logic here is that the use of such balls will create more long hits and more home runs, and lead to higher-scoring games that will attract more and more fans to live games.

And not only did speed clap skates create controversy, as many felt that the sport should be about skill and strength rather than technology (most skaters and coaches have accepted them as long as they are available to all skaters), but the full-body swimsuit also created contention. The Australian Olympic Committee challenged, unsuccessfully, the use of the suits, and they were banned from the U.S. Olympic swimming trials on the basis of their inaccessibility to all swimmers.

A High-Tech Dilemma

At issue is the relationship of sports organizations with technology. Engineers, with the development of new materials, are creating sports equipment that is dramatically changing performance; that is, the cost of participation, the skills necessary to succeed in a particular sport, and the injuries associated with that sport.

Sports organizations must continue to meet the needs of sport as a business. At the same time, they must allow innovation and encourage the growth of the sport to meet the needs of the athletes and the fans, as well as the media, while determining and then protecting the particular skills and traditions that are essential to their sport – a tough balancing act.

COMPUTER TECHNOLOGY IN SPORT

Over the last two decades the revolution in computer technology has become increasingly involved in sport, from the creation of sophisticated timing and measurement devices to online support for coaches. Strength, stamina, and motivation will always play a crucial role in a champion athlete's performance. However, as improved training regimes bring athletes closer to the limits of what is physically possible, winning or losing often hinges on technique, which today is being fine tuned by computer analysis and virtual practice.

Timing and Measurement Devices

In the first ever Olympic Games of 776 B.C., no times were recorded (as far as we know). In the 1912 Olympic Games, the first recorded times were for the 100-yard dash, made with a manual stopwatch that only timed to a fifth of a second. Now, timing device systems use video images and a "slit video" system positioned in line with the finish line, which scans this image 2000 times every second. This is linked to the starting pistols and blocks, and digital clocks, which enables an athlete's time to be measured to the nearest thousandth of a second.

At the 2002 Salt Lake City Winter Olympic Games, Seiko's timing teams took between 90,000 and 95,000 timing measurements. Among the new devices used by the biathlon and cross-country timing teams was a transponder system, whereby antennae laid under the snow registered the time of the passing of a transponder strapped to an athlete's leg. That time was communicated to the timing room and out to broadcasters, results services, and scoreboards in real time. The two contacts of the start gate in Alpine skiing also utilized new timing technology and were tuned to open within one-thousandth of a second. Seiko also used more speed traps and intermediate times on the course. For the first time ever, Seiko instituted what it called "Olympic time" – every PC, venue, and scoreboard was fully synchronized.

Personal Equipment

Computer technology has also provided an array of personal measurement and timing devices. Heart rate monitors are now available, consisting of a heart rate electrode placed around the chest. The information is transmitted to a watch-like device, some models of which can be plugged into a computer. Others can remotely transmit the data to a computer.

Pedometers are available to measure hip undulations or strides and thereby measure distance travelled. Most clip onto a belt or are worn around the ankle. A pedometer known as the Speed and Distance

Monitor measures not only the distance travelled but the speed at which it was covered. It is worn on a running shoe and works with a watch worn on the wrist. Yet another pedometer, known as SportBrain, measures hip undulations and calculates the number of steps taken. If worn with the heart rate device, heart rate is also recorded and all information collected is stored and can be accessed on a free website.

More serious athletes can choose from an array of electronic sport-specific measurement and timing devices. For runners, a timing gate system records lap and split times during performance testing, complete with database and analysis software. High jumpers can measure their vertical jump height. For swimmers, technology is available that offers precise control over stroke rate and pace as well as an audible training partner for solo swimmers. Radar guns offer a velocity profile and acceleration tests of any moving object, and a real-time system measures a cyclist's power output from both sides to help identify asymmetry in pedalling.

A hand-held, battery-operated timing computer system is available and is used in such sports as inline speed skating, swimming, track, athletics, and cross-country running. This system can be used with almost any device that is used to signal the start and finish of a race. Results can be sent to a PC or a scoreboard, or both, and is effective for races with staggered or common starts and for speed traps. This system can also be used for such sports as rally racing and skiing.

Coaching

Traditional coaching methods can now be enhanced with products from companies such as CANCoach Systems Inc., which has created a series of interactive multimedia coach and player education products that are available over the Internet. CANCoach Sport Planner is a library of computer-based sport resources for coaches and players. Sport-specific sets of drills and practice plans can be imported. Each drill can be viewed in stop-action or full-motion video, and is accompanied by a description of organization and key coaching points and diagrams that can be printed out and used at practice.

After developing and publishing two market versions of the Sport Planner for hockey, basketball, softball, netball, soccer, and rugby, CANCoach is currently creating new titles in the sports of cricket, yoga, and volleyball, with more to follow.

Yet now, even the human touch of the sports coach is being challenged by technology. International hockey player turned computer programmer Andrew Silver has developed the "computer coach," which will deliver information on diet and fitness over the Internet. Individual training schedules and methods to improve performance are given in response to the details of how much an athlete is exercising and attempting to train and how much he or she is eating.

Motion Analysis

Until recently, athletes' movements were scrutinized only by their coach. Now, the video camera with its slow-motion playback feature has provided a new motion analysis tool for analyzing the minutest movements that affect performance. Recent improvements in the speed and graphics capabilities of computers have taken this even further – a computer can now analyze a video film of an athlete.

For example, the Movement Analysis Company offers the NEAT (Never Ending Athletic Trainer) System to help actualize athletic performance using a video capture card and motion analysis software. The capture card translates the analog of video cameras, VCRs, and television to the digital of the computer and allows the inputting of footage directly into a PC. The software permits digital video clips to be manipulated, instantly retrieved, viewed in real time or frame by frame, and compared side by side or in sequence format for evaluation and comparison.

The graphics capabilities of the system allows the user to compute angles, sketch freehand, draw lines and circles or create stick figures, place a grid over the subject, and create a "swing trace" of relevant activity, a function which can also calculate velocity, such as golf club head speed or bat head speed. All computer analyses can be outputted to a VCR for home study.

In soccer, a software product known as Second Look 3P's (Player, Performance, Profile) can apparently analyze a player's performance throughout the match and provide details, such as completed and lost passes. Data can be input on an individual player during a live game or from a video, to any level of specification, and the events are graphically displayed on the field where they actually occurred. This technology is being used by some of the world's top soccer teams.

Similarly, a tracking system devised by Polhemus allows the capture of movement of any subject or object in real time using from one to thirty-two receivers. The motion data can then be used to interface with a computer or for real-time analysis. Applications include the analysis of physical limitations and optimizing movement, and is useful in rehabilitation. It can also be applied to the adjustment of such sports equipment as tennis racquets and golf clubs. It can provide quantitative data on acceleration, force, momentum, body posture, deformations, calculation of joint angles, and balance. In addition to biomechanical studies, this system has also been used to study how the performance, balance, and

Montreal Canadiens' goalie Jacques Plante prepares to don the face mask that helped him retain his 1959 title as the league's best goalie (CP PHOTO/Montreal Star).

movement ability of a goalkeeper and penalty kicker in soccer are affected by external noise, particularly the uni-directional movements of the goalkeeper.

Precision Analysis

The computer can also construct a detailed three-dimensional (3D) simulation of how the human body moves. The computer models an athlete's body as a linked system of segments. In an activity such as hurdle jumping or shot putting, the athlete's movements can be compared with the optimum movements needed for the perfect throw, jump, or hurdle until he or she has perfected the technique. Computer models of complex gymnastic movements can be used to help develop exercises that will increase the coordination and movement skills necessary for the athlete to perform the movement. These exercises can be mastered before trying the final movement, thereby reducing the risk of injury.

Innovative Sports Training has developed such a real-time 3D motion capture system, trademarked The MotionMonitor, for use in medical research and sports medicine labs, as well as in the performance evaluation of athletes at all levels. The 3D allows views of motion from every angle, and the system provides quantitative feedback to assist in training. According to the manufacturers, athletes can reference a prior optimum movement and then enter the graphic representation to experience its correct mechanics or focus on problem areas by isolating movements of certain parts of the body. The system aids in the analysis of performance by graphing the acceleration and velocity of body segments, by tracking the body's centre of mass, and by displaying not only the path of any point of the player's body or equipment but also the translucent planes that trace these paths.

Baseball players can use the system to analyze batting and pitching; golfers, to analyze their game as well as club rotation, club head speed, and 3D cocking angle; and football players, to analyze defensive and offensive drills as well as kicking and passing.

Computational Fluid Dynamics Computer Simulations

Shaved bodies and full-body swimsuits have been joined by advanced modelling and simulation software for USA Swimming in designing and helping their elite swimmers to achieve their perfect stroke.

When USA Swimming became aware of ground-breaking research that was being done to analyze a swimmer's strokes by using computational fluid dynamics (CFD) software, which is used to analyze fluid flow, they quickly consulted with the engineer to conduct research for them. Using software from Fluent Inc., computer simulations of a swimmer's hand and arm were run while altering certain variables, such as position of the hand and arm during a swim stroke, and water turbulence. Preliminary CFD results compared well with traditional physical experimental data developed using a flume, a wind tunnel, and a tow tank. Not only does CFD software allow the analysis of the rotation, acceleration, and deceleration of a swimmer's stroke, USA Swimming is hoping it will reveal how a swimmer's propulsion is generated.

Fluent's CFD software has been used by Team New Zealand to design the hull of their winning yacht in the 2000 America's Cup, by Benetton Formula 1 and Team Rahal in designing their race cars, and by Quicksilver (WRS) Ltd. in designing their craft. It has been used to analyze the trajectories of a soccer ball to determine optimum ball design and to analyze the benefits of V-style versus parallel ski jumping. USA Swimming is hoping that this research will help their swimmers gain an edge in the 2004 Olympics.

Virtual Reality

By the year 2010, if you want to learn how to do a triple backflip, you will slip into your virtual reality bodysuit and allow a computer to take you through the movements. You will practise your performance to perfection by adjusting your head a mere fraction or pulling in your elbows a little. The computer will allow for your adjustments and avoid any virtual accidents. And if you do injure yourself when doing it for real, then you need not lose any of your motivation while you recuperate. You can simply continue to practise in pain-free virtual reality.

Virtual reality technologies are already being used in athletic and gymnastic training. The Tectrix VR Bike, for example, combines state-of-the-art virtual reality software with aerobic fitness equipment. The machine integrates a 20-inch colour monitor, a recumbent exercise bike, and virtual reality software to provide a high level of interactivity. Resistance in pedalling increases or decreases depending on the terrain explored by the cyclist, whose weight is used to steer and lean in the virtual reality world. The system is also able to network groups of VR bikes, allowing cyclists to compete against one another.

The controls are located on the handlebars and are thumb operated. The cyclist can break, shift gears, and also view his or her statistics, which include the number of calories burned, length of workout, distance travelled, and elapsed time. Both a ground view and an aerial view of the route is available, which is useful to monitor the progress of the other racers.

The U.S. Olympic bobsled team also uses a virtual reality simulator to help them train. A computer runs code that calculates the dynamics of the sled in real time. The program is fed track data, such as that of Lillehammer or Salt Lake City, and driver steering input. It then solves the equations of motion and draws a picture on the screen from the driver's viewpoint. Data is also sent from the workstation to a motion control system, which plays a CD of the sounds of a bobsled going down a real run, rolls the cockpit, and provides force feedback to the driver through the steering handles. The simulator allows team members to practise on different tracks without travelling, to work on one particular section of a track, to make as many practice runs in a day as they choose, and to receive feedback on their performance after each run.

Augmented virtual reality brings computer-aided 3D-interactivity one step further. This virtual world allows for the interaction with and preparation for the "unknown," offers insight into product design for human interaction, and allows training for and maintenance of specific tasks. This system uses cyberware such as a head- or face-mounted display, software rendering, and, where finger movements are required, data gloves, all integrated using Vicon's motion-tracking technology.

"Virtualized" Reality

Television can give us a view into another part of the real world, such as a sporting event, but each viewer sees the event from the same viewpoint. Virtual reality immerses viewers in virtual worlds even though their bodies are still in the real world. Although each viewer can move independently in virtual reality, what has been created is not real but virtual. Computer Vision, however, offers virtual models of real-world events, trademarked as Virtualized Reality. With these virtual models, photorealistic views of a real event can be constructed from any viewpoint.

The position of video cameras is calibrated to capture the events. Then, by applying a computer vision technique called stereo, the shapes of the objects in each image are determined. This technique seeks corresponding features in the images and then triangulates them to determine the distance to the three-dimensional feature. The image-based shape models are then integrated into a complete single-shape model of the entire scene.

These models can be used to create totally new views of real events. The shape model is coloured by the information captured in the camera images. What is visible and what is not from a particular viewpoint is determined from the shape model, and what is visible is then projected or rendered into a virtual camera to create a new image of the real event. Each viewer, in effect, has a virtual camera under his or her control and can view an event from, for example, the middle of a baseball field or on a basketball court. For training purposes, Virtualized Reality dynamic event modelling offers a complete model of an event rather than a mere instructional video.

WHERE DO WE GO FROM HERE?

In this section, we have looked at some of the ways in which technology has been used to improve human performance on the playing field. The next time you watch participants in a sporting event use a piece of equipment, you will be able to consider some of the factors that went into the design of these items and why they are constructed the way they are.

In the next section, we will look at the role of training in human performance, by which the human body is made more efficient and better able to perform sports-related tasks. A number of important principles we have covered thus far, particularly those in Unit 1, are pertinent to the following discussion. Due to the many connections between training principles and the body's skeletal, muscular, cardiorespiratory, and energy systems, it is recommended that you review these sections briefly before continuing.

Donovan Bailey in the men's 100-metre semi-final at the World Track and Field Championships in Edmonton, Alberta, in 2001. After the race, Bailey did a lap carrying a Canadian flag to a huge ovation from the crowd at Commonwealth Stadium (CP PHOTO/Chuck Stoody).

13
Training Principles and Methods

**"With just under 2 weeks to go, I would have to change my plans. I wasn't getting fit fast enough....
Speed work was what I needed, and what I gave myself."**
— Ron Hill, marathon winner, as he attempted to qualify for the 1968 British Olympic team

KEY CONCEPTS

- Resting heart rate (RHR)
- Target heart rate (THR)
- Maximal heart rate (MHR)
- Heart rate reserve (HRR)
- Borg Scale of Perceived Exertion
- F.I.T.T. Principle
- One repetition maximum (1RM)
- Repetition maximum (RM)
- Principle of Overload
- Principle of Progression

- Specificity Principle (the S.A.I.D. Principle)
- Principle of Individual Differences
- Principle of Reversibility
- Principle of Diminishing Returns
- Periodization
- The General Adaptation Syndrome (GAS)
- Concurrent training
- Interval training

- Fartlek training
- Resistance training
- Plyometrics training
- Cold stress and heat stress
- Thermoregulation
- Heat exchange
- Acclimatization
- Proprioceptive neuromuscular facilitation
- Burnout and overtraining

Over the years, there have been tremendous reductions in the times of world-record performances in such sports as track and field, swimming, and cycling, due in large part to the increasingly sophisticated methods of preparing athletes for competition.

In 1954, for example, the Englishman Sir Roger Bannister became the first person to run a mile in less than 4 minutes, an achievement that is still hailed as one of the groundbreaking accomplishments in all of sport. Today, dozens of athletes break that barrier. An examination of Bannister's training log, as set forth in his autobiography, *The First Four Minutes*, is revelatory: although he was on the cutting edge of training techniques in his day, his regimen – both in terms of volume and intensity – seems almost primitive by modern standards.

What Is Training?

But what is training? In its simplest definition, training is a vehicle by which the human body is made more efficient. In the context of sports and physical activity, that means making the body better able to complete certain tasks – running, jumping, lifting, shooting a basketball, and the like – than it currently is. The process by which we accomplish this change is known as training.

This process and the changes it effects can take many forms, depending on the individual who is training, and on his or her goals. An individual's training needs could range from preparing for national- or Olympic-level competition, to gaining muscle in order to perform more effectively on the job or to improve one's appearance, to reducing fat and losing body weight, or to achieving a personal best time in swimming, running, or another individual sport at the recreational level.

Training needs vary greatly depending on both the objectives and the physical attributes of the individual involved. Given the wide number of variables that can come into play, the basics of training can become very complicated. As well, there seem to be several schools of thought about the best way to train for a certain sport or physical task.

One way of gaining a clear understanding of training is to use the analogy of a recipe. For example, there are many different recipes for preparing chocolate chip cookies. All have variations in ingredients, different baking instructions, and nuances in preparation. In the same way, there are certain aspects of training that are common and others that amount to variations in ingredients and instructions.

In designing any type of training program, the basic recipe that is widely used in the sports and fitness

Measuring Cardiorespiratory Fitness
Using heart rate and exertion to estimate exercise intensity levels

In order to set appropriate aerobic intensity, we must first find out how well our bodies consume oxygen.

Historically, if we did not have the luxury of being tested in a human performance laboratory, research suggested that we take a percentage of our VO_2max (how well the body uses oxygen during maximal exercise) based on a maximal or sub-maximal test (such as the 12-minute run, the step test, or by using the Borg Scale of Perceived Exertion). However, there are now various ways of establishing heart rate and estimating training intensity without having the use of a human performance laboratory.

Heart Rate

Resting heart rate (RHR) is the number of times the heart beats per minute during a resting state. The heart is most at rest when we are asleep; the best time to determine our heart rate is when we first awake. Record your resting heart rate for three days and then add these together and divide by three. This will give you an accurate average resting heart rate.

For example, morning one, RHR = 70; morning two, RHR = 68; and morning three, RHR = 66. RHR in this case can be fixed at 70 + 68 + 66 = (204/3) = 68. Detecting your pulse and therefore your heart rate is most easily done at your radial artery (which is located at the distal end of your radius) or at your carotid artery (which is located on the lateral sides of your hyoid bone in your neck).

Percentage of Maximal Heart Rate

This method is by far the most popular and widely used to determine a target heart rate range (THR), which is the number of beats per minute (bpm) at which your heart should be beating during aerobic exercise in order to facilitate cardiorespiratory improvement. For healthy individuals, this range is from 60 to 90 percent of maximal heart rate (MHR). The range within which an individual will train will of course vary,

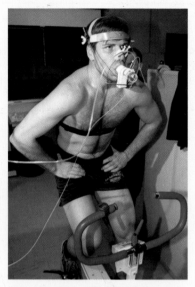

NHL player Doug Weight has his aerobic fitness level tested (CP PHOTO/ Edmonton Sun-Brendon Dlouhy).

depending on the individual's fitness level and training needs.

In order to obtain an estimate of your maximal heart rate (MHR), subtract your age from 220. For example, an eighteen-year-old may have a MHR of 220 − 18 = 202 bpm. To determine THR, this individual would take a percentage of his or her MHR, and target aerobic work between 60 percent on the lower end to 90 percent on the upper end. This calculation would be expressed as follows:

THR of 60% = 121 bpm
THR of 90% = 181 bpm

The American College of Sports Medicine (ACSM) recommends the following method for older individuals.

Karvonen or Heart Rate Reserve Method (HRR)

The Karvonen or heart rate reserve method (HRR) takes into account resting heart rate and is defined as the difference between MHR and RHR (MHR − RHR). The ACSM recommends the use of this method over the percentage of maximal heart rate

because it correlates well with laboratory values of VO_2 Reserve, which is the difference between VO_2max and VO_2 at rest.

Using this method, RHR is initially subtracted from MHR. Once the exercise intensity has been determined, RHR is simply added back on.

Using our example of the eighteen-year-old who has a RHR of 72 bpm and a MHR of 202, the application of the HRR formula would be as follows:

HRR = 202 − 72 = 130 bpm

Therefore, using the heart rate reserve method, a THR set at 50 percent of HRR would be

(130 x .50) + 72 = 65 + 72 = 137 bpm

whereas, a THR set at 85 percent of HRR would be

(130 x .85) + 72 = 110 + 72 = 182 bpm

Borg Scale of Perceived Exertion

The Borg Scale of Perceived Exertion is yet another way of determining one's level of exercise intensity. The scale starts at level 6 (no exertion at all) and finishes at level 20 (maximal exertion). Levels 12-14 on the Borg Scale correlate to 70-85 percent of MHR.

Although the Borg Scale lacks the empirical precision of HHR percentage calculations, it is a useful tool for people who are "in tune" with the relative exertion levels of different types of exercise.

Final Word

Current research tells us that individuals who are in poor aerobic condition will benefit more from working on the lower end of the percentage of their HRR and vice versa. Also, keep in mind that, whatever method you use to determine intensity, it is only an estimation of appropriate intensity levels − if you feel as if you are exercising too hard or too little, you probably are. The best advice is to reduce or increase your intensity and find a heart rate range that works best for you.

world is known as the F.I.T.T. Principle. Tied closely to this is the need for any good training program to take into account the body's three major energy systems – the anaerobic alactic, anaerobic lactic, and aerobic systems – and the specific energy demands of any particular sport. Finally, continuing the analogy just a bit further, the ingredients and instructions of any sound training program consist of several specific principles pertaining to training for physical activity (Overload, Progression, Specificity, Individual Differences, Reversibility, and Diminishing Returns).

THE F.I.T.T. PRINCIPLE

The F.I.T.T. Principle captures the four basic building blocks of any exercise plan:

- Frequency
- Intensity
- Type
- Time

These four dimensions apply to and need to be addressed when devising any fitness or training program. The acronym (F.I.T.T.), coined by David M. Chisholm, M.D., makes it easy to remember.

Frequency

The frequency of training sessions within an overall plan depends on several factors, including an athlete's age, conditioning, and competitive aspirations. For example, the Canadian Society for Exercise Physiology (CSEP), in its 1996 report "Personal Plan for Healthy Active Living," recommends from three to five sessions a week as the basis for aerobic fitness, with beginners starting at three sessions and building from there. However, this is clearly not enough for top-level athletes. For example, long-distance cyclists or runners often follow, during the heaviest periods of their training, a program that calls for more than fifteen sessions per week, including twice-daily runs or rides, plus from three to four weekly sessions in the weight room.

Clearly, the number of sessions a person is able to fit into their training schedule will be influenced by other commitments, and the amount of time he or she is able to devote to training. This means that people who design training schedules for themselves or others must take into account this big picture before plotting out a training plan that may be impossible given a person's work, school, or family schedule. Although the same exercise plan cannot be recommended for everyone, the concept of regularity should also be kept in mind when considering training frequency. It is far less beneficial, for example, to embark on a vigorous, seven-day program for a couple of weeks, followed by several months of inactivity, than it is to exercise a few times a week for many consecutive months.

Intensity

There are several ways of prescribing aerobic intensity levels within a training schedule. These include a percentage of VO_2max, the Borg Scale of Perceived Exertion, a percentage of maximal heart rate, and the Karvonen method or heart rate reserve (see the information box on page 188 for an in-depth look at how to use these methods).

The most accurate way of determining training intensity is to undergo a laboratory test to find out one's VO_2max or, more precisely, VO_2R, which is the difference of VO_2max and VO_2 at rest. Although this method is accurate, for most situations it is not practical as it requires a qualified instructor and expensive, sophisticated equipment. In Section 14, "Personal Fitness and Training," we will look at various ways of estimating VO_2max, using sub-maximal and maximal tests. VO_2max is also discussed in greater detail in "The Cardiovascular and Respiratory Systems" beginning on page 109.

Training intensities can also be determined by utilizing a basic assumption that is well recognized in the physiological community – that heart rate (HR) has a linear function with exercise intensity. Simply put, higher intensities equal higher HRs and also higher oxygen consumption. It should be noted that, while HR data is simple and easy to determine, it does have some inaccuracies. Exceptional and elite athletes should consider laboratory methods of assessing exercise intensity.

One of the most popular ways of determining weight-training intensity is to derive a percentage of an individual's one repetition maximum (1RM), which is the maximal amount of weight an individual can lift for one repetition. This method is very taxing on the body and should only be performed by experienced athletes under the supervision of a qualified fitness professional.

A less taxing variation requires an individual to complete a higher number of repetitions until they can no longer perform that particular exercise. This is known as a repetition maximum (RM). For example, a 10RM means that an individual can lift that particular weight ten times maximally. Once this number has been determined, a trainer can consult various tables to design appropriate programs for that athlete based on percentages of their projected 1RM throughout the training year. (See Table 13.1 and 13.2 for the procedure for performing a one or multiple repetition maximum test.)

Repetition Maximums

How to determine weight training intensity

The easiest way to determine how much weight you should lift is to carry a journal with a list of all the exercises that you would like to perform, then go to the weight room and experiment with each exercise, finding the appropriate loads and recording your findings. Although this sounds quite easy, it is extremely time consuming. Also, if proper rest times are not adhered to, inaccurate information will result.

An easier approach would be to calculate your one repetition maximum (1RM) or your multiple repetition maximum (e.g., lifting a weight eight or ten times maximally equals a 8RM or 10RM, respectively). Once you have determined your maximum intensity (i.e., how much weight you can lift once), you can then use a percentage of this to determine which loads to use and when to use them.

Here is the breakdown of the proper execution of these two methods of determining weight-training intensity. Keep in mind that your intensity level should reflect your current level of experience with weight training. For elite and exceptional athletes, the level of intensity will be based on the stage of periodization they are in and also on the demands of their sport.

For the average individual seeking to start or improve their current strength level, some of the same principles can be used when designing a program. Please refer to Table 13.1 for the ACSM recommended resistance-training guidelines. This will not only ensure quicker results, but it will also lead to less injury and a more knowledgeable approach to your weight-training program.

Once loads have been established, intensities can be determined and a program may be designed to work either muscle strength or endurance. This is accomplished by lifting low repetitions with high intensity (loads) or high repetitions with low intensity (loads), respectively. This, of course, will depend on your level of competence in weight training.

It is important that you consult a physician to obtain medical clearance before embarking on a weight-training program.

Table 13.1: Suggested procedure for determining one repetition maximum

Instructions: Before beginning, perform a total body warm-up followed by an exercise-specific warm-up of which you can easily perform 5 to 10 repetitions. Rest 1 minute then move on to Stage #1. For Stages #1 to #3, add 4-9 kg (10-20 lbs.) for upper body exercises, and 14-18 kg (30-40 lbs.) for lower body exercises.

Stage #1	Stage #2	Stage #3	Stage #4
Estimate a load of which the athlete can perform 3-5 repetitions. Allow a 2-minute rest. Move to Stage #2.	Estimate a load of which the athlete can perform 2-3 repetitions. Allow a 2-4 minute rest. Move to Stage #3.	Estimate a load of which the athlete can perform 1 repetition. If successful add 2-4 kg (5-10 lbs.) for upper body or 5-7 kg (15-20 lbs.) for lower body exercises. Allow a 2-4 minute rest. Move to Stage #4.	Continue adding or subtracting weight until the athlete can, with proper technique, complete 1 repetition. 1RM should be found within 5 attempts.

*This test should be conducted by a qualified fitness professional, and used by experienced athletes who have passed linear growth, especially when performing exercises that place a direct load on the spine.

Reprinted, by permission, from Baechle, T.R., Earle, R.W., & Wathen, D. (2000). Resistance training. In Baechle, T.R., & Earle, R.W. (Eds.), *Essentials of strength training and conditioning*, NSCA (p. 409). Champaign, Il.: Human Kinetics.

Table 13.2: Suggested procedure for multiple repetition maximum for projected 1RM

Instructions: When 1RM is not an option, then testing to find a 10-repetition maximum is a safe alternative for most athletes, as long as proper technique is used for the exercise tested. Before beginning, perform a total body warm-up, followed by an exercise-specific warm-up of 12-15 repetitions.

Stage #1	Stage #2
Estimate a load of which the athlete can perform 10 repetitions. If successful, allow a 2-4 minute rest and add 2-4 kg (5-10 lbs.) for upper body exercises and 7-10 kg (15-20 lbs.) for lower body exercises. If successful, allow a 2-4 minute rest. Move to Stage #2.	Continue adding or subtracting weight, as in Stage #1, until the athlete can, with proper technique, complete 10 repetitions. 10RM should be found within 5 attempts.

*This test should be conducted by a qualified fitness professional.

Reprinted, by permission, from Baechle, T.R., Earle, R.W., & Wathen, D. (2000). Resistance training. In Baechle, T.R., & Earle, R.W. (Eds.), *Essentials of strength training and conditioning*, NSCA (p. 409). Champaign, Il.: Human Kinetics.

Although the 10RM is a useful tool, it should only be used as a guideline as some values may be too low or high. Increase or decrease the load slightly until the desired repetitions are met. Refer to the guidelines recommended by ACSM on page 192 for novice and advanced-level weight-training.

Type

In Unit 1, we looked at the body's three basic energy systems ("Energy Systems and Muscle Fibre Types," beginning on page 81). The extent to which an athlete uses one or more of these systems determines his or her training needs, and depending on the needs of the athlete, the prescription for exercise will be either aerobic or anaerobic. In many sports, some combination of aerobic and anaerobic training is required in a proportion that is governed by the needs of the athlete and the requirements of the sport. As we will see in some of the principles of training outlined below, an athlete can train by performing activities directly related to his or her sport (i.e., ball-control drills in soccer, stick-handling exercises in hockey, sessions with a blocking dummy in football, or repeatedly shooting free throws in basketball) or activities that build strength and endurance without actually mimicking the skills needed in certain sports, such as weightlifting, resistance training, and plyometrics.

Time

Generally speaking, if an exercise is not maintained for long enough, it will not do the body much good physiologically. But how long one should perform a certain exercise within a training schedule will depend on a number of factors, including one's previous conditioning and overall goals. The CSEP paper recommends 20-60 minutes of continuous activity. People just beginning to exercise are often advised to keep early sessions of jogging or walking to 20 minutes or less until they can build up to longer durations. But elite or experienced athletes with certain training needs will often go beyond the 60-minute limit. Experienced marathon runners, for example, can complete 2 hours or more of continuous aerobic activity in preparation for the long haul that these endurance races demand. The same principle applies for those looking to build muscular mass through strength training: as the body adapts, athletes can take less time between sets, while enduring longer and longer workout sessions to increase conditioning.

Perhaps more than any other element of F.I.T.T., the amount of time one can devote to training is related to one's lifestyle. Attempting to fit exercise into a busy schedule can often be difficult, but it can pay dividends in terms of overall fitness and health that, in turn, will make other aspects of life easier. When designing a training program, however, it is crucial to be honest about the amount of time one has to actually complete the training on a day-by-day basis. Nothing is more discouraging than attempting to meet a pre-set time goal in training (e.g., "I will exercise for 30 minutes a day") only to discover that one simply cannot make sufficient time.

THE ROLE OF ENERGY SYSTEMS IN TRAINING

While some sports rely mainly on one energy system, many of them make heavy use of a combination of two or even three. Consequently, when it comes to training, different types of exercises and training methods will be needed in order to maximize an athlete's use of the required system.

- **The anaerobic alactic system.** This is the system from which the body gets most of its energy for quick bursts of about 10 seconds or less. It is best suited for providing energy for high-speed, explosive movements, such as short sprints; heavy, short-duration lifting; and explosive jumping. The energy is produced from the breakdown of ATP (adenosine triphosphate) and CP (creatine phosphate). Once the athlete has developed a level of aerobic base fitness, he or she can begin this type of training. Following the F.I.T.T. Principle, training for the anaerobic alactic system takes on the form of interval training, with no one repetition taking more than 10 seconds. Therefore, the energy stores of ATP and CP are depleted, and sufficient time must be allowed for ATP and CP to be regenerated. In general, it is recommended that the recovery time between work periods be equal to about five or six times the work period itself, with no more than 60 seconds total of work per set of repetitions (i.e., six bursts of 10 seconds), with, again, a pause long enough (3-10 minutes) between sets to rebuild energy stores.

- **The anaerobic lactic system.** This energy system is fuelled by glucose and glycogen, which the body relies upon for energy in bursts from between 10 seconds and 2 minutes, with a peak output of about 30 seconds. When this energy system is put into play, it produces lactic acid, which impedes athletic performance until it is dissipated. Athletes who hit their anaerobic threshold will quickly become familiar with its signs – very rapid breathing and a heavy feeling in the limbs are the two most recognizable. Again, athletes looking to train this system need a solid aerobic base and, in interval training, need to follow the F.I.T.T. Principle by using repeti-

Table 13.3: Resistance training guidelines

Individuals	Frequency	Recommended intensity	Number of sets	Number of repetitions	Duration of program
Strength (beginner)	3 times per week	70-80% of 1RM or 8-12RM	Greater or equal to 1	8-12	6 weeks or more
Strength (expert)	5-6 times per week	85-100% of 1RM or 1-6RM	Greater or equal to 3	1-6	12 weeks or more
Toning	3 times per week	60-70% of 1RM or 12-15RM	Greater or equal to 1	12-15	6 weeks or more
Endurance	3 times per week	Less or equal to 60% of 1RM or 12-20RM	Greater or equal to 1	15-20	6 weeks or more
Hypertrophy (expert)	5-6 times per week	70-75% of 1RM or 10-12RM	Greater or equal to 3	10-20	12 weeks or more

The American College of Sports Medicine recommends that older adults and children use multi-joint exercises, and exercise programs for children and adolescents should be supervised by qualified fitness personnel.

Adapted, by permission, from Heyward, V.H. (2000). *Advanced fitness assessment and exercise prescription* (4th ed., p. 137). Champaign, Il: Human Kenetics.

tions of between 10 seconds and 2 minutes. Recovery between repetitions and sets (with a total volume of 10-12 minutes recommended for most athletes) can be sped up greatly by gentle aerobic activity such as jogging and walking, as this has the effect of reducing the lactic acid buildup in the muscles.

- **The aerobic system.** The aerobic system supplies the body with the energy for long-term, steady exercise such as jogging, walking, long-distance cycling, and other endurance exercises. Since the aerobic system relies on the blood to bring energy – from carbohydrates, proteins, and fats – to the muscles, these muscles and the systems that support them need to be changed if aerobic improvements are to occur. Athletes can work on increasing the length of aerobic sessions and their intensity. These sessions can take the form of continuous, steady-state exercise of about 20 minutes or more, and aerobic interval training in which the intensity of the work periods is less

than is needed when working the two anaerobic systems, while featuring relatively longer work periods. As recommended above, athletes should do a certain amount of aerobic training to build a base of this kind of fitness before moving on to work on the anaerobic systems. Many coaches pay particular attention to the ability of their athletes to take up and use oxygen for aerobic exercise – in other words, their endurance. Known as the VO_2max, it is defined as the highest rate of oxygen consumed during maximal exercise. Clearly, the more intense aerobic exercise becomes, the higher the rate of oxygen consumption; as aerobic intensity reaches the point where an athlete can no longer take in increasing levels of oxygen, he or she reaches his or her maximal aerobic capacity. From a clinical view, then, the goal of every endurance athlete is to increase his or her VO_2max, as this will allow more and more oxygen to be utilized by the aerobic energy system to enhance performance.

OTHER PRINCIPLES OF TRAINING

Now that we have established the basic recipe for athletic training, we can look at the actual ingredients and instructions of sound training programs – in other words, how the F.I.T.T. Principle can be put into action. Although approaches vary somewhat, most experts agree that there are six basic training principles that complement F.I.T.T.:

- The Principle of Overload
- The Principle of Progression
- The Specificity Principle
- The Principle of Individual Differences
- The Principle of Reversibility
- The Principle of Diminishing Returns

The Principle of Overload

In order for physiological change to occur, the human body must be subjected to greater stresses than the ones to which it is accustomed. This is known as the Principle of Overload. Over time, all types of muscles – and especially the skeletal and cardiac muscles – will adapt to this overload, making the body able to perform more and more efficiently while handling greater and greater loads. (This principle, in fact, runs throughout our lives, as we adapt to a range of mental, emotional, and psychological factors.)

In the training context, the Principle of Overload applies to both aerobic and anaerobic exercise – the specific exercise one chooses, and just how much muscle overload one is subjected to, depends on one's training needs. For example, a person looking to train aerobically by beginning a modest jogging routine will, after a while, find that his or her body is able to run for longer and longer periods of time, and at greater and greater speeds as well. The same basic idea is true of a person attempting to train anaerobically by developing a weight-training regimen, as they discover their strength increasing after repeated lifting sessions. Of course, the opposite is also true – decreased exercise will mean that the gains achieved through overload sessions will start to disappear.

The Principle of Progression

When we examined the Principle of Overload above, we noted that a person engaged in regular training will gradually find his or her muscles adapting to more and more stress. Consequently, the Principle of Progression holds that in order for the overall – or absolute – effect of training to progress, an athlete must be subjected to greater and greater overloads, over time. Simply put, after an athlete has had the chance to adapt to a certain level of training, it will take increased stresses to effect a performance improvement. Merely staying at the same level will not lead to any kind of training – or competitive – progress.

For example, an athlete who begins a portion of their weight-training program by bench pressing a certain weight at a certain number of repetitions will not experience any progress unless one or both of those variables is raised. If all other factors remain constant, just doing the same reps at the same weight, week after week, may lead to an initial gain in strength, but will not yield any long-term progress. Since progression and overload are so closely combined in training theory, experts often refer to the Principle of Progressive Overload.

The Specificity Principle

The Specificity Principle, which at times is referred to as the S.A.I.D. (Specific Adaptation to Imposed Demand) Principle, holds that, in order for specific outcomes to occur, training exercises must be specific to those outcomes. Muscle adaptations will occur in athletes if their training regimen imposes a specific demand for improvement in a given skill. It is not enough to train generally by working on a certain set of muscles or a certain skill. In order to reach maximum training effect, the loads placed on the body have to mimic the actual sport as closely as possible.

Using an example of the Specificity Principle in action in aerobically based sports, one can look at the different training needs of long-distance swimmers and runners. Clearly, athletes competing in both sports need to have an extremely high degree of aerobic conditioning, because of the huge demands that both sports place on the cardiovascular system. But, according to this principle, simply working on becoming more and more aerobically fit is not enough. Because of the specific requirements of the sport, swimmers must train by swimming (developing upper-body strength, for example, to an extent not required by runners) and distance runners by running (developing strength in the load-bearing muscles of the leg) in order to achieve their best results.

An anaerobic example can be found in the training of someone attempting to develop the ability to dunk a basketball. Performing exercises in the weight room such as squats would go a long way towards building the explosive power needed to execute a basketball dunk, but squats would not mimic the footwork, hand-eye coordination, and ball-handling skills needed to perform the manoeuvre on the court. Only when each of these skills is combined with the leg-strength exercises is a person likely to get the full training effect.

The Principle of Individual Differences

The Principle of Individual Differences (also known as the Individuality Principle) rests on the fact that every athlete has a different physical and psychological makeup, which means that every athlete will have different needs when it comes to training. Several factors come into play in ascertaining these needs, including pre-training fitness level, specific requirements within a sport (e.g., the different requirements in football of a quarterback and a linebacker), age, gender, the ability of an athlete to recover from intense workouts, and previous susceptibility to injury.

In many sports, the training schedules of top athletes are published in magazines and books. While these schedules can be inspiring to younger athletes looking to learn more about how to train like the pros, they can also have another, more deleterious effect — one that further emphasizes the Principle of Individual Differences. In attempting to copy these advanced schedules, athletes at a lower training or competition level will often find themselves unable to complete even the simplest workouts, leading to frustration and, in some cases, injury.

The Principle of Reversibility

Have you ever heard the expression "Use it or lose it"? That is exactly the dynamic at play in the Principle of Reversibility – namely, that when a muscle or muscle group has undergone a period of training, and then has that training effect removed, the muscle(s) will, over a period of time, begin to lose the benefits the training brought to it in the first place. This is a fairly intuitive concept; anyone who has ever spent time attaining a certain level of fitness or strength, only to stop for a while, can attest to the fact that it does not take long to lose one's edge or to become out of shape.

The Principle of Reversibility also leads to two important and related concepts: atrophy and detraining. *Atrophy* occurs when muscles undergo periods of complete or near-complete inactivity. Not only does the muscle lose strength with disuse, but it can also lose size — as anyone who has even seen a limb that has been immobilized in a cast after an injury can attest. *Detraining* is the term used to describe a time period in which someone who has undergone a significant amount of training removes or reduces the effects of that training. This can occur for a number of reasons, including the inability to train because of an injury, lack of motivation, and the encroachment of other commitments on one's training time. Also, many athletes who compete year-round will take some time between competitive seasons to intentionally detrain as a way of avoiding the psychological burnout that can come with several months of intense training and competition, such as the multi-sport athlete who takes a couple of weeks of active rest between hockey and baseball seasons. While the physical effects of this detraining period may come into play, such athletes often find that the mental freshness that accompanies a limited period of detraining are worth a slight loss of fitness.

The Principle of Diminishing Returns

The Principle of Diminishing Returns is based on the fact that a person's training gains will reflect that person's prior level of training. Although it can sometimes be frustrating to an experienced athlete, in reality this principle describes the fact that a person who has had no, or relatively little, training is usually able to make significant gains in their levels of fitness, strength, and so forth while highly trained individuals usually make relatively small incremental gains in their performance through repeated training. Again, this scenario will be commonplace to anyone who has observed athletes at varying levels of training and experience.

Beginning joggers, for instance, often seem to make big gains in their fitness levels – they can, over a relatively short time, develop the ability to run farther and faster in their first year at the sport, especially if these early efforts involve significant weight loss. But an experienced distance runner can spend an entire training and racing season attempting to shave just a few seconds off his or her time in a long-distance race.

As an athlete's training experience accumulates, he or she often reaches what is called a performance plateau; that is, his or her progress in training and results in competition tend to level off, with improvements being minor or non-existent. When that occurs, many athletes begin looking for ways to go beyond that plateau, including ethical ones, such as adopting new training methods or developing a relationship with a new coach, and unethical ones, such as the use of anabolic steroids or illegal equipment to enhance performance.

TRAINING METHODS

Once athletes and coaches have established an understanding of the building blocks of training involving the F.I.T.T. Principle, the ways in which certain forms of training affect one or more of the three energy systems and the other essential principles of training, they can move on to an exploration of the actual methods of training. In other words, once the foundations are in place, it is possible to look at some of the ways in which these theoretical principles can actually be implemented by athletes.

Demonstration of the overload principle. The individual begins with body-weight squats.

The level of difficulty of the exercise is then increased by adding weights.

Essentially, athletes can train to increase speed, endurance, strength, agility, and flexibility. Indeed, most competitive sports require a mix of all of these traits. These are the main methods used in achieving these objectives through training:

- Periodization
- Concurrent Training
- Interval Training
- Fartlek Training
- Resistance Training
- Plyometrics Training

In Section 14, "Personal Fitness and Training," we will examine just how these methods can be utilized – and in many cases combined – to compile a customized program to suit an individual's training needs. But for the purposes of rounding out our look at physical training, let us examine some of the most commonly used training methods, with a brief explanation of how each one works and what training benefits it brings.

Periodization

Just a few generations ago, it was common for athletes, even those at the professional levels of competition, to approach their sports in almost a part-time fashion, with athletic commitments consisting only of a pre-season conditioning period, followed by their competitive season. Then, for the rest of the year, many North American professional hockey, football, baseball, and basketball players, for example, did not follow any kind of structured off-season regimen at all. That has all changed, as most serious athletes at all levels have elevated competitive sports training to a year-round endeavour in order to maintain a competitive edge. This does not mean, however, that training should be maintained at the same intensity, or be of the same type, for the whole year. Most athletes, after all, seek to hit some kind of a peak at a certain part or parts of the year, coinciding with the major championships at their level of sport.

Consequently, the concept of periodization comes into play – the breakdown of the overall training plan into distinct training periods in an attempt to maximize performances at peak times and to reduce the risk of injury and mental burnout. In seasonal sports, periodization occurs when coaches and athletes divide training periods into three major seasons: the off-season, the pre-season, and the in-season (or competition) periods. These three periods, when combined in the context of a seasonal sport such as hockey or football, are known as the macrocycle, but for Olympic

The General Adaptation Syndrome (GAS)
The basis of periodization theory

In the mid-1950s, stress researcher Hans Selye devised the theory of the General Adaptation Syndrome, also known simply as GAS.

This theory holds that, as humans, we have what Selye called, a "non-specific response to stress," meaning essentially that our responses to any kind of stress are more or less the same, regardless of exactly what that stress is. Selye's GAS theory incorporates three stages:

- the alarm reaction;
- the stage of resistance; and
- the stage of exhaustion.

The alarm reaction stage is the one that prompts what is often known as the "fight or flight" response from our central nervous system. In athletic training, this alarm stage is usually manifested in the body's initial "shock" at increased loads and, in competition, is usually represented by a drop in performance.

The stage of resistance is often called the "adaptation" phase, reflected in competition by a relative increase in performance, as the body becomes accustomed to increased loads.

In the stage of exhaustion, the body is finally no longer capable of adapting to increased loads of stress, meaning that performance will hit a "plateau" and can even decrease due to injury or sheer physical exhaustion and overtraining.

Hans Selye discovered that humans need adequate levels of stress in order to enhance performance. This is clear in the Overload Principle, which states that, in order for adaptation to occur, the body must be stressed incrementally. When you become accustomed to that level, then you move on to more difficult problems. With each move, the mind is stressed and challenged to adapt to greater "loads." Over time, if you have the desire and progressively overload, you will achieve a high level of competency. For athletes, the trick is to ascertain what the right level of stress is for each individual, as everyone handles stress differently.

The two types of stress are eustress (the good one), which is the ideal amount of stress to initiate adaptation, and distress (the bad one), which overtaxes and injures the body. Some athletes can handle a large amount of stress while others crumple under the same amount. In the "Psychology of Sport" section on page 267, we look at various ways of combating and handling stressful sporting situations. In order to become a great athlete, one must know what one's stressful limits are for physical, psychological, emotional, and mental well-being and work at increasing those levels.

athletes, the macrocycle could be as long as four years. It is even possible to conceive of an athlete's entire career in terms of periodization with skill and/or motor development early in life; followed by gradual improvements in skill, strength, and endurance as the athlete gets older; culminating in the athlete's competitive peak years as an adult.

Within these macrocycles are smaller mesocycles, shorter periods of time (typically measured in weeks or months), which are, in turn, divided into transition, preparatory, and competition periods. The transition period takes place after the last in-season competition has taken place, at the beginning of the off-season. Many coaches call this the active rest period, since athletes entering it have usually just completed a tough competitive season. The emphasis is on unstructured, recreational exercise – maintaining some level of fitness while allowing some downtime from a structured training and/or competition schedule.

The preparatory period takes place during a sports off-season, when competition generally does not occur. This period has three phases in itself: (1) the hypertrophy/endurance phase, which is also known as the base phase, when high-volume, low-intensity training occurs in an effort to establish an endurance base for further higher-intensity training; (2) the strength phase, also occurring in the off-season and characterized by increased intensity and volume; and (3) the power phase, now in the pre-season, when training reaches near-competition levels, and as training intensity increases while volume begins to drop.

Then, in the competition phase, training moves to an even higher intensity, with volumes dropping even further. Also, an emphasis is usually placed on training sessions that emphasize strategy and tactical planning. In sports such as track and field and rowing, the competition phase is relatively short; in the major professional sports, it can last for many months. Typically, within the competition period, coaches advocate developing training microcyles – short periods that usually last from one to seven days. During a seven-day cycle leading up to a major competition, an athlete's most intense training will occur in the first three to four days, with a tapering, and possibly a complete rest, just prior to the competition.

Concurrent Training

Throughout this section, we have looked at ways in which the body's energy systems come into play during training – for example, how steady-paced swimming or running is a good way to further aerobic conditioning. But it is possible to train multiple energy systems by performing different types of training simultaneously. Known as concurrent training, this practice refutes much of the conventional wisdom of earlier generations, when it was believed by many coaches that endurance athletes could not benefit from strength or power training, and athletes who trained primarily to improve strength and power should avoid all endurance training.

What is more, concurrent training can be of special benefit to people who are training more for general fitness than for a specific sport, since combining resistance and endurance training appears to maintain and improve lean muscle mass while decreasing fat. In short, concurrent training is an ideal way of losing and keeping off weight and, in general, toning up.

Interval Training

Interval training is based on the idea that the body's energy systems can make both aerobic and anaerobic gains, not only by steady, uninterrupted exercise, but also by alternating periods of relatively intense exercise with periods of recovery within the same workout. In many endurance sports such as swimming, cycling, and running, interval training is the preferred method of allowing the body to become accustomed to lactic acid buildup and anaerobic loads.

In general, interval training involves variables: the length of the intense period, its intensity, the length of the rest interval, and the number of repetitions to be done. All of these factors can be varied in accordance with the athlete's training needs. For example, a typical interval workout for a recreational runner looking to improve his or her 10-kilometre performance would be from six to eight repetitions of 1,000 metres (usually done on a running track or measured course for accuracy) at the athlete's goal pace (calculated by taking their goal time for the 10-kiometre race and dividing by ten to get the training pace for 1 kilometre), with a 2-minute jogging break between the repetitions. Of course, it is easy to see how a sprinter or middle-distance runner would vary this workout so that he or she would be running many more repetitions of much shorter segments, much faster and with probably less rest in between the sprints. Depending on what stage in the athlete's season the interval workout comes (see "Periodization" above), athletes and coaches will change these variables to develop speed, endurance, and so forth as needed.

Fartlek Training

For many athletes, interval training can be an overly intense form of athletic preparation, especially when used repeatedly, week in and week out, within a comprehensive training schedule. In response to this, the Fartlek training method was developed in the 1940s by Swedish runners; the term literally means "speed play."

In its general form, Fartlek accomplishes the same basic physical goals as interval training, but without the latter method's rigid numerical controls. In this form of training, the emphasis is on alternating intense bursts of effort with recovery periods. But unlike interval training, where the intensity and length of the hard effort, the length of the rest interval, the number of repetitions, and so on are all predetermined, Fartlek encourages a more free-form session, with athletes changing these variables according to the terrain or simply according to how they feel.

For example, a cross-country runner may run a Fartlek session through the woods by deciding to sprint the uphills, recover on the downhills, and then run at near-maximum effort on certain flat stretches while slowing to a steady pace on other flat sections.

Resistance Training

The most common form of resistance training is weightlifting — where the weight literally provides resistance to the muscles, which in turn work to move the weight, thereby gaining strength in accordance with the Principle of Overload, which we examined above. Not only can this form of training lead to muscle mass gain and strength, but when it is done properly, it can lead to improved flexibility and range of motion and prevent injury to key muscles and tendons. Coaches and athletes choose resistance exercises based on the desire to work either several muscle groups (known as structural exercises) or specific ones, which isolate a single joint or muscle group (known as body-part exercises).

There are a number of variables to take into account when considering a weight-training program, including:

- the order in which exercises are to be done (most experts suggest moving from the large muscle groups to the smaller ones);

- the number of repetitions to be done in each lifting set;

- the number of sets of each exercise;

- the amount of rest to be taken between each set;

- the intensity of the exercises (the training load, or amount of weight lifted in each repetition);

- the volume of each workout (the total amount of weight lifted); and

- the number of training sessions in a given period (the frequency).

Emil Zatopek
Interval training pioneer

Today, an intense, varied training program is a must for any world-class athlete. But just two sporting generations ago, even elite athletes lacked a proper understanding of what constituted the right kind of training, both in terms of intensity and in terms of the methods that could be used to achieve improved results in competition.

A champion runner of the 1940s and 1950s went a long way towards increasing much of this understanding in his sport. His name was Emil Zatopek, and he represented the country then known as Czechoslovakia (now two separate countries, the Czech Republic and Slovakia). Born in 1922, he tasted his first Olympic glory in 1948, finishing second in the 5,000-metre, and winning the 10,000-metre event.

But that was just the beginning. He became a national hero and an international running legend with his wins in the 5,000-metre, the 10,000-metre, and the marathon race at the 1952 Olympic Games in Helsinki, Finland. To this day, he is the only runner to have won all three events at the same Games. By the end of his career in 1958, he had set eighteen world records. (As an historical note, Zatopek's wife, the javelin thrower Dana Zatopekova, also won her event at the 1952 Olympics, making the pair the first married couple to win gold medals at the same Games.)

Surprise Tactics

He also gave the running scene a boost in popularity with his characteristic running style – from the hips down, he was an efficient running machine, but above the waist, Zatopek ploughed around the track with his head rocking from side to side, grimacing as if in complete agony, with arms pumping furiously. Fans loved the show, and the veteran American sportswriter Red Smith once wrote that Zatopek "ran like a man with a noose around his neck," and called him "the most frightful horror spectacle since Frankenstein ... on the verge of strangulation; his hatchet face was crimson; his tongue lolled out."

Emil Zatopek, shown at Amsterdam's Olympic Stadium, revolutionized the world of long-distance running through his innovative – and demanding – interval training methods (AP PHOTO).

The reason for Zatopek's success is explained partly by his tremendous determination in competition, but also by his tremendous innovations in training. Although the distance running world had known about interval training since it was developed for athletes in that sport by German researchers in the 1930s, it was not widely used until Zatopek began achieving success through a training regimen that revolved primarily around this form of serious preparation.

Zatopek's interval training regimen not only changed the way long-distance runners prepare for competition, it also revolutionized the way they actually ran during their races. Before his time, most distance runners used one of two tactics: they either outran their rivals right from the start, taking the lead from the starter's gun and never relinquishing it, or they remained directly behind the leader of a given race for most of the distance, and then sprinted past the leader some time during the final lap of a 5,000- or 10,000-metre track race. Zatopek introduced a new approach.

Because Zatopek experimented with so many changes of pace in his training – from sprinting to jogging and at speeds ranging from flat-out to slow recoveries – he became used to a wide range of paces, which he then incorporated into competition. Imagine the surprise of his rivals who were used to running at a relatively steady pace for most of their events, when they saw this grimacing Czech surging past them, virtually sprinting for an entire lap in the middle of a race and building a big lead, only to slow to a jog for a while, followed by another sprint.

If tales of Zatopek's huge training loads did not intimidate them, this on-again, off-again tactical approach, made possible by his radical training methods, certainly would have.

National Hero and International Legend

Zatopek became a national hero among his fellow Czechoslovakians. Sporting legend has it that, in the years following his retirement from competitive running, Zatopek opposed the Communist government in his country, he was stripped of the prestigious military title he had be given, and was forced to work as a garbage collector.

When his horrified countrymen saw him hoisting cans into the back of sanitation trucks, they ran into the street and insisted on loading their own garbage. After the fall of Communism, Zatopek was restored to his former glory, and even appeared, courtesy of archival footage, in a television commercial for Adidas footwear in the late 1990s.

In the decades that followed, runners, coaches, and exercise physiologists would refine Zatopek's pioneering work with the help of advances in science and increased understanding of how the human body responds to stress. But it took this early champion runner (who passed away in 2000) to pave the way with his revolutionary training methods – backed up with tremendous results on the track.

Plyometrics Training

Also known as stretch-shortening exercises because of its ability to stretch and then shorten the muscles through exercise, plyometrics training is a form of resistance training that its advocates use for its potential to develop strength and power. In Unit 1 (Section 3), we looked at how muscle fibre can both expand and contract when the limbs are put through a range of motion. This expansion and contraction is the basis of plyometrics, which utilizes a series of drills, usually using the body's own weight (although sometimes weights such as a medicine ball or weighted vests are used) as the overload.

Squat-jumps, box drills, bounding, hopping, and ballistic medicine ball drills are examples of plyometric exercises, all of which use a pre-stretch, or countermovement to build up muscular energy before an explosive movement releases it. Plyometrics training should be performed only after the athlete has developed a solid resistance training base.

THE EFFECT OF ENVIRONMENTAL FACTORS ON TRAINING

Many books and articles on training seem to assume that all exercise regimens will take place in ideal conditions. But in reality, environmental factors – such as extreme temperatures, high humidity, high altitude, or air quality – need to be taken into consideration when it comes to athletic training.

In some cases, exercising in certain extreme environmental conditions can be very dangerous and even fatal. Let us examine a number of ways in which the environment can have an impact on training.

Body Temperature Regulation and the Environment

Under normal circumstances, the human body maintains a fairly normal temperature range, with core (rectal) measurements fluctuating between 36°C upon waking from a night's sleep or in cold weather and 40°C during hard exercise or in very hot weather. Generally, the average human temperature is about 37°C. But the body cannot adapt to vast fluctuations in temperature, which are often the result of extremes in external, or environmental, temperatures. A person can withstand a drop in core body temperature of about 10°C, but a rise of only 5°C. Beyond these levels, conditions known as cold stress and heat stress can set in, and both have proven fatal in many cases directly related to sport situations. There have been several highly publicized cases, for example, of football players, who practice wearing heavy protective equipment, collapsing in extreme heat (one such player, the Minnesota Viking's Korey Stringer, died during a hot-weather practice session in the summer of 2002), and of marathon runners who have also collapsed in hot conditions. In other words, the body's ability to regulate its core temperature – known as thermoregulation, or maintaining a thermal balance – is essential to our survival.

Heat Transfer

The body's temperature is maintained by a group of neurons located at the base of the brain, called the hypothalamus. Essentially the hypothalamus is able to regulate body temperature by means of thermal receptors in the skin and the blood. Heat generally passes from the body to the outside environment, and in most cases, the hypothalamus is able to regulate core temperature easily. But in extremely cold weather, massive heat loss can occur, causing the core temperature to drop to dangerous levels unless the body can increase heat production and decrease heat loss – both of which can be stimulated by exercise, and which do not occur as steadily when the body is at rest.

In extremely hot conditions, the opposite danger is present – the body may "overheat" so that the core temperature soars to dangerously high levels, preventing key organs in the body from functioning and causing an overall "shut down" in bodily functions, including respiration and heartbeat. In order to combat this, the body promotes a process called heat exchange, which can be accomplished by radiation (the emission of radiant heat from the body into the cooler environment); conduction (the transfer of heat through a liquid, solid, or gas – in the case of exercising in the heat, this can be accomplished by dousing oneself in cool water); convection (air movement around the skin); and evaporation (water – i.e., sweat – vaporization from the skin into the environment).

In most cases, evaporation is the body's major mechanism for cooling off in the heat. But special care should be taken while attempting to train in conditions that combine high temperatures with high humidity levels. In these conditions, the air vapour pressure is close to that of sweat- or water-covered skin, and this means that perspiration does not have a chance to vaporize and thus cool the skin. In such conditions, excessive moisture loss, known as dehydration, and overheating can easily occur.

The Role of Clothing

In most sporting situations, clothing plays a key role, including protecting the athlete against cold, rain, or sun, and as a means of identifying teammates and opponents. But in terms of temperature regulation in extreme conditions, clothing can sometimes have an adverse effect on an athlete. In the heat, excessive clothing and equipment can block the body's cooling mechanisms, preventing the dissipation of heat and impeding the evaporation of perspiration. Some studies have shown, for example, that the tremendous amount of gear worn by football players can effectively block 50 percent of the body's surface from cooling itself. In hot weather, loose clothing – which promotes moisture evaporation from the skin – is recommended, as is lighter-coloured clothing, which reflects heat rays more effectively than dark gear.

People whose sport training program or exercise regimen calls for working out in cold weather need to be especially careful when the temperature drops, and conditions are made even more extreme by high wind-chill values. Consequently, clothing becomes a real concern, and many experts recommend a "layered" approach – the wearing of a few, thin layers over the legs and trunks. It is especially helpful if these layers are made of fabric (such as polypropylene) that "wicks" moisture away from the skin to the outside of the garment, where it can evaporate quickly. If moisture is absorbed by a dense fabric such as cotton, it can lose up to 90 percent of its insulating capacity. At the same time, a multiple-layered approach can create "pockets" of warmth and allow an athlete simply to strip off layer after layer as he or she starts to heat up.

Exercise, Atmospheric Pressure, and Altitude

The air we breathe is not the same throughout the world. That is because the density of oxygen molecules found in the ambient air around us can change considerably as the barometric pressure decreases at increasingly higher elevations. In other words, as we start to climb above sea level, there is less and less oxygen in the air. Consequently, there will also be less oxygen in the blood of an exercising individual, and thus less chance of him or her achieving full performance results.

Even a small rise in altitude will cause a decrease in athletic performance in oxygen-dependent endurance events. A rise in elevation of about 2,000 metres above sea level, for example, allows the hemoglobin in the blood to retain 90 percent of the oxygen it can use at sea level – a reduction that has very little effect on a resting person. But as was borne out at the 1968 Mexico City Olympic Games, such a relatively minor rise (Mexico City is approximately 2,300 metres above sea level) has the potential to adversely affect the performance of endurance athletes, a result that is invariably borne out in international competitions at high altitudes. To this day, for example, not a single world running record for men or women at distances of 800 metres or greater has ever been set at high altitude. Interestingly, though, athletes competing in anaerobic events in which the body's capacity to utilize oxygen is not crucial – such as a sprint in track and

field – tend to record faster times at higher altitudes, due to the decreased air pressure and thus decreased resistance to their bodies as they speed along.

Altitude Acclimatization and Training

There has long been a debate as to whether athletes who have spent their lives at sea level can adjust, through training, to conditions at higher altitudes. This adjustment, over time, is known as acclimatization, and added to this debate is the speculation as to whether or not sea-level athletes can increase their oxygen-carrying capacities by training at higher altitudes. If, the theory goes, a sea-level athlete trains at a higher altitude, adapting physiologically to conditions in which the air is "thinner" and then returning to sea level to compete, the increased oxygen-carrying capacity he or she has developed during the acclimatization process should allow him or her to realize improved performance.

Certainly, training at higher altitudes has been shown to improve an athlete's ability to compete at such an altitude. But the results of returning to sea level to compete after a period of altitude training are inconclusive, based on tests that have been conducted on athletes' VO_2max (maximal oxygen uptake) levels. Since it is simply impossible to train as hard at higher altitudes as it is at sea level (with reduced oxygen, a person cannot run or cycle as fast or as far with the same output of energy), this reduction in absolute intensity will have negative effects (such as a reduction in muscular power and endurance) that cannot be offset by gains in increased oxygen-processing ability. Some athletes refer to this as a "detraining" effect.

Consequently, some endurance athletes adopt what is known as the "live high, train low" approach, reasoning that, while spending their non-training time at altitude can still have acclimatization benefits, it is better to realize the full physiological benefits of training at sea level. Combining the two approaches can take place in areas where it is easy for an athlete to travel back and forth between higher and lower altitudes, or the "live high, train low" strategy can be simulated by various devices that simulate altitude conditions. Many endurance cyclists and runners, for example, sleep in hyperbaric chambers and "altitude tents" that simulate the barometric pressure and reduced oxygen of high altitudes, while training in normal sea-level venues.

Air Pollution

While training and living at differing altitudes offers an important example of how the composition of the air we breathe can have a direct impact on the effects of training, a much more pressing concern for most athletes is having to train in air that is in some way contaminated by pollutants, such as lead, ozone, nitrogen dioxide, carbon monoxide, and sulphur dioxide.

Those who exercise in conditions in which levels of these and other chemicals in the ambient air are high suffer a much greater health risk from these pollutants than those who are not active, because they are taking in, through respiration, more air – up to ten times more than a stationary person – and therefore breathing in higher amounts of pollutants. Added to the risk is the fact that, while exercising, we tend to "gulp" air more freely through the mouth and not the nose, which is a much better filter of pollutants. Worse still, groups such as children, the elderly, and people with asthma and heart and lung problems – already at high risk in polluted environments – are increasingly vulnerable when they are exercising, especially when high temperatures and extreme humidity prevail.

Health problems can arise when excessive amounts of pollutants are brought into the body through respiration and passed into the lungs, heart, and other key organs. These include diminished breathing ability, chest pain, coughing and wheezing, a reduction in the body's ability to fight infection, an aggravation of asthma, emphysema, and other breathing problems, heart disease and other physical irritations.

In all, the picture looks bleak for those hoping to train in environments in which air pollution is a problem – especially when you consider a recent survey in which one in every five Canadians was found to have some kind of respiratory ailment, and approximately one in four Canadians believed that air pollution was causing them serious health problems.

Several organizations devoted to lung and cardio-respiratory health – such as the Canadian Lung Association and the American Lung Association – however, suggest that people who live in polluted areas and want to train for sport or exercise outdoors can follow a set of guidelines that will reduce their health risks. These include:

- training during cooler weather, avoiding the May-to-September "smog season" if possible;

- training during times when there is less vehicular traffic, thus reducing exposure to carbon monoxide levels; also avoiding training during afternoon hours, when the sun is at its highest and ozone smog formation is at its peak;

- keeping informed by news and radio reports regarding high-risk days when the "air quality index" is considered too high to exercise; and

- whenever feasible, exercise in an appropriate indoor location (a gym or exercise club). This might change the workout significantly (i.e., running on a treadmill instead of outdoors), but you may benefit from better quality air.

OTHER IMPORTANT FACTORS

In addition to the various training principles we have examined above, there are a number of other key factors that must be taken into consideration in any sound training regimen.

Rest, Recovery, and Avoiding Injury

Even though many highly motivated athletes would like to, it is impossible in most sports to train at full intensity every day. In high-impact sports, such as running, basketball, or soccer, the body's weight is borne by the legs. The constant pounding on the muscles and joints means that, without a rest component built into a training schedule, some form of injury is almost inevitable. Even in non-weight-bearing sports such as swimming or rowing, it is impossible to train intensively every day without a break to rejuvenate tired, overworked muscles.

Physical injury is likely in a training regimen that does not contain a rest component, as is mental fatigue. Since both of these factors have to be avoided, coaches – especially those in the endurance sports – often design training schedules that revolve around one high-intensity day, followed by one rest day. This hard-easy schedule is based on the physiological principle that at least one day of recovery is needed for every intense workout. Some coaches suggest that two easy days are necessary after each hard day.

There is a well-known saying in the sports world in relation to injuries: "It is better to be 90 percent fit than the best-trained spectator in the stands." In other words, too much stress on the body in preparation for competition can lead to injuries or illness, and all of the athlete's training will have been wasted. In addition to rest, there are several complements to a training program that can reduce, although likely never eliminate, the risk of injury.

- **Stretching.** Most athletes follow a routine of stretching exercises to increase muscle flexibility. Flexibility is crucial for an athlete participating in a sport that involves muscles that are put through a wide range of motion; for example, diving or hurdling. However, in all cases, flexibility leads to muscles that are more supple and less prone to injury.

  Stretching is generally divided into three major styles: ballistic stretching, static stretching, and what is known as PNF, or proprioceptive neuromuscular facilitation. Ballistic stretching is done by means of bouncing motions in which the muscles are rapidly stretched and then immediately relaxed. Static stretching represents the opposite kind of muscle activity, as the muscles are slowly stretched, then maintained in the

Jennifer Robinson competes in the ladies short program during the World Figure Skating Championships in Vancouver, March 2001 (CP PHOTO/Chuck Stoody).

stretched position for several seconds (exactly how long it should be held is a matter of considerable debate – some exercise physiologists maintain that a "hold" of 5-10 seconds is sufficient, while others contend that 30-60 seconds represents the correct length of stretch). Finally, **proprioceptive neuromuscular facilitation (PNF)** involves intense isometric contractions – involving no movement of the bones connected by the muscle about to be stressed – followed by static stretching. Research has shown that each of these stretching techniques can increase the range of motion of a muscle's or group of muscles. It is worth noting, though, that from an injury-prevention perspective, ballistic stretching is considered to be the riskiest because of the stress it puts on the muscles being stretched.

- **Warm-up and cool-down session.** Most coaches also advocate a warm-up period to prepare the muscles for strenuous activity, and a cool-down period following a workout to dissipate lactic acid buildup.

- **Weight training.** Many athletes also follow a weight-training regimen, even though they may not be involved in an explosive, power-driven sport. Even for endurance athletes, the principle is the same: a body with well-toned, balanced muscles is better insured against injury than an unbalanced one in which only certain sets of muscles are developed.

- **Physical therapy.** Finally, many competitive and non-competitive athletes alike avail themselves of some form of physical therapy to prevent, or treat, injury. Professional athletes have access to top-level facilities for the treatment of injuries and minor aches and pains. These include X-rays to examine possible broken bones, whirlpool baths to treat inflamed tendons, massage, and even surgical procedures if the injury is serious enough. Less serious athletes partake of a wide range of treatments as well, including massage, physiotherapy, ultrasound, and chiropractic care. A certain amount of joint stiffness, muscle strain, or just plain fatigue is to be expected from a regular training regimen, especially an intense one designed to prepare an athlete for competition. It is not always easy to determine whether it is wise to train through or to ease back on a pre-set workout schedule. For the athlete and coach, the trick is to know when to reduce the intensity of the athlete's training before serious injury occurs. Hindsight, as the saying goes, is always 20/20.

Maintaining an Interest Level

Along with finding the right levels of frequency, intensity, time, and the right type of training (as per the F.I.T.T. Principle), those who wish to remain active need to ensure that the activity corresponds to their psychological needs. Some participants are content, for example, to jog or skate alone several times a week, relishing the solitude of this activity. Others, however, may find themselves growing bored and are unlikely to continue the activity unless they can do so in the company of friends. Some people are attracted to the camaraderie of group activities, while others prefer to exercise alone, and many enjoy a mix of solo and group exercise. Also, while many enjoy relatively time-consuming, repetitive activities such as running, cross-country skiing, rollerblading, and cycling, others prefer more varied pastimes.

The key is to find an activity or a program of varied activities that will maintain the participant's interest and allow for a high level of enthusiasm.

Sleep and Rest

Anyone who has tried burning the candle at both ends knows that exercise and activity are not effective if they are not accompanied by a sufficient amount of recovery time, including sleep. It is generally considered crucial for people to get regular, uninterrupted sleep at night in sufficient quantity to regenerate the key bodily systems that are needed during the day.

In smaller children, sleep is a process that stimulates bodily growth. For adults, lack of sleep can lead to various symptoms, including slowed reaction time, general irritability, difficulty in performing regular tasks, and overall fatigue. There is also some evidence to suggest that lack of regular sleep can lead to insomnia, weight gain, and possibly even irregular heartbeat patterns.

Just how much sleep an individual requires is not always easy to establish. Many people seemingly have to fit sleep into a busy schedule of work and other activities. Others find their sleep interrupted, and still others find themselves awake at odd hours due to shift work. Most experts agree, though, that if a person does not usually wake up feeling refreshed after a regular night's sleep, he or she is not getting enough sleep.

AVOIDING BURNOUT AND OVERTRAINING

Anyone who is familiar with training practices at just about any level of sport will also be familiar with the concept of **burnout and overtraining** – the situation in which many athletes find themselves after long periods of training and competition. In this condition, the very act of training and competition can seem like an unendurable chore, injuries can occur, and performance, understandably, drops off. (In the context of training alone, this phenomenon is often known simply as "overtraining.")

There have long been two schools of thought about the nature of athletic burnout. One considers it to be a purely physiological phenomenon; the other, a psychological one. The former school of thought holds that, after long periods of accumulated fatigue (i.e., repeated training sessions and competitions without proper in-between rest), the body simply "gives up" and can no longer operate on a high level. Adherents to the latter school maintain that, after similarly long periods of tough physical demands, athletes cannot maintain a high enough level of enthusiasm and motivation, causing them to "give up" in the psychological sense. It is simply too difficult to "get psyched up."

Today, most experts agree that burnout is caused by a combination of these two factors. Indeed, current trends in advice for athletes who are attempting to prevent burnout seek to take both physical and psychological factors into account. These include

- detecting early signs of physical and/or mental fatigue and incorporating extra rest periods into training and racing schedules;
- using the principle of periodization, breaking the athlete's training and/or competitive schedule down to allow for "off-seasons" in between periods of intense work;
- revising training and competitive goals to offer new challenges;
- altering the specific demands of competition to allow the athlete to continue to work towards long-term goals while introducing an element of "freshness" into his or her competitive participation (e.g., allowing a long-distance runner to compete in middle-distance races as a way of honing his or her speed in a competitive situation, or allowing a basketball forward to play at the guard position for a limited time as a way of working on ball-handling skills); and
- working on ways to develop awareness among coaches and athletes that burnout may be setting in by encouraging dialogue about fatigue, nagging injuries, lack of enthusiasm, and/or motivation, and so on.

Adding to the confusion about athletic burnout are numerous examples of athletes who, year after year, season after season, seem to keep coming back to record ever-improving performances while showing no signs of slowing down. One likely reason for the success of the "anti-burnout" athlete is that he or she may have developed certain mental strategies for keeping their enthusiasm levels high. These might include setting a relatively large set of personal goals that act as "signposts" along the path to athletic progress. Another popular strategy among these veteran athletes who never seem to suffer from burnout is the adoption of a philosophy of achievement that stresses lowered expectations – they seek a more gradual pattern of improvement, as opposed to a "shoot-for-the-stars" approach.

WHERE DO WE GO FROM HERE?

In this section, we have covered the basics of how the body responds to differing stresses, all of which come into play in a comprehensive training program designed to maximize an athlete's performance.

The next section explains how personal trainers and others assess an individual's readiness for fitness training and the stages they go through in creating personalized fitness plans.

Dallas Mavericks' guard Steve Nash of Victoria, B.C., makes the pass as Toronto Raptors' forward Jerome Williams (left) looks on during first-half NBA action in Toronto (CP PHOTO/Kevin Frayer).

14
Personal Fitness and Training

"To exercise at or near capacity is the best way I know of reaching a true introspective state. If you do it right, it can open all kinds of inner doors."

– Al Oerter, four-time Olympic gold medallist in discus

KEY CONCEPTS

- Fitness objectives
- Motivational readiness
- FANTASTIC Lifestyle Checklist
- Performance-related fitness
- Health-related fitness

- The Canadian Physical Activity, Fitness and Lifestyle Appraisal (CPAFLA)
- Cardiovascular endurance
- Body composition
- Muscular strength

- Muscular endurance
- Flexibility
- Léger "Beep Test"

Just as an understanding of the effects of physical activity on human health has advanced in recent years, so too have the number of people seeking advice from personal trainers, coaches, and others with specialized skills in the area of personal training and exercise design. Personal training and the design of exercise programs is about helping people adopt, enjoy, and maintain an active lifestyle.

Whether it is for yourself or for others, developing a sound fitness training program involves three basic stages. The first stage is to get a comprehensive picture of the objectives of the individual concerned – why he or she decided to undertake physical fitness training and his or her history, needs, and hopes for achievement. The second stage involves gathering detailed information through an assessment of the individual's current physical fitness and conditioning. The final stage involves selecting appropriate exercises from a wide menu of available choices according to how well they fit with the agreed-upon goals.

Whether you aspire to be a kinesiologist, a personal trainer, a coach, a fitness specialist, or simply to help yourself or a friend, this section will introduce you to ways in which fitness training programs are developed, and it will provide specific examples of such programs. It draws on applied exercise physiology, the art of counselling, and training principles to provide you with some of the basic knowledge and skills involved with safe, effective, and enjoyable physical activities.

STAGE 1: COUNSELLING AND OBJECTIVES

Above all, exercise design involves pursuing clear fitness objectives, whether they include developing a more active lifestyle, recovering from an injury, or improving athletic performance. One of the first challenges, therefore, is to acquire a picture of the exercise history of the individual, and his or her needs and hopes for achievement. This picture will fill in and perhaps change as the program progresses, so it is crucial that clear priorities are established. This will assist in developing objectives that are measurable.

Designing personalized exercise programs involves helping the individual choose exercise elements that suit their goals. It is important not only to set the objectives carefully but to follow up afterwards to verify that the program is meeting his or her needs and that he or she is comfortable and pleased with the results.

Discovering the Level of Commitment

Early discussions should clarify what the individual hopes to gain or learn. Determining this will aid in choosing the best strategy for helping him or her to do so. The Canadian Society for Exercise Physiology has developed a Stages of Change Questionnaire designed to establish the individual's stage of motivational readiness for physical fitness training. The questionnaire identifies five stages (see Table 14.1). Once you know the stage that the individual is at, you can choose strategies that are effective for that specific stage.

Table 14.1: Stages of change questionnaire

Physical activity can include such activities as walking, cycling, swimming, climbing stairs, dancing, active gardening, walking to work, aerobics, sports, etc. Regular physical activity is 30 minutes of moderate activity accumulated over the day, almost every day, or vigorous activity done at least three times per week for 20 minutes each time.

1. Here are a number of statements describing various levels of physical activity. Please select the one that most closely describes your own level:

❏	I am not physically active and I do not plan on becoming so.
❏	I have been thinking about becoming physically active, but I haven't done anything about it yet.
❏	I am physically active once in a while, but not regularly.
❏	I have become involved in regular physical activity within the past six months.
❏	I participate in regular physical activity and have done so for more than six months.

2. (Answer if not currently active)

❏	I was physically active in the past, but not now.

Reprinted from The Canadian Society for Exercise Physiology. (1998). *The Canadian physical activity, fitness & lifestyle appraisal: CSEP's plan for healthy active living* (2nd ed., Tool #4). Adapted with permission from the Canadian Society for Exercise Physiology.

Setting Priorities and Measurable Objectives

The value of an exercise program will depend on the degree the individual is able to set priorities for actions that will satisfy his or her needs and wants within his or her lifestyle limitations. It is important to recognize that needs are not the same as wants. Needs originate in human biology (such as the need for nourishment) and in the human social condition (such as the need for affection and social interaction). In the context of exercise, needs are basic requirements related to an injury, a specific weakness in an area of fitness, a health risk factor, or some other personal situation (such as wanting to participate in a sport or a problem with motivation). Wants are desires to meet these needs in specific ways. Wants often determine our choices about how to address needs, and are, of course, influenced by social forces.

The requirements of a person's lifestyle must also be considered, including available time and facilities, as well as other aspects of one's life (such as partners, family demands, financial resources, travel, employment, and so on). The areas of overlap – where a need and a want coincide and the lifestyle is compatible – are the areas of greatest potential for success. It is on these overlapping areas that trainers and individuals seeking improved physical fitness should focus.

Goals provide a visual picture of a future outcome. The process of setting a goal can lead to even more focused objectives that describe the desired outcome more precisely. Objectives are action-oriented and indicate how well and under what conditions the outcome should be performed. Small, measurable time frames obviously will result in more frequent success.

Health and Lifestyle Appraisal

The major causes of disability and death are no longer infectious diseases but rather diseases of lifestyle. Health status and lifestyle should be assessed during the early phase of counselling, before other fitness assessments.

Behaviours that contribute to various chronic illnesses include alcohol and drug abuse, smoking, inappropriate diet, and insufficient physical activity. Elements of a healthy lifestyle include a positive attitude towards self and others, an ability to cope with stress, a zeal for life, and the practice of healthy behaviours. A health risk appraisal or, more positively, a health and lifestyle appraisal – may be a first step to behaviour change.

One such questionnaire that considers a variety of factors affecting health and well-being is what is known as the FANTASTIC Lifestyle Checklist. The questionnaire includes health factors such as family and friends, physical activity, proper nutrition, tobacco and other toxics, alcohol consumption, sleep, stress and safety, type of behaviour, insight, and career. The issues raised in the checklist have a major influence on health and allow one to reflect on these habits and attitudes.

Table 14.2: FANTASTIC lifestyle checklist

Instructions: Unless otherwise specified, place an "X" beside the box that best describes your behaviour or situation in the past month.

Family Friends	I have someone to talk to about things that are important to me	Almost never		Seldom		Some of the time		Fairly often		Almost always	
	I give and receive affection	Almost never		Seldom		Some of the time		Fairly often		Almost always	
Activity	I am vigorously active for at least 30 minutes per day (e.g., running, cycling, etc.)	Less than once a week		1-2 times/ week		3 times/ week		4 times/ week		5 or more times/ week	
	I am moderately active (e.g., gardening, climbing stairs, walking, housework)	Less than once a week		1-2 times/ week		3 times/ week		4 times/ week		5 or more times/ week	
Nutrition	I eat a balanced diet	Almost never		Seldom		Some of the time		Fairly often		Almost always	
	I often eat excess: 10 sugar, or 12 salt or 16 animal fats or 14 junk foods	4 of these		3 of these		2 of these		1 of these		None of these	
	I am within ____ kg of my healthy weight	Not within 8 kg (20 lbs.)		8 kg (20 lbs.)		6 kg (15 lbs.)		4 kg (10 lbs.)		2 kg (5 lbs.)	
Tobacco Toxics	I smoke tobacco	More than 10 times/ week		1-10 times/week		None in the past 6 months		None in the past year		None in the past 5 years	
	I use drugs such as marijuana, cocaine	Sometimes								Never	
	I overuse prescribed drugs or over-the-counter medicine	Almost daily		Fairly often		Only occasionally		Almost never		Never	
	I drink caffeine-containing coffee, tea, or cola	More than 10 times/ week		7-10/day		3-6/day		1-2/day		Never	
Alcohol	My average alcohol intake per week is _____	More than 20 drinks		13-20 drinks		11-12 drinks		8-10 drinks		0-7 drinks	
	I drink more than 4 drinks on an occasion	Almost daily		Fairly often		Only occasionally		Almost never		Never	
	I drive after drinking	Sometimes								Never	
Sleep Seatbelts Stress Safe Sex	I sleep well and feel rested	Almost never		Seldom		Some of the time		Fairly often		Almost always	
	I use seatbelts	Never		Seldom		Some of the time		Most of the time		Always	
	I am able to cope with the stresses in my life	Almost never		Seldom		Some of the time		Fairly often		Almost always	
	I relax and enjoy leisure time	Almost never		Seldom		Some of the time		Fairly often		Almost always	
	I practise safe sex	Almost never		Seldom		Some of the time		Fairly often		Always	
Type of behaviour	I seem to be in a hurry	Almost always		Fairly often		Some of the time		Seldom		Almost never	
	I feel angry or hostile	Almost always		Fairly often		Some of the time		Seldom		Almost never	
Insight	I am a positive or optimistic thinker	Almost never		Seldom		Some of the time		Fairly often		Almost always	
	I feel tense or uptight	Almost always		Fairly often		Some of the time		Seldom		Almost never	
	I feel sad or depressed	Almost always		Fairly often		Some of the time		Seldom		Almost never	
Career	I am satisfied with my job or role	Almost never		Seldom		Some of the time		Fairly often		Almost always	

Step 1: Total each column

Step 2: Multiply the totals by the number indicated — 0 — 1 — 2 — 3 — 4

Subtotal

Step 3: Add your scores across bottom for your grand total — GRAND TOTAL

Scores: 80-100 excellent; 70-79 good; 60-69 fair.

From Wilson, Dr. Douglas. (1995). FANTASTIC lifestyle assessments. Hamilton: Department of Family Medicine, McMaster University. Reproduced by permission.

Table 14.3: Health-related fitness appraisal: Items and sequence

Screening

- ❏ PAR-Q (Physical Activity Readiness Questionnaire)
- ❏ Consent Form
- ❏ Observations
- ❏ Resting Heart Rate Measurement
- ❏ Resting Blood Pressure Measurement

Healthy Body Composition

- ❏ Standing Height
- ❏ Body Mass (Weight)
- ❏ Waist (Abdomen) Girth
- ❏ Skinfolds: triceps

  biceps

  subscapula

  iliac crest

  medial calf

Healthy Aerobic Fitness

- ❏ Modified Canadian Aerobic Fitness Test (mCAFT)
- ❏ Post-Exercise Heart Rate
- ❏ Post-Exercise Blood Pressure

Healthy Musculoskeletal Fitness

- ❏ Grip Strength
- ❏ Push-Ups
- ❏ Trunk Forward Flexion
- ❏ Partial Curl-Ups
- ❏ Vertical Jump

Reprinted from The Canadian Society for Exercise Physiology. (1998). *The Canadian physical activity, fitness & lifestyle appraisal: CSEP's plan for healthy active living* (2nd ed., Figure 7-3). Adapted with permission from the Canadian Society for Exercise Physiology.

STAGE 2: FITNESS ASSESSMENT

The counselling and objectives stage has, thus far, provided us with a picture of the history, needs, and hopes of the individual wishing to improve his or her physical conditioning. The second stage of designing an exercise program involves gathering more detailed information through the assessment of physical fitness.

Physiological measurements are necessary to set guidelines and monitor progress, and a variety of training methods (discussed in Section 13) will allow us to match potential benefits to desired outcomes. Issues of preference and equipment availability will also be important in this context. Exercise strategies are created based in large part on an interpretation of these assessment results.

Why and What to Assess?

Fitness assessment helps one to identify physical abilities and areas that need improvement. Baseline measures are useful in setting goals and can be used to monitor progress and adjust exercise programs. The test process and results can also help to educate, motivate, and stimulate interest in exercise and other health-related issues.

Test selection should also be based upon the objectives and components of concern to the client. Before we can develop an exercise prescription, we must assess baseline values for selected components of fitness (e.g., cardiovascular, body composition, muscular strength and endurance, and flexibility). It is important to remember that, while some individuals will be looking simply to improve their general fitness, others may seek more performance-related or health-related fitness.

- **Performance-related fitness** is necessary for higher levels of sport performance or optimal work performance. This includes: motor skills (e.g., speed, agility, balance, and coordination); cardiovascular endurance; muscular power; strength and endurance; body composition; size; skill acquisition; and motivation.

- **Health-related fitness** includes: body composition (e.g., subcutaneous fat distribution, abdominal visceral fat, body mass relative to height); muscle balance (strength, endurance, and flexibility, particularly of the postural muscles); cardiovascular functions (e.g., sub-maximal exercise capacity, blood pressure, lung functions); and metabolic components (e.g., blood lipids, glucose tolerance).

The question of what exactly to assess and which tests are most appropriate depends upon equipment

Physical Activity Readiness
Questionnaire - PAR-Q
(revised 2002)

PAR-Q & YOU

(A Questionnaire for People Aged 15 to 69)

Regular physical activity is fun and healthy, and increasingly more people are starting to become more active every day. Being more active is very safe for most people. However, some people should check with their doctor before they start becoming much more physically active.

If you are planning to become much more physically active than you are now, start by answering the seven questions in the box below. If you are between the ages of 15 and 69, the PAR-Q will tell you if you should check with your doctor before you start. If you are over 69 years of age, and you are not used to being very active, check with your doctor.

Common sense is your best guide when you answer these questions. Please read the questions carefully and answer each one honestly: check YES or NO.

YES	NO		
☐	☐	1.	Has your doctor ever said that you have a heart condition <u>and</u> that you should only do physical activity recommended by a doctor?
☐	☐	2.	Do you feel pain in your chest when you do physical activity?
☐	☐	3.	In the past month, have you had chest pain when you were not doing physical activity?
☐	☐	4.	Do you lose your balance because of dizziness or do you ever lose consciousness?
☐	☐	5.	Do you have a bone or joint problem (for example, back, knee or hip) that could be made worse by a change in your physical activity?
☐	☐	6.	Is your doctor currently prescribing drugs (for example, water pills) for your blood pressure or heart condition?
☐	☐	7.	Do you know of <u>any other reason</u> why you should not do physical activity?

If

you

answered

YES to one or more questions

Talk with your doctor by phone or in person BEFORE you start becoming much more physically active or BEFORE you have a fitness appraisal. Tell your doctor about the PAR-Q and which questions you answered YES.

- You may be able to do any activity you want — as long as you start slowly and build up gradually. Or, you may need to restrict your activities to those which are safe for you. Talk with your doctor about the kinds of activities you wish to participate in and follow his/her advice.
- Find out which community programs are safe and helpful for you.

NO to all questions

If you answered NO honestly to <u>all</u> PAR-Q questions, you can be reasonably sure that you can:
- start becoming much more physically active — begin slowly and build up gradually. This is the safest and easiest way to go.
- take part in a fitness appraisal — this is an excellent way to determine your basic fitness so that you can plan the best way for you to live actively. It is also highly recommended that you have your blood pressure evaluated. If your reading is over 144/94, talk with your doctor before you start becoming much more physically active.

DELAY BECOMING MUCH MORE ACTIVE:
- if you are not feeling well because of a temporary illness such as a cold or a fever — wait until you feel better; or
- if you are or may be pregnant — talk to your doctor before you start becoming more active.

PLEASE NOTE: If your health changes so that you then answer YES to any of the above questions, tell your fitness or health professional. Ask whether you should change your physical activity plan.

<u>Informed Use of the PAR-Q</u>: The Canadian Society for Exercise Physiology, Health Canada, and their agents assume no liability for persons who undertake physical activity, and if in doubt after completing this questionnaire, consult your doctor prior to physical activity.

No changes permitted. You are encouraged to photocopy the PAR-Q but only if you use the entire form.

NOTE: If the PAR-Q is being given to a person before he or she participates in a physical activity program or a fitness appraisal, this section may be used for legal or administrative purposes.

"I have read, understood and completed this questionnaire. Any questions I had were answered to my full satisfaction."

NAME _____

SIGNATURE _____   DATE _____

SIGNATURE OF PARENT _____   WITNESS _____
or GUARDIAN (for participants under the age of majority)

Note: This physical activity clearance is valid for a maximum of 12 months from the date it is completed and becomes invalid if your condition changes so that you would answer YES to any of the seven questions.

CSEP
SCPE © Canadian Society for Exercise Physiology   Supported by: [🍁] Health Santé
                                                                          Canada Canada

Figure 14.1: CPAFLA's Physical Activity Readiness Questionnaire (PAR-Q).

Source: CPAFLA's Physical Activity Readiness Questionnaire (PAR-Q) © 2002. Reprinted with permission from the Canadian Society for Exercise Physiology (www.csep.ca/forms.asp).

Table 14.4: Recommendations for fitness training in healthy adults

Various organizations, including CPAFLA and the American College of Sports Medicine, have developed the following recommendations for the quantity and quality of training for developing and maintaining overall fitness in healthy adults.

1. Frequency of training (F)
3-5 days per week.

2. Intensity of training (I)
60-90 percent of maximum heart rate or 50-85 percent of maximum oxygen uptake or heart rate reserve.

3. Duration of training (T)
20-60 minutes of continuous aerobic activity. Duration is dependent on the intensity of the activity. Lower intensity activity should be done for a longer period of time.

4. Mode of activity (T)

Aerobic activity: Any activity that uses large muscle groups, can be maintained continuously, and is rhythmical and aerobic in nature, e.g., walking-hiking, running-jogging, cycling-bicycling, cross-country skiing, dancing, skipping rope, rowing, stair climbing, swimming, skating, and various endurance game activities.

Resistance activity: Strength training of a moderate intensity, sufficient to develop and maintain fat-free weight (FFW), should be an integral part of an adult fitness program. One set of 8-12 repetitions of 8-10 exercises that condition the major muscle groups at least 2 days per week is the recommended minimum.

When incorporating any or all of these recommendations, the activities that you choose must be fun, enjoyable, and, above all, safe. Adding a variety of exercises and a balance of both resistance and aerobic activity will help deter the boredom that can result if your program selection is repetitive and monotonous. Ideally, your program should be changed or altered every 6-12 weeks, depending on your needs. In the case of elite athletes, these time frames may need to be changed or altered frequently, depending on your sporting needs.

The above recommendations apply mostly to healthy adults, but before engaging in any fitness program, regardless of age, it is advisable to consult your doctor. A fitness professional can assess your current level of fitness while helping you start and design a fitness program to insure proper implementation. They can also help to make sure that proper safety guidelines and exercising techniques are followed.

Reprinted from The Canadian Society for Exercise Physiology. (1998). *The Canadian physical activity, fitness & lifestyle appraisal: CSEP's plan for healthy active living* (2nd ed.). Adapted with permission from the Canadian Society for Exercise Physiology. (F.I.T.T. acronym courtesy of David M. Chisholm, M.D.)

availability, knowledge of how to use it, time, and expertise. Many good fitness tests do not require expensive testing instruments, nor do they demand advanced technical skills or advanced knowledge of anatomy and physiology. Test selection should also be based upon the objectives and issues of concern to the individual.

Canada's Own Standardized Test of Fitness

Screening procedures bring a measure of safety to the fitness appraisal. They can help reduce the risk involved with attempting to design programs for individuals who, because of health problems, may be at risk if they engage in certain activities. The Physical Activity Readiness Questionnaire (PAR-Q) can help determine whether an individual should provide a detailed medical history before entering an exercise program (see Figure 14.1). You can use PAR-Q as a screening device both for sub-maximal aerobic assessment and for beginning moderate and progressively advanced exercise programs.

The Canadian Standardized Test of Fitness was originally developed in 1979 as a consistent approach to appraisal. Now called The Canadian Physical Activity, Fitness and Lifestyle Appraisal (CPAFLA), it continues to provide a simple, safe, and standardized approach to assessing the major components of fitness in apparently healthy individuals. Developed by the Canadian Society for Exercise Physiology, it also allows for interpretation based on norms and health benefit zones for Canadians fifteen to sixty-nine years of age.

The CPAFLA has a very clear health-related focus with scoring for each test item within one of five "health-benefit zones," ranging from "needs improvement" to "excellent." The entire CPAFLA test (or protocol) involves a single 60-90 minute session, with minimal equipment and facility requirements.

In addition to CPAFLA, there are a number of other fitness tests for each of the components of fitness areas. In many cases, results from relatively simple field-based tests may be adequate to identify and quantify an individual's needs. Field-based tests are usually less expensive and more easily administered than laboratory tests. Indeed, for the personal trainer, coach, or small facility director, they may be the only option.

Table 14.6 on page 216 lists a series of additional tests that can be used to assess various components of fitness. It is recommended that you find out how to administer the tests and pay particular attention to any safety guidelines or measures in order to reduce the risk of injury to the athlete. Some of the tests are designed for elite level athletes and may not be appropriate for beginner or novice athletes.

Cardiovascular Assessment

Arguably, the most important component of physical fitness and the best indicator of overall health is **cardiovascular endurance**. This is the ability of the lungs, heart, and blood vessels to deliver adequate amounts of oxygen to the cells to meet the demands of prolonged physical activity. The level of cardiovascular endurance, cardiovascular fitness, or aerobic capacity is determined by the maximal amount of oxygen (VO_2max) that the human body is able to utilize per minute of physical activity.

The most precise way to determine **maximal oxygen uptake** is through direct gas analysis under laboratory conditions. Although not as accurate, several field-test methods are often used. Cardiovascular fitness can be assessed by using a step test, walk-run test, bicycle ergometer, treadmill test, or even a swimming test. Whatever the case, an assessment device should be selected that is suitable for the age of the individual concerned, the anticipated mode of exercise or sport, and general health and fitness status. These tests can be especially helpful if the method of monitoring is similar to that used for the test itself.

We will look at two examples, the first from the CPAFLA protocol (the Modified Canadian Aerobic Fitness Test) and a second, more easily administered run-walk field test.

The Modified Canadian Aerobic Fitness Test (mCAFT)

The mCAFT test is structured so that individuals complete one or more sessions of 3 minutes of stepping (double 20.3 centimetre steps) at predetermined speeds based on their age and gender. Instructions and time signals are given on the CD/cassette tape as to when to start and stop and for the counting of the 10-second measurement of post-exercise heart rate.

Individuals complete these 3-minute bouts, which are progressively more demanding, until they reach 85 percent of their predicted maximum heart rate. An aerobic fitness score is then calculated using the mCAFT formula, and the health-benefit rating is established.

The Modified Canadian Aerobic Fitness Test is designed principally for individuals seeking to start a fitness training program or to improve on their general fitness level. It is not a test that lends itself well to individuals who are in superior aerobic condition. Athletes that are in superior aerobic condition should use a test, preferably in a fitness laboratory under the supervision of a PFLC (Professional Fitness and Lifestyle Consultant). A PFLC can administer a maximal aerobic test in order to determine the athletes's maximal usage of oxygen (VO_2max).

A demonstration of the procedure for the Modified Canadian Aerobic Fitness Test (mCAFT).

Table 14.5: Estimated maximal oxygen uptake in mL/kg/min for 1.5-mile run test

Time	Max VO$_2$	Time	Max VO$_2$
6:10	80.0	12:40	39.8
6:20	79.0	12:50	39.2
6:30	77.9	13:00	38.6
6:40	76.7	13:10	38.1
6:50	75.5	13:20	37.8
7:00	74.0	13:30	37.2
7:10	72.6	13:40	36.8
7:20	71.3	13:50	36.3
7:30	69.9	14:00	35.9
7:40	68.3	14:10	35.5
7:50	66.8	14:20	35.1
8:00	65.2	14:30	34.7
8:10	63.9	14:40	34.3
8:20	62.5	14:50	34.0
8:30	61.2	15:00	33.6
8:40	60.2	15:10	33.1
8:50	59.1	15:20	32.7
9:00	58.1	15:30	32.2
9:10	56.9	15:40	31.8
9:20	55.9	15:50	31.4
9:30	54.7	16:00	30.9
9:40	53.5	16:10	30.5
9:50	52.3	16:20	30.2
10:00	51.1	16:30	29.8
10:10	50.4	16:40	29.5
10:20	49.5	16:50	29.1
10:30	48.6	17:00	28.9
10:40	48.0	17:10	28.5
10:50	47.4	17:20	28.3
11:00	46.6	17:30	28.0
11:10	45.8	17:40	27.7
11:20	45.1	17:50	27.4
11:30	44.4	18:00	27.1
11:40	43.7	18:10	26.8
11:50	43.2	18:20	26.6
12:00	42.3	18:30	26.3
12:10	41.7	18:40	26.0
12:20	41.0	18:50	25.7
12:30	40.4	19:00	25.4

The 1.5-Mile Run Test

With only a stopwatch and a pre-measured 1.5-mile (2.41 km) course, this test can be very efficient for mass testing. It predicts cardiovascular fitness according to the time the person takes to run or walk the course. Maximal oxygen uptake is estimated based on the time it takes to cover the distance.

Here are the basic stages:

1. Make sure that you or the individual concerned qualifies for this test. This test is contraindicated for unconditioned beginners, individuals with symptoms of heart disease, and those with known heart disease.

2. Select the testing site. Find a school track or a pre-measured course.

3. Have a stopwatch available to determine your time.

4. Conduct a few warm-up exercises prior to the test. Do some stretching exercises, some walking, and slow jogging.

5. Initiate the test and try to cover the distance in the fastest time possible (walking or jogging). Time yourself during the run to see how fast you have covered the distance. If any unusual symptoms arise during the test, do not continue. Stop immediately and retake the test after another six weeks of aerobic training.

6. At the end of the test, cool down by walking or jogging slowly for another 3-5 minutes. Do not sit or lie down after the test.

7. According to your performance time, look up your estimated maximal oxygen uptake in Table 14.5. For example, if one runs the 1.5-mile course in 12 minutes and 40 seconds, Table 14.5 shows a maximal oxygen uptake of 39.8 mL/kg/min.

This test lends itself to maximal effort by its participants. As a result, care must be given when instructing athletes. They should work within their limits, and if they feel nauseous or sick, they should inform the instructor and terminate the test.

Source: Adapted from Cooper, K.H. (1968). A means of assessing maximal oxygen intake. *Journal of the American Medical Association, 203,* 201-204. Reprinted with permission from the American Medical Association.

The term **body composition** is often used in reference to the fat mass and lean body mass (non-fat). The total fat in the body is either essential fat or storage fat. Essential fat is needed for normal physiological functions. Storage fat is stored in adipose tissue, mostly beneath the skin (subcutaneous), around major organs and the visceral areas. Recent research indicates that it is the distribution of adipose tissue that determines the health risk of obesity, with visceral fat posing a greater health risk than subcutaneous fat.

Body composition can be determined through several procedures. The most common are: hydrostatic or underwater weighing, bioelectrical impedance, skinfold thickness, and girth measurements. Hydrostatic weighing is the most accurate test of body composition, although this is a laboratory-based assessment and is less practical. The use of skinfold calipers is based on the principle that about half of the body's fat tissue is located directly beneath the skin. Girth measures at various body sites can be quite accurate. Measures such as waist girth and skinfolds can be done quickly and can be good indicators of progress.

Although a popular practice, recording a client's overall percentage of body fat has significant risk of error and provides no specific information on fat distribution. For this reason, it may be more valuable to report individual anthropometric measurements (skinfold or girth) at particular sites.

CPAFLA's Healthy Body Composition Test

Although the calculation of body fat percentage and ideal weight may be useful in performance-related fitness appraisals, the CPAFLA approach is more health related and deals with body weight, adiposity, and fat distribution. Four specific indicators are measured:

- body mass index (BMI);
- sum of (five) skinfolds (SO5S);
- waist girth (WG); and
- sum of (two) trunk skinfolds (SO2S).

The BMI and SO5S provide an indication of the amount of body fat. The WG and SO2S measures focus on the concerns related to trunk versus a general pattern of fat distribution. A healthy or unhealthy rating is established for each indicator and then results are combined for a comprehensive score and corresponding health-benefit zone.

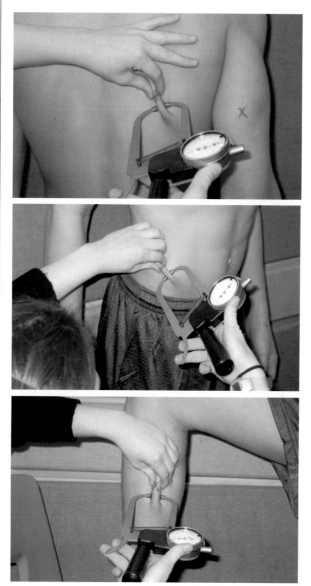

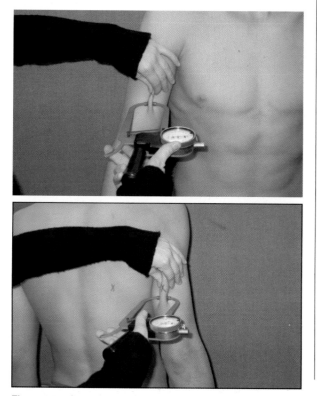

Figure 14.2: Skinfold test at five locations: subscapular, biceps, suprailiac, triceps, and medial-calf.

Muscular Strength and Endurance Assessment

Muscular strength and muscular endurance are two different qualities of muscle performance. **Muscular strength** is the maximum tension or force a muscle can exert in a single contraction. **Muscular endurance** is the ability of the muscle to perform repeated or sustained contractions over a period of time. Both components are critical for individuals who participate in competitive sports, and for those looking to enhance performance-related fitness. However, substantial health benefits include optimal performance in daily activities, reduced injuries, healthy aging, healthy back, posture, and an increase in resting metabolism. Both age and gender can significantly affect muscular strength and endurance.

Strength and muscular endurance can be measured using dynamometers, cable tensiometers, electromechanical devices, and constant-resistance as well as variable-resistance exercise machines. Electromechanical, hydraulic devices (such as force platforms), and dynamometers are used to assess static and dynamic strength, endurance, and power. Because these instruments are quite sophisticated and relatively expensive, they typically are found only in research laboratories. Field-based assessments of muscular strength and endurance, on the other hand, can closely simulate the training conditions. These tests are usually cheap and easy to administer, and often can be modified to suit desired resistance levels.

Muscular strength is usually determined by the maximal amount of resistance that an individual can lift in a single effort (known as one repetition maximum or simply 1RM). A true 1RM for the chest muscles, for example, during a bench press may be difficult to obtain because earlier trials will leave the client fatigued. A strength profile should also include several selected body areas. Traditionally, a representative strength measure is the Hand Grip Test, using a device called a grip dynamometer. CPAFLA's Healthy Musculoskeletal Fitness Test uses grip strength and vertical jump measures as indicators of muscular strength and power respectively.

Muscular endurance is commonly assessed by the number of repetitions that an individual can perform against a sub-maximal resistance, or by the length of time a contraction can be sustained. Tests that could be used include the amount of weight lifted "to failure" (i.e., until unable to continue) for 5-10 repetitions (5-10 RM), the total number of push-ups or sit-ups, or how long a person can hold a chin-up. Again, muscular endurance is usually specific to the body part or muscle groups.

CPAFLA's Healthy Musculoskeletal Fitness Test uses push-up and partial curl-up tests to assess muscular endurance.

Partial Curl-Up Test (CPAFLA)

This test should also be conducted by a qualified fitness trainer, but here is a description of the basic test. The individual lies in a supine position with his or her head resting on the mat, with arms straight at sides and parallel to the trunk. The middle finger tips of both hands are located at the zero mark on a piece of tape adhered to the mat. Ten centimetres from this is another tape mark. The arms should be fully extended when the finger tips are at the zero mark. The individual bends his or her knees at an angle of 90°, keeping the heels in contact with the mat.

During the curl-up, the palms and heels must remain in contact with the mat. Anchoring of the feet is not permitted. On the return, the shoulder blades and head must contact the mat and the finger tips of both hands must touch the zero mark. The movement is performed in a slow, controlled manner so that the time to perform the lifting and lowering stages of the curl-up is the same at a rate of 25 curl-ups per minute. The subject performs as many consecutive curl-ups as possible, without pausing, to a maximum of 25 in the 1-minute time period. The test is terminated if the individual is experiencing undue discomfort, is unable to maintain required cadence, or is unable to maintain the proper curl-up technique. The number of partial curl-ups completed is recorded.

CPAFLA's partial curl-up test, beginning and end positions.

Flexibility and/or Muscle Tightness Assessment

Flexibility refers to the ability of a joint to move freely through its full range of motion (ROM). Improving and maintaining this component of fitness has been gaining greater recognition in the performance arena and in athletic injury prevention. It has also been gaining recognition in terms of preventative health care, including postural alignment, spine and pelvic mobility, reduced tension, and improved self-image. Again, both gender and age have a major influence on joint flexibility.

Because flexibility is specific to each joint, it is difficult to have one general flexibility test. To assess flexibility and identify tight muscles, a battery of flexibility tests suited to the needs and demands of the individual is the best approach. Has a joint area been overworked, possibly causing muscle tightness? For example, clients who plan a weight-bearing or locomotion activity should have their ankle flexibility assessed. Clients who sit for long periods of time should be checked for muscle tightness of the hip flexors and trunk extensors. Many manual workers tend to have tight anterior chest muscles, such as the pectoralis major and minor. Overuse or underuse of back muscles may leave them tight and the joints inflexible.

There are good Canadian standards (or "norms") for the CPAFLA Trunk Forward Flexion Test, which rates the relative tightness of the hamstrings and lower back. The better of two trials on the flexometer is given a health-zone rating. Combined with the results of CPAFLA's partial Curl-Up Test, the results from the Trunk Forward Flexion Test can provide some insight into back fitness.

Most athletes forsake working on their flexibility as they feel it cuts into their training time. Stretching should never be ignored or underestimated. It not only enhances the joints' ROM, but it also helps to nourish the joints' connective tissue while enhancing muscle length.

Trunk Forward Flexion Test (CPAFLA)

Again, this test should be conducted by a qualified fitness trainer. Consult the CPAFLA manual for details, but the basic procedure is as follows:

1. The individual warms up for this test by performing slow stretching movements (modified hurdle stretch held for 20 seconds, repeated twice on each leg) before taking the actual measurements. He or she, without shoes, sits with legs fully extended and the soles of the feet placed flat against the flexometer. The flexometer is adjusted to a height at which the balls of the feet rest against the upper crossboards. The inner edge of the soles are placed 2 centimetres from the edge of the scale. Keeping the knees fully extended, arms evenly stretched, and palms down, the individual bends and reaches forward (without jerking), pushing the sliding marker along the scale with the fingertips as far forward as possible.

2. The position of maximum flexion must be held for approximately two seconds. The individual is advised that lowering the head will maximize the distance reached. If the knees flex, the trial is not counted. There is no attempt to hold the knees down. In addition, a bouncing or jerking motion is avoided.

3. The test is repeated twice. Record both readings and record the maximum reading to the nearest 0.5 centimetres.

The results of this test will give you a good benchmark that can be used to measure your progress. Once you have developed a sound flexibility program and have incorporated it into your normal exercise regime, re-test yourself. After several weeks, your results will have improved.

CPAFLA's trunk forward flexion test, showing the beginning and end positions.

Table 14.6: Fitness tests

Fitness Component	Types of Tests	Relevant to These Sports
SPEED AND REACTION TESTS Measures all out linear speed.	• Metre stick drop • 5-33 metre (10-40 yd.) sprints • Dynavision board	Football, track and field, hockey, soccer, lacrosse, baseball, bobsledding
POWER AND STRENGTH TESTS Measures explosiveness.	• Standing long jump • Vertical jump • One repetition maximums • 8-12 repetition maximums • Dynamometers • Cable tensiometers • Cybex (isokinetic resistance)	Football, martial arts, track and field, basketball, gymnastics, volleyball, hockey, Olympic lifting and wrestling, rowing, rugby, cycling
AGILITY AND COORDINATION TESTS Measures change of direction.	• Illinois agility • Hexagon drill • Line test • T-test • Wall ball toss (eye-hand coordination test)	Hockey, field hockey, soccer, volleyball, basketball, wrestling, football, skiing (slalom, moguls), rugby, tennis, squash
FLEXIBILITY TESTS Measures range of motion of joints.	• Goniometer (this protractor-like device is used to measure the flexibility of most joints) • Sit and reach • Trunk rotation test	All sports that benefit from maximal range of joint motion
ENDURANCE TESTS Measures how well the body uses oxygen.	• Luc Léger "Beep Test" • Multistage shuttle test • Copper 12-minute run • 2.4 km (1.5-mile) run • Step tests • Rockport walking test • Graded exercise tests • Bike ergometer test	Long-distance running events, cross-country events, 10 km events, marathons, triathlons, soccer, cross-country skiing, lacrosse, water polo, tennis, mountain biking, cycling, squash, and similar sports that need a solid aerobic base
BODY COMPOSITION TESTS Measures body fat and tissue distribution.	• 3- to 7-site caliper tests • Hydrostatic weight • Bioelectrical impedance analysis (BIA) • Anthropometric measurements (body segment measurements) • Air displacement "Body Pod"	Useful for sports where body composition might affect performance level. Norms are available for various sports; if used, caution should be practised when assessing and interpreting results for younger athletes to avoid body image sensitivities

Important note: This table gives a list of tests that could be used to determine athletic performance levels. However, these tests must be administered by a qualified fitness leader. It should also be noted that each test is specific to certain outcomes and may not be beneficial for all athletes. When selecting which test to use, consider the athlete's needs, current fitness level, and the relevance, reliability, and validity of the test itself.

STAGE 3: GUIDELINES FOR DEVELOPING AN EXERCISE PROGRAM

The third stage of designing an exercise program involves the actual process in which appropriate exercises are selected. These decisions are based on two main criteria: the physiological rationale, and how that goal will work for the exerciser.

For every individual, a trainer can judge the specific benefits provided by weight training, flexibility training, aerobic training, and anaerobic training. An exercise program will take into consideration not only optimal training outcomes, but also preferences and equipment or facilities.

Designing Aerobic Exercise Programs

Continuous aerobic training is safe and well suited for many different individuals and activities. Frequent workouts are possible and fewer injuries reported. The F.I.T.T. Principle should be used to map out the variables of an individualized aerobic program.

A proper warm-up must be incorporated, which prepares the body for exercise. A warm-up traditionally includes a 5-10-minute jog followed by 10-20 minutes of total body stretching. Circuit training is effective for the development of the cardiorespiratory system and is less stressful for the individual both mentally and physiologically. This type of training lays a solid foundation for more sports-specific aerobic activity later.

Depending on the individual's cardiorespiratory fitness assessment, he or she may begin at 50-65 percent HRR (heart rate reserve) to 70-75 percent of HRR for a more fit individual. A highly fit individual may train at 80-95 percent of their HRR depending on their specific needs and goals. Duration should be increased before intensity; although intensity is the most important part of an aerobic program, it is also the most taxing on the body. Intensity should not be increased until an individual can train continuously at 75 percent of their HRR. The most important factor for the beginner is that the type or mode of training be fun and enjoyable. It should involve several large muscle groups such as those used in walking, jogging, running, biking, hiking, cross-country skiing, swimming, using a treadmill or other aerobic training machines – all are suitable as long as the desired intensity and time are achieved.

By adjusting the duration of high-intensity exercise and the alternate relief periods, interval training (IT) is effective in working any energy system. Interval training achieves the greatest amount of work with the least fatigue. It can be tailored to suit a specific demand (e.g., a sport), yet it is also adaptable for individuals who are in poor condition. A typical IT program involves: (1) determining the energy system; (2) selecting the type of exercise; and (3) selecting work interval, number of repetitions and sets, work-relief ratio, and type of relief. Elite athletes require interval training and more sport-specific aerobic training to meet their goals. The cool-down period traditionally includes a 5-10-minute jog followed by a total body stretch in order to return the body to a resting state.

Designing Anaerobic Exercise Programs

Most anaerobic training programs require an aerobic base. Anaerobic training is used mostly for recreational, intercollegiate, elite, and professional athletes whose sport involves the use of the two anaerobic energy systems. Individuals interested in general fitness may incorporate low levels of resistance training but may not want to expose their bodies to high loads or intensities.

This type of training does not necessarily enhance cardiorespiratory health for the average person. Highly skilled aerobic athletes do benefit from anaerobic training, specifically from high-lactate threshold training, but this is not required of those who are merely trying to improve their fitness level. Anaerobic training programs may include speed, agility, strength, and power development. Select the ones that apply to the individual's needs and goals. As with aerobic program design, use the F.I.T.T. Principle as a guide to map out the variables of the program.

As anaerobic training is extremely taxing both physiologically and mentally, it is important to avoid overtraining. This is best avoided by incorporating off-season, pre-season, and in-season training programs (periodization). This model slows down detraining and helps to maintain the gains made during the off-season.

The type of training will vary greatly with the needs of each athlete. Those of a football player will differ drastically from those of a swimmer, for example. Proper selection of interval, Fartlek, resistance, and plyometric training must meet the needs of each specific athlete, as individuals should train the specific anaerobic energy system that pertains to their sport or activity. Caution and care must be taken when selecting high-load or volume training to avoid overtraining and injury, depending on the individual's sport and the periodization that has been developed. It is neither recommended nor possible for an athlete to train at maximal or near maximal levels for months at a time.

A cool-down period is extremely important after anaerobic training as this type of training can elicit high levels of blood lactic acid that can impede muscle activity. Cooling down can help to lower lactic acid levels in muscles.

SPECIALIZED EXERCISE PLANS

Plan for Cardiovascular Conditioning

Intensity, as stated earlier, is the most important and most involved factor in designing a cardiovascular exercise program. Trainers can vary the prescribed intensity level for different individuals depending on their fitness level and/or exercise history, their objectives, and level of risk factors. Often it is helpful to start at a lower intensity and increase the volume of work gradually. High-intensity intervals will produce aerobic and anaerobic benefits; moderate, steady intensities improve stamina and aerobic endurance. Progress will need to be monitored in order to verify that the workload is eliciting the desired heart rate.

The optimal duration of an exercise session depends on the desired intensity. Generally, the higher the intensity, the shorter the duration. If the individual's objective is cardiovascular improvement, "duration" should refer to the time within the training zone. (Activity below the training zone may still positively affect body composition or decrease risk factors). For those involved in sports that demand high levels of cardiovascular endurance, the individual and his or her trainer must determine the typical duration of high-intensity "spurts" of activity required in those sports, and then design interval training programs with similar durations. Duration is an important consideration for those who have intensity restrictions

Table 14.7: Tips for setting cardiovascular intensity	
Low fitness status/inactive/several risk factors/wants lower intensity, longer duration	50%-65% of HRR
Average fitness status/normal activity/few risk factors	65%-85% of HRR
Excellent fitness status/very active/low risk/an athlete/intervals	85%-90% of HRR

(i.e., symptoms that limit their level of intensity). If recovery is incomplete within one hour, or heart rate is still more than twenty beats per minute above the pre-exercise level after 10 minutes of recovery, then intensity, duration, or both may be too high.

The frequency of exercise depends on the duration and intensity of the session. If the intensity is kept low and duration is short, plan more sessions per week. If aerobic improvement is a primary objective, there should be no more than two days between workouts. If the individual is just beginning a weight-bearing activity such as jogging or aerobic classes, 36-48 hours of relative rest between aerobic workouts is often recommended to prevent overuse injuries.

Table 14.8: Cardiovascular prescription model	
Step 1: Consider Assessment Information	• Heart rate, blood pressure, and perceived exertion • Recovery rate • Visual signs and symptoms Note: Although recommended, Step 1 may not be possible. A detailed history and subsequent monitoring and follow-up checks are increasingly important.
Step 2: Establish Intensity	• Recommend a training zone (% HRmax, %HR reserve, %VO₂max, perceived exertion)
Step 3: Establish Mode	• Primary activity and alternate or cross-training activities • Special needs and/or problems
Establish Workload	• As related to the training zone (Step 2)
Establish Method of Training	• For example, continuous versus interval
Step 4: Establish Duration of Work (and Rest)	• May include total work and/or session (cal/session)
Step 5: Establish Frequency	• Calculate weekly work (kcal/week)
Step 6: Establish Progression	• Stage or progression (periodization) • Method of progression • Monitoring and follow-up check
Step 7: Design Warm-Up and Cool Down	• Consider the previous steps

Plan for Weight Management

Bearing in mind that there is a large range of healthy weights and variations in body size, aerobic exercise is the best type of fitness program for losing body fat. It involves large muscle groups, so recommended exercises can go beyond "typical" activities such as walking, jogging, stair climbing, and bicycling to ones that incorporate shoulder and trunk muscles. Remember that the action should be continuous, so that the energy expenditure level is maintained. Weight training can prevent significant losses of lean body mass and decreases in resting energy expenditure. The optimal solution is a combination of aerobic exercise and light resistance training. The bottom line, of course, is to select activities that are convenient and enjoyable, since adherence is the most important factor in any program.

During light exercise, about 30 percent to 50 percent of the total energy cost is derived from carbohydrates, while the other 50 percent to 70 percent comes from free fatty acids. Our bodies predominately use carbohydrates as an energy source during high-intensity exercise (65 percent to 70 percent of VO_2max and above). When we exercise at higher intensity levels, we burn more calories than during low-intensity exercise. However, depending on your fitness level, you may not be able to exercise at high-intensity levels or, if you can, you may not be able to sustain that effort for very long. Everyone has an optimal intensity, depending on his or her condition, and the intensity must be adapted to the duration of the exercise. This will ensure safety and enjoyment in your program.

One of the initial challenges for the individual is to reach a point of sufficient aerobic fitness that he or she can sustain moderate-intensity exercise for enough time to burn a large number of calories. However, duration and total distance are more important than speed (intensity) alone. The benefits of avoiding labour-saving devices – taking the stairs, walking to work, and generally living more actively – can accumulate during the day and effectively extend the daily energy expenditure. Frequent, short bouts of moderate day-to-day activities can burn the equivalent of a kilogram of body fat per month. In this case, there does seem to be some truth in the old saying that "every little bit counts."

The more a person exercises, the greater his or her caloric expenditure. A daily program is more likely to establish a behavioural habit and thereby promote adherence. Four sessions per week are satisfactory, provided duration and intensity are adequate. An active lifestyle can effectively complement a more formal exercise program and make a significant difference in the speed of weight loss or the ease of weight maintenance.

Dr. Luc Léger
The "Beep Test"

In 1982, Dr. Luc Léger of the University of Montreal and his associates developed the Léger 20-metre multi-stage shuttle run test for aerobic fitness that quickly became an industry standard.

This test, commonly referred to as the Beep Test, is simple to use, especially when assessing large groups. It has been field tested by the physiological community, which found it to be as accurate in assessing maximal oxygen consumption (VO_2max) as laboratory testing.

This test is unique in that it can be used on healthy children and healthy adults of different sexes without a change in protocol. The same CD or cassette is used for all healthy individuals and can be purchased from Canadienne de la Physiologie de l'Exercice Programme National de Certification et d'Accréditation d'Évaluateurs de la Condition Physique (CAECP) at caecpquebec@kinesiologue.com.

About the Test

The test starts off with a brisk walk of 8.5 kilometres per hour (5 mph) and increases each minute by .5 kilometres per minute. The distance of the course is 20 metres, and it can be performed in a gymnasium or on a tennis court surface. The pace is set by the instructions of the CD or cassette, and the advancement of shuttles are indicated by a "beep" sound. The more fit you are, the longer the test will take.

The test measures maximal aerobic power for each individual by announcing, after each 30-second increment, the level reached. This is expressed in metabolic equivalents (METS). The amount of oxygen your body needs is proportional to the amount of energy you need during any physical activity. At rest our bodies use 3.5 mL/kg/minute, which is equivalent to 1 MET.

If you reach level 10 during the Beep Test, it would mean that you are working at ten times your resting oxygen needs or 10 METS.

Consult the age- and sex-appropriate tables to determine your VO_2max.

Test Precautions

- Any individual with joint injuries or cardiorespiratory illness should not partake in this test without a doctor's clearance.

- Do not eat for 2 hours and drink no fluids 15 minutes prior to the test.

- Do no heavy exercise, or drink alcohol or take any drugs, prescription or non-prescription, the day before.

- Do not smoke for an hour prior, and do not run the test in hot and humid weather.

Plan for Muscle Flexibility

Although flexibility is often defined as a range of motion of a joint, it involves both the length and strength of muscles. Flexibility plays a major role in the maintenance of muscle balance. As we saw in Unit 1, a short muscle restricts the normal range of motion. Muscles that are too short are usually strong and hold the opposite muscle in a lengthened position. Excessively long muscles are usually weak and allow adaptive shortening of their antagonists.

In order to increase flexibility, it is advisable to choose movements that lengthen short muscles (by increasing the distance between the muscle's origin and insertion opposite to the direction of the muscle action), and strengthen weak muscles that have been elongated by strong antagonist muscles. The individual's exercise objectives will determine how, where, and through what technique flexibility should be integrated into the program.

Plan for Resistance Training

Developing or maintaining muscular endurance, strength, hypertrophy, power, muscle balance, or body composition are all objectives of resistance training whether the individual is primarily concerned with fitness, health, or performance. Basically, designing a resistance exercise program involves a relatively sequential series of decisions. The sequence may vary slightly between clients depending on preference, situation, or special circumstances. Each stage is always dependent upon prior selections and the trainer should often go back to consider earlier decisions.

The very basics of the individual's needs are addressed first, such as the limitations of injuries or cardiovascular risk. Available facilities, equipment, and time will also affect the ultimate program design.

With many different brands and types of equipment available, the pros and cons of each should be matched to the individual concerned. Free weights and some stack weights are a "constant-resistance" and require the joint to stabilize itself. Some machine designs and those that use a cam are "variable-resistance" and will match more closely the strength of the muscle through its range of motion. Small, affordable equipment, such as bands, tubes, balls, and boards can be very versatile in meeting specific needs.

Exercises such as a knee extension that are simple, isolated, and single joint are better suited for such goals as bodybuilding or rehabilitation. Complex multi-joint exercises such as a squat are more functional and cover several muscle groups at once. Specific exercises may be coordinated around the available equipment or be designed to target certain muscles or joint movements. Always do a quick safety check to assure there are no contraindications and the level or difficulty suits the individual's experience and strength.

The order of the exercises can affect fatigue, safety, and results. Generally, the order should be from large to small muscle groups. Alternating agonist and antagonist (push-pull) or upper body and lower body can achieve rest and balance. Complex and sport-specific exercises are better performed early when freshness gives the best form. Working stabilizers such as the trunk should be done later to maintain the safety of good form. Most beginning and intermediate programs are a standard (simple) set design involving a number of sets of one exercise at the same intensity and then moving on to the next exercise. A circuit will involve moving from one exercise station to the next in a balanced sequence, usually at lower loads. Table 14.9 gives an idea of how load, repetitions, and rest combine to meet various goals and stages of training.

Table 14.9: Volume overloads for resistance training

	Preparation	Hypertrophy	Strength Hypertrophy	Power/ Strength	Strength Endurance
Intensity/ Load	Low 60-69% of 1RM	Moderate 70-76% of 1RM	Mod-High 77-84% of 1RM	High 85-100% of 1RM	Low-Mod 60-69% of 1RM
Reps	13-20	9-12	6-8	1-5	13-20
Sets	1-4	3-5	3-5	1-3	1-3
Rest b/w Sets	60-120 sec	30-90 sec	30-120 sec	1.5-3 min	0-60 sec
Volume	Medium	High	Medium	Low	Med-High

Adapted from Stone, M.H., O'Bryant, H., & Garhammer, J. (1981). A hypothetical model for strength training. *Journal of Sports Medicine 21*, 344.

PERSONALIZED EXERCISE PLANS

There are several approaches that one can take when it comes to putting together an exercise program. Let us examine the design of training programs for three different individuals. Individual 1 is interested in overall fitness and staying in shape. Individual 2 has a number of cardiovascular risk factors and has set a goal of health-related fitness. Individual 3 is an athlete interested in enhanced performance.

Overall Fitness (Individual 1)

Individual 1 wants primarily to be able to perform moderate to vigorous levels of physical activity without undue fatigue and to maintain such ability throughout life. He or she wants to see improvements in cardiovascular condition (VO_2max), body composition, flexibility, and muscular strength and endurance. The American College of Sports Medicine recommendations (see Table 14.4) summarize suggested optimal intensity, duration, and frequency, and give general exercise prescription guidance for most of the training components.

Health-Related Fitness (Individual 2)

Physical fitness and health-related fitness, while not synonymous, are complementary. Although an individual may experience the health benefits of exercise along with improvements in fitness and performance capacity, health benefits may also come from frequent performance of low-intensity exercise. Very inactive people will benefit most from even low-intensity exercise, because the detrimental health-related consequences of extreme inactivity are rapidly reversed.

Given equal total energy expenditure, lower intensity, longer duration exercise will benefit older or less fit persons as much as high-intensity, shorter duration exercise. Moderate-intensity exercise carries lower cardiovascular risk and lower probability of orthopaedic injury, and it enjoys higher compliance. If an individual is concerned about weight loss, it is recommended that he or she could exercise at a moderate to low intensity sufficient to burn 300 Calories, three days per week, or 200 Calories per day, four days per week. Using frequent, short bouts of moderate activity, he or she may progress up to a target of 1,500 Calories per week.

Less active persons may prefer 8-10 minute bouts of moderate intensity exercise, several times per day, most days of the week. For resistance training, an individual may prefer to use higher volume training (i.e., multiple sets, moderate intensity, large muscle groups) and avoid exhaustive sets.

Personal trainer Todd Matthews looks on as Kathryn McChesney runs on the treadmill in Toronto, 2002. McChesney runs indoors about four months of the year (CP PHOTO/Aaron Harris).

Performance-Related Fitness (Individual 3)

For the "serious" exerciser or athlete, it is the upper levels of intensity and volume that are required in a personal periodized training program. As noted, the components include motor skills (e.g., speed, agility, balance, and coordination), cardiovascular endurance, muscular power, strength and endurance, body composition, size, skill acquisition, and motivation.

For this type of person, optimal training can be achieved only by maintaining a fine balance between intense training and rest; therefore, recognition of overtraining is critically important, yet difficult (see page 203). Prevention of overtraining is achieved by

- **Adequate short-term recovery.** If a person's workout is 90 minutes or longer, and is more vigorous and high impact, he or she may need to wait two or three days before a similar workout.

- **Proper variation.** Periodic changes in training technique, volume, intensity, venue, the use of massage, or stress management techniques can prove to be rejuvenating.

- **Careful monitoring.** Careful observation and keeping a training diary or log are essential.

Table 14.10: Sample program for individuals #1 and #2

	Aerobic		Anaerobic/Resistance Training	
	Weeks 1-8	Weeks 9-16	Weeks 1-8	Weeks 9-16
INDIVIDUAL 1				
Frequency	3 x/wk	3 x/wk	3 x/wk	3 x/wk
Intensity	50-55% of heart rate reserve (HRR)	60-75% of HRR	50-55% of 1RM 3 sets of 15-20 repetitions (reps) Rest: 20-30 seconds	60-75% of 1RM 3 sets of 12-15 repetitions (reps) Rest: 30-45 seconds
Type	walking (or any other aerobic activity of their choice, as long as it is 50-55% of their HHR)	jog, walk (or any other aerobic activity of their choice, as long as it is 60-65% of their HHR)	**Circuit:** resistance training using tubing, medicine balls or machines for: bench press, lat pull down, biceps curl, triceps extensions, abdominal curls, squats, hamstring curls, calf raises	**Circuit:** resistance training using machines and free weights for: bench press, lat pull down, biceps curl, triceps extensions, abdominal curls, squats, hamstring curls, calf raises
Time	20 minutes	20 minutes	20 minutes (circuit)	20 minutes (circuit)
INDIVIDUAL 2				
Frequency	3-4 x/wk	3-4 x/wk	3 x/wk	3-4 x/wk
Intensity	60-70% of heart rate reserve (HRR)	70-80% of HRR	65-75% of 1RM 3-5 sets of 9-12 repetitions (reps) Rest: 45-60 seconds	80-85% of 1RM 2-4 sets of 5-8 repetitions (reps) Rest: 60-120 seconds
Type	jogging (or any other aerobic activity of their choice, as long as it is 60-70% of their HHR)	jog, run (or any other aerobic activity of their choice, as long as it is 70-80% of their HHR)	**Hypertrophy:** resistance training using machines, free weights including dumbbells for: bench press, lat pull down, biceps curl, triceps extensions, abdominal curls, squats, hamstring curls, calf raises	**Strength:** resistance training using a variety of resistance training methods and techniques: bench press, lat pull down, biceps curl, triceps extensions, abdominal curls, squats, hamstring curls, calf raises
Time	20-30 minutes	30-40 minutes	60+ minutes	60+ minutes

Note: Individuals #1 and #2 should incorporate a combination of both resistance and aerobic training. This will help them to build a solid aerobic and strength base in order to progress to a more advanced program in the future.

Table 14.11: Sample program for individual #3

Name:				Month:				Season:			
Sept	Oct	Nov	Dec	Jan	Feb	Mar	Apr	May	Jun	Jul	Aug
Pre-season (6 weeks)		In-season (24 weeks)						Off-season (22 weeks)			
				Competition		Play Offs					
Number of workouts per week: 3-5		2 times per week during in-season plus practices				1-2		3	3	3-4	3-4
• Workouts • Plyometrics • Sports-specific skills • Sports-specific resistance training • Mental preparation • Nutritional modifications		• Maintenance phase • Mental preparation • Nutritional modification, pre-game and post-game meals				• Maintenance phase • Mental preparation • Nutritional modification, pre-game and post-game meals		• New fitness testing • Hypertrophy/strength • Low loads (weight) high reps • High loads (weight) low reps in last four to six weeks • Design nutritional modifications			

GENERAL PROGRAM DESIGN – SAFETY ISSUES

Most advice you will read or hear about personal training programs tends to deal with exercise regimens in "ideal" terms. That is, they contain prescriptions that assume that, on a mental and physical level, the person doing the training is always ready to train, and that he or she has no physical problems such as lingering fatigue or injuries. But any good exercise or training program must incorporate a concern for safety issues in order to avoid injuries, muscle soreness, feelings of burnout, or reduced performance levels. Not to do so is simply to ignore one of the fundamental aspects of any training program: that people are not machines and they cannot be expected to perform without experiencing some negative side-effects.

The following exercise program segments identify safety issues that are prominent during each segment.

Preparation (Warm-Up) Segment

Beginning with range-of-motion (ROM) movements of major joints will increase joint lubrication from synovial fluid secretion, give some flexibility gains, and serve as a first check on how the body feels before work. As the individual moves into a light aerobic circulatory warm-up (ideally the same mode as the upcoming cardiovascular [CV] work), the heart and circulatory system will be gradually prepared and increases in tissue temperature and synovial fluid will facilitate stretching.

Flexibility gains will come from primarily static stretching that targets muscles to be used, especially if used eccentrically. Moderate dynamic stretches may be used for sport preparation. There is a natural transition into the aerobic segment with a progressive overload in the aerobic activity to follow.

Aerobic Segment

Most aerobic programs, whether continuous or interval, will build up and ease gradually, avoiding sprints or sudden stops. This allows for better cardiovascular adaptation. Monitoring of heart rate, perceived exertion, talk test, muscle tightness, joint soreness, or adequate relief (if intervals) can verify an appropriate intensity. An athlete needs to look for opportunities to do a mini-warm-up and skill practice (especially in intermittent sports, e.g., baseball) and tend immediately to any minor injuries.

Resistance Segment

Progressive overloads with resistance training can be enhanced with the incorporation of warm-up set(s) (e.g., 60 percent of training weight) and adequate relief between sets and exercises. You and/or the individual in question should always follow weight-room safety rules, especially spotting guidelines. The guidelines for specific training methods should be followed for optimum and safe results. Traditional weight-room practices often do not check for a "balanced" program with respect to agonists and antagonists, and therefore there may be a need for specific muscle stretching or strengthening. As with the aerobic segment, monitor correct breathing techniques, speed of movement, base of support, muscle tightness and alignment, such as pelvic stabilization, and avoidance of extreme ROM. Differentiate between fatigue, soreness, and inflammation and modify exercises around minor injuries (including avoidance).

Cool-Down Segment

This is probably the time, with the tissues warm, for maximum flexibility gains. Target those muscles used in the workout, especially if they were used eccentrically. Emphasis is usually on static stretching but consider PNF (proprioceptive neuromuscular facilitation; see page 202) if flexibility is a priority. At this point, cardiovascular indicators (e.g., heart rate, depth of breathing, blood pressure) should be well down. Muscles should feel worked but not sore or tight, and if there are any "hot spots" or minor injuries, ice them – and do not underestimate the effect of a relaxing shower.

As anyone who has ever suffered the next-day effects of a particularly hard workout or training session can attest, spending a little extra time during the cool-down phases is well worth the effort, given the potential for diminished training due to soreness and fatigue. Even though you may be extremely tired after a workout, it is wise not to cut corners on this cooldown phase.

WHERE DO WE GO FROM HERE?

In order to design effective exercise programs, we must be able to analyze various exercises, sport skills, and work tasks. The next section will present and apply biomechanical principles that not only relate to fitness and personal training, but facilitate performance improvement and injury prevention.

When combined with the material we have covered in the last two sections – on basic training principles and the more specific adaptation of these principles into a personal training program – you now have a thorough grounding in the fundamental elements of exercise and physical activity, and how the human body performs in myriad ways while exercising. This material will prepare you for the topics covered in Unit 3, as we examine the basics of how people develop motor abilities and learn the skills necessary to participate in sport and other physical activities.

New York Giants' quarterback Jesse Palmer of Ottawa (Nepean), Ontario, drops back during action in Atlanta, August 2002. Named Canadian Player of the Year in 1996, Palmer received a scholarship to the University of Florida (AP Photo/Alan Mothner).

15

Biomechanical Principles and Applications

"Nature and Nature's laws lay hid in night. God said, 'Let Newton be!' and all was light."
— Alexander Pope, epitaph intended for Sir Isaac Newton

KEY CONCEPTS

- Biomechanics
- Scientific models
- Equilibrium
- Conservation of energy
- Newton's Three Laws of Motion
- Centre of mass
- Linear (or translational) motion

- Rotational motion
- Acceleration
- Force as a vector
- Angular acceleration
- Moment of force (torque)
- Moment of inertia
- Radius of gyration

- Classes of levers
- Seven principles of biomechanics
- Applied biomechanics

In previous sections of this unit, we have looked at factors that can influence our ability to perform, such as the foods we eat, the chemicals we ingest, and the equipment we use to assist us. In this section, we will take a look at a slightly different area – namely, how physical forces affect human performance. This broad field is known as biomechanics.

Biomechanics plays an indispensable but little-recognized role in the various sub-fields of health and physical education. In particular, clinical practitioners of biomechanics play a vital role in isolating the physical causes and corrective actions required for serious physical injuries. Practitioners are also prominent in the design of sport and office equipment as well as prosthetic devices, such as artificial hips and limbs and orthopedic footwear. Biomechanics is a field too vast to cover fully here. Nevertheless, the material in this section will give you an idea as to what this exciting subject is all about.

MODELS, THEORIES, AND LAWS IN SCIENCE

"Models" (and theories and laws) are what scientists ultimately strive for. Scientific models reduce things to their essentials and establish a basis, not only for understanding how things work, but also for predicting how they will behave and, ultimately, for influencing them to behave in the ways we want. Recall, for example, the "anatomical position" discussed at the beginning of Unit 1. This is a simplified "model" used worldwide as a starting point for describing and analyzing human anatomy and movement.

Any discussion of biomechanics (not to mention physics) must begin with a tribute to Sir Isaac Newton and his famous three "Laws of Motion." This book is no exception. From Newton's simple statement (model) of the nature of physical relationships of three hundred years ago, a great deal has followed. It is probably safe to say that few other scientific theories have had such far-reaching implications as Newton's Laws of Motion.

For all intents, Newton's "model" explained the workings of physical forces in the universe and laid the basis for modern physics (and thereby biomechanics as well).

Equilibrium and the Conservation of Energy

Newton's theory (and biomechanics) rests on two assumptions: physical equilibrium and the conservation of energy. Equilibrium is posited in his First Law and the conservation of energy in his Third Law. The rest follows from these assumptions.

Normally, a force acting on a body results in acceleration. Equilibrium can be thought of as kind of a "perfect" situation where more than one force acts on a body but, because the sum of forces is zero, no change in velocity results. The conservation of energy principle, on the other hand, states that energy can never be created or destroyed, but can only be converted from one form to another.

Isaac Newton's "Model Universe"
The Laws of Motion

In 1687, Sir Isaac Newton published his two-volume *Philosophiae Naturalis Principia Mathematica*, which laid out his famous Three Laws of Motion. At the heart of Newton's model was the idea of physical equilibrium, with things resting (or possibly moving) in a uninfluenced state (inertia, his First Law).

1. The Law of Inertia

Every object in a state of uniform motion tends to remain in that state of motion unless an external force is applied to it.

Newton's First Law asserts that a body will remain at rest or in a state of constant velocity unless acted upon by an external force.

This law (known as the Law of Inertia) would apply, for example, to an athlete in a stationary position or to someone moving at a constant speed in a particular direction (say, a downhill skier).

2. The Law of Acceleration

The relationship between an object's mass (m), its acceleration (a), and the applied force (F) is F=ma.

Newton's Second Law states that a force applied to a body causes an acceleration of that body of a

Sir Isaac Newton (1642-1727).

magnitude proportional to the force, in the direction of the force, and inversely proportional to the body's mass.

This law (known as the Law of Acceleration) could be applied to a projectile, such as a javelin or a baseball, where it would be possible to compute acceleration from measurement of the changing speeds.

3. The Law of Reaction

For every action there is an equal and opposite reaction.

Newton's Third Law asserts that, when one body exerts a force on a second body, the second body exerts a reactive force on the first body that is equal in magnitude and opposite in direction.

This law (known as the Law of Reaction) would apply, for example, to a basketball player leaping to make a jump shot. The action of pushing against the court floor leads to a reaction (i.e., the floor pushing back) and, ultimately, the athlete's body leaving the ground.

Newton's Relevance to Exercise

As a material object, the human body is, of course, not exempt from Newton's three laws. Just as biomechanics can be defined as "the application of the principles of physics to the analysis of movement," it is necessary to view our bodies at rest and in motion as we would any other object. It is thus subject to inertia, acceleration, and reaction. A football player sprinting down the field obeys the Law of Acceleration, for example, and the Law of Reaction when he or she is tackled.

Jordan Jovtchev (Bulgaria) in the Gymnastics World Cup Final, Stuttgart, Germany, 2002 (AP Photo/Thomas Kienzle).

From these two starting principles, or theoretical assumptions, one can go on to examine, concretely, what happens when an external force (F – a push or a pull) enters the picture, causing a change in movement (a – acceleration) of a mass (m). In fact, this is the purpose of Newton's Second Law as expressed in the famous formula:

$F = ma$ (Force equals mass times acceleration)

The standard unit of measurement for force is, appropriately enough, the **Newton**, (abbreviated as N). An object of about 102 grams (such as a lunch-box sized container of yogurt) would have the weight of about 1N on Earth. This unit, however, is not a basic unit but a derived one. Its relation to the basic units – seconds (s), mass (m) and kilogram (kg) – follows from Newton's basic law of mechanics: $F = ma$.

Thus: $1 \, [N] = 1 \, [kg] \, [m] / [s^2]$.

It should be pointed out that the two terms *mass* and *weight* are not synonymous. On the moon, you would have the same mass as you do on Earth, but you would have less weight (due to the reduced gravity). Likewise, the term "centre of gravity," commonly used to describe the point at which the mass of a body seems to be focused, is a misnomer. The correct term is centre of mass since it is not really dependent on gravity.

TYPES OF MOTION

Before going on, let us also distinguish two types of motion: linear (or translational) motion and rotational motion. The physical principles (Newtonian physics) are the same, but they need to be analyzed differently.

- Linear (or translational) motion is movement in a particular direction (and would include the resultant of more than one linear force acting on an object). Linear movement is when a sprinter accelerates down a track or, to use a more complicated example, a hockey player quickly veers to go around another player. In such cases, force is generated by the athlete's muscles and the resulting motion is in a straight line (or can be resolved in a straight line).

- Rotational motion, on the other hand, refers to movement about an axis. Unlike with linear motion, in rotational motion the force does not act through the centre of mass, but rather is "off-centre," and this results in rotation. Kick a soccer ball through the centre of mass and it goes in a straight line; kick it "off-centre" and the ball rotates. Examples commonly used to illustrate rotational motion are the gymnast's somersault and the ice-skater's spin.

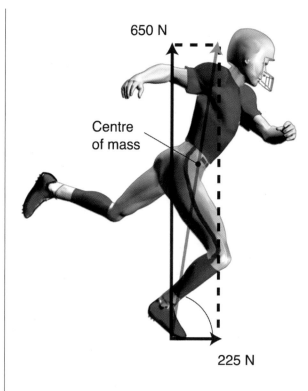

650 N

Centre of mass

225 N

Figure 15.1: Basic vector analysis.

Linear Motion

Take the simplified example of a wide receiver in football, where the motion involves acceleration (that is, a change in velocity) in a straight line. Because the athlete starts from a stationary position and accelerates down the field, the basic physics involved ($F = ma$) are relatively straightforward.

Of course, human movements are not in a straight line, as in the case of the wide receiver. Thus, it is necessary to introduce the notion of a force as a vector – that is, force as a push or a pull of a certain magnitude in a particular direction. The forward movement of the wide receiver is a combination of a vertical force and a forward force, resulting in a vector force somewhere in between. The working out of such resultant forces follows the basic laws of trigonometry. This notion of force as a vector, as in this simplified example, can help to shed light on the factors affecting the movement's outcome.

The illustration above (Figure 15.1), for example, shows a vector analysis of a wide receiver's movement. The vertical force of 650 N combines with the forward force of 225 N, resulting in a diagonal force vector acting on the centre of mass that can be computed using basic trigonometry.

Biomechanical Innovations
The "Fosbury Flop" and the "Jump Serve"

No introduction to biomechanics would be complete without examples of where biomechanical analysis has led to a breakthrough of one kind or another.

The "Fosbury Flop"

Until the mid-1960s, athletes who participated in the popular track-and-field discipline of the high jump attempted to clear the bar by running towards it, "straddling" it by lifting one leg and then the other quickly over the bar, in a forward position that almost resembled a sideways roll in mid-air. That all changed with Dick Fosbury, an American jumper, who, as a young high-school student, started experimenting with a technique that saw him run to the bar, twist his body upon take-off, and then clear the bar headfirst while flying through the air on his back.

Although Fosbury initially attempted his "Fosbury Flop" as an experiment, he soon perfected the technique to the point where he won the gold medal in the high jump in the 1968 Olympics in Mexico City, setting a world record in the process. Since then, every high jumper at the national and world level has used Fosbury's jumping style.

From a biomechanical perspective, the technique has an advantage over the older "western roll" approach (as it was called at the time). As the athlete approaches the bar, he or she arches the neck and back, keeping the centre of mass relatively low in comparison to the other method. This allows the jumper to apply the ground reaction force over a longer period of time and to achieve greater vertical velocity and a higher jump.

This jumping style has also only been made possible due to the development of high-tech foam pits. It would have been dangerous to land on one's back (the end result of a flop jump) from heights of more than 2 metres in old-fashioned sand or sawdust.

The "Jump Serve"

The sport of volleyball also saw the introduction of an important innovation in the 1980s in the form of the "jump serve." Prior to this, players serving in volleyball games would stand in a stationary position, and with an overhead, side-arm, or underhanded motion, serve the ball to the opposing team. But with the jump serve, players began standing well behind the service line, lobbing the ball forward, and then running and jumping high into the air to "spike" the ball to the opposing team.

Clearly, this transfer of forward momentum makes the service zip through the air at a much faster speed – clocked among top players at up to 120 km/h – making it much more difficult for opposing players to receive than the stationary service. In addition, the fact that the ball is travelling from a much higher point – i.e., well above net level – makes it harder to return than one served from just above a player's head.

While the jump serve is not as widely adopted in volleyball as the Fosbury flop is in high jumping, it is still common at all levels, including international, professional, and Olympic competition, and in beach volleyball.

Both the Fosbury Flop and the jump serve tell us something important about innovations in sports technique; namely, that while it may be good to follow conventional wisdom, it is sometimes wise to question why coaches and manuals recommend certain ways of performing a skill. A grounding in biomechanics can help us understand how techniques can be improved.

Rotational Motion

In cases of rotational motion, the same Newtonian laws apply. If the two kinds of motion are kept separate – linear (or translational) and rotational – the application of the physical principles, or at least the idea behind them, is fairly straightforward.

Rotational motion is comparable to linear motion (see Table 15.1). In the case of rotational motion, however, the object in question (say, the body or a body part) spins around an axis. With rotational motion, instead of the acceleration (change in velocity) of a mass, there is **angular acceleration**. Similarly, instead of force, there is what is known as the **moment of force (torque)**. Finally, rather than mass as a measure of inertia, there is what is referred to as the **moment of inertia** (rotational inertia).

A key concept in the case of rotational motion is the "moment of inertia." This is a difficult concept to grasp, but is central to the other concepts. Recall Newton's "model universe" and his First and Third Laws regarding equilibrium (inertia) and the conservation of energy (reaction). As in the case of linear or translational motion, the rotating object will be unmoved providing there is no additional moment of force that would cause an angular acceleration (a change in angular velocity per unit of time). The moment of inertia refers to the resistance to rotation. The larger the moment of inertia, the larger the moment of force needed to maintain the same angular acceleration.

In rotational systems, the moment of inertia depends on the distribution of the mass in relation to the axis of rotation. In effect, the further the mass is from the axis, the greater the moment of inertia (and therefore the harder it is to cause it to spin or to stop it from spinning). The closer it is to the axis of rotation, the easier it is to rotate it or to stop it from rotating. The average distance from the axis of rotation is known as the **radius of gyration**.

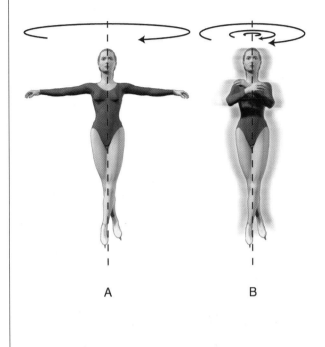

Figure 15.2: Manipulating the moment of inertia. Illustration A represents a strategy of increasing and illustration B represents a strategy of decreasing the moment of inertia during an ice-skating spin.

Examples of Rotation Principles

Because all human movement, especially in physical exercise and sport, involves rotation of one kind or another, there are many examples that could be used to demonstrate the biomechanical principles involved, some more obvious than others.

- **Ice-skating.** The ice-skater begins to spin with arms spread apart then suddenly brings them closer to the body. The end result of tightening up is that the skater's spin (angular velocity) increases, seemingly miraculously.

- **Gymnastics.** Following a series of rapid somersaults in a tight position, the gymnast does a forward flip with the body positioned more or less straight. By opening up, the gymnast increases the moment of inertia, thereby resulting in a decrease in angular velocity.

- **Diving.** After leaving the high diving board, the diver curls tightly and then opens up just before entering the water. By opening up before entry, the diver increases the moment of inertia, thereby slowing down the angular velocity (and, one hopes, ensures a smooth and safe entry).

Table 15.1: Linear and rotational motion: comparable concepts

LINEAR MOTION	ROTATIONAL MOTION
Displacement	Angular displacement
Velocity	Angular velocity
Acceleration of a mass	Angular acceleration
Force	Moment of force (torque)
Mass	Moment of inertia

LEVER SYSTEMS

In introductory physics texts, a lever is affectionately referred to as the simplest mechanical device that can be rightly called a "machine" (an instrument for performing work). Every movable bone in the human body, acting alone or in concert with others, is part of a lever system that facilitates movement.

The Human Muscle Machine

Physicists identify three **classes of levers** based on the location of the fulcrum (the triangle in the illustrations) in relation to the force.

- In a **Class I lever** (e.g., a teeter-totter), the fulcrum (or axis) is located between the force (effort) and the resistance (load).

- In a **Class II lever** (e.g., a wheelbarrow), the resistance is between the force and the fulcrum.

- In a **Class III lever** (e.g., snow shovelling) the force is between the fulcrum and the resistance.

An example of a Class I (teeter-totter) lever in the human body is the neck moving from a position of flexion to a position of extension. The contraction of the trapezius muscle permits extension of the head. This is the weakest of all the levers.

There are very few cases of Class II (wheelbarrow) levers in the human body – the ankle joint, shown in the illustration below, is one example. The gastrocnemius muscle pulls on the calcaneus to plantar flex the foot. Because of its arrangement, this second-class lever can lift a large amount of weight.

The most common type of lever in the human body is the Class III (snow shovelling) lever. With such levers, the muscle force can be near the joint (fulcrum) but the force is always between the joint and the resistance. The most obvious of these is the biceps-elbow complex (shown in Figure 15.3). In the human body, this type of lever mechanism permits speed of movement (in, say, the forearm) in return for a sacrifice of muscle force (in the biceps).

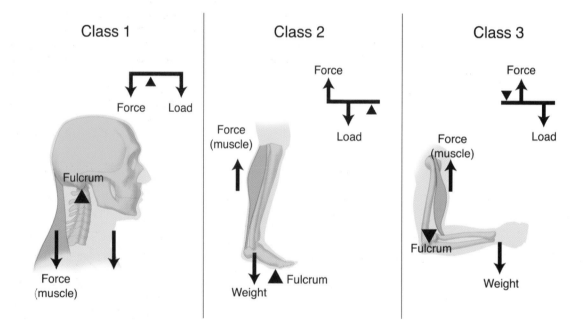

Figure 15.3: Physicists have identified three classes of levers based on the location of the fulcrum (indicated by a triangle). Levers play a critical part in human movement and in the biomechanics of the musculoskeletal system.

Seven Principles of Biomechanical Analysis
The building blocks of exercise

You can gain insight into movement dynamics and begin to apply biomechanical analysis by utilizing the seven principles of biomechanics. The Coaching Association of Canada's National Coaching Certification Program (NCCP) Level 2 Theory course sets forward these seven principles, which can be grouped into four broad categories: (1) stability, (2) maximum effort, (3) linear motion, and (4) angular motion.

Stability

The ability to maintain one's balance is crucial in just about any sport, whether one is on skates, a balance beam, or the football field (for example, in the case of a ball-carrier trying to fend off a tackler).

Principle 1: The lower the centre of mass, the larger the base of support, the closer the centre of mass to the base of support, and the greater the mass, the more stability increases.

This principle has, in itself, four subcomponents:

The height of the centre of mass. The imaginary point at which a person or an object's mass is concentrated.

Principle 1: Stability.

The line of gravity. An imaginary vertical line that passes straight down the centre of mass to the ground.

The base of support. The area between the supporting limbs.

Mass. Mass is defined as a measure of resistance to linear motion, with greater mass representing greater resistance – i.e., a more massive athlete (usually referred to as a "heavier" one) can offer greater resistance to linear motion than can a lighter one.

An extreme example of the stability principle can be seen in the sport of Sumo wrestling, which, while often the source of some puzzlement in Western culture, is taken very seriously in Japan. As a group, Sumo wrestlers are the most massive of all athletes. In competition against each other, they adopt a legs-spread-wide-apart stance to increase their base of support and ensure a lower centre of mass. Since the object of the sport is to force your opponent outside a relatively small ring and/or to topple the opponent over, it is clear that a wrestler's stability is the most important aspect of the sport (along with the muscular strength needed to push against and gain leverage over your opponent).

In some sports, athletes are rendered totally unstable when they lose contact with the ground for short stretches of time. Anyone who has seen a football receiver receive a hit while taking to the air to catch a ball, or a high-flying basketball player being undercut when he or she jumps to execute a lay-up, can attest to just how vulnerable these athletes are while in an unstable position in mid-air.

Maximum Effort

In many sports, athletes are required to use skills that enable them to go "all out" during competition or training, such as attempting to run at top speed or to lift heavier weights than ever before.

Principle 2: The production of maximum force requires the use of all possible joint movements that contribute to the task's objective.

In a sense, this principle is self-evident: with more joints coming into play in a given skill, the more muscles there will be to contract – leading to a greater force being exerted (thus lending an air of truth to the old sayings, "Give it your all!" or "Put everything you've got into it!"). Consequently, when performing activities where maximum force is required, coaches encourage athletes to use slow, controlled, high-intensity movements, while moving body segments at more or less the same time.

When coaches encourage athletes to adopt a slow, controlled approach to lifting weights such as during Olympic lifts, squats, or the bench press, they are following this biomechanical principle as a way of ensuring that the muscles that these exercises are designed to help are actually being helped. (It is also a good way to avoid injury.) Added to that is the fact that, for maximum force, all the potential joints that can be used can take part in the exercise. In accordance with the Principle of Overload (see page 193), this also means

Principle 2: Maximum force.

Principle 3: Maximum velocity.

that maximum training can take place over time.

In golf, beginners often try to rely too much on their arm strength as a way of hitting the ball a great distance without using the joints of the pelvis, legs, back, and other body parts in their swing. If an experienced golfer can instruct the beginner in an "integrated swing" – one that uses many joints as opposed to just a few – the novice can often see his or her swing improve quickly.

Principle 3: The production of maximum velocity requires the use of joints in order – from largest to smallest.

Although high-velocity skills are often performed so quickly that it is difficult to notice the intricacies of what is going on, it is usually the case that, in performing them, the larger, slower joints (i.e., those in the leg) begin the movement while the smaller joints play their role when the preceding joint has reached its peak speed. With some skills – such as hitting a tennis or golf ball, or a hockey slapshot – the aim is to have reached maximum velocity of movement at the exact moment of impact with the ball, puck, and so forth. Participants try to combine the velocity of previous movements and transfer them into the final skill segment, which often requires a stick, club, or racquet, so that this implement is moving at

maximum velocity when it strikes. A related principle holds that, the longer the implement, the faster the impact, providing the athlete can actually swing a longer (i.e., heavier) implement with greater velocity.

When basketball coaches tell players that their jump shots should "come from the legs," they are merely restating this third principle. The large joints in the leg begin the shooting motion as the player pushes off the court. Then, other joints further the shooting motion in sequence (the pelvis, the trunk, the shoulder, the elbow, the wrist, and the fingers) until the proper follow-through is complete.

In theory, a longer hockey stick with a longer handle should help a young player shoot the puck harder and farther because it will enable the player to generate more velocity. But this theory does not always work out in practice. It is only the case if the player can duplicate the shooting motion of the shorter stick with the longer one – which would be tough to do with a longer, heavier stick. Also, the move to a longer hockey stick will mean a likely sacrifice in accuracy, as the heavier implement would be harder to control.

Linear Motion

Linear motion is simply movement in a straight line. It can be broken down into several aspects.

Momentum refers to the amount of motion developed by an athlete (or object). Linear momentum is the amount of momentum developed in a straight line, a quantity that can be calculated by multiplying the mass of an athlete (or object) by its velocity. If you think of a football player or hockey player, there is certainly a component of linear motion and a significant momentum in the actions of these athletes — indeed, the outcomes of collisions is a direct consequence of momentum.

Impulse refers to the application of force over a segment of time that results in a change of momentum. Impulse can be calculated by multiplying the average force applied by the length of time during which it is applied to bring about the change in momentum.

Principle 4: Impulse.

Joint range of motion refers to the amount of movement a joint can undergo, as measured in degrees.

Streamlining refers to minimizing the surface area of an object in the direction of motion. Streamlining also involves making this surface area as smooth as possible so that the flow of air (or water) past the object is also smooth.

Principle 4: The greater the applied impulse, the greater the increase in velocity.

Also known as the "principle of impulse," this principle comes into play when joint range of motion is relevant. Basically, when an activity requires a maximal application of force, it follows that the joint involved will go through a longer range of motion.

The principle of impulse often occurs in reverse – when forces have to be absorbed. Many sports require a "soft touch" in catching or controlling a puck or ball. In such a case, the athlete has to dissipate the momentum he or she has built up in order to prevent the object from eluding his or her control.

When attempting to dunk a basketball, it is often the players who bend their knees the deepest while gathering themselves for takeoff who end up furthest above the rim when dunking – and the same has been noted with high jumpers whose crouch phase in the run-up to the bar is pronounced. This is because these athletes are going through the greatest range of motion as they attempt to attain maximum height. Note, though, that simply making the deepest crouch does not guarantee maximum height. That is because being able to go through this maximal range of motion also implies a great deal of leg strength. Simply going into a deep crouch will not work unless you have the leg strength to pull off the full jump.

Inexperienced soccer players often stick out one of their feet stiffly in an attempt to control a rolling ball or one sailing through the air, only to see it bounce away. But an experienced player will, with a deft movement of the leg and foot, draw inward, taking back some of the force and allowing the ball's force to be dissipated over a slightly longer instant than would be the case if the ball was to hit the foot dead-on.

Principle 5: **Movement usually occurs in the direction opposite that of the applied force.**

Known as the principle of the direction of the application of force, this principle is closely related to Newton's Third Law of Motion which, stated briefly, holds that every action has an equal and opposite reaction. In sports, this principle is relevant whenever an athlete pushes against any playing surface or piece of equipment. When the athlete exerts a force, the surface pushes back with the same force and in the opposite direction. Since an athlete usually directs his or her force in more than one direction (i.e., the high jumper who is trying to move up while gaining height and forward while clearing the bar), this force usually has a diagonal component to it.

Coaches often recommend that beginner runners try to avoid bouncing when they run – that is, they should attempt to reduce the vertical force they are exerting, producing an up-and-down motion, and concentrate instead on developing an efficient stride that moves them forward while cutting down on the "bobbing" motion.

In many sports, athletes try to cut down on forces that oppose movement

Principle 5: Reaction.

according to Newton's Third Law – for example, resistance from water or air currents. This is why many swimmers have turned to streamlined full-body swimsuits similar to those worn by speed skaters and skiers. In sports where the merest fractions of a second can make all the difference, these high-tech methods of countering opposing forces are crucial.

In the same way, cyclists and runners will often try to use the tactic of "tucking in" behind opponents when facing a stiff head-wind. Not only do these athletes have to overcome the usual opposing forces of the ground pushing against their legs and wheels, but they also have to overcome the increased air resistance that comes with competing on a windy day. If an athlete can "hide" from an oncoming wind by allowing an opponent to face most of the resistance, and thereby deflect it, it is estimated that energy savings of between 20 and 40 percent can occur.

Angular Motion

In every sport, angular motion plays a key part. Defined simply, it is the circular motion that occurs around an imaginary line called the axis of rotation. As discussed at the beginning of this book (Unit 1, Section 1), the body is usually described as having three main axes: a vertical one running through the centre

of the body from head to toe (longitudinal axis); a horizontal one passing from side to side through the centre of the body (horizontal axis); and another horizontal one that passes from back to front (antero-posterior axis).

The axis of rotation passes through the middle of a joint when a body point moves around the joint. When the whole body rotates (as in a somersault), the axis of rotation is the body's point of contact with the ground (in a somersault, first the hands and then the back of the neck/head). And when the body is airborne, all of its axes pass through the centre of mass, with all body parts rotating around it. There are also three key terms relating to angular motion.

Angular velocity. Usually measured in degrees per second, angular velocity is the rotational velocity of an athlete or his/her body segment in the performance of a movement – i.e., a measurement of just how fast that body part is rotating.

Moment of force or torque. The product of the applied force and the perpendicular distance to a pivot (or hinge) is called the torque (or the moment). Torques produce rotations in the same way that forces produce translational (linear) motion.

Moment of inertia. In the same way that we defined mass above as resistance to linear motion, the moment of inertia is the resistance to angular motion. The moment of inertia is computed as the mass multiplied by the square of the perpendicular distance to the axis of rotation.

Principle 6: **Angular motion is produced by the application of a force acting at some distance from an axis, that is, by torque.**

This principle is also known as the principle of the production of angular motion. In the same way that the application of force produces changes in linear motion, the application of torque produces changes in angular motion.

Athletes are concerned with three kinds of rotations produced through torque: rotations of their entire body, rotations of individual body segments, and

Principle 6: Torque.

Principle 7: Angular momentum.

BIOMECHANICAL FORMULAE

We have examined a number of ways in which the principles of biomechanics can be used to analyze "real-life" sports. To aid in this, a number of formulae are utilized by biomechanists. Following are several key ones.

Force: As derived by Newton, the force acting on an object (what causes it to accelerate) can be expressed as follows:

Force = ma

where m is the mass of the object and a represents acceleration.

Acceleration: The acceleration of an object is measured as follows:

Acceleration = (v-u) / t

where v is the object's final velocity, u is its starting velocity, and t is the time it takes an object to travel a set distance.

Momentum: Momentum represents the product of the object's mass and its velocity. It can be expressed as follows:

Momentum = mv

where m is mass and v is velocity.

Impulse: Impulse refers to the product of a force applied over a time interval. It can be expressed as follows:

Impulse = $F(t_f - t_i)$

where t_f and t_i are the final and initial limits of the time interval.

Impulse-momentum relationship: In order for an object to experience a change in momentum, an impulse must be applied. It can be expressed as follows:

$F(t_f - t_i)$ = mv-mu

where t_f and t_i are the final and initial limits of the time interval, m is mass, v is the final velocity at t_f and u is the initial velocity at t_i.

The above material is based on the National Coaching Certification Program (NCCP) Level 2 Theory course guide, pages 5-5 to 5-35, published by The Coaching Association of Canada (2000). For more on the work of The Coaching Association of Canada and the NCCP, see pages 279, 284-85, 288-89, and 373.

rotations of projectiles. The entire body is rotated by the application of some off-centre force – i.e., one that does not go through the centre of mass. Body segments rotate when muscles produce torque around a certain axis of rotation. In the case of projectiles, the natural flight of objects such as a baseball, basketball, or javelin is in a parabola. But in many sports, being able to impart spin on a projectile is a key component of strategy – i.e., throwing a curve ball in baseball or using back- or top-spin in tennis and golf. Spins occur when off-centre forces are imparted at the moment of release and/or impact.

One of the most common injuries found in baseball pitchers is to the rotator cuff – the group of muscles in the shoulder that play a major part in the delivery of a pitch, particularly those such as curve balls and "sliders" that have considerable spin imparted to them. After hundreds of thousands of such pitches, these muscles can become worn down by the constant torque placed on them in an effort to begin the necessary spinning motion. Interestingly, the delivery of such pitches includes both the rotation of the arm and the rotation of the projectile (i.e., the baseball).

In sports, it is often the opponent who tries to impart the off-centre force in the form of body contact. In a hockey body-check, or a football or rugby tackle, for example, the idea is to knock an opponent off his or her centre of mass and thereby cause a loss of balance.

Principle 7: Angular momentum is constant when an athlete or object is free in the air.

This principle is also known as the principle of conservation of angular momentum, and its key component is the fact that, once an athlete is airborne, he or she will travel with a constant angular momentum.

The example of a diver is often used to illustrate the principle of the conservation of angular momentum. When the diver rotates in the air after leaving the diving board, his or her angular momentum is constant while in the air. As angular momentum is the product of both the diver's moment of inertia and his or her rate of rotation (the angular velocity), changes in the rate of rotation will result as the diver repositions his or her limbs and trunk to change how far the mass of the body is distributed from the axis of rotation.

In order to ensure a controlled entry into the water, towards the end of the dive the athlete must "open up" from the "tuck" position (thereby increasing the moment of inertia) so as to reduce the rate of rotation.

APPLICATIONS IN BIOMECHANICS

In view of ever greater demands for better performance results by elite athletes and their coaches, it is not surprising that the field of **applied biomechanics** has grown incrementally in recent years. But it is not only coaches who have been involved in the application of biomechanical theory. A whole range of health-care professionals – physiotherapists, sport physicians, rehabilitation medical professionals, and design engineers charged with creating new prosthetic devices – are involved as well. Behind them is an army of research institutes and scholars carrying out scientific experiments that they hope will add to the knowledge of movement and lead to applications for those suffering from various kinds of physical injury.

The principles of biomechanics have been applied to every sport – from baseball pitching and batting, to kicking and "heading" a soccer ball, to improving the mechanics of swimming and cycling, to name just a few – and probably to most kinds of human movement. As a field of analysis and practical intervention, biomechanics has already proved its value to athletes and to the wider public. As sports and the treatment of physical injury become more and more "scientific," and as the difference between a first and second place finish becomes smaller and smaller, it can only be expected that the role of biomechanical analysis will become more important.

The ultimate goal of applied biomechanics depends on your area of interest.

- **Performance improvement.** Coaches and athletes are focused on "performance improvement" within the aspects of technique and sport training.

- **Injury prevention and rehabilitation.** A high level of interest in biomechanics has come from sports medicine specialists, trainers, and injured athletes in relation to "injury prevention and rehabilitation."

- **Fitness and personal training.** In the burgeoning field of "fitness and personal training," biomechanical analysis can be applied both to exercise and to equipment.

Let us end this section on biomechanical principles by examining some practical applications in each of these three areas.

PERFORMANCE IMPROVEMENT

Many biomechanists feel that the greatest value of their discipline lies within the area of performance improvement. Coaches, athletes, and equipment manufacturers who have been willing to apply the principles and experiment with traditional techniques, training regimens, and strategies have accounted for many improvements in sports performances. Below we will see how the performance of athletes is a function of (1) their technique, (2) training, and, in some cases, (3) the design of their equipment.

Application I – The Pre-Stretch

The swing of a batter, the serve of a tennis player, or the slap shot of a hockey player are all powerful sport skills that require large forces in the direction of the ball or puck (Newton's Second Law). Upon closer analysis of each of these skills, it is apparent that the athlete's first action is, in fact, in the opposite direction. What is the purpose of this wind-up or preparatory phase? Is it a good thing or could it be a potential cause of injury?

The first thing you notice about this preparatory or pre-stretch phase is that it places the muscle(s) in a stretch prior to using the muscle(s) for a joint action. The amount of force produced by a muscle is related to its length. The optimum tension that can be generated will occur when the active muscle is slightly greater than its resting length (usually between 100 and 120 percent of the resting length).

The tension or force that the athlete is able to generate is not only dependent upon the muscle's ability to contract. As the muscle lengthens beyond its resting length, "passive" tension is also generated. The connective tissue in the muscle and tendon offers resistance to the stretch, thereby contributing stored elastic energy, much like the elastic recoil of a stretched rubber band.

The total tension increases after the "active" (muscular) tension starts to drop off. This total tension includes both the active and passive components, demonstrating how influential the pre-stretch phase can be in order to facilitate force output from the muscle in the movement. Effective batting, serving, and shooting is significantly dependent upon the athlete's use of this preparatory phase of the skill.

This pre-stretch is obviously achieved through a greater range of motion of the joint. Two words of caution before we think that more range of motion is better. Firstly, remember that when the muscle is lengthened further, the tension generated by muscle contraction will drop off. This may mean that if you bounce a little at the bottom of your bench press (to gain passive tension), it does little to increase the training effect on the muscle. You would be wiser to get slight assistance on the up phase from a partner. Secondly, there is a "yield" point or point of tissue failure. Many muscle strain injuries are a result of this extreme length-tension situation.

Application 2 – Training: Plyometrics

Essential to athletes who jump, lift, sprint, or throw is a training technique called plyometrics. Plyometrics are exercises that enable a muscle to reach maximal strength in as short as time as possible (power). Plyometric training can take on various forms such as bounding, multiple hops and jumps, box and/or depth jumps, and medicine ball exercises for the upper body.

For an exercise to be truly plyometric, it must be a movement preceded by an eccentric (lengthening) contraction. This stretch-shortening of muscle tissue combines two training factors: (1) the pre-stretch elastic recoil from the connective tissue; and, (2) the sensors in the muscle spindle (proprioceptors) that activate the stretch reflex after a rapid lengthening.

Because of chemical, mechanical, and neurological factors that influence the force of the contracting muscle, eccentric lengthening (before rapid concentric shortening) produces the greatest force and power capabilities. Specific plyometric training changes the strength of the response in terms of muscle contraction. The faster the muscle is lengthened (eccentric phase), the greater the concentric force after the stretch. Thus, training with pre-stretch and activating neuromuscular components improves the efficiency of neural actions and will allow for faster and more powerful changes in direction. Plyometric training allows the athlete to mimic, to a greater extent than most strength training methods, the forces and specific joint involvement of any given sport action.

Application 3 – Equipment Design

Perhaps in no other sport than golf has the evolution of equipment had so much impact on the athlete's ability to perform. One of the first applications of biomechanics to golf is that of lever arm length and golf shaft length. Given the same force and club velocity, the longer the club, the farther the ball will travel. Longer clubs naturally put the golfer farther away from the ball. At this distance, it is the angular speed of the club head that transfers velocity to the ball (the application of Newton's First and Second Laws).

Recall, from earlier in this section, that linear velocity equals angular velocity times the radius of rotation (club length). Therefore, the angular acceleration of a longer club head will produce greater linear velocity to the ball than will a shorter club. What would the effect be if the golfer stood farther from the ball by slightly extending the shoulders and elbows?

Earlier in this section we learned that the moment of inertia depends on the position of the mass in relation to the axis of rotation. The manufacture of a golf club's weight distribution or swing weight can be adjusted to move the weight farther from the grip end of the club. This increase in the club's moment of inertia requires an increase in the moment of force to maintain the same angular acceleration. If the golfer is strong and skilled enough to provide this, the performance will improve. If the golfer cannot generate a sufficient moment of force, the performance will probably be jeopardized.

INJURY PREVENTION AND REHABILITATION

Physicians and physiotherapists have long known that a good knowledge of biomechanics will help in diagnosing the causes of an injury. It can provide the mechanical basis that athletic therapists need to tape a joint, or assess the value of a brace or orthotic device. Coaches and athletes need to recognize when fatigue or minor injuries are affecting the mechanics of a skill or when a drill may produce excessive or dangerous forces.

From a preventative and rehabilitative perspective, proper training principles should be followed.

- Progressive resistance training to improve muscular endurance, size, and tensile strength of both muscle and connective tissue can be integrated into the off- and pre-season schedule.

- Specific design of aerobic and muscular warm-up tailored to the activities planned for the workout will bring more injury prevention value to the session.

- All key muscles to be used must be stretched once warm.

- Finally, muscle imbalance needs to be addressed. (Check your own sport or activity. Are there muscles that are used heavily and, therefore, are probably overly tight? Conversely, their antagonists may be disproportionately weak.)

Application 4 – Injury Risk Assessment

Injuries to muscles, tendons, ligaments, and joints can occur when the muscle is overloaded rapidly, during an eccentric contraction to control momentum, when it is fatigued, or when used over a long duration.

Just as we can identify people at high risk of cardiovascular disease, it is important to identify those who are at risk for muscle and/or tendon strain. Athletes and coaches should go through a mental checklist before every practice or game.

- Are the muscles recovered or do they remain weak from previous workouts? Remember that it takes much longer to recover from a plyometric workout or intense game than it does from a moderate jog.

- Is there an existing injury that may be aggravated?

- Many athletes continue to play and practice when injured by substituting joint actions, which leaves them susceptible to an injury or muscle imbalance elsewhere.

- Is the athlete fatigued from the previous drill or activity? With fatigue, the neuromuscular system loses its ability to control the forces imposed on the muscles and/or joints. Performance and the ability to absorb shock are sacrificed.

Muscles (and their tendons) at greatest risk of strain are biarticular muscles or muscles that cross two joints. These muscles are not long enough to allow a full range of motion at both joints at the same time. For example, once the knee is pulled close to the chest, the hamstrings cannot be stretched long enough to allow full extension of the knee.

Consider the hurdler who drives the hip into flexion (lead leg), then immediately extends the knee to have the heel clear the hurdle. Effective hamstring stretching will allow the hurdler to stay low while still clearing the hurdle. Those athletes who excessively raise their centre of mass over the hurdle could improve their time significantly with focused stretching.

Application 5 – Controlling Momentum

Muscles are responsible for routine joint movements but they also generate great speed in the body, slow down a fast-moving segment, and stabilize a joint position. The tension developed by muscles applies compression to the joints, enhancing their stability along with ligaments and joint capsules. However, in some joint positions, the tensions created by the muscles can act to pull the segments apart and create instability. As well, in some circumstances, the tension of the muscle may not be sufficient to withstand its attempt to stabilize the moving joint.

Muscles used to terminate a range of motion are at risk because they are used eccentrically to slow or "brake" a limb or body segment that is moving very quickly. It is not simply the speed or velocity of the limb, but it is the "momentum" of the limb. Momentum is a product of the segment's mass times its velocity *(momentum = m x v)*.

We see examples of this with the posterior rotator cuff muscles as they slow the arm in the follow-through phase of a throw or the hamstrings slowing the hip flexion of a soccer or football kick.

An individual may also experience such risk during a trunk twist when the velocity is not as great but the mass of the trunk is large, resulting in significant momentum. The trunk muscles would strain

Denis Garon competing in the weightlifting event at the 1988 Olympic Games in Seoul, South Korea (CP PHOTO/COA/Tim O'Lett).

eccentrically to control this action. We see that to change the momentum of an object (e.g., a body segment), an external force (eccentric muscle contraction) must be applied to the object.

Application 6 – Lifting an Object

By looking at movement mechanics, practitioners of biomechanics can reduce the risk of physical injury and design safer performance mechanics.

Lifting an object from the ground represents a mechanical action we face many times in a day. We must create a series of torques *(force x distance to axis of rotation)* within several lever systems. Let us focus on one of them – movement of the upper body as it rotates at the hip. If the spine and pelvis are stable, the force created by the hip extensors (gluteals) is transmitted by the erector spinae along the length of the spine to the upper limb, which then delivers the force to the object being lifted.

Recall that, in rotary systems, the moment of inertia depends on the position of the mass in relation to the axis of rotation. In effect, the farther the mass is from the axis, the greater the moment of inertia and the greater the torque needed to cause the rotation. Positioning the object to be lifted closer to the body (and the fulcrum) requires less torque during the lift.

The spinal column itself is not strong enough to bear the compression force from lifting heavy objects. The force created by the torque of lifting heavy weights can be many times the force of the weight itself. The muscles and connective tissues of the lumbar spine must bear the large majority of the forces involved. If these soft tissues are not sufficiently trained, severe injury can result.

FITNESS AND PERSONAL TRAINING

From individual exercise design to large group fitness classes, there are a large range of body types, sizes, and levels of fitness. As a result, some individuals inevitably overexert themselves, and others do not work as hard as they should. This is particularly true during strength training exercises. The application of biomechanical principles can allow one to make small adjustments in exercise design so that one's efforts are optimized while taking into account whatever limitations that may exist.

Biomechanical analysis begins by examining the method of execution of an exercise. Such analyses enable one to give advice concerning:

- the position of joints to isolate specific muscles;
- how to align the movement to the muscle;
- how to combine muscles for optimal results;
- the optimal speed for the objective;
- the best starting position and range of motion for an exercise; and
- how to modify the leverage to gain a greater strength output.

Application 7 – Gaining Leverage

Lever systems can help you to modify exercises and optimize the effort. If you are having difficulty with an exercise or want to make it more challenging, you can adjust the intensity by changing the lever system(s).

To view the body as a series of lever systems, consider the joint as the fulcrum and the bones as lever arms that move around the fulcrum. Muscle contraction is the force applied to the lever (at a point where the tendon attaches to the bone), while the weight of the body part(s) plus any external weight being lifted represent resistance to the force.

The majority of levers in the body are Class III (as discussed earlier in this section), which means that the force is applied between the resistance and fulcrum. The classic example of a third-class lever is the biceps acting around the elbow joint in which the elbow is the fulcrum, the radius bone is the lever arm, the biceps exerts the force, and the weight of the forearm (and object) is the resistance. The tendon of the biceps inserts just below the elbow. The distance from the fulcrum (elbow) to the force (biceps tendon) is called the muscle movement arm. The distance from the fulcrum (elbow) to the resistance is the load movement arm.

You can modify the intensity or difficulty of an exercise by changing aspects of the lever system. Changing the distance between the joint and the resistance (RA) is the most versatile way to modify an exercise. As the resistance moves closer to the joint, the muscle will have an easier time moving it. The challenge is to recognize the parts of the lever system in question: Which joint is the acting fulcrum? What is the best way to adjust the resistance arm? With calisthenics (body weight resistance exercises), you can use this knowledge to change the position of certain body segments and create changes in loading or difficulty.

For example, curl-ups can use a modified hand position to change the resistance arm (RA). Level one hand position has arms at the sides just above the floor. Level two has the arms crossed on the chest. Eventually the arms can be extended straight upwards beside the side of the head. If the fulcrum is the lower back, by moving the arms progressively farther away from the fulcrum, the resistance is also moving farther from the fulcrum. The increase in difficulty is quite noticeable as a result of the increased resistance arm (RA).

Application 8 – Generating Tensile Force

The maximum force that a muscle is capable of developing depends on several factors, including the length of the muscle, the type of contraction, and the velocity of the muscle contraction. When you are in the weight room, can you lift a greater weight than you can lower? Is the amount of weight that you can lift affected by how fast you lift it?

The mechanics of muscle force generation are dependent on the velocity of shortening as well as on muscle length. The mechanics of contraction within the sarcomere (the functional units that make up voluntary muscle) determine the relationship between the velocity of a muscle's contraction and its maximum force of contraction. As discussed in Unit 1 (beginning on page 40), the tension of a muscular contraction is the result of the attachment of crossbridges of the myosin filament to the actin filament within the sarcomere. This tensile force is proportional to the number of crossbridges attached and pulling on the actin filaments. When a muscle is shortening, some crossbridges will have been released. However, if the velocity of shortening is slow, only a small proportion will not be contributing to the tension. Therefore, in the sarcomere, higher tension is developed at slower velocities of shortening. This holds true for the whole muscle.

Let us say we are doing a biceps curl exercise. We may be able to lift 5 kilograms very quickly, but 15 kilograms cannot be lifted as quickly. Newton's First Law tells us that this is partly due to the inertia of the weight, but it is also because large forces cannot be produced if the muscle is shortened quickly.

Now, what about our ability to lower that weight or to hold it stationary? A muscle contracting eccentrically or isometrically is capable of producing more force than a muscle contracting concentrically. This means that you may need some help lifting 20 kilograms for the biceps curl, but you may be able to hold it steady (isometric). In fact, with 25 kilograms, after assistance during the concentric (up) phase, you may not be able to hold it stationary, but you may still maintain control during the lowering (eccentric) phase.

The tension developed in the eccentric contraction is greater than the maximum tension that could be developed in the isometric or concentric contractions. By understanding this concept, a spotter can anticipate when a lifter may fail and when they may need assistance.

Application 9 – Evaluating Resistance Machines

The basis for the design of resistance training equipment is rooted in many principles of mechanics. Above all, the resistance machine should closely replicate the path of motion of the body and add appropriate resistance throughout the range of safe motion.

An examination of equipment should consider the following mechanical issues:

- **Type of lever.** If the weight machine uses a Class III lever, the force is between the resistance and the axis of rotation. In this design, the weight has to move through a greater distance, which leads to greater inertia. The lifter has a harder time starting the move and stopping it once it is moving.

- **Axis of rotation.** The axis of rotation of the machine must match the axis of rotation of the joint in use. If not aligned, there are undue forces on the joint that can result in injury. Look for adjustments on machines that accommodate for differences in body size and limb length.

- **Path and range of motion.** Machines should follow the normal path of motion of the joints that they are trying to work. Is the joint path straight or curvilinear? Does the machine provide a fixed path of motion or does it allow some

freedom of movement, like a pulley system? As well, when analyzing a machine, make sure it does not take a person to extreme ranges of motion where the resistance can be difficult to control.

- **Machine resistance matching joint strength.** Each joint movement has an associated strength curve. In the earlier example of the biceps curl, the lifter is strongest around 90 degrees and weaker at the start and end of the range of motion. To accommodate these unique strength curves, equipment designers often use "cams." The cam is an elliptically shaped pulley-like mechanism on which the cable or belt travels. The cam changes how heavy the weight feels through the range of motion. It varies the resistance as the person naturally varies in strength.

Well-designed resistance exercise equipment will take into account these kinds of factors, and a knowledge of these biomechanical considerations will enable one to make better choices from the many types of fitness and training equipment available in the marketplace today.

WHERE DO WE GO FROM HERE?

In this section, we looked at Newton's Three Laws of Motion, the differences between linear and rotational motion, and human lever systems. We also examined the seven basic principles of biomechanical analysis and a few areas where biomechanical analysis can be applied to particular problems relating to improving performance, preventing injuries, and increasing personal fitness. This ends Unit 2 on "Human Performance." Many of the ideas presented here will recur throughout the rest of the book, so it is worth taking the time to ensure you have a good command of this material.

In the following Unit, we will refine what we have learned thus far about anatomy and physiology, and biomechanics and human performance by examining how humans utilize these systems and principles for the development of increasingly complex skills, including those needed to participate in sport and other physical activities. Many students have some prior experience with young athletes at an early stage of development – or have moved up through the ranks of organized sport themselves – and are therefore aware of the varied levels of ability and coordination – from the beginner's level to the most advanced.

In Unit 3, we will see just how these abilities can develop and change over time, and how sport and physical activity educators can further this process.

Careers and Websites

"Movement represents more than just a convenience; it is fundamental to our evolutionary development — no less important than the complexities of intellect and emotion."
— from the preface to *Essentials of Exercise Physiology* (2000) by William McArdle, Frank Katch, and Victor Katch

Below is a guide to the many career choices that are available to those who are interested in specializing in one or more of the areas covered in this unit. On the following page are website links that you will find useful in connection with the many topics touched on in the unit.

CAREER OPPORTUNITIES

- **Kinesiologist**
Experts in the study of human movement, kinesiologists combine the fields of anatomy, physiology, and biomechanics, as well as related studies such as sociology, ethics, and the history of sport. In one branch of this broad field, kinesiologists aim to correct human movement where physical deficiencies exist. One example is gait correction, for which the kinesiologist can design and construct orthotics to both comfort and minimize injury.

- **Ergonomist**
An ergonomist participates in the design of systems – such as the layout and set-up of an office environment or a factory assembly line – to optimize overall performance. Hence, the ergonomist needs to understand the range of anatomical and physiological factors, as well as the needs and requirements of the system (i.e., a factory looking to increase productivity or office managers seeking to reduce repetitive stress injuries among keyboard users).

- **Biomechanist**
Biomechanists are often trained in injury or impact biomechanics, which involves an understanding of the loads and thresholds required for specific types of injuries in bone, muscle tendons, ligaments, and joints.

- **Certified Personal Trainer/Certified Fitness Instructor**
These individuals design and monitor fitness programs for individuals seeking a better quality of life. They do not require a university degree, although many employers require trainers to possess some official designation.

- **Strength and Conditioning Specialist**
Specialists in this field work with a range of clients looking to improve their strength and overall conditioning. Duties can include conducting pre-training assessments, developing fitness programs, and implementing continuing measurements of fitness. The National Strength and Conditioning Association in the U.S. offers a Certified Strength and Conditioning Specialist designation.

- **Nutritionist/Dietician**
Nutritionists and dieticians plan food programs in a number of institutional settings, such as schools, hospitals, seniors' centres, and correctional facilities. A large part of their work involves educating people regarding correct eating habits, and implementing food programs that can improve health through better diet. Within this field, the position of sports nutritionist is also common. In this position, one works with teams, athletes, and coaches to assess the nutritional requirements of athletes and, in many cases, to suggest nutritional improvements that can be made to improve performance.

- **Health and Physical Education Teacher**
At all levels of primary and secondary education, schools require teachers to instruct students in health and physical education. In most cases, this learning involves both a classroom and a "hands-on" participatory component, and in many schools, a health and physical education teacher's responsibilities can be extended to include coaching school teams, after-school sports, intramural competition, and so forth.

- **Corporate Fitness Instructor**
Many companies enlist the help of trained fitness instructors to work with employees at all levels of fitness, to promote overall health, to reduce stress, and to implement a "healthy workplace." In many cases, these instructors are also responsible for the development and maintenance of an on-site corporate fitness centre. Many firms believe that having a healthy workforce is in their best interest.

USEFUL WEB LINKS

The URLs for these websites were active at the time this book went to press. For an up-to-date listing check the supporting student workbook or the website for this textbook: www.thompsonbooks.com/hpe.

- **Canada Food Guide**
  http://www.hc-sc.gc.ca/english/lifestyles/food_nutr.html
  Official Health Canada site explaining the Canada Food Guide; includes related links on nutrition.

- **Gatorade Sports Science Institute (GSSI)**
  www.gssiweb.com
  The GSSI is a free, subscription-based site that deals with all the current research findings that pertain to professional audiences such as scientists, coaches, medical professionals, athletic trainers, nutritionists, and health and physical education professionals who have a fundamental understanding of human physiology.

- **ExRx (Exercise Prescription)**
  www.exrx.net
  ExRx is a resource for the exercise professional, coach, teacher, or fitness enthusiast. This site consists of over 1,000 pages, most of which deal with personal fitness improvement.

- **Nutritional Analysis Tool**
  www.nat.uiuc.edu/mainnat.html
  This free online tool helps users record their daily nutrient intake and breaks down the percentages of each nutrient consumed.

- **Canadian Health Networks (CHN)**
  www.canadian-health-network.ca
  CHN's site helps Canadians find information on how to stay healthy and prevent disease. This network of health information providers includes Health Canada; national, provincial and/or territorial non-profit organizations; and universities, hospitals, libraries, and community organizations.

- **Ontario Association of Sport and Exercise Sciences (OASES)**
  www.oases.on.ca
  The official site of the OASES provides information on how the association promotes the training and certification of fitness consultants and personal trainers through the national organization, the Canadian Society for Exercise Physiology (CSEP).

- **The Canadian Society for Exercise Physiology**
  www.csep.ca
  This site offers many links to Canadian-based research and information on human performance.

- **Biomechanics World Wide**
  www.per.ualberta.ca/biomechanics
  This branch of the University of Alberta's department of physical education site is designed to assist all persons in the search for information on the broad topic of biomechanics. It is an excellent resource for finding other biomechanic-related sites as well as files of relevant information.

- **Environmental Factors and Exercise**
  http://jan.ucc.nau.edu/~kkt/EXS300/Environmental_Factors.html
  This site describes the wide range of environmental factors (thermoregulation in extremely hot and cold conditions, dehydration, altitude, and so on) that can have an impact on exercise.

- **ExRx: Fitness Testing**
  www.exrx.net/Testing.html
  The Exercise Prescription site's comprehensive resource for those interested in enhancing their knowledge of testing practices and procedures.

- **Canadian Fitness and Lifestyle Research Institute**
  www.cflri.ca
  The Institute's mission is "to enhance the well-being of Canadians through research and communication of information about physically active lifestyles to the public and private sectors." To that end, the website contains a vast amount of information about human performance-related topics, including statistics on the state of overall fitness in Canada and research projects that are assessing Canadian fitness and health levels.

- **Sports Science**
  www.sportsci.org
  Includes all areas of study in the field of exercise science, including medical journals and current research.

- **The Medical Basis of Stress, Depression, Anxiety, Sleep Problems, and Drug Use**
  www.teachhealth.com
  A comprehensive description of stress, designed specifically for high-school and college-level students. Includes a "checklist for handling over-stress," and the site's developers have presented it copyright-free for in-class distribution

- **Sportquest**
  www.sportquest.com
  SIRC is the world's leading bibliographic database producer of sport, fitness, and sports medicine information. It provides access to resources on all sports and exercise science topics, including a listing of all the universities in Canada that offer kinesiology programs.

Scott Shaw of Calgary jumps to a men's silver medal during the International Snowboarding Federation pro quarterpipe invitational competition, March 2001, in Stoneham, Quebec (CP PHOTO/Jacques Boissinot).

UNIT 3
MOTOR LEARNING AND SKILLS DEVELOPMENT

Victor Davis competes at the 1984 Olympic Games in Los Angeles, California (CP PHOTO/COA/Ted Grant).

17
Principles & Terminology

"The will to win is important, but the will to prepare is vital."
— legendary football coach Joe Paterno

Have you ever watched a group of youngsters playing an organized team sport, such as soccer, hockey or baseball, and then compared these participants' abilities to those of older, more experienced players? While the activity of the former group often appears chaotic compared to that of the latter, such a comparison has tremendous value from the standpoint of allowing the observer some significant insight into the area of human development.

Unlike the relatively uniform nature of adult sport, young participants can come in all shapes and sizes, and represent a wide range of ability levels. Some youngsters might be physically small in stature, but fleet of foot and seemingly well coordinated compared to their peers. Others might be larger in size and less agile, but physically more powerful. Some may be able to concentrate on – and complete – difficult sporting tasks, while others are not yet able to grasp either the mental or physical concepts necessary to stop a soccer ball successfully using only their feet, to execute a hockey slap shot, or to hit a baseball off a tee on the first swing. However, as these young players find continued opportunities to practice and compete, they will improve in all aspects of their sport until their progress closely matches that of their older counterparts, many of whom seem able to execute complicated sports activities such as shooting a jump shot in basketball, executing complicated manoeuvres in figure skating, or mastering difficult freestyle wrestling moves in a seemingly "automatic" fashion.

After watching youngsters at play, one does come away with a few key ideas about human development. For one thing, it becomes clear that humans grow physically in very different ways and at different rates from one another. And it is evident that people develop the ability to master certain skills, such as the ones necessary to participate in sports, at varying rates and with varying degrees of aptitude.

This kind of comparative observation of youth in sport settings can reveal a lot about more than physical factors. It is easy to see, for example, that mental factors such as determination, motivation, and psychological preparation play an enormous part in how both young and more experienced athletes take part in sport and physical activity. And in addition to the role

that physical and mental factors play in sport at any level, there is another crucial element to consider – the role of the coach in both training and competition.

We will begin this Unit by examining how human beings grow and change, following fairly unified patterns based on factors such as age, nutrition, and heredity. In the context of this book's major themes – how sport and physical activity can be influenced by a wide range of human factors – we will also look at why an understanding of these growth patterns is crucial for both participants in, and organizers of, sports and physical activity, exploring why an understanding of the variables that affect the way people grow and change over time can help us immensely in helping people of any age lead healthier and more active lives.

In Section 19, we will go beyond a consideration of basic human physical growth patterns to explore the ways in which people develop so-called "motor skills" – that is, the ability to master increasingly difficult tasks. Knowing the ways in which people develop these skills is critical to an understanding of the larger topic of sport and physical activity for two important reasons. First, athletes, coaches, and instructors who comprehend the stages at which people develop motor skills can, in turn, adapt both training schedules and competitive objectives to appropriate levels. Second, the realization that just about every sports skill (the slap shot in hockey, the serve in tennis, the sprinter's running motion, and so on) can be analyzed and refined allows participants and their coaches to hone and improve individual skills.

As anyone who has ever faced a tough challenge on the practice field or in the heat of competition knows, mental factors also play a huge role as well. Consequently, in Section 20, we will examine how physical skill development can be augmented by working to develop one's mental skills. In addition, we will see how, in the same way as training methods and principles have evolved over the years, the techniques that sport psychologists use to help athletes enhance their performance have progressed as well.

If positive outcomes are indeed the result of a successful mixture of both physical and mental factors, it is also true that success cannot be achieved without a high level of expert guidance. In other words, most athletes discover early that a good coach is a necessary component to success in competition and overall enjoyment in sport. In Section 21, we will look at the role of the coach, and how he or she can maximize athletic development while adhering to certain philosophical principles that make the sporting experience a rewarding one for the athlete as well as his or her parents, family, and friends.

IMPORTANT TERMINOLOGY

Before moving ahead, it is necessary to define a few basic terms that will reoccur throughout this Unit.

Human Growth

There are numerous ways to describe how the human body grows and changes. But for the purposes of this section, it is important to emphasize that humans grow primarily through the release of chemicals released by various glands (such as the pituitary). These chemicals are known as hormones, and, in combination with proper nutrition and exercise, will lead to many changes within the body, especially during puberty. Hormones stimulate the growth of facial hair and the development of sex organs. They can also – again, in combination with other factors, such as exercise and diet – increase muscle size and lead to overall gains in weight. Clearly, any kind of significant physical changes will have an impact on one's participation in sport and physical activity. It is also important to remember that physical changes represent only one type of growth. Other forms of growth, which we will examine in subsequent sections, include the development of cognitive (or mental) and emotional abilities.

Skills

The term skills covers a wide range of human abilities. As we will see in the sections that follow, some skills – such as using utensils to eat – are developed early in life, take a relatively short time to master, and are retained by a person for his or her entire life to the point where performing them is almost an unconscious matter. Others – such as driving a golf ball off a tee – demand an extremely high degree of coordination and can only really be mastered after hundreds or even thousands of hours of practice. The differences in skills will be examined in the sections that follow, as well as an examination of why the old adage "practice makes perfect" does hold true in most skill-development contexts.

Motor Learning

In much the same way that humans can master complicated skills such as the abstract representation of ideas by means of symbols, physical or "motor" skills can be learned as well. The development of these motor skills is usually a case of repetition and practice, and involves a blend of physical development and the neurological system's ability to send commands to the muscles and joints in a sequence, which becomes easier and easier with each successive trial.

Sport Psychology

Although there are many branches of psychology – often defined as the scientific study of the thought processes and behaviour of humans and other animals in their interaction with the environment – one segment of the discipline deals exclusively with the endeavours of athletes and coaches. As we will see, there are many ways of practicing the psychology of sport, but each has one major objective as its goal: to enhance performance. Of course, there are many different ways of defining this enhancement. Some athletes define their goals in terms of race times or places, some wish only to win, others to win large amounts of prize money, and still others look for more abstract outcomes, such as enjoyment, the fulfillment of personal goals, and so on. But the bottom line is that, with the recognized techniques used by sport psychologists, athletes and their coaches have come to realize that working on the mental aspects is as important as the physical ones.

Coaching

A coach is any person who supports the efforts of an athlete or team by direct involvement, without actually assisting those athletes directly in competition, as a teammate would. Coaches help athletes in numerous ways, such as by designing training schedules, providing encouragement and motivation during competition and practice, formulating strategies for competition, resolving conflict, and by working through many of the logistics of an athlete's endeavours. But coaches also play a critical role in determining an athlete's or team's philosophy or approach to sport. As such, coaches hold an important position in the sports world. Not only do they possess the technical knowledge to help athletes succeed, but they also determine the tone for their competitive careers as far as ethics and "fair play" are concerned.

One of the interesting things about coaching is that, no matter what the sport, there are certain principles that can be applied to the ways in which coaches work with athletes in any sporting field. A broad body of theory has been developed that will enable coaches in any sport to understand their role with individual athletes and/or teams. In Section 21, we will examine the basics of this theory. Once these very general principles are understood, it is time to move on to the specifics of coaching on a sport-by-sport basis.

Wayne Gretzky, executive director of the Canadian Hockey Association, with minor hockey players following a press conference in Toronto, March 2001 (CP PHOTO/Aaron Harris).

Human Growth and Development

"Be strong in body, clean in mind, lofty in ideals."
— Dr. James Naismith, the father of basketball

In the previous two Units, we examined the physical structure and the basic functions of the human body (Unit 1) and the principles governing how our bodies operate in the context of physical activity (Unit 2). But it is important to bear in mind that neither of these important areas are fixed or static – in reality, the human body undergoes considerable change over time, beginning from birth and continuing through childhood, puberty, adulthood, and into old age.

It is also clear that, except in circumstances where disease or poor nutrition have a negative impact, humans follow fairly standard patterns of growth and development. Furthermore, while we go through these established stages, our rate of growth is not constant. Rather, the body's development seems to occur in "spurts" of rapid change.

Within the context of sports and physical activity, knowledge of how the human body grows and develops is important because it allows us to understand how people respond to the demands of exercise at different stages in the development process. We would naturally expect children to respond to exercise in a very different way than an adult – the rates at which they can learn a new skill, for example, will differ widely. In this section, we will examine the stages of physical, cognitive, and social human growth and development. In the section that follows, we will focus on changes in our ability to accomplish tasks – that is, the process by which we develop the capacity to learn and enhance a wide range of human skills.

AREAS OF HUMAN DEVELOPMENT

It is easy to assume that in referring to "human development," we are speaking only about physical growth and change. But, in fact, there are four basic areas of human development, and each of them plays a key role in the ways in which people progress to increasingly complicated levels of sport and physical activity. Adapting to more and more complex challenges in the context of exercise involves developing skills beyond merely physical ones, including the ability to take in and process information and the ability to interact with teammates and opponents in an appropriate way. These four key components of human development are:

- **Physical development.** The growth and development of the body's muscles, bones, energy systems, and the nervous system.

- **Cognitive development.** An individual's ability to interpret and process information; emotional development, or the development of a person's self-concept, or awareness of one's self.

- **Motor or skills development.** A combination of cognitive and physical development, whereby humans develop the ability to perform a wide range of tasks (see the following section).

- **Social development.** The development of relationships with peers, friends, relatives, adults, and others in the "outside world."

AGE AND PHYSICAL DEVELOPMENT

In the course of normal conversation, there is little doubt what a person means when they refer to someone's age. But when it comes to talking about age in terms of human growth and development, the term has three important meanings:

- **Chronological age.** Age measured in years, months and days; that is, the "standard" use of the term.

- **Skeletal age.** Age as indicated by the physical maturity of the skeleton; that is, the degree of ossification of bones, usually measured by an X-ray of the hand and wrist. Standard skeletal ages can be predicted and charted according to chronological age, But a number of factors – including nutrition and diet, disease and major bone injuries – can cause a person's skeletal age to lag behind their chronological age.

- **Developmental age.** Age as expressed in one's ability to perform certain tasks; that is, when someone says something like, "He's a seven-year-old kid with the tennis serve of a teenager," they are making a rough distinction between a youngster's chronological and developmental ages.

Human Morphology

During the growth phases, people tend to develop into one of three key body types (see Figure 18.1), which researchers have identified to help classify both people's appearance and physical structure. This type of categorization is known as morphology, and one often comes across the designations below to describe body shapes and how humans grow physically.

- **The endomorphic type.** People with this body type tend generally to have more fatty tissue and thicker body parts.

- **The mesomorphic type.** Often maturing early as children, people with this body type tend to develop stocky, heavily muscled, and broader bodies.

- **The ectomorphic type.** Generally later to reach maturity, people with this body type develop a thinner body, characterized by narrow hips and longer legs and arms.

It is important to remember that these three types are theoretical constructs only; very few people fall into only one category, and most are a mix of two or even all three types.

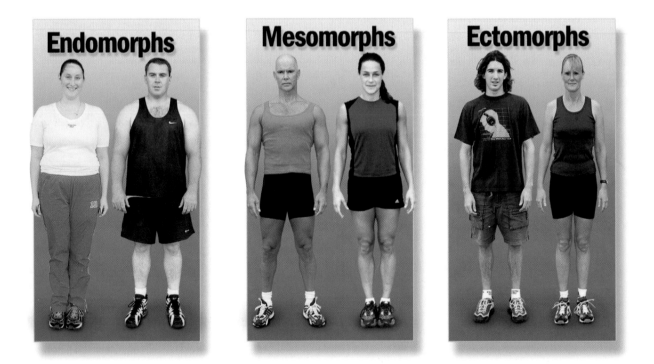

Figure 18.1: The three main body types are shown in this recent photo illustration: the Endomorphs are Karina Chenard and Craig Murray, the Mesomorphs are Roger Richard and Robin Niderost and the Ectomorphs are Joey Sadler and Sherry Armstrong. These three body-type categories were created in the early 1940s by U.S. psychologist William Sheldon, who developed the theory after studying the photographs of 4,000 college-age men (CP PHOTO/Moncton Times &Transcript/Ron Ward/Viktor Pivovarov).

THE STAGES OF PHYSICAL HUMAN GROWTH AND DEVELOPMENT

Human growth and development continues throughout a person's life, but takes place at different rates during different stages. Males and females also develop at different rates and in varied ways. Specialists in this field usually divide human growth and development into four basic stages, each with its own fundamental aspects and characteristics and its own particular relationship to gender. Although perhaps not relevant to the issues of physical activity and exercise, a fifth stage is often also included in this continuum, known as the pre-natal stage, which incorporates human growth from conception through the development of the fetus.

It is important to keep in mind that, in any description of the stages of human development, the age ranges for each stage should not be taken as exact, but rather as rough upper and lower age limits. For example, a nineteen-year-old may still lack many of the physical characteristics typical of someone in the adult stage of development, even though they have reached an age generally considered to be within the adult range.

With this in mind, let us take a look at the four basic stages of human growth and development.

(1) Infancy/Toddler (zero to two to three years)

In general, infancy – the period between birth and one year of age – marks the time of the most marked growth in humans, relative to all the other stages. For example, normal babies will double their birth weight in six months and triple it in a year. The head and chest grow rapidly, allowing the brain, heart, and lungs to develop quickly. The bones harden considerably during this time. Brain weight also increases rapidly during infancy: by the end of the second year, the brain has already reached approximately 75 percent of its adult weight.

From the time of birth to the upper age limit of this stage, a person's weight will typically increase by about 300 percent. Furthermore, his or her height, also often referred to as "body length," will increase by about 50 percent. In the earliest phase of this stage, usually during the first year of life, humans also experience considerable muscular development and considerable gains in their ability to perform basic tasks. Infants begin to grasp things, crawl, pull themselves up to a standing position, and even start to walk. Although boys are slightly heavier and taller than girls at birth, these discrepancies soon even out until adolescence and puberty.

Although the rate of growth slows considerably during the toddler period, this is still a time of marked gains in body length and mass, as well as the development of a huge range of motor skills. By age two, most children have mastered walking, have begun to run, and have started to perfect more complex motor skills such as using a spoon and fork, turning the pages of a book, kicking a ball, and climbing and descending stairs on their own. By age three, motor skills have improved even further, so that the child has mastered running and has developed the ability to balance on one foot for short periods and to ride a tricycle.

(2) Childhood (four to ten years)

Researchers have long noted that, compared to other animals, the human period of childhood is a relatively long one. From about four until six years of age (a period often called early childhood), young people still maintain a fairly rapid rate of growth, though it slows considerably when compared to the infancy and toddler stages. From about six to ten years, or mid-childhood, the body undergoes something of a stabilizing period in which a uniform relationship between bone and tissue growth and development occurs. This allows the child to begin to establish an important base of motor skills.

Certainly, the childhood stage represents a fertile field of study from the exercise science perspective. Because the human body is in such a rapid state of growth and development – especially in the four-to-six-year-old phase – and because this is often the age at which children are introduced to some form of organized sports or games, those who work with young people in this age group are faced with a particular challenge: how to accommodate a wide range of sizes and ability and/or development levels in the same unified activity. In Section 21, "Coaching Principles and Practices," we will examine how this kind of accommodation can occur.

(3) Puberty/Adolescence (eleven to eighteen years)

Although growth and development solidifies somewhat during late childhood, growth speeds up again during the period of puberty and adolescence. During puberty, a whole range of changes takes place, both physical and psychological. This period is marked by a pronounced "growth spurt," in fact, the most pronounced since the infancy stage. By most definitions, this is the time in which boys are considered to grow into men, and girls into women; in other words, both genders begin to grow into sexual maturity. Puberty usually takes place between the ages of ten and fifteen in both sexes but, in general, occurs slightly earlier in females. On a physiological level, puberty occurs when the pituitary gland – the small endocrine gland that lies at the base of the brain (sometimes known as

Phases of Movement
The basics

As humans grow and develop, their ability to perform an increasingly complex set of motor skills changes profoundly. Those who study human movement – especially as it relates to sport and physical activity – have developed four distinct phases of human movement that most people go through from birth to adulthood: the reflexive, rudimentary, fundamental, and sport-related movement phases. Below, we will look at the basic elements of each.

It is important to keep in mind that the age ranges given represent rough guidelines rather than firm divisions. As anyone who is familiar with youth sport can attest, the levels of skill and human movement among any group of children of the same age can vary widely. What follows is a description of each basic phase:

- **Reflexive Movement Phase:** Occurring very early in life (zero to four months), this newborn phase is the first instance in which humans show controlled motor development. In this phase, the brain's sub-cortex controls all reflexive movement.

- **Rudimentary Movement Phase:** This phase also comes very early in life, from birth to two years of age, and overlaps with the reflexive movement phase. Locomotor activity (crawling, walking), basic manipulation (picking up and releasing objects), and stability movements (gaining control of the head and neck; sitting and standing unassisted) all begin in this phase.

- **Fundamental Movement Phase:** At two to seven years of age, humans begin to develop basic movement skills that evolve into sports-related skills in the following phase. This stage actually includes three progressive phases – initial, elementary, and mature – all of which witness the development of basic skills (running, throwing, kicking) that humans need to develop more complicated sport skills.

- **Sport-Related Movement Phase:** Beginning at age seven and moving into adulthood, this phase is divided into three distinct sub-phases – general, specific, and specialized.

  - In the general phase (seven to ten years), the skills developed in the latter fundamental phase become refined into sport skills, such as an underhand ball toss that evolves into an underhand tennis serve.

  - In the specific stage (eleven to thirteen years) the young athlete develops more accuracy in his or her skill (e.g., the ability to consistently kick a ball on target) and complexity.

  - In the specialized phase (fourteen to early adulthood), the skills that have been built during the previous stages are refined even further, in many cases to the point where they will remain throughout a person's life, such as golf or bowling stroke.

the body's "master gland" because of the way in which it triggers this crucial growth stage) – secretes chemicals known as hormones that, in turn, cause the sex organs to grow and develop, making them capable of reproduction.

This stage also witnesses the development of marked changes in physical appearance and body function. In both sexes, pubic hair appears. In females, breasts begin to develop along with other pronounced body contours, accompanied by the onset of the reproductive cycle and menstruation. Males begin to produce semen, grow facial and body hair, and experience a deepening of the voice. The average age range for puberty in girls is from twelve to thirteen years, and from thirteen to fourteen years of age for boys. Due to this difference, girls are, on average, taller and heavier than boys from about ten to thirteen years of age. Once boys have "caught up," this trend reverses.

During adolescence, the body adjusts to the rapid changes experienced during puberty. This is often considered a time when people "grow into their bodies" without undergoing actual measurable gains in height and physical structure after about midway through the adolescent period. It is also a time of considerable psychological adjustment, as many of the changes brought on by puberty – the appearance of bodily hair, a deepening voice in males, development of sex and gender characteristics – take on a social and behavioural context.

(4) Adulthood (eighteen years and older)

By the time humans reach adulthood, most of the body's growth has taken place. Except in very rare instances, for example, humans do not gain in height during this period. Clearly, though, adults do go through a wide range of physical changes as they grow older. These can include relatively large gains in weight, a reduced capacity to take in and utilize oxygen, a rise in blood pressure and resting heart rate, and various deteriorations in joints of the lower body, such as the knees and hips. Many of these conditions cannot be attributed simply to the fact that the body is getting older since, for many North Americans, adulthood represents a relatively long period during which exercise is diminished, diet and nutrition are ignored, and the varied stress factors in life increase with added responsibilities such as work, family, and so forth.

As we will see in the following section, it is clear that adulthood is an important stage for the continued development of a huge range of complicated motor skills. And although regular exercise, a healthy diet, and other positive steps can slow the aging process, it does seem inevitable that some physical deterioration occurs as people age.

DIFFERENT RATES OF GROWTH FOR DIFFERENT BODY PARTS

Another key aspect of human growth and development is the fact that not all body parts and systems undergo change at the same rate. For example, during the average human lifespan, the arms and legs generally grow from four to five times their original size, while the size of the head only doubles from birth, with a large part of this growth occurring early in the growth period. Infants' heads appear to be large in proportion to the rest of their bodies, just as an awkward-looking early teen may appear to have arms and legs that are slightly longer in proportion to the rest of the body. The flip side of these varying rates of growth is that, at a certain age, growth seems to even out so that the body attains a fairly uniform proportion at some point in late adolescence or early adulthood.

In general, the human body is considered to grow and develop according to two main sequences, both of which describe the ways in which certain body parts develop faster than others. In the **cephalocaudal sequence**, growth progresses fastest in the head, followed by the trunk, and then the extremities. In other words, as infants, people develop fastest and mature earliest in the brain and skull, followed by the heart, lungs, and organs of the trunk, followed by the limbs. The other important human movement development sequence is called the **proximodistal sequence**, which describes how body movements that originate close to the centre of the body seem to develop earlier than those that originate further away from the centre. One obvious example of this sequence lies in the way in which entire arm or leg movements – such as those used in running – tend to develop faster than the movements of the extremities, such as the precise finger movements needed to play the piano or type.

Variations in Growth

Beyond the basic generalizations we have examined, there really is no such thing as "uniform" or "standard" patterns of human growth; that is, the variation among individuals is fairly wide. The field of sports and physical activity provides an excellent context in which to view this variance. Some athletes seem to excel in certain sports because, even after they have finished growing, they have long arms and legs (e.g., the "classic" physique for a basketball player) while others are stockier, with shorter legs and a relatively long trunk (i.e., the "classic" rugby player or weightlifter). However, there are many exceptions to these standard sporting body types and growth patterns, which reminds one of the old adage about size and athletes: "If your feet can touch the ground, you're the right size for whatever sport you want to play."

FACTORS AFFECTING PHYSICAL GROWTH

Up to this point, we have been discussing human growth in general terms, noting how people move through the various stages of physical development from infancy to adulthood at certain "average" ages. However, there are a number of key **factors affecting physical growth**.

Glandular/Hormonal Activity

Through the endocrine system, numerous glands secrete hormones that travel in the blood to the body's various organs and tissues. Once these hormones arrive, they affect the metabolism of the tissue. As we saw above, the pituitary is the prime gland for secreting the necessary hormones for growth and development during puberty; others include the thyroid (which secretes thyroxine, a hormone that regulates important metabolic functions), the ovaries (which secrete estrogen and progesterone, important hormones for the development of female sex characteristics) and the testes (which secrete testosterone, crucial for the development of male sex characteristics). The glands, however, can suffer from various diseases, which in turn can affect their production of hormones and, ultimately, human growth. One example of such a condition is known as acromegaly, an endocrine disorder caused by an oversecretion of growth hormone produced by the pituitary gland. In adults, this leads to an excessive thickening of bones, predominantly in the skull and the small bones of the hands and feet. In children, this disorder leads to a condition known as gigantism, in which a person grows to well above normal size – and often leads to a much shortened lifespan.

Heredity

Although attempting to draw definite links between a person's genetic heritage and his or her growth is difficult, there does seem to be some connection between, for example, people having tall genetic descendants, and their growing to be tall themselves. Indeed, it is intuitively appealing to suggest that traits such as height, muscularity, and so forth tend to "run in families." There is a problem, however, in attempting to predict many areas of genetically inherited growth and development. For example, it is easy to assume that there must be a genetic cause to obesity upon observing a family with overweight parents and overweight children. But is there really an "obesity gene" at play here, or is the children's physical condition a factor of environmental factors, such as poor diet or a dislike of physical activity? As we will see, external forces can play a large role in an individual's development.

International Paralympic Games
The democratization of sport

For many people, the classic models of human growth and the development of sports skills do not apply. Some athletes, for example, have experienced serious physical trauma, resulting in the loss of, or diminished capabilities in, the use of their limbs. For these athletes, the development of muscle strength, endurance, and motor skills are very different processes than they are for persons who have full use of their arms and legs. For others, certain neurological or spinal dysfunctions – whether present at birth or caused through injury – cause the processes of physical development and the acquisition of skills to differ from the "standard."

The Paralympic Games

Fortunately, there are many athletes, coaches, and organizers who welcome the opportunity to participate in sport despite the presence of different human growth and motor-learning models. Indeed, large gatherings of athletes come together from around the world for multi-sport competitions that celebrate the fact that sport can be played by persons who are either physically or mentally challenged.

In 1948, a man named Ludwig Guttmann organized a sports competition involving Second World War veterans with spinal cord injuries in Stoke Mandeville, England. In 1952, the number of competitors grew, and an international movement, now called the Paralympics, was underway.

The first Olympic-style games for athletes with a disability were organized in Rome in 1960. By 1976, Toronto was playing host to larger games, with other disability groups being added to the mix. Also in 1976, the first Paralympic Winter Games were held in Sweden.

The Paralympic Games are held in the same year as the "regular" Olympic Games, and since the 1988 Seoul Summer Games and the 1992 Albertville Winter Games, they have also taken place at the same locales as the Olympics.

Stephan Putnam competes in the bocce event at the 1992 Paralympic Games in Barcelona, Spain (CPC Photo/Christine Chew).

The current Paralympics – the last of which were the winter version, held in Salt Lake City in 2002 just after the regular Winter Games at the U.S. Venue – play host to thousands of elite athletes from around the world.

In Sydney, Australia, in 2000, the summer version of the Games – also held in concert with that year's Olympics – welcomed participants from 123 countries. In 2004, the Summer Paralympic Games will be held in Athens, Greece. Turin, Italy, is slated to host the 2006 Olympic and Paralympic Winter Games.

In the Summer Paralympic Games, athletes compete in seventeen sports: archery, athletics, bocce, cycling, equestrian, goalball, judo, bowls, powerlifting, sailing, shooting, soccer, swimming, table tennis, wheelchair basketball, wheelchair rugby, and wheelchair tennis.

In the Winter Games, four Paralympic sports are contested: alpine skiing, cross-country skiing, ice sledge hockey, and wheelchair dance sport.

Furthermore, Paralympic participants compete within subcategories, based on their disabilities. These categories are: athletes with cerebral palsy; athletes with spinal cord lesion, spina bifida and polio; athletes with blindness; and athletes with amputations.

In 2002, the Paralympic Games achieved a major breakthrough in public awareness with a large televised package of highlights from the event's four sports being aired on the Arts and Entertainment cable network in the U.S. and on CBC in Canada. Although the Summer Paralympic Games two years earlier in Sydney were held in conjunction with the regular Olympic competition, and thus received only sporadic television coverage, the fact that the Winter Paralympics followed the regular Games in Salt Lake City meant that television coverage of the Games could air without the "competition" of the regular Games.

The 2004 Paralympic Games

As mentioned above, the 2004 Paralympics are scheduled to be held in Athens, Greece. Organizers of the event, which will run from September 17 to 28, expect a huge influx of visitors. These include about 4,000 Paralympic athletes from about 130 countries, who will convene at the Paralympic Village in the Greek capital. Also, more than 2,000 team officials will accompany them, and approximately 3,000 media representatives are expected to be on hand to cover the event.

On the technical side, about 1,000 event officials and 15,000 volunteers will provide assistance. And added to these numbers will be about 2,500 members of what is known as the "Paralympic Family" – representatives of the International Paralympic Committee (IPC), the National Paralympic Committees (NPCs), and so forth. Consequently, with some 21,000 people involved with these Games, it is easy to see how the Paralympics have come to be a major world sports event.

Nutrition/Diet

A factor that is important to growth and development is diet. As we saw in Section 10 ("Nutrition for Performance"), what we eat and drink can have a strong bearing on our ability to perform both regular, day-to-day tasks and more complicated, strenuous activities. Diet also affects human physical growth – an inadequate or unbalanced diet can lead to serious problems in physical development. Malnourishment early in life can lead to reduced growth and diminished intellectual capacity, for example, although there is some evidence that a young person can "recover" with an improved diet and resume normal growth patterns. On the other side of the dietary equation, researchers are now finding that excessive weight gain at a young age can have marked effects on body shape for the rest of a person's life, and evidence suggests that it is difficult to reverse physical patterns such as obesity or rapid weight gain.

Physical Activity

Clearly, a lack of physical activity can influence a person's growth, since it can lead to weight gain at an early age, poor cardiorespiratory development, underdeveloped muscle strength, and diminished motor skills. There is considerable evidence to suggest that physical activity performed from a young age can enhance these factors and promote an individual's growth and development. However, an excess of physical activity can have a negative effect. Although many long-held preconceptions about physical training and youngsters and its effects on their development – such as the idea that weight training for pre-teens can "stunt their growth" – have been shown to be inaccurate, it is still true that overtraining, especially during childhood and early adolescence, can have an adverse effect on aspects of human development, such as muscle growth and bone formation.

Sociocultural Factors

It is sometimes difficult to assess how social forces influence human growth and development. For instance, a person from a low-income household may have had a poor diet from infancy or may not have had opportunities to exercise regularly. On the other hand, many social and/or cultural groups bring other factors into play that work in the opposite direction – to promote rapid growth and development. For example, some communities encourage achievement in sports, and this encouragement – through the existence of role models, coaching, and so forth – can promote early and rapid development of the skills needed to succeed in those sports on a widespread level.

COGNITIVE DEVELOPMENT

As noted above, cognitive development is defined as the changes that take place in a person's ability to interpret and process information, as well as alterations in their emotional development, and the introduction and establishment of a person's self-concept or awareness of one's self. Just as the human body changes in ways that allow it to master increasingly complex tasks and skills, our ability to think also changes over time. But what, exactly, is taking place? It is easy to observe physical development through changes in a person's physical structure. As cognitive development occurs, however, many of the changes are far more subtle.

Although there have been many attempts to categorize the ways in which humans develop cognitively, the most widely accepted one is the model developed by the Swiss psychologist Jean Piaget (1896-1980). Based on his study of thousands of young children, Piaget's four stages of cognitive development describe the ways in which cognitive development occurs in children. Piaget referred to these as the sensorimotor stage, pre-operational stage, concrete operational stage, and formal operational stage.

Piaget laid out these four steps in a progressive model. At its centre is a person's ability to adapt to his or her environment – what Piaget called intelligence. He characterized each stage as follows:

- **Sensorimotor stage** (infancy, or approximately zero to two years of age). This stage is characterized by an infant demonstrating intelligence by means of motor activity without the use of symbols. In other words, infants can crawl, but cannot read or recognize letters, numbers, and other symbols. In this stage, an infant's knowledge is based purely on his or her own immediate experience. Piaget demonstrated that during this stage (at about seven to nine months) children acquire what is known as "object permanence," or the ability to use their memory to recall objects and events. As noted above, this stage involves some development of physical mobility, which in turn allows children to begin developing new experiences and new intellectual abilities. The later part of this sensorimotor stage is also characterized by the development of early language abilities.

- **Pre-operational stage** (toddler/early childhood, or approximately two to seven years of age). In this stage, children demonstrate intelligence through the use of symbols, such as letters, numbers, and pictorial representations of real-life objects, all of which they can both recognize and reproduce. Also, in the pre-operational stage, language abilities begin to develop considerably. Children in this stage are also characterized by significant growth in their memory and imagination. Although children are able to begin thinking in a linear fashion during this stage and can "think through" events from start to finish, they are usually not able to reverse the process. Also, the phenomenon of what Piaget called "egocentric" thinking is prevalent during this stage, as youngsters are largely incapable of understanding another person's point of view or sacrificing their own interests for those of another person.

- **Concrete operational stage** (elementary/early adolescence, or approximately seven to eleven years of age). Piaget characterized this stage as the one in which logical thinking develops, and children become able to solve concrete, hands-on problems in a logical fashion. Also, children in this stage begin to develop an understanding of the concept of "conservation" – that is, the fact that number, length, liquid, mass, weight, area, and volume can all be manipulated, added to, and subtracted from – and can start to classify objects and put them into lists based on a standard criterion (i.e., arranging family members according to age). Children in this stage can understand logical sequences in reverse, which is also known as reversibility or "operational thinking." During this stage, most children also begin to limit egocentric thought and start to develop a capacity for empathy with the feelings of others.

- **Formal operational stage** (adolescence/early adulthood, or eleven to fifteen years of age). In this stage, children demonstrate intelligence through their ability to solve increasingly complicated abstract problems using logic, and by understanding how to use symbols related to abstract concepts. Paradoxically, Piaget found that youngsters often return to egocentric thinking patterns early in this stage, and begin thinking about social issues and their own identity and appearance.

Although Piaget's four-part classification of cognitive development is a useful model, many critics have reacted against the seeming rigidity of its age divisions. Others hold that Piaget's framework places too little emphasis on the cognitive abilities of pre-schoolers, while overemphasizing the cognitive skills of adolescents and adults. Some studies, for example, have attempted to show that only about 30 percent of adults would actually qualify for the formal operations stage. Also, critics of Piaget's model assert that he does not explain exactly why these stages occur – that is, what impels humans to move through them.

SOCIAL DEVELOPMENT

People who study human development have always been interested in the ways in which, from a young age, humans form attachments with others. Indeed, this process of socialization has many similarities with the cognitive development model outlined above. As a young person moves from early stages in which he or she is essentially capable of functioning only within his or her "own universe" into ones in which he or she is able to understand the needs and characteristics of others (as outlined by Piaget), that person will also be increasingly able to form personal attachments with other people. In this process, young children gradually move away from the relative isolation (and near-total emotional dependence on a parent, usually the mother) of infancy and toddlerhood into a time in which making close friends is common.

Within the last two decades, however, just how important that process of making friends really is for young people has become a subject of considerable study. The consensus seems to be that early social development is extremely significant because of its impact on us in later life. In 1992, the psychologist Willard Hartup summed up many of the important aspects of this area:

> Indeed, the single best childhood predictor of adult adaptation is not school grades, and not classroom behavior, but rather, the adequacy with which the child gets along with other children. Children who are generally disliked, who are aggressive and disruptive, who are unable to sustain close relationships with other children, and who cannot establish a place for themselves in the peer culture, are seriously at risk. (Hartup, W., Having friends, making friends and keeping friends. *ERIC Digest*, 1992, EDO-PS-92-4).

But what is friendship? Most definitions suggest that in order for two people – no matter what their age – to become friends, two major factors must occur: the people must be engaged in a reciprocal relationship (i.e., doing things for one another in roughly equal measures), and they must be committed to doing so over an extended period of time. Also prevalent in most definitions of friendship among young people is the notion that two people must share common interests for friendship to develop. As people grow older, concepts such as understanding, empathy, and trust also enter into friendships. Clearly, sports teams for even very young children fill these qualifications, as does being in the same class in school, living in the same neighbourhood, and so on.

It is possible to observe the beginnings of social development even in very young children. Two American educational researchers, Diane McLellan and Lilian Katz, developed a checklist as a way of helping educators and parents chart the social progress of pre-schoolers. This checklist is as follows:

Individual Attributes

The child:

❏ is usually in a positive mood;

❏ is not excessively dependent on the teacher, assistant, or other adults;

❏ usually comes to the program or setting willingly;

❏ usually copes with rebuffs and reverses adequately;

❏ shows the capacity to empathize;

❏ has a positive relationship with one or two peers; shows capacity to really care about them, miss them if absent, and so forth;

❏ displays the capacity for humour; and

❏ does not seem to be acutely or chronically lonely.

Social Skill Attributes

The child usually:

❏ approaches others positively;

❏ expresses wishes and preferences clearly; gives reasons for actions and positions;

❏ asserts own rights and needs appropriately;

❏ is not easily intimidated by bullies;

❏ expresses frustrations and anger effectively and without harming others or property;

❏ gains access to ongoing groups at play and work;

❏ enters ongoing discussion on the subject; makes relevant contributions to ongoing activities;

❏ takes turns fairly easily;

❏ shows interest in others; exchanges information with and requests information from others appropriately;

❏ negotiates and compromises with others appropriately;

❏ does not draw inappropriate attention to self;

❏ accepts and enjoys peers and adults of ethnic groups other than his or her own; and

❏ interacts non-verbally with other children with smiles, waves, nods, and so forth.

Peer Relationship Attributes

The child is:

❏ usually accepted versus neglected or rejected by other children; and

❏ sometimes invited by other children to join them in play, friendship, and work.

This checklist is described in McClellan, D., & Katz, L., Assessing young children's social competence. *ERIC Digest*, March 2001.

The Role of Sport Participation and Team Play

The context of sports and physical activity can provide one of the best ways of establishing – and continuing – friendships. Whether it is as members of an elite sports organization or as participants in recreational activities, people who build friendships in these settings often find they continue for a very long time.

There is also another important way in which the development of social skills is influenced by the involvement of young people in sports – namely, the way in which sports can further the development of co-operation among young athletes in team sports such as soccer, hockey, and basketball. Although it may be obvious to older observers that one of the best way for teams to succeed is to "share" the responsibilities on the field or court by passing the ball or puck and working together as a team (as opposed to relying on the individual efforts of one player), this is an extremely difficult concept for young athletes, especially those younger than eight or nine years of age. Through patient coaching, youngsters can develop the ability to work with teammates in search of team goals, which represents an invaluable lesson in social interaction and building relationships with peers.

WHERE DO WE GO FROM HERE?

In this section, we have looked at the basics of human growth and development, examining how people move from the youngest stages of infancy, to full development as adults. But alongside this physical, cognitive, and social growth comes another form of development – our increasing ability to perform a wide range of skills, and to "learn" these skills on both a mental and physical level.

In the following section on motor learning and skills development, we will take what we have learned about human growth and apply it to an examination of how we learn – and ultimately master – the skills we need both to survive and to participate in a vast number of sports and physical activity.

Jean-Luc Brassard, of Grand-Ile, Quebec, performs his trademark cossack jump during an honourary run before the final moguls event at the XIX Olympic Winter Games held in Deer Valley, Utah, February 2002 (CP PHOTO/Adrian Wyld).

Motor Learning and Skill Acquisition

"It's not necessarily the amount of time you spend at practice that counts;
it's what you put into the practice."

— Eric Lindros, Canadian NHL hockey player

Human beings have the ability to perform a wide range of skills. Some of these activities – such as balancing ourselves, picking things up with our hands, or seating ourselves in a chair – are so natural that we consider them to be innate; that is, most people seem to be born with the ability to perform these skills and only need a little time and practice before they can perform them. On the other hand, many other, more complex skills – such as riding a bike, typing, hitting a golf ball, driving a car, drawing, or skating – can only be accomplished after a relatively large amount of practice.

When we think about the wide range of skills that humans can accomplish, however, two things are clear: First, the more we perform almost any skill, the better we become at it. Second, as human beings physically grow and develop, our ability to master increasingly complicated skills is enhanced, from the first efforts of infants and toddlers, to the refined abilities of adults.

In this section, we will examine how humans acquire both simple and complex motor skills. We will look at how these skills can also change over time, and how athletes can work to develop their skills, by means of training, in highly specialized ways. Finally, in conjunction with an examination of the ways in which humans develop these skills, we will look at several factors that can affect skill development, and explore the ways in which coaches and physical education instructors and teachers can modify activities in order to better match them with the skill level of participants.

BASIC PRINCIPLES OF MOTOR LEARNING AND SKILL ACQUISITION

The most basic definition of motor learning is the process by which a person develops, through a combination of physical and psychological factors, the ability to perform a task. Anyone who has had experience with small children will have witnessed the very basic stages of motor learning in action. The smallest infants first gradually develop the ability to push things with their fingers, then grasp smaller objects with increasing dexterity, followed soon by an increasing facility at drawing, printing, and writing. In the same way, most infants begin moving themselves about by pulling and pushing themselves across the floor with their arms and legs, followed by crawling, then unsteady walking, followed by an increased stability while they are "on their feet," and eventually running. A similar progression can be noted among those of all ages who are first learning a sport skill. Initially, the person's movements will often seem jerky and uncoordinated. With practice, however, they gradually become smoother and more fluid, leading, in highly trained individuals, to movements that seem almost seamless in their execution. In all of these cases, the body and the mind are working together to allow this progression to occur. But how does it happen?

The most important body parts involved in any motor activity would, upon first consideration, seem to be the ones, such as muscles, tendons and limbs, that actually perform these tasks (e.g., the legs and feet in running, or the arm in throwing a football). But a closer examination of the way in which motor skills

Ten-year-old soccer player Ali Roberts of the Lakeshore Lions learns to head a ball during a game in 1997 (CP PHOTO/*Ottawa Citizen*-Rod MacIvor).

are learned and developed reveals that the root of any motor activity lies in the sensory and nervous systems. Before we can complete any motor task, we need to be aware of its context: the nature of the activity, the characteristics of the person performing it, and the external environment in which the act is to be performed.

It is only when the senses gather information about the context of any given activity that the brain can begin directing the body to perform the appropriate actions. It is at this stage, moreover, that the concept of pattern recognition plays an important part: by comparing the requirements of an activity to those performed in the past, we are able to decide what actions are required. Having learned how to perform a certain action and having practised that action repeatedly, it becomes easier to perform that task time and time again. As the perceptual system takes in information for processing, our memories recall similar events that allow us to react in what we remember as having been successful ways – often referred to as the decision mechanism. Yet, once that decision has been made, it is the effector mechanism, or the coordination between the mind and the body, that actually ensures

the action is performed. Consequently, a well-trained basketball player, for example, can make the act of shooting a jump shot seem almost effortless, especially to someone who is trying to master the shot for the first time. This is because he or she has performed the action so many times that the mechanics of it have become ingrained in memory, making the execution of this skill an almost "automatic" matter.

Another important concept in the theory of motor learning is the division of motor activity into two basic divisions: automatic and controlled. As its name suggests, **automatic motor activity** involves very little thought, and results in movement that appears to be an almost unconscious reflex action. For example, a baseball batter who, in a split second, sees that an out-of-control pitch is heading right for his or her head, makes an involuntary move to duck out of the way. **Controlled motor activity** needs relatively more thought and time to perform. A soccer player weaving in and out of traffic during a game is processing a lot more information than is the baseball player above, though still rapidly, including his or her own speed and control of the ball, the challenges of opponents, and so on.

A further key principle in the area of motor learning and skills development is one which may well be the most self-evident. It is known as the **principle of individual differences**, and it holds that, in the same way that people have different anatomical and physiological makeups and appearances, so too do individuals differ widely in terms of how quickly and easily they learn new motor skills.

STAGES OF MOTOR LEARNING

In the previous section, we examined the four basic phases of human development, known as the reflexive, rudimentary, fundamental, and specialized and/or sport-related phases. But what happens when a person moves beyond these basic steps and attempts to master a complicated sports skill, such as an adult learner trying to put together the various skills needed to successfully execute a tennis serve for the first time? Or a youngster who, having mastered the basics of swimming, attempts to perfect a complicated stroke such as the butterfly or breaststroke?

As anyone who has either coached another or attempted to master such skills themselves can attest, it is clear that people who are learning a skill go through certain stages (also known in the theory of motor learning as "phases") as they develop a mastery of the skill. Specialists in the field of motor learning and skills development have attempted to develop models by which we can describe and explain each of these important steps.

One of the earliest and still widely embraced models of human learning was developed by two American researchers, Paul Fitts and Michael Posner in their landmark 1967 book *Human Performance* (Belmont, CA: Brook-Cole). Today, this is often referred to as the "classic" stages-of-learning model. In seeking to explain how people acquire new skills, Fitts and Posner came up with a three-stage description. When thinking about the three stages outlined below, it is important to consider that people do not suddenly shift from one stage to another; rather, the change in learning stages is a gradual one.

In the first, or **cognitive, stage**, people must come to some basic understanding of the task, or tasks, at hand. In the case of a youngster learning to play soccer, for example, some simple cognitive problems have to be addressed, such as understanding the basics of playing the game (i.e., avoid touching the ball with the hands and arms for most of the game, moving the ball mainly by kicking it in the most effective way, the basic idea of scoring a goal, what the most effective way is to kick the ball, how the game's rules are slightly different for goaltenders because they are permitted to handle the ball, and so forth). Fitts and Posner also pointed out that, in this stage, learners will often commit relatively large errors in performing their tasks. In soccer, these errors might include youngsters who will often miss the ball entirely when trying to kick it, or may blithely pick up the ball or attempt to throw it, or may frequently "score" on their own nets. Fitts and Posner indicated that beginners moving through the cognitive stage may be vaguely aware that they are doing something "wrong" when they commit these fairly major errors but that they may need some specific instruction on how to improve.

The second stage of learning identified by Fitts and Posner is what they called the **associative stage**. In general, this can be considered the stage in which learners begin to refine the skill they had been trying to master during the cognitive stage. During the associative period, learners go beyond the basic mechanics of the skill and develop some awareness of the mistakes they are making, which to some extent leads to fewer, and less pronounced, errors. In this stage, for example, the soccer player may not be able to kick a ball "on target" all of the time, but will develop an awareness that the reason his or her shots and passes are going astray is that the non-kicking foot is being placed too far away from the ball when "planting" before a kick, or that he or she is not following through after the kick. And despite the continued presence of errors, in general, the associative period is characterized by more and more consistent efforts.

Fitts and Posner identified a third and final stage of motor learning, which they called the **autonomous stage**. In this stage, a skill becomes, as the name suggests, an almost "automatic" undertaking. Someone who has reached this level will not spend much time actually thinking about the basic fundamentals of their activity. They are able to "just do" that activity, while concentrating on certain specialized and highly refined aspects of the skill. In soccer, a player's skill in kicking a ball will be so highly developed that the player will be able to concentrate on attempting to "curve" or "bend" a shot on goal, or to impart a certain spin on a pass to make it easier for a teammate to control. The other important aspect of the autonomous skill phase is its high level of self-awareness. People who have reached this level of skill development – almost always following a tremendous amount of practice – are both supremely aware of the mistakes they are making (which are, in fact, quite small in relation to those made by learners at the two previous levels), and highly aware of what they have to do to correct them.

Factors Affecting Skill Development

In the development of motor skills, factors outside the control of the teacher and/or coach and learner can change rapidly, leading to errors in decision making and subsequent actions. Also, due to a wide range of factors affecting skill development such as fatigue, nervousness, weather, distractions, and so on, information can be misprocessed and even experienced competitors can make mistakes.

British track-and-field coach Brian Mackenzie (www.brianmac.demon.uk) has identified the following reasons for faults and errors in a given skill:

- Incorrect understanding of the movement
- Poor physical abilities
- Poor coordination of movement
- Incorrect application of power
- Lack of concentration
- Inappropriate equipment, clothing or footwear
- External factors, e.g., weather conditions

Other factors that inhibit performance can include physical and psychological fatigue, distractions such as audience noise or unusual environmental factors, and poor motivation. The successful execution of skills can also be more difficult in competitive situations, where opponents are going all-out to impede them. It is one thing to execute a hockey slapshot in practice under a coach's watchful eye, but another altogether to do so with an opposing defender checking you! As athletes progress in their skill levels, it becomes increasingly necessary to do drills that simulate competitive situations by introducing pressure from opponents, or the fast-paced environment of competition.

Canadian Basketball Coach, Jack Donohue (1930-2003)
Mentor, friend, instructor, and legend

It may be difficult to comprehend today, but for a long time, Canadians had a fairly ambivalent relationship with the sport of basketball. The 1990s, after all, saw a tremendous surge of interest in the game with the arrival of two NBA franchises to this country. And most Canadian sports fans can tell you the story of Dr. James Naismith, a Canadian physical education specialist who was living in the Massachusetts in the mid-1800s when he came up with the idea of an indoor sport in which players scored points by throwing a round ball through a peach basket, and could only advance that ball by bouncing it on the floor.

There are many who argue that the recent surge of NBA-fuelled interest in the game would never have happened in Canada if it had not been for an extremely influential figure in the sporting history of this country who came along in the mid-1970s and paved the way for the growth of the sport. His name was Jack Donohue, a man who passed away in April 2003 at the age of seventy.

As a long-time coach of the Canadian men's national team (and a short-time coach of the women's squad), Donohue almost single-handedly turned around international-level basketball in this country, and contributed hugely to the growth of grassroots programs for younger players as well.

An American from New York City, Donohue arrived in Canada in 1972 and almost immediately began improving the national team program. The holder of a master's degree in health education, he built on his experience coaching in the highly competitive New York high-school system (he coached the legendary Lew Alcindor – who later changed his name to Kareem Abdul-Jabbar – at Power Memorial High, a team that won seventy-one straight games under his guidance) and in U.S. colleges. After his arrival, Donohue soon had the Canadian players, whom

Basketball coach Jack Donohue at the 1988 Olympic Games in Seoul, South Korea (CP PHOTO/COA/S. Grant).

he said at first had a "negative attitude," competing among the world's best.

In 1983, the Donohue-coached squads won the World University Games after achieving a huge upset over the heavily favoured U.S. and Yugoslavian teams; in Olympic competition they recorded excellent fourth-place finishes in both 1976 and 1984 (Canada boycotted the 1980 Games in Moscow), and also won the 1978 Commonwealth Games title. In 1988, he concluded his official duties as the Canadian men's coach by leading the team to a sixth-place finish at the Seoul Olympics, although he continued to be involved with the program as a consultant and adviser, and travelled across the country giving motivational speeches in his crusty, good-natured style, always wearing one of his trademark outlandish neckties.

The key to Donohue's success was twofold: he combined impeccable technical knowledge of all aspects of the game with an amazing ability to motivate players. One of his former national team players, Jay Triano of Niagara Falls, has gone on to become the

current Canadian men's coach and an assistant with the NBA's Toronto Raptors. "He played a huge role in my life. Obviously basketball was the way it started, and then friendship grew from that," Triano told the Canadian Press just after Donohue's death. "What makes him so special is that it was beyond the basketball that he was so effective at teaching. He taught me so much about life."

Part of the Donohue influence came from the fact that he was able to contribute over such a long period – his seventeen years at the helm of Team Canada make him the longest-serving head coach in amateur or professional sport in Canada. For this service, Donohue, who lived in Ottawa, was inducted into the Olympic Hall of Fame and the Canadian, Ontario, and New York basketball halls of fame, and was also well known to basketball fans for his role as a television commentator and analyst.

In an interview with CBC Radio just after Donohue's death, Eli Pasquale, one of the mainstays of Donohue's teams of the 1970s and 1980s and a team leader in international basketball, recalled that, when the American-born coach arrived in Canada, he set about trying to change the players' outlook on the game. "He told us that if we were going to go out there and put on the uniforms and represent our country, we had better do it with pride," said Pasquale. "For him, it was all a question of attitude."

Indeed, Donohue's coaching style – he was nicknamed "Jack Don't-know-who" because of his legendary habit of forgetting players' names – was based, first and foremost, on his athlete's perceptions of themselves and their abilities. "It's all a matter of attitude," he told reporters before the 1984 Olympic Games. "A guy leaves the house wearing his new, expensive suit for the first time, trips and falls in a puddle. He can get up and curse; or he can get up and check his pockets to see if he caught any fish."

TEACHING AND LEARNING A SKILL

In many cases, people are unable to learn complex skills on their own. Some other person is required to teach and work with them, usually a coach, instructor, or teacher with some training in the area of instructing people using the basics of motor learning.

Singer's Five-Step Process

One of the most popular models for describing the ways in which people learn skills was developed by the University of Florida psychologist Robert Singer in a series of research papers published in the 1980s and 1990s. Singer developed what is now known as the five-step method of skills teaching. As its name suggests, this method utilizes five basic building blocks in the teaching (and learning) of a skill, and has been found to be successful across a wide range of motor activities. According to Singer, these five steps are:

- Readying
- Imaging
- Focusing
- Executing
- Evaluating

In the following section (Section 20, "The Psychology of Sport") we will look at these and similar approaches in greater detail as they relate to athletes seeking success in competitive sport.

In the case of teaching and learning a skill, however, the progression from each of the five steps to the one that follows is key. One often hears the expression "learning curve" to describe the rate of progress one makes in developing a new skill or learning something new. The curve or slope is initially steep when the learning is difficult and less steep as the learning become easier.

The following describes Singer's five steps in more detail:

- In the readying (also known as the preparatory) state, the teacher and learner work to attain the ideal mental and emotional state for learning a skill. This might involve making sure the learner has the correct equipment, feels ready to begin a practice session, and has completed a proper warm-up.

- In the imaging step, the learner must develop a "picture" in his or her mind of the correct execution of the skill components. The teacher or coach can assist in this process by demonstrating the skill or having an experienced athlete do so. It is often also useful for learners to watch the skill being performed on videotape.

- The focusing step requires teaching the learner to block out all internal and external distractions, and thereby "zeroing in" on learning the skill or skill components.

- Executing occurs when the learner actually attempts the desired skill after completing the three previous preparatory steps and using them to perform the task with what Singer calls a "quiet mind."

- Finally, in the evaluating step, the learner and coach attempt to assess which aspects of the skill were performed successfully, and which need improvement. Clearly, athletes at all levels engage in this latter step; even those at the highest levels work to refine their abilities.

The Role of Evaluation

Feedback, or the information a learner obtains regarding how he or she is progressing in learning to perform a skill, can assist in performance improvement. When a gymnastics coach watches a young athlete performing a routine and offers suggestions on how to correct balance or to perform manoeuvres more explosively, the coach is offering one type of feedback. Similarly, a football team watching a tape of a particular offensive sequence that did not work out successfully in a game situation is benefitting from another type of feedback.

Essentially there are two kinds of feedback: that gained by the knowledge of the results of an action (or **KR feedback**), and that gained by the knowledge of performance (**KP feedback**), also known as kinematic feedback. In its simplest form, KR feedback comes simply from seeing the final outcome of an action. Someone working on their golf swing can get KR feedback just by noting the outcome of their swing; that is, how far the ball travelled after each shot.

With KP feedback, the emphasis is not on the outcome of an activity, but rather on how the body performed during the activity. A person practising his or her golf shot would not concentrate so much on where the ball was landing, but rather on their swing, such as how far the club head was travelling on the back-swing, keeping the head down during the swing, and following through after making contact with the ball.

The input of an outside observer or instructor is critical in KP feedback; for example, "Your ball only travelled a short distance because you jerked your head up at the last instant, and that caused you to hit the ball only partially." A video recording of the practice session would also be helpful in showing a learner where they are going wrong on the driving range.

Transferability

One key aspect of teaching and learning a skill hinges on a concept known as **skill transferability** – that is, the fact that skills, when learned in the context of improving performance in one sport or activity, can often be applied, or transferred, to a different sport. For example, someone learning a skill that emphasizes hand-eye coordination, such as a serve in volleyball, will, after practising, be able to transfer this skill to the slapshot in hockey or the lay-up in basketball.

SKILL CATEGORIES

Humans can perform a wide range of skills, and it is obvious that some of them, shuffling a deck of cards, for example, draw on a very different set of physical and mental resources than others, such as running a 100-metre sprint. In fact, the huge variety of human skills require such radically different motor-learning abilities that it is useful to divide them up into three **basic skill categories**, according to what they enable us to accomplish.

In general, specialists in the study of human skills acquisition use three categories, which are not necessarily independent of one anther:

- Locomotor-moving skills
- Manipulative-handling skills
- Stability-balancing skills

Physiologist Ann Gentile established in the 1970s what has come to be known as a two-dimensional system for classifying skills. It is based on two key factors: the requirements of an action, and the demands of the environment in which the person is performing that action. (Initially, Gentile established these categories as a way for physical therapists to evaluate their clients' motor skills, but the system works well for people in almost every sport or physical activity setting.)

Essentially, the possible requirements of an action will depend on what degree of body transport (known as locomotor-moving skills), object manipulation (manipulative-handling), or balancing skills the action entails. For instance, balancing oneself on two feet (i.e., standing still) requires neither body transport skills nor any object manipulation, and it can be performed more or less regardless of context or environment. But stickhandling a puck past opponents in a hockey game requires both body transport (skating) and object manipulation (controlling the stick) in an environment that varies according to the position of both one's teammates and opponents. And clearly, many skills would involve a combination of all three skills.

Within the framework set forward by Gentile, it is possible to classify many skills as a combination of both body transport and object manipulation characteristics, while also combining varying environmental demands. Here it is important to point out two other ways that skills are often classified by researchers; namely, as open skills and closed skills. An **open skill** is one that is performed in an unpredictable environment, which requires participants to adapt their movements to the changing nature of that environment. A **closed skill** is one that takes place in an environment that is predictable and permits participants to plan their movements in advance.

Thus, the environmental conditions needed for closed skills are stationary, while those required for open skills are in motion. A baseball diamond can offer us examples of both open and closed skills. When a young T-ball player hits a stationary baseball from a tee, he or she exhibits one type of closed skill, since one important environmental condition – that is, the placement of the ball – would be constant, at least as long as the tee was placed at the same height each time the youngster stepped up to bat. But an older player hitting a ball thrown by a pitcher would be demonstrating one kind of open skill, since he or she would have to adapt his or her swing to a number of factors, including the velocity of the ball, whether or not the pitcher had imparted spin on the ball to make it curve or "slide," and whether the pitcher was using a left- or right-handed delivery.

SKILLS ANALYSIS

As we have seen thus far, skills can be classified in a number of ways. All of these classifications are useful from the theoretical standpoint, because they allow us to understand certain types of activities in relation to one another – as a way of comparing basic and more advanced skills, for example, or ones that take place in a relatively distraction-free environment versus one with constantly shifting contexts. But being able to classify skills in this way is only part of the larger goals of understanding motor development. Anyone who wants to comprehend skills in order to refine them (either one's own or those of others) must also observe and analyze these skills.

Anyone who attempts to impart knowledge of a skill or skills – usually a coach or teacher of some kind – needs to possess not only a knowledge of that skill in all its phases and be able to demonstrate it, but also know how to observe others attempting to perform the skill and how to evaluate their performance. In doing so, it is crucial to be able to detect errors, to know how to point them out in a constructive way, and to be able to suggest ways in which these errors can be corrected.

Skills Observation

The National Coaching Certification Program (NCCP) identifies two distinct stages of skill observation: a pre-observation stage and an observation stage. In the pre-observation stage, coaches are encouraged to:

- **Identify the purpose of the skill.** Because each skill has an overall purpose within its sport, knowing this purpose goes a long way towards being able to observe the skill. In other words, if both the athlete and teacher or coach are clear that the purpose of, say, a jump shot in basketball is to score points within the rules of the game, it will give both of them a framework from which to observe and analyze the skill.

- **Break the skill into phases.** The NCCP identifies five general phases for each skill:

  Preliminary movements. The movements needed to get ready for a skill, including the necessary footwork, balancing, body positioning, and so forth.

  Back-swing or recovery movements. Movements that usually take place just before the force-producing movements, such as the back-swing in golf, or the arm-recovery movement in a repetitive activity such as swimming.

  Force-producing movements. The movements executed to produce force for impact or propulsion, such as the forward swing of the leg and foot in a soccer kick.

  The critical instant. The point that determines how effective the execution of a skill is ultimately going to be, such as the instant a driver makes contact with a golf ball, or a field-goal kicker's boot hits a football, or the final foot-plant of a long jumper after sprinting down the runway. Paradoxically, as the NCCP manual on skills analysis points out, "participants cannot do anything at the critical instant to alter its effectiveness; instead, they must make any necessary changes before the critical instant, but the most significant part of the skill is the force-producing phase." In other words, it is the preliminary work done before the critical instant that allows it to be completed successfully. And what is more, the critical instant of most skills usually passes so quickly as to be almost unobservable (but certainly observable after the fact using video tape or photography).

  The follow-through. The movements that take place after the critical instant. These are key because, in many sports, they are crucial to a skill being completed successfully (think of the bas-ketball jump-shooter's follow-through of the arm and wrist as a key aspect of the total shooting skill). They also slow body parts down, and are therefore important in preventing injuries that can occur when abruptly stopping.

- **Identify key elements of each phase.** Not only is it important to break down each skill into phases, but also to break each phase into distinct, observable elements. Although such compartmentalizing might seem excessive, it is worth noting that the key elements of each phase usually have a lot to do with the execution of other phases of a skill. For example, the way in which a tennis player sets her feet before tossing the ball in the air to serve will eventually have a lot to do with the way in which she strikes the ball and follows through later in the skill's execution.

- **Develop an observation plan.** Because there are so many different elements in most sports skills, observers need to decide before watching just how they are going to perform the observation process. In most cases, this plan has to take into account that an observer usually cannot take in every aspect of a skill – or even a skill phase – at once. Consequently, an observation plan should include a determination of what key elements will be observed, a scanning strategy that includes first obtaining a general picture of a participant's execution of a skill before honing in on specific elements, choosing a varied number of positions for observation, and determining just how many observations will be needed. (It is a good idea to develop some kind of chart outlining the observation plan, which can then be filled out during the observation itself.)

It is crucial that the observations occur without distractions, meaning that observers should take every measure possible to eliminate any obstacles to a clear observation session.

One example of skill-observation techniques occurs in youth leagues for sports such as hockey, basketball, or soccer. In order to divide the players into their respective teams while evenly dispersing the highly skilled players, these leagues will often hold evaluation sessions in which large numbers of young athletes go through a series of drills designed to allow coaches to obtain a quick reading on what level of skill each youngster possesses. In these instances, it is important for observers to be able to identify both the component parts of a skill and skills as a whole, and to make a fairly rapid evaluation of each – that is, to assign a rough numerical value on how a player handles the puck or ball, how he or she shoots at a target, passes to a teammate, and so on.

Shaquille O'Neal
Sometimes you can teach an old dog new tricks...

Although we usually think about young or beginning athletes when we talk about skills development and the progression of motor learning capabilities, it is not always kids and novices who need help when it comes to working on their sports skills. Sometimes even veteran athletes are forced, for a number of reasons, to completely relearn one aspect of their game, or even a whole range of sports skills.

In fact, one of the world's best-known professional athletes found himself turning, late in his career, to a specialist in skills analysis for help with one specific part of his game.

For the past several seasons, Shaquille O'Neal has been one of the dominant players in the National Basketball Association (NBA). The Los Angeles Lakers centre combines tremendous size with exceptional quickness and power, and is an especially dangerous player close to the basket. Under O'Neal's leadership, the Lakers won three consecutive NBA championships, in the 1999-2000, 2000-01 and 2001-02 seasons, leading many basketball experts to begin calling "Shaq" one of the best athletes ever to play the game, and labelling him as the man who truly revolutionized the way that the sport's "big men" can control the action in NBA contests.

But as dominant as O'Neal can be, there has always been one glaring weakness in his otherwise near-perfect game: his ability to shoot free throws. Although the concept of a seven-foot-tall, 300-pound player converting a shot from a foul line that is a relatively short distance away from the basket – with no opposing players trying to block him – seems simple, that was not the case for O'Neal, whose percentage of successful free throws often dipped well below 40 percent. (The NBA's best shooters routinely average above 90 percent.)

Things got so bad that, in the 2000 NBA playoffs, the Lakers' opponents started resorting to an annoying tactic that reporters soon began calling the

Shaquille O'Neil shoots over Dallas Mavericks' centre Raef LaFrentz (AP Photo/Donna McWilliam).

"Hack-a-Shaq" – fouling or "hacking" O'Neal in the hope that he would be unsuccessful when he went to the free-throw line. And to add insult to injury, opposing fans started putting on hard-hats whenever O'Neal stepped to the foul line, in reference to his tendency to shoot "bricks" or awkward-looking shots that bounced gracelessly off the rim of the backboard.

Luckily for O'Neal, help arrived in the form of a man who calls himself "The Free Throw Surgeon" because of the way in which he "dissects" the mechanics of poor shooters and coaches them into better ones. Ed Palubinskas, a former Australian Olympic basketball player and a man who has won numerous foul-shooting competitions himself (including one in Winnipeg, where he shot a perfect 75-for-75 from the line), began working with O'Neal in 2000 in an effort to correct his mechanically disastrous form.

The two started practising at a high-school gym, and Palubinskas quickly figured out what was wrong – O'Neal was flaring his elbows out when he shot in an attempt to compensate for

an old wrist injury. Under the guidance of "the Surgeon," Shaq started shooting 300 to 350 free throws a day, with Palubinskas watching his every move.

"We've made his shot more mechanical," Palubinas said in a 2001 *USA Today* article about their work together. "We're taking it away from him and giving it to science. We've realigned all the angles, speeded up his release and taken the ball out of the palm and onto his fingertips. He's finally getting a grip on it, pardon the pun."

Things quickly got better for O'Neal. His percentage, while still far below that of the NBA's leaders, jumped into the high-50s after a few months of practicing. "I told Shaq his shooting wouldn't really take off until he started dreaming about me," said the coach. "Three or four weeks later, he said, 'Ed I'm finally dreaming about you.'"

Despite the success that O'Neal and Palubinskas had in refining the younger man's free-throw shooting style, the Lakers player will never match the record of the all-time leading free-throw ace in the NBA, Rick Barry. The Hall of Fame star compiled a career record of exactly 90 percent of made free throws during his long basketball career.

From a skills development perspective, Barry's feat is even more significant because of the way Barry shot his free throws. Unlike almost every player in NBA history, Barry used an underhand technique (often called the "granny shot" by playground basketball players) and release the ball with considerable backspin from below his waist.

Although he used a decidedly "un-cool" way of free-throw shooting, Barry achieved the necessary results to silence the critics. To this day, many commentators are mystified as to the reasons why more players – especially those struggling from the free-throw line – have not tried to copy his style.

Source: www.freethrowmaster.com/Freethrow/News/news.html

ADAPTING SKILL DEVELOPMENT TO MATCH ABILITY LEVELS

There are certain ideal ways of both teaching and learning every skill. But these ideals assume that an athlete is fully able to understand all of the elements of the skill, to perform all of those elements, and, finally, to put them all together to the completion of the skill.

Beginners – especially young ones – however, rarely possess all three of these abilities. Consequently, coaches need to adapt the development of skills to match ability levels. One of the main ways of doing so is by taking complicated or complex skills and breaking them down into elements that can be mastered (or at least practised and repeated) separately, before they are combined as a whole.

There are several ways of making a complex skill simpler in order to teach the steps a learner needs to eventually master the complex skill. One way to simplify a complex action is by leaving out some of its parts. The learner can first practise only a few of the skill's elements and others can be added later. Another is to practice the skill in a situation that eliminates some of the external complications likely to be faced in competition. When soccer players dribble the ball around pylons in practice, they are using a simplified version of the dribbling they will need in a game against mobile opponents who will want to take the ball away from them.

Yet another way of simplifying a complex skill is by slowing it down. The learner is allowed to "go through the motions" time after time in an effort to master the skill's elements correctly before speeding them up to competitive speed. This is a common teaching tool in basketball, for example, where young players learning the lay-up for the first time go through a slow one-two-three motion needed to make the shot successfully before attempting it at faster speeds.

The NCCP identifies two other key ways of teaching complex skills, known as shaping and chaining.

Shaping

Shaping encourages learners to develop, or "shape," a skill gradually. The coach briefly demonstrates the skill and includes only the most important actions. The athletes practise the simplified skill, and the coach then adds the missing parts gradually until the whole skill is learned. It is important to note that the shaping process is a very gradual one, and should take several practice sessions before it is complete.

Learning to hit a golf ball off a tee offers an example of how shaping can be used to teach a skill. In stage one, the coach teaches the golfer the basics of the swing – without yet using a golf ball – and covers the basics of hand position on the club, the mechanics of the swing, keeping the head down while swinging, and following through. In stage two, the golfer tries the steps of stage one, repeating it until it becomes a smooth action with all of the elements in place.

In stage three, the coach adds a ball, encouraging the learner to attempt to hit it with only moderate force ("Don't try to kill it!" is an oft-heard form of encouragement at this stage). At this point, the coach can offer some encouragement regarding accuracy – i.e., reminding the learner that, at this stage, hitting the ball straight is the general goal. Finally, in stage four, the learner practises the drive over and over, working to simultaneously increase the force of the shot, the distance the ball travels, and the straightness of the drive while keeping in mind all of the skill elements previously learned.

Chaining

Since complex skills are made up of separate and distinct parts, this approach uses the metaphor of the links of a chain to break a skill down, and encourages athletes to join – or "chain" – these elements together. The most common approach to chaining is called forward chaining; that is, learners start at the beginning of an action, learning the first phase first, the second phase second, and then chaining those two phases together before moving on to learn the third phase, which is then chained to the first two. In other words, learners develop mastery over the parts in the same order as they are executed in the finished skill.

The other chaining approach is called backward chaining, in which an athlete begins at the end of a complex skill and works backward. One of the advantages to this approach is that it begins with the skill elements that are usually the most rewarding (the successful shot's follow-through and the release of the ball in a basketball jump-shot) before moving backward to the "hard parts" (the foot-plant and drive from the legs).

WHERE DO WE GO FROM HERE?

The physical aspect of motor development is only one part of a larger puzzle. At a fundamental level, sensory perception is crucial to the development of motor skills, and as these skills become more and more complex – especially within the context of sport and physical activity – biomechanical, psychological, and mental factors are important as well.

In the following section, we will look at the relationship between psychology and sport – how the motor skills we have examined thus far can be combined with the mental aspects of training and competition as a way of enhancing physical performance even further.

Quebec's Dominique Bilodeau prepares to throw the javelin in the finals at the Canada Summer Games in London, Ontario, August 2001. She went on to win the event (CP PHOTO/Jonathan Hayward).

20

The Psychology of Sport

"Baseball is 90 per cent mental. The other half is physical."
— Yogi Berra, baseball Hall of Fame player

Until now, the material in this book has concentrated almost entirely on the physical aspects of sport and physical activity – how the various body parts and systems function, both individually and in conjunction with each other, to allow us to accomplish and eventually master a huge range of skills and abilities.

In the present Unit on motor development, we have been looking at the question of how physical skills can be developed over time, allowing people to move from the beginning stages of learning to increasing their expertise and ability. Implied in this model is the fact that, as humans, our bodies can "learn" skills. At the same time, improvements in the sensory perceptions occur that allow this physical progress. Thus, it would seem logical that the more time an individual spends on developing the physical side of sport expertise – what we usually refer to as "training" (detailed in Sections 13 and 14) – the better he or she will become at the skills needed to succeed at that sport.

But, as everyone involved in competitive sport quickly realizes, the physical side of athletic competition is only part of the picture. For athletes who want to succeed at any level, physical training is only one component of the preparation they need to attain higher levels of excellence. That is because the mental – or psychological – aspects of training and competition form a key component of the efforts of the successful athlete. In fact, in the last decade or so, when many observers of the sporting world have referred to advances in athletic training, they have cited progress in the area of sport psychology as being the most significant. Even in the days before the term *sport psychology* was in vogue, coaches and athletes realized the importance of motivation, goal setting, and relaxation as aids to top-level training and competition. Within the last three decades, however, the study of sport psychology has emerged as a recognized field with an important impact on a wide range of sport disciplines.

Many fans of competitive sports can relate stories in which, for example, athletes with apparently limitless physical gifts fell short of expectations because they were unable to "pull it all together" for the big race or game. Sports lore is filled with examples of favoured athletes "choking" during a big competition, and supposed pre-competition "underdogs" who "came out of nowhere" to win a major event.

Certainly, at the highest levels of sport, in which many of the physical aspects of the competitors are more or less equal – most athletes follow more or less the same training regimen and meet roughly the same standards of height, weight, speed, strength, and so forth – the one major factor that separates those who succeed and those who do not is often said to be psychological. But, like many other aspects of performance enhancement we have previously examined, sport psychology is far from being the exclusive domain of elite competitors alone. Athletes at all levels, and those who simply engage in exercise for non-competitive reasons such as improved health and overall fitness, can also benefit from the basic principles of sport psychology.

The Mental Component

You may have heard the old adage that sports are "90 percent mental and only 10 percent physical." With all things being more or less equal on the physical side, the theory goes, it is the participants who have developed the mental side of their sport who will carry the day.

In this section, we will look at key aspects of the psychology of sport, as well as examining the ways in which sport psychologists use various techniques and concepts to help athletes achieve increased levels of performance.

Sport Psychology: A Definition

Psychology is the scientific study of the thought processes, feelings, and behaviour of humans in their interaction with the environment. **Sport psychology** is this field of study within the context of sports – how people think, feel, and behave in sporting situations, and what mental processes motivate the way they behave in training and competition.

But sport psychology is more than just an academic pursuit. Sport psychologists try to make sense of a wide range of behaviours that take place in actual sporting situations by seeking answers to such questions as: Why do certain athletes perform well under pressure, while others succeed in unimportant competitions and fail in important ones? Why does one athlete with apparently less physical ability constantly defeat a seemingly physically superior one? Why can some athletes maintain a consistent training regimen, week in and week out, while others have serious (and regular) motivational problems, and still others take training too seriously, exhausting themselves in preparation for competition so that they "have nothing left" when the big race or match comes along? And why are some coaches and competitors compelled to adopt a "win-at-all-costs" attitude, while others seem content to take a more introspective approach, such as striving for personal bests or the sheer enjoyment of competition and training?

All of these questions (and many more) are the domain of sport psychologists. They use a number of tools to do their job, including observing athletes in action to see what patterns emerge in their performance, interviewing participants and coaches to get their feedback on how and why certain performances were successful and others were not, and applying recognized principles and research methods in psychology.

In this way, sport psychologists consult and work with athletes and coaches to assist the athletes in achieving desired levels of performance.

THE MENTAL AND PHYSICAL CONNECTION

In order for sport psychology to have any relevance at all to the world of competition, there must be some actual connection between the activity of the brain and the workings of the muscles, joints and limbs, as well as the systems our bodies use for breathing and creating energy. In Unit 1, Section 6 ("The Nervous System and the Control of Movement"), we examined this mind-body connection – how the brain sends out commands through the nervous system that in turn allow body parts to operate.

In the case of athletic performance, the brain's cerebral cortex plays a key role. As the source of thought, it generates the general mental state that a person finds him or herself in prior to an athletic event – extreme nervousness, to cite a common example. This leads to extra stimulus being placed on the muscles, which can make them harder to control in the case of what is commonly known as "nervous tension" or "tightening up under pressure." This increased cortical activity can also lead to a range of other involuntary muscle and glandular activity, such as rapid breathing, sweating, nausea, dry mouth, and a general loss of coordination. All of this activity is controllable, however, as we will see below, utilizing a number of relaxation exercises and techniques that have been developed by sport psychologists. Indeed, the annals of sports history are filled with stories of various champion athletes who learned, in one way or another, to control or channel their extreme nervousness and did not permit it to affect their performance adversely.

One such athlete, the Australian middle-distance runner Herb Elliot, habitually vomited from sheer nervousness before every race and ended up retiring from his sport in his mid-twenties. But Elliot also won the Olympic 1,500-metre run, was world record holder in two events, and remained undefeated throughout his career in the 1,500-metre and 1-mile races – track's highest-profile middle-distance events – suggesting that he and his coach had developed some fairly successful methods of coping with pre-race anxiety.

PERFORMANCE STATES

How many times have you heard a successful athlete tell interviewers that he or she was "in the zone" during a particularly good performance? We have all seen examples at all levels of sport where competitors seemingly could not miss a shot in basketball, aced numerous serves in tennis, or "nailed" all the elements of their gymnastics routine. In these instances, it is almost as if the athlete were operating on "auto-pilot," combining the right mental commands with flawless physical execution.

Sport psychologists have a formal term for what many athletes refer to as "the zone" – they call it the **ideal performance state**. (Another common term for this state in the scientific/psychological literature is *flow*.) Researchers have summarized the narratives of several athletes in which they describe their own experiences into the following areas, all representative of this ideal performance state:

- the complete absence of doubt and fear of failure, and a general lack of inhibition;
- a lack of self-analysis or critical thought of performance during competition;
- a very narrow focus of attention with little or no signs of distraction from the goals of competition;
- a sense of effortlessness and simply "letting it happen";
- powerful feelings of being "in control" of one's performance; and
- the feeling that time has "stood still," without any feeling of urgency or being "rushed" by opponents, the game clock, and so on.

In other words, achieving this ideal performance state represents the ultimate psychological achievement in sport – the perfect mix of physical and mental forces in just the right combination.

Interestingly, while the physical effort needed to succeed in sport is tremendous, athletes who speak of performing "in the zone" often talk of just how little effort such performances seem to take. Some studies have indicated that athletes who attain this mental state during competition experience reduced activity in the left (or analytical) hemisphere of the brain, therefore succeeding in what sport psychologists call "quieting" critical or self-doubting mental activity during competition. But how do athletes – and the coaches and psychologists who work with them – work towards this ideal performance state? The first step lies in understanding a number of key terms and concepts, along with how they can be applied in a sporting context.

KEY TERMS IN SPORT PSYCHOLOGY

Sport psychologists use a number of core terms when referring to the mental aspects of sports.

Arousal

Often referred to as "being psyched up," **arousal** is the state in which an athlete feels ready both psychologically and physically to do his or her very best in

Kelley Law gets a hug from sports psychologist David Cox after winning the bronze medal in women's curling at the 2002 Winter Olympics (CP PHOTO/COA/Mike Ridewood).

competition. This mind-body relationship allows the athlete to perform at the highest levels in competition. At its worst, extreme arousal can impede physical and mental pathways, leading to poor performance as a result of overexcitement or an "out-of-control" state of mind. Sport psychologists work with athletes to make them aware of their arousal levels, and to help them control and channel it into top performances.

Anxiety

Every athlete – even those performing at the highest levels of international sport – gets nervous before a competition. As the popular saying among athletes and coaches goes, "If you don't get nervous, you're not human." But strong feelings of **anxiety** can be manifested in apprehension, a general sense of uncertainty about what lies ahead, and a range of physical and mental reactions such as sweating, "the butterflies," and muscular tension, all of which can seriously inhibit athletic performance. As we will see below, sport psychologists work with athletes to limit and control anxiety prior to competitions and/or to channel these anxious feelings into a mental state that actually enhances performance.

From Athlete to Psychologist
Helping athletes get motivated

Canadian sports fans who follow rowing will recognize Kirsten Barnes as the woman who won two gold medals for her country in the 1992 Olympics in Barcelona. But in recent years, the Vancouver native has used her sports savvy in a different way – as a sport psychologist.

A graduate of the University of Victoria, Barnes – who in addition to her 1992 golds, was a part of the Canadian team that won four world titles at the 1989 World Rowing Championships – moved on to Bristol University in England, where she took the knowledge she had gained about competitive sport during her time as a rower and channeled it into a doctorate in sport psychology. In England, Barnes met up with a number of rowers she had met during her competitive days (one of whom is now her husband) and ended up being hired to assist the legendary rowing team at Oxford University.

In fact, Barnes signed on to help Oxford with a particular problem: how to beat its bitter rivals, Cambridge University, in the two schools' traditional rowing race. Oxford had a seven-year losing streak, and was hiring Barnes as the university's first-ever sport psychologist for the 2000 contest. Apparently the decision was a good one, because under Barnes' guidance, Oxford won.

"A lot of people connect my profession with mystical, magical stuff," Barnes told Ann McMillan after the race in an article that appears on the CBC's website. "But my philosophy involves a lot of common sense. The athletes I work with are good. My job is how to make them better by putting them in the right frame of mind."

To that end, Barnes stresses visualization in her rowers, asking them to "rehearse" a big event in their mind, with the help of videotapes of prior competitions. And since the Oxford-Cambridge race is a huge event in Britain, watched by millions live and on TV, Barnes prepares her crew for the pressure, too.

"When we get distracted, we get nervous and self-doubts creep in," she says of her attempts to maintain the crew's focus. "If you have a structure or plan to step into, you can concentrate on that instead of worrying about things going wrong."

Part of that structure is a "charter" that Barnes asks rowers to develop, which lists key words that help them hone in on what is important to them as they train. That list includes words such as "hunger," "commitment," and "belief" with "victory" topping the charter.

Macmillan, A. (2001). Kirsten Barnes: Keeping athletes in top mental shape. *CBC Television News* (www.cbc.ca).

Relaxation

In sport, relaxation refers to the mind-body state in which an athlete has no feelings of anxiety, and is feeling "loose" and ready to do his or her best. (This is distinct from what we mean by relaxation in the general, non-athletic sense – i.e., de-stressing from life's daily pressures.) A large part of the role played in sport by psychologists lies in assisting highly trained but often over-anxious athletes to relax mind and body to the point where they are able to compete effectively.

Concentration

Defined broadly as the ability to keep one's focus on the task at hand without being distracted from it by changes in the surrounding environment, concentration is a key part of athletic success. Generally, the highest levels of competition demand that an athlete's powers of concentration be extremely highly developed – there is often no room for distracting thoughts about other aspects of life. The other key factor regarding concentration and focus in an athletic sense is that the actual environmental contexts of competition usually change frequently and rapidly, forcing an athlete to shift concentration and attention as well. Further adding to the problem is the fact that athletes are often required to sort out, very rapidly, which external information (such as distractions in the crowd) and internal feelings (such as self-doubt) or "cues" are relevant to their performance and which are irrelevant to it. For example, a batter in baseball must quickly sort out all the visual cues supplied by a pitcher – wrist rotation, arm speed, the angle at which the pitch is being delivered – followed by other cues, such as the spin of the ball and the velocity and direction at which it is travelling, in order to make a quick decision as to whether the pitch is worth swinging at, followed by a judgment as to how to swing the bat. In the professional ranks, these pitches are approaching the batter's box at speeds close to 150 km/h, making it abundantly clear that a huge amount of concentration is required. Using mental exercises that improve concentration, sport psychologists help athletes to develop this ability, along with the mental tools needed to filter out external factors such as distractions from fans and attempts by opponents to "psyche out" their rivals.

Motivation

How many times have you heard an athlete say, "I'm having a hard time getting motivated," or a sports commentator tell an audience that a team coach is particularly good at getting his players motivated for a big game? In its general sense, motivation is simply defined as the "direction and intensity of effort." This definition has two components: (1) the direction of effort refers to the tendency of a person to be attracted to certain sport situations, such as deciding to run on a regular basis, or train for a specific championship swim meet; and (2) the intensity of one's efforts is a measure of how much actual physical and mental energy one is willing to put into a sporting endeavour.

Clearly, this twofold definition has, in turn, two implications for athletes and their motivation. The first lies in the area of training, where sport psychologists can help an athlete to maintain a vigorous, regular, and intense training regimen day after day, and week after week. The other is in competition, where psychologists can assist competitors in sustaining the mental drive they need to achieve the desired results. Sport psychologists have defined motivation both as an internal trait, often called "self-motivation," in which an individual is able to direct the intensity of his or her own efforts towards a competitive or training goal, and as an external force, in which a person looks to some other person (such as a coach or friend) for motivation.

AUDIENCE AND FATIGUE

Two important physical and mental factors also come into consideration when we look at the role psychological tools can play in sport. One of these is the role of the audience and its impact on performance. Many athletes, for example, react positively to large crowds and the encouragement they can provide. Others, however, seem to succeed better in settings where they are relatively isolated from spectators, and still others find that they can become extremely discouraged or distracted by crowd noise. Many sport psychologists work with athletes to help them control their response to audiences – for example, working on developing the ability to screen out crowd noise or to channel it into enhanced performance.

Another key area in which sports psychologists work with athletes is in attempting to mitigate the influence of fatigue. Clearly, the onset of physical fatigue in any sport leads to a mental state where feelings of tiredness can lead to a decrease in performance. But through a variety of techniques, psychologists can help athletes to understand that fatigue, while inevitable, can be overcome, and that "pushing through the pain barrier" can lead to previously unrealized performance levels.

SPORT PSYCHOLOGY: FACTORS AFFECTING PERFORMANCE

Sport psychologists work with athletes to allow them to achieve peak performance. People in the field often refer to this interaction between sport and psychology as psychological skills training, or PST, in which sport psychologists and athletes use specific tools to improve athletic performance.

Self-Talk

As anyone who has trained for and competed in sporting events will attest, a big part of "getting psyched up" for them lies in the internal monologue or self-talk that goes through one's mind, exhorting oneself to achieve success. Unfortunately, much of an athlete's self-talk can be negative and discouraging, as the pressures of competition give way to thoughts such as "I'll never be able to succeed" or "My fellow competitors are much more talented than I am."

One of the major tasks of a sport psychologist is to teach athletes how to regulate and control this internal "talk" in a positive way, and how to use it to achieve peak performance by enabling relaxation and the optimal direction of intensity and effort. Often, psychologists will develop basic "scripts" or lines of dialogue that an athlete can recite prior to competition as a way of reinforcing positive self-talk.

Imagery/Visualization

Many people ascribe to the saying "Seeing is believing." It is often true that, if an athlete can see him or herself succeeding, this will be a powerful impetus for further success. But athletes do not necessarily have to witness themselves competing successfully, at least not in the traditional sense (e.g., on videotape or on television), to gain this inspiration. This is where imagery and visualization come into play.

Sport psychologists can work with athletes to help them visualize or imagine themselves succeeding – almost like writing their own movie script, with them in the starring role – or to recall powerful images of past triumphs, all as ways of improving future performance. Within these scripts, athletes will often attempt to bring in a wide range of sensory tools as well – such as hearing, smell, touch, and so on – to develop a broad picture of what success "feels" like.

Psychologists often ask athletes to visualize scenarios that are completely unrelated to sport situations as a way of achieving certain mental states. For example, athletes who have a hard time relaxing before competition may be encouraged to imagine themselves sitting or lying down in a quiet room, thinking about some positive experience from their past. But whether the visualization takes on a sport or a non-sport aspect, researchers in this field stress one major fact: the only athletes who seem to benefit from these common imagery techniques are the ones who actually believe it is a powerful tool for athletic enhancement.

Hypnosis

In the popular imagination, hypnosis conjures up images of people doing all sorts of potentially silly things under the "control" of a hypnotist or circus magician. But in the sporting sense, the increasingly popular technique of hypnosis has come to refer to a state of intense concentration in which the mind directs the body to perform certain acts while blocking out all external stimuli except the ones that are essential to the completion of the ultimate goal. (Because of the widespread misunderstanding of hypnosis in general, it is likely the least understood of all sport psychology tools.)

Although it is hard to concretely define the term, one of the key elements of hypnosis is the willingness of a person (in the sporting context, an athlete) to respond to suggestions and to act on them. Once that receptiveness is in place, a therapist trained in hypnotism has a chance to work with a subject, usually in three phases: the induction phase, the hypnotic phase, and the wake-up phase.

In the induction phase, the therapist attempts to create in the subject an overall feeling of relaxation, lethargy, and confidence in the hypnotic process. The subject usually begins to feel sleepy during this phase as well, and is generally receptive to the suggestions of the therapist. In the hypnotic phase, the subject can then move from the relaxed state of neutral hypnosis to one of waking hypnosis – that is, he or she will be able to carry out suggestions while in a trance-like state. These suggestions can also revolve around remaining relaxed while in the waking-hypnosis state.

The final part of the hypnotic phase is based on suggestions that the therapist gives to the subject to carry out once he or she has awakened – known as post-hypnotic suggestions. This is the phase that is most relevant to sport psychology, since it is the suggestions that a therapist imparts during this phase that can be acted on during competition, such as "When the starter's gun goes off, you will leave the starting line feeling fast and relaxed," or "You will be able to stop any puck the opposition shoots at you." Finally, the wake-up phase sees the subject "coming out" of the trance, usually on an agreed-upon signal from the therapist.

Although a person can be placed under hypnosis by someone else (known as heterohypnosis), he or she can also undergo self-hypnosis. The basic elements of self-hypnosis are fixation – zeroing the conscious attention in on a certain point, say, a spot on the wall, to the exclusion of all else – and relaxation. Once a person has mastered these elements, he or she combines them with a pre-set message or "script" that is repeated over and over, often visualizing success in competitive situations. When these elements are combined to allow athletes to focus in a relaxed and total way on the goal at hand, they are said to be in a state of self-hypnosis – one that can be consistently improved upon over time, with practice. In both types of hypnosis, researchers have generally found that, the more willing an athlete is to be influenced by suggestion, the more likely he or she is to benefit.

Relaxation/Arousal Regulation

People who study sport psychology have noted that nervousness and anxiety are accompanied by changes in a range of autonomic nervous functions, including changes in heart rate, breathing patterns, muscle tension, blood pressure, body temperature, and other physical reactions. But sport psychologists have also looked for ways to control these reactions voluntarily – in a basic sense, to enforce a state of relaxation over the mind and body that will lead to enhanced performance through the removal of these inhibiting physical reactions to anxiety. And although popular lore is full of tales of coaches delivering powerful motivational speeches to inspire their athletes, the opposite is often true: many athletes require help in simply relaxing and focusing prior to competition.

To that end, psychologists have developed a range of activities that can be done prior to and during competition. These include breathing control exercises, progressive relaxation exercises (which teach athletes to relax specific muscle groups in a virtually unconscious way), meditation, and imagery. Suggested techniques for helping typically over-aroused athletes to relax include asking them to recall previous successful performances in which they remained "in control" and able to deal with the pressure they felt to succeed. For athletes who seem to lack in arousal – i.e., ones who complain that they cannot "get psyched" for competition – psychologists suggest imagining themselves competing aggressively, perhaps to loud cheers from fans and friends. Other recommended forms of relaxation include listening to music, some form of physical activity, and carefully reviewing one's goals.

Improving Motivation

Some degree of motivation is required for anyone competing at any level of sport – otherwise, no one would be at the starting line or at practice sessions. Motivation comes from a huge number of sources, such as a desire to gain the recognition of one's peers, a wish to please one's parents, or just a willingness to set a goal and then achieve it. But as important as motivation is in sport, psychologists recognize the need to define the word in terms that relate to athletes. In other words, although it is easy for a coach or a parent to say, "Come on, get motivated!" or "What this team really needs is some motivation!", its outcomes must first be defined.

Researchers have developed four basic principles around which motivation can revolve.

- **Personal traits versus the environment.** People who attempt to motivate others are often careless in the way they assess motivation, leading to the belief that a lack of motivation is the result of innate behaviour. "She just doesn't have the discipline to improve," or "He's lacking in determination" are two such statements, which tend to produce the feeling that a failure to become motivated to achieve a certain goal is the result of some personal shortcoming. Usually, though, an athlete's particular environment or background has as much to do with motivation as any innate traits. In fact, coaches often fail to consider whether their own influence, as part of the environment of the athlete, has anything to do with an athlete's lack of motivation.

- **Multiple motives.** It is very rare that a single factor is responsible for an athlete's motivation. While a female athlete might outwardly declare that she is "training to win the Olympic gold medal," the underlying reasons are usually much more complex. Built into the Olympic athlete's rationale for spending most of her waking life in athletic preparation and competition could be related factors such as potential financial gain, a desire for fame and recognition, the desire to please family or a coach, or the wish to leave her historical mark in her chosen sport. Consequently, sport psychologists contend that it is crucial for a coach and the athlete to be clear on the motives an athlete has for participation in sport. It is also vital that both athlete and coach understand that motivating factors can change considerably over time – what motivates a younger athlete, for example, can be very different from what keeps her competing in the latter stages of her career. The issue of multiple motives becomes even more complex for coaches who are involved with several athletes, since personal motivational factors have to be considered as part of larger team goals.

- **Staying motivated.** One of the biggest obstacles to motivation in the sporting context is what is often referred to as "staleness" – a feeling of boredom and general "burnout" that accompanies training programs, which, after all, are characterized by regular, intense exercise. After weeks, months, and even years of training, athletes at any level can become bored with the "same old thing" in their training. Changing factors in the athlete's environment can go a long way towards keeping athletes motivated, whether it is an occasional change of training venue, the introduction of sessions designed more for fun than for physiological benefit, or the development of social activities related to the sport, such as informal get-togethers away from the practice field.

- **Leadership.** In any sport, there are coaches who, at first glance, seem to be able to train successful athletes despite a limited amount of technical knowledge. One reasons for this may lie in their ability to motivate their athletes. Some coaches are able to engender great loyalty simply because they are excellent motivators, and are able to get the most from their teams and/or individual athletes because of their personal style. This usually involves a great deal of loyalty on their part, in turn, for their athletes.

Setting Goals

Strongly implied in any discussion of motivation is the notion of goal setting. There are as many athletic goals as there are athletes and, as we have seen, many sports-related goals spill over into areas related to other areas of psychology, such as relationships with family and friends, self-esteem, and the like.

But while goals can vary widely depending on the individual, one thing seems certain: athletes need to have a clear idea of what they want to achieve before they can build up the motivation to achieve it. Although this seems like an obvious maxim, it is nevertheless true that goal setting can be confused somewhat by the fact that there are a number of possible types of goals an athlete can strive for. These include objective ones, goals that are empirically quantifiable, such as wanting to break a certain time barrier in a given event or achieve a certain numerical ranking on an official list. Subjective goals, while no less important, hinge on outcomes that are harder to quantify, such as "I want to become a better player this season."

Psychologists also speak of "extrinsic" and "intrinsic" motivational factors. The former refer to material rewards – medals, trophies, money – that participants can strive for. The latter refers to goals that are more self-oriented, such as a desire to master a skill, the love of competition, or a focus on having fun.

Psychologists agree that any sound coach-athlete relationship requires some basic discussion of what the aims are of the sporting endeavour. One basic framework for establishing goals is known as the S.M.A.R.T. principle. This is the principle that goals should be:

- **Specific** – able to be precisely defined;
- **Measurable** – able to be quantified;
- **Attainable** – within an athlete's limitations;
- **Realistic** – attainable within constraints; and
- **Timely** – achievable within a set time frame.

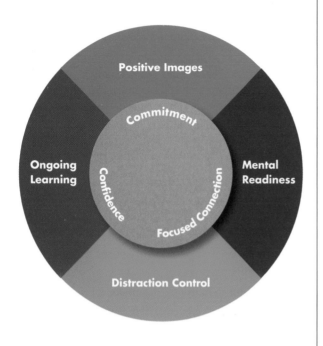

Figure 20.1: Orlick's "Wheel of Excellence."

Reprinted, by permission, from Orlick, T. (2000). *In pursuit of excellence* (3rd ed., p. 4). Champaign, Il: Human Kinetics.

Developing Concentration

As we saw above, concentration in the athletic sense hinges on being able to maintain one's focus in the face of distractions. In psychological terms, this is known as maintaining one's attentional focus, or developing selective attention. In many sports settings, this ability is made all the more difficult by the fact that it must be done over relatively long periods of time – and while dealing with high levels of fatigue, the opposing efforts of opponents, and distracting efforts by fans.

One of the worst things that can be said of any athlete is that he or she "choked" – that is, under a pressure-filled situation, but one in which the athlete could have reasonably expected to succeed, he or she failed to achieve the desired result. All areas of sport see such events unfold on an almost daily basis, and from the standpoint of concentration, they can be interpreted as failures to maintain attentional focus for long enough – or in the right way – to achieve success.

Psychologists recommend various techniques for improving concentration, including positive self-talk and exercises in which distractions are duplicated in practice settings to teach athletes to better cope with them when they arise in competitive settings. In basketball, for example, many fans will sit directly behind an opposing team's basket, waving their arms and banners in an attempt to distract the other team's

free-throw shooters. Therefore coaches, in order to prepare players for such a situation in games, will attempt to distract shooters in a similar way during practice, putting trainers and other players behind the practice basket and exhorting them to make noise and jump around while instructing shooters on how to calmly execute their free throws in the face of such pressure. Other psychologists encourage the use of "cue words" to help athletes stay focused. For instance, a speed skater who finds her stride getting choppy during the sections of the race in which she feels extreme fatigue might repeat the word "smooth" to herself during a race in order to keep up the desired pattern.

THE QUEST FOR EXCELLENCE

A large part of any sport psychology program is the concept of "excellence." The term itself has as many definitions as there are athletes – for example, for some people, excellence is defined in terms of attaining personal goals, such as improving one's best time in a 10-kilometre road race. For others, excellence is predicated on winning certain competitions or achieving a high ranking at the end of a season. For still others, excellence is measured by gains in finance or prestige. And for many, simply achieving consistency in training is a mark of excellence.

Whatever the definition, there are certain aspects of the pursuit of excellence that remain consistent, regardless of sport contexts or individual goals. Canadian author Terry Orlick, for example, has developed a concept known as the wheel of excellence that suggests seven key elements of excellence, all of which relate to concepts we have touched on thus far (see Figure 20.1):

- Commitment
- Focused connection
- Confidence
- Positive images
- Mental readiness
- Distraction control
- Ongoing learning

In Orlick's "wheel," the first three key concepts – commitment, confidence, and focused connection – lie at the centre of the wheel, with the four other elements revolving around them. Taken as a whole, Orlick writes, they "provide the mental keys that empower you to excel and free you to become the person and performer you really want to be." Furthermore, according to Orlick, "[t]he great news is that each of these elements of excellence is within your potential control."

SPORT PSYCHOLOGY AND CHILDREN

Often, discussion of sport psychology revolves around the exploits of elite adult athletes. But top-level adult competitors are far from being the only people who can benefit from the relationship between sport and psychology. Given the millions of Canadian youth who participate in a huge range of sporting activities, sport psychology can have a significant impact on their approach to sport from a physical, social, and mental perspective. This importance is underscored by the fact that kids tend to drop out of organized sports as they reach their late teens, leaving the ranks of many sports full of only elite young athletes.

In general, young people who perceive themselves as "athletes" and have a positive perception of their own abilities in sports are more likely to continue to participate as they get older. Some kids enrol in early stage organized sports because of their own interest; others are encouraged to do so by a parent or other adult. But why do many youngsters drop out? Some develop interests other than sports, while others are interested in "doing what their friends are doing" – which may not involve sports at all. Still others are "put off" by poor coaching, which can include an overemphasis on winning or a lack of encouragement for anyone but the top goal-scorers or fastest runners.

Consequently, if keeping youth interested in sports until they grow into adults is a major goal, there is a need for sport psychology to address young, developing athletes to much the same extent as older, high-performance competitors. This application, however, cannot take the form of simply applying the psychological principles that work in the world of adult sport to kids – because of their different psychological makeup, children have different needs in this area.

In general, children respond well to praise and encouragement, and enjoyment of – especially at the early levels – activities that will help them build skills and confidence as opposed to games that centre entirely on winning and losing. Also, children seem to benefit from lots of participation during games and practices – sitting on the bench or standing around waiting for others to finish a practice drill leads to boredom and distraction.

ROLES AND CAREERS IN SPORT PSYCHOLOGY

In general, there are three main avenues open to someone interested in pursuing a career in the sport psychology field: research, teaching, and consulting. Often these roles are interconnected, and sport psychologists can find themselves occupied in all three fields.

Research. Sports psychologists try to further what is known in the field by studying its various aspects in an attempt to come up with new ideas, concepts, and techniques about its application to sport. The research they conduct can take a number of forms, ranging from experiments conducted in a laboratory, to wide-ranging surveys in which participants in a certain sport are interviewed for information about how they prepare for competition and compete. Most sport psychology researchers work in a university setting and usually publish the results of their inquiries in specialized journals devoted to the field, although in many cases, topics in sport psychology can spill over into the popular media as well.

Teaching. Since much of the research done on contemporary sport psychology is conducted in universities, many sport psychologists teach students interested about the subject in courses that cover various aspects of the field. These can include courses taught in departments of psychology, kinesiology, and sociology.

Consulting. Perhaps the most "glamourous" aspect of a career in sport psychology is that experts in the field are often called on by athletes and coaches to assist in psychological preparation for competition and training. Around the world, many national Olympic associations, professional and university sports teams, and individual athletes and coaches consult sport psychologists on matters such as motivation, pre-competition nervousness, visualization, "choking" during competition, consistency during training, and many others.

WHERE DO WE GO FROM HERE?

In this section, we have examined several concepts related to the application of psychological principles to sport. But in sports, most competitors are not expected to "go it alone." Coaches also play a valuable role in the application of the various athletic-enhancement techniques available. Often, because of their greater experience and knowledge, they are instrumental in introducing athletes to many of the ideas that in turn can help competitors become better at their sport while increasing their enjoyment of it. For athletes from the beginning stages of sport development all the way to the advanced levels of professional sport, coaches are crucial figures on the sporting scene because of their ability to teach, motivate, and guide.

In the following section, we will look at the role of coaches in sport, analyzing the important role they play in determining the overall outlook of their athletes, before moving on to specific techniques and concepts that are crucial to coaching success.

Canada's women's basketball team (red and white) competes at the 2000 Paralympic Games in Sydney, Australia (CP PHOTO/Don Gaudette).

21
Coaching Principles and Practices

**"Great coaches don't make great athletes. It's the other way around –
the coaches owe their reputation to their athletes."**
— legendary Canadian athletics coach Donald Mills (1927-2003)

KEY CONCEPTS		
• Coaching styles • Autocratic coach • Democratic coach • National Coaching Certification Program (NCCP)	• Fair play • Role of a coach • Age-appropriate coaching strategies • Strategy/tactics	• Standards of ethics and behaviour for coaches • Coach-athlete relationship

Anatomy and physiology, biomechanics, the evolution of motor skills, the principles of sport psychology – the sport coach, at any level of competition, must have a basic knowledge of the role these (and other aspects) play in athletic development. To some degree, coaches must serve as experts in physiology, training methods, motivational techniques, the practice of adapting physical activity to appropriate stages of development, along with a large range of other requirements.

In this section, we will look at the fundamentals of coaching by exploring the central roles and responsibilities of coaches, and examining and assessing a number of differing coaching styles. Central to our discussion of coaching will be many of the concepts concerning human growth and development, the progressive development of motor skills, and the fundamentals of sport psychology.

COACHING STYLES

Many athletes report that sport coaches have been among the most influential figures in their personal lives, on and off the playing field. The successful coach has, at all levels of sport, often been referred to by athletes and outside observers as a "friend," a "mentor," and an "inspiration" to his or her athletes. Clearly, although knowing the technical aspects of a sport is crucial, there is a lot more to coaching than an ability to impart knowledge of rules and basic skills.

There are as many different kinds of coaches as there are types of athletes. Certainly, anyone who has

seen the coach-athlete dynamic in action will recognize a number of distinct coaching styles.

Some coaches, for instance, seem to be constantly exhorting their athletes in training and competition, often yelling and cajoling in an attempt to induce maximal performance. Others, in both the professional and youth ranks, adopt a win-at-all-costs philosophy, stressing discipline in training and results above all in competition. Still other coaches stress enjoyment and the social aspect of sport first and foremost. And still others focus on the development of skills and a long-term approach that seeks to maximize the length of time an athlete remains in a given sport, while minimizing the factors that can lead to dropping out. And many coaches adopt an approach that is a combination of these styles.

In the same vein, there is a huge variation in the personalities and training requirements of athletes. Certain one-on-one fitness training techniques that prove to be extremely successful for one person might not work at all for another – and the same is true for the relationship that exists between a coach and the athletes he or she is attempting to prepare for competition in a team or individual sport. Consequently, depending on the athlete(s) involved in the relationship, any of the coaching styles mentioned above (and many others) could be effective. But there are certain basic principles that apply to any coach-athlete dynamic – concepts upon which any sound relationship will rest.

The approach and style a coach adopts is determined to a large extent by the age and level of development of the athlete. In many cases, there are other people who enter into the equation. For example,

Canadian women's head coach Karen Hughes and Assistant Coach Mike Pelino watch a play during practice in Calgary, Alberta, March 2003 (CP PHOTO/Adrian Wyld).

since the involvement of parents is usually a key factor in the development and continued participation of young athletes, coaches are also faced with the added responsibility of making sport a positive experience for both young athletes and parents. And for older athletes, other family members such as spouses or partners play a key role in the competitor's sporting career.

Although it is difficult to establish concrete categories of coaching styles, there have been several studies that have attempted to establish those into which the majority of coaches will fall. Although these categories contain many generalities, anyone who has been or has worked with a sport coach will recognize many of the characteristics mentioned. It is important to remember that any one coaching style is rarely successful on its own, and that most successful coaches in fact combine several of the styles and approaches as outlined below.

Furthermore, since a coaching style is often a reflection of an individual coach's personality, coaches usually succeed when they adopt a style that most closely mirrors their demeanour away from the playing field.

In other words, a fun-loving, "laid back" person would be ill-advised to attempt to adopt a tough, disciplinarian approach when he or she is coaching.

One recent Australian survey of five hundred sport coaches, for example, identified five distinct coaching styles, each with its own unique characteristics:

Authoritarian
- Emphasizes discipline in practice and competition
- Well organized in all aspects
- Teams are characterized by good team spirit when winning, but by dissension when losing
- May be feared or disliked by some athletes

Business-like
- Adopts a logical, "professional" approach to training and competition
- Plans and organizes practices and competitions thoroughly
- Remains current on new technologies
- Expects top effort from athletes, at all times
- May set goals too high for some team members

"Nice Guy/Gal"
- Is usually well liked by athletes
- Players may take advantage of his or her co-operative nature
- Works particularly well with athletes of similar temperament; may alienate those with more intense personalities

Intense
- Emphasizes winning above all
- His or her high anxiety often translated to players
- May alienate easy-going athletes

"Easy-Going"
- "Casual" approach to training and competition
- Often gives impression of not taking sport seriously
- May not be prepared to "push" athletes in training
- Usually well liked by athletes but some may find his or her approach not serious enough

In the same way that coaches are advised to adopt a coaching style that suits their personality, it is also a good idea for them to be aware of the importance of adapting their style to suit the personality of the athlete. Many competitors, for example, will respond well to a "nice guy/gal" approach, while others may be looking for a more authoritarian approach to motivate them. In all cases, it is crucial that coaches get to know their athletes' unique personalities – not always an easy task in team sports when the ratio of athletes to coaches can often be quite high, and when opportunities to actually spend the time to fully understand a player's specific traits can be limited.

Autocratic and Democratic Coaches

On a more basic level, people who study this field have established a simpler way of categorizing coaching styles, comprised of just two groups: autocratic and democratic coaches.

In general, the autocratic coach adopts a "do-as-I-say" approach. This type of coaching style can further be broken down into two sub-categories – "telling" and "selling." The autocratic-telling coach is content simply to instruct his or her athletes, defining the rules and parameters of a given activity and seeking no input from the athlete at all. The autocratic-selling coach will provide an explanation of what the athlete should do, but then will encourage questions and feedback regarding the correct execution of the activity. Ultimately, though, the final decisions rest with the coach.

The democratic coach takes a different approach, encouraging his or her athletes to be fully involved in the decisions being made about training and competition. Similar to the autocratic coaching style, it is possible to divide the democratic style into two subgroups, "sharing" and "allowing." The democratic-sharing coach typically begins by making suggestions about training or competition, then follows up by seeking input from athletes. The end result is that the coach develops his or her training and competition plans based on what the athletes have suggested. And finally, the democratic-allowing coach is involved only in making suggestions about training and competition to his or her athletes, then allows the athletes to brainstorm possible approaches, and, ultimately, to implement those suggestions themselves.

Clearly, each of these approaches has its own merits, depending on the athletes involved, their level of experience, and their athletic goals. For instance, the autocratic-telling approach may be the most successful when working with very young or totally inexperienced athletes, since these athletes do not have any prior experience to draw upon in making their own decisions – they are looking, primarily, for basic instruction regarding training and competition upon which to build further knowledge and skills. On the other hand, a group of experienced adult athletes may respond best to the democratic-allowing approach, because, after long experience in a sport, they may simply be looking for a little direction in advance of developing their own training and/or competition schedules.

THE PHILOSOPHY OF FAIR PLAY: A KEY CONCEPT FOR COACHES

In many countries, coaches from across the sporting spectrum share information to develop guidelines for all levels of competition. While the requirements of various sports are different, the fundamentals of coaching are similar. In Canada, the Coaching Association of Canada offers the National Coaching Certification Program (NCCP), a series of instructional courses for coaches. The NCCP instructs sport coaches in the basics of coaching and progresses all the way to advanced coaching theory and technique, and recognizes coaching competence by awarding certificates at various levels. (For more on the NCCP and its coaching skills development program, see "The NCCP: Coaching the Coaches" below.)

As one of its fundamental tenets, the NCCP espouses an underlying philosophy of fair play. In the organization's first-level coaches guide, the NCCP asserts that this philosophy is grounded in the belief that sport is a moral pursuit and emphasizes participation. The NCCP has developed five key principles that are key to the fair-play philosophy:

- respecting the rules of the game;
- respecting officials and accepting their decisions;
- respecting the opponent;
- providing all participants with equal opportunities; and
- maintaining dignity under all circumstances.

The NCCP's idea of fair play is an approach to sport and coaching that requires the total participation by everyone involved in sport at the youth level:

> These principles apply in all circumstances, and they apply to everyone in sport: participants, officials, parents, sponsors, etc. Parents, for example, can uphold this philosophy by asking children about their sport experiences, by never forcing their children to participate in sport, and by never publicly questioning an official's judgment.

Clearly, much of the responsibility for promoting fair play lies with coaches, who stand in the centre of a small but often complicated world made up of young athletes, their parents, and officials. The importance of this responsibility is made all the more vivid when one considers that the vast majority of youth sport coaches in leagues and schools across Canada are strictly voluntary. Given much of the recent publicity surrounding the behaviour of "ugly sports parents" who abuse – verbally and sometimes physically – both coaches and officials, it would appear that the role of youth-sports coaches in furthering the principles of fair play is more difficult than ever.

Women's Hockey Coach, Danièle Sauvageau
Despite her successes, women's hockey coach faces an uphill battle

She is a coach who led her players to an Olympic gold medal against long odds, defeating a powerful squad from the United States. In doing so, she proved all the critics wrong who said, time and again, that she had no business being chosen to coach her team in the first place. But even after having reached the highest possible level of success in international women's hockey, Canada's Danièle Sauvageau found herself unable to remain at the helm of the national women's team.

Despite leading the women's squad to a dramatic win over their American rivals at the Salt Lake City Games in early 2002, Sauvageau found herself forced to resign her position as head coach and general manager of the national women's team in September 2002, as it prepared for the 2003 World Championships. Sauvageau's position was taken over by former assistant coach Karen Hughes, as the now ex-coach returned to her old job as a police officer in Montreal, where she also planned on contributing to the French-language version of CBC's *Hockey Night in Canada* broadcasts. In early 2003, she also agreed to help Canada's national water polo team as a motivational coach.

So what happened? Are not successful coaches in every sport supposed to continue at the helms of the teams they have helped succeed?

Part-time Coach

Sauvageau's return to the Montreal police force was the result of a decision by the Canadian Hockey Association (CHA), which was unable to offer her a full-time coaching position, and was asking her to relocate to Calgary to coach the national team at the training centre there.

"I had a vision for the women's team all along – I could have handled the job from Montreal in the future, but I was reluctant to move to Calgary," Sauvageau told the *Toronto Sun*. "I wasn't turning down the job, I was

Danièle Sauvageau, former coach of Canada's women's hockey team (CP PHOTO/Mike Sturk).

turning down the location. Also, I don't believe in part-time coaching. I've been associated with the women's hockey program for eight years and doing it for next to nothing ... However, I'm prepared to help the Canadian women's program at any time."

Sauvageau's departure, at least for now, from the national women's hockey program – easily the world's most successful (in addition to the 2002 Olympic gold, the Canadian women have won eight consecutive World Championships) – must be a bittersweet one for her. After all, her success coaching the national team in Salt Lake City occurred amidst criticism by sportswriters that she was far less qualified for the job than any number of male candidates.

"There are few female coaches in the country – including Sauvageau – who even would be considered candidates for anything as meaningful as a junior hockey appointment," wrote nationally syndicated columnist Steve Simmons before the Games. "So why, other than the fact she happens to be a female, should she be put in a position to coach at the highest possible level?"

Of course, Sauvageau's success at Salt Lake City, and the classy way she handled the post-tournament press, proved this criticism to be unfounded.

Is the NHL Ready for a Female Coach?

After deciding to part ways with the CHA, several experts said they believed they would see Sauvageau behind a hockey bench again soon, perhaps even in the males-only coaching ranks of the NHL.

"I can see a day when a woman could be an assistant coach on an NHL team. Then, when a certain confidence and trust developed, she could be promoted," Ken Dryden, former NHL goalie and now the general manager of the Toronto Maple Leafs, told *Toronto Sun* columnist George Gross in a February 2002 interview.

"And it was impressive how she handled the team after all the penalties they had incurred in the final. Most people would have been preparing excuses for why the team lost. Also impressive was her speech after the gold medal win. It was a speech any male coach would have been proud of. She obviously has what it takes to coach."

The current attitude that prevails in leagues such as the NHL is that women are simply not knowledgeable enough to hold authority over a team of professional male athletes. People such as Danièle Sauvageau are beginning to change that perception.

For now, the comments of well-known hockey analyst and former coach Don Cherry regarding the likelihood of a female coach in the NHL probably – and sadly – reflect the opinions of most of the league's owners, players, and fans. "To be politically correct, as one should be these days, I would say that women should have a chance to coach in the NHL," says Cherry. "But being who I really am, I would say there will never ever be a woman coach in the NHL."

THE ROLE OF THE COACH

How can coaches promote the ideals of fair play? What is the essential role of a coach?

The following list, as suggested by the NCCP and several other sources, are ways in which coaches can develop successful relationships with their athletes within the fair-play context.

- **Keeping it positive.** It does not take an advanced degree in psychology to understand that the best way to motivate young people is by encouraging them when they do something that is viewed as positive within a given situation. Conversely, punishing or scolding a young athlete for actions considered undesirable is suspect. For example, a coach seeking to teach a young runner the benefit of a relaxed, economical stride would do far better to avoid comments such as "You're way too tense, and it's slowing you down! Relax!" in favour of ones such as "Okay, let's not worry about speed for a while. Let's just see you take a nice, slow lap of the track, focusing in on maintaining a steady, relaxed stride, and see how that feels."

- **Self-esteem.** Building an athlete's self-esteem is not always an easy task when athletes of varied skill levels participate within the same group, or when less-skilled young athletes observe that they are not as successful as their peers. Coaches, however, can work to build this self-esteem by finding something to praise in every athlete's efforts. For example, many youth soccer coaches encourage young players who may have trouble with ball control by using comments such as "Nice hustle!" or "That's great running!", even if the athlete's attempts to kick and pass are not yet successful.

- **The team-based approach.** Clearly, team sports provide a context in which it is easier for a coach to promote the concepts of teamwork and co-operation. Yet even individual sports such as swimming, tennis, track and field, and cycling (in which athletes compete most often as individuals yet train and travel to competitions in groups) offer an opportunity for coaches to encourage a feeling of shared effort among the athletes. These include drills or warm-ups that can be done in pairs or groups, regular team meetings, group strategy and planning sessions, constructive criticism among team members, social events (which can also include parents) and the like.

- **Balance.** Coaches can help athletes to understand that participation in sports – and, consequently, success at them – is only one part of a larger picture of personal development. Certainly many young athletes will feel pressure from other sources, such as media, family, and friends, to overemphasize success at sports. Attempting to stress that sports has an important, but not all-important, place within a healthy overall lifestyle can be extremely difficult for coaches, especially when dealing with an athlete who shows considerable promise at a young age, but it is a key component of the overall fair-play approach.

- **Participation.** Most coaches agree that, whatever an athlete's age and/or development level, he or she derives the most enjoyment and skill development from actually performing the physical activities involved in a given sport. While this sounds obvious, consider the average practice session of a team sport in which coaches attempt to build skills by involving athletes in a number of drills. In many case, these drills are performed by a handful of athletes while the remainder simply stand around, waiting for their turn. Given the theory that learning and enjoyment increase through performance, however, most successful coaches (especially of younger athletes) incorporate drills that maximize involvement for the largest number of participants.

- **Staleness and burnout.** Tied in with the concept of maximum participation is the realization that athletes respond negatively to performing the same old thing in practice and competition. At one level, this can be known as athletic staleness; at another, more severe, level, all but the most highly motivated athletes often complain of the burnout that comes from doing the same practice drills after the same warm-up or competition strategy, time after time. Consequently, the wise coach will build some flexibility into his or her approach when preparing a training and/or competition plan for an upcoming season so that tiresome repetition is avoided before it can discourage athletes.

- **Coaching personality and style.** Most experts on the subject suggest that every coach should develop a style that best fits his or her personality and general approach to life. Contrary to popular belief, it is not necessary to be a hard-driving extrovert or a fiery motivational speaker to be a successful coach. Many of the best coaches at all levels of sport are soft-spoken and introspective. They lead by their example of quiet determination, dedication, thorough preparation, and sheer knowledge of a sport.

- **Working with parents**. Parental liaison – especially with those of younger athletes – is crucial for coaches. Anything coaches can do to keep the lines of communication open between the coach (or coaching staff), athletes, and their parents or caregivers is a step in the right direction.

At the beginning of a season, many successful coaches assemble parents and athletes for a general information session in which the coach's overall philosophy is set forward and everyone becomes aware of their responsibilities (time commitment, equipment, specific game and practice times, and so forth). This gives everyone a chance to ask questions and voice concerns, right from the beginning.

At this stage, parents should not only be made aware of the coach's philosophy towards practice and competition, but should also be told what the coach's expectations are of them. Within the fair-play framework, this includes making parents and caregivers aware of the principle of showing respect for opponents and officials, the idea that winning within the sports arena is not the ultimate goal of the athlete-coach relationship, and that open, two-way communication is encouraged. Many coaches invite feedback from parents throughout the season, fielding a range of concerns, comments, and so forth from parents on a wide range of issues.

Coaching Skills

Because of their central role in so many areas of sport development, coaches must know much more than the technical aspects of their sport. The British athletics (track and field) coach Brian MacDonald (www.brianmac.uk) has developed a list of crucial skills that coaches in all sports and at all levels should be expected to develop, such as those in skills and motor development, nutrition, training methods, and so forth. These include:

- Knowing how to communicate with athletes;
- Understanding how athletes learn, and having a grasp of basic training principles;
- Realizing that various coaching styles exist, and knowing which ones are the most effective for specific athletes;
- Understanding the physical and motor-skill limitations of young athletes;
- Being aware of all aspects of safety, and teaching athletes about safe practices;
- Recognizing the causes and symptoms of over-training and staleness;
- Knowing how to reduce the risk of injury;
- Developing training schedules that meet the needs of each athlete;

- Helping athletes in the development of new skills;
- Evaluating athletes to monitor progress;
- Advising athletes on diet and nutrition;
- Knowing how to develop the basic energy systems;
- Helping athletes with relaxation and imagery skills;
- Advising athletes on the use of legal and illegal supplements; and
- Continually evaluating the coach-athlete relationship.

THE WINNING AND/OR LOSING PARADOX: A DILEMMA FOR COACHES

One of the most common sports quotations is the one attributed to the American professional football coach Vince Lombardi (1913-70), who led the Green Bay Packers to two Super Bowl victories in the 1960s, compiled a 98-30-4 record as head coach, and is generally regarded as one of his sport's great motivators. "Winning isn't everything," Lombardi is often quoted as saying. "It's the only thing."

While his opinion that winning is the only thing that matters in sport is certainly questionable on many levels, it is worth remembering that Lombardi was speaking of a world in which paid coaches and paid athletes worried much less about the players' overall moral and skills development than about simply winning football games. And while a win-at-all-costs philosophy certainly has many flaws, one can at least see how it could be applied to highly trained professionals who are competing, not for the love of the game, but for the spoils that big-business sport can bring them.

The problem with this philosophy, though, lies in its application at the developing levels of sport. Young athletes should be encouraged by coaches to follow the principles of fair play as illustrated above while honing their skills and developing a life-long enjoyment of sports. Paradoxically, those who espouse the "winning" philosophy often say that, of course young people should have fun in sports, but nothing is more fun than winning. But coaches, by the example they set, can demonstrate to the youngsters with whom they work that winning can in fact take a back seat to other factors such as the attainment of personal goals, getting along with teammates and opponents, and developing respect for officials.

When coaches encourage participation in sports within this context, they are building a framework in which people will want to continue sport participation for a lifetime, regardless of their win-loss results.

AGE-APPROPRIATE COACHING STRATEGIES

Many of the coaching concepts outlined above apply to athletes at the beginning or early stages of physical and sport development. However, an appreciation of the stages of human growth and the phases of skills development can allow coaches to adapt these basic principles into age-appropriate coaching strategies that work for athletes of different ages and stages.

For example, while close communication with parents is always important in a relationship between a young athlete and a coach, this relationship will usually change as an athlete becomes more mature and responsible for his or her own actions. By the same token, the coach of the older player needs to take into account a whole different set of issues. For example, advanced players of seventeen may be thinking of ways to continue their athletic careers after secondary school through athletic scholarships to the United States, meaning that the coach will be called upon to be aware of the options available to his or her soon-to-be-former player. Coaches may also find themselves challenged when it comes to making practice sessions enjoyable as athletes grow older. For example, coaches of young basketball players often use a version of the traditional game of tag to further ball-control skills – an approach that is inappropriate for older athletes.

Coaching Advanced Athletes

Coaches need to be aware of the motivational requirements of advanced competitors as well. Many of the simple, "fun" approaches may need to be changed if they are to have an effect on such athletes. The following are other aspects for coaches to keep in mind when working with these athletes:

- **Motivation**. As we saw in Section 20, there are a number of key ways to achieve – and maintain – athletic motivation. Again, knowledge of an athlete, his or her personality, and personal circumstances are crucial in this regard, since motivation to participate (and in some cases to excel) can be both a product of an athlete's internal or intrinsic desires for self-improvement, or of his or her extrinsic desires for rewards such as recognition, trophies, and the like. Athletes are also motivated by the particulars of their competitive events or practice sessions ("She's 10 metres ahead of me, but I'm going to catch up!") and their particular personal factors, such as home life ("My dad says he'll buy me a bike if I score thirty goals this season.") Clearly, coaches can have far more impact on the former motivating factor.

- **Ethics.** In the discussion on fair play above, we saw how a straightforward philosophical approach that promotes good sportsmanship has a direct bearing on all aspects of the coach-athlete dynamic. But as athletes progress up the ranks in accordance with their increasing skill levels, it becomes clear that there are a large number of factors that can enter into the ethical decisions that they – and their coaches – need to make (for more on the ways in which questionable ethics have affected the sporting world, see Section 31, "Social and Ethical Problems in Sport"). These ethical issues can include the use of performance-enhancing drugs and illegal equipment, along with attempting to influence the decisions of officials and general "dirty play" in an attempt to injure opponents. In this area, the example coaches set is paramount – if coaches are seen to cheat, or even cut corners, their athletes are likely to think it is okay to do so as well.

- **Goal setting and independence.** Many people involved in sport remember the old saying that the ultimate goal of every coach should be to render him- or herself obsolete. While this might be a slightly extreme position – especially as it relates to younger athletes – it is nevertheless true that one of the central aims of coaching should be to develop an increasing spirit of independence in athletes. Often this results in athletes managing one aspect of their sporting development while turning to a coach for another. For example, advanced figure skaters may find that they can motivate themselves sufficiently for competition, but may still require the help of a coach to perfect the technical aspects of the increasingly difficult routines. To that end, coaches need to work with the more advanced athletes to set long- and short-term goals that cover both training and competition. Clearly, these goals cannot be arrived at independently: they cannot simply be the coach's goals alone, or ones set by the athlete without consideration of the coach's input. It is true, however, that, in keeping with the psychological aspects of sport, coaches may attempt to participate in this goal-setting process by framing their view of appropriate goals in such a way as to inspire their athletes according to their personality. For example, a certain type of athlete might respond to a goal suggestion such as "Why don't we look at trying to run the 1,500-metre this season in under 4 minutes? I'm really not sure you'll be able to pull it off" with the kind of defiance that will go a long way towards success ("Hey, I'll show her! She doesn't think I can do it, but I will!").

STRATEGY, TACTICS, AND PLANNING

While setting goals, building skills, and motivating athletes are all crucial aspects of a coach's role, they are all essentially part of the process by which athletes prepare for competition. Coaches have another important job when it comes to working with athletes – the role they play during the actual competition itself.

How many times, for example, have you seen the following during a sporting event?

- After calling a "time out" in the waning seconds of a close game, a basketball coach pulls the players into a huddle and diagrams an intricate play using Xs and Os on a white board, designed to win the contest if it is executed properly.

- Following a consultation with the team's manager, a baseball pitcher intentionally walks a star batter in order to "pitch to" a weaker hitter who is next in the batting order.

- Realizing its strength is on the defensive side of the ball, a football team elects to punt the ball to the opposition in the closing minutes of a close game, confident that they can stop the rivals' offensive march down the field.

- In a middle-distance running race, a competitor "shadows" the leaders, only taking the lead in the final few hundred metres, confident that his or her finishing "kick" will lead to victory.

- A soccer squad, trailing in an important game, sends in a forward to replace a defender, hoping that the extra attacker will help it notch a tying, and perhaps winning, goal.

- Every time a hockey team's star goal scorer steps onto the ice, the opposing coach sends out his ace defensive player to "neutralize" the offensive player's ability.

- Realizing that her opponent returns serve far less successfully with her backhand, a tennis star continually hits her serve to the "weak side" in an attempt to exploit this aspect of her opponent's game.

- In a championship bout, the taller of two boxers is determined to keep his opponent "at arm's length," attempting to use his greater reach to keep the shorter man at bay while connecting with his own punches.

- On a gruelling road course, a team's star cyclist rides within a pack of his teammates, allowing them to shield him from the wind and lead him up tough inclines before breaking away on his own to victory.

Certainly, many of these and other scenarios are familiar to sports fans. But they all have one thing in common – in each case, an athlete is attempting to secure a competitive advantage over his or her opponents through some form of planning. When these plans are formed in advance and executed in competition, they are often known as strategy. And when a competitor comes up with a competitive plan during the heat of an athletic contest, such plans are usually referred to as tactics.

In both cases, however, coaches are a crucial part of the strategic and/or tactical planning process. No matter what the sport, coaches can bring a number of resources into play in order to help their athletes. These can include:

- adapting experience of similar competitive situations from the past to the race, game, match, or so on at hand;

- scouting the opponents in advance of competition to discover weaknesses in their approach, and developing strategies to exploit these weaknesses;

- understanding the strengths of a team or individual athlete, and designing a "game plan" to maximize those strengths;

- encouraging athletes to try new approaches to competitive situations when staleness or frustration has set in with the "same old ways";

- realizing that certain pre-established strategies are proving unsuccessful and changing them "on the fly" to adapt to unexpected competitive changes (i.e., weather conditions, unanticipated approaches by opponents);

- motivating tired, fearful, or frustrated athletes from the sidelines during difficult moments of games or races; and

- encouraging defeated athletes to react gracefully, and victorious competitors to accept victory appropriately.

THE NCCP: COACHING THE COACHES

Canadians who are interested in furthering their ability to coach athletes of all ages and at all levels of development can participate in the National Coaching Certification Program. It is the national standard for coaching in this country and is sponsored by the Coaching Association of Canada (CAC). Since the program began in 1974, almost 900,000 coaches have received instruction and certification through the program.

In many cases, sports associations and leagues will make NCCP instruction available to their coaches,

Table 21.1: NCCP Certification: Coaching level 4/5 tasks

1	Energy Systems	11	Practical Coaching: Strategy and Tactics
2	Strength Training for Elite Athletes	12	Planning and Periodization (Advanced Program Design)
3	Sport-Specific Performance Factors	13	Analyzing Performance Factors
4	Nutrition for Optimal Performance	14	Practical Coaching: Training Camps
5	Environmental Factors and Performance	15	Practical Coaching: Competitive Tour
6	Recovery and Regeneration	16	Athlete Long-Term Development
7	Psychological Preparation for Coaches	17	Leadership and Ethics
8	Psychological Preparation for Elite Athletes	18	Individual Studies
9	Practical Coaching: Skill Training	19	Canadian Sport System
10	Biomechanical Analysis of Advanced Skills	20	National Team Program

especially those with no prior formal coaching experience. In others, coaches are required to have attained some degree of NCCP certification before they can work with athletes. The NCCP instruction is delivered to coaches at five levels. Levels 1, 2, and 3 are geared towards coaches at the community, regional, and provincial sport levels, such as those who work with community, school, or club-level athletes, and teach participants the fundamentals of coaching.

At these first three levels, coaches must complete three distinct components for each level:

- **Theory.** These courses cover the basic principles of coaching, including planning, sport safety, skill analysis and development, mental preparation, training methodology, and leadership.

- **Technical.** Courses related to coaching a particular sport. More than sixty sports offer what are known as Approved Technical Programs within the NCCP. The courses present sport-specific information on skills and drills, rules of play, equipment, training methods, and preparation for competition.

- **Practical.** This component provides instruction on the actual "hands-on" aspect of coaching, providing coaches with input on how effective they are at working with athletes. For example, coaches working towards Levels 1 and 2 are evaluated on their ability to run practice sessions and their competence at explaining and demonstrating skills. Throughout Canada, the various national sport federations set criteria for the practical component.

In most instances, coaches with prior experience but no formal training can apply for "equivalency" credit and, in all, about one hundred hours of instruction and testing are required for the completion of each of these first three coaching levels.

Levels 4 and 5 (see Table 21.1), however, are far more advanced – what the CAC call "the highest levels of professional training for coaches." Designed for coaches of national- and international-level, high-performance athletes and for people looking to pursue careers in coaching, participants at these levels must have attained Level 3 certification, a minimum of three years coaching experience, and approval from their national sport federation. These levels require coaches to complete a rigorous study program of twenty tasks, similar to the credit system used in universities, as outlined in the table above. To receive Level 4 certification, coaches must complete at least twelve of twenty tasks (including mandatory tasks nine to twelve) with the remaining tasks to be completed for Level 5 certification.

ETHICAL AND LEGAL ISSUES FOR COACHES

As we have seen, there is far more to coaching than knowing the technical aspects of a sport and how to motivate athletes. As we examined in our discussion of "fair play" above, it is clear that coaches also must contend with a sizeable range of ethical issues when they deal with athletes. Luckily, most leagues and sport associations have fairly well-defined standards of ethics and behaviour for coaches; in some instances, these are highly detailed statements to which all coaches must agree before working with athletes. In the United States, for instance, coaches working with Olympic athletes must agree to the United States Olympic Committee's (USOC) "Coaching Ethics

Code." But even at less advanced levels of sport, coaches are usually required to agree to some minimum standards of ethical behaviour.

Although many legal and/or ethical issues involving coaching are relevant only to sport at higher levels, youth sport has its own standards of behaviour. In some cases, this can even include some disclosure about a prospective coach's legal history. In Canada, it is common for youth sport leagues to "screen" applicants for volunteer coaching positions in order to gain information about possible past arrests, convictions, and so on. Often, coaches are asked to submit to voluntary "police checks" into their background, and can only sign on as coaches once these checks are completed.

Parents of young athletes and coaches alike should ensure that youth leagues maintain a policy of ethical conduct for coaching. Some of the key questions to consider for coaches, parents and athletes alike are:

- What guidelines exist regarding discipline and coaches?
- What safety/emergency/injury treatment training must coaches possess?
- What is the overall philosophy of the team/league (i.e., to have fun, develop skills, prepare athletes for provincial-level competition, and so forth)?
- What guidelines exist for coaches to deal with an athlete's personal and/or family problems?
- What input can parents have regarding the management of practices and competition?
- If team activities include travel and overnight stays, what is the supervisory policy?

COACHES AND ATHLETES: FINDING THE RIGHT COMBINATION

For many athletes, there is very little choice in the coach with whom they end up working. In community leagues and school sports, coaches are often assigned to certain teams or sports. But for others, such as athletes looking beyond school or local-league competition, some opportunity does exist to choose from among a group of well-qualified coaches. For example, a young athlete looking to join a sport club during the summer months to intensify his or her training and competition towards a provincial or national level, or to attend university or college in the hopes of competing on an inter-collegiate level, will likely need to assess a number of coaches before making his or her choice.

In Section 14 ("Personal Fitness and Training"), we looked at ways in which personal trainers and individuals can work together in order to establish a "good fit" in terms of the specific exercise needs of that person. In the same way, the **coach-athlete relationship** is an essential part of any successful athletic career. It is important to note here that, in many cases, people who function in a supporting role for the athlete – parent, guardian, partner, spouse – should be involved in this assessment process as well.

The following is a list of some of the questions that can be asked when an athlete is looking for a coach:

- What background experiences have led you to become a coach?
- How long have you been a coach? What did you do before that? Did you ever compete in this sport?
- How would you and I go about setting goals (individual and, if applicable, team goals)?
- What do you expect from me as an athlete? Are there any financial expectations attached to our relationship?
- What opportunities will I have for feedback on how our coach-athlete relationship is progressing?
- How much input will I have in my daily/weekly/monthly training and competition schedules?
- What will be the primary way we interact as athlete and coach (i.e., one-on-one workouts; team training sessions; training and/or competitive advice given over the phone, by mail or e-mail, and so on)?
- Beyond strictly athletic commitments (i.e., attendance at training sessions and competitions), are there other requirements such as participation in fund raising, charity events, and so forth?
- As a coach, what is your policy regarding punctuality for practices and other meetings? If there is a strict policy in place regarding being "on time," is there a system of "warnings" or discipline in place (i.e., you can be late for two practices before being suspended for the next scheduled game)?
- Can you tell me of any "success stories" in which an athlete you coached had a similar background to mine? What about not-so-successful instances?
- What methods have you developed for resolving conflicts with athletes you have coached?
- What if things do not work out between us? How have you terminated relationships with athletes in the past?
- What are you hoping to gain from our relationship?

Monitoring Coaches

Most sport leagues, regardless of their level, have a set of policies in place for monitoring the behaviour of their coaches. These policies go hand-in-hand with a league's overall philosophy of sport, and reflect the type of service that coaches are expected to provide to athletes, their families, and the community. For example, a coach supervising athletes in a "fun" league will be subjected to a very different set of expectations than the coach of an elite travelling team.

But no matter what the level of competition, all coaches are expected to obey community laws and policies regarding issues such as harassment, verbal and sexual abuse, and safety. Since this is the case, most leagues also have policies in place for warning, disciplining, and even dismissing coaches who fail to comply. For the most part, though, coaches at all levels of Canadian sport comply in a highly competent way with all the rules and regulation governing their behaviour and relations with athletes.

COACHING OPPORTUNITIES

Essentially, anyone who has a basic knowledge of sport and a desire to work with athletes can find some opportunity to coach in Canada. In most cases, coaches throughout the country work as unpaid volunteers, helping young athletes develop their skills and a sense of fair competition in a variety of school and local league sports. For the most part, these coaches volunteer their time and energy simply for the love of their chosen sport and, in many cases, as a way of returning some of the effort that coaches spent on their development when they were young athletes. As well, in many communities, coaches act as sport organizers, often establishing clubs and even entire leagues that did not exist previously, especially in the so-called "minor sports." Many communities have also adopted programs in which high-school, college, and university students can earn academic credits by coaching youth sports.

But what happens when a coach wants to move beyond the basics of working on a volunteer basis with young athletes and into the role of coaching experienced athletes for national-level and even international-level competition? Canadian coaches who move through the ranks of the National Coaching Certification Program (NCCP) will find that their opportunities for coaching increase along with their experience and knowledge; in fact, as we saw above, Canadian sport associations require coaches to have attained a minimum of Level 4 certification (or equivalent experience) before they can qualify as national or international coaches, and the same is true of most professional or semi-professional sports leagues.

Many successful coaches at the youth and high-school level have found success within the university sports system in Canada. At most post-secondary institutions in Canada where the "major" sports (i.e., hockey, basketball, football) are offered for men and women at an inter-collegiate level, there is some financial support for full- or part-time coaches. Coaches of other sports, however, such as tennis, cross-country running, track and field, fencing, and swimming, often find themselves working with university athletes on a volunteer basis. There is some level of government-supplied financial support available to club coaches in Canada in these sports who work with elite athletes in preparation for international competition, such as the Olympics or the Commonwealth Games. But more often than not, even top-level club coaches function on a volunteer basis, supporting their efforts with other forms of income, such as full-time jobs or private fitness consulting.

Paradoxically, many Canadians in a wide range of sports often find coaching opportunities are more widely available in the United States, especially on the collegiate level. As there are hundreds of schools who field teams for competition at various levels of the National Collegiate Athletic Association (NCAA) in the U.S., there is also a need for coaches to work with these athletes. Consequently, many Canadians have found the opportunity to work as a paid coach at an American university or college, often achieving the "best of both worlds" by combining this activity with enrolment in an academic program.

WHERE DO WE GO FROM HERE?

This section on coaching ends the Unit on motor learning and skills development, in which we have examined a wide range of topics related to the enhancement of athletic performance and physical activity in general.

By studying how the human body grows and develops, and how we acquire the ability to perform a wide and increasingly complex range of skills, we have completed the progression that we began in Unit 1 and continued with in Unit 2. With these three pieces of the physical activity "puzzle" in place, you should now have a clear picture of how humans are able to go beyond the basics of movement and into the often challenging world of sports and exercise.

In the following Unit, we will begin to look at exercise as a collective phenomenon. We will examine many of the ways in which individual participation in sport and physical activity has changed over the years, and how it has affected large groups due to its important role in many societies – including our own.

22
Careers and Websites

"They're actually going to pay me to play hockey. I can't believe it."
— Manon Rheaume, signing her contract to play in the men's professional hockey league

Below is a guide to the many career choices that are available to those who are interested in specializing in one or more of the areas covered in this unit. On the following page are website links that you will find useful in connection with the many topics touched on in the unit.

CAREER OPPORTUNITIES

• Coach

At all levels of Canadian sport and recreation, coaches work with athletes to develop skills, further an understanding of physical activity, and enhance the enjoyment of participation. Although much of the coaching done in Canadian schools and youth leagues is done by enthusiastic volunteers, the Coaching Association of Canada (CAC) offers certification programs for ascending levels of coaching expertise.

• Professional Coach

In contrast to volunteer coaches, professional coaches obtain a fee for their services in working with athletes. In Canada, coaches of national and provincial teams must obtain at least a Level 4 designation from the CAC. Professional coaches work with teams and individual athletes at these levels, as well as with college and university teams, sports clubs and, of course, professional athletes in sports such as hockey, football, basketball, baseball, and soccer.

• Athletic Director

In many scholastic institutions such as colleges and universities, the infrastructure of coaches and sport administrators is overseen by an athletic director who coordinates the efforts of the athletic department as a whole. Athletic directors often attain their position after holding other administrative or academic positions; many are also former coaches.

• Sport Psychologist

Working with athletes and coaches to address sport's mental aspects, sport psychologists perform assessment and counselling to enhance performance utilizing motivation, relaxation, and other techniques. As members of a field that is growing rapidly in acceptance, many sport psychologists also conduct research and publish their findings.

• Social and/or Outreach Worker

In many communities, sport plays a large part in programs that assist "at risk" youth through such activities as drop-in basketball games, and motivational initiatives through boxing or martial arts. In these instances, social and/or outreach workers need a grounding in sport-related skills and coaching to function effectively.

• Occupational Therapist

After an serious injury, many people need to relearn certain skills in order to be able to return to the workplace or simply to function effectively in everyday life. Occupational therapists bring a wide range of therapeutic practices and a comprehensive knowledge of motor learning and skills development to their work with those seeking rehabilitation.

• Community Sports Administration Director

Many communities offer a variety of sport and physical activity programs to citizens of all ages, and require individuals who can promote these programs. The director must also ensure the participation of qualified coaches, coordinate event schedules, and make certain that proper equipment and safety equipment is in place.

• Adapted Equipment Designer

Through their knowledge of skills development and biomechanics, these designers are able to modify and/or adapt standard sporting equipment for use by disabled or injured athletes. In most cases, this involves assessing the specific needs of the athlete while being aware of the design factors that go into building standard sports equipment, and then modifying and/or designing equipment accordingly.

• ECE Specialist

Early childhood education professionals work with young children in all areas of their early development. Included in this mandate is the responsibility to help them refine some basic motor skills, including those that are best developed by exercise, such as running, jumping, throwing, catching and kicking a ball, and balanced-based activities. A solid grounding in the basics of exercise science will assist ECE specialists in these tasks.

Life Coach

An increasingly popular role, the life coach assists people in working through various transition periods in their life (e.g., job changes) as well as helping people feel generally more "in control" of their lives. A large part of the work of many life coaches is the promotion of exercise and physical activity as an important step towards overall well-being, and as such, many life coaches have developed knowledge in this area to better serve their clients.

Human Development/Motor Learning Researcher

Although much is known about the way the human body develops and performs, there is still information to be gained in these fields. Consequently, research in human development and motor learning requires professionals with extensive knowledge of exercise science and biomechanics as well as all areas of human development. Their published findings benefit both athletes and the population in general.

USEFUL WEB LINKS

The URLs for these websites were active at the time this book went to press. For an up-to-date listing check the supporting student workbook or the website for this textbook: www.thompsonbooks.com/hpe.

Coaching Association of Canada (CAC)
www.coach.ca
The CAC's website contains information of interest to coaches at all levels, including a guide to the organization's rigorous certification program.

Ophea (Ontario Physical and Health Education Association)
www.ophea.net
This site offers a comprehensive guide to the teaching of health and physical education in Ontario, including in-depth curriculum resources for teachers and students. One of the site's best features is the highlighting of key feature articles and resources. For teachers, the Ophea site also contains updates on the latest conferences and professional development events. The site requires free registration, and Ophea sends out regular news bulletins by e-mail.

Women in Coaching
www.coach.ca/women/e/index.htm
A vast resource of interest to anyone interested in coaching women athletes, this branch of the Coaching Association of Canada site contains technical information, resources (books, tapes, videos, and so on), news updates, conference and event announcements, and profiles. The site also includes the online version of the Canadian Journal for Women in Coaching.

Athletic Insight: The Online Journal of Sport Psychology
www.athleticinsight.com
For anyone looking to further their understanding of the concepts involved in sport psychology - both basic and advanced - this is the place to start. The journal covers both theoretical and practical applications of the field, and contains a comprehensive set of links to other related sites.

AAASP Online
www.aaasponline.org/index2.html
The website of the Association for the Advancement of Applied Sport Psychology, this site is wide-ranging, with an enormous amount of information geared to all levels of interest. For those just beginning to study the subject, the site's "What is Sport Psychology" link attempts to answer the question using practical applications in real-life sporting situations.

Introduction to Motor Behaviour and Control
http://plato.acadiau.ca/courses/kine/bmcleod/kine2013/ppoint/a/index.htm
Provided by Acadia University in Nova Scotia, this site contains a presentation (in PowerPoint format) on motor learning and skill acquisition.

Sports Media
www.sports-media.org
This site has numerous topics associated with the coaching and teaching of all sports. It includes a database of physical and health education lesson plans on all sports.

The Canadian Association for Health, Physical Education, Recreation and Dance (CAHPERD)
www.cahperd.ca
The Canadian Association for Health, Physical Education, Recreation and Dance (CAHPERD) is a "national, charitable, voluntary-sector organization whose primary concern is to influence the healthy development of children and youth by advocating for quality, school-based physical and health education." CAHPERD is active in developing numerous initiatives within schools and communities throughout Canada, and makes resource material available on the Internet and in print form. CAHPERD also works closely with various provincial organizations that are active in the promotion of physical activity and sport.

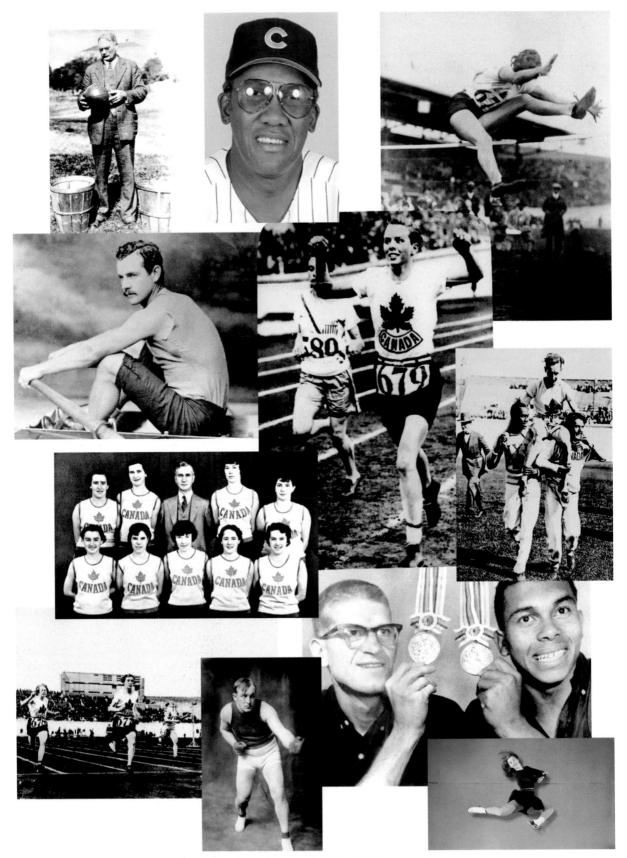

Canadian sport heroes. *Clockwise from top left:* Dr. James Naismith (CP PHOTO/OTTC); Ferguson "Fergie" Jenkins (AP Photo); Ethel Catherwood (CP PHOTO/NATARK); Jean Thompson (CP PHOTO/NATARK); Percy Williams (CP PHOTO/NATARK); Bill Crothers and Harry Jerome (CP PHOTO/COA); Barbara Ann Scott (CP PHOTO/NATARK); Tommy Burns (CP PHOTO/NATARK); Ethel Smith and Fanny Rosenfeld (CP PHOTO/NATARK); Edmonton Graduates Commercial Basketball Team (CP PHOTO/COA); Edward "Ned" Hanlan (CP PHOTO/STR-TRSTR).

UNIT 4

THE EVOLUTION OF PHYSICAL ACTIVITY AND SPORT

Fans show Canadian pride during the Canada-Denmark match at the FIFA U-19 Women's World Soccer Championships at Commonwealth Stadium, August 18, 2002, in Edmonton, Alberta. Canada won 3-2 (CP PHOTO/*Edmonton Sun*/Darryl Dyck).

23
Principles & Terminology

"It is impossible to describe modern life accurately without some account of sports."
— Bruce Kidd, *The Struggle for Canadian Sport*, 1996

To this point, we have examined sport and physical activity by looking at the ways in which the human body functions – from the most basic anatomical and physiological aspects, to more complex biomechanical and motor-skill elements – as a single, self-contained unit. We have also analyzed the ways in which coaches, training practices, nutrition, and performance-enhancing drugs can influence training and competition.

It is also obvious that sport and physical activity can have immense social significance. The ways in which members of a society or community choose to spend their leisure time reveals as much about them as more serious collective pursuits, such as politics, military activity, literature, or labour. Even the most casual observer will notice that during times of major sporting events – such as soccer's World Cup or the Winter and Summer Olympic Games – most other news is pushed to the margins as "sporting fever" takes over.

Those who look for trends in the relationship between sport and society have, over the centuries, noted that this relationship can play out in a "chicken-and-egg" fashion. Historians, journalists, and sports fans often ask whether sport really has an influence on society, or whether it is larger social trends that are influencing events in the sports world.

For example, the popular media is filled with claims that hockey is "Canada's game." Certainly, the success of both the men's and women's Olympic teams at the 2002 Winter Games in Salt Lake City went a long way towards helping many Canadians sports fans define themselves as members of a nation that possesses a powerful hockey tradition. During – and since – the Games, many Canadians have invested in commemorative jerseys, coins, medallions, videos, and many other objects as concrete ways of remembering these international successes and reinforcing what it means to "be Canadian," at least in the sporting sense. In this way, sport has had a major impact on Canadian society.

But looking at the double Olympic hockey wins in another way, it is possible to see them as the reverse – that is, as ways in which society has had a major impact on sport. Clearly, larger social trends were already well established by 2002 – for example, trends in merchandising, media publicity, and the creation of sporting heroes into recognizable figures in day-to-day life, to name just a few. These all came into play when the two "Team Canadas" won their golds. In addition, it is possible to see the Canadian women's win as the result of a larger trend in our society over the last fifty years. Until relatively recently, women did not play ice hockey at the international competitive level. The fact that Canada was able to field such a strong national team can be interpreted as a representation of larger social gains that women's rights activists have fought for and won.

In this Unit, then, we will begin to explore some of these questions. We will look at how sport and physical activity affects communities, societies, and entire nations and vice versa. Beginning with an overview of how sport and physical education have evolved over the centuries to their present form (Section 24), we will proceed to an examination of the role – both past and present – of women in organized sport (Section 25). We will follow this with a look at the influence that governments in Canada and other countries have had on national sport policies and competition on the domestic and international fronts (Section 26).

IMPORTANT TERMINOLOGY

In this Unit, we will discuss a number of key concepts related to sport and the evolution of physical activity to its current state. These concepts occur both in this Unit and in the following one.

Amateur versus professional sport. Of all the important ways in which the study of sport in large groups can be organized, the distinction between amateur and professional sport is perhaps the most fundamental. Sport performed by amateurs is that which is done strictly for enjoyment, without promise of any material or financial reward. The opposite of this kind of sporting activity, professional sport, is that which is performed with the hope of some kind of material reimbursement – usually money or some other kind of prize.

Historically, the Olympic Games were contested (at least in theory) only by amateur athletes. Those who had accepted any form of prize – or even financial or material support to allow them to train and compete – were vigorously excluded from the Olympics and other amateurs-only competitions. But within the last decade or so, most governing bodies of sport have relaxed their rules considerably and have allowed professionals to compete in championship events. Olympic basketball, hockey, and baseball now allow highly paid professionals, and international track-and-field organizers – once the sports world's staunchest defenders of the "no professionals" standpoint – have been allowing competitors to accept prize money and endorsement fees for the last decade.

Sport and culture. There are many definitions as to what comprises a society's culture, but most agree that, to some extent or another, the term culture refers to the common elements of day-to-day life among a given people. The culture of a community, nation, or society can consist of the food its members eat, how patterns of work shape their daily lives, what music they create and listen to, how they raise their children, and how they spend their leisure time. As a part of the latter, sport plays a large part in the daily life of many people – whether as spectators, participants, or simply through being aware of "what's going on" in the sporting world. As well, stories about the exploits of well-known teams and athletes are often embedded in the history of a given culture (such as the 1972 Canadian hockey victory over the Soviet team).

Gender roles. A key social division for most sport historians and scholars is the different ways in which males and females are involved with sporting activities. Increasingly, young girls and women are becoming involved in organized and informal sports. Some observers have pointed out that gains made by women in sport have mirrored similar gains in other areas of life. Others point out that male-dominated sports settings perpetuate gender-based inequalities. Whatever the case, an analysis and understanding of the roles of males and females in the context of sport is crucial.

Competitive versus non-competitive sport. Not all people who engage in physical activity do so for competitive reasons. Recreational joggers, bikers, hikers, or those who participate in aerobics or yoga classes or practice tai chi are often not seeking to beat the performance of others or to improve their own prior efforts. Instead, they seek to challenge themselves, socialize with people who have similar interests, and to take advantage of the health benefits that physical activity can provide. Indeed, many who participate in these kinds of non-competitive activities do so because they oppose the "couch potato" mentality of those who watch sports but rarely play them.

Many who find themselves drawn to non-competitive activities have had bad experiences with people who have taken competition too seriously. As you read through this Unit, recall that many people prefer participating in non-competitive activity, in which participation, and not winning, is the main factor.

The concept of "governmental support." In Section 26, we will examine the concept of government support for sport and physical activity. In sports, this term essentially refers to some kind of assistance provided to an athlete or group of athletes (or coach[es]) that will aid them in their sporting endeavours. This can take on the direct form of financial support, which will allow competitors to purchase the food and lodging they need to train, funds to cover travel to competitions, or the money needed to buy proper equipment. On a broader scale, governments can "support" sports through initiatives such as youth leagues, community centres, and promoting physical activity in schools.

Sports and nationalism. In the following section – and in reports in the media – you will encounter many instances of claims linking a country's so-called "national identity" to sport. For the most part, these links between a nation's favourite pastime and the way its citizens define themselves are fairly harmless. For instance, much has been made of hockey's position as the "Canadian game" or baseball's uniquely "American" status. Consequently, nations sometimes develop rivalries against others based on their shared love of a given sport – one such rivalry exists between Italy and Brazil over soccer. These rivalries are essentially friendly ones, with emotions and conflict kept largely to the playing surfaces. At times, however, violence can erupt on the field and in the stands.

Because of the popularity of sport in Canada and around the world, people feel passionately about it. Often, different sides of a particular issue – the issue of violence or the participation of women in men's sporting events, just to take two examples – are hotly debated. As you develop an understanding of many of these topics, you will likely be asked – by classmates, friends, family, and so on – to "take a stand" on some of these sports issues. In all cases, an informed opinion is always the best one.

WHERE DO WE GO FROM HERE?

We can now begin to look at the historical context of sport and physical activity. Keep in mind that the trends and events described here would not have been possible were it not for the efforts of many outstanding individuals – athletes, coaches, organizers, and innovators. The Unit that follows contains profiles of many Canadians and their achievements as athletes or as catalysts for larger sporting trends.

Former Edmonton Grads basketball members (left to right) Edith Stone Sutton (played 1930-34), Margaret MacBurney Vasheresse (1926-36), and Helen Northup Alexander (1934-40) pose with a modern rubber version of the ball that made them legends. At the time, the Grads were toasted by thousands but disparaged as destroyers of feminine grace and beauty (CP PHOTO/John Ulan).

24
History of Physical Education and Sport

"Mens sana in corpore sano." (A sound mind in a sound body.)
— Juvenal, A.D. 60-130; a Latin expression that captures the essence of amateur sport

KEY CONCEPTS

- Olympic Games
- Renaissance man
- Calisthenics
- Olympic Charter
- Olympic Movement
- International Olympic Committee

- National Hockey League
- Edmonton Commercial Graduates Basketball Club
- Canadian Football League
- Commonwealth Games
- Canada Games
- Crazy Canucks

- ParticipAction
- Marathon of Hope
- Terry Fox Run
- Man in Motion World Tour
- Role models
- Exploitation
- Sport equity

The history of people gathering to take part in sporting competition and physical activity is a long one. Most historians contend that, for a time, humans were so concerned with gathering food and securing shelter that they had no time for leisure activities. But as these concerns about basic survival became less pressing, some humans began to get together for athletic competition.

In ancient times, people began to articulate what anyone who has engaged in worthwhile sporting activities knows well: physical activity can have immense benefits, not only in terms of physical fitness, but in psychological well-being as well. In this section, we will examine how physical education and sport have evolved from ancient times to the present day, with a particular focus on how Canadians have participated and contributed to this evolution.

THE GREEKS AND ROMANS

Though previous civilizations may have participated in organized sports, no early peoples documented their sport as well as the Greeks did. They were the first to derive an idea of how the pursuit of physical activity could also go a long way towards promoting a person's mental health.

To that end, the ancient Greeks developed the sporting events that formed the early Olympic Games. Though the original Olympic Games only included one sporting event, a foot race, or *stade*, of

approximately 200 yards, other sports were later added, including wrestling, long distance running, discus, boxing, long jump, and javelin. The first recorded Olympic Games took place in 776 B.C., although the competition probably started long before then. The Greeks had a time measurement of four years, termed an Olympiad, and the Olympics were held at the beginning of each new Olympiad in homage to Zeus. The Greeks believed that the gods bestowed extraordinary physical abilities upon the athletes, and the winners would often present offerings to the temples of the gods. One month before the Olympics started, an Olympic truce, or peace, would be called that allowed the athletes to journey to Olympia without fear of travelling through a warring state. The "Olympic Peace" is a concept that is still embraced by the modern Olympics.

When the mainland of Greece was integrated into the Roman Empire (between about 50 B.C. and A.D. 500), the Romans continued on with the Olympic tradition. When the Romans adapted the Greek philosophy of sport, they developed the Latin saying "a sound mind in a sound body" (or *mens sana in corpore sano*), which reflects the idea that physical and mental health go hand in hand.

The Greeks and Romans had a similar admiration of athletics; both considered them to be an important part of a young man's education. The Romans embraced boxing, as they favoured more brutal sporting events. Boxing was first mentioned in Homer's

Iliad, written around 1800 B.C. Boxing evolved in the hands of the Romans to a gladiator sport; gladiators wore leather coverings over their hands and arms that were often coated with metal spikes. The participants (usually slaves, prisoners, and later, Christians) usually fought until one of them was either mortally wounded or dead. Once a gladiator had overpowered his opponent, the audience was allowed to decide if the loser lived or died. If they waved their handkerchiefs, it meant that the man should be spared; if they turned their thumbs down, it meant that he should be killed.

THE AMERICAS

The Aztecs, the native American people who dominated northern Mexico at the time of the Spanish conquest led by Hernán Cortés in the early sixteenth century, played a game that is considered to be a forerunner to modern basketball, called Tlachtli. Legend has it that the winners of the game could claim all of the clothes and jewelry from the spectators, and that the losers, normally prisoners of war, were decapitated and offered as sacrifice to the Aztec gods. The players had to get a ball through a hoop at the end of the court without using their hands; this task was so difficult that the first one to score won the game.

Sports were important to Native Canadian culture as well. Like the Greeks, many of the athletic games were part of religious ceremonies. Physical fitness was seen to help participants gain spiritual fitness, and was important to a young warrior. Depending on the nation, some of the games played included wrestling, archery, foot races, horse races, and a game often referred to as hoop-and-pole. The hoop-and-pole game required participants to stop a rolling hoop with a pole. Played with two players or two teams, the game required excellent hand-eye coordination, quickness, and spear-throwing ability.

The greatest contribution of Native Canadians to Canadian – and international – sport is the game of lacrosse. Lacrosse was originally called *baggataway* and was more violent than the sport we know today. The game served as training for warriors in peaceful times. The early French settlers picked up the game, tamed it to their liking, and named it *la crosse*, because it was thought that the netted sticks used to play the game looked like crosses.

In fact, Native Canadians still have an impact on the world lacrosse community. The Six Nations sends a team to compete as an independent nation in the World Championships, held every four years. Although their inclusion in the Worlds was thought by some to be a symbolic gesture, the performance of the Six Nations team has proven they belong in the tournament on a strictly competitive basis.

THE EUROPEANS

As the Roman Empire declined (about A.D. 500), the athleticism of the age declined as well. Any real athletic events were left to the elite. Sword fighting, horseback riding, jousting, and archery were pursuits performed by those who had leisure time, such as noblemen aiming for knighthood, rather than the average peasant.

The idea that physical activity was an important part of life and education made a resurgence during the Renaissance period (roughly 1400-1650), when people began to look back at Greek and Roman culture and beauty as an ideal. The Renaissance was a time of expanding knowledge about art, language, science, and history. Ancient Greek statues began to be unearthed and appreciated for their beauty and skill, much of which had been lost during the Dark Ages. The majority of Greek statues display the subject as very athletic, and thus, this again became the ideal.

The concept of the **Renaissance man**, a person who is equally good at and interested in multiple things, began at this time. It was not unusual for the intellectuals of the day to be scientists, poets, painters, historians, and sculptors all at once. This list also began to include athletes as more people began to acknowledge the benefits of physical activity on the body and the mind. Because of the progression of science in western Europe during the Renaissance, the study of human anatomy and physiology progressed at the time as well, thanks to persons such as Leonardo da Vinci, the consummate Renaissance man.

In response to this change in view, an Italian physician began the first childhood physical education classes in 1420. New sports were developed around this time throughout Europe. Scotland advanced two major sports that are still popular today: the first written references to golf were made in 1457 and to curling in 1541. Versions of ice and field hockey popped up in England and France about this time as well. The earliest references to "folk football" games come from the 1400s. These rough-and-tumble team ball games were the predecessors of modern games such as soccer, rugby, field hockey, and American football.

Athletics and the Victorian Era

The world changed greatly during the reign of Queen Victoria in England in the 1800s. Despite the horrors of child labour, a middle class developed, blurring the line between rich and poor. The population grew, especially in urban centres, where new industrialized jobs were located. The middle class was eager to join the upper class in their leisure activities. However, unlike their upper-class contemporaries in England, the urban middle class had no sprawling country estates where sport could take place, and with little space in the growing urban areas, large clubs, fields, and arenas had to be created to house the activities. The development of the middle class also meant that there was extra money available for many to spend on leisure. Clubs and arenas could be created for sports because the owners were able to charge spectators an admission fee. Though both the middle- and lower-class workers wanted to watch the spectator sports that were being developed at the time, most worked long hours for relatively low wages. There was not a lot of time to set aside for recreation. It is because of this that clearly set rules and time limits were placed on most games that we still enjoy today.

Another important factor in sport at that time was the Victorian ideal of the gentleman athlete and amateur. The well-rounded and refined British gentleman was also a sportsman, who believed that fair play and participation in sporting events were more important than winning. Fair play remains a strong concept in sport today. Amateurism was also important to the Victorian sportsman, because it excluded the lower classes from participating. Rules preventing teams from compensating players for time lost while playing sports effectively limited sport to the middle and upper classes. The Victorian sportsman also believed that sports were a reflection of life and that the same values that held true in sports held true in life. It was a commonly held belief that sports developed manly character and camaraderie amongst men. Unfortunately, it was commonly thought at this time that athletics had the opposite effects on women; it was believed by many that too much physical activity was harmful to a woman's delicate constitution.

The Victorians believed that physical education and sport were a large part of a young man's education. The qualities necessary for sports were deemed to be desirable – hence the contemporary notion that "sport builds character." Physical education and organized sports programs were implemented in the growing British public school system. Cricket, rugby, soccer, calisthenics, rowing, and netball were all played in the schools. These young men then travelled to the British colonies of Canada, Australia, India, South Africa, and New Zealand, taking their sports and games with them and implementing them in the colonies' schools. But the growth of sports education was not limited to British colonies. Germany, France, Russia, and the United States all emulated the British model of physical education.

Calisthenics

Calisthenics became a prominent method of keeping physically fit in Britain during Queen Victoria's reign, though the origin of calisthenics, which means beauty and strength in Greek, is unclear. There is a strong connection between calisthenics and early gymnastics, which began in Germany in the late 1700s. Calisthenics are a series of vigorous exercises and stretches often done as a group, sometimes set to music. The British school system used calisthenics in its physical education programs on a regular basis. Calisthenics enabled the average citizen, if so inclined, to keep fit and healthy. This series of movements, sometimes called drills, are the basis for many of the exercises that are still done in classes, both in schools and in gyms, today.

"RESTRICTED" AND SEGREGATED SPORT

Sport has often mirrored the restrictive or segregationist practices of societies in which certain cultural, racial, or ethnic groups have been denied equal access to social benefits. One well-known international example was the case of South Africa, which for many years denied blacks, Asians, and mixed-race athletes the right to compete in the same sporting events as whites as a manifestation of the country's official practice of apartheid. The international sporting community responded by banning South Africa from world events such as the Olympics. (The country was allowed to return to the Summer Olympics in 1996.)

Another example of restrictive sport arose in North America, with the rise of the so-called "Negro Leagues." These baseball leagues flourished during the 1920s and 1930s, when much of society in the United States prevented African-Americans from equal access to public facilities (such as washrooms and swimming pools), private institutions (such as restaurants and hotels), and even to employment and the right to vote. In sport, African-Americans (known at the time as "Negroes") responded by forming their own teams and a loosely organized league. The teams travelled around the country to play one another in front of African-American audiences. Despite the fact that teams such as the Homestead Grays, Brooklyn Royal Giants, and Baltimore Black Sox boasted many excellent players, they were never permitted to test their skills against the much more highly paid (and publicized) stars of the white major league teams.

Many baseball historians believe that Negro League stars, such as pitcher Satchel Paige, home-run hitting ace Josh Gibson, and all-around star James "Cool Papa" Bell, were in fact much better players than their white contemporaries, and bemoan the fact that they never had the chance to compete in the "official" major leagues while in their prime. (Some, like Paige, were able to play for major league teams once race restrictions had been relaxed, but long after their best playing days were over.)

The Olympic Movement
"All sports for all people." — Pierre de Coubertin

While working as an educator in France, Baron Pierre de Coubertin (1863-1937) decided to re-create the ancient Olympics with modern sport. After de Coubertin founded the International Olympic Committee, or IOC, in June of 1894, athletes from fourteen countries participated in the first modern Olympics, held in Athens, Greece, in 1896. There were forty-three different events, including cycling, track and field, fencing, lawn tennis, weightlifting, shooting, gymnastics, swimming, and wrestling.

Because of the nature of Victorian sporting ideals, no women competed in the first Olympics and no non-European countries competed (i.e., there were no Asian, South American, or African countries invited). Only "gentlemen" were allowed to compete in the Games, meaning that people who made their living doing physical work were excluded from competing. Two hundred and forty-five athletes competed in those first Games.

Despite the drawbacks of the first Games, the principles of competing against the best and focusing on the competition rather than the prize has since influenced the youth of the world in a profound manner. The Olympic Charter, first penned by de Coubertin, details the goals for the Olympic Movement, of which competitive sports are only a portion. The Charter emphasizes peace, tolerance, education, fair play, international understanding, and amateurism. De Coubertin believed that physical activity led to the development of character, as well as mental and spiritual growth.

The goal of the Olympic Movement has evolved to help create a better world by educating through sport without discrimination, and fostering understanding, friendship, and fair play. The actual manifestations of the Olympic Movement have changed considerably over the years, as the Games have seen changes in countries, sports, participants, and sporting rules.

Elizabeth Manley celebrates her silver medal in figure skating at the 1988 Winter Olympics in Calgary (CP PHOTO/ COA/C. McNeil).

The International Olympic Committee is a non-profit, non-governmental body of international members who represent the Olympic Movement in their respective countries. Members are elected through a nominations committee and serve an eight-year renewable term. The members meet once a year, and their main responsibility is to govern the Winter and Summer Olympics.

Summer and Winter Olympic Locations

Summer Games

The Summer Games are held every four years; other than interruptions due to war, the only exception to this pattern came in 1906, when a special Games was held.
- 1896: Athens, Greece
- 1900: Paris, France
- 1904: St. Louis, USA
- 1906: Athens, Greece
- 1908: London, England
- 1912: Stockholm, Sweden
- 1916: Not held (World World I)
- 1920: Antwerp, Belgium
- 1924: Paris, France

- 1928: Amsterdam, Netherlands
- 1932: Los Angeles, USA
- 1936: Berlin, Germany
- 1940: Not held (World War II)
- 1944: Not held (World War II)
- 1948: London, England
- 1952: Helsinki, Finland
- 1956: Melbourne, Australia
- 1960: Rome, Italy
- 1964: Tokyo, Japan
- 1968: Mexico City, Mexico
- 1972: Munich, Germany
- 1976: Montreal, Canada
- 1980: Moscow, USSR
- 1984: Los Angeles, USA
- 1988: Seoul, South Korea
- 1992: Barcelona, Spain
- 1996: Atlanta, USA
- 2000: Sydney, Australia
- 2004: Athens, Greece

Winter Games

Beginning in 1924 and until 1994, the Winter Olympics were held in the same year as the Summer Games; in 1994 they began to be held in the middle of the Summer Games' four-year cycle.
- 1924: Chamonix, France
- 1928: St. Moritz, Switzerland
- 1932: Lake Placid, USA
- 1936: Garmisch-Partenkirchen, Germany
- 1948: St. Moritz, Switzerland
- 1952: Oslo, Norway
- 1956: Cortina d'Ampezzo, Italy
- 1960: Squaw Valley, USA
- 1964: Innsbruck, Austria
- 1968: Genoble, France
- 1972: Sapporo, Japan
- 1976: Innsbruck, Austria
- 1980: Lake Placid, USA
- 1984: Sarajevo, Yugoslavia
- 1988: Calgary, Canada
- 1992: Albertville, France
- 1994: Lillehammer, Norway
- 1998: Nagano, Japan
- 2002: Salt Lake City, USA
- 2006: Torino, Italy
- 2010: Vancouver-Whistler, Canada

CANADIANS AT THE OLYMPICS

Canada has always maintained an excellent team for the Winter Olympics. In the first Winter Olympics in 1924, Canada's hockey team came home with the gold medal, scoring 104 goals over four games. The Canadian Olympic hockey team continued to win gold in 1928, 1932, 1948, and 1952. In the 2002 Winter Games in Salt Lake City, both the men's and women's Canadian hockey teams overcame obstacles to win gold, making the entire country proud. Canada's athletes have continued to win medals at both the Winter and Summer Olympics since Etienne Desmarteau won our first gold medal in 1904.

Ethel Catherwood

Ethel Catherwood, nicknamed the "Saskatoon Lily," is the only Canadian woman to win gold in an individual track-and-field event in the Olympics. The 1928 Amsterdam Games were the first Olympics in which women were able to compete in track-and-field events. The Canadian women's track-and-field team won four medals and the women's team title. Catherwood made history by winning the gold medal for the high jump. Her Olympic success helped to redefine the role of women in sport.

Barbara Ann Scott

Barbara Ann Scott, or the "Queen of Blades," is one of Canada's greatest skating talents. At the age of only thirteen, she became the first woman to land a double lutz in a competition. Judges were impressed with Scott's athleticism; in the 1947 World Championships, Scott executed turns, spins, and jumps that were normally only performed by men. After several international medals, Scott won the gold medal in the women's singles event at the 1948 St. Moritz Games. To this day, she remains the only Canadian woman in Olympic history to win the event. Her win helped to boost the morale of Canadians still struggling from the effects of the Second World War. As a show of gratitude, the City of Ottawa tried to give Scott a convertible, but she declined the gift so that she could maintain her amateur status under the rules of the day.

Nancy Greene

Nancy Greene, though gentle and pleasant in public, started her competitive skiing career as a very tough, aggressive, and ambitious skier. In fact, her teammates called her "Tiger." Her skiing style got her to the Olympics (Greene competed in the games in 1960, 1964, and 1968); however, she was unable to earn a medal. Nancy developed a new mental attitude and focused on controlling her skiing rather than attacking the course. The hard work paid off. At the 1968 Games in Grenoble, France, Nancy Greene won Olympic gold in the giant slalom and earned a silver medal for her performance in the slalom event. Nancy inspired many young Canadians to follow their Olympic dreams and was part of the Federal Task Force on Sport for Canadians in the 1970s.

Gaetan Boucher

Gaetan Boucher began winning Olympic medals for speed skating at the 1980 winter games in Lake Placid. That year he earned the silver medal in the 1,000-metre race. Four years later, after shattering his ankle in an accident during a short-track practice, the shy Boucher was back at the Olympics, carrying the Canadian flag in the opening ceremonies. Gaetan had to change his attitude about competition; he started expecting to win rather than just hoping he would. The new attitude and the hard work that accompanied it earned Boucher the bronze medal in the 500-metre race, and he carried on to win the gold in both the 1,000- and 1,500-metre races. Canada won four medals at the Sarajevo Games, three of which were courtesy of Gaetan Boucher.

Elizabeth Manley

Elizabeth Manley was not a favourite to win at the Calgary Winter Olympics in 1988. Katarina Witt of East Germany and Debbi Thomas of the United States were expected to be fighting for the gold medal; the others would be left with the silver. However, Elizabeth Manley's free skate, the final skating portion, was the best of the night, and her win inspired patriotism throughout the country. Manley was the first Canadian woman to land a triple combination in a competition. Her free skate raised her overall marks enough to earn her the silver medal. Because of her cheerful demeanor and medal win when no one expected it of her, Elizabeth was labelled a winner. She became a professional figure skater shortly after her silver medal win in Calgary.

Myriam Bedard

Myriam Bedard won the bronze medal for the women's 15-kilometre biathlon – a combination of target shooting and cross-country skiing – in the 1992 Winter Games, the first time the sport was included in the Games. At the next Winter Olympics, in Lillehammer, she came home with the gold medal in the same event. While competing in the 7.5-kilometre race that year, Bedard realized that she was wearing two different skis and that one was improperly waxed. Despite the adversity, she successfully struggled through the race and won a second gold medal.

Marathon Swimmers
Marilyn Bell, Vicki Keith, and Ashley Cowan

In 1954, the Canadian National Exhibition offered a well-known marathon swimmer $10,000 to swim across Lake Ontario. Marilyn Bell, a sixteen-year-old, decided to try to complete the swim herself, without any offer of money. The swimmers went into the water in Youngstown, New York, at 11 p.m. on September 8. Marilyn swam on through extreme fatigue and cold water with the help of her coach, Gus Ryder.

As Bell swam, the public in Toronto became more excited. Around 8 p.m. on September 9, Marilyn had conquered Lake Ontario and a large crowd had gathered to cheer her. Bell, the first person to swim across Lake Ontario, shattered the myth of the fragile schoolgirl. The Canadian National Exhibition announced that Bell would receive the $10,000 prize. The area close to where she finished the swim is now called Marilyn Bell Park. The next year, Marilyn became the youngest person to swim the English Channel. In 1956, she swam across British Columbia's Juan de Fuca Strait. Marilyn is now a member of Canada's Sports Hall of Fame.

One of Marilyn Bell's biggest fans was Vicki Keith. In a two-month period, Vicki became the first Canadian to swim across all of the Great Lakes. She also swam across Lake Ontario more than any other person with five crossings. In 1989, she became the first person to cross the English Channel using the butterfly stroke. She continued her marathon achievements by swimming the Catalina Channel the same year. Keith's marathons raised a great deal of money for disabled children's foundations. Vicki received the Order of Canada in 1992 and a point of the Toronto harbour was named after her in 1998.

In addition to being a superb endurance athlete, Keith has also served as a tremendous inspiration and coach to another very special long-distance swimmer. Her name is Ashley Cowan, and at the age of eight, she watched a documentary about Keith's aquatic exploits and decided that she too could be a long-distance swimming star. Such dreams seemed unlikely, however. Due to a bout of meningitis as a toddler, Cowan had lost the bottom half of her arms and legs.

When she approached Keith, who was coaching at Toronto's Variety Village, to ask her to be her coach, Keith told her she would only do so if Ashley could swim eight consecutive lengths. Even though the youngster had at that point not even completed one length on her own, she managed the eight-lap challenge and never looked back. Working with her new coach, she trained diligently for seven years before becoming the first person with a disability – and the youngest person in history – to cross one of the Great Lakes, traversing Erie in 14 hours and 20 minutes at only fifteen years of age.

Silken Laumann

Silken Laumann competed in her first Olympics in 1984 and earned a bronze medal in the double sculls with her sister and rowing partner, Danielle. Despite her skill and success in her sport, Silken had a hard time finding funding because rowing received limited attention. As World Cup Series Champion in 1991, Silken was the favourite to win gold in the 1992 Olympics. However, during a practice race, she was seriously injured when a German double sculls team hit her scull, and Silken had to undergo five operations in a ten-day period. She rehabilitated herself, and after three weeks, she was back in her racing shell. In her final Olympic Games in 1996, Laumann earned the silver medal in single sculls.

Donovan Bailey

In 1996, Donovan Bailey carried the Olympic hopes of all Canadians with him. Donovan's main event was the 100-metre race, the same race in which Ben Johnson had won the gold medal in 1988. Johnson's medal was taken away because of his use of anabolic steroids. Not only did Bailey win the gold medal in the 100-metre race, he also set a world record with his time of 9.84 seconds. Bailey was also part of the gold-medal-winning 4 x 100-metre Canadian relay team. In 1996, Bailey was the fastest man in the world and the most admired Olympic athlete in Canada.

Catriona Le May Doan

Catriona Le May Doan first received a gold medal for her performance in the 500-metre speed-skating race in the 1998 Nagano Games. Her time also became an Olympic record. In the 2002 Salt Lake City Games, Catriona carried the Canadian flag in the opening ceremony, and won gold again. Once again she broke the Olympic record, although this time it was her own – one that she had set four years earlier. Catriona continued to push herself to do better; she competed in four Olympic Games and broke the world record in her event eight times before retiring in 2003.

Marnie McBean and Kathleen Heddle

When you talk about Canadian achievement at the Olympic Games, it is impossible not to talk about rowing's "odd couple," Marnie McBean and Kathleen Heddle. The outgoing, outspoken McBean and the quieter Heddle have combined for three gold medals, the most received by any Canadian athlete in the Summer Games. In 1992 and 1996, the duo teamed up for golds in the coxless pairs event and both rowed on an eight-woman team that also nabbed gold at the 1996 Games.

EARLY CANADIAN SPORTS PIONEERS

Today, Canadian sports fans follow the adventures of their athletic heroes on television, on the radio, over the Internet, and in newspapers. Many keep track of the most minute details of these athletes' lives, both on and off the playing surface. But this has not always been the case; many Canadian athletes of years gone by are little more than a footnote in the sporting history of this country. This is because of the limited news media of their time and because the records of their achievements have not been passed down to today's sports fans. The following is a look at some of the great Canadian athletes and sport innovators who have made their mark over the past two centuries.

George Beers

George Beers (1843-1900) was a Montreal dentist who founded the Montreal Lacrosse Club in 1856. He made a standardized set of rules for the game in 1860. These rules still govern the sport today. In 1867, he organized the National Lacrosse Association, which was the first national Canadian lacrosse organization. George also campaigned for lacrosse to be named Canada's national sport. Because of his promotion of the game, Beers became known as the "father of lacrosse."

Edward "Ned" Hanlan

Edward Hanlan (1855-1908) is often described as the best sculler of all time. He began competing when he was sixteen in Toronto regattas, and when he was eighteen, he won the Toronto amateur sculling championship. "Ned" Hanlan had developed a new style of rowing; he was smaller than most of his competitors and he used that to his advantage. His rowing style was graceful, with smooth strokes and a sharp catch.

At the international level, he could not be beaten. At the age of only twenty-one, Ned won the Philadelphia Centennial Regatta, setting a new world record for a three-mile course. Two years later, he won the U.S. title and, a year after that, he defeated Britain's premier rower by eleven lengths.

Sculling was popular at this point (during the height of Victorian-era sportsmanship) and large crowds were normal for the sport. Hanlan played up to the crowds by stopping to wash his face, wave to the crowd, or waiting until the other competitors caught up to him and then dashing off to the finish line.

After defeating the Australian champion, Hanlan officially became the world's champion sculler, a title he would defend six times. Ned won more than 300 races before he died at the age of fifty-two. After his death, a statue was erected at the Canadian National Exhibition and a section of the Toronto Islands was named after him. He is still remembered as the best sculler in the history of the sport.

Tom Longboat

Tom Longboat (1887-1949), an Onondaga Indian from the Caledonia Reservation, was one of the few prominent Native Canadians in early twentieth-century sports. Longboat was a long-distance runner, coached by Six Nations runner Bill Davis, and he ran his first race in 1906. When Longboat started the race, dressed in an old bathing suit and cheap sneakers, spectators laughed at him, but they did not laugh for long. Tom won the 19-mile race by 3 minutes. Following that win, he entered the Ward Marathon and won again by a lengthy distance.

Longboat started his international career by entering the Boston Marathon in 1907. Tom won his first Boston Marathon, breaking the course record by 5.5 minutes. The record was not beaten until the course was changed to make the race easier. After protests against Longboat's attempt to claim amateur status, he was allowed to compete in the 1908 Olympic Games. However, after maintaining second place through much of the race, he collapsed at the twentieth mile, leading to rumours that he had been using stimulants.

Longboat soon turned professional, winning several more races, and was regarded by most as the fastest runner in the world. After serving in the First World War, Longboat returned to Canada, his winnings spent, moving from job to job. He died on the Caledonia Reservation in 1949.

Dr. James Naismith

When James Naismith was away from his native Canada, studying Physical Education in Massachusetts, his professor gave the class an assignment to come up with a new game to provide relief from the typical late-nineteenth century physical education class of calisthenics. As Naismith worked out the details of his game, some rules became clear. Running had to be limited because of the space constraints of an indoor game. Tackling and rough contact had to be eliminated for the same reasons. James borrowed rules from other games and looked to a game he and his friends had played at McGill called "duck on the rock," in which the players had to throw balls into empty boxes to develop their aim.

When the rules were set, James asked the janitor if he had any boxes the players could use for the game. The janitor produced two peach baskets that Naismith nailed to the balconies at the opposite ends of the gym. After picking teams and explaining the rules, the first game of basketball, the American game invented by a Canadian, was played in 1891.

The NBA Comes to Canada
Raptors shine while Grizzlies fade

Although most basketball fans consider the National Basketball Association (NBA) to have been an all-American league up until 1995 when it admitted franchises from Toronto and Vancouver to its ranks, that assumption is not exactly true. Back in the early days of pro basketball, a Canadian team was very much a part of the scene.

They were called the Toronto Huskies, and they took part in the Basketball Association of America (BAA), the league that began in 1946 and, a few years after that, would become the NBA. In fact, the very first BAA game ever played took place in Toronto, as the Huskies lost a close game to the New York Knicks. The Canadian squad did not last long, though – by the end of the 1946-47 season, the franchise's owners realized that it would be too tough to compete with the Toronto Maple Leafs for fans, and dissolved the franchise.

It would be almost fifty years before pro basketball at its highest level returned to Canada. For the 1995-96 season, the NBA, led by its high-profile commissioner David Stern, decided to allow two new franchises in Canada – the Vancouver Grizzlies and the Toronto Raptors. The league was convinced that these cities were full of basketball fans who would support teams, and, perhaps just as importantly, provide a fertile market for the huge array of NBA-branded products. At least in Toronto, this suspicion proved accurate. Before the Raptors had even played a single game, sales of the team's distinctive dinosaur-emblazoned products had vaulted to sixth in the twenty-nine-team league.

The Toronto Raptors

The story of the Toronto Raptors and their entry into the NBA is, for the most part, one of success. The franchise, in keeping with the league's overall plan, aimed most of its promotional efforts at young fans, and built a solid base that was rewarded, after a few years of poor

Vancouver fans during a match against the Toronto Raptors in Toronto, March 2001 (CP PHOTO/Aaron Harris).

performances on the court (typical for expansion teams who usually require five to six years to build a competitive team through player drafts and trades) and a significant ownership change, with a team that emerged as a playoff contender. Certainly, the Raptors' 2002 signing of its top player, Vince Carter, to a long-term contract (estimated to be worth about CDN$25 million a year for seven years) proved to fans that the franchise had come to stay.

The signing of Carter was all the more significant because it showed players and agents around the league that the Raptors were willing to spend large amounts of money to keep a top player such as Carter in Canada – not an easy task considering the relatively poor value of the Canadian dollar and the fairly high income taxation rates in Canada compared to tax rates in many U.S. states.

The Vancouver Grizzlies

Things did not go as smoothly for the Vancouver Grizzlies, however – and the difference between the two Canadian franchises' short histories is instructive for those who study the business of

sport and the history of professional league expansion.

Simply put, the NBA's Grizzlies experiment was a failure, and, according to many observers and sports historians, one of the worst attempts at professional-league expansion that was ever attempted. By the end of the 2001-02 season, the Grizzlies had not even come close to compiling a winning record in six seasons, and had made a particularly questionable long-term signing of a player named Bryant Reeves, who never fulfilled his promise yet ended up being paid so much money that the team was unable to sign other top-quality players to improve efforts on the court.

Of course, the Grizzlies' on-court woes led to frustrations on the part of fans, who, while they enjoyed seeing top-notch pro basketball, became disillusioned with a team that could not win. Citing poor attendance, Vancouver owner Michael Heisley (who had just bought the team from its original owners the year before) sold the team to an ownership group in Memphis, Tennessee, where the Grizzlies began playing at the start of the 2002-03 season.

With the Grizzlies now based in the United States, it is up to the Toronto Raptors to carry Canada's NBA torch. But what does the future hold for them? If the 2002-03 season is any indication, the team still has a lot of work to do, both on and off the court. The Raptors failed to make the playoffs for the first time in four seasons, and injuries to key players such as Carter and Davis generally hurt team morale and led to a decidedly sub-par season overall. With a losing record in 2002-03, a drop in fan attendance, and the eventual firing of coach Lenny Wilkens, it will be tough for the team to regain dwindling fan support. Since professional sports fans clearly prefer supporting – and spending money on – winning teams, it is apparent that the Raptors will need to improve significantly during 2003-04 if they want to put fans back in the seats.

THE RISE OF PROFESSIONAL SPORTS

In the early years of the twentieth century, the Victorian age of sports ended, but the love of sports that had evolved the century before did not. It was around this time that professional sports teams and leagues began to develop. Amateurism was still greatly valued, to which the growth of the modern Olympics, begun in 1896, can attest, but not all sports lent themselves to maintaining an amateur status. Sports that were included in the Olympic games, such as cycling, track and field, fencing, gymnastics, and swimming, were easy to maintain as amateur sports because the majority of the participants at the time were upper-class enthusiasts and did not require full-time jobs. However, sports that had become associated with the common man and the well-established middle class did not need to remain amateur – as most of these athletes were from middle-class families, and amateurism had initially been popular as a way to keep athletics restricted to the upper class.

In the early stages of pro sport, athletes competing in sports such as baseball, football, soccer, basketball, and hockey needed to be employed if they were not going to be paid for their work on the team. The working man was also now paying to see these sports played, making field and arena owners very wealthy. However, in order to keep patrons returning to see games, teams needed to have the best players available. Many teams started paying their athletes in order to keep them, and professional teams were born. When multiple professional teams were created in one sport, professional leagues sprang up in order to keep the games fair; an amateur team had little chance of winning against a professional team that could pay to keep the best players.

The National Hockey League

In 1917, the National Hockey League began its first season with five teams – the Montreal Canadiens, the Montreal Wanderers, the Ottawa Senators, the Quebec Bulldogs, and the Toronto Arenas. The Toronto team won that first season, and they played the winner of the Pacific Coast League for the Stanley Cup, created in 1893 by Governor General Lord Stanley to encourage the growth of hockey. The Pacific Coast League would eventually go out of business and, in 1926, the ten teams were divided into two divisions, and the NHL took control of the Stanley Cup.

In the mid-1940s, the NHL had a taste of what superstar players could bring to the game. After sitting out most of his rookie season with the Montreal Canadiens after breaking an ankle, Maurice Richard grabbed the attention of the nation by achieving the first fifty-goal season in NHL history in 1944-45. At

Edmonton Oiler Wayne Gretzky screams with joy as he hoists the Stanley Cup following a win over the New York Islanders in Edmonton in 1984 (CP PHOTO/STF-Mike Ridewood).

the time, there were only fifty games in a season and his record was not beaten until the season was lengthened to seventy games. Every boy in Quebec wanted to be "the Rocket" and wear the number nine on their Montreal Canadiens jersey. Richard spent his entire career, eighteen years, with the Montreal Canadiens, and when he retired in 1960, he had scored 544 regular season goals and 82 playoff goals.

Gordie Howe started his career shortly after Richard. The Second World War had just ended and Howe was a rookie with Detroit. Howe was a large man, and when he played his first game against the Montreal Canadiens, he knocked the tough Maurice Richard out cold. No other player in the NHL has matched Howe in longevity and consistency. He has played in games over six decades (including a one-shift game in the 1990s) and set several records.

In 1952, Canada was introduced to *Hockey Night in Canada*, an instant television classic that united the country with a passion for hockey. This coverage changed the way hockey was viewed; professional hockey was now for everyone in the country, regardless of how far you were from the rink.

Mike Weir: History-Making Golfer
Canadian's win at the Masters was a record-breaking feat

When Canadian golfer Mike Weir won what is generally considered to be the most prestigious golf tournament in the world in April 2003, he entered the sports history books in two important ways.

By firing the lowest total score on the famous Masters course in Augusta, Georgia, and outpacing a top-notch collection of rivals that included Tiger Woods – the man largely regarded to be the greatest golfer of all time – Weir became the first left-handed golfer ever to become Masters champion. And more significantly, the pride of Bright's Grove, Ontario, entered the record books as the only Canadian ever to wear the famous green jacket that is given to every Masters winner.

Born in 1970, he won the 1986 Canadian Juvenile Championship and the Canadian Junior Championship in 1988. Following those successes, Weir moved into the adult ranks and won the Ontario Amateur Championships in 1990 and 1992, and qualified for the Canadian Tour, where he was named Rookie of the Year in 1993 after winning the Infinity Tournament Players Championship. From there, Weir progressed rapidly on the Canadian Tour and eventually won the 1998 PGA Tour's "Q School" – the series of tournaments that qualifies players for the highest level of Professional Golf Association competition.

Following that, Weir's rise was even more meteoric: he won his first PGA tournament, the Air Canada Championship in 1999, becoming the first Canadian to win on native soil since 1954, and the first Canadian golfer to win any event on the Tour since 1992.

In 2000, Weir kept on going, winning the World Golf Championships in Spain and finishing the season twenty-first in the world rankings. For his efforts, Weir was named Male Athlete of the Year by the Canadian Press, an accolade he captured the following year (2001), as well, on the strength of his top-ten finish in the world rankings.

Mike Weir is the first Canadian to win a Major on the PGA Tour. (CP PHOTO/ Frank Gunn).

But as fast as Weir's progress into the upper echelons of golf has been since his junior days in Canada, 2002 was a disappointing season for a golfer who appeared to be poised to become one of the game's truly great players. Weir could only compile a season in which he finished forty-second in the world rankings, and seventy-eighth on the money list.

As a testament to his tremendous determination and focus, Weir retrenched and prepared for the 2003 season. Right off the tee, his fortune improved. He began 2003 with a ninth-place finish at the Phoenix Open, winning $112,000, and followed that with a win at the Bob Hope Classic, which netted him $810,000. As Weir joked to the press following that triumph, he had already earned more in his first two tournaments of 2003 than he had in all of the previous season.

But although 2003 started well for Weir, things soon looked as though they were reverting to 2002's disastrous form – he finished in a tie for third in his next event, followed by four horrible finishes leading up to the Masters. Certainly, Weir did not look as though he would be

a top contender for the annual Augusta classic. But he took an early lead and never looked back, despite a tremendous charge from Woods and other rivals. When it was all over, Weir had made Canadian sports history.

While Weir's tremendous success at the 2003 Masters, and indeed, his superb accomplishments thus far in his golfing career, have rightly been interpreted as a great Canadian sporting success, one must be careful about considering him to be a completely "home-grown product" of our system. He competes, after all, primarily in the United States, where the huge prizes offered, and the accompanying sponsorships and endorsement opportunities, dwarf comparable Canadian ones. It is also where serious golf can be played year-round in places such as Florida, California, and Arizona, unlike the climactic restrictions that exist in most of Canada.

What is more, part of the important development of his skills while he was a young player took place in the U.S., since Weir played college golf on scholarship at Brigham Young University in Utah and was able to raise his game to the competitive NCAA level there. Indeed, Weir – who is married and has two young children – still lives in Utah, where he has been wholly embraced by the sporting community and the general public. Utah Governor Mike Leavitt recently announced that, in recognition of his Masters win, May 12 (Weir's birthday) would be known as "Mike Weir Day."

Nevertheless, Weir has always been quick to identify himself as a Canadian first and foremost when he competes on the international golfing circuit. In addition, his website regularly publicizes the efforts of other Canadian golfers (www.mikeweir.com). And, perhaps most significantly, Weir was quick to return home to celebrate the big Masters win. The day after, he was joined by friends, family, and 3,000 golf fans at an autograph session in Toronto.

In 1966, the Boston Bruins had a rookie who would make hockey history. Bobby Orr won the Calder Trophy that season and, much like Gordie Howe, was a great scorer, team player, and, when he needed to be, a fighter. Bobby was an offensive-minded defenceman, changing the way the position had been traditionally viewed. Orr was also a member of the 1972 Team Canada Summit Series, a team that thrilled the country with their win over the USSR. Orr won several NHL trophies and is remembered as one of the best players the game of hockey has ever seen.

The best player in NHL history is, of course, Wayne Gretzky. Gretzky holds or shares sixty-one records, and broke nearly all of the records that had been set by his hero Gordie Howe. Trained by his father from the age of six, Gretzky was an immediate success when he started playing in the NHL with the Edmonton Oilers; in his first season he won the Hart Trophy, the first time it had ever been given to a rookie player. He would win it, and many other awards, several more times. Wayne was routinely the leading scorer for the entire NHL during his twenty-year career and has been named the greatest hockey player of all time.

The Edmonton Grads

From 1915 to 1940, the **Edmonton Commercial Graduates Basketball Club**, or the Grads, had an unequalled winning streak. The women's basketball team started as a high-school squad consisting of students and graduates of McDougall Commercial High School. The Grads won more than 500 games over twenty-five years and lost only 20 games. In 1923, they won their first Canadian title and started competing on an international level. That same year, they beat the American champions and won the Underwood Trophy. For seventeen consecutive years, the Grads held the trophy. The Grads represented Canada at the Olympics, winning all of their games, but since women's basketball was not an official sport, the team did not bring home any medals.

Despite the changing team members over the years, the Grads remained strong due to their high standards, consistent practice, and a series of farm teams under the Grads that supplied fresh talent, allowing women to develop their skills before joining the main team. The Grads were also well known for their sportsmanship and fair play. Their success helped dismiss the idea that women should not participate in sports or physical activity. Based on their overall win-loss record, the Grads are the most successful sports team in Canada's Sports Hall of Fame.

The Canadian Football League

Canadian football evolved in the late 1800s and early 1900s from rugby, which had been invented in Britain in 1823. In 1909, Governor General Earl Grey decided to donate a trophy to a Canadian rugby championship, much like Lord Stanley had done for hockey. The first Grey Cup game was played in Toronto in December 1909. Despite the popularity of Canadian football across the country, the teams remained amateur until 1958. In that year, the **Canadian Football League** (CFL) was formed, the teams became professional, and they were able to recruit players from outside the country. Today, the CFL is the only professional sports league to operate solely within Canada.

The National Lacrosse League

Although lacrosse has deep historical roots in Canada, the sport has had a tough time drawing fans to professional games. That has changed in recent years, however, with the formation of the National Lacrosse League (NLL; originally called the Eagle Pro Box Lacrosse League) in 1986. The league currently has twelve teams playing the indoor (or "box") version of the game, including four Canadians teams based in Toronto, Calgary, Vancouver, and Ottawa. In much the same way as with the NHL, many outstanding Canadians compete for U.S.-based teams. But one Canadian franchise, the Toronto Rock, has been particularly successful in NLL competition. In May 2003, the Rock – who play home games at Toronto's Air Canada Centre – defeated the Rochester Knighthawks by 8-6 to capture their fourth league championship

The Canadian Professional Soccer League

Despite its continued growth on the grassroots level of youth and recreational leagues and as a school sport, professional soccer has had a hard time establishing itself in Canada. During the 1970s and 1980s, both Vancouver and Toronto had successful franchises in the **North American Soccer League** (NASL), but this organization was short-lived. A number of attempts to rejuvenate the professional version of the game were also not very successful, but, recently, the **Canadian Professional Soccer League** (CPSL) has achieved considerable success in drawing fans and promoting the sport.

The CPSL was formed in 1997 as the result of a study that pointed out the need for a pro league with close ties to a club program for developing players, similar to the models that have been in place for many years in Europe. The league began play in 1998 and today there are there are thirteen teams competing – twelve in Ontario and one in Quebec. The CPSL season begins in May, with the league championships taking place in October. The CPSL teams also contest the Open Canada Cup.

The Original Six and NHL Expansion
The emergence of today's National Hockey League

As amazing as it might seem to anyone who has begun to follow North American professional hockey in recent years, today's thirty-team NHL is something of an anomaly, at least as far as the history of the league is concerned.

This is because, for most of its existence, the NHL has featured far fewer franchises than it does today. And, contrary to popular belief – even among die-hard hockey fans – the league did not begin play with the half-dozen teams now known nostalgically as the "Original Six." (For the record, these are the Toronto Maple Leafs, Montreal Canadiens, Boston Bruins, New York Rangers, Detroit Red Wings, and Chicago Black Hawks.) In fact, the story of how the current NHL came to be – after several decades of expansion and franchise changes – is one of the most fascinating tales in Canadian sport history.

A group of teams that called itself the National Hockey League actually banded together in 1917. The five (the real "original" NHL squads) were the Montreal Canadiens, Montreal Wanderers, Ottawa Senators, Quebec Bulldogs, and the Toronto Arenas. The following year, though, the Bulldogs did not play, and in 1918, Montreal also pulled out because their arena had been destroyed by fire – meaning that, in 1918, the NHL had only three teams.

By the 1919-20 season, the Quebec Bulldogs had moved and were competing as the Toronto St. Patricks. The league added a team in Hamilton, and in the 1923-24 season, it added its first American team, the Boston Bruins. The following season, the NHL welcomed another franchise from Montreal called the Maroons.

In the 1925-26 season the Hamilton franchise left the league, and its players were signed by a new team called the New York Americans. Several teams were soon added – the New York Rangers, the Chicago Blackhawks and the Detroit Cougars – with the Toronto St. Patricks changing their name to the Toronto Maple Leafs in 1926-27.

Montreal Canadiens' Maurice Richard in a 1954 match against the Toronto Maple Leafs (CP PHOTO/STF-CP).

After a series of name changes, geographical team shifts, and new owners throughout the league, by the 1942-43 season, the six teams we now know as the "original" six squads were in place. Even though the NHL had been in existence for more than twenty-five years, there is a good reason most sports historians call the Maple Leafs, Canadiens, Red Wings, Blackhawks, Bruins, and Rangers the "Original Six" – it was upon this foundation that the NHL launched its first wide-scale "expansion" or simultaneous addition of franchises.

After the six had played against each other exclusively for another twenty-five seasons, the league doubled in size to twelve teams in 1967-68. Added to the NHL schedule were the Minnesota North Stars, California Seals, Los Angeles Kings, Philadelphia Flyers, Pittsburgh Penguins, and St. Louis Blues. Then, in 1970-71, two more teams joined the fray, the Buffalo Sabres and the Vancouver Canucks, followed in 1972-73 by the Atlanta Flames, and, in 1974-75, the Kansas City Scouts and the Washington

Capitols – bringing the league total to seventeen. After a few more changes through mergers and teams changing cities, the NHL absorbed, in 1979-80, four franchises from another league – the World Hockey Association, or WHA – the Edmonton Oilers, Quebec Nordiques, Hartford Whalers and Winnipeg Jets, making a twenty-one-team NHL. In the 1991-92 season, another new franchise joined, the San Jose Sharks, followed by the Tampa Bay Lightning and Ottawa Senators (1992-93), and the Mighty Ducks of Anaheim and the Florida Panthers (1993-94).

After several more team moves and name changes, the Nashville Predator franchise in 1998-99 brought the league to twenty-seven teams, with the Atlanta Thrashers joining in 1999-2000, and the Minnesota Wild and the Columbus Bluejackets teams coming on board in 2000-01, bringing the current total to thirty teams.

Those who support NHL expansion – especially in its recent form during the past decade – argue that it has brought professional hockey to many communities throughout North America, thereby expanding the game's fan base. Advocates of an expanded league say that more teams simply means that more highly skilled foreign players are able to sign with NHL teams, and more young Canadian and American players can be developed into professionals. Those who oppose it say that it has had a detrimental effect on pro hockey, because it has diluted the pool of talent playing in the NHL.

Opponents of expansion also argue that because of the intense competition among teams for fans, the owners of so-called "small-market" teams in Canada are overly tempted to sell their franchises to high-paying American owners. This did indeed happen in two controversial instances in 1995-96, when the Quebec franchise moved to Colorado, and the Winnipeg Jets became the Phoenix Coyotes.

TWENTIETH-CENTURY CANADIAN ACHIEVEMENTS IN SPORT

The twentieth century saw even more growth in physical education and sport. With the invention of television, everyone, regardless of their location, could see sports taking place around the world. The Olympics became accessible to all classes of people, uniting countries in pride for the achievements of their athletes.

In addition to the myriad of national sports competitions, international tournaments were created for soccer, cricket, hockey, skiing, and many other sports, allowing athletes to travel and meet competitors from other countries.

The 1972 Canada-USSR "Summit Series"

No event in Canadian sporting history has drawn as much national attention – and, more than thirty years later, continues to receive attention from fans and scholars alike – as the so-called "Summit Series" of hockey games that took place between a team of Canadian professional players and an all-star squad of athletes from the former Soviet Union. Indeed, few have not heard at least a snippet of the famous final seconds of the broadcast of the series' eighth and final game. The voice of the legendary announcer Foster Hewitt, describing the last-ditch goal by Canadian Paul Henderson with only 34 seconds remaining, is likely the best-known "sound bite" in our country's history.

Although many fans recall the series as an example of the finest competitive hockey ever played, Henderson's winning goal and the overall series win for Canada were significant from more than a sporting perspective. The four games that took place in Canada and the four that were hosted by the Soviet Union's hockey federation represented a clash of sporting ideologies between the two best hockey nations in the world.

At a time when the so-called "Cold War" was near its height, Canada's team represented the free-market capitalist society, and its players, all well-paid NHL professionals, represented the hopes and dreams of many Canadian youth growing up within this socioeconomic system. On the other side, the Soviet squad consisted of state-supported players who were nominally amateurs (although most held symbolic positions in the USSR's military and actually devoted themselves full time to hockey).

In the end, Canada's win was hailed by many as a triumph for "our way of life" over the one that existed in the communist USSR. Today, that analysis seems somewhat simplistic. It is true, though, that when these two hockey juggernauts clashed, the level of play on the ice was superb.

Yvon Cournoyer of Team Canada hugs Paul Henderson after Henderson scored the winning goal in the Canada-U.S.S.R. hockey series on September 28, 1972 (CP PHOTO/*Toronto Star*/STF-Frank Lennon).

The Canada Games

The first Canada Games were held in Quebec in the winter of 1967 to coincide with Canada's centennial celebrations. The idea of having a series of games that celebrated Canada's athletes and allowed young athletes to compete against their fellow Canadians first arose in 1924, and though it was frequently discussed, it was more than forty years before the Games came into being. The Canada Games alternate between winter and summer every two years. Every province has hosted the Games and many have hosted them more than once. Forty-five thousand young Canadians, from all of Canada's thirteen provinces and territories, have qualified and participated in the Games since they began. Many now-prominent athletes can claim that the Canada Games were one of the first national competitions that they were able to compete in, including curling champion Colleen Jones, speed skater Susan Auch, and figure skater Brian Orser.

The games are a springboard for international-level athletes to start competing in their respective sports in

The Commonwealth Games
"The friendly games"

In 2006, the Commonwealth Games will be held in Melbourne, Australia. Like the Olympics, this large sporting event is contested every four years – unlike the Olympics, not every country in the world can send athletes to compete.

That is because the Commonwealth Games are contested only by countries – such as Canada, India, and Australia – with direct political and cultural ties to the former British Empire. Although they are now removed from direct British control, these nations still maintain symbolic ties to the English crown (such as the presence of the Governor General in Canada), and, in general, hold similar values about both government and the role of sport in their respective societies.

The Friendly Games

This system of holding multi-sport events based on certain shared characteristics of countries is not unusual. The world sporting scene also witnesses events such as the Pan-Am Games (for athletes in North, South, and Central America), the African Games, the Asian Games, and La Francophonie, a worldwide sporting competition for athletes from nations (including Canada) in which French is spoken.

Besides a common cultural past, the athletes in the Commonwealth Games all come from countries in which English is an official language. The joyous atmosphere long surrounding the Commonwealth Games has led them to be referred to as the "Friendly Games."

Like most international sporting events, the Commonwealth Games has a mission statement and an overall philosophy. According to the Commonwealth Games Federation (CGF), the aim of the Games is to "promote a unique, friendly world-class Games and to develop sport for the benefit of the people, the nations and the territories of the Commonwealth, and thereby strengthen the Commonwealth."

Calgary's Kyle Shewfelt wins gold in men's floor gymnastics at the 2002 Commonwealth Games (CP PHOTO/ Andrew Vaughan).

The First Commonwealth Games in Hamilton, 1930

Canada, in fact, has played an important role in the development of the Commonwealth Games, since it was in this country that the first Games were held, in 1930, in Hamilton. (Interestingly, Hamilton is making a strong bid to hold the 2010 Games, having been chosen the official Canadian city to make a bid for the competition.)

In those days, the Games were known as "The British Empire Games," and this first edition saw eleven countries and four hundred athletes participating. Since those first Games, the event has been held every four years with the exception of 1942 and 1946, due to the Second World War. In 2002, more than 6,000 athletes competed in the Games when they were held in Manchester, England – making it the largest sports event ever held in the United Kingdom.

In 1950, the Games changed their name slightly, to the British Empire and Commonwealth Games. Then, in 1974, they took on the title of British Commonwealth Games, changing once

again in 1978 (when Edmonton played host) to simply the Commonwealth Games.

In Melbourne, seventy-two nations and territories will compete

- **Africa:** 19
- **Asia:** 8
- **The Americas:** 6
- **The Caribbean:** 15
- **Europe:** 10
- **Oceania:** 14

These nations and territories will contest twenty-four different sports. These include the standard Olympic sports such as track and field, gymnastics, wrestling, boxing and weightlifting, and several non-Olympic events, such as lawn bowling and seven-a-side rugby.

As a nation, Canada has always done well at the Commonwealth Games. At the Manchester Games of 2002, it finished third in the overall medal count (behind Australia and England); at the 1998 event in Kuala Lumpur, Malaysia, Canadian athletes again finished third, behind the same two nations. And, at the 1994 Games – which Canada hosted in Victoria – it managed a second-place showing, behind Australia.

These are the host cities for the Commonwealth Games since 1930:

- **1930:** Hamilton, Canada
- **1934:** London, England
- **1938:** Sydney, Australia
- **1942:** not held
- **1946:** not held
- **1950:** Auckland, New Zealand
- **1954:** Vancouver, Canada
- **1958:** Cardiff, Wales
- **1962:** Perth, Australia
- **1966:** Kingston, Jamaica
- **1970:** Edinburgh, Scotland
- **1974:** Christchurch, New Zealand
- **1978:** Edmonton, Canada
- **1982:** Brisbane, Australia
- **1986:** Edinburgh, Scotland
- **1990:** Auckland, New Zealand
- **1994:** Victoria, Canada
- **1998:** Kuala Lumpur, Malaysia
- **2002:** Manchester, U.K.

a friendly and encouraging environment. Over forty sports have been played in the winter and summer Canada Games, and there is a movement to introduce more sports development. The Games encourage young people to compete and host cities to build more sports facilities, which further encourages growth of public sports programs. The next summer Canada Games will be held in Regina, Saskatchewan, in 2005, and the next winter Canada Games will be held in Whitehorse, Yukon, in 2007.

The Crazy Canucks

The 1970s were a great time for Canadian downhill skiers. To that point, European athletes had dominated the World Cup circuit and all major downhill skiing competitions. In 1974, four Canadians started making it harder for the Europeans to maintain control of the standings in the World Cup. Dubbed the Crazy Canucks by the European skiing media for their kamikaze, fearless, high-speed skiing style, Ken Read, Dave Irwin, David Murray, and Steve Podborski captured the imagination of Canadians and the international skiing world. Young and wild, the Canadians not only seemed comfortable on the challenging European slopes, they were bored with the seemingly straightforward ones. In 1975, Ken Read became the first non-European to win a race in the World Cup circuit.

Steve Podborski, only eighteen years of age when he skied his first World Cup circuit, was the youngest and most successful member of the Crazy Canucks. In 1980, he was the first Canadian male to win an Olympic medal in alpine skiing, winning a bronze medal at the Winter Olympics in Lake Placid. He became the first North American man to win a World Cup Championship in 1982, making him the best skier in the world at the time.

Major League Baseball

Although baseball and its many variations – such as softball, slow-pitch, and T-Ball – have always been popular in Canada, the big-league, professional brand of the game did not arrive in this country until 1969, when Major League Baseball admitted the Montreal Expos franchise to the National League. "Les Expos" first played their home games in Montreal's venerable Jarry Park before moving into the stadium built for the 1976 Summer Olympic Games.

It was not until 1977 that the American League admitted a Canadian team, the Toronto Blue Jays. This team may have helped to convince American baseball fans and players that Canada was indeed too cold a place for baseball by playing their first ever home game at Exhibition Stadium against the Chicago White Sox on April 7 of that year – amidst snow flurries.

Nancy Greene in the Women's Special Slalom during the 1968 Winter Olympics. Greene was voted "Female Athlete of the Century" by Canadian radio news directors and newspapers editors in a poll conducted by The Canadian Press (AP Photo).

On the field, the Jays have had much more success than their Montreal counterparts. After a few rocky years in the late 1970s and early 1980s, the team hit its stride in the mid-1980s. In 1992, the Jays achieved the pinnacle of success, winning the World Series, a feat that they repeated in 1993.

No discussion of pro baseball and Canada would be complete without a mention of Ferguson Jenkins, the pitcher from Chatham, Ontario, who starred in the Major Leagues from 1965 to 1983. Born in 1943, "Fergie" played for the Philadelphia Phillies, Chicago Cubs, Texas Rangers, and Boston Red Sox during his nineteen-year career in the Majors. Most significantly, he compiled an impressive record of six consecutive twenty-win seasons from 1967 to 1972. In 1971, Jenkins's 24-13 record on the mound for the Cubs, combined with 263 strikeouts, earned him the Cy Young Award as the National League's top pitcher. In 1991, Jenkins became the first Canadian to be inducted into the Baseball Hall of Fame in Cooperstown, N.Y.

MODERN DEVELOPMENT OF PHYSICAL EDUCATION AND SPORT IN CANADA

In the twentieth century, local sports clubs and all levels of amateur leagues were created in cities and counties across Canada. Curling and hockey rinks, golf clubs, tennis courts, bowling alleys, and soccer fields popped up everywhere, creating a space where people could participate in friendly competition.

Physical education was expanded in schools throughout the country, and children's sports teams and outside-school physical education classes, such as gymnastics, martial arts, and dance, grew at great speed in the last quarter of the century. Calisthenics were the primary form of school exercise, especially for girls, at the beginning of the century. However, as women became more liberated, more sports were added to the physical education curriculum.

ParticipAction

By the second half of the century, much of the population had become sedentary after they had finished school. The Trudeau administration decided to create a non-profit organization to address the problem. ParticipAction was created in 1971 to encourage the public to become more physically active on a regular basis. It was estimated that, when ParticipAction started their first campaign, only 5 percent of the population exercised enough to reap any health benefits. In 1973, ParticipAction ran advertisements stating that a sixty-year-old Swede was more physically fit than a thirty-year-old Canadian. Even though there was no study to prove this, the reaction from the Canadian public was great.

ParticipAction urged Canadians to incorporate some form of activity into their lives every day. Operations such as Canada's Fitweek and SummerActive encouraged communities and individuals to compete with each other by completing and reporting any physical activity. ParticipAction also encouraged competition within schools that awarded badges and pins for participating in track-and-field events. Body Break television segments, featuring easy tips to help Canadians incorporate activity into their daily lives, were also created by the organization and hosted by athletes Hal Johnson and Joanne McLeod.

ParticipAction shut down in 2000 due to lack of funding. Unfortunately, the number of obese people in Canada, including many children, has grown as people spend more time in front of computers, televisions, and video games rather than participating in sports. At this point, Canadians have relatively few public resources available to help them increase their levels of physical activity.

Twentieth-Century Challenges

The second half of the century also saw a greater acceptance of and an appreciation for challenged individuals. Clear benefits, both physically and mentally, could already be seen in people who participated in sports and physical activity, so would this not extend to children and adults overcoming illnesses or physical and mental challenges? For example, Terry Fox has become a Canadian hero, not just to children with illnesses, but for anyone looking for an example of how to overcome a seemingly insurmountable challenge.

While he was growing up in British Columbia, Terry Fox was very physically active, playing many sports. At the age of eighteen, Terry was diagnosed with bone cancer. One of his legs was amputated in 1977. Terry was a young victim of cancer, but he saw many younger cancer patients while he was in the hospital for treatment. He made an inspirational decision to help others suffering from cancer. Fox decided to run across Canada, raising money for cancer research as he went. He called his run the Marathon of Hope. Terry started his run in St. John's, Newfoundland, in 1980. At first it was difficult to get the media attention necessary to raise money and increase cancer awareness, but the more he ran, the more the media started to cover the story.

Terry ran 42 kilometres – the equivalent of an official marathon – every day through the Maritimes, Quebec, and Ontario. Public enthusiasm grew for Terry's quest, and more and more people could be found lining the route that he was running. However, after 143 days, Terry had to stop his run because the cancer had spread to his lungs. Everyone in Canada was deeply saddened when Terry passed away in 1981 at the age of twenty-two. Even though Terry was gone, his legacy lived on. The Terry Fox Run was founded across Canada, and to date the annual run has raised almost $300 million for cancer research in honour of the brave young Canadian. The money raised has helped researchers treating cancer so much that, if Fox were alive today, he probably would not have lost his leg or his life to the disease.

Over the past thirty years, wheelchair sports have grown tremendously by both the number of sports and the number of participants. Some of the newest additions include powerlifting and wheelchair rugby. The Canadian Wheelchair Sports Association was founded in 1967 to promote wheelchair sports in Canada, and it continues to represent Canadian athletes today. One Canadian in particular was able to bring wheelchair sports to the forefront and show that people with disabilities are able to accomplish great things.

As a teenager, Rick Hansen loved sports. While returning from a fishing trip in 1973, the car he was in went out of control and crashed. At the age of fifteen,

Rick was told he was paraplegic and would never walk again. Rick remained positive and viewed his position as a challenge to be overcome. He remained athletic and focused his attention on wheelchair sports. Rick became a world-class wheelchair athlete, winning nineteen international marathons and competing in the 1984 Olympics. He also became the first physically disabled Physical Education graduate of the University of British Columbia.

However, Rick's biggest accomplishment came in 1985 when he gained international recognition with his **Man in Motion World Tour**. Rick's goal was to raise money for spinal cord injury research, but he also inspired many to follow their dreams regardless of the obstacles that challenged them. The tour spanned four continents, thirty-four countries, and more than 40,000 kilometres. The last leg of Hansen's tour was through Canada, where thousands of people lined the route to support him, back to his home in Vancouver. The Man in Motion Tour raised $24 million for spinal cord injury research and inspired thousands.

THE CONTRIBUTION OF SPORT AND PHYSICAL ACTIVITY TO CANADIAN SOCIETY

Anyone who is familiar with the study of sport and how it influences – and is influenced by – social trends will be familiar with two essential issues that inform any such discussion: sport role models, and the issue of exploitation and equal access in sport.

The Influence of Sport Role Models

When examining the impact that sport has had on society, it is important to consider the significance of role models for young people in any given community. Essentially, **role models** are persons who occupy certain positions or "roles" in a society, and upon whom others (often young people) try to base – or "model" – certain aspects of their behaviour.

Modern society is filled with countless potential role models. Many young people try to emulate, for example, their parents, other relatives, and a wide range of other, often highly visible figures, such as film and television stars or characters, pop musicians, doctors, lawyers, and many others. Given the tremendous degree of publicity that professional athletes receive in all forms of media, it is also the case that sports heroes – both male and female – have come to be regarded as some of the most influential role models in the modern world.

The fact that young people "look up to" athletes in Canada and other countries is the subject of considerable discussion. Many people feel that, for the most part, high-visibility participants in sport represent an excellent ideal towards which youngsters can strive,

Terry Fox during his run across Canada to raise money for cancer research. He did not finish the run and died in a Vancouver hospital in 1981(CP PHOTO).

since they exemplify positive traits such as discipline, courage, determination, a commitment to an overall healthy lifestyle, the ability to function at a high level as part of a team or other organizational structure, and a high degree of mental focus and concentration. Furthermore, those who believe that athletes offer sound role models for youngsters maintain that, in many cases, they provide the most realistic persons to emulate in pursuit of further success – that in many socio-economic cases, it may not be possible for a young person to become a successful professional in a field such as law or medicine, whereas dreams of athletic success are at least plausible.

Certainly, there have been many inspirational athletic examples of this type of role modelling. Golfer Eldrick "Tiger" Woods almost single-handedly caused a huge explosion in the popularity of golf with his successes in the late 1990s. What is significant about Woods, at least from a role-model perspective, is that as an athlete of mixed ethnic background (his father is Afro-American, his mother is from Thailand) his success created a "boom" in interest in golf among groups

Sport Participation
Which sports are the most popular?

Most Canadians, if asked in the course of a casual conversation, would likely be able to venture a fairly accurate guess at the most popular sports played and watched by their fellow citizens. But for any national government involved in the day-to-day responsibility of organizing and funding sport, it is necessary to have much more than a general idea of how many citizens get involved in all sports. In this way, government agencies that deal with sport funding and the support of physical activity programs will know how to allot money in proportion to participation.

The Canadian government has long been involved in the compilation of statistics regarding how its citizens participate in sport. In 1998, its data-collection branch undertook a comprehensive study to see just what sports Canadians over the age of fifteen were playing, and in what numbers. The following, taken from the Statistics Canada website (http://www.statcan.ca/english/Pgdb/arts16.htm) represents some of the most popular sports, on a participation basis, among approximately 25 million Canadians (11.937 million male and 12.323 million female) surveyed. Keep in mind that many respondents play more than one sport in the course of a year.

	000's	%
Golf	1,802	7.4
Hockey (ice)	1,499	6.2
Baseball	1,339	5.5
Swimming	1,120	4.6
Basketball	787	3.2
Volleyball	744	3.1
Soccer	739	3.0
Tennis	658	2.7
Skiing, downhill/alpine	657	2.7
Cycling	608	2.5
Skiing	512	2.1
Weightlifting	435	1.8
Badminton	403	1.7
Football	387	1.6
Curling	312	1.3
Bowling, 10 pin	282	1.2
Softball	210	0.9
Bowling, 5 pin	200	0.8
Squash	163	0.7
Karate	129	0.5
Figure skating	121	0.5
Rugby	104	0.4
Ball hockey	91	0.4
Snowboarding	81	0.3
In-line skating	70	0.3
Racquetball	58	0.2
Other sports	323	1.3

Source: Statistics Canada, General Social Survey, 1998.

who had not been drawn to a sport previously dominated by upper- and middle-class whites around the world. When Woods looked into the camera in a Nike commercial and asked "Hello, world. Are you ready for me?", he was asking a two-part question: Was the world ready for a golfer with his never-before-seen abilities? And was the world ready for a golfing role model who did not look like one of the sport's traditional superstars?

Opponents of the athlete-as-role-model scenario argue that an overemphasis on sports prevents the development of successful people in non-sports fields – the arts, medicine, music, business, and so forth. If youngsters were made aware of a broader range of career choices that included options outside sport, the argument goes, they would be able to succeed in many other worthwhile fields.

Providing fuel to this argument is the undeniable fact that, while hopes and dreams are one thing, the odds of any one person making it into the ranks of professional sports are incredibly long – and they only increase when it comes to actually becoming a superstar, multi-million dollar athlete. Consequently, those who support this side of the argument maintain that instead of ignoring, or downplaying, one's education and the development of non-sport skills, these areas of life should be emphasized by means of appropriate role models, since it is this modelling that will likely be much more useful later in life.

People who contend that athletes do not always make the best role models for young people have had another major argument to draw on in the last decade, one based on the increasingly common news reports about high-profile athletes whose off-the-field behaviour is less than exemplary. Along with television, radio, and newspaper reports of game scores and race results, sports fans of all ages have become accustomed to stories of athletes who have committed illegal acts, including drug and alcohol abuse, domestic violence, vehicular offences, fraud, assault, weapons possession, and even murder. Of course, the vast majority of athletes do not commit such crimes, and those who do often have done so for reasons that are mainly unrelated to sport. Nevertheless, athletes who do commit such offences are often held up as examples of poor role models for young people.

Perhaps the most logical approach for coaches, parents, and others who are responsible for the continuing development of young people involved in sport is to stress athletic role models in balance with those who are high achievers in other fields. Certainly, many Canadian youth have been able to draw inspiration from the examples – both on the playing surface and off it – of such stars as hockey hero Wayne Gretzky, Toronto Raptors star Vince Carter, Mike "Pinball"

Clemons, and the Toronto Blue Jays' Joe Carter. But it is necessary keep the sporting success of such athletes in perspective, stressing that their careers represent the exceptions rather than the rule, and that there are other successful people in many other walks of life who are also worthy of emulation.

Exploitation and Sport Equity

In a general sense, the term exploitation refers to any relationship in which one party engages in the majority of the effort without receiving a fair share of the results. In a sporting context, exploitation has the same connotation: any athlete who is performing an excessive amount of work (i.e., competing or training) without garnering an appropriate benefit (i.e., prize money, publicity, athletic advancement, and so on) can be said to be in an "exploitive" relationship.

Unfortunately, youth sport – especially on a high-performance level – provides many possibilities for an exploitive relationship to develop. Commenting on this trend, University of Toronto sports sociologist Peter Donnelly has written that, although child labour laws protect young workers in most of the world's advanced societies, and despite the fact that the entertainment world has long had legislation in place to prevent against the exploitation of young actors and musical performers, the sports world does not have such protections. This is the case, Donnelly argues, even though "adult careers and incomes may be contingent on the performances of children." Although many adult professional athletes have protection through membership in players' unions, youngsters appear to have no such safety net (Young athletes need child law protection. In *Taking sport seriously: Social issues in Canadian sport.* Toronto: Thompson Educational Publishing, 2000).

Sport equity occurs whenever the same athletic opportunities are afforded to one group of people as they are to another. Normally this involves simply allowing people to take part in sport (such as the use of equipment, access to membership on a team or in a league, or the availability of top-notch coaching), but it may also include equal access to publicity, government funding, or simply the ability to participate in a sports setting without harassment.

Historically, a number of distinct groups in Canadian society have had to struggle for equal access to sport. These include women who have long argued for equality in all aspects of sport (including the right to compete on men's teams), persons with disabilities who have won the right to have special equipment installed at sports facilities so that they may compete, and visible minorities who have fought to be allowed to play for teams at all levels of sport. While many barriers have been eliminated, many still remain.

Canada's Hugh Fisher and Alwyn Morris celebrate a gold medal win in the men's doubles kayak event at the 1984 Olympic Games in Los Angeles. California (CP PHOTO/COA).

In many cases, it has been the athletes themselves who, by their remarkable achievements, have brought about a change in public attitudes. For example, the Native long-distance running champion Tom Longboat in the early years of the twentieth century, Afro-Canadian sprinter Harry Jerome in the 1950s and 1960s, and the champion Native Olympic canoeist Alwyn Morris in the 1980s and 1990s are just three examples of pioneering athletes who have helped to break down racial and ethnic barriers in sport in Canadian society.

WHERE DO WE GO FROM HERE?

In this section we have looked at the development of physical education and sport, both professional and amateur, with a primary focus on Canada. From early sports pioneers to physically challenged athletes who have inspired the world, Canadian athletes have contributed much to the history of sport.

In the next section, we will look at the remarkable achievements of women in sport in recent years and we will celebrate their victories.

Kara Lang of Oakville, Ontario, in close pursuit as the Brazil player clears the ball during semifinal action at the Under-19 FIFA Women's World Championship in Edmonton, August 2002 (CP PHOTO/Adrian Wyld).

25
Women in Sport

"The solemn periodic manifestation of male sport based on internationalism, on loyalty as a means, on arts as a background and the applause of women as a recompense."

— The world has changed almost beyond recognition since Baron de Coubertin, founder of the modern Olympics, uttered these disparaging words about the role of women in sport.

KEY CONCEPTS

- Femininity
- Women's Amateur Athletic Federation
- Title IX
- Gender representation in leadership positions

- Media coverage of women's sports
- Body image
- Female triad

- Canadian Association for the Advancement of Women in Sport (CAAWS)
- On The Move
- ACTive
- Girls @ Play

It may be difficult for many people to believe, but just a few decades ago, women's participation in all aspects of sports was seriously limited. Today, women of all ages compete in a wide range of sports at all levels, from local recreational soccer, baseball, and hockey teams, to intercollegiate competition, to the Olympic and professional ranks.

There is perhaps no area in which development in sport mirrors developments within society as a whole as closely as that of women in sport. In the following section, we will look at some of these developments and at several Canadian women athletes who have helped – or are currently helping – to establish a true culture of women's sports around the world.

AN HISTORICAL OVERVIEW

In the last hundred years, societal expectations of women have changed drastically, as has the concept of femininity: the word *feminine* is no longer equated with weak, silent, unthinking, corset-waisted waifs who know nothing of the world but can mean strength, endurance, knowledge, muscles, and a fiercely competitive attitude. The role of women in society has changed from subservient wife, mother, and daughter, to voting woman, to educated woman, to working woman, and finally to completely independent woman. With each of these strides, women gained more ground and could see what they and their daughters would someday accomplish – equality. And athletically minded women pushed open doors in the sports world that had previously been closed and saw

the direction that they and future generations needed to follow to reach equality.

In the nineteenth century and early part of the twentieth century, women had to fight against the so-called feminine ideal to enter certain sports. The role of women was strictly a reproductive one; in order to keep women from venturing into the male-dominated world of sports, women were told that physical activity would inhibit their ability to have children, that their bones were weaker than men's and therefore they would experience more injuries, that intense exercise would cause menstrual problems, and that sports would cause them to develop large muscles that would make them unattractive to men. To maintain decorum, women were expected to participate in the few sports open to them while wearing long, heavy skirts and long sleeves.

In 1849, bloomers were invented in New York to aid in female sports participation, especially bicycling. Bloomers and split skirts were not quick to be accepted by either sex. Many women who dared to wear these baggy, non-revealing sports pants in public were ridiculed and often had items thrown at them as they cycled down the street. Those who were against women participating in sports led the campaign to keep women in impractical clothing during physical activity because it was impossible to play sports in heavy skirts. Bloomers became accepted as bicycling became more common, but well into the 1920s, women were still fighting for the right to wear sleeveless shirts, shorts, and to bare their legs while participating in sports.

Playing with the Boys
Blainey, Rheaume, and Wickenheiser

In Canada, we can turn to the sport of hockey for three inspiring tales of women who excelled because their abilities as athletes – and determination as human beings – allowed them to compete successfully against men.

Justine Blainey

Today, Justine Blainey is best remembered among Canadian sports fans as the young woman who, in 1987, won a landmark sexual discrimination case in the Supreme Court. At the age of eleven, Blainey and her parents felt she was ready to compete against boys of her age in organized hockey – a decision with which coaches and officials in the Metro Toronto Hockey League (MTHL) did not agree. Despite Blainey's advanced level of play, the MTHL felt that Blainey should remain in girls' competition, no matter what her desires were for tougher competition.

Blainey lodged a complaint with Ontario's Human Rights Commission, which ruled that, for all intents and purposes, gender-based discrimination was allowed in sport. Undaunted, Blainey kept making her case upward through the province's legal system, all the way to Canada's Supreme Court. (Although her case took four years to make it to the Supreme Court, it was in fact the fastest to be considered by Canada's highest judicial body.).

In 1987, Blainey was finally granted the right to compete on a boys team and did so despite tremendous opposition in the press, among hockey coaches and officials, and on the part of opposing players who wanted to prove that she did not "belong."

Manon Rheaume

Manon Rheaume was the first female athlete to play a game in a major men's professional sports league anywhere in the world.

On September 23, 1992, the Lac Beauport, Quebec, native took her place as the goalie for the NHL's Tampa

Hayley Wickenheiser after victory against USA at 2002 Olympic Winter Games (CP PHOTO/Tom Hanson).

Bay Lightning in a pre-season game against the St. Louis Blues. But that is not the only "first" recorded by Rheaume – not by a long shot. She was also the first woman to sign a professional hockey contract, and the first to play in a regular season professional hockey game (although not in the NHL). In addition, her stellar goaltending helped the Canadian women's team to win the 1992 and 1994 World Championships, and to capture the silver medal at the 1988 Olympics.

Rheaume started to play hockey at the age of five and quickly rose through the ranks of women's hockey, becoming the first girl ever to play in the prestigious Quebec International Pee Wee tournament for youngsters. At nineteen, she broke the first of her many hockey barriers at the pro level, playing for the Trois-Rivières Draveurs, a major men's junior hockey team. And after the record-breaking game with Tampa Bay in the NHL, she continued her professional hockey career with several teams in the International Hockey League, the East Coast Hockey

League, and the West Coast Hockey League, all professional organizations.

Rheaume, who is the mother of a young son and whose brother Pascal is an NHL player, is the subject of a 2000 documentary film called *Behind the Mask*. Rheaume earned her place in Canadian sports history because of one main reason – she was a great hockey goalie.

Hayley Wickenheiser

Shaunavon, Saskatchewan, native Hayley Wickenheiser is famous in Canada and around the world for a number of reasons. As a softball player, she has competed many times for her country in international competition, including at the 2000 Summer Olympics in Sydney, Australia.

But it is in hockey that Wickenheiser has really shone. In 1998, she was one of the stars on the Canadian Olympic team that placed second at Nagano, and, in 2002, she was one of the leaders of the Canadian team that won the gold, a tournament for which she was named Most Valuable Player.

All of that international ice experience was enough to impress scouts for the Kirkkonummi Salamat men's team in the Finnish professional league, who invited her (after an unsuccessful attempt on her part to catch on with a team in the Italian men's league) for a one-month tryout in December 2002 and January 2003. Evidently, Wickenheiser impressed the team's coaching staff during that trial period, because she was signed to a four-month contract that would take her to the end of the 2002-03 season with the Finnish club. This meant that she would get to play in twenty-two regular-season games (after three in the tryout stint), in which she was expected to play about 10-15 minutes per contest.

By February 1 of her first season, Wickenheiser had made her mark, scoring her first goal for Kirkkonummi Salamat.

Nor was physical education widely available to women in the nineteenth and early twentieth centuries. As more women gained admission to university, however, they sought to bring physical education to all young girls and women. One of the first crusaders for female physical education was Dorothea Beale. Beale, a British teacher and headmistress of Cheltenham Ladies College in the mid- to late 1800s, was one of the first people committed to education for girls, including physical education. She encouraged her students to walk and perform calisthenics in the school gym; calisthenics at this time, like all physical activity, was believed by most to be harmful for girls and women. Perhaps because of the period in which Beale began teaching, she did not believe in competitive sports for women. It would take some acceptance of her beliefs before the world would be ready to take that leap.

Mary G. Hamilton was one Canadian who was ready to make that leap. Hamilton was one of Canada's first teachers of physical education for girls, as well as a champion of camping and sports for women and girls. She was the head of physical education programs for several prominent girls' schools in Toronto, including Bishop Strachan School, Branksome Hall, and Margaret Eaton School. It was at Margaret Eaton, where she began teaching in 1910, that Hamilton created a diploma course in physical education. The government did not recognize the course, but the graduates took up positions teaching physical education to other girls across the country. The talent from the program was in high demand at private schools and YWCAs.

Hamilton started dance classes for Toronto women and co-created Camp Tanamakoon in Algonquin Park. The camp for Margaret Eaton students was ideal for swimming, canoe instruction, and the teaching and practice of leadership skills. In 1933, the Canadian Physical Education Association was created, with help from Mary, who was vice-president of the association for two years. In 1941, after Hamilton had retired, Margaret Eaton School amalgamated with the University of Toronto, creating Canada's first physical education bachelor's degree. This encouraged women to regard physical education as a possible career as it enabled graduates to teach physical education in public schools for the first time.

As women gained more freedom throughout the twentieth century, they created more physical education opportunities for themselves and pushed the boundaries of the sports world. Many Canadian women were pioneers in both the national and international sports world. When basketball was still a relatively new sport, the Edmonton Grads women's basketball team was setting world records. When track-and-field events were introduced in the

Marilyn Bell entered Lake Ontario on September 8, 1954. After 20 hours and 57 minutes she touched ground west of the CNE, greeted by an estimated crowd of 300,000 people who had gathered to give her an emotional welcome (CP PHOTO).

Olympics, the Canadian team won gold medals and displayed remarkable team spirit to the world. In the 1950s, Marilyn Bell swam across Lake Ontario, a feat no man had been able to accomplish. These are sports accomplishments, not just Canadian women's sports accomplishments. Unfortunately, many female sports pioneers and women's sports groups are not as well remembered or regularly celebrated as this group.

Fortunately, there are several groups dedicated to redressing this imbalance, including the Canadian Association for the Advancement of Women in Sport (CAAWS), described on page 327. In addition, there are a number of Canadian female athletes who have emerged during the last decade as role models for young girls and women in sports that have previously not seen high-visibility female competitors. These include Stacy Dales-Schuman and Tammy Sutton-Brown, both star Canadian-born basketball players who played first on scholarships at U.S. universities, and now compete in the relatively new (founded in 1996) WNBA, the Women's National Basketball Association.

THE WOMEN'S AMATEUR ATHLETIC FEDERATION

The Women's Amateur Athletic Federation (or WAAF) was the first national body where Canadian women could address issues in sports and gain the support they needed. Created in 1926 by Alexandrine Gibb and several other sports pioneers, the federation was commonly called the Canadian Parliament of Women's Sport. WAAF encouraged women to participate in sporting events, especially in international competitions. With coast-to-coast operations, WAAF instilled a women-friendly environment in the sports they coached and helped to build the first Canadian, and very successful, track-and-field team for the 1928 Olympics. The federation continuously fought to add sports and events to competitions specifically for women.

Before the outbreak of the Second World War, WAAF had more members than the Amateur Athletic Union of Canada, its male counterpart. All of the WAAF board members were volunteers who balanced their work with fund raising, running a household, and raising a family. The majority of the athletes that benefitted from their work were working-class or poor women. WAAF broadened the scope of the world for these women, allowing them to travel for competitions and experience all that the sports world had to offer. The Women's Amateur Athletic Federation created many opportunities for women and encouraged generations to participate in sports in its time. However, after thirty-seven years, the federation, after many setbacks, decided to merge with the Amateur Athletic Union of Canada.

PIONEERING CANADIAN SPORTSWOMEN

Many of the members of the Women's Amateur Athletic Federation became prominent sports writers, including Fanny Rosenfeld and Alexandrine Gibb. Along with Abby Hoffman, these pioneers did much to further the position of women in various aspects of sport.

Alexandrine Gibb

Alexandrine Gibb was a true sports pioneer. Gibb helped start the Women's Amateur Athletic Federation and served as its first president. She believed that women should govern women's sports. Gibb was an avid athlete, competing in several different sports, including basketball. The school that she attended as a girl encouraged physical activity for women and her teachers were trained in Britain, where sports had become an integral part of education. In order for women to participate in sports at the time, they needed to have a place where they could be active

without men present. To this end, Gibb and her athletic friends created the Toronto Ladies Club, which included teams coached by women. At the same time that Gibb pushed WAAF into existence, she also created the Canadian Ladies, a new club for women to participate in hockey, softball, track and field, and basketball. She travelled across the country raising awareness of the federation and challenging women to join. Alexandrine also became a well-respected sports journalist for the *Toronto Star*, writing a column entitled "No Man's Land of Sports."

Fanny Rosenfeld

Fanny Rosenfeld (1903-69), nicknamed "Bobbie" by her family, was one of the first and best track-and-field athletes ever to compete for Canada. Fanny excelled in all sports, but as a young woman in her early twenties, she began equalling and breaking world records in track-and-field sports. In 1925, at the Ontario Ladies Track and Field Championship, she won the 220-yard race, 120-yard low hurdles, discus, long jump, and shot put. During the trials for the Canadian women's Olympic team, Rosenfeld set three Canadian records. Unable to enter all the events at the 1928 Amsterdam Olympics, Fanny placed second, by a thin margin, in the 100-yard dash. But, more remarkable than Fanny's silver medal win was her incredible team spirit and selflessness. After a teammate experienced a leg injury in practice, Fanny spent an entire race running beside her and encouraging her on. The teammate, Jean Thompson, came in fourth place in the 800-yard race, and Fanny came in fifth, forsaking her own glory to encourage a friend.

After a bout of arthritis, Fanny had to retire from competition, but her love of sports did not diminish. Rosenfeld became a sportswriter for *The Globe and Mail*. In 1949, Fanny was named Canadian Woman Athlete for the Half-Century. She helped encourage Canadian women to take part in sports throughout her life, in both her actions and her words.

Abby Hoffman

Abby Hoffman admired Canadian sportswomen including Fanny Rosenfeld and the Edmonton Grads and, in turn, became a Canadian sports pioneer herself. In 1956, at the age of nine, Abby cut her hair off and posed as a boy in order to join a hockey team. After her identity was discovered, she turned to track and field and became a world-class middle-distance runner. She competed in four Olympic Games and brought home the gold medal for the 880-yard event in both the 1963 and 1966 Commonwealth Games. After competing in the Olympics and while still a student and a competitive athlete, Abby was thrown out of Hart House in the University of Toronto for

Title IX and its Aftermath
Equal-opportunity legislation in the U.S. affects Canadian athletes

Title IX is a section of the landmark Educational Amendments of 1972. This piece of American legislation prohibits gender discrimination of any kind in schools and was particularly influential regarding athletic policies at all levels of educational institutions. Title IX allowed girls and women the same sports and physical education opportunities that men had taken for granted. This piece of legislation was very controversial when it was released. Many schools falsely believed that they were being forced to eliminate programs for men, rather than create new opportunities for women.

Pre-1971

In the United States in 1971, less than 300,000 girls played high-school sports and very few sports were available that girls were allowed to participate in. Now, more than thirty years after Title IX was passed, millions of girls participate in high-school sports and the number continues to rise. In order to be in compliance with Title IX, schools need to look at whether financial assistance is being divided equally, whether sports are divided equally in terms of interest and skill, and whether equality exists in several other areas, including equipment, supplies, scheduling, travel, academic tutoring, coaching, locker rooms, facilities, medical services, housing, dining, publicity, and recruitment. Since the legislation was passed, girls and women are participating in increasingly more sports that were formerly known as "male," such as hockey, lacrosse, rugby, and soccer.

Before 1972, athletic college scholarships were non-existent for women. Donna de Varona, a two-time gold medal Olympic swimmer, was unable to get an athletic scholarship because there were not any available to women. Though the change in scholarship disbursement took time, today the ratio is much closer to the ratio of male and female athletes. Statistics show that girls who participate in sports are less likely to smoke, drink alcohol, become

Abby Hoffman competes in an athletics event at the 1976 Olympic Games in Montreal (CP PHOTO/COA/RW).

pregnant, or drop out of school. A large number of highly placed women in corporate business today played sports in high school and university due to Title IX. Because of the legislation, more women are graduating from high school and universities than ever before.

Canadian Policy Initiatives

Title IX has forced other countries to look at how women and girls are treated in schools and particularly in athletics. The Canadian Charter of Rights and Freedoms was passed in 1982 and sets out similar laws against discrimination as Title IX does. Most notably, Canadian sport is governed by the Canada Sport Policy, developed by our national Canadian Heritage Ministry over several years and released in 2002 (for a comprehensive look at this policy, see page 330). As many commentators have noted, this initiative is significant because it sets forward a clear, government-supported plan to make sport more inclusive. Groups that have previously had a hard time being "accepted" in organized sport can point to it as a clear reference mandating their inclusion.

In much the same way that Title IX has legislated that American post-secondary institutions need to give equal weight to scholarships for both male and female athletes, the Canada Sport Policy provides governmental guidance regarding the inclusion of women and others. Also, many observers of the links between government and sport worldwide have indicated that Canada is one of the only countries to have received a clear statement on this issue from its federal legislative body.

Concerned with how things are, and determined to make things better, the Canadian Sport Policy reflects a new approach to shared leadership and collaboration amongst all stakeholders to achieve the goals of enhanced participation, excellence, capacity and interaction in sport.

Title IX's Direct Impact in canada

Title IX itself might seem to be a piece of legislation with little immediate relevance to Canadian athletes. This, however, is not entirely the case, for one important reason: the opportunities it affords to women athletes through increased funding and scholarships are not limited to American athletes. Scholarships offered by U.S. universities and colleges are available to athletes from other countries, including Canada – and, indeed, many young female competitors from this country have benefitted from sports scholarships "down south" in a wide range of sports.

Although official statistics are not kept on just how many high-school graduates attend U.S. schools with some form of financial assistance, it is safe to assume that, among women, the number is somewhere close to one hundred each year, in sports that include basketball, volleyball, track and field, cross country, soccer, rowing, and ice hockey.

Without Title IX, the number of Canadian women who benefit from these scholarships would likely have been considerably less.

attempting to use its indoor track, the only one in Canada at the time. When her competing days were over, Abby turned her attention to championing women's rights to participate in sports. She became executive secretary for the Ontario Human Rights Commission, the first woman director general of Sport Canada, and the first woman ever elected to the Executive of the Canadian Olympic Association. She was recognized for her work in sports in 1982 when she was given the Order of Canada.

WOMEN IN SPORT TODAY

When the first modern Olympic Games took place, no women competed; in 1996 at the Atlanta games, one hundred years after the first Olympics and for the first time in history, Canada's Olympic team consisted of more women than men. In the 2002 Commonwealth Games, the female athletes won 58 percent of the medals that Canada's team received. Today, women compete in and excel at every sport that men do. Though there are still steps to take to ensure that women are on an equal playing field with men, things appear to be headed in the right direction. Many women still have to deal with the issue of remaining "feminine" while playing sports, and because of this there is often more interest in participating in "female" sports, such as figure skating and gymnastics than in "male" sports, such as hockey, rugby, or weightlifting. There are still more boys and men competing and coaching than there are women, but the gap is closing. Society has overcome several gender-related barriers and stereotypes, and the athletic girls and women of today are gaining respect and admiration in their respective sports. With more and more female sports heroes for girls to look to for inspiration, the gap in women's sports participation will close completely.

Chantal Petitclerc

Chantal Petitclerc is a very special athlete. Petitclerc has been in a wheelchair since she was in a very serious accident when she was in her early teens, and it was at that point that Chantal became interested in sports. After racing for many years, Chantal competed in the Paralympics in 1992, bringing home two bronze medals. Petitclerc challenged herself over the next four years and her hard work paid off. She won two gold medals and three silver medals in the Paralympic Games in 1996. But her biggest accomplishment came in 2002 at the Commonwealth Games. For the first time in history, the Commonwealth Games included an 800-metre wheelchair race and Petitclerc won, becoming the first disabled athlete to win a fully recognized gold medal in a multi-sport competition. Petitclerc was excited to win the medal for Canada and

looks forward to the day when her sport is added to the Olympic roster as more than a demonstration sport.

Clara Hughes

As a champion cyclist and speed skater, Clara Hughes has competed in several Olympic games, both Winter and Summer. She started to speed skate after seeing Gaetan Boucher win in the 1984 Winter Olympics. As a teenager, Clara skated competitively for two years. In the off-season, she began cycling as a means of cross-training and keeping herself in top physical condition. She soon discovered that she was also very good at cycling, and when her cycling career took off, Clara retired from speed skating. Clara cycled in two Summer Olympics and won two bronze medals. In 1999, she won at the national level, but failed to win the Pan Am Games a month later. That same year, one week before the world championships, a car hit her while she was training. But Clara still competed in the Pan Ams and finished in seventh place. She decided that her competitive cycling career was nearing an end and decided to return to her first love, speed skating. Clara practised hard and qualified to join the national speed-skating team. After only a short time on the national team, Clara qualified for the Winter Olympics. One of a few Canadian athletes who have competed in both Summer and Winter Olympics, Clara placed third in the 5,000-metre race, bringing home yet another bronze medal. Clara Hughes had triumphed over adversity and fulfilled her Olympic dreams.

Scott Tournament of Hearts

Women's curling has grown immensely in terms of both participants and viewers over the past twenty years. Canadian women and girls are very active in curling; girls', women's, and mixed leagues are opening at curling rinks across the country. Though only 35 percent of the curlers in the country are female, that number is growing and is much larger than it was in the past. Team spirit, co-operation, balance, and coordination make curling an ideal introduction to sports participation for girls. There are over 1,250 curling rinks in Canada, making the sport accessible to nearly everyone in the country. Curling is one of the largest amateur sports in Canada, and though television ratings tend to still favour the Nokia Brier men's tournament, the women's curling fan base has been steadily growing. Women's curling has been attracting more media attention every year. When it is time for the championships, it is easy to find women's curling articles and features in the sports section of the newspaper, the Internet sports databases, and television sports news. In 2001, The Scott Tournament of Hearts won a Gemini award for the best live sporting event on television that year. The final game of the tournament that year reached more than three million viewers, and actually beat the television ratings of the Nokia Brier for men.

The Scott Tournament of Hearts, or the Canadian Women's Curling Championship, has been a highlight of the Canadian curling scene since 1982. Each province and territory sends a team to the competition, though competition to represent one's province can be fierce. The winner of the tournament then represents Canada at the World Championships, at which Canadian women excel. The symbol of the tournament is four hearts joined together, representing both the four members of a curling team and the spirit of camaraderie, friendship, and fair play that exists among competitors.

Colleen Jones

Colleen Jones is currently one of Canada's best curlers with a record to prove it. She is the first woman to win the Canadian Women's Curling Championship five times – in 1982, 1999, 2001, 2002, and 2003 – the last four times with the same team. In 2001, she and her team won the World Championship title. Jones is not only an incredible role model on the ice, but also in her professional life. She is the weather and sports reporter on CBC's *Newsworld Morning* and has covered several Olympic Games and Commonwealth Games for the CBC. Jones helps promote women's sports both on and off the curling rink.

Sandra Schmirler

Sandra Schmirler was one of Canada's best curlers in her time. She won three Canadian championships and three world championships. But Schmirler's biggest success was a gold medal win in the first Olympics in which women's curling was a medal sport. After her win in 1998 in Nagano, Sandra was dubbed "the Queen of Curling." However, her success was short lived. Only a few years after her gold medal win, Sandra Schmirler was diagnosed with cancer. She died in March 2000 leaving behind a husband and two daughters. The Sandra Schmirler Foundation was created in her honour to help families with seriously ill children.

Team Canada Hockey

The Canadian women's national team is the best female hockey team in the world. Team Canada has represented the country at every Women's World Hockey Championship, started in 1990, and they have won the gold medal at each tournament. In fact, Team Canada has never lost a game in the championships. The hockey players have fifty-six gold medals

Team Canada skip Colleen Jones and third Kim Kelly celebrate after defeating Newfoundland to win the 2003 Scott Tournament of Hearts in Kitchener, Ontario (CP PHOTO/Kevin Frayer).

between them from the Women's World Hockey Championships. The national women's team also competed in the Women's Pacific Rim Championships. These games included Canada, the United States, Japan, and China, and took place in 1995 and 1996. The Canadian women won first place at both events. The success of Team Canada led the Canadian Hockey Association in 1999 to create the National Women's Under 22 Hockey Team. The team grooms women to play at an international level and allows talented young players to compete with others at their age and skill level. The young women compete in exhibition games against the best players from the United States, and they also play in the Christmas Cup in Europe.

Team Canada has also competed at two winter Olympics. Women's hockey became an Olympic sport in 1998 in Nagano, Japan. Despite a hard-fought final game, the Canadian team took home the silver medal while the United States won gold. The team members were disappointed but vowed that they would win at the next Olympics. Danièle Sauvageau, the assistant coach in Nagano, was chosen as the head

Alison Sydor from North Vancouver makes her way through a stumpy wooded section of the cross-country course at the National Mountain Bike Championships in Kamloops, B.C. in August 2001 (CP PHOTO/*Kamloops Daily News*/Keith Anderson).

coach for the 2002 Games and she trained her players hard, strengthening their weak spots and ensuring that they played their best through all three periods. Ten players from the 1998 Olympics returned for the 2002 Games. The United States were the favourite team to win gold, as they had won all of their games for the season before the Olympics, including eight wins over the Canadian team. The two teams met again in the final game, but four years after their Nagano disappointment, the Canadian team was not going to go home with a silver medal. In a closely fought and intense game, Canada beat the United States three goals to two. Caroline Ouellette, Hayley Wickenheiser, and Jayna Hefford all managed to score goals during the final game, and goaltender Kim St. Pierre made several great saves while her team was short handed.

The gold medal game was watched by more than five million Canadians and inspired both girls and women at all levels of hockey.

Women's Under 19 National Soccer Team

Canadian girls and women have embraced soccer, and in the last decade, the number of females playing the sport has increased significantly. The Canadian Soccer Association estimates that there are almost 300,000 females playing soccer in the country. And with the success of the Under 19 Canadian Women's Soccer Team, that number is bound to increase greatly.

In 2002, the Fédération International de Football Association (or FIFA) held its first Under 19 World Cup championship for women in Edmonton. The Canadian team was selected over an eighteen-month period beginning in early 2001 and worked as a team for three months before the tournament began. Though all the women on the team were young, they had many years of soccer experience between them, as most had started playing before they were six years old.

The eighteen women chosen for the team accomplished something that no other Canadian soccer team had been able to do – they played in a World Cup final game. The final game of the tournament was played against the United States and was watched live by 47,000 fans in Edmonton and by over 900,000 Canadians on television. The determined Canadian team lost in a close 1-0 game against the United States, but they had made history and impressed and inspired the entire country.

In 2003, the team was selected as a finalist for the Female Team of the Year in the Annual Canadian Sports Awards (an award ultimately won by the gold-medal Olympic hockey squad).

Alison Sydor

If there is a single Canadian athlete who is responsible for the growth of interest in his or her sport, cross-country and mountain bike racer Alison Sydor may well be the one. Sydor has won three World Championships in the sport and also captured an Olympic silver medal in Atlanta in 1996.

Based in Vancouver, Sydor was born in Edmonton in 1966 and was a successful triathlete (Alberta junior champion) and multi-sport athlete (she played volleyball, hockey, and basketball in high school) before turning her talents to road-race cycling. Many athletes have attempted to make the transition from road to cross-country riding, but few have done it as well as Sydor – as her three consecutive world titles (in 1994, 1995, and 1996) attest. A graduate of the University of Victoria, Sydor spends a lot of her time in Europe competing in races under the sponsorship of the Volvo automotive company and Cannondale bikes.

WOMEN IN LEADERSHIP POSITIONS IN SPORTS

The **gender representation in leadership positions** in sports – coaches, officials, committee, league, or tournament members – is still disproportionately in favour of men. Women have had a difficult time breaking down this barrier, but as more former athletes look for post-competitive careers in sports, this field is opening up. There are not enough female officials in any sport despite a great need for them.

Many professional female leagues have difficulty finding officials for their games, and because of this, the few females referees that exist are often dealing with a bigger work load than they can handle, or male officials end up stepping in to fill the gap. The same is true of female coaches. The majority of female sports teams are coached by men. Many of the female pioneers that are currently in sports leadership positions are often paid much less than their male counterparts. In view of these problems, many people are advocating for a change in the Canadian sporting system that will pay women enough to make full-time careers of these positions. Former female athletes are a largely untapped source of coaching, officiating, and organizational expertise.

A new system to promote these roles to athletes as a post-competitive career – with a monetary incentive and a comprehensive educational component to help them get started – would increase the numbers of women in leadership positions. As more women hold these leadership positions, the numbers should continue to increase and sustain themselves, as more women follow in their footsteps.

Sonia Denoncourt

Refereeing has remained a male-dominated aspect of sport – few females have ventured into the world of officiating until recently. Sonia Denoncourt decided to forgo her soccer career in order to work on her refereeing skills. Denoncourt started refereeing soccer games at the age of fourteen. While she was working towards her degree in physical education, she decided that she should focus her attention on refereeing rather than playing, despite being one of the best soccer midfielders in Canada. Sonia was the first Canadian woman to officiate an "A" level international men's game. In 1994, the Fédération International de Football Association (or FIFA) for the first time appointed three women, including Denoncourt, to the list of game officials. Sonia became the first woman to referee an Olympic soccer game in 1996. She has also become the first female official in Brazilian professional soccer. FIFA officials must maintain a high level of fitness in order to remain on the list of possible referees. All games are monitored for the performance of the official, and mistakes are not tolerated. Referees must have an excellent knowledge of their sport and the ability to deal with all different kinds of players. Denoncourt is an inspiration to female soccer players and to all women interested in officiating in any sport.

Danièle Sauvageau

Danièle Sauvageau is a Montreal police officer who worked undercover for years in the narcotics division. She was also part of the security team at the 1988 Calgary Olympics. Ten years later, when women's hockey was added to the Olympics, Danièle was appointed assistant coach for Team Canada. That year, the American team won the gold medal and a disappointed Team Canada vowed that they would win next time.

Danièle was head coach of the national team in 1999 and 2001, winning world championships both years. She was also the first female to coach in the Quebec Major Junior Hockey League with the Montreal Rockets in the 1999 and 2000 season. Named head coach for Team Canada for the 2002 Winter Olympics, Sauvageau took a leave of absence from the Montreal Police force to concentrate her efforts on coaching the team. Her hard work paid off. Danièle used all the team's players and helped the women on the team remain focused on the game. Team Canada won the final game and the gold medal. After the game, Sauvageau praised the team members and their fair play.

Danièle's strong leadership skills make her and her team members great role models for young girls across Canada. As noted earlier, in 2003, Sauvageau was picked to help Canada's Olympic water polo team as a motivational coach.

Carol Anne Letheren

A former badminton champion and Olympic gymnastics official, Carol Anne Letheren made an impact on Canada and the world as an International Olympic Committee (IOC) member. Carol became a director of the Canadian Olympic Association (COA) in 1981 and is often remembered in Canada as the official who had to take Ben Johnson's ill-gotten gold medal away at the 1988 Olympics in Seoul, Korea. Her handling of this issue caught the attention of the IOC, and in 1990 she was awarded a seat on the committee. Carol was appointed president of the COA in 1994 and was a member of the IOC coordinating committee for the 2002 Olympics. Letheren suffered a fatal brain aneurysm in 2001, before the Olympics took place. After her death, a scholarship was created in her honour to help support young Canadian women with excellent leadership, athletic, and scholarly skills. Letheren was an excellent role model for anyone wanting to work in a leadership role.

MEDIA AND WOMEN'S SPORTS

Though there have been significant increases in women's sports participation, media coverage of women's sports has not increased by the same percentage. In general, women's sports receive less than 10 percent of the total sports coverage of most networks and newspapers. The sad reality is that media shapes our perceptions, particularly those of impressionable young minds. With such a lack of media coverage of women's sports teams, leagues, and athletes, the media is sending the message that women's sports and athletic accomplishments are unimportant compared to men's sports. The consequence of this underreporting, besides the general public's ignorance of women's sports, is that young girls have a difficult time finding athletic heroes to look up to. Also, with little media coverage, female athletes and teams often have a difficult time finding funding and sponsorship from corporations.

The argument against reporting on more women's sports is that there is no demand for it. However, the public cannot demand to see something that they do not know exists. The dilemma facing broadcasters is whether they should cover women's sports to create an interest or wait until the public requests it. Women's sports that the public have been exposed to often receive excellent television ratings, suggesting that there is a demand for media coverage of similar events. Women's curling, golf, and tennis have all seen increases in television ratings when they are aired.

Unfortunately, when women's sports do receive media coverage, the story is often on the last pages of a newspaper's sports section or in the final minutes of a television broadcast. With the diminishing attention spans of viewers and readers, these reports are often overlooked. The same impact on consumers is achieved with this poor positioning as is with no reporting at all – women's sports are unimportant. Part of the problem is that many journalists, the majority of whom are male, view women's sports stories as secondary or junior assignments. Professional league women's sports are perceived as being on the same level as high-school sports, worthy to participate in but not to report on. In fact, in many local television markets, men's high-school basketball and hockey are often more widely reported than women's sports.

The media also often has a tendency to focus on a female athlete's appearance rather than her skill and talent. Women are objectified in a way that male athletes are not. Attractive female athletes have a greater chance of getting media attention than the best athlete in the same sport. Anna Kournikova is an excellent example of this. While Kournikova has yet to win a tournament, she receives a great deal more media attention than the top female tennis players. This type of reporting trivializes women's sports into a sort of peep show for male spectators. The media often portrays muscular women as masculine or tomboyish, and not as well-trained athletes.

Female Sports Broadcasters

Female sportscasting has come a long way in the last twenty-five years. Many of the first women to work in sports broadcasting were merely co-anchors or hosts of television shows who knew very little or nothing about sports. In an effort to get more men to watch a program, these women were hired for the way they looked, not for their knowledge. Women were not given the same rights that male reporters took for granted.

However, many female sports reporters began to challenge the sports world in the 1960s and 1970s. In the 1970s, well-respected reporter Jeannine Morris was not permitted to report on a football game from the press box because she was a woman. When she was eventually allowed to work in the press box, no women's washroom facilities were provided.

Women reporters have had a difficult time reporting from locker rooms after games. In the mid-1980s, after they were allowed to report from locker rooms, they were, and still are, not readily welcomed. Female reporters that enter locker rooms for post-game interviews have been accused of being perverted, have been verbally abused, have had jock straps thrown at them, and have been subject to inappropriate, aggressive, and vulgar sexual advances. The attitudes of many professional male athletes are products of outmoded stereotypes that portray women as sexual objects. These attitudes need to change for total equality to be achieved.

Female sportscasters still do not generally make the same amount of money as their male counterparts, and male reporters still have a much larger presence in television sports broadcasting than do women. Networks argue that male reporters are more popular and often have more experience reporting sports than women do and that this is the reason for the discrepancy in salaries. However, if more women are not hired to report on sports, how will any build a loyal viewer base and gain experience? There are several knowledgeable female sportscasters on Canadian television, but an attractive appearance still seems to be more important for a female sportscaster to maintain than for a male sportscaster. Male sportscasters are less likely to be physically fit and well groomed than a female reporter. Once again, a small shift in attitude from the networks would help women sportscasters to continue to move forward.

BODY IMAGE

Women and girls are now under more pressure to look a certain way than ever before. Women feel pressured to stay thin and do everything in their power to maintain what has been deemed "beautiful" regardless of their age, experience, genetics, and nature. Many experts believe that this pressure originates in the images of women in the media. After years of looking at these images, often computer-enhanced, girls develop low self-esteem because they can never achieve such unrealistic ideals. Hearing similar things from their friends and mothers often compounds their low self-esteem. The result of these unrealistic expectations is sometimes an unhealthy diet, which often leads to eating disorders – compulsive overeating, anorexia nervosa, and bulimia nervosa – and excessive exercise.

The "Beauty Myth"

Girls are beginning to develop unrealistic beauty expectations for themselves at a very young age. Girls as young as seven or eight are dieting and exercising to aerobic-style home videos aimed at young girls. Nor are athletic girls and women immune to these pressures – many young female athletes try to maintain unhealthily low levels of body fat and exercise far too much for their food intake. Low self-esteem often grows in these young girls because they feel extra pressure to remain "feminine" (many female athletes are teased that they are too "tomboyish"), at least according to the ideals they see presented in the media.

Female athletes, both amateur and elite, face the same body image concerns that most women and girls face. Pressure to be thin comes from an even greater number of sources for the athlete. In endurance events, thinness and low body-fat levels are associated with better athletic performance – however, if taken to a dangerous level, the opposite is true. In the so-called "aesthetic sports" – such as gymnastics, synchronized swimming, and figure skating – there is also pressure to be thin. Serious health risks due to too low levels of body fat and weight can lead to injuries, disease, poor physical performance, and long-term psychological problems.

Unfortunately, many female athletes do not recognize when their weight loss and exercise have passed into dangerous territory. Many believe that it does not matter how weight is lost so long as it is achieved. This leads them into the phenomenon known as the female triad (see box on page 326).

Weight loss and problems arising from the associated female triad are not the only issues that concern those who study the concept of female body image as it relates to sport. Another issue is how a woman

Catriona Le May Doan of Saskatoon waves the flag (upside down) after winning gold in the women's 500-metre speed-skating event at the 2002 Salt Lake City Olympics (CP PHOTO/Frank Gunn).

"should" look. At the beginning of this section, we referred to the concept of femininity and how it has changed, and is changing, over time. Recently, to some controversy, some female athletes have reverted to a fairly traditional representation of women in an effort to raise money for their sports. Just before the 2002 Summer Olympics, a number of top-notch women's sports teams – including the Australian women's soccer squad and the New Zealand eight-woman rowing team – posed nude for calendars designed to be sold to a mostly male audience. Team members, citing a lack of government support for women's sport, said that other avenues of funding had been exhausted. In the lead up to the 2000 Winter Games, members of the Canadian women's Nordic ski team also released a similar calendar.

Those who opposed these calendars said that, instead of portraying these athletes in their best light (that is, as dedicated, extremely fit, and highly accomplished practitioners of difficult physical pursuits), they showed women in ways that were more in line with "old-fashioned" values – objects to be admired only for their looks, and not their achievements.

The Female Triad
Disordered eating habits, amenorrhea, and osteoporosis

The female triad is a syndrome that includes disordered eating habits, amenorrhea, and osteoporosis. Like many male athletes, many athletic women are perfectionists and have a drive to excel (a trait that helps them succeed in sports). This in turn leads some female athletes to try to achieve weight goals – goals that they genuinely believe to be realistic – by any means necessary. In order to reach these weight levels, these women resort to eating disorders, which in turn lead to the other aspects of the triad. The syndrome is also related to the unique cultural and social pressures on females in our society (see the discussion on the "beauty myth" on the previous page).

Disordered eating

Disordered eating can include anorexia nervosa, bulimia nervosa, and the restriction of certain kinds of food, particularly fats and carbohydrates. Eating disorders often occur because an individual is so frightened of gaining weight that any means of keeping the weight off becomes acceptable. Many psychological factors can contribute to disordered eating including low self-esteem, a need to be in control, self-loathing, perfectionism, and the desire for acceptance. Many people who suffer from eating disorders have a distorted self-image and do not see themselves as they truly are.

Amenorrhea

Amenorrhea, the absence of regular menstrual periods, occurs when a woman's weight or body fat is too low or when there is poor nutritional practice. Overexercise alone can lead to amenorrhea – athletes need to consume enough calories to make up those they burn during exercise; the energy taken in must at least equal the energy expended. The female body should never drop below 12 percent body fat; any percentage below this is not conducive to good health and can cause illnesses, injuries with slow

Outstanding female athletes, whose careers have not been complicated by these illnesses, can serve as powerful role models for young women. Above, Marnie McBean wins gold in the 1999 Pan American Games women's single sculls (CP PHOTO/Frank Gunn).

recovery, and a lack of physical ability. Amenorrhea often has serious effects on bone density and calcium absorption. Bone density may never return to its previous levels after a drop. Athletes with amenorrhea risk fractures and early onset osteoporosis.

Osteoporosis

Osteoporosis, the third component of the female triad, is a bone disease, normally occurring in menopausal women, caused by poor bone density. Individuals with this disease break bones easily and healing is slow. Lack of calcium is a key factor in the disease. Teenage female athletes require a minimum of 1,300 milligrams of calcium daily.

Many of the symptoms of the female triad are similar to the symptoms of an eating disorder, such as inability to concentrate, fatigue, anemia, erosion of teeth enamel from the acids produced in vomiting, abdominal pain, bloating, chest pain, light-headedness, and intolerance to cold. Unfortunately, many

athletes who experience the symptoms of the triad do not report them.

Though amenorrhea is the most easily recognizable aspect of the triad, many women believe the absence of their periods to be a blessing rather than a problem, and they do not believe that there is a need to talk to their doctor or coach about it. With increased education for athletes, coaches, and parents, there will be a greater awareness of the need for early intervention.

Breaking the triad

Although a knowledge of the causes and results of the female triad is important for anyone involved with women in sports, knowing how to overcome it is perhaps more crucial. It is possible to "break" the triad and return a female athlete to healthier eating habits and more realistic perceptions of her body weight and image. But, given the complexity of this condition, the process must be undertaken with the guidance of trained medical professionals, including a physician, a dietician, and a psychologist, and also requires the full involvement of coaches, parents, and, of course, the athlete herself.

As is the case with similar conditions, early identification and intervention are especially important. Many experts suggest that, when a concerned parent or coach approaches an athlete concerning an eating disorder, the best way is to express concern for the athlete's overall health, without explicitly discussing weight or eating habits.

Despite the many pressures to succeed, behaviour that is dangerous to one's health should never be engaged in, even in the pursuit of sporting excellence. Certainly, there is a fine line between maintaining a weight and body shape that is appropriate for many sports and entering into unhealthy dietary habits. No matter how important winning might seem, it is never a good idea to try to do so at the risk of permanently damaging one's health.

CANADIAN ASSOCIATION FOR THE ADVANCEMENT OF WOMEN IN SPORT (CAAWS)

The **Canadian Association for the Advancement of Women in Sport (CAAWS)** was founded in 1981 as a non-profit organization to promote sports and physical activity for women across Canada. With a small staff and a large network of volunteers, CAAWS works in communities across the country, in partnership with Sport Canada, to gain gender equality in sports. While working towards making women and girls active sports participants rather than just viewers, CAAWS also encourages females to break down all sports-related barriers including those in coaching and officiating.

Females are still not as physically active as males in Canada. With obesity, heart disease, and osteoporosis on the rise rather than on the decline, the promotion of physical activity for girls and women is more important than ever. Though CAAWS has a number of programs devoted to new mothers and women, their programs aimed at girls are very important. If girls start good exercise practices at a young age, including fun sports, these practices will become a part of their lives and remain with them throughout life. The programs ACTive, On the Move, and Girls @ Play are progressive strategies to help females become more active in their lives.

On The Move

On The Move (OTM) is a program developed by CAAWS for implementation in communities across the country. The goal of OTM is to make sports and physical activity available to females who might normally miss out on opportunities and the physical and psychological benefits of activity due to social barriers. The participants are female only and include pre-teens, teens, recent immigrants, women living in poverty, and any other women who want to be involved. The program is different in each community as it is tailored to the wants, needs, and talents of the local participants. Fun physical and social activities, participant input, and a safe and supportive environment are just some of the things that help make OTM a success in the communities that adopt the program.

ACTive

ACTive is a program created by CAAWS in association with Sport Canada and Health Canada based on the Brighton Declaration on Women and Sport and the Windhoek Call for Action. ACTive is a coordinated effort between government and local organizations to promote physical activity for women and girls and provide opportunities for them to participate. The strategy will provide more opportunities for women to become involved in sports at the level of coaching, officiating, and volunteer leadership. Governments will help to ensure that programs are in place in local communities and that they are closely monitored for their success. ACTive brings a number of different groups together – sport organizations, YWCAs, cultural clubs, health organizations, and any other organization with programs for women's physical activity – for support and development of ideas and practices. With ACTive, Canada should see an increase of women and girls participating in sports, an increased skill level in women's sports, and an equal footing between men and women in sports.

Girls @ Play

In an attempt to fulfil its mandate of "getting more girls in the game" by "encourag[ing] girls and women to get off the bleachers and sidelines and onto the playing fields as participants and leaders," CAAWS has teamed up with Nike Canada to develop the **Girls @ Play** program. Among other initiatives, Girls @ Play offers a $500 grant each month to a deserving young athlete, sponsors the Nike Youth Achievement Award, and makes a wide range of resources, such as workshops, articles, and handbooks (available to interested parents, teachers, coaches, and athletes through the CAAWS website at www.caaws.ca).

Addressing Harassment and Abuse

CAAWS is also active in attempting to prevent harassment and abuse of all kinds in sport, and in educating those who may be confronting such issues as to how to deal with them. In 1997, the organization combined with forty other National Sport Organizations – including the Canadian Hockey Association, the Coaching Association of Canada, and the Canadian Centre for Ethics in Sport – to form a group called the Harassment and Abuse in Sport Collective. The following year, the collective released a handbook (and website) called *Speak Out! Act Now!* This resource offers a comprehensive program that sport organizations and clubs can follow in pursuit of the prevention and proper response to harassment and abuse.

WHERE DO WE GO FROM HERE?

In this section, we have examined the experience of women in sport with an emphasis on exploring the achievements of Canadian athletes. We have also looked at gender inequities that still need to be addressed.

In the next section, we will look at what may be part of the solution – governmental support for sport and physical activity, from local to federal levels.

A 2000-square foot mural overlooks the Gardiner Expressway advertising Toronto's 2008 Olympic bid. However, Beijing, China, won the bid to be the host city for the 2008 Summer Olympic Games (CP PHOTO/Aaron Harris).

26

Government Support for Sport and Physical Activity

"We cannot work, or eat, or drink; we cannot buy or sell or own anything; we cannot go to a ball game or a hockey game or watch TV without feeling the effects of government."
—E.A. Forsey, *How Canadians Govern Themselves*, 1982

KEY CONCEPTS

- Mills Report
- Sport Dispute Resolution Centre
- Canadian Sport Policy
- Sport Canada
- Canadian Olympic Committee
- Canadian Sport Centres
- National Sport Organizations (NSOs)

- Provincial Sport Organizations (PSOs)
- Multi-Sport Service Organizations (MSOs)
- Games of La Francophonie
- Athlete Assistance Program
- Royal Commission on the Status of Women in Canada
- Sport Participation Development Program

- Aboriginal Sports Circle
- Artic Winter Games
- Canadian Paralympic Committee
- Special Olympics
- Sports Select and PRO-LINE
- Inter-Provincial Lottery Corporation

Sports are an important part of the cultural life of a country. They can galvanize large crowds, and can unify communities and even entire nations as people rally their support behind the achievements of their favourite athletes. And in doing so, they promote a common identity, pride, and self-esteem and engage the interest of a population in a common, usually peaceful enterprise.

Whether through funding (which is currently shrinking) or by organizational contributions, governments at all levels today are influential in fostering a more liberal, expansive, and inclusive growth in the environment in which sporting events take place in Canada. These initiatives take the form of supportive financial programs for men and women, the disabled, Aboriginal people, and especially for young people everywhere in the country. This section describes some of the programs and policies that Canadian governments at all levels pursue in this area.

WHEN WINNING MATTERS

It is often said that hockey represents Canada's "national passion." Nowhere was this as evident as at the 2002 Winter Olympic Games in Salt Lake City, Utah, in which Team Canada captured the gold medals in both men's and women's competition. Both final matches, which featured the Canadians taking on the host teams from the United States, drew record

television audiences for men's and women's hockey in Canada, touched off celebrations across the country, and were hailed in the media as crowning achievements of both Canadian sport and culture.

Such events, however, can have an impact on a level that goes much deeper than simply a sporting one. Governments are also interested in promoting sports achievement as a nation-building activity, as a means of promoting exercise among the general population, and as a way of securing future electoral support. To this end, both at the federal and provincial levels, departments and agencies staffed by public employees have been established to administer the work. Far from being mere "games," sports now have a formal presence in the apparatus of government.

Part of this interest in sport is based on the view that, if more citizens spent more time in physical activities, they would spend less time in medical care. But there are also political motives for governments to become involved in the promotion of sport. During the so-called "Cold War," which followed the Second World War and continued until the fall of most of the regime of Eastern Europe in the late 1980s and early 1990s, much was said and written about the desire of the leaders of those nations to illustrate the ideological superiority of their systems through success in international sport. As evidenced by the 2002 Winter Olympic hockey finals, Canada and Canadians are not immune to this pressure.

The Mills Report

The Mills Report revealed several significant things about the widespread influence of sport in Canada. For example, the study found that sport in Canada represents an $8.9 billion contribution to Gross Domestic Product, and accounts for 262,326 jobs in Canada. Here are more highlights:

Professional Hockey (NHL)

- Six teams (Vancouver, Edmonton, Calgary, Toronto, Ottawa, and Montreal) and 8,689 jobs plus 3,839 indirect jobs, with direct wages of about $300.7 million.

- $211 million in tax monies per year paid to all levels of government in Canada.

Professional Baseball

- The Toronto Blue Jays and the Skydome combined account for 2,700 full-time and part-time jobs – that is a contribution to Gross Domestic Product (GDP) of $97.3 million.

- Montreal Expos account for 1,252 jobs, which is a contribution to GDP of $105.3 million.

Impact on Health

- A 10 percent increase in the fitness of Canadians will result in health care savings of $5 billion. If all Canadians were active, annual savings for heart disease alone would be $776 million.

- Physical activity can reduce the risk of colon cancer by as much as 50 percent and may help to protect women against breast cancer.

Impact on Tourism

- Twenty-six percent of all person-trips by Canadians in 1996 were for sport activity.

- Thirty-eight percent of all international person-trips to Canada include sport or outdoor activity.

- Sport tourism represents $4 billion in spending (10 percent of total tourism spending).

Impact on Youth at Risk

- In Quebec, children who participated in 5 hours of sport per week had significantly higher school marks than children who did not.

- More than 80 percent of Canadians between the ages of 10 and 20 who are active have never smoked.

- In Northern Manitoba, there was a 17.3 percent crime reduction in communities with a sports program.

- Girls who are active in sports are 92 percent less likely to use drugs and 80 percent less likely to have an unwanted pregnancy.

- It costs 100 times more to incarcerate a young person than it does to provide recreation programs.

THE MILLS REPORT: WHY GOVERNMENTS ARE INTERESTED IN SPORT

For governments to become involved in sport funding, they must first become aware of the specific needs that exist in this area. This is usually done by means of a comprehensive survey and can take on a number of forms. In Canada, we have an excellent recent example of such a fact-finding survey and sufficient time has passed since the survey to evaluate its impact on government policy.

The Mills Report: Sport in Canada, was published in December of 1998. It was the work of the members of Parliament on the Sub-Committee on the Study of Sport in Canada chaired by Dennis Mills, Member of Parliament for the Danforth riding in Toronto. *Sport in Canada* represents the most comprehensive parliamentary review of the Canadian sports scene in thirty years since the 1969 *Task Force Report on Sport*. Though many of the specific recommendations in the report were not followed by the government, one concrete result was the appointment of a cabinet minister for sport, now known as the Secretary of State for Amateur Sport. The first such official was Denis Coderre, who was appointed on August 2, 1999.

In addition to the creation of this position, the other significant result of the Mills Report was the introduction of a new piece of legislation governing Sport Canada and associated agencies, *Bill C-54, An Act to Promote Physical Activity and Sport*, which was ultimately passed by the House of Commons on June 18, 2002. Among other things, the Bill also establishes the Sport Dispute Resolution Centre of Canada, an independent organization whose mission is to provide the sport community with a national alternative-dispute-resolution service for sports disputes, and expertise and assistance in that regard.

The "life" of Bill C-54 is significant in the context of the ways in which government action actually becomes implemented. After Bill C-54's passage by the House of Commons, Bill C-12 (October 9, 2002) replaced Bill C-54 because the original Bill had not been passed by the Senate when Parliament adjourned for the fall. In its new form as Bill C-12, it received royal assent on March 19, 2003.

NATIONAL SPORT POLICY

The Canadian Sport Policy was developed by the federal government in 2002, after two years of consultation with various members of the sport community. They sought a general consensus on the purpose of a Canadian sport policy – how to manage and promote sport in such a vast and diverse country.

Consultation meetings were held to analyze and discuss related papers and surveys in order to cover all aspects of sport. These talks resulted in a general consensus that all levels and forms of sport are interrelated and therefore promoting one level or form would affect all others. It was also concluded that the development of sport relies on its promotion, in formal settings such as schools and community programs, as well as the promotion of physical activity in general.

The consultations also focused on several key issues in Canadian sport. Among these were the decline of physical activity in youth and the need to improve school sport programs. The policy reports revealed that participation decreases beginning at age twelve and the proportion of overweight boys and girls increases accordingly. Governments need to assess the quality and extent of physical education, the accessibility and use of sport facilities, and the environment for physical activity in schools across Canada. Moreover, the focus is on inclusion – where students from all social, linguistic, cultural, and economic backgrounds are encouraged to participate.

The policymakers identified four key areas that require promotion and support from all participants.

- *Enhanced participation.* To increase the level and quality of participation in school, community and sport organizations. The agreed-upon goal is to attain the broadest possible participation – with the inclusion of the full community – in high-quality, accessible sport programs. To do this, it will be necessary to:

  - promote physical activity through sport, with all its personal and social benefits;

  - support sport organization;

  - increase youth participation in school sports;

  - promote participation in community sports; and

  - ensure that all groups (especially those that are currently underrepresented) have access to sport programs.

- *Enhanced excellence.* To increase the number of talented athletes and teams performing at the highest levels of competition with consistently successful results. The goal is to establish a constant supply of world-class athletes, coaches, and officials competing under the highest standards of ethics.

- *Enhanced capacity.* It was also agreed that it was necessary to establish a sport system that allows for ongoing change as required. All levels of government will need to ensure that the services they provide meet the needs of their community and that sport is constantly being developed.

Cyclists ride past advertisement from the federal and provincial governments at the 2002 Women's Cycling World Cup Challenge in Montreal, Quebec (CP PHOTO/Paul Chiasson).

- *Enhanced interaction.* To create an interconnected sport system that benefits from collaboration among its participants, organizations, communities, and government. The policy states that all levels of sport are connected. To achieve this goal, the entire sport community will need to develop stronger relationships and partnerships.

The goal for full implementation of the Canada Sport Policy was set for 2012, but in the twenty-six-page policy document, only one page is devoted to how to go about doing this. The provincial and territorial governments have all agreed to the policy and are expected to devise action plans (both individually and collectively) to implement these lofty ideals. Progress will be monitored by each provincial minister responsible for sport. Following the Mills Report and the legislation, much remains to be done. The enormous amount of coordination of all the levels and forms of sport organizations and participants that would be involved in carrying through the sport policy's goals is yet to be realized.

The Sport Community

The sport system in Canada is made up of a number of organizations that provide sport programming and services at the national, provincial/territorial, and municipal levels. These groups serve either individual sports (single sport organizations), or cater to numerous sports sharing common needs (multi-sport and multi-service organizations). Basketball Canada would be an example of the former, while the Coaching Association of Canada or the Canadian Wheelchair Sport Association are examples of the latter.

These organizations receive support from various levels of government, according to the scope of their programs and services. For example, a local swim club may be funded by the municipality and participant fees, whereas the national swim team would be eligible to receive federal government funding. National sport organizations also obtain corporate financing through sponsorship agreements and generate revenue themselves through other sources including fundraising and membership fees.

National Sport Organizations (NSOs) are members of International Federations (IFs) that establish the rules of the sport and, among other things, determine where their respective international competitions will be held.

National Games Organizations, such as the Canadian Olympic Association (COC), belong to international games organizations (in the COC case, the International Olympic Committee), which are in turn the franchise holders for major games.

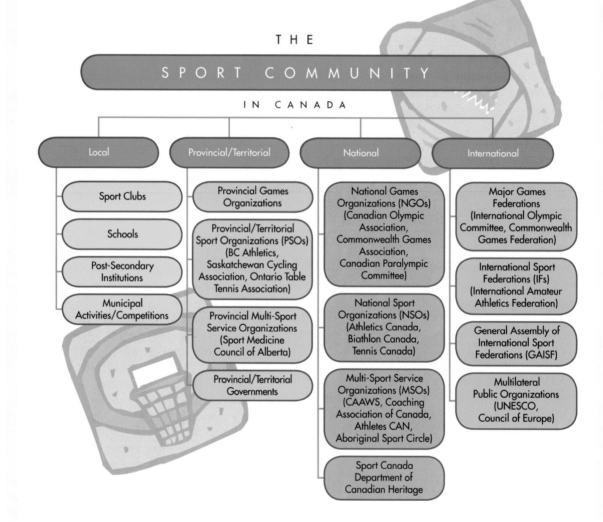

Figure 26.1: The sport community in Canada.

Adapted from *The Mills Report: Sport in Canada*, 1998.

ORGANIZATION OF SPORT IN CANADA

At the federal and provincial levels, the network or organizations through which sport is administered are complex and varied. The governance and management of sport in Canada is based on a complex and decentralized system that cuts across sport organizations and jurisdictional lines. While this system allows for far-reaching networks and opportunities for innovation and customized approaches at all levels, it also presents challenges with respect to concerted and coordinated efforts to get results.

One of the main thrusts of the recently adopted Canadian Sport Policy is that, for sport participation and high levels of athletic performance to flourish in Canada, the various administrative bodies charged with this responsibility will need to develop new and stronger partnerships among themselves and with the other stakeholders in sport. The main organizations are Sport Canada, the Canadian Olympic Committee, and the many national and provincial sport organizations and associations.

Sport Canada

Sport Canada, the major granting agency for sports in Canada, is located within the bureaucracy of the International and Intergovernmental Affairs Sector of Heritage Canada. Its major funding programs include the Athlete Assistance Program, which is "aimed at enhancing the Canadian high performance sport system" by funding athletes on a system known as carding. This means that, depending on the world ranking they have achieved, athletes qualify for financial support on a sliding scale.

Sport Canada is a permanent part of the Government of Canada. Its goals are to promote excellence in sports competition in order to demonstrate both the role of sports in maintaining a positive Canadian identity and also the positive role of culturally contributing athletic events. In order to achieve these goals, financial and policy support is provided to elite athletes and their coaches. Financing is also available for the system of sports achievement screening and development in partnership with community groups so that the athletes of tomorrow will be identified and trained for future competitions.

Sport Canada also seeks to portray sports in a favourable light for the Canadian population in order to maximize participation by ordinary citizens and thus to realize any potential health benefits that might be had. Sport Canada is also concerned with increasing access and equity in sports participation and, with this in mind, delivers support to targeted underrepresented social groups.

As already noted, in the Canadian Sports Policy, published in May 2002, the federal, provincial, and territorial governments and many other sports federations and agencies that stage, influence, and benefit from Canadian sports indicated a desire to open sports in Canada to participation by everyone who has the potential and the desire to contribute. The policy underlines the intention to improve the sports experience for all Canadians, and the coordinated efforts of all levels of government and the sports organizations themselves would be necessary. Sport Canada, the federal government's main instrument in this area, is at the forefront of this campaign across the country.

Canadian Olympic Committee

The Canadian Olympic Committee (COC), first recognized by the International Olympic Committee in 1907, is a private, non-profit corporation that represents Canada in the international Olympic sports movement. It is also the largest private-sector funder of elite sports in Canada.

The COC is responsible for all aspects of Canada's involvement in the Olympic Games as well as the Pan American Games. It manages a wide variety of programs that promote successful Canadian participation in these Games and also grassroots programs within Canadian communities that promote Olympic values and the sports careers of future national sporting representatives. The Committee also selects and supports Canadian sites for future Olympic Games such as the candidacy of Vancouver for the 2010 Winter Olympic Games.

The COC is one of the founding partners of the Canadian Sports Centres established by Sport Canada across the country in eight separate locations. These Centres serve to support elite athletes in many ways so that they can attain their highest potential in important international competitions. The Committee also promotes sport in general to the Canadian population as a positive and health-giving force for everyone.

The Canadian Olympic Committee has a large Board of Directors on which fifty-one Olympic and Pan American sports federation representatives are members, in addition to six members from the Athlete's Council Executive Committee (athletes elected by fellow athletes) and also a representative of coaches. Two members of the athlete representation are also members of the Board's sixteen-member Executive Committee.

According to its latest annual report, for the 2001-04 "Quadrennial" or four-year Olympic cycle, the Canadian Olympic Committee expected to give about $24 million to the National Sports Centres, National Sports

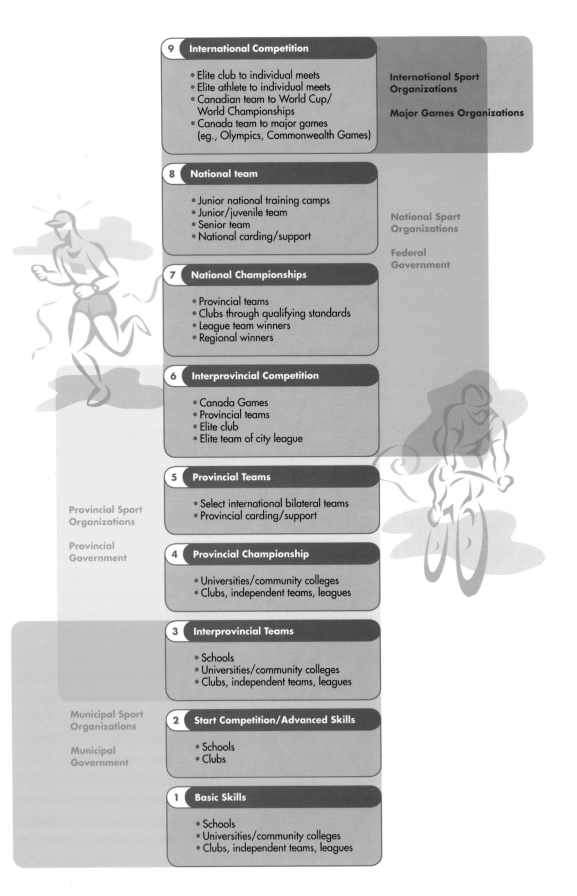

Figure 26.2: The sport delivery system in Canada.

Adapted from *The Mills Report: Sport in Canada*, 1998.

Federations, athletes, and coaches. During the same period, costs associated with Games Missions for the Olympic Winter Games, Pan American Games, and the Olympic Games are expected to be about $15 million. This money is raised from Olympic brand licensing, an endowment fund, and from private corporate donors for the most part.

The Canadian Olympic Committee received just over $53 million in surplus funds from the XV Olympic Winter Organizing Committee, which staged the 1988 Winter Games in Calgary. This fund is managed to provide ongoing revenues that are used in support of athletes and sport in general. As of the end of December 2000, the fund balance was $91 million.

National Sport Organizations (NSOs)

At the federal level, it is the National Sport Organizations (NSOs) that provide administrative expertise and technical support for the development of athletes and their participation in international competitions. These are not-for-profit organizations that service the various sports and are the principal means through which Sport Canada fosters sport, and especially elite sport, in Canada. Each NSO is responsible for performing its role to the best of its ability.

All major and many minor sports are represented at this level – for example, Skate Canada, Volleyball Canada, Tennis Canada, Judo Canada, Bobsleigh Canada, the Canadian Amateur Wrestling Association, Canada Basketball, the Canadian Table Tennis Association, and so on.

The NSOs are members of their respective International Federations and have leadership responsibility for sport participation and excellence throughout the country. Their main responsibilities are as follows:

- to organize, govern and regulate their sport;
- to provide essential services for athlete and coach development;
- to determine participation by Canadian athletes in international competitions;
- to represent Canadian sport in the international arena; and
- to collaborate with their provincial counterparts in the international development of their sport.

While the NSOs are autonomous in principle, in practice there is considerable federal government influence on the operations of the NSOs. This occurs because the federal government is a major source of revenue for these organizations. Between 1992 and 1996, for example, there were substantial funding cutbacks for sport at the federal level, following a 1992 task force that addressed sport funding and related issues. More recently, the federal government has arrived at a new approach to funding NSOs, which is referred to as the Sport Funding and Accountability Framework.

The Sport Funding and Accountability Framework (SFAF) has added an element of stability to federal funding, but the new framework has shifted the emphasis of government policy from funding all NSOs to funding only those meeting more stringent criteria. This, in turn, has placed pressure on many NSOs to find creative new ways to supplement their finances, such as corporate sponsorships and a more commercial focus to their operations.

Provincial Sports Organizations (PSOs)

Working in close liaison with the NSOs are the various provincial and territorial sport organizations. These Provincial Sport Organizations (PSOs) are volunteer-managed entities that form an intermediary between community sport organizations and national sport organizations. At the provincial level, they represent a critical link in sport development for athletes and participants in specific sports.

The provincial ministries work with these organizations to increase their self-reliance and organizational autonomy. They deliver coaching-theory training, leadership training, and other services to the sport and recreation community. They also foster measures to promote sport safety and minimize injuries, and provide resources to assist with equal opportunity and anti-harassment initiatives.

The functions of a PSO are normally outlined in policy documents developed by the various provincial governments. In the case of Ontario, for example, the role and functions of a PSO are outlined as follows:

- organize, coordinate and/or conduct training or certification for coaches (National Coaching Certification Program – Technical and Practical components), instructors, officials, trainers, club leaders, volunteers, and so on;
- oversee team selection processes, especially relating to Ontario and Canada Games;
- schedule, coordinate and/or organize sport competitions (competitions exist at house, club, district, regional, provincial, national, and international levels – the roles of any given PSO will vary according to the level and capacity of the PSO and the structure of the specific sport;
- coordinate and/or deliver athlete development programs, including clinics, training camps, coaching by provincial coaches and so forth, for levels from novice to national team (the degree of PSO involvement in each level varies according to the structure of the sport);

- coordinate and/or conduct information-sharing activities and advocacy for their sport;

- conduct public-information campaigns aimed at barrier removal, equal access, anti-harassment, drug free sport, or safety activities at the club and/or regional level;

- coordinate and/or deliver broad-based participation or grassroots development programs, including local and regional recruitment, talent identification programs, skills programs, "get started" programs, and so forth (again, the extent to which PSOs offer these programs will vary;

- maintain the capacity to deliver sport opportunities and to conduct the business of their sport – including planning, democratic decision-making processes (such as open annual meetings and elections), membership registration, fundraising, marketing, accounting, volunteer recruitment, development and awards, staff management, results management, and so on;

- provide differing levels of administrative support for their networks of clubs and/or regions and act as funding conduits to these levels (some PSOs also provide other support, such as equipment loans, to clubs and/or regional levels;

- act as focal points for volunteer activity in their sport and as clearing houses for all sport-specific information – volunteers, members, athletes, and coaches typically contact the PSO office first when seeking information beyond that which may be obtainable at a local club level; and

- act as a link between municipal, regional, and the national sport organizations who deal with Sport Canada.

Each of the provinces and territories in Canada has agencies that administer sports in their jurisdictions:

- Newfoundland and Labrador Department of Tourism, Culture and Recreation;

- Prince Edward Island Department of Education;

- Nova Scotia Sport and Recreation Commission;

- New Brunswick Department of Municipalities;

- Quebec Ministry of Health and Social Services;

- Ontario Department of Tourism and Recreation;

- Manitoba Department of Culture, Heritage and Recreation;

- Saskatchewan Department of Municipal Affairs, Culture and Housing;

- Alberta Department of Community Development;

- British Columbia Department of Small Business, Tourism and Culture;

- Yukon Department of Community and Transportation Services;

- Northwest Territories Department of Municipal and Community Affairs; and

- Nunavut Department of Community, Government and Transportation.

Again, taking Ontario as an example, responsibility for sports is located in the Sport and Recreation Division of the Ontario Department of Tourism and Recreation. Its interest is in promoting amateur sport in Ontario as an aspect of quality of life that builds personal excellence, teamwork, and generally better health, leading to, according to the Department, "higher productivity and a stronger social fabric." The PSOs are recognized by the provincial government and funded accordingly. In turn, these provincial sport associations serve over three million registered members and other participants.

Through the PSOs, the Province of Ontario supports a system of competitions from the community to national levels. Outstanding Ontario athletes and coaches are also recognized annually through the Ontario Sports Awards. Also honoured are the volunteers and corporate sponsors for their contributions to amateur sports in Ontario. The PSOs also sponsor coaching clinics and seminars, training for volunteers to work with young people, and preparation of new training materials.

Multi-Sport Service Organizations (MSOs)

Somewhat underrecognized, but critically important in the complex Canadian sport system, are the various Multi-Sport Service Organizations (MSOs) that exist to provide support and services across the various sport organizations. These important bodies, also funded mainly through Sport Canada, address the common needs of the different sport bodies and act in various ways to educate the general public and the sport community about issues and achievements.

Multi-Sport Service Organizations, such as the Coaching Association of Canada, the Canadian Centre for Ethics in Sport, and the Canadian Association for the Advancement of Women and Sport (CAAWS) work with international and provincial and/or territorial counterparts in the development and delivery of specific programs and levels of expertise in priority areas for sport in Canada. (The Coaching Association of Canada is discussed in more detail on page 373; the Centre for Ethics in Sport is described on page 168; and the objectives and work of the Canadian Association for the Advancement of Women and Sport are described on page 327.)

THE GAMES OF LA FRANCOPHONIE

La Francophonie is the international community of peoples who speak French or who may use it to various degrees, either in their own country or internationally. The Games of La Francophonie (Jeux de la Francophonie) are an international cultural and sporting event in which the states and governments of La Francophonie participate. It includes fifty-five participating states and governments. The Canadian participation in the Games of La Francophonie consists of three teams: Canada, Canada-Quebec, and Canada-New Brunswick. Canada's threefold representation is evidence of the historical and traditional importance that Quebec and New Brunswick attach to their Francophone roots.

The Games have a number of features that distinguish them from similar events. They are the only major international games where sports and cultural activities are presented in a competitive context – the Games of La Francophonie are the only international games where medals are awarded both for athletic and artistic competitions. This uniqueness showcases the originality of Francophone culture and the excellence of athletes from member states.

Francophonie must not be confused with Francophone. As in the case of the Commonwealth Games, the choice of athletes and artists who participate is based exclusively on excellence, regardless of whether they are Francophones, Anglophones, or Allophones (with neither French nor English as their mother tongue). The Games of La Francophonie are an international cultural and sporting event in which athletes and artists from Francophone, Anglophone, or Allophone countries participate.

There have been four Games of La Francophonie held to date:

- July 1989 Morocco (Rabat and Casablanca). Thirty states and governments of La Francophonie, with 1,800 participants.
- July 1994 France (Paris). Forty-three states and governments of La Francophonie, with 3,000 participants; Canadian delegation: 400.
- August 1997 Madagascar (Antananarivo). Thirty-six states and governments of La Francophonie, with 1,700 participants.
- July 2001, Canada (Ottawa-Hull). Fifty states and governments of La Francophonie, with 2,600 participants.

Building on the success of these previous Games, a fifth Games has been scheduled for Niger (Niamey) in 2004. The representative organizations in Canada will again be well represented at these games.

Jeux de La Francophonie Ottawa-Hull, 2001

Canada hosted the fourth Games of La Francophonie from July 14 to 24, 2001, in the Ottawa-Hull region. Over 3,000 athletes and artists from fifty-one states and governments attended the event. In addition to providing an exceptional platform for Canadian artists and athletes, the IV Games of La Francophonie in Canada provided an opportunity to combine Canadian Francophonie and the cultural wealth of the Francophone world.

The 2001 Games were a celebration of the French fact in North America – a forum for cultural and sport exchanges with the world. The Games also illustrated the benefits Canadians derive from their linguistic duality (official bilingualism) and from belonging to the International Francophonie.

As with previous Games, Canada's participation was ensured by three teams: Canada, Canada-Quebec, and Canada-New Brunswick. Nearly six hundred athletes, artists, coaches, health-care professionals, and team attendants were part of the Canadian delegation. Team Canada alone accounted for 300 people and won a record of forty-six medals.

As set in the Régles des Jeux de la Francophonie, the 2001 Games were organized and coordinated by a non-profit organization, the Committee of the La Francophonie Organizing Committee (COJF). The COJF was responsible for organizing sports and athletic competitions; hosting, providing accommodations and food; coordinating health services; local transportation; organizing the press centre, media relations, and public relations; organizing the opening and closing ceremonies; tourism promotion, promoting the Games in Canada; preparing competition sites, ensuring technical support; and accreditation and securing funding.

Events at the 2001 IV Jeux de la Francophonie, Ottawa-Hull

Sporting competitions	Cultural competitions
Handisport (men and women) (demonstration)	Busking (demonstration)
Athletics (men and women)	Song
Basketball (women)	Storytelling
Boxing (men)	Traditionally inspired dance
Judo (men and women)	Literature (poetry)
Soccer (men)	Painting
Table tennis (men and women)	Photography
Beach volleyball (men and women) (demonstration)	Sculpture

THE FEDERAL SPORT BUDGET

But just how much money does the federal government really spend in support of sport? In Canada, a look at the budget year 2000-01 is revealing. During that time, the federal government gave about $67 million to a wide variety of sports organizations in Canada. Some of these organizations were very small, and consequently received relatively small amounts of money.

In addition, Sport Canada gave approximately $15 million to individual athletes through the Athlete Assistance Program to help meet their living, training, and travel expenses. Without these support payments, many of the athletes who represent Canada in international competition would have to work at part- and full-time jobs unrelated to their sport, rely on the support of their parents, families, partners or spouses, or even drop out of their sport completely. Indeed, even with government funding, the sporting press is still filled with admissions by many amateur athletes that trying to forge a career in sports such as archery, canoe racing, cross-country skiing, or judo is very difficult in Canada and cannot be done without additional sources of income such as part-time work.

Other Funding Initiatives

The Canadian government is also behind a number of other funding initiatives, including:

- the National Sport Organization Support Program: "targeted to priority areas such as national team programming and the development of coaches and officials";
- the Sport Participation Development Program: "to help National Sport Organizations (NSOs) to increase ongoing participation and reduce the drop-out rates";
- the Multi-Sport/Multi-Service Organization Support Program, which assists delivery of programs and services to eligible sports organizations in their "pursuit of the sports objectives they share with the federal government." Recipients of this funding include such organizations as the Coaching Association of Canada and the Canadian Centre for Ethics in Sport.

Also receiving federal funds are the National Sports Centres Program in at least eight cities across the country and the Sport Hosting Program, which assists with operating funds for Canadian sport organizations that host single sport events in Canada.

In addition, Sport Canada funds major international sport gatherings, such as the Pan Am Games, the North American Indigenous Games, and the Arctic Winter Games.

In addition to these activities, which are directed towards Canadian success in international competition, Sport Canada is also charged with promoting athletic exercise among the Canadian population in order to realize health benefits. Most Canadians will have seen television commercials and heard radio spots for government-supported health and fitness initiatives such as "ParticipACTION," which aim to raise awareness of the importance of healthy living and exercise.

Hosting International Events

Governments also promote sport by hosting international events, helping organizations that promote awareness of sport and social issues, and providing support for international teams competing in events in other countries. The many events and initiatives promoted by Sport Canada in 2001-02 include:

- 2002 Olympic Winter and Paralympic Games (Salt Lake City, Utah);
- 2001 World Athletic Championships (Edmonton);
- Jeux de la Francophonie (Ottawa-Hull);
- the 18th Canada Games (London, Ontario);
- 2002 Arctic Winter Games (Iqaluit, jointly hosted with Nuuk, Greenland);
- Helping establish the headquarters of the World Anti-Doping Agency (Montreal) in 2001;
- National Summit of Sport, April 2001;
- Canadian Sport Policy and Federal-Provincial/Territorial Action Plan, April 2002; and
- Erection of a statue of Maurice (Rocket) Richard, Jacques Cartier Park in Gatineau, Quebec.

Sport Canada Finances

For the budget year 2001-02, Heritage Canada had 1,834 full-time employees and spent $1.1 billion, of which $850 million (78 percent) was dispersed as grants. Of this total departmental expenditure, the allocation to Sport Canada was $103 million in 2001-02, or about 10 percent of the total.

Among the Sport Canada non-program expenditures were $6.6 million to the Vancouver 2010 Bid Corporation to assist in planning for and promoting the bid for the 2010 Vancouver/Whistler Winter Olympic Games. In order to support its Sport Canada budget, Heritage Canada received $57 million in Federal-Provincial Lottery Agreement funds in 2001-02. Expenditure estimates for the fiscal year 2002-03 for Heritage Canada suggest a modest decline in total to $1.0373 billion in total, so it is safe to assume that Sport Canada's spending patterns remain about the same for the current period of time.

PROMOTING WOMEN IN CANADIAN SPORT

Prior to the 1920s, women only appeared in strictly limited sporting contexts such as fox hunting, croquet, golf, curling, and tennis, often as "lady associates" in predominantly male clubs and facilities. These ideas about the inappropriateness of sports for women have gradually faded away. For instance, women became prominent in figure skating, basketball, and softball beginning in the 1920s. The first female Canadian athlete appeared in the 1924 Winter Olympic Games in Chamonix France – figure skater Cecile Eustace Smith. The Women's Amateur Athletic Federation of Canada was formed in 1926.

The process was not without setbacks however. In the 1928 Amsterdam Olympic Games, which were boycotted by British women athletes protesting the small number of women's Olympic events, several women competitors in the 800-metre race collapsed at its conclusion. The event was then declared to be dangerous to women and was not run again by women competitors until 1960.

Royal Commission on the Status of Women

In 1970, the Report of the Royal Commission on the Status of Women in Canada was published. It contained recommendations addressing the lack of equal opportunity for girls in school sports programs. In 1972, Fitness and Amateur Sport Canada commissioned research on defining and solving these problems. But it was not until 1974 that the first National Conference on Women and Sport was held.

Throughout the 1970s provincial Human Rights legislation was used as a basis of equality-promoting lawsuits by several girls wishing to play on all-male teams. These cases raised public awareness. Finally, in 1980, the Government of Canada created a Women's Program within Sport Canada. Its first female Director was former Olympic athlete Abby Hoffman. Today, many of the barriers to athletic competition for women have been removed, though sports competition remains gender segregated for the most part.

One of the policy objectives that Sport Canada has in its mandate is to increase the participation of women in Canadian sport. It has attempted to use its influence whenever appropriate to draw in greater numbers of women athletes and officials at all levels from high visibility elite sports right down to community-based sports activities. These efforts are beginning to pay off, as shown in a study commissioned by Sport Canada in 1999. The following box provides some of the highlights of this survey. The full results are provided in the Sport Canada website listed at the end of this Unit.

Gender Representation
National team athletes

Overall, for thirty-seven federally funded NSOs, it was reported that there are 3,511 athletes on Canada's national teams:

- Women represent 47 percent (1,647 athletes) of the national teams.
- Men represent 53 percent (1,864 athletes) of the national teams.

Gender Distribution by Team Level

- **Senior teams:** (1,566 senior team members): 4 percent more are men than women – 816 (52 percent) are men; 750 (48 percent) are women.
- **Junior teams:** (715 junior team members): 2 percent more are men than women: 364 (51 percent) are men; 351 (49 percent) are women.
- **Developmental teams:** (1,230 team members): 12 percent more are men than women: 684 (56 percent) are men; 546 (44 percent) are women.

Coaching

NSOs were also surveyed on the gender representation in coaching. Equal representation of women and men is far from the case in any category. It is, however, closest for part-time and for non-head coaches.

- **Overall:** NSOs reported 257 coaches of which 83 percent (213) are men, and 17 percent (44) are women.
- **Head Coaches:** NSOs reported 107 full-time and part-time head coaches of which 84 percent (90) are men, and 16 percent (17) are women.
- **Other Coaches:** NSOs reported 150 full-time and part-time other coaches of which 82 percent (123) are men, and 18 percent (27) are women.
- **Full-Time Coaches:** NSOs reported 77 full-time coaches of which 91 percent (70) are men, and 9 percent (7) are women.
- **Part-Time Coaches:** NSOs reported 180 part-time coaches of which 79 percent (143) are men, and 21 percent (37) are women.

Canadian Women and Men as International Officials

NSOs were asked to provide information about types of officials and certification level for Canadian women and men. Essentially, the study found that Canadian men are more frequently represented than Canadian women at the international level as both head and other officials in international competition. Women are more likely to be represented as other officials rather than as head officials in international competition.

Youthful Talent
Great Canadians in sport

Canadian sports history is filled with tales of great competitors who have excelled while still young. Here is a look at just two of them.

Carling Bassett Seguso (tennis)

Born in 1967, Carling Bassett Seguso (who, before her 1987 marriage to fellow player Robert Seguso, competed as Carling Bassett) took the world of adult tennis by storm in the 1980s. She hailed from a prominent Canadian sports family (her father, the late John F. Bassett, formerly owned the Toronto Argonauts and Maple Leafs and played on Canada's Davis Cup tennis team in the 1950s), and, as a nine-year-old, cut her hair short and dressed in boys' clothes so she could sneak into an all-male competition.

Once Carling showed some early aptitude for the sport, her father enrolled her in the famous Nick Bollettieri Tennis Academy in Florida. By the age of fifteen, she had turned professional and soon competed in Wimbledon and other top women's tennis tournaments in North America and Europe. In 1984, she played two well-publicized matches in major tournaments against the American Chris Evert, then the world's number-two ranked player. She lost both matches but gained rave reviews from tennis experts worldwide for her gritty performances. In 1985, she attained her highest-ever world ranking with an eighth-place spot on the world chart. She was also the top-rated player in Canada from 1982 to 1986.

In 2001, Bassett Seguso was inducted into Canada's Sports Hall of Fame, becoming only the second tennis player ever to attain that honour.

Gajan Sivabalasingham (golf)

Since he is only eight years old, one might excuse Gajan Sivabalasingham for having dreams of becoming the next Tiger Woods, on the grounds that he is only indulging in a bit of youthful dreaming. Then again, you might consider the fact that the Markham, Ontario, resident – already known in golfing circles as "Little Tiger" – first broke par at the age of six.

Actually, Sivabalasingham has a number of excellent accomplishments that warrant comparison with the great American golfer. He learned the game from his accountant father, Marimuthu, and by the age of four, he had played his first eighteen-hole course. At six, he won the tournament that qualified Canadian players for the World Junior Championships – in the under-twelve division, no less – and already seems poised to be one of the country's top junior players even though he will not move into the senior ranks for about a decade.

GOVERNMENT SUPPORT FOR YOUTH IN SPORT

Leaving aside the performance of elite athletes in high-visibility international competition, the most important aspects of government programs for promoting sport are directed at young people. The hope is that a higher level of sports participation will encourage active and healthy lifestyles across the entire population through habits of exercise learned in childhood, and that uniquely talented individuals can be identified for further high-performance training with a view to improving Canada's national and international sports achievements.

To accomplish these goals, programs must be broad and involve all levels of government (school programs, municipal recreation programs, provincial competitions, and national team training and competition). All levels of government are thus involved in program delivery right down to the local school phys-ed program. Equipment budgets, teacher and coach salaries, and travel budgets are accounted for in many ways in the various government budgets involved.

At Sport Canada, the main program involved with spreading a sports culture in younger age groups is the Sport Participation Development Program. This program is intended to provide financial support to National Sports Organizations in their efforts to increase participation levels, recruit new participants, and reduce drop-out rates. Preference is given to projects that target children and youth, girls and young women, and underrepresented groups including Aboriginal people, people with disabilities, youth at risk, visible minorities, and economically disadvantaged individuals.

Examples of supported activities include the Jackrabbit program, which seeks to increase participation in cross-country skiing; flag football Outreach, which exists in more than 1,100 schools across the country with about 300,000 participants; a national youth rowing program; and Volleyball at School. Other examples include Aqua Fun, a synchronized swimming program for teens and adults; the Baseball School Initiation Program, currently being tested in 200 schools in Ontario and Quebec; Run Jump Throw, which is an introductory athletics program for young people in Alberta; and Kids of Steel, a triathlon program for children aged seven to nineteen.

Because Sport Canada aims to promote long-term sport when funding a program, it takes into consideration its sustainability, the possibility for "strategic partnerships," and its impact on participation levels. Consequently, successful programs need to have an official evaluation process – what Sport Canada calls performance indicators, targets, and outcomes.

ABORIGINALS AND SPORT

Sport Canada also supports a number of initiatives to encourage and foster sports participation among Canada's rapidly growing and very young Aboriginal population. For instance, there is the Aboriginal Sports Circle, Canada's national voice for Aboriginal sport. Established in 1995, the Aboriginal Sports Circle promotes indigenous games and traditional approaches to amateur sport. Although most Canadians are familiar with lacrosse, other pre-Columbian sports survive to this day and have been revived and fostered as a result of the Circle's work. The Circle pays to bring Aboriginal athletes together from across the country each year to participate in training in a high-performance environment. It also sponsors the National Aboriginal Hockey Championships and the National Aboriginal High Performance Hockey Camp. It brings together the interests of First Nations, Inuit and Métis peoples, and fosters more accessible and equitable sport and recreation opportunities for Aboriginal peoples in Canada (see box).

Arctic Winter Games

The Arctic Winter Games are another such initiative. The idea for the games began in 1967 in conjunction with the Canada Winter Games held that year in Quebec City, in which athletes from the Yukon and Northwest Territories faired poorly as a result of inadequate facilities and training in northern communities. As a consequence, the governments of Canada, Yukon, and the State of Alaska organized a Winter Games in Yellowknife in 1968. Northern Quebec joined the games in 1972 for a few years, and Northern Alberta joined in 1986. The site of the Games typically rotated between Yellowknife, Whitehorse, and Fairbanks, Alaska. Representatives from other countries started to attend in 1990. Athletes and cultural performers have attended from Russia and Greenland.

In 2002, the XVII Arctic Winter Games were co-hosted by Nuuk, Greenland, and Iqaluit, Nunavut. Over 1,600 athletes, coaches, mission staff, officials and cultural performers took part.

Other departments of government and private donors have undertaken supportive projects as well. One such initiative was a grant of $409,000 from Human Resources Development Canada (HRDC) made to the Manitoba Aboriginal Sports and Recreation Council in 1999. Private companies such as UPS have been heavily involved too. Through the UPS Olympic Sports Legacy Program, thousands of pieces of sports equipment have been delivered to recreation organizations including many in rural Aboriginal communities across Canada.

Voices of Aboriginal Sport
Native success stories

Since the days of the champion long-distance runner Tom Longboat at the turn of the century (see page 301), there have been a number of great Canadian sporting figures of Native descent. Let us look at two recent examples.

Ted Nolan (hockey coach)

As a hockey coach, it was always Ted Nolan's dream to make it to the big time; that is, to coach an NHL team. As the highly successful coach of the junior powerhouse team the Sault Ste. Marie Greyhounds in the early 1990s, it certainly looked as though that dream would one day come true. And indeed it did – Nolan was signed on by the NHL's Buffalo Sabres and was given charge of the team. He responded brilliantly, and, in 1996-97, won the Jack Adams Award as the league's coach of the year as a result of guiding the Sabres to the Northeast Division title before losing to the Flyers in the Eastern semifinals. At the end of that season, however, he was offered a one-year contract extension that he declined, since he found such a short-term offer "insulting." Certainly, most coach-of-the-year award winners have been able to parlay their successes into more lucrative deals. Nolan, though, was not so lucky – and has not coached in the professional ranks since leaving the Sabres. He still has an impact on the game, though, as he awaits his next NHL assignment. He maintains a full schedule of motivational speaking, often to Native audiences, works with a First Nations hockey program, and helps to run a foundation that assists Canadian Aboriginal women.

Alwyn Morris (kayak)

Olympic champion in kayaking at the 1984 Summer Games in Los Angeles, Alwyn Morris celebrated his win by holding aloft an eagle feather to honour his Mohawk heritage. Born in 1957 in the Mohawk community of Kahnawake, Morris was profoundly influenced by his grandfather, who had been an outstanding lacrosse and hockey player. Canadian kayaking legend has it that, in 1968, when the two watched action from the 1968 Mexico City Olympics together, the eleven-year-old Alwyn "promised" his grandfather that he would one day compete in the Games. However, as a youth, Morris was considered to be too small and thin to be a good kayaker, and several coaches and athletes told him to forget about a career in the sport. He persevered, though, eventually making the 1980 Olympic team (though not travelling to the Games because of the American-led boycott that year) and then winning the gold in 1984, along with a bronze in the two-man race. Now retired, Morris still lives in Kahnawake and is active in politics and community affairs in the Mohawk community.

Arnold "Arnie" Boldt
Canadian disabled sport pioneer

Sport for people with disabilities has advanced tremendously over the past three decades. But it is likely that this branch of sport would not be nearly as advanced – in Canada and the rest of the world – without the efforts of a farm boy-turned-high jumper named Arnold "Arnie" Boldt.

Born on September 16, 1957, Boldt lost his right leg at the age of three in an accident with farm equipment. He will always be remembered as the man who high-jumped an incredible 2.08 metres – on only one leg. No other amputee jumper has come anywhere close.

In his prime in the mid-1970s and early-1980s, Boldt competed in Canadian university meets (he attended the universities of Saskatchewan and Manitoba) and in international competition against able-bodied athletes to find the right level of competition. He always maintained that the only way to improve as an athlete is to compete against those who are better.

Boldt won his first Paralympic gold medal in 1976. That year, the Games (then known as the Olympiad for the Disabled) were held in Toronto, and in addition to winning the high jump, he also set a world record in that event. What is more, Boldt captured the gold medal in the long jump with another world record in the 1976 event.

Boldt also won gold in these jumping events at the Canadian Games for the Physically Disabled in 1977 and 1978. By 1980, he was clearing the incredible height of 2 metres, and jumped 2.08 metres at an indoor meet that year. In the same year, Boldt won both jumping events in the Olympiad in the Netherlands.

During his extensive athletic career, Arnie Boldt also competed in wheelchair basketball and volleyball, where his superb jumping ability was a huge asset. He went on to a career in educational administration when his competitive days ended.

As one of the very few athletes – indeed, he is perhaps the only one in sporting history – who have competed at the top levels of both disabled and able-bodied sport, Boldt is in a unique position to comment on the value of disabled sport. "The quality of the training and the dedication of the athlete has really improved," he told *Amputee-Online* magazine. "People take things a lot more seriously especially at the international level." Boldt also notes that governments – such as Canada's – are much more willing to support disabled athletes in training and international competition, unlike in his day.

For his amazing achievements in sport, Arnie Boldt has been inducted into both the Saskatchewan Sports Hall of Fame and the Canadian Sports Hall of Fame.

SPORTS AND THE DISABLED

The Canadian Paralympic Committee (CPC), a private non-profit charitable corporation, is the Canadian representative to the International Paralympic Committee that organizes world games for the disabled in parallel to the Olympic Games. Its foundations were laid in 1976 when the federal government first donated funds for the fifth Paralympic Games in Toronto. The money was to be used for the purpose of developing competitive sports events for athletes with a disability. The World Paralympics, like the Olympic Games, are held every four years and attract disabled competitors from around the world.

National multi-sport games for Canadian disabled athletes began in 1987 in Brantford, Ontario, and are now held every two years. Winter Paralympic Games were added in 1988 and involve sports such as skiing. In 1993, disabled athletes were included in the regular Canada Winter Games for the first time in Kamloops, B.C. The CPC continues to be a social movement that works on behalf of the community of athletes with a disability with the financial support of governments and private donors.

The Special Olympics

Another entirely separate organization, Special Olympics Canada, runs counterpart Games for persons with mental disabilities. Each province and territory has its own local organization and sports events. Originally formed as an activity of the Joseph P. Kennedy Jr. Foundation, Special Olympics organizations can now be found in many countries.

In the summer of 2003, approximately 7,000 mentally disabled athletes from around the world are expected to gather in Dublin, Ireland. Participation in sports clearly enriches the lives of these Canadians and encouraging such participation receives financial support from Sport Canada.

In fact, Special Olympics programs help more than one million people in more than one hundred and fifty countries to compete and train year-round in sports. The organization's Olympic Oath, "Let me win. But if I cannot win, let me be brave in the attempt," illustrates its underlying spirit and commitment to helping mentally handicapped athletes to become physically fit and respected members of society. By 2005, Special Olympics organizers estimate that the number of people helped by these training and competition programs will have doubled to more than two million. Currently, the worldwide Olympics competition consists of twenty-six Olympic or "Olympic-type" (events modified for people with disabilities) events, a number that is also constantly on the rise as persons with disabilities develop more and more athletic skills.

Government Impacts on Sport
Advertising, taxation, subsidies, and extensive regulation

As a matter of policy, Sport Canada seeks to involve as many young people, women, and Aboriginal people as possible in active sports activities in the various communities across Canada. But beyond this policy role, government is in evidence in the world of sport in many ways, some more obvious than others.

Image Advertising

Through its various image advertising campaigns, the familiar Canada wordmark (the word Canada with a flag flying from the "d"), appears at various sporting events across the country. Sometimes it is on the boards at hockey rinks and sometimes on the barriers at Formula 1 and CART car races. It has become a familiar presence, which the federal government hopes will remind citizens of Canada that their government is an active participant in support of sporting events of all sorts.

Tax Revenues for Governments

The relationship between government and sporting organizations is not entirely one way. Various levels of government receive tax revenues from sales of tickets at the gate, from special amusements taxes, from sales tax at the food and beverage concessions, and tax revenues from the sale of team memorabilia and replica uniform clothing. In addition, the salaries of professional athletes, like those of everyone else, are subjected to personal income taxation, though, for the elite athlete, the tax bite might be incomparably larger than for the average citizen. (One common complaint of American professional athletes who sign on to play with a Canadian professional team is that their taxes are much higher, proportionally, than those of their counterparts who play for teams based in U.S. cities.)

Governments also benefit directly from sports betting, through the various government lottery monopolies that have branched out into such vehicles as Sports Select and PRO-LINE.

Montreal's heavily subsidized Olympic Stadium, home of the 1976 Summer Olympics and the Expos (CP PHOTO/Andre Forget).

Violence on the Playing Surface

Another overlap between government and sport occurs in the criminal courts. Occasionally, the violence in places such as hockey rinks rises to the level necessary for criminal charges to be laid, especially when serious injuries occur or where the assault was particularly vicious or dire threats were made.

This level has been exceeded in player-on-player fights, player-on-spectator battles, and of course, fan-on-fan assaults.

Advertising Regulation

Tobacco advertising is another area of overlap. Where once tobacco and alcoholic beverage advertisers happily provided the secure financial backbone of commercial sponsorships for sporting events (and nowhere were they more in evidence than at car races), legal restrictions on the advertising of tobacco and alcoholic beverages both at athletic events and on television coverage of those sporting spectacles have had a serious effect on the budgets of sports promoters.

While breweries and distillers can still advertise brands and the corporate image (if not displayed on an actual bottle or can, and if not showing actual human consumption), tobacco manufacturers have been subject to a much more severe regulation verging on total prohibition. These restrictions were put in place in the interests of promoting public health by removing tobacco brand logos from any positive association with potential role models such as elite professional athletes.

Subsidies and Tax Expenditures

Governments participate in the economics of sport in other ways too, sometimes by providing public investment in stadium facilities (e.g., installing the water and sewer connections, building access roads and parking lots), sometimes by granting forgivable loans, which do not have to be repaid if certain conditions are met, or by guaranteeing loans that would not be granted otherwise, and sometimes by providing favourable property evaluations on team facilities. Buildings may be exempt from city property taxes, for instance, if the organization is charitable in nature.

Crossing the Border to Play

Yet another dimension in which the federal government has a presence is in the area of immigration law and the issuing of work permits. Citizens of other countries are often invited to play their sports in Canada. In many cases, especially where amateur sports are involved, an application for a tourist visa may be all that is involved. But with elite athletes, that is often not the case.

An American football player coming to play in the CFL, for instance, may not only be subject to league quotas on foreign nationals on the team but also to immigration regulations. Any previous conviction for a criminal charge can put anyone applying for temporary or permanent residence for the purposes of playing in Canada in some difficulty.

Wagering on Sports
A Canadian timeline

Canada has a tradition of sports wagering, which includes betting that has been sponsored – or at least permitted – by provincial and federal governments for the purposes of raising revenue.

- **Pre-1969:** All gambling on sporting events (with the exception of pari-mutuel betting at horse racing tracks where bettors have to be physically present) were illegal. However, Canadians bet on sporting events discretely on a personal basis or with small illicit book-making businesses. Governments and sports organizations did not share in the take, except at horse racing tracks.

- **1969:** Amendments to the Criminal Code of Canada legalize gambling and give provinces authority to operate lottery schemes and casinos, to license charitable or religious organizations to operate specific lottery schemes. It is intended that sports organizations amongst others should benefit from revenue generated.

- **1970-73:** Provinces establish lottery licensing boards.

- **1974-76:** The Western Canada Lottery Foundation is established (Manitoba, Alberta, Saskatchewan and British Columbia) to jointly administer betting activities. The Inter-Provincial Lottery Corporation is created through an act of the Ontario legislature, and shortly after receives a federal corporate charter.

- **1978-79:** The province of Quebec joins the Inter-Provincial Lottery Corporation in 1978. The Atlantic Provinces join in 1979. The federal government withdraws from the lottery field altogether. Licensing is broadened to include more charitable organizations.

- **1980:** All provincial lotteries brought under one administrative roof.

- **1985:** An agreement is signed between provincial and federal governments whereby the provinces pay the federal government a continuing annual fee from gaming revenues. The Criminal Code is amended removing the legal right of the federal government to operate lotteries.

- **1989:** North America's first year-round continental-style casino, the Crystal Casino, opens in the Fort Garry Hotel in Winnipeg.

- **1990:** Sports wagering introduced.

- **1990-present:** Sports wagering is introduced in the form of games such as Sports Select and PRO-LINE.

SPORTS FINANCE: THE GOVERNMENT LOTTERY AND SPORTS WAGERING BUSINESS

An important source of funds for Sport Canada – some 55 percent of its entire budget in fact – is the annual transfer of lottery revenues from the provincial lotteries to the federal government. Internationally, this is nothing unusual, as many countries around the world rely on lottery money to support sport on all levels. In Canada, these transfers are paid in return for the withdrawal of the federal government from the lotteries field and for the liberalization of the Criminal Code provisions on gambling, both of which occurred many years ago. However, the history of how lotteries, sport, and the government interact reveals a lot about how these sources of sport funding have been managed over time (see box on this page).

PRO-LINE

In publicly available games such as **Sports Select** and **PRO-LINE**, Canadian bettors can place bets online on a limited selection of hockey, football, basketball, and baseball games. These "games" are run by the government lottery boards and generate funds for the lottery commissions and thus indirectly for sports organizations. No such money goes directly to professional sports teams, at least for now. The province of Alberta did raise the possibility of holding a special lottery for the benefit of the two Alberta NHL hockey teams that are both in financial difficulties.

Straightforward "sports book" betting of a commercial non-charitable nature, though not legal in Canada, is available to online bettors on the Internet. The books are run from places where bookmaking is legal, such as the State of Nevada.

Lotto Dollars for Sport

The federal government, under an agreement dated September 23, 1979, with the **Inter-Provincial Lottery Corporation**, withdrew from the lottery field in exchange for payment of $24 million annually beginning in 1979. In other words, the Canadian government agreed to allow private corporations to run lotteries, in exchange for a remittance of funds by these private lottery organizations.

The value of this grant has been increased over time to reflect the effects of price inflation, so that by 2001, the amount of the transfer was $56.8 million. A large part of the gaming revenue that remains after the transfer to Sport Canada is paid to the general revenue funds of each of the provinces.

For instance, the Saskatchewan Lotteries Trust Fund for Sport, Culture and Recreation received net profits from the Western Canada Lottery of $45 million on total gaming sales of $128.5 million in 2001. Of this total, $15 million was paid to the federal government ($1.8 million), former distributors ($1.5 million), the general revenue fund of Saskatchewan ($12.2 million), and the Saskatchewan Exhibition Association ($310,000). Of the remainder, $26.1 million was approved (but not necessarily paid out) as grants. Actual grants paid out to Saskatchewan sports organizations totaled $10.1 million in 2001.

In other provinces, the distribution of gaming revenues can be quite different. For example, in New Brunswick, most of the net proceeds go directly into general government revenues with only a small amount (in this province, $500,000) going to the Sports Development Trust Fund. This amount was less in total than the Lotteries Commission of New Brunswick spent for gambling addiction education and treatment ($558,570).

NOT A SIMPLE GAME TO PLAY

In this section, we have seen a number of ways in which governments can – and do – have an impact on the sporting life of a nation. In particular, we have examined many of the ways in which the Canadian government has influenced sport and sport policy in this country.

This section by no means exhausts the list of the various ways in which economic and policy-based advantages can be conveyed to or withdrawn from sports organizations by governments. But whether through various programs that support sport, foregone tax revenue, the conveyance of lottery funds, direct subsidies, or the rental of advertising space, the public through its governments does participate in supporting sport in a multitude of ways, some obvious and some not so obvious. Most Canadians are pleased and proud when a national team or an elite athlete does well in international competition. But many do not realize that their tax dollars contributed in no small way to making those successes and also the inevitable spectacular failures possible.

Without government financial and organizational support, most of what we now know as a thriving sporting culture in Canada would collapse. Even at the community level, assistance, perhaps for the most part unseen and unacknowledged, is at work keeping facilities in playing condition, paying to keep the lights on, paying for officials to supervise games and safeguard the well-being of the players, and keeping the necessary equipment in good working order.

Whether these funds come from a city government as part of a recreation budget, from a grant from Sport Canada, or from a provincial lottery authority, governments underwrite and organize the unpaid work of sports volunteers as well.

Kenyan runner Joseph Maina wins the Casino Niagara International Marathon in 2002 (CP PHOTO/Dan Dakin).

Government aid to sport in Canada is not only seen at international competitions or in the arenas and stadiums of professional sport. It is everywhere where games are played in Canada – in the public tennis and basketball courts, in community arenas across the country, and in all the other places where Canadians follow their favourite sporting pastimes.

WHERE DO WE GO FROM HERE?

This section on the role of governments and sport concludes this examination of the evolution of sport and physical activity, but it does not mark the end of the exploration of the role of exercise in a larger, collective context.

In the following Unit, we will examine several key aspects of how sport has an impact on society in the areas of economics and commerce, community and school initiatives, and ethical and/or moral dilemmas that affect individuals and groups. Keep in mind many of the concepts you have learned in this section as you move into the final Unit on social issues in sport and physical activity.

27
Careers and Websites

"Serious sport has nothing to do with fair play. It is bound up with hatred, jealousy, boastfulness, disregard of all rules and sadistic pleasure in witnessing violence: in other words it is war minus the shooting."
— George Orwell, British novelist, *The Sporting Spirit,* 1945

Below is a guide to the many career choices that are available to those who are interested in specializing in one or more of the areas covered in this unit. On the following page are website links that you will find useful in connection with the many topics touched on in the unit.

CAREER OPPORTUNITIES

- **Sports Journalist**

  Given the vast array of sporting events available through media, it is not surprising that there are many ways in which people can contribute to the dissemination of information about them. Reporters, photographers, website developers, editors, and many others play central roles in ensuring that information about sports reaches wide audiences through TV, newspapers, radio, the Internet, and magazines.

- **Sports Historian/Archivist**

  As a key aspect of Canadian culture, it is important to maintain a record of sport's statistics and stories. Sports historians and archivists are employed by sport leagues, halls of fame, and institutions such as universities to keep an accurate record of sporting events and personalities, and to organize and make these records available to those wishing to access them for research purposes.

- **Sports Agents/Lawyers**

  As intermediaries in the financial dealings of large sport organizations (i.e., professional teams and leagues) and athletes, agents and lawyers play a key role in negotiating contracts, endorsement deals, and collective agreements between players' unions and owners.

- **Advocates/Activists**

  For some groups in Canadian society, many sports remain inaccessible. Sport advocates and activists work on behalf of these groups to raise awareness of their exclusion from sport, or simply to encourage sport organizers to include them. While many advocates and/or activists work alone (i.e., a young girl struggling to be allowed to play on a boy's team), many attempt to represent large numbers in excluded groups.

- **University and/or College Professor**

  In many areas of academic life, there is a need for researchers and instructors who specialize in aspects of sports, health, and physical activity. These professors further understanding in their fields by publishing their findings in books and journals, and introduce students in Canada each year to new concepts in fields such as kinesiology, sport history, and physiology.

- **Government Sport Agency Staff**

  In Canada, provincial and federal agencies take care of most of the administrative details of Olympic and amateur sport. These agencies require directors and other staff who work in such areas as providing funding for athletes, securing corporate sponsorship, hiring coaches and trainers, and promoting a given sport to both participants and spectators.

- **Facility Manager/Director**

  Any large sports facility, such as a tennis club or skating rink, requires a manager or director to coordinate community programs and special events. These individuals must serve both the needs of the athletes and coaches who use the facilities, and those of the larger community.

- **Sports/Adventure Tourism Managers**

  An increasingly popular field of tourism, sports/adventure tourism brings people together for excursions that have some form of physical activity – hiking, mountain climbing, cycling, and so forth – as their focus. Those who organize, manage, and lead such tours need a thorough knowledge of the sports involved, both from the physical and social perspective, to ensure the safety and enjoyment of tourists.

- **Multi-Sport Competition Organizers**

  Communities benefit from large, multi-sport competitions, such as the Canada Games, Commonwealth Games, the Olympics, and many other events of a smaller scale, but require an enormous number of people, both paid and volunteer, to organize them. As such, these organizing teams need to comprise persons with a wide range of expertise, from technical specialists in the actual sports, to those skilled in sport promotion, media relations, facilities management and maintenance, and food and beverage supply.

USEFUL WEB LINKS

The URLs for these websites were active at the time this book went to press. For an up-to-date listing check the supporting student workbook or the website for this textbook: www.thompsonbooks.com/hpe.

- **Canadian Hertiage – Sport Canada**
  www.pch.gc.ca
  The official site of the Canadian government's heritage department, the section dealing with sport covers almost every aspect of the Canadian government's involvement in sport, from its history to current government policy. Although it is extremely heavy in content, this site is well-organized by topic and easy to navigate.

- **Canadian Association for the Advancement of Women and Sport and Physical Activity**
  www.caaws.ca
  "CAAWS is in business to encourage girls and women to get out of the bleachers, off the sidelines, and onto the fields and rinks, into the pools, locker rooms and board rooms of Canada." To that end, this site contains a vast array of information about women's sport in Canada and around the world, including an excellent archive of profiles, news items, and historical narratives, and highlights of the latest resources pertaining to women's sport.

- **AthletesCAN**
  www.athletescan.com
  AthletesCAN is the organization that represents Canadian national team athletes in all sports. As such, its official website contains a large amount of information on government support for elite athletes, the history of Canadian participation in international competition (Olympics, Commonwealth Games, and so on), and details on how athletes can qualify and compete for various government- and private-sector funding initiatives that support training and competition.

- **North American Society for Sport History (NASSH)**
  www.nassh.org
  The mission of NASSH is to "to promote, stimulate, and encourage study and research and writing of the history of sport." Consequently, the organiza-

tion's website provides information for those studying sport at all levels. Especially useful to those doing online research is the site's "Related Links" component.

- **The Olympic Movement (Official Site)**
  www.olympic.org
  Billing itself as the "Official website of the Olympic Movement" this site covers – in an especially thorough way – all aspects of the Olympic experience, from its guiding philosophy, to organizing principles, to the more "hands-on" aspects of individual sports, athlete profiles, and lists of sports and Games locations throughout history. Of course, a good deal of the site is currently devoted to providing information about the upcoming 2004 Games in Athens.

- **The Commonwealth Games (Official Site)**
  www.commonwealthgames.com
  This site, the official presence of the Commonwealth Games on the Internet, contains a vast array of information about the Games, including its history, a list of countries that compete in them, and a comprehensive explanation of the basic philosophy behind the event. For those interested in a more detailed, sport-by-sport breakdown of results, the site also has records of individual events arranged chronologically, from the first Games in 1930 to the present.

- **The Special Olympics Public Website**
  www.specialolympics.org
  The Special Olympics website has information about all aspects of this worldwide initiative. This includes the Special Olympics mission statement, its overall philosophy of competition and participation, as well as information about Special Olympics activities around the world, from competition on a community level to international events run by the organization. Specific information about the 2003 Special Olympics international games – to be held in Ireland – can be found at: www.specialolympics.com.

- **Canadian Sports Halls of Fame**
  www.canadiansport.com/halloffame.html
  There are many sports halls of fame throughout Canada, for which this site acts as a comprehensive clearinghouse. Users can search by sport or by province, and each site offers a varying degree of historical information on both the halls themselves, and the athletes who have been inducted into them. Of particular interest is the website of the Canadian Hockey Hall of Fame and Museum, located in Toronto (www.hhof.com), a virtual online "shrine" to Canada's favourite sport.

Pierre Leuders (front) and Giulio Zardo push off their sled during the third run of the two-man bobsled event at Utah Olympic Park during the 2002 Winter Olympics (CP PHOTO/HO/COA/Mike Ridewood).

UNIT 5

SOCIAL ISSUES IN PHYSICAL ACTIVITY AND SPORT

Silken Laumann competing in the singles rowing event at the 1992 Olympic Games in Barcelona, Spain (CP PHOTO/ COA/Ted Grant).

28
Principles & Terminology

"Sport has infiltrated the great social institutions of family, school, municipality, and private enterprise, and it has ... become one of the great social phenomena of the twentieth century."
— Gaston Marcotte and René Larouche, *Coaching: A Profession in the Making*, 1991

In Unit 4, we began to look at how sport and physical activity can have far-reaching community and social effects, beginning with an historical overview of the field, and progressing through an analysis of the role of women in, and government support for, these areas. In doing so, we created a basic framework for looking at sport and physical activity as a collective phenomenon – that is, as something that has broad implications for communities, societies, and even nations.

In this Unit, we will continue our examination of sport and physical activity, beginning with an analysis of the ways in which sport has combined with the powerful forces of business and the media (Section 29), to produce a situation in which unprecedented levels of information are available to the sports fan – a scenario in which enormous amounts of money are changing hands through player salaries, endorsement contracts, and the sale of broadcasting rights to television networks.

In contrast to this profit-driven system, we will also examine the status of sport in schools and at the community level (Section 30). These non-profit sectors are organized differently than the business-driven models of sporting organizations and we will examine their impact on the larger society.

Finally, in Section 31, we will take a look at some of the "tough issues" of sport in examining how social problems have spilled over into sports – and witness how sport can, in turn, further problems in society through violence (both among players and fans); cheating (in a wide array of forms); and drug use.

IMPORTANT TERMINOLOGY

There are several important concepts and terms that are introduced in this unit. Before continuing, let us examine some of them.

Community. Although it is difficult to precisely define the term, "community" is a concept that defines any group of people that gather because of a common interest – which includes, of course, sports and activities. Sports can define and unify a community; when young people and their families get together on a regular basis for hockey, baseball, or soccer, for example, they can be said to be forming a community around their chosen sport. Facilities such as community playing fields or a swimming pool can provide an important source of interaction within that community.

Entertainment and/or leisure. A certain amount of time of our lives each day must be devoted to certain obligatory tasks, with work, school, and family obligations being the three most common. Since the early part of this century, however, most study and work schedules have evolved to allow time for activities undertaken for the purposes of entertainment, recreation, or relaxation. Leisure activities play an important role in any society as they offer an opportunity for members to improve their health and fitness, to de-stress from the pressures of daily life, and to interact with like-minded individuals in a positive way. An examination of whether people choose to spend their leisure time as spectators or as participants, for example, tells us something about their communities and what these communities generally regard as being important.

Social mobility and class. One of the enduring concepts within the study of sport and society is the idea that, through success in sport, individuals or groups can increase their standing in society in terms of social class and wealth. This is a particularly prevalent notion in the context of the relationship between sport and big business (examined in Section 29), where entrepreneurs set out to use sport specifically to make money for themselves. It also applies at the level of the individual athlete, who if successful in a popular sport stands to earn large sums of money. Unfortunately, although it is possible for this to happen, the odds are very long that any one person will actually become a highly paid professional athlete. Dreams of these huge boosts in social class or income from sport participation are a lot more common than their occurrence.

Sport can and does, however, often act as a great social equalizer by bringing together people from all walks of life in support of a common sporting goal, such as the desire to urge on a favourite pro team.

While this is true in the sense of an entire country rallying to cheer for a World Cup soccer team (or a city such as Toronto, Edmonton, or Vancouver unifying to support a NHL hockey team in the playoffs), it should also be remembered that this can also help to obscure persistent economic or class differences in society. For example, people attending a live sporting event at the Air Canada Centre, the Northlands Coliseum, or General Motors Place will quickly find that the "best" seats in the stadium – those closest to the action – cost the most and are affordable only to a small fraction of the crowd.

Ethical behaviour. Throughout this Unit, and most notably in Section 31, we will examine a number of what are termed "ethical problems" in sport. Although most people understand what is meant by "ethical" behaviour, sport is a field in which its has a wide range of meanings. For example, one definition of ethics as it pertains to sport holds that obeying the rules of a sport – both on the playing surface and off it – represents ethical behaviour. All sports have both regulations that govern the way in which they are played (e.g., do not touch the ball with your hands in soccer; a touchdown is worth six points in football; you cannot run with the ball in basketball; and so forth) and other rules about conduct that takes place off the playing surface (e.g., you cannot ingest performance-enhancing drugs; athletes in strictly amateur sports cannot accept prize money; and so on). In this definition, you are acting ethically as long as you do not contravene these rules.

Another definition of ethics as it pertains to sport stipulates that the rules of sports are far less relevant than other considerations. In Section 21, "Coaching Principles and Practices," we looked at the concept of fair play and examined how it influences athletes and coaches. In this context, the treatment of one's teammates and opponents is the most important yardstick with which to measure ethical behaviour. For example, the practice of "trash talking" – insulting your opponent – is not expressly prohibited in many sports, and there is no penalty for it. But in the principle of fair play, such an approach demonstrates a lack of respect for the opponent, and by implication, for one's teammate and the competitive endeavour in general. Such an action is considered "unethical" in this definition.

The athlete as worker. Given the publicity that surrounds the world of high-profile sport in the various professional sports leagues in North America and Europe, or in the Winter and Summer Olympic Games, it is sometimes difficult to remember that, in the strictest sense, athletes fill the role of "worker" or "labourer" in the system of economic exchange that governs many sports. Through their training and competition, athletes expend considerable energy,

develop highly honed skills, and are faced with the daily responsibility of keeping themselves in top condition so that they may continue to ply their trade – all characteristics of modern workers in "regular" jobs in factories, offices, and the like. Professional athletes also find their day-to-day activities governed to some extent by their employers (usually team owners or sponsors) and supervisors (managers or coaches), and many have been organized into unions or similar labour groups who negotiate the terms and conditions of their work, post-retirement benefits, safety conditions, and health benefits and the like, usually in the form of written contracts.

The main difference between "ordinary" workers and athletes is often the terms of compensation – top pro athletes can receive reimbursements that total in the millions of dollars, a salary level that is not common in the workplace. Yet the athletes we see on television and read about in the newspapers represent a very small percentage of all the athletes who compete in a given sport. The salaries of these less famous athletes are not all that out of line from those earned by the elite portion of the business world, such as the president of a large corporation or a highly paid lawyer. As well, in contrast to most workers who can continue to earn a salary well into their mid-sixties, most professional athletes have relatively short careers – meaning that they have a need to earn high salaries for a short period of time, as compared to an office or factory worker who can spread his or her earnings over a much longer period.

Business models. Generally speaking, any transaction that involves the exchange of money or other method of payment for a good or service provided can be considered to be a form of business. Of course, there are a number of variables involved in any business transaction, such as the sum of money that changes hands, the price of a good or service, and the length of time it actually takes to complete the exchange. The point here – one that will be made a number of times in the sections that follow, in particular in Section 29, "The (Big) Business of Sport Entertainment" – is that in its modern, professional form, sport is just one of the many businesses that exist in our society today. Although many people who feel that sport should somehow remain "above" the world of business react negatively to this idea, it is only realistic to view professional sports in these terms.

WHERE DO WE GO FROM HERE?

With these concepts in mind, let us continue our examination of the important role sport plays in society with a look at the interplay between it and two key elements of modern life: big business and the media.

Canadian beach volleyball player Jody Holden of Toronto dives for the ball during a qualifying match against Germany during the 2000 Summer Olympics in Sydney, Australia (CP PHOTO/Scott Grant).

29
The (Big) Business of Sport Entertainment

There's no business like show business — except for sports business."
— William Baker, *Sports in the Western World* (1982)

KEY CONCEPTS

- For-profit/not-for-profit sport
- Amateur/professional athletes
- Media
- Sports-as-entertainment industry
- Broadcasting rights
- Endorsement
- Sport franchises
- Player's agent
- Fan loyalty
- Players' strikes
- Stadium concessions
- Charitable activities

As we saw in Section 24, "History of Physical Education and Sport," elite sport, as it is played today, has changed considerably from its early days. In the twentieth century, sport left the confines of local, not-for-profit pastimes to become an important part of the global entertainment business. The invention of the electronic media of mass communication led to unparalleled growth in sport of all kinds, along with an equally huge boom in advertising in those media. These factors have made modern professional sport into a truly "big business."

Sport is now an important part of the economic system of most Western countries and operates along the same lines as any big business. In this section, we will examine the major changes that have helped to bring about this relatively recent transformation.

THE ECONOMICS OF SPORT

The world of sport is divided between for-profit and not-for-profit sport, and between sport on amateur and professional levels.

For-Profit versus Not-for-Profit Sport

The distinction between for-profit sport and not-for-profit sport is based on the economic motivation behind those who organize and provide financial support for sport teams. The organized sport we are accustomed to watching on television or in large stadiums is run primarily as a business by corporate owners, and played by athletes who are under contract to them. Although most owners are sports fans to some

degree, they and others, such as sponsors, athletes, and coaches, are involved with organized sport first and foremost for one reason: to make money. This does not mean that for-profit sport is not enjoyable or exciting — indeed, athletes involved in it are among the best, if not the best, at what they do.

Others are involved in sport for other reasons, such as enjoyment, personal development, physical fitness, the chance to socialize with others who have similar interests, and a sense of personal accomplishment. Sports that are played in schools, communities, and local clubs are primarily for enjoyment and not for profit. Although a great deal of money is raised and spent on equipment, facilities, local coaches, and so on, this kind of sport is primarily driven by the enjoyment of playing and achieving, or coaching, or watching your friends and family members play.

Amateur versus Professional Sport

The historical roots of the division between amateur and professional athletes were examined in Section 24 ("History of Physical Education and Sport"). Essentially, amateurs derive no direct financial or material rewards from their sporting efforts; professionals do. In terms of our analysis of the big business of sport, however, the importance of this amateur or professional divide lies in the amount of compensation which professional athletes stand to gain for the labour they put into sport. Today, this is accomplished through player contracts, endorsement deals, the sale of merchandise and tickets, and other ways, all of which we will examine in greater depth.

Why Are Sport Salaries So High?
Winner take all

There is probably no single subject (other than perhaps the use of performance-enhancing drugs by athletes) that inflames the passions of long-time observers of sport as much as the question of the salaries that are now being paid to modern professional athletes. Old-time fans can recall – and not all that long ago – when the amounts earned by big-league hockey, baseball, basketball, soccer, and football players were within the same range as other professionals.

But during the last decade or so, the sports pages and television reports have been full of stories about the rising amounts that pro athletes stand to earn from both team contracts and endorsement deals. Even though some increase in these salaries can be attributed to inflation, this is an extremely small factor in why athletes make so much more money than they did just a few decades ago.

In Perspective

To begin, it is important to place these athletic incomes in context by comparing them to the amounts that people in North America earn through other forms of labour.

In Canada, the latest census data compiled by Statistics Canada during 2000 reveals that, among the more than 16.4 million people aged fifteen and over who had income from employment, the average annual earnings were about $32,000 (in Canadian dollars), with the Ontario average a bit higher, at about $35,000. In the United States, the figure is about $42,000 per year (in U.S. dollars) according U.S. government statistics in September 2002.

Consider the following average salaries for professional athletes in North America (all figures are in U.S. dollars):

- NBA basketball: $4.0 million;
- Major League baseball: $2.3 million;
- NHL hockey: $1.6 million;
- NFL football: $1.2 million.

The CFL's highest earner, Blue Bombers quarterback Khari Jones, during CFL action in 2002 (CP PHOTO/John Ulan).

In other words, these annual rates of pay are many times higher than the average worker's salary in both Canada and the U.S.

Keep in mind that these figures represent only the average amounts earned in each league. At the extreme margins of all of these sports, top athletes can make much, much more. A few examples of these mega-earning superstars (again, with figures in U.S. dollars) are:

- Kevin Garnett, Minnesota Timberwolves (NBA): $25.2 million per season;
- Alex Rodriguez, Texas Rangers (Major League Baseball): $22 million per season;
- Donovan McNab, Philadephia Eagles (NFL): $11.3 million per season;
- Peter Forsberg, Colorado Avalanche (NHL): $11 million per season.

The main exception to all of this is the Canadian Football League (CFL), Canada's only professional football league. Players in the CFL earn, on average, about $50,000 per season (in Canadian dollars), a lot closer to the average Canadian income; the league's highest-paid player, quarterback Khari Jones of the Winnipeg Blue Bombers, makes about $300,000 per season.

When Supply Meets Demand

It is appropriate to ask why pro sports salaries are so high. Indeed, numerous sports writers, television commentators, and academic researchers have posed this very question. In general, their answers fall into the broad framework of "supply and demand."

Basically, this theory holds that, at any given moment, any product or service has a "correct" price. If, in reality, the price placed on the product or service is too high, consumers will not purchase it, and producers will be forced to adjust the price if they want to sell. In the same manner, a price that is too low will mean that there will be no incentive to produce the product or service. But the "correct" price is one at which all those who wish to buy can find sellers willing to sell, and all those who wish to sell can find buyers willing to buy.

Given the varying levels of athletic talent available in any league, players will be paid more or less according to a sliding scale of how productive they are (i.e., scoring goals, hitting home runs, and so forth). The best players are generally paid the highest salaries, and the "correct price" for each ability level is set based on this performance.

Many argue that pro sports salaries simply reflect the money-making world of sport today, and that the spending on players' salaries is a reasonable way for the owners to invest in a team's success. Since the supply of talent matches the demand for these athletes' services, they maintain that all works out in the end. Moreover, given the large revenues going to team owners from television rights, it is hard to argue that the players should not receive their fair share.

From the perspective of the athlete, it is important to remember that, in contrast to today's multi-million dollar salaries, even well into the 1960s and 1970s elite professional athletes in sports such hockey, baseball, and basketball typically were paid so little that many needed to find other kinds of regular employment during their sport's off-season. World-class participants in other sports such as track and field, rowing, and archery could not afford – and today in many cases still cannot afford – even to compete in their sports without working at "outside" jobs to pay for travel, food, and equipment.

Even though the distinction between amateur and professional sport is a fundamental one, for many athletes it is not a rigid dividing line. It is not uncommon for an athlete's career to be a blend of these two types of sport, since top amateur athletes, who have developed their skills in a not-for-profit context, usually want to move up to the "big leagues" where the financial rewards are plentiful. As well, many sports have, during the last decade or so, relaxed their rules considerably to the point where, for example, professional hockey and basketball players are permitted to compete in the formerly amateurs-only Olympic Games.

Winning Is Everything

Winning is important beyond the final score between two teams on the field or rink. In the business sense, winning is crucial. It reinforces fan loyalty, which in turn results in bigger gate receipts, more sales of products featuring the team's logo or "brand," higher fees for more widely watched television broadcasts of games, and a steady supply of talented young people wishing to join the team. In most professional sports, this increased revenue can lead to teams having more and more money available to sign superstar players to huge contracts.

Sport on this scale is utterly reliant on the support of a massive, often worldwide, fan base. Players in such sports are more akin to entertainment celebrities than to amateur athletes of previous eras – those who played for fun and some small bit of local prestige. Those who accumulate stellar career records often go on to a lifetime of endorsement fees, television commentary positions, professional coaching, and continuing prominence in their communities long after their active sports careers are finished.

Today elite athletes earn salaries of millions of dollars a year (see "Why Are Sports Salaries So High?" on page 354). Certainly, it is logical to assume that team owners will pay athletes salaries that are in proportion to the overall profits they make from the total team operations – that is, as pro teams make money, the salaries of star players will rise accordingly. But where does all this money come from?

Ten-year-old Andrew Richler holds up a sign with his views on a strike during action between the Toronto Blue Jays and the NY Yankees, August 2002 (CP PHOTO/Aaron Harris).

The answer lies in an analysis of what are known as "revenue streams" – that is, the various ways in which money can be brought into the coffers of a pro sports team. In the pages that follow, we will examine a number of these, but it is important to remember that, in most instances, while the game action is a starting point for this income, the money that fans spend on tickets to see a live game is only one piece of a much larger revenue puzzle. It is only when teams use these games for the sale of various rights – such as the right to broadcast games on television, or the right to manufacture products such as T-shirts or mugs – that the real profits start rolling in.

Live sports events are really no different from concerts, films, or even craft fairs or trade shows in that the basic concept of revenue generation is the same. Organizers first charge attendees a fee to be a part of the main event. They then attempt to find other ways of making money from these fans while they are at the event. They also try to find ways of making money from those who did not attend in person yet still want to be a part of the event.

Hockey Night in Canada

How sports and the media combined to form a national institution

Canada's national broadcaster, CBC Television, has held the exclusive rights to show NHL hockey games to Canadians on Saturday nights since *Hockey Night in Canada* (HNIC) began in 1952.

This is not to say that the CBC holds a monopoly on hockey broadcasting in Canada – far from it. In the cable universe, for example, The Sports Network (TSN), the cable all-sports channel, has a national broadcast contract with the NHL that allows it to show a limited number of games on weeknights. Sportsnet, another all-sports cable network with regional divisions across Canada, has another agreement to televise dozens of other games.

However, none of the hockey action on other networks attracts as many fans as the decades-old Saturday night tradition that is HNIC, which draws an estimated average of 1.2 million viewers every week. All of the telecasts include pre-game programming, including feature reports about significant hockey stories from across Canada, highlights from other games going on around the NHL that night, reams of analysis from CBC's large studio team of experts (mostly ex-coaches and former players) and interviews from rinkside.

To keep all of this information flowing, the CBC employs a huge staff. This workforce includes announcers, reporters, camera operators, and sound and lighting technicians who operate from the rink itself, and a group of producers, directors, and assistants who work out of a mobile production unit that is usually parked in the bowels of a stadium, or just outside. This mobile unit – affectionately called "the truck" by CBC staff – is packed with video screens, editing equipment, and all manner of computerized equipment that allows the production crew to control which images and sounds actually make it to the television sets of the viewers at home. To spend a couple of hours in the truck is to experience an absolutely frantic pandemonium of shouted instructions, fast-paced shifts by directors from one

Hockey Night in Canada's Ron MacLean and Don Cherry (photo courtesy of the Canadian Broadcasting Company).

camera angle to another, a slew of instant replays and quick jumps back and forth from the game at hand to highlights from another one being played an entire continent away, and the coordination of a host of on-air voices offering commentary and analysis. Amazingly, though, it all comes through to the viewer at home as a single, essentially seamless, package.

Along with the production crews that operate close to the game are an equally formidable numbers of CBC employees who staff the network's permanent studios in Toronto. And although there have always been a number of well-respected hockey commentators and analysts sporting whatever colour of CBC blazer happens to be in vogue, it is safe to say that none have even come close to attaining the status of the legendary HNIC duo, Don Cherry and Ron MacLean.

For all of his irascible demeanour and gruff mannerisms – not to mention his outlandish suits and controversial views – Cherry has emerged as the best-known non-player in the hockey world.

In addition to his work in front of CBC cameras, Cherry is easily recognizable as a spokesman for a number of products and services on television and radio commercials, and the ex-NHL coach has also secured a wide audience for the many hockey videos and short radio commentary spots he has created.

While MacLean's role on the "Coach's Corner" spots in which both men appear between game periods is that of the reasonable "straight man" to Cherry's more bombastic approach, it appears to be no less successful.

In 2002, when the Alberta native announced that he would not be continuing after sixteen years with HNIC because of a contract dispute with the CBC, viewers responded with outrage, arguing that MacLean's knowledge of the game (he is generally regarded by colleagues as one of hockey's most thorough researchers) was too valuable to lose. In the end, CBC Sports head Nancy Lee rethought the position of "the corporation" and settled with MacLean.

THE ROLE OF THE MEDIA

It is important that people who follow sport on any level understand the role of the media – television, radio, the Internet, newspapers, magazines, and all the forms of advertising that appear in these media outlets – in the world of professional sport.

In the "old days," if you did not attend the sporting event in person, next-day print reports of game action were essentially the only way of following sports. Today, fans can avail themselves of a 24-hours-a-day sports information barrage on cable television and through the Internet.

Newspapers have long included sports coverage, but, because of the nature of print reporting, fans would have to wait until well after the action had ended to find out who won, who scored, and other important game details. In the 1930s and 1940s, radio sports broadcasts broke that pattern by allowing live coverage, and by increasing the traditional audience size limitations. This began in the early decades of the twentieth century, first with accounts of hockey games and then baseball and football games. Radio listeners in remote locations could now partake of important sporting events. Radio allowed the game to grow beyond the bounds of a physical arena and developed fan loyalty to the extent that people could support a team avidly without actually living in the geographical area in which it was based.

The Influence of Television

While the influence of radio was significant, it pales in comparison to that of the television camera. While the first broadcasts were primitive (NHL hockey games first came to home viewers in Canada in 1952), and tended to adopt the conventions of the radio sports play-by-play commentary, they had the effect of taking the action to an even wider audience of families gathered in their own homes, free of direct charges. The potential audience was now huge, had free access to the broadcast, and perhaps most importantly, could be made to listen to and watch interspersed advertisements. The audience was also relatively unified – there were few channels and fewer alternative programs.

Far from being just a passive spectator at sporting events, the television camera has, in the years since the first primitive broadcasts of hockey and football games in the 1950s, gradually reshaped the rules of sport, caused the redesign of uniforms and equipment worn by the players, and has even affected the duration and tempo of sporting events since sports television began. These effects have been worldwide in scope, and sport organizers and broadcasters have worked together to refashion the elite sporting event, both in the stadiums

The CBC's omnipresent Brian Williams after winning an award for best sports broadcaster at the 13th Gemini Awards in 1998 (CP PHOTO/STF-Frank Gunn).

and the broadcast versions, as a fast-paced, advertisement-interspersed entertainment vehicle.

No longer limited to simple game coverage, this relatively recent explosion of the sporting media includes reams of statistics at the touch of a computer key through the Internet, plus round-the-clock cable feeds of athlete interviews, press conferences, and sport-by-sport highlight packages. All manner of analysis by experts is available. And in the midst of all this coverage, which, for the most part, represents a fairly objective branch of the news-and-information-gathering industry, advertisers of every kind of product have lined up to sell their wares to spectators of both live and televised sports.

In many cases, this involves recruiting top athletes to act as spokespersons for these products, which include sports-related items and non-sports related items, such as cars, food and beverages, and personal grooming products. Certainly, this level of exposure would not be possible without television and its dual impact of making live events available to a wide audience, and providing a vehicle for advertisers.

The WWE Phenomenon
Entertaining, perhaps — but is it sport?

To anyone who followed professional wrestling just a few decades ago, the modern form of this worldwide entertainment spectacle would be all but unrecognizable. Pro wrestling has become the epitome of the sports-as-entertainment genre.

Televised matches attract millions of viewers and showcase the athletic and theatrical talents of male and, increasingly, female competitors, who don all manner of costumes and employ all kinds of shady tactics to conquer their opponents. Pro wrestling's largest governing body, World Wrestling Entertainment, or WWE (formerly known as the World Wrestling Federation, or WWF, until a much-publicized lawsuit by the World Wildlife Federation forced the wrestling group to change its acronym) is now a recognized logo around the globe, and its high-profile leader, the outspoken Vince McMahon, is widely considered to be one of the world's leading entertainment promoters.

Actually, terms such as "competitors" and "winning" used in reference to pro wrestling matches have a much different meaning than when used to describe more conventional sport. That is because the outcome of these matches has, for the most part, been determined beforehand, as has the way that much of the action unfolds. Although just a generation ago, most pro wrestlers, organizers, and fans would never admit that the matches were "staged," this suspension of disbelief has largely disappeared since the phenomenal rise of pro wrestling in the 1990s. Still, fans show up for the action, and action is what they get.

Although this very different dynamic prevents wrestling from attaining the status of a true sport, it is nevertheless the case that those who participate in it can still be considered athletes. Many of them, such as the popular American wrestler Bill Goldberg (who competes as simply "Goldberg"), played professional football before turning to WWE action. Others, such as the Canadian

A 2002 WWE cruiserweight title bout at the Halifax Metro Centre (CP PHOTO/ *The Halifax Daily News*/Scott Dunlop).

superstar Trish Stratus, took part in bodybuilding or fitness competitions before launching their wrestling careers. All pro wrestlers today exhibit a high level of muscle tone and definition as the result of serious strength and flexibility training regimes. As anyone who has ever seen pro wrestling knows, the competitors need to be able to undergo some pretty strenuous physical activity in plying their trade.

Their considerable physical accomplishments, however, still do not qualify them as "athletes" in the strictest sense of the term. Since pro wrestlers are working to a pre-established "script" in their matches, it might be best to consider them as one-part actor and one-part athlete. Indeed, it is hard not to ascribe a certain talent to this odd blend of athlete and performer, especially when you look at the accomplishments of someone such as Jesse Ventura. Ventura was a champion wrestler when he competed as "The Body." He parlayed his popularity into a successful career in U.S. politics, rising to the position of governor of the state of Minnesota.

Regardless of the definition you choose to apply to those who take part in pro wrestling, it is impossible to argue with the impact the WWE has had on the sports-as-entertainment field. The merchandising of licensed products has been combined with a carefully crafted television rights package.

All live, high-profile WWE events, such as the "Smackdown" or "Wrestlemania" series are broadcast not as regular over-the-air telecasts or through conventional cable presentations, but as exclusive, pay-per-view engagements. This enables WWE to both control access to the action and to charge fans for the right to see the events, thereby eliminating the need to seek advertising dollars to fund the broadcasts. For example, recent WWE "Wrestlemania" events held throughout 2002 resulted in about $1 million pay-per-view "buys," bringing the action to living rooms of people who paid from $10 to $35 to view each event.

Those who study pro wrestling as a way of trying to understand what its popularity says about social trends often point out the fact that in most WWE matches – and, in fact, most pro wrestling bouts since the sport's "golden age" in the 1950s – there is usually one competitor who is easily recognizable as the "good" wrestler, and one who is "bad." Observers point out that this clear good-versus-bad battle appeals to fans who enjoy seeing both roles played out so clearly, which is very different from most ambiguous scenarios in daily life. Supporters also argue that, while this action might not be to everyone's taste, it does offer one sports (or, perhaps pseudo-sports) arena in which males and females seem to compete with near-equal publicity, and without being separated into matches in different venues and on different nights.

But is pro wrestling a sport? Like many such questions, the answer will depend on your definition of the term at hand – in this case, what it means for a certain type of activity to be a genuine "sport."

THE SPORTS-AS-ENTERTAINMENT INDUSTRY

Many technical advances in television broadcasting have led to the immense growth of what is popularly known as the **sports-as-entertainment industry**. In this context, the actual action involved in a game, race, or contest is just one part of the overall entertainment package that is presented to the viewers as part of the telecast. Although they seem common today, sports "extras," such as teams of celebrity play-by-play announcers, pre- and post-game analysis sessions, interviews with players, highlights from other games being played simultaneously, replays (often illustrated with a "Telestrater" pen), in-depth player profiles and the like were unheard of even twenty years ago.

Television advertisers now electronically place phantom product signs on the stadium walls or giant corporate logos on the field of play itself, or, in the case of car racing, in the grassy infields of race tracks. Corporate logos adorn sports uniforms and stadiums alike. All of these instances simply underscore the fact that advertising is an integral part of professional sport, to the point where sports action and advertising are now completely inseparable. The reason for this close union lies in the reliable ability of sports broadcasting to deliver young and middle-aged male viewers and listeners to the advertisers and their corporate clients. In return, the corporate advertisers deliver the advertising dollars that are the lifeblood of all elite sports, whether they are professional or amateur.

Broadcasting Rights

The relationship between professional sports teams (and leagues) and the media – through the sale of **broadcasting rights** to games – is key to the extremely large amounts of money that change hands in the business side of professional sports.

It is in this context, for example, that the National Football League in the United States receives at least $18 billion a year from the U.S. television networks for the rights to telecast its games, and the American CBS network has reportedly entered into a contract with the National Collegiate Athletic Association (NCAA) that will see $500 million being paid to the NCAA for the rights to broadcast the annual "March Madness" men's basketball tournament – an event that lasts all of three weeks.

Typically, the broadcasters attempt to recoup these fees – and turn a profit besides – from advertising revenues. Also, broadcasters hope that viewers who watch games on their network will leave the television on and watch other entertainment broadcasting (promoted during the game telecast) which follows the game, thus raising the ratings for other non-sports programming.

The retail manager of Maple Leaf Gardens, Jeff Newman, displays the new-look Toronto Maple Leafs' jersey – the numbers, names and fabric were to be changed as part of an arrangement between six NHL teams and Nike (CP PHOTO/*Toronto Sun*-Greig Reekie).

In print journalism – that is, newspaper and magazines – a vastly higher ratio of income is earned through advertising than through the sales of subscriptions or single copies. In other words, when people say that a good sports section "sells newspapers" to the public, the revenue they are talking about is very small compared to the revenues that advertising – in sports or any other section – brings to the publisher.

Endorsement

The **endorsement** by sports celebrities of particular products – often for a sizeable fee – is an important part of promoting seemingly unrelated products. Although it seems logical to find athletes endorsing the kind of products they would use in the course of training and competition – skates, baseball bats, basketball shoes or sports drinks, for example – it has always been common to see sports celebrities appearing in advertisements for items and services that are seemingly unrelated to their sporting careers. In recent years, these have included the Tiger Woods Buick and the Wayne Gretzky Ford car advertisements.

Vancouver-Whistler to Hold Winter Olympics in 2010
The risks and the glory of Olympic bids

In the sports business arena, competing for the honour of hosting the Summer and Winter Olympic Games is taken extremely seriously. In these competitions, city organizing committees must put together elaborate proposals for how they plan to accommodate the thousands of athletes – and hundreds of thousands of spectators – who assemble every four years to take part in the Games.

As the International Olympic Committee (IOC) narrows down its choices to pick the winning city well in advance of the actual Games, the cost of submitting detailed proposals gets higher and higher – from the millions of dollars it costs simply to offer an early bid to the IOC, to the billions it costs to actually host a Summer or Winter Games.

Indeed, in most cities that bid to host the Olympic Games, there regularly emerges a sizeable protest movement that opposes the bid – as was the case when Toronto was seeking to host the 2008 Summer Olympics – by citizens who argue that, if a city can afford the huge sums of money involved in playing host to this sports festival, it should be able to spend similar amounts on trying to solve social problems such as poverty and homelessness.

Financial Incentive to Playing Host

So why is there this immense outpouring of money, especially when one considers that of the many serious bids set forward to hold each Games, only one will be chosen by the IOC?

Hotels, restaurants, public transport systems, and many other local businesses stand to earn a considerable income during the actual three weeks of the Games, to say nothing of the post-Olympic tourism that can accompany the good publicity an Olympic Games can bring.

What is more, advocates of such hosting bids argue that there is a tremendous "leave-behind" effect that follows one of these global competitions. Olympic-calibre pools, soccer stadiums,

Heritage Minister Sheila Copps celebrates at GM Place in Vancouver, July 2, 2003 (CP PHOTO/Chuck Stoody).

cycling venues, and track-and-field sites will remain for many years after the Games have been held. In addition, civic infrastructure improvements – better roads, improved water delivery systems, and so forth – can continue to benefit communities long after the Olympics.

Vancouver's Successful Bid

In 2002, organizers in Vancouver submitted a bid to the IOC for the right to host the 2010 Winter Olympics in that city and in nearby Whistler, B.C. The cost of preparing and submitting the bid was estimated at $34 million. As a further example of the way in which such bids can aid sport at a grassroots level, it is worth noting that, of this total, $5 million was spent on provincial government sponsorships of sports programs in British Columbia as a way of attempting to ensure the support of citizens for the bid. The remainder was spent on advertising, promotion, travel, and the actual preparation of the detailed bid submission to the IOC.

Even with all of this expenditure of money and effort, there was no guarantee of success, as was proven by the

recent failure of Toronto to secure the 2008 Summer Games. (The winning city, Beijing, reportedly paid more than $60 million just to prepare its bid.) Furthermore, the high-stakes nature of the competition for hosting rights has led to many allegations – such as those surrounding the successful Salt Lake City bid to host the 2002 Winter Games – that IOC officials are targets for bribes and other shady practices on the part of would-be Games organizers.

A Close Decision

All of this did not deter Vancouver's attempts. In early 2003, after it had made the IOC's short list of cities in the running for the privilege of hosting the 2010 games, hopeful organizers submitted a formal offer to the IOC. Following that, however, the bid received a major blow, as high-ranking IOC officials visited Vancouver and declared that the distance between Vancouver and Whistler – the proposed site for many of the 2010 events – was simply too great and serviced by an inadequate road system.

Vancouver organizers managed to overcome these objections, and by July, 2003, the stage was set for a showdown between Vancouver, Salzburg, Austria, and Pyeongchang, South Korea, the final three cities under IOC's consideration. In a tense, two-stage ballot held in Prague in the Czech Republic, Salzburg was eliminated in the first round, leaving only Vancouver and Pyeongchang to battle it out. After the final count was in, it was time to rejoice: by a narrow margin of 56 to 53, Vancouver had won the right to host the 2010 Winter Games.

The city has its work cut out for it, though. The operating costs alone for the Games are estimated at $1 billion, with road, infrastructure, and facilities costs pegged at several hundred millions of dollars more. Nevertheless, all the signs point to a huge and highly successful Winter Olympics in 2010.

Sales of branded sporting goods, videotapes, and computer games endorsed by sports celebrities are a very important part of "lifestyle marketing" and consumption patterns, since the companies that produce and market them assume that sports fans will transfer the admiration they have for these athletes into a desire to purchase things their heroes endorse. It was no accident that one of the most successful athlete endorsement initiatives of all time – basketball star Michael Jordan's television ads for the Gatorade sports drink – hinged on the slogan "I wanna be like Mike!" In fact, Jordan himself ushered in an important trend in athlete endorsement and marketing, becoming the first in a long line of athletes who earned more from endorsements (in Jordan's case, Gatorade, Nike athletic apparel, and several other products) than they did from the salaries they earned to play their sport.

Promotional Success: The Nike story

The Nike "swoosh" is now emblazoned on all manner of sports clothing and equipment, both on players and fans alike. The company was started in 1964 (taking its name from the goddess who represented victory in Greek mythology) to manufacture and distribute athletic footwear primarily to runners and other track-and-field athletes. In the years since, the brand has expanded hugely, to include shoes and apparel for every sport imaginable, as well as clothing, bags, caps, and so forth for the leisure-wear market.

From a manufacturing perspective, Nike has been remarkably successful worldwide, in part because it shifted actual manufacture of its products to low-wage Third World countries. This fact has garnered both tremendous support and opposition from economists who have studied this trend in "remote" manufacturing. Nike has aimed its marketing efforts at a young audience, and, with the aid of top-level spokespersons such as Tiger Woods, Michael Jordan, and soccer star Mia Hamm, has portrayed its products as ways for ordinary people to identify with successful elite athletes. These athletes endorse the company's products – with their unifying brand hallmark, the "swoosh" – in all forms of media, such as television commercials, print ads in magazines, and giant billboards – for a substantial fee. The company, for example paid US$40 million to Tiger Woods to wear the branded hat and shirts during competition, and US$7 million to the University of Michigan football team to place the logo on its uniforms. Nike spent a reported US$100 million on advertising at the Olympic Games in Atlanta, even though it was not an official sponsor. The swoosh seemed to be everywhere in the Atlanta urban landscape for the three-week duration of the Olympic Games.

Tiger Woods during the final round of the 1996 Greater Milwaukee Open, sporting the trademark Nike "swoosh" on his hat (AP Photo/ Morry Gash).

Ironically, one unfortunate consequence of these huge endorsement fees is that the ultimate level of achievement in sports is often seen not as athletic excellence but as huge endorsement contracts. These may dwarf athletic salaries; for many elite athletes, this is now typically the case.

The Nike story has not received completely favourable attention from those who study sport on a global level. For one thing, the company's aforementioned labour practices have come under serious scrutiny from those who see the farming-out of shoe and apparel manufacturing to Third World factories as little more than a "sweatshop" initiative, with unsafe working conditions and low wages. Critics also point to the reluctance of Nike spokespersons such as Jordan or Woods to comment on these labour practices.

Many have also noted that the Nike promotional campaign has taken attention away from the actual purpose of high-tech sports equipment – to help a person train and compete more effectively – and placed it on the equipment itself. Young athletes may focus too much on the acquisition of shoes, jerseys, and the like, and not enough on training, fitness, and overall health.

Sport Business of a Different Kind

Eastern Europe and Cuba

There have been many instances in which champion international competitors have emerged from nations where the means of generating money differ greatly from that of capitalist countries. In the world of sport, two such examples stand out: pre-1990 Eastern Europe and Cuba.

Eastern Europe

Following the Second World War, the former Soviet Union and its so-called "satellite states," such as East Germany, Czechoslovakia, Romania, Bulgaria, Yugoslavia, and Poland, functioned under communist systems of government. On an economic level, this meant that all industry and commerce within those countries was under state, or government, control. On a sporting level, this meant that top-level athletes trained and competed under government-funded programs that supported them to the point that most did not require any other employment.

In many cases, these athletes – such as the majority of the Soviet hockey players that took on Canada in the famous "Summit Series" in 1972 – were nominally members of their nation's armed forces, but were in fact full-time athletes. The success of the Soviet hockey team, the tremendous collective performance of the East German men's and women's Olympic teams in the Summer Games of 1972, 1976, and 1980 (notably in swimming and track and field), and the dominance of the Romanian women's gymnastics teams in 1976 are just a few examples of the way in which this state-supported sport system found success in its heyday.

World politics, from after the Second World War until the fall of communist governments in Eastern Europe in the late-1980s and early 1990s, was dominated by the so-called "Cold War" – an ideological battle between the communist nations of Eastern Europe and China, and the capitalist countries of the West. This clash of political ideologies also spilled over into the world of

Canadian athletes at the 1991 Pan American Games in Havana, Cuba (CP Photo/COA/Tim O'Lett).

sport. In many instances, Olympic athletes and coaches from the so-called "Soviet Bloc" of nations openly declared that their sporting success had come as a direct result of their countries' superior political systems – with Western athletes countering that it was impossible to compete against rivals who were, in effect, state-sponsored professionals and who had been "manufactured" for success by the communist system.

This convergence of world sport and world politics came to a head in the early 1980s, as the United States, supported by most Western nations (with the exception of Great Britain) did not send any competitors to participate in the 1980 Olympics, held in Moscow, as a protest against the Soviet invasion of Afghanistan. In retaliation, the Soviet Union and its allies did not attend the 1984 Games in Los Angeles.

The fall of most Eastern European communist regimes in the late 1980s and early 1990s put an end to this state of affairs. With state-supported sport systems crumbling, and regulations governing the financial rewards open to athletes in the former "amateur" sports

relaxing considerably (track-and-field competitors, for example, began to be permitted to accept prize money around this time), athletes from the former Soviet Union and its allies now found themselves competing on the "open market," battling for corporate sponsorships and lucrative professional contracts.

Cuba

Although it is located only about 150 kilometres from the U.S., Cuba has, since about the early 1970s, held steadfast to the system of government support for athletes – with excellent success in all kinds of international competition.

Although it has only about 11 million inhabitants, Cuba has been a world-beating nation in boxing, track and field, and baseball, among other sports. Always among the top medal-winning nations in the Summer Olympic games since 1972 – and easily the top country in terms of medals won per total population – Cuba has boasted such superstars as Olympic boxers Teofilio Stevenson (triple heavyweight gold medallist in 1972, 1976, and 1980) and Felix Savon (Olympic heavyweight champion in 1992 and 1996); 1976 Olympic double gold-medal-winning runner (in the 400- and 800-metre) Alberto Juantorena; double world champion (1993 and 1997), Olympic gold medallist (1992), and current world-record high jumper Javier Sotomayor; and double world champion (1995 and 1997) 800-metre runner Anna Quirot.

In baseball, Cuba has long been a world leader. The country's long-time president, Fidel Castro, is an ex-player and an avid fan, and games there draw huge crowds. Cuba handily won the first two unofficial Olympic baseball competitions (in 1992 and 1996) and was runner-up to the U.S. in 2000 after compiling an 18-0 record in international competition before the Sydney Summer Games.

KEY PLAYERS ON THE SPORTS BUSINESS FIELD

Modern sports fans need to understand the roles played by the key figures in the big business of sport. These include a team's owners, its players, the players' agents, and, of course, its fans.

The Owner's Role

People who own professional sports teams have many non-economic reasons for wanting to do so, including making a contribution to the life of their community and indulging in a life-long passion for sport on a grand scale. But if a sports franchise owner – or a corporation that wants to invest in a professional sports team – is looking to make large profits on their investment, they will be forced to explore a number of ways to draw revenue, beyond simply collecting money from ticket-holders.

Many clubs operate at a substantial loss even though the value of the franchise itself may still be climbing. If a particular team is struggling to attract fans and can be sold by one owner to another in a city with a better climate for generating revenue, the original owner can usually realize a large profit from the sale, especially if the franchise can be moved to a larger city with a better television deal or a free-of-charge stadium to play in. Recent figures indicate that a professional sports franchise in North America is worth 2.8 times the average annual revenue for NBA teams, 2.5 times for hockey franchises, and baseball teams 2.2 times the average earnings. Indeed, many professional sports teams are now owned by large media conglomerates (AOL-Time Warner or Disney, for example) who may not object to the team itself losing money so long as it continues to contribute to the conglomerates "branding" and thereby the corporation's financial success overall.

The Athlete's Role

Although the world of big-business sports is comprised of many facets, some form of sporting competition must exist at the heart of it all. When commentators talk about the "product," what they are really talking about is the action that is produced by athletes. As the main drivers of this action, athletes stand at the very centre of sport as a business, and, as such, play a unique and sometimes conflicted role.

Professional athletes find themselves continually called upon to perform at a consistently high level in order to remain competitive, game after game, race after race, and season after season, both as athletes and as members of a workforce in which performance is the one criterion upon which all members are judged. An oft-repeated sports maxim holds that "you are only as good as your last game," and with the high degree of

Mario Lemieux and Wayne Gretzky celebrate Canada's gold-medal victory over the U.S. at the 2002 Olympic Winter Games. Both Lemieux and Gretzky are also now team owners (CP PHOTO/Frank Gunn).

scrutiny to which athletes are subjected – by both the media and fans – this mindset holds especially true, and can lead to an environment in which the pressure to perform is extreme. Although many feel that this represents a "pure" way of judging talent – "statistics don't lie," as another saying goes – it is nevertheless true that in the world of big-business sports, athletes are required to perform to ever-increasing standards if they wish to earn higher and higher salaries.

Just how high these salaries should go, however, is the subject of some debate. Salaries have skyrocketed to the point where yearly compensation is routinely measured in millions of dollars. Aided by the growing role of the sports agent (see below), professional athletes have seen their salaries – and the money they earn from endorsement deals – climb higher and higher. In the NBA, for example, any first-year player who manages to sign a contract with one of the leagues' teams will earn a guaranteed minimum of US$1.5 million in a contract that will last for no less than three seasons; the Toronto Raptors star player Vince Carter reportedly earns a cool CDN$25 million

Advertising Awareness
Caveat emptor

Many people who study the messages we receive from the media urge consumers to be wary of what they are seeing and hearing. In the context of sports-driven advertising, for example, there are many instances to adopt a buyer-beware approach. Can the latest abdominal-exercising machine really make the kind of muscular improvements its manufacturers – and perhaps its celebrity spokesperson – says it will? Can a sports electrolyte-replacement drink really enhance performance? Will the latest (and likely quite expensive) pair of super-shoes actually help you to play basketball like the all-star player endorsing them?

Often, it is easy to believe that the promises made by advertisers are true – especially when a well-liked athlete is making them on behalf of a company. Luckily, though, there are a number of resources available to consumers that can help in getting to the truth about advertiser claims – adding truth to the oft-repeated aphorism that research is often a consumer's best friend in the face of an advertising barrage.

Knowledge Is the Best Defence

Since many of the claims made by sports advertisers are in support of various products that can enhance the user's prowess at some form of sport or physical activity – such as exercise equipment or apparel – some knowledge of basic anatomy, physiology, biomechanics, training principles, and motor development (such as the material presented in the first three units of this book) can go a long way towards assessing the truth in this kind of advertising.

If, for example, you are familiar with the basic principles of physical training, you will be able to decide whether typical claims that a certain piece of equipment can increase the size of a certain muscle group in a very short time are true, or just a lot of "advertising hype" designed to get you to spend your money.

Toronto Raptors' Vince Carter and Jerome Williams during game three NBA Eastern Conference semi-final action in May 2001 (CP PHOTO/Frank Gunn).

To their credit, several sport advertisers have recently begun bucking this trend by creating ads in which they openly admit that consuming their product will not make one a better athlete. In this way, advertisers can score points with viewers by appearing to be taking an honest approach to marketing their product, by, in effect, exposing an advertising myth that most viewers already know to be untrue.

Canadian basketball fans, for example, became accustomed to a television ad in which Toronto Raptors superstar Vince Carter appeared on screen, executing an high-flying maneuver in a commercial for Sprite soft drink. A short while later, Carter's teammate Jerome Williams – also an excellent player, but considered to be a more workmanlike and far less spectacular than Carter – appeared in a similar ad in which, at the last instant before his super slam-dunk, the camera peeled back to reveal that Williams was suspended in the air by pulleys. The implication was equally clear: Sprite cannot make you jump higher, but it is fun to believe it can.

"Lifestyle" Advertising: Whom to Trust?

Things become a little more difficult in the area of "lifestyle advertising." In this case, the advertiser enlists the aid of a well-known sports figure to promote a product or service not directly related to his or her sport – say an automobile, personal grooming product, or fast food. In this case, the advertiser is again looking to capitalize on the loyalty a potential consumer might have for a certain famous athlete or team. But again, the consumer has to take certain factors into account, not the least of which is the fact that, while "player X" might be saying he or she supports a certain brand of car, he or she is, in all likelihood, doing so because he or she is receiving a lot of money for doing so – perhaps more than he or she makes in actually playing his or her sport.

In fact, there is one particular product that forms the basis for one of the oddest alliances between the world of modern, professional sport and the products it endorses. That product is beer, and, as anyone who has spent time watching pro sports on television can attest, North American broadcasts of pro hockey, basketball, baseball, and football are filled with advertisements for numerous brands of beer. Although athletes do not appear as frequently as they once did on these spots, the implication is clear – the sports fan and the beer drinker are one and the same person.

The paradox, however, lies in the logical conclusion of this thinking. Although many highly trained athletes may drink some alcohol occasionally, a steady consumption of beer cannot be part of a serious competitor's diet, because of alcohol's dehydrating effects and the "empty calories" beer contains. Yet the attempt to promote beer among sports fans is undeniable, leading to a further paradox: the more of it that spectators consume, the less likely they are to be able to emulate the sporting heroes they admire.

per season for playing with the NBA team, not including endorsement payments.

Advocates of high salaries for players argue that, given the relatively short careers of professionals, these huge per annum amounts are justified; players' union supporters also hold that the compensation their members receive is not out of line compared to the total earnings of the teams that pay them. After all, they maintain, if it were not for the players – and particularly the team stars – fans would have nothing to watch, and teams would soon face bankruptcy.

The Agent's Role

The last two decades of big-business sport have been characterized by the emergence of another figure who, just a few sporting generations ago, was almost an unknown. Far from being a presence on the playing surface, however, the person in this role exerts a tremendous influence on professional sports from a distance. This is the player's representative, or **player's agent**, a person, often with a legal background, who represents athletes in all levels of business dealings.

Agents are instrumental in negotiating player salaries with team owners, in developing collective agreements between player unions and leagues, and in arranging sponsorships and endorsement deals with agents and companies. In many cases, agents also act as money managers for professional athletes, recommending ways of investing the large sums of money that professionals earn during their careers.

Generally, the sporting world is of two minds regarding sports agents and their roles. Supporters argue that, without expert representation, athletes could be taken advantage of in negotiating with owners and suppliers of products and services. Certainly, in the pre-agent days of pro sports, many top-notch stars played for salaries that were paltry – even when you factor in inflation – when compared to sums earned today. And without the assistance of sports agents, many athletes found that, once their careers in sport had ended, they were unable to fall back on any "nest eggs" that they might have been able to build had they received sound financial advise. Consequently, it is not uncommon to hear agents and their supporters arguing that these representatives are "just trying to get the best deal possible for the player" when negotiating with wealthy owners.

But some oppose the increasingly powerful role played by sports agents. They argue that, because agents make their living by charging a commission – a pre-arranged percentage of the value of each contract signed by a player – it is in their interest to sell their client's services to the highest bidder, without considering larger implications, such as a player's long-term goals or the overall needs of a team or league.

Canadian fans show their support during a hockey game at the 1994 Lillehammer Winter Olympics (CP PHOTO/COA).

Whatever one's position, one thing seems clear: in the big-business world of professional sports, agents will continue to play a role for quite some time to come.

The Fan's Role

In the same way that consumer loyalty – a buyer's preference for one brand of soft drink over another, for example – is the key to success in the business world, **fan loyalty** is the central asset for a sports franchise. Dedicated fans will support a team through many lean years of mediocre success and even through periods of suspension of play due to labour disputes. They buy season tickets, watch televised games and related sports programming, and come out to games, all in support of their favourite team.

In an era in which many media commentators and fans alike have noted the tremendous rise in ticket prices, this loyalty can be undermined if team management does not make efforts to improve the results of the team and its athletes. Fans may reach the conclusion that they are being manipulated and that the owners have no intention of paying the high price to put a winning team on the field.

FIFA World Cup
"The beautiful game"

Every four years, there is a tournament featuring the best national soccer teams in the world. Although the event has always been contested at several venues within one host nation, in 2002 Korea and Japan shared the hosting duties. As was the case in 1998, the 2002 World Cup produced huge television audiences worldwide.

In fact, except for the Olympics, there is no other televised event of any nature that has ever approached this series in audience attraction. Television broadcasts of the games, all of which were shown in Canada – though, in many cases, on a delayed basis – reached 213 countries with about 41,100 hours of programming including commentary in many languages. According to the organizing body, FIFA (the world-governing organization for international soccer), the amount of programming was 38 percent greater than for the previous World Cup in France in 1998.

In 2002, the total number of worldwide viewer-hours was 49.2 billion. This is a truly global audience of unprecedented proportions. Some of these hours were spent in large public spaces where screens had been set up, or in bars and restaurants. Experimental programming was also provided for some types of advanced mobile phones. For one game in which their national team took part, 4.2 million Koreans took to the streets to watch large outdoor screens. For the final match of the tournament, open air viewing boosted the total viewers worldwide to 1.1 billion persons (or a little more than 18 percent of all human beings alive on the planet at that moment).

The audited cumulative television audience over the twenty-five days of the games in 2002 reached a total of 28.8 billion game viewers. Each viewer in this total represents one person watching all or part of one game. Since there were only 6 billion human beings alive in 2002, the figures strongly suggest that many people made a point of watching some or all of the games. The highest viewership figure in the World Cup 2002 was in Brazil. During the England versus Brazil quarter-final game, out of a total population of about 170 million people, there were 46 million Brazilian viewers tuned in (at 3:30 a.m. local time).

The Germany versus Brazil final game (which had a more civilized 8 a.m. starting time in Brazil) attracted 52.3 million Brazilian viewers and 26.5 million German viewers (or about 9 or every 10 German television watchers at that time). The final game also attracted 54 million viewers in Japan or about ten times the total of those who watched the 1998 final held in France. (For the record, Brazil convincingly defeated Germany in the 2002 final; in 1998, France thrilled the home crowd by winning the final over Brazil.)

As a FIFA press release indicates, "soccer has long been seen as the perfect vehicle for sponsors to deliver messages to the dream male demographic."

In the same vein, however, players and their representatives must also work to maintain their image – again through the media – among fans, many of whom see a direct correlation between rising ticket prices and the huge increases in player salaries. Further adding to fan disapproval is the fact that a number of professional leagues (most notably Major League Baseball and the National Basketball Association) have had play disrupted by **players' strikes** and/or lockouts over the past decade. In some cases, these "work stoppages" have been caused by players – through their agents or players unions – disputing clauses in their contracts, such as salary, pensions, or details regarding their status as "free agents" once a contract has expired. In others, owners have refused to back down in the face of agent and/or union demands and have simply shut down their operations. These stoppages have seriously undermined fan loyalty, as sports buffs begin pondering the ethical implications of millionaire players and owners squabbling over huge salaries.

SPORTS SPIN-OFFS

Today, sports enterprises have much the same objectives as other types of for-profit corporations: revenue growth, the accumulation of assets and their best use for the benefit of the owners, preserving a good public reputation, control of their environments, and having quality "products" to sell to trusting customers. In the context of sports as business, these products include the team itself, and the entire experience of seeing it play live or on television. But the actual game-day action is only part of the package. We have already examined the importance of advertising and broadcasting rights in this equation – the following are some of the ways in which professional sports teams seek to make money both within their community and on a much larger, worldwide scale.

Replica Products

All professional sports teams – and many minor league and even amateur teams – have websites that promote their activities and replica products such as team jerseys, coffee mugs, supporter banners, scarves, and so on. Organized baseball has taken this a step farther with a uniform format at a central website and has attempted to sell RealAudio streams of radio play-by-play commentary to distant club supporters who have no other way of following their club's games. In the future, streaming video of sporting events in far away locations will be possible.

Food and Beverage Sales

Food and beverage sales in **stadium concessions** during games are another important source of revenue for stadium owners and clubs. The rights to establish such restaurants are sold for substantial sums. In order to recoup these costs, the price of foods and beverages for sale is typically much higher than those at a restaurant across the street from the stadium. While a neighbouring restaurant may lose sales during games, it may gain them back – and actually see an increase in business – when the crowd spills out into the street and decides to wait until the street traffic gridlock and overloaded public transit become more accessible.

Alternative Use of Sport Stadiums

Sports stadiums are only used for their principal purpose – as sites for sports events – for a fraction of the time, although in many large North American cities, joint organization of two or more professional teams in different sports allows single stadiums to serve as "homes" for these teams concurrently. (A prime example of this occurs in Toronto, where the NHL's Maple Leafs and the NBA's Raptors both play their home games on alternating nights at the downtown Air Canada Centre.) But during non-game nights, or during the off-season, the owners of the stadium (very often the public) can defray some of the construction and operation costs if the other time can be used commercially. Thus, sports stadiums have become a common site for musical concerts, religious gatherings, trade shows, and as sites for amateur sports such as high-school and university football playoffs. In Canada, attempts have been recently made to use hockey stadiums for professional lacrosse games and even roller hockey games during the summer.

Charities

Most professional sports teams sponsor charitable activities directly, such as having special game days for donations to a worthy cause or charitable organization, or indirectly by establishing their own charitable institution whose activities team players are expected to support in their off hours. In this role, sports celebrities can serve as positive role models in the wider community and dispel somewhat the notion that they are greedy and insensitive to the fans, thereby generating favourable publicity for the team. Charitable organizations gain access to funds which would not otherwise be available while gate receipts may be increased for the clubs.

Contribution to Local Economies

From a strictly economic standpoint, professional sports teams contribute to the local economy in which they are situated. For instance, clubs pay taxes to all levels of government and employ scores of people in support roles. Sporting events are also tourist attractions. They draw visitors who spend their money in local businesses, such as hotels, taxi companies, and restaurants. Sports teams also buy services in local communities. For instance, sporting events must be advertised in order to build up a dedicated fan base. Many people are employed in the advertising business and in the customer fulfilment area (such as taking phone reservations and distributing tickets). The tickets and programs themselves must be produced as well. In addition, sports coverage provides media at all levels – from local newspapers, radio stations and television networks – with important content.

In a less economically driven way, pro sports franchises play a unifying role in bringing large numbers of people together to rally behind a common goal. In Canada, there are many notable instances of the ways in which large-scale sporting events can unify communities, such as the support and enthusiasm shown for professional hockey teams, or our national hockey squads when they compete in Olympic or World Championship competition.

Indeed, the landmark deciding game of the 1972 "Summit Series" between Canada and the USSR – and the winning goal netted by Canada's Paul Henderson – are still, more than thirty years later, hailed as "great Canadian moments" in history books and documentary films. And, more recently, the largest audience ever to watch a hockey game in Canada sat down – and likely stood up and cheered – to see Canada defeat the United States at the 2002 Winter Games in Salt Lake City, another experience that brought a sense of national pride to millions.

WHERE DO WE GO FROM HERE?

In this section, we have looked at the way in which the big business of sport has many important implications for society as a whole. We have examined the numerous ways in which the popular media plays a part in this impact, and how the role of money (i.e., profit) has changed sport over the years.

We have also examined how much of the professional sport we come into contact with in the course of a day – on television, in the newspaper, on the Internet, and in the form of the myriad products we see being worn and consumed – is organized and presented to us.

In the following section, we will take a look at a very different kind of sport – the sport that is played in schools and communities. In the context of communities and schools, sporting events take on a very different social meaning than they do in professional sport. Participants – coaches, athletes, spectators – take part in sports for reasons that have little to do with financial gain and everything to do with fun and enjoyment.

Francois-Louis Tremblay, Eric Bedard, and Mathieu Turcotte celebrate after setting a new Olympic record during competition in the men's 5000-metre relay semifinals short-track speed-skating race in the Winter Olympics in Salt Lake City, 2002 (AP PHOTO/Doug Mills).

30
School and Community Sport Programs

"By choosing to take part, you're already a winner."
— popular community-sport saying

Physical education and amateur sport in Canada have evolved over the last two centuries. From the struggle to legitimize sport in the Canadian school curriculum to the establishment of youth and recreational leagues in our communities, the structure and goals of sports programs have changed dramatically.

Now, with childhood obesity on the rise, establishing physical activity as a positive element in young people's lives seems more important than ever. School and community athletic programs can help youth build and maintain a lifelong relationship with sport. However, the ways in which physical education is administered can vary greatly from one organization to the next.

In this section, we will look at the development of sport in Canadian schools and the way in which governments and communities support these programs, sometimes with different (and conflicting) goals and results. Finally, we will explore the benefits – both personal and social – arising from community and school sport programs.

PHYSICAL EDUCATION IN SCHOOLS

Physical education now seems as natural a part of the school curriculum as math or English classes, but it was not always this way. Physical education has come a long way from the elite English private schools of the nineteenth century to the Canadian public school system we know today. Its purpose has also changed dramatically. Once a means for training society's future leaders or military commanders, sport is now recognized as inherently valuable and a vital part of every student's life. Despite the acceptance it has gained as a legitimate academic course, it still lurks on the margins of the curriculum and is often the first subject to suffer when schools undergo funding cuts.

Early Timeline of Physical Education in Canadian Schools

- 1830 – Upper Canada College, the first private school in Ontario, is founded in Toronto. It carries over the British games tradition of physical education in private schools, starting with a cricket team.

- 1846 – Egerton Ryerson introduces his public education plan. Physical education becomes part of the curriculum, but it is not mandatory; individual teachers and school boards are left to decide whether or not to teach it.

- 1852 – The Normal School is established in Toronto. Physical training is included in the curriculum, but classes focus mainly on gymnastics and calisthenics.

- 1872 – *The Ontario Education Act*, which recognizes physical education as a school subject, is introduced.

- 1878 – The first teachers' certificates recognizing proficiency in physical training are awarded.
- 1880 – Public schools begin to organize extracurricular games.
- 1889 – Physical training becomes compulsory.
- 1909 – The Strathcona Trust is established, providing future funding for physical education.

Rugby College: The Victorian Ideal of Sport

Invented in 1823 at Rugby College in England, the sport of rugby was enormously popular with students and eventually spawned Australian rugby and Canadian and American football. Thomas Arnold, headmaster of Rugby from 1828 to 1842, worked to diversify the college's curriculum to include previously neglected subjects, such as science and physical activity. But he did not consider team sports such as rugby as important as physical activity; it was not until after Arnold's time that they gained so much attention.

Arnold's son, Matthew, went on to become a school inspector and, like his father, a strong advocate for school reform. Although he is best known as a poet and literary critic, he had strong ideas regarding democratic education in England that greatly affected the school system there and furthered the cause for physical education.

His fellow student, Thomas Hughes, was also greatly influenced by the senior Arnold's philosophy. He went on to write *Tom Brown's Schooldays*, a novel chronicling life in a college similar to Rugby. Cricket and rugby featured prominently in the book, which coined the phrase muscular Christianity. This term was used to describe the popular idea that physical activity was directly linked to moral righteousness. Muscular Christianity equated physical strength with spiritual fortitude. To engage in physical activity was to be a good Christian – or at least be on the path towards being one. This attitude was meant to inspire spiritual and patriotic fervour, and it was no coincidence that the skills learned on the football field – strength, discipline, teamwork – were transferable to the military battlefield.

Early Private Schools in Canada

Before the development of a public school system in Canada, physical education was available only to those with access to private education. As descendants of British private schools, these early Canadian counterparts also equated team sports with manliness and moral development. The promotion of British sports in the upper-class private schools in Canada was a means of supporting the British Empire. By propagating the British ideals of manliness and gentility, England was grooming future Canadian leaders.

Dr. Egerton Ryerson: A Canadian Community Sport Pioneer

Born in 1803 in Norfolk County in what was then Upper Canada, Egerton Ryerson is widely recognized as the founder of Canadian public education. He began as a travelling Methodist preacher at the age of eighteen. For many years he lived as a missionary and dedicated his professional life to religion and politics.

In 1844 he was offered the post of chief superintendent of education for Upper Canada. His goal was to make education accessible to all. After reviewing American and European education models, he developed an extensive plan for public education that became the foundation for the education system we know today. Physical education gained ground as an important component in this new system.

In 1852, the Normal School for teacher training was established in Toronto. Physical education attained professional status as teachers were schooled in this new subject. The emphasis was still on building character and skill, rather than on sport, but the stage was set for further development.

The University of Toronto was the first university in the British Empire to establish a degree program for training in physical and health education. In the fall of 1940 six men and eleven women began the program. Finally, with the recognition that physical education was a true profession, it started to gain some serious attention in the school curriculum.

Strathcona Trust: An Early Model for Sport Funding

In 1910, Lord Strathcona established a trust fund of $500,000 for physical education. Impressed by the British physical education system, Lord Strathcona intended for the money to be administered by the Canadian government and distributed to schools for the express purpose of building similar programs in Canada. Lord Strathcona stipulated that the money be used to promote physical training and to establish a military cadet corps in public schools. At this time, most teachers were retired military officers who used drills, calisthenics, and gymnastics to instil a sense of discipline in their students. If private education was preparing the elite for leadership, the public schools were preparing the masses for a lifetime of hard work and discipline.

In the 1920s and 1930s, this style of physical education came under fire for being too rigid and militaristic. Team sports and games remained largely extracurricular. Track and field was popular, but the emphasis was still on discipline and training, not play and sport.

PHYSICAL EDUCATION IN TODAY'S SCHOOLS

The aim of physical education in the school curriculum is to promote physical activity in all students, regardless of social or economic differences. Sport in school is supposed to present a "level playing field," where all students are encouraged to participate.

The Canadian Association for Health, Physical Education, Recreation and Dance (CAHPERD) recommends a minimum of 150 instructional minutes per week of physical education. Although provincial standards vary, most schools do not offer anywhere near that amount of time. Physical education programs vary from school to school – even from year to year within a school – because funding for sport is dependent upon provincial government education spending and, as a consequence, individual school board budgets.

Budget cuts in the 1990s have left many school boards across the country scrambling for cash. As administrators struggle to compile their budgets, money previously allocated for sport programs is often diverted to satisfy academic demands. Not only has the amount of time devoted to sport been decreased dramatically in some provinces, but there is currently a shortage of qualified instructors and consultants available, and a severe lack of facilities and equipment necessary for sport activities.

In the face of these cuts, schools have been forced to adapt their programs in an effort to provide some level of physical education to their students. Some schools share equipment with other schools and make use of community facilities, such as parks, skating rinks, and swimming pools. They attempt to compensate for the lack of staff by training students to be peer leaders in classes and intramural competitions, and they invite community members, such as coaches, into the classroom to share their expertise with the students and teachers. Fundraising has also become an important aspect of administering a physical education program. Bake sales and car washes now fund new hockey equipment or uniforms for the volleyball team. Corporate sponsors are becoming another sports-funding option for cash-strapped schools.

Despite the measures schools undertake to keep physical education alive and well, the programs have suffered, proven by current participation rates. Teachers now have less time than ever for extracurricular events. In 2000 the Ontario government introduced controversial Bill 74, the *Education Accountability Act*, which defined extracurricular activities as mandatory for teachers. This caused a massive uproar in the teaching community and a year-long work-to-rule campaign, during which time teachers offered no services outside of class time. These sometimes bitter labour disputes – not at all unique to Ontario – have not served to foster a positive environment for sport in schools. Organizations do exist, however, to create and support positive sport experiences for students. What follows is a few examples.

Canadian Intramural Recreation Association

The Canadian Intramural Recreation Association seeks to reduce physical inactivity through sport in education. A national organization, it works in partnership with the federal government as well as its provincial and territorial affiliates to encourage all children to participate in school sports. Volunteers are active on all levels – from working directly with students to training other volunteers and teachers in how to develop fun physical activity programs for all students, regardless of age, gender, size, skill, culture, or socioeconomic status.

Canadian School Sport Federation

Each province in Canada has its own student sport federation, and these are gathered under the umbrella of the Canadian School Sport Federation. The branches comprise volunteer coaches, students, and administrators dedicated to the promotion of sport in education. Aside from offering leadership and resources to sport educators, each federation organizes provincial championships.

In Ontario, the Ontario Federation of School Athletic Associations, or OFSAA, consists of approximately 300,000 members – athletes, coaches, teachers and administrators – devoted to the promotion of education through sport. OFSAA regulates Ontario sport competitions. To date, it sponsors competitions in over twenty sports, not counting all the divisions and levels within each sport. The association has formulated a constitution to govern issues such as drugs, gender equity, and rules of behaviour. Ontario tournaments that host teams from outside the province must apply for OFSAA sanction to ensure that the competition meets all of OFSAA's rules and guidelines for fair play.

OFSAA also keeps statistics on student sport in Ontario. For example, the most recent set of statistics (www.ofsaa.on.ca) indicates that, for the 2001-02 school year, a total of about 245,000 Ontario high-school students competed in inter-school events, a rise of 62 percent from the previous year. Of this total, approximately 110,000 of the athletes were girls and 135,000 were boys, representing respective rises of 61 and 63 percent. The most popular interscholastic sport for girls was volleyball (with about 15,000 players across the province), followed by basketball and soccer; for boys, the top choice was basketball (about 16,000 participants), followed by soccer and football.

Sport Scholarships

A worthwhile goal for Canadian high-school athletes?

Anyone who has spent time in a secondary school athletic setting is familiar with sports scholarships. Many Canadian high-school athletes have decided to travel to the United States to pursue both their post-secondary studies and to further their athletic careers at the intercollegiate level, mostly in competition sponsored by the National Collegiate Athletic Association (NCAA) in track and field, football, basketball, hockey, tennis, and other sports.

The system does have its detractors. Opponents of athletic scholarships say that student athletes are forced to over-emphasize the sporting side of collegiate life, thereby compromising their educational priorities. Also, the tremendous emphasis placed on sports means that coaches can force athletes to overtrain and overcompete in an attempt to further team goals while sacrificing individual development.

In recent years, Canadian universities have begun considering the possibility of offering them to student athletes in an attempt to stop the southward flow of talent while raising the level of competition in Canada. For example, the University of Toronto has been working to raise money from alumni and corporations since the mid-1990s in an effort to develop an endowment that will allow qualified student athletes to compete at an intercollegiate level with some financial assistance.

In other parts of Canada, universities are actively looking to attract athletes who are also qualified students. One such institution, the University of Alberta in Edmonton, gave out almost $800,000 in athletic scholarships in the 2002-03 school year, $533,000 of which came from provincial scholarships paid by the Alberta government. These scholarships require the student to have lived in Alberta for two years and to maintain a 5.7 (out of 9) grade average in their university studies.

Whether a Canadian high-school athlete is considering a sports scholarship in the United States or in their home

Kevin Sullivan of Brantford, Ontario, after finishing the 1500-metre final at the 2000 Olympics in Sydney. Sullivan attended the University of Michigan on an athletic scholarship (CP PHOTO/Kevin Frayer).

country, there are a number of factors that coaches, athletes, and advisors recommend that they consider.

What are the conditions of the scholarship I am being offered?

This includes the length of the scholarship (guaranteed for the full four years of an undergraduate degree, or renewal evaluated on a year-by-year basis), as well as what financial aspects it covers, such as tuition fees, residence fees, cost of books and academic materials, food allowance, travel expenses, athletic equipment, and so on.

What is expected of me as a scholarship recipient?

Many coaches have performance expectations upon which continuation of the scholarship is based, such as recording certain times in competitions or qualifying for certain levels of competition. Coaches also often have academic standards that must be met for an athlete to be eligible for competition. All of these should be clear to both the athlete and coach from the outset.

What is the school's position on mixing academics with sport?

Student athletes must remember that success in sports alone will not ensure a successful scholarship experience. Obtaining a university degree is invaluable, and both coach and athlete must work together to ensure that this becomes a reality. Often, academic and athletic schedules come into conflict, so the athlete should ascertain how these will be handled. Some university sport programs offer academic assistance to athletes as well.

What is the school's record with athletes from a similar background?

Although a university team in a given sport may have compiled a winning record, it is still necessary to ascertain whether this success is relevant to a specific athlete's goals. For example, has a successful track-and-field team developed great athletes in all disciplines, or only in the sprints and field events but not in middle- and long-distance running? Also, Canadians attending university in the U.S. should determine whether other athletes from their province have attended a given school and enjoyed success.

What will the student athlete's overall role be on the team?

Many athletes who have been highly successful in high-school competition find themselves somewhat overwhelmed when they begin competing at a university level. Although they were successful enough to have attained an athletic scholarship and likely excelled at the provincial or even national level, on entering collegiate competition, they may find themselves far from being the best athlete on their own team, struggling to qualify even for their university's varsity team. The athlete and his or her prospective coach should establish exactly how this transition will be managed. Will the first-year athlete be expected to move in and take on the role of "star" right away, or is there room for development in later seasons?

COMMUNITY PROGRAMS

Community programs strive to fill the gaps and pick up where larger government programs leave off. For many community members, local sport organizations provide an important resource for physical activity and socialization. Although paid administrators and coaches enter the picture at higher levels of sport, in most Canadian youth leagues and associations, the organizational responsibilities fall to unpaid volunteers, such as parents, high-school and university students looking to gain practical experience as part of their academic studies in physical education, and other willing volunteers.

Regardless of who is organizing the program, there are a number of key areas for organizers to consider, including policy, infrastructure, coaching, accessibility, and liability.

- *Community sport policy.* Logically, this is where the planning should begin, but this aspect sometimes gets sidestepped. Despite the lack of attention it receives, it is important to articulate the goals of any sport program. Administrators, coaches, and volunteers should agree on a sport philosophy so that all aspects of planning can reflect the policy developed for the program. Most community programs strive for maximum participation, so inclusion is key. Organizers determine what participants will want and need, what barriers to accessibility exist, and how they can overcome them. They also develop an ethical code of conduct to govern the behaviour of all the organization's participants – coaches and players alike.

- *Organizational infrastructure.* Many community programs – whether formal leagues with hired coaches, or a collective of parent-run youth teams – create an organizational structure to manage the group and ensure that it lasts beyond the first season. In order to manage volunteers, players and cash flow, all participants – coaches, treasurers, and executives alike – need to have defined roles.

- *Coaching.* Coaches are undoubtedly a vital part of any community sport program. They have perhaps the closest connection with the players, providing encouragement, support, and guidance as well as professional instruction in technique and skill. A good coach is key to providing a positive sport experience to participants.

  The Coaching Association of Canada (CAC) offers programs for training and certification of coaches in over sixty sports. The National Coaching Certification Program (NCCP) was developed in close collaboration with the federal, provincial, and territorial levels of both government and sports federations. The program is useful for all levels of sport – from coaches working with young kids who may be experiencing sport for the first time to those working with professional athletes. It teaches coaches how to recognize and meet the needs of participants, how to create a positive sport experience, and how to help participants meet their full potential as athletes.

  The NCCP differentiates between coach training and coach certification. Coach training is geared primarily towards community and volunteer coaches looking to expand and improve their skills. The program teaches them how to create sound practice sessions and develop the basic skills of their participants through sport.

  The Coaching Association of Canada also offers workshops and online resources for community coaches just starting out in the field. The Sport Leadership Program is designed specifically for the community sport environment and advises in such areas as liability, financial management, marketing, and volunteering screening practices.

- *Accessibility.* When organizing a community club, accessibility becomes a key issue. This includes fees charged for registration and any equipment, such as uniforms, that may be needed. Organizations that strive to be inclusive will need to determine what fees they can charge for facilities and equipment. Also, inclusive organizations need to develop policies for individuals whose access to sport or recreation may be impeded by certain barriers, such as physical disability or language. This may involve adapting existing community policies, such as local regulations concerning the use of facilities for people with disabilities.

- *Liability.* Liability is an important issue at any level of sport; in a community program without a formal structure, it can often be an afterthought. Participants need to be aware of potential risks and be prepared to accept responsibility for behaviour and actions. At the same time, community sport program administrators should be informed about the different types of insurance available to sports and recreation programs. Coverage for individuals and small groups can often be obtained through provincial sport organizations, depending on the type of sport and level of competition. Regardless of insurance coverage, though, the best way to avoid insurance and liability issues is for parents, volunteers, coaches, and participants to promote safe practices and injury prevention.

"Thin Ice" in Winnipeg
Community involvement in professional sport

That Canadians are passionate about hockey is something well known the world over. With that popularity comes another oft-repeated idea about hockey in Canada – its ability to act as a unifying force for many communities as people share in the exploits of their local teams. But in 1995, this ability of hockey to unite a community came under serious scrutiny by the Canadian media.

In the spring of that year, it appeared as though the NHL's Winnipeg Jets would no longer be able to remain in the Manitoba capital. The team was playing poorly, and consequently, had a dismal attendance record – leading to a significant loss of revenue.

Several years before, the Jets had appealed to the city and provincial governments for financial support, which they received. But by the mid-1990s, team owner Barry Shenkarow was again claiming that unless his team received some substantial federal, provincial and city government help – this time in the form of a $120-million new arena, built with public funds – he would have to move it to a community with a wider fan base.

This situation has, in fact, arisen in many instances in so-called "small-market" cities across North America, as professional sport teams look to move into playing facilities that can support a large number of "luxury boxes" for use by corporations who will pay large sums of money – and very little taxes – for the use of these areas to entertain business clients.

The community of Winnipeg rallied against the possible departure of the Jets to another (likely American) city, including public demonstrations, a flood of calls to radio phone-in shows, virulent newspaper editorials, and speeches by politicians at all levels of government. But what at first glance seemed to be a unified movement to keep the team in Winnipeg actually turned out to be a point of significant contention on the city's political scene. This was the result of two professors at

Jets players do a lap around the arena after their last game in Winnipeg, 1996 (CP PHOTO/STR-Joe Bryksa).

the University of Winnipeg, Carl Ridd and Jim Silver, who launched a competing initiative in an attempt to remind Winnipeggers that, despite their loyalty to the team and their desire that their city and provincial governments take action to keep it from leaving, there were more pressing and important social and economic problems than keeping an NHL franchise in Winnipeg, a city with its fair share of social woes.

Thin Ice

Known as the "Thin Ice" movement, Ridd and Silver worked, as writer Doug Smith put it, to remind Canadians that "in the nation's child-poverty capital, the public bail-out of a team of millionaires and neo-millionaires, owned by a group of hyper-millionaires, represented a rather skewed ordering of priorities."

Adding to the community interest was the fact that, as the threat of the Jets' departure became more and more serious, a provincial election loomed near. In early April 1995, Scott Taylor, a sports columnist for the Winnipeg Free Press, appeared on a national broadcast of Hockey Night in Canada. He told

viewers that, since the Liberal party had gone on record as saying that they had not decided whether to support the building of a new arena, and the NDP was claiming that it definitely would not, the Tories, under Premier Gary Filmon – who had publicly committed themselves to putting $10 million towards the new stadium – were the party to vote for if Manitobans wanted to keep the Jets in the province. Indeed, Filmon and the PCs did win the election.

Taylor later – and probably correctly – said that his views as aired on Hockey Night in Canada could hardly have been said to have been responsible for the Conservative's election win. But his involvement did highlight another important aspect of the way in which the "Save the Jets" campaign was played out in the Winnipeg community – while all the local media backed efforts to prevent the team from moving, at the same time they attempted to discredit the important role of the Thin Ice activist group.

In the midst of all of the public gatherings, one of which saw close to 35,000 people assemble for a benefit concert, and a huge outpouring of donations to the team from private citizens estimated at about $12 million, with $62 million coming from the private sector, the drive to keep the Jets from leaving Winnipeg suffered a big setback. The city and provincial governments gave $37 million to the proposed new stadium, but the federal government would not commit to this amount. (It eventually committed to "only" $20 million.)

Ultimately, the Jets relocated to Phoenix, Arizona, and were reborn as the Phoenix Coyotes. For many people in the Winnipeg capital, the failure of the franchise to remain there is just another example of a small-market team losing out in the high-dollar world of pro sports. But from the perspective of community issues, the 1995 Jets controversy reveals much more – namely, the fact that while sports can unite a community, they can also pull it apart.

LEAGUES AND CLUBS

Organized sports leagues and clubs often focus on formal skill development and competition. The development of the sport is a concern so future stars are sought out to keep the level of competition up to perceived standards of excellence. There is a marked difference between these types of clubs and more inclusive community-centred sports clubs in terms of organization, the facilities and funds available, the type of participants they attract, and their ultimate goals. In comparison to the volunteer-run community teams, organized clubs are usually well-structured, open only to those who can afford the administration and equipment costs, and are concerned mainly with grooming top athletes for advancement in sport.

Minor Hockey in Canada

A sport that is played from coast to coast, hockey is the quintessential Canadian sport. It is played on frozen lakes, at community rinks, and even on suburban streets around the country. So, of course, there exists a well-established system of leagues in every city, town, and province. Young players who take the sport seriously (and their parents) can look forward to investing in expensive sports equipment and getting up at the crack of dawn for early morning games, but for many it all seems worthwhile. Most professional hockey players started out in community leagues and progressed to the NHL, becoming well-paid Canadian heroes. Maybe it is for this reason that the focus of amateur hockey leagues is less on the individual and more about breeding talent and maintaining or improving the competitive level of the sport as these players eventually filter into the professional leagues.

Canadian Hockey Association

The Canadian Hockey Association (CHA) held its first meeting on December 4, 1914. It began with an eye towards promoting senior hockey in Canada and establishing a national championship at that level. However, through the years it has had an on-again, off-again relationship with the NHL and, with the creation of the World Hockey Association in 1971, the two groups finally severed their ties. Now the association's mandate is to support amateur hockey in Canada. Most recently, minor hockey has expanded greatly. The CHA organizes provincial and regional playoffs and established Minor Hockey Week – a major promotional project held annually in January – making minor hockey even more popular.

Although the CHA focuses on amateur hockey, it still retains a strong connection to the professional game through its players – some of whom will go on to NHL careers – and through the Hockey Hall of Fame, at which the association is responsible for creating the amateur hockey displays. Over the years, they have showcased the different national trophies sponsored by the CHA – the Allan Cup, the Hardy Cup, the OHA Memorial Cup – and the teams who have won them. Also on display are the winners of the CHA's award for coaches, players, and association members who have made outstanding contributions to Canadian amateur hockey. Celebrating the dedication and achievement of amateur hockey within the walls of the Hockey Hall of Fame legitimizes the Canadian Hockey Association's place as a training ground for professional hockey.

Community Centres

Community recreation centres act as a common meeting ground where people from different social, economic, and cultural backgrounds can interact and support one another. Physical activity and sport are often seen as a means by which individuals can get involved in their community, interact with and support one another, and pursue a healthy lifestyle. Community sport programs support the belief that healthy individuals create a healthy society. Their services are therefore geared towards this end – they are meant to be inclusive, educational, and fun.

Fun Leagues

In many communities across Canada, sport organizers for youth have developed the idea of the "fun league" in sports such as basketball, soccer, and baseball. In these leagues, coaches, parents, and players agree by their participation to abide by the principles of fair play and inclusion – that is, maximum playing time for everyone – while limiting competitive aspects. For example, most fun soccer leagues have an overall rule against keeping score in individual games, and the leagues themselves do not have final standings. Instead, each player receives a trophy at the end of the year.

Coaches place an emphasis on the development of skills, especially in young players, and attempt to develop a love of the particular sport that will last a lifetime. In addition, fun leagues generally adopt a zero-tolerance policy on issues such as violence, harassment, and abuse. Generally, parents and athletes looking for a more "intense" sporting atmosphere for youngsters are encouraged to move to a more competitive league if the opportunities offered in fun leagues do not seem appropriate. This should not suggest that the level of play in such low-key leagues is necessarily sub-par; on the contrary, the relaxed atmosphere often brings out the best in players, parents, and coaches, with excellent results on the sporting level.

Health and Physical Education Associations
Promoting exercise in schools and communities across Canada

At the national and provincial levels there are a number of noteworthy organizations that put a great deal of time and effort into encouraging sport and physical activity among young people. These include CAHPERD (Canadian Association for Health, Physical Education Recreation and Dance) and Ophea (Ontario Physical and Health Education Association) – the two largest organizations – as well as similar advocacy organizations across the country.

CAHPERD

The Canadian Association for Health, Physical Education Recreation and Dance (CAHPERD) is a national charitable organization, based in Ottawa.

CAHPERD's roots were established in 1933, when a McGill University scholar, Dr. Arthur S. Lamb, founded a group called The Canadian Physical Education Association (CPEA). In 1948, the association changed its name to the Canadian Association for Health, Physical Education and Recreation (CAHPER) and, in 1994, to incorporate the increasing role that dance education had come to play in Canada, the organization's name was changed to its current acronym.

CAHPERD offers an array of teaching and learning resources for students and teachers, and supports and promotes research (notably through its bilingual journal *Avante*). It also sponsors and organizes health and physical education conferences and workshops across Canada (www.cahperd.ca).

At the school level, CAHPERD's key initiative is QDPE (Quality Daily Physical Education), a program supported by resources such as the "QDPE Report Card" and the "School Recognition Award Program," to help students to become more active in school and to assist teachers in helping them along.

Information about CAHPERD and its initiatives, as well as support material and resources, can be found on the world wide web at www.cahperd.ca.

Ontario's Laura Roberts battles against Quebec's Helene Couture during the under-15 Canadian Girls Soccer Championship, July 2000 (CP PHOTO/ *Winnipeg Free Press*-Phil Hossack).

Ophea

Ophea (Ontario Physical and Health Education Association) is a leading authority on the health of children and youth.

Ophea is a not-for-profit organization dedicated to supporting school communities through advocacy, quality programs and services, and partnership building. Ophea is led by the vision that all children and youth will value, participate in, and make a lifelong commitment to, active healthy living.

Ophea provides quality programs, services, resources, training, and support to school communities to help enable children and youth to lead active healthy lives. Ophea works strategically to develop active healthy school communities, addressing such areas as physical activity, nutrition, health and physical education curriculum, substance use and abuse, safety and injury prevention, as well as other health-related issues pertaining to children and youth.

Ophea has long-standing and well-developed relationships with leaders in education and health promotion. Ophea also hosts and organizes a number of conferences, workshops, and information sessions throughout the province for education and health professionals.

Information about Ophea and its initiatives, as well as articles, activity ideas, resources and more, is available at www.ophea.net.

Provincial Associations

CAHPERD also acts as a central source of information on the various provincial and territorial organizations:

- Newfoundland: Physical Education Special Interest Council (PESIC)
- Prince Edward Island: Prince Edward Island Physical Education Association (PEIPA)
- Nova Scotia: Teachers Association – Physical and Health Education (TAPHE)
- New Brunswick (English language): New Brunswick Physical Education Society
- New Brunswick (French language): Association des professionnel(le)s de l'education physique
- Quebec (French language): Federation des educateurs et educatrices physiques enseignant du Quebec (FEEPEQ)
- Quebec (English language): Association for Physical Education in Quebec (APEQ)
- Ontario (French language): Association franco-ontariens des educatrices et educateurs physiques (AFOEEP)
- Manitoba: Manitoba Physical Education Teachers Association (MPETA)
- Saskatchewan: Saskatchewan Physical Education Association (SPEA)
- Alberta: Health and Physical Education Council (HPEC)
- British Columbia: Physical Education Provincial Specialist Association British Columbia (PEPSABC).

YMCA IN CANADA

In the 1840s, England was in the throes of the Industrial Revolution. Like many young men of his age, George Williams, a young draper's assistant, moved to London from a small town in rural England in order to learn his trade. He worked in a factory that employed 140 men and found that many of them were in the same situation – alone and struggling in the big city. In response to his situation, Williams founded the Young Men's Christian Association (YMCA) in 1844. In the beginning it consisted only of George and eleven of his friends, all of whom felt the need for a supportive Christian group in a city that offered too many unhealthy diversions. The group, which centred its activities around Bible study and recreational pursuits, quickly grew.

In 1851 a group of Canadians who were familiar with the British organization decided to start their own YMCA in Montreal, Quebec. It was only two years later that they hired their first professional worker, Samuel Massey, from Manchester, England. Under his guidance, the group focused on education, socializing, and religious studies. Eventually, physical activity officially became another priority for the Montreal YMCA. By this time, there were many other YMCA organizations across Canada, also providing physical education along with religious and social support to their respective communities.

In the early days, physical education classes were offered in wrestling, fencing, track and field, and gymnastics; swimming and lifesaving followed shortly after. Other games and team sports were also played, including basketball, lacrosse, baseball, and football. All lessons promoted the values of the YMCA, such as fair play and respect, and encouraged leadership skills, character building, and camaraderie with fellow members.

The popularity of the YMCA in Canada continued to grow. As a result, finding places to offer all of its programs became increasing difficult. In the early days, meetings were held in schools, churches, and people's homes, but soon permanent buildings seemed an inevitable part of the YMCA's progress. The first Canadian YMCA buildings were established in the Maritimes where towns with considerable wealth could afford them. Eventually these community centres dotted the Canadian landscape from coast to coast, and now they are practically indispensable to the YMCA's services.

Permanent homes allowed the YMCA to develop consistent and quality programs. The YMCA has undertaken many major initiatives since its inception, always with a proven commitment to physical education and the development of strong and healthy individuals and communities.

Leaders' Corps

Established in 1892 in Montreal, the Leaders' Corp trained YMCA members to express the Y's core values of kindness and community involvement through physical education. Students learned about anatomy, physiology, and first aid; attended morality lectures, Bible study, and prayer meetings; and participated in the community by officiating at sport events, initiating athletic leagues, and operating playgrounds or gymnasiums. A similar corps was developed for youth in 1908, but women were not welcomed with their own leadership program until 1948. Now many organizations outside of the YMCA also participate in the program, which has since moved beyond its original focus on physical education.

Military Work

From the Boer War to the Second World War, YMCA members have supported Canadian troops overseas. The YMCA tradition of combining sports and recreational programs with vital community support did not change during times of war. Military support services provided food, medical attention, religious services, entertainment, and education, along with sports and athletics programs to Canadian soldiers. By 1943 almost 70 million soldiers had participated in YMCA Military Service Programs.

YMCA Camps

The first YMCA camping trip took place in Nova Scotia in 1890. The program took off and other camps were quickly established across the country. These camps maintained the focus of the YMCA, fostering spiritual and social growth through sport and physical activity. More than a century later, the camping programs are still going strong and new, innovative programs have been developed. Larger day camps created in the 1980s to reach out to the whole community are still hugely popular. And, like the city programs, the YMCA day camps strive to be inclusive; financial assistance is available to ensure that the camp experience is accessible to all youth.

Aquatics Program

In 1888 the Toronto YMCA built the organization's first swimming pool. Swimming, once seen as a distraction from real physical exercise, began to grow in popularity. In 1906 a radical new swimming program was implemented. It differed in two ways from previous strategies: it was taught by a group of instructors rather than an individual, and it began with land drills, allowing the students to practice their stroke techniques before entering the water. Many regionalized programs were initiated to promote swimming

More than one thousand runners are shown at the start of the 21-km race during the 22nd Gatorade Half-Marathon held in Peterborough, Ontario, February 2000. The event is a fund raiser for the YMCA and part of the Great Canadian Race series (CP PHOTO/*The Peterborough Examiner* -Ray Bourgeois).

instruction. In 1909 a North American learn-to-swim campaign was launched, and the following year, a national YMCA swimming instruction program was developed in which 30,000 boys enrolled. The YMCA even trained military soldiers to swim in the First World War by using land drills and survival swimming – an exercise that required soldiers to swim in deep water while carrying heavy packs of gear. The YMCA has since proved to be a popular provider of swimming instruction to Canadians. By 1984, the collective YMCA was the largest operator of swimming pools in the world.

The YWCA

The female counterpart to the YMCA, the Young Women's Christian Association (YWCA) began in England in the mid-1850s when nurses, who were the first women to serve at the front of major battles, began returning home after the Crimean War. (One of them was the well-known nurse Florence Nightingale, who was instrumental in setting up hospitals for English soldiers on the battlegrounds.) During this time, the Industrial Revolution saw women as well as men leaving family farms to look for work in the industrializing cities.

This combination of empowerment and a need for urban shelter led to the opening of the first YWCA in England in 1855, and the initial chapter in the U.S., in 1858. In 1870, a woman named Agnes Blizzard organized the first Canadian YWCA in two rooms she had rented in Saint John, New Brunswick. Soon after, YWCAs opened in Toronto (1873), Montreal (1874), and Quebec City and Halifax (1875).

From the outset, there have been two main strains of activity in the YWCA's mandate – one that promotes the spreading of a religious message, and one that advocates social activism, such as aid for the poor and better housing for all. Today, the YWCA is active around the world, combining service and social action programming with a wide array of sports and physical activities in its sites in large urban areas. In keeping with its early commitment to housing and shelter, most YWCA chapters provide affordable places to stay for women and their families.

DROP-IN CENTRES

As after-school activities are being reduced or cut altogether from many schools in Canada, drop-in centres have grown in importance. The centres usually focus on sports and recreational activities, and it is these activities that usually initially attract its main clientele. Once there, however, youth generally find a range of support services, from homework help to job search resources.

Drop-in centre programs are meant to be inclusive – they are available to the whole community, regardless of race, gender, language, and economic or social status. As such, they provide an opportunity for cross-cultural interaction, resulting in greater communication and understanding in diverse and sometimes divided communities.

Perhaps most importantly, drop-in centres reach out to those who would not otherwise have access to sport facilities or programs. Youth at risk of violence, crime, or drugs often feel excluded from mainstream culture and activities. In an effort to create their own cultural meaning, they often choose to rebel against mainstream society in negative and destructive ways. Drop-in centres offer a welcoming environment and an opportunity for youth at risk to create or contribute to an alternative culture that recognizes and responds to their needs. They promote self-confidence by providing self-directed sport activities to a portion of the population who often otherwise feel a sense of powerlessness in their lives.

Midnight Basketball: A Success Story

While serving as town manager of a Washington, D.C., suburb in the mid-1980s, G. Van Standifer became concerned about the high crime rate in his town. He determined that some of this crime was a result of the lack of programs for youth at risk. Consequently, Standifer created the Midnight Basketball League (MBL) as an alternative activity for youth between the ages of fourteen and twenty-six during the "high-crime" hours of 10:00 p.m. and 2:00 a.m.

The league is now a national program supported by local businesses, law enforcement, and political and community leaders in over fifty cities across the U.S. The MBL hosts organized basketball games in an effort to reach out to youth at risk, but it also offers counselling and workshops on education, employment, personal development and responsibility, health, and conflict resolution.

In 2000, two existing Toronto basketball clubs merged to form the Grass Roots Canada Basketball, or GRC, a group that follows the MBL model of using basketball to attract and motivate youth. The program is overseen by the GRC in co-operation with different

"Zero Ceiling" instructors Liz Christy and James Roelofsen teach disadvantaged young people to snowboard at Whistler, B.C. Some of these students go on to become instructors themselves. (CP PHOTO/Bonny Makararewicz).

agencies such as the police department, local school boards, the Toronto Parks and Recreation Department, and the Toronto Correctional Department. Workshops are offered on various topics such as drug and alcohol abuse prevention, anger management, employment preparedness, nutrition, and sexually transmitted diseases. GRC believes that athletic competition helps youth to become more disciplined, focused, and self-confident. Sport motivates students to set goals and strive to achieve them, teaching them important leadership and teamwork skills along the way.

Just a few years after its inception, the program boasted eighty Canadian student athletes who were former participants of GRC, and who had become post-secondary students, the majority on full scholarship. Such success helps perpetuate the program, as former participants become future role models and examples of GRC's positive work in the community. Many of the former participants played on an elite team, representing GRC at various North American tournaments.

Recreational Programs Make a Difference
Community Sport "Knockout"

Boxing has long been considered one of the most violent of the major sports. In its professional form, it also has a long history of corruption and shady dealings on the part of promoters, trainers, and athletes alike in conjunction with the sports-gambling industry. Even in its amateur form – most notably in Olympic competition – the sport of boxing has suffered from several high-profile instances of corrupt judging.

But boxing has a much more honourable reputation from the perspective of community-based sport. Throughout the world, various boxing programs have helped at-risk urban youth escape many social problems through "learn-to-box" and more advanced programs at local gyms. These programs serve both to train youth and to teach them important lessons about life. Often a well-known fighter or trainer will be at the centre of such initiatives, using prize money to fund the program.

Although the U.S. provides the best-known examples of these youth boxing initiatives, there are several excellent examples of this kind of program in Canada.

PRYDE: Kitchener-Waterloo, Ontario

Based in Ontario's Kitchener-Waterloo region, PRYDE is the brainchild of world-ranked Canadian super-middleweight boxer Syd Vanderpool, known in boxing circles as "Syd the Jewel." Based on his work at another youth centre, Vanderpool decided to start the program in 2000 in order to fulfil his desire to teach kids about the sport he loves and as a means of combating what he saw as the increasing inactivity of young people aged ten to seventeen in his area.

Many Canadian boxing champions have grown up and developed their skills in the Kitchener-Waterloo area, and one of them, Lennox Lewis, who trained at the Waterloo Regional Boxing Academy, is the current world

PRYDE founder Syd Vanderpool, left, takes a tumble during his world super-middleweight championship bout in May 2000 (AP Photo/Tom Strattman).

heavyweight champion, the most prestigious title in the sport.

Through its clinics, PRYDE leaders teach young people both skills in sport – which it promotes in furthering muscle conditioning, building stamina, and increasing coordination – and "life skills," including discipline, self-esteem, confidence, leadership, and sportsmanship, while promoting an active approach to life. As a means of developing strong ties with the community, the program has also implemented relationships with local businesses that help to sponsor the clinics.

The Cabbagetown Boxing Club and Youth Centre: Toronto

Founded in 1972 in the east end of Toronto, the Cabbagetown Boxing Club began as a program geared to local youth. From an initial membership of just six, the club has gone on to produce several Canadian champions and Olympians, including Canadian boxing icon Shawn O'Sullivan.

The club now holds a virtually round-the-clock program of boxing training, and exercise and weight

training for male and female participants of all ages, and has been particularly innovative in the field of women's boxing. One of the club's coaches, Peter Wylie, is currently the Canadian National Women's team coach.

While the Cabbagetown centre began as sports-based community facility, it has expanded into something with a much broader reach – there is a lot more to this community-based initiative than boxing.

The "youth centre" part of the club's name is actually a misnomer, since the facility now offers a wide array of programs for people of all ages, from pre-school to seniors. In fact, a look at just some of programs that are offered (www.cabbagetownboxing.on.ca) is an indication of just how much community-based expansion has occurred since the club started in the early 1970s:

Programs for families:
- Drug prevention programs
- Family Literacy, Hearing, Vision and Speech Programs

Programs for children:
- Children's dance
- Active games after school
- Team-related sports leagues (basketball, hockey, soccer, and volleyball)

Programs for youth:
- Boxing Club
- Judo and wrestling
- Daycare
- Parent-Child programs
- Winter basketball league
- Homework Club
- Bluewater Camp for At-Risk Youth
- Pool and weight room
- Summer Sports Program
- Summer Day Camp

Programs for adults:
- English as a Second Language
- Computer training
- Job readiness and search
- Micro business support
- Drop-In Social Club

PHYSICAL HEALTH AND SPORT

Studies show that Canadian children are significantly less active today than they were only thirty years ago. Children spend more time watching television than any other activity, with the sole exception of sleeping. Those who spend most of their time watching television or sitting in front of a computer, both known commonly as "screen time," are less likely to engage in physical activity. Girls face other obstacles to establishing an active lifestyle. Studies have shown that they are often less active than boys, especially after the age of twelve, when sport begins to focus on competency rather than participation. It has been found that adolescent girls often underestimate their performance in sport and so are less inclined to participate, assuming that they are not sufficiently competent. Sport that encourages participation regardless of skill, ability, age, gender or other factors helps instil a love for sport in children at an early age.

Physical inactivity can become a lifestyle for many youth, and so a large percentage of obese children grow up to be overweight adults. In fact, the majority of Canadians, obese or not, are not active enough even to gain health benefits. For optimal health benefits, Canadian adults need 30 to 60 minutes of physical activity every day. Ideally, this should involve a combination of endurance, flexibility, and strengthening exercises.

There are many health risks associated with physical inactivity, including heart disease, high blood pressure, adult-onset diabetes, osteoporosis, stroke, depression, and colon cancer. Heart disease and stroke together rank as the number one cause of death in Canada, among both men and women. Physical activity, even moderate amounts, can help to greatly reduce the incidence of heart disease. Regular physical activity also helps to increase bone mass, preventing osteoporosis in older adults, especially in women.

Personal Development

From the British tradition of muscular Christianity to the midnight basketball teams of urban Toronto, athletic programs have always supported the idea that the benefits of sport extend beyond the physical. Sport builds character and creates healthy, responsible adults. Healthy competition teaches young athletes that success is possible through hard work, discipline, and determination. Even defeat on the playing field is useful if it is not equated with failure, but proves that every experience offers the opportunity to learn and grow. Consequently, sport spurs young athletes on in other areas of life. It motivates and allows participants to see the potential for growth and success in other circumstances. This leads to an increased sense of self-confidence and self-empowerment as young people realize that they can overcome obstacles and attain success through their own efforts.

Sport also fosters co-operation and teaches leadership skills. Working on a team presents challenges for every player, but in the end, success depends on their trust in one another and on their individual efforts to work co-operatively. Those who assume leadership roles must learn how to effectively manage a team while maintaining a sense of equality, camaraderie, and respect among its members.

While youth crime remains a problem in most of Canada – from large urban centres to small northern towns – community and political leaders are starting to recognize that physical activity is a viable solution. Programs such as Grass Roots Canada Basketball have proven that sport and recreation activities can help divert youth from crime and drugs. They offer a supportive environment where young people can release pent up physical energy and resolve conflicts on the court or field. These programs are sometimes the only ones available to youth from lower-income families – the ones who are often labelled as being "at risk" – when mainstream physical activity programs are geared towards those with the resources to pay registration fees and uniform or equipment costs.

ESTEEM Team

Created from a small British Colombia program in 1993, the ESTEEM Team is now a national not-for-profit organization that seeks to motivate and inspire youth across the country to become active in sport. Professional athletes tour Canadian schools, speaking to students about the lessons they have learned and the challenges they have faced throughout their sport careers. Athletes who have participated in the program include Jeff Adams (Paralympic gold medallist); Veronica Brenner (Olympic silver medallist in freestyle skiing); Clair Carver-Dias and Catherine Garceau (Olympic medallists, synchronized swimming); Karen Furneaux (world champion, kayak); Steve Giles (Olympic medallist, canoe); Ljiljana Ljubisic (Paralympian, athletics); and Isabelle Turcotte Baird (Olympian, triathlon).

These athletes visit schools, community centres and sport clubs, talking to youth from eight to eighteen years of age. The presenters use personal anecdotes to advise students to maintain a positive attitude, set and achieve their goals, accept both victory and failure, take responsibility for decisions, overcome obstacles, and persist on the path they have chosen. The experiences they share are meant to be relevant to all youth and easily transferable to other life situations. The focus of the ESTEEM Team is not on sport itself, but on the lessons and experiences sport offers. Again, sport is used to attract youth and motivate them to transfer the skills and values that sport promotes to other areas of life.

CREATING SOCIAL NETWORKS

Family is perhaps the most fundamental social network. Relationships within families depend on trust, respect, support and co-operation. Sport nurtures these kinds of values and relationships, and at the same time provides an opportunity for shared experiences. As families grow and individual interests change, sport can be a unifying activity that helps to strengthen bonds within the family.

The negotiation and co-operation skills learned in family sport experiences can be transferred to the community context as well. Communities are made up of individuals from different backgrounds. Sometimes these differences – social, economic, racial, religious, and political, to name but a few – seem infinite and insurmountable. But whether it is the players on a team striving to win a game or reach the playoffs, or a group of parents, volunteers, and coaches working together to build a successful soccer league for local youth, everyone is obliged to put aside differences and co-operate in pursuit of a common goal.

Each person can offer a different skill or resource to the sports program. As such, every individual has a vested interest in the success of the program and in the health of the community. This creates room for responsive and responsible citizenship to grow – responsive in that those engaged in community or school sport listen to and care about the needs and interests of its participants; responsible in that they are willing and committed to setting goals and taking action to achieve those goals.

By engaging members of the community in social interaction, sport and recreation help to reduce the feeling of loneliness and isolation so many people experience in today's individual-centred society. Whether it is in the school or in the community, sport aids in the development of social skills and encourages individuals to take active, leading roles in their lives and communities.

The facilities created for sport and recreation in neighbourhoods serve to bring the community together. Parks and recreational centres function, not only as sport facilities, but also as community meeting places where people can interact and build relationships. In larger urban areas, they also often serve as the only green space available to city inhabitants. Indeed, community spaces that are conducive to sport and leisure activities are an integral part of the health and quality of life of every neighbourhood.

RAISING AWARENESS THROUGH SPORT

Many top athletes have realized that their public visibility puts them in a position to influence people on issues that go beyond the playing surface. The work of Rick Hansen and Terry Fox has been mentioned (pages 98 and 310 respectively), but there are many more such outstanding athletes.

Bruce Kidd

In the 1960s Bruce Kidd was well known as a distance runner. An accomplished athlete, he won the 6 mile at the 1962 Commonwealth Games in Perth and was elected Male Athlete of the Year by the Canadian Press in both 1961 and 1962. At the 1966 Commonwealth Games in Kingston, he was chosen to receive the baton from the Queen as the Lead Runner in the Queen's Message Relay. He has since been inducted into the Canada's Sports Hall of Fame, the Canadian Olympic Hall of Fame, and the University of Toronto Sports Hall of Fame.

It was at the 1964 Tokyo Olympics – the first major games to exclude South Africa due to Apartheid – where Kidd felt inspired towards activism. He discovered that he could engage in the struggle for human rights through his love for sport. He became a participant in the international campaign to exclude South Africa from sport as a way of increasing awareness about the appalling ideology of Apartheid. Through letter-writing campaigns, demonstrations, and tireless lobbying efforts, things finally began to change. Canada severed its strong sporting ties with South Africa, and in 1986, the United National Committee Against Apartheid awarded Kidd a special citation "for his valuable contribution as a sportsperson to the campaign for the elimination of Apartheid and the establishment of a non-racial and democratic society in South Africa." Kidd was the first Canadian sportsperson to be invited to South Africa by the non-racial National Olympic Committee of South Africa once apartheid was abolished in 1992.

Simon Ibell

In 2002 Simon Ibell set out to cycle the length of Vancouver Island to raise awareness and funds for Mucopolysaccharidosis (MPS). Simon himself is affected by this serious and rare genetic condition of enzyme deficiency. Recent advancements in enzyme replacement technology could help the 1 in 125,000 children affected by this disease, many of whom may not live to see their tenth birthday.

It was Simon's goal to bring MPS into the public consciousness and to raise funds for this important research during his two-week trek, which received widespread media attention. In the tradition of Terry

Fox and Rick Hansen, Simon Ibell set a difficult physical goal for himself and achieved it, proving that most obstacles can be overcome with hard work and determination.

Simon's journey was meant to inspire and give hope to those living with his condition, or any difficulty – physical or otherwise. It also served as Simon's way to give back to his community, proving in the process that physical activity can bring people together in pursuit of a common goal.

HEALTH, SOCIAL, AND ECONOMIC BENEFITS

The benefits of a physically active population are far reaching. Studies have shown that people who are active are healthier both physically and mentally, and the social networks that support them as individuals are stronger as well. Accordingly, the costs of inactivity are evident in all areas of life. People who are not physically active are at a greater risk for heart disease, stroke, cancer, and other related illnesses. They generally require more medical attention than those who participate regularly in sport and other physical activities. That means increased health-care costs for visits to the physician or hospital, and costly medical procedures required for unhealthy individuals. If the population of inactive Canadians could be reduced by just 10 percent, it is estimated that we could save $5 billion in health-care costs.

Physical activity is also associated with other healthy lifestyle choices. Because of the demands of exercise, people who participate in regular physical activity usually choose a healthy diet and are less likely to smoke. Their incidence of illness and injury is decreased, which affects productivity as well as health-care costs since healthy individuals are less likely to be absent from work.

Aside from health-care costs, there are social costs incurred by inactivity. As previously discussed, physical activity reduces the incidence of youth delinquency and crime. Regular participation in sport and physical activity in youth results in reduced incidence of drug and alcohol use and smoking. This sets a foundation for a healthier lifestyle in adulthood and reduces the amount of money society will spend on drug and alcohol programs, health costs associated with the risks of smoking, and the crime that many frustrated, restless youth turn to when no alternatives exist.

Sport and recreation activities promote more than a healthy lifestyle – they serve as a means for individuals to interact socially and become involved in their communities. Sport engenders a sense of purpose and responsibility for the well-being of all members of the community. It attracts those who might otherwise fall through the cracks of our social system to community programs where they can receive an array of support services. Without the midnight basketball leagues, or the YMCA/YWCA, or even physical education in the classroom, we would be lacking a vital social networking opportunity.

The economic benefits of sport extend beyond preventative costs; sport contributes money directly to our economy as well. In addition, volunteers contribute millions of unpaid hours of service every year to sport activities in their communities. All of this work is estimated to be worth over a billion dollars.

Quality of Life for Individuals and Communities

Every year the United Nations releases a Human Development Report, which ranks the world's countries in terms of quality of life. Canada usually ranks near the top of this list, though our exact position changes from year to year. For most of us, quality of life depends on many factors, including our economic status, personal and political freedom, level of education, access to health care, and physical security. Sport can be a great contributor to our quality of life on individual, family, community, and national levels.

It is easy to see how a mutually beneficial relationship develops between those who participate in community sport and their community at large. For instance, many people identify strongly as participants in community-based sports or exercise programs. Organizers of such activities as youth leagues in soccer, hockey, or baseball, or local, recreational-level jogging, rowing, or cycling clubs often provide uniforms, T-shirts, or other items to strengthen feelings of identification. Such groups also attempt to be an integral part of their larger community. Many sponsor events that actively seek to include the participation of family members or the community at large, such as fundraising drives, special exhibition events at fairs or community gatherings, efforts to collect money on behalf of charity, or car washes or park clean-up events. All of this helps to give one a sense of belonging and strengthens our communities.

WHERE DO WE GO FROM HERE?

In this section, we have looked at the development of physical education and sport programs in schools and examined the many benefits arising from both community and school sport programs.

In the next section, we will explore some of the ethical problems that can arise in sports and in the sports community at large, such as violence, gambling, alcohol and drug abuse, and cheating.

Judges during the 2003 European Figure Skating Championships in Sweden – the first time that the new Interim Judging System was used. From the panel of fourteen judges, nine are randomly drawn, and their marks form the results (AP Photo/Martin Meissner).

31
Social and Ethical Problems in Sport

"It is the essence of athletic competition that it should be conducted fairly in accordance with the underlying principles of ethics and morality. That is what sport is all about."
— The Commission of Inquiry into the Use of Drugs and Banned Practices Intended to Increase Athletics Performance (the Dubin Inquiry), 1990

KEY CONCEPTS

- Canadian Strategy for Ethical Conduct in Sport
- Canadian Centre for Ethics in Sport
- Instrumental aggression
- Hostile aggression

- Cheating
- Recruiting violations
- Corruption of judges and officials
- World Anti-Doping Agency
- World Anti-Doping Code

- Athlete's Passport Program
- "Recreational" drug use
- Sports gambling

Fair play is a concept that has been with the world of sports since sports began. During the Victorian era, the British gentleman athlete perfected the idea of fair play and those high ideals are still with us today. The Olympics, the Commonwealth Games, and many of the sports that we play today were created with ethics in mind. As we have seen in several of the preceding sections, much of Canadian youth and amateur sport hinges on the fair-play philosophy as well. However, fair play, or ethical conduct that adheres strictly to the rules of a given sport, is unfortunately often just a concept. While the majority of the sports world believes in playing by the rules, many others believe in winning at any cost.

In this section, we will look at a national strategy that urges a return to ethical conduct and examine the issues of violence, cheating, drug and alcohol abuse, and gambling in the world of sport.

A STRATEGY FOR ETHICAL CONDUCT IN SPORT

The sports community and Canadian governments have been calling for more attention to be paid to ethical issues in sports. The Canadian Strategy for Ethical Conduct in Sport was created to ensure that participation in sports at all levels and ages is safe; to prevent doping, violence, and harassment in sport; to create a place where sports disputes can be dealt with fairly; to encourage rewards for good sportsmanship; and to promote fair play to all sports participants. The Canadian Centre for Ethics in Sport determined the strategy jointly with Sport Canada, and it is a large undertaking that encompasses all these aspects of fair play and ethical conduct. By 2012, all the stages of the implementation of the strategy will be complete and will hopefully result in a firm commitment to ethical conduct by athletes, coaches, parents, and officials; safe, non-abusive, and welcoming sports environments; the advancement of athletes regardless of their disability, gender, race, or personal circumstances; a safe environment for spectators to view events; a recognition and respect for volunteers, officials, and coaches; the accountability of organizations that receive funding; and a system that provides resolution of disputes in a fair and timely manner. Both the Canadian government and many within the sports world believe that, if all of these things are accomplished through education and promotion in the allotted time period, there will be a system set up to create the next generation of fair-play-based sports leaders.

In addition to assisting in the creation of the Canadian Strategy for Ethical Conduct in Sport, the Ottawa-based Canadian Centre for Ethics in Sport is active in a wide range of initiatives to fulfil its mission of promoting ethical conduct in all aspects of sport in Canada. As well as providing information on topics that include fair play, non-violence, and drug-free sport, the CCES is responsible for administering Canada's domestic drug-free sport program, and is an international leader in policy making in the promotion of drug-free, fair, and ethical sport around the world. (For more information on the Centre, see the list of sport-related websites at the end of this Unit.)

Hockey Violence: Brashear versus McSorley
What lessons have we learned?

For many fans, players, and commentators, on-ice fighting in North American professional hockey is considered to be "part of the game" and is actually encouraged as a strategic way of intimidating one's opponents. Indeed, most NHL teams boast one or more players who are known as "enforcers" and whose main role on their team is to intimidate the opposing team while protecting his own team's star. And for advocates of rough-and-tumble pro hockey, the presence of these enforcers – and the fighting that their presence promotes – is perfectly acceptable.

But even the staunchest defender of fighting in hockey had to be horrified at the events that transpired on February 21, 2000, in Vancouver, during a game between the hometown Canucks and the visiting Boston Bruins. Both teams had well-known enforcers on their rosters: the Vancouver Canucks' Donald Brashear and the Boston Bruins' Marty McSorley had established reputations as two of the NHL's top "tough guys," and both engaged in minor skirmishes throughout the game. Brashear seemed to have gotten the better of his opponent through most of the fighting, and many eyewitnesses reported that the Canuck player had openly taunted the Bruins' bench as he skated by.

But in the waning seconds of the game, McSorley decided to have his revenge, smashing Brashear over the head with his stick – although he later said he'd been aiming for his rival's shoulder – and sending him crumpling to the ice. Brashear's head hit the ice hard when he fell, leaving him unconscious and twitching, with blood pouring from his nose. Brashear suffered a concussion when his head hit the ice after he'd been struck. Luckily he recovered after several weeks away from the game, although he continued to have frequent headaches for some time after. "I never thought I'd see a player acting like that toward another player," Brashear told the Associated Press shortly after his recovery.

Marty McSorley and Donald Brashear in an encounter in Vancouver in 1999, the year before the stick-swinging incident (CP PHOTO/STF-Chuck Stoody).

For his part, McSorley was suspended for one full year from the NHL without pay – the longest such suspension in the league's history. Although McSorley apologized for the attack, Brashear, not surprisingly, refused to accept it. What was surprising, though, was Brashear's insistence that fighting – and intimidation – was still part of the game for professional enforcers such as him.

"That was a game that I had to play hard, where I was just doing my job. I remember we got into a fight right off the start. Those are all things that I have to do during a game," Brashear later recalled.

"In a game you try to make people lose their focus by any different way," he said. "[But] certainly not hitting someone in the head with your stick. I'm just happy that I can walk right now and be on my feet and see my 4-month-old son, and keep living. But I'm not going to feel as good as when I'm going to be able to put my skates back on, give a hit or take a hit or get into a fight for my teammates. I'm not going to change the way I play the game in any way."

Criminal Liability

More significant than the suspension-from-play penalty levelled against McSorley was the fact that criminal charges were brought against him – the first to stem from on-ice action in an NHL game since 1988. (In that case, a player named Dino Ciccarelli was slapped with a $1,000 fine plus a day in jail after hitting Toronto Maple Leaf defenseman Luke Richardson on the head with his stick.)

British Columbia Provincial Court Judge William Kitchen did not accept McSorley's contention that the hit had really been intended for Brashear's shoulder. "He slashed for the head," Kitchen said after finding McSorley guilty in court of assault with a weapon.

"A child swinging as at a tee-ball would not miss. A housekeeper swinging a carpetbeater would not miss. An NHL player would never miss. Brashear was struck as intended."

Anti-violence advocates approved of the action taken against McSorley, but many were critical of the lenient sentence. The Bruins' player did have to miss one year of NHL play – and salary – but the assault on Brashear did not leave him with a criminal record, and carried no jail time.

While the entire event was, in the end, deplorable, it did raise an important question about sports violence: Is it allowable for police to charge an athlete who commits what, outside an arena, would be considered assault, with a criminal offence? After all, as advocates of this view argue, anyone who hits a fellow citizen with a hockey stick would be thus charged in the "real world," and the fact that it happened in a hockey game does not make it any different.

"If the game is to become less violent," wrote Kitchen in his decision, "it will likely only be in response to pressure brought by the fans. If this is the trial of Canadian hockey, then [the] judge and jury are the Canadian public."

VIOLENCE AND AGGRESSION IN SPORTS

Most people would agree that, for an athlete to be successful, he or she must be aggressive in training, and in his or her drive to succeed when competing. However, the aggression needed to perform well in a sport is very different from aggression related to hostility.

There are two different kinds of aggressive behaviour in sport: instrumental aggression and hostile aggression. Instrumental aggression is when another player is injured as a side effect of the aggressor's attempt to achieve something else, for example, a football tackle. Hostile aggression, or affective aggression, is the deliberate intent to harm another player fuelled by anger and hostility, such as a baseball brawl or a hockey fight. Many athletes, coaches, and parents believe that hostile aggression is simply a part of sports and that this kind of aggression pushes athletes to excel. However, many sport psychologists feel that the two types of aggression are not related and an elevation in hostile aggression does not help the athlete achieve better results. In fact, hostile aggression shifts the focus of the athlete from the sport to the non-game issue of harming the opponent.

The line between the two different types of aggression is often blurred, and it is sometimes difficult to determine the difference between appropriate and inappropriate aggression. Young hockey players in non-competitive leagues are more often than not encouraged by coaches and parents to body check, start fights, and win at any cost – the development of aggression seems to be more important than skating skills and scoring ability.

Young hockey players across the country look up to National Hockey League players as role models. But many NHL hockey players are paid millions of dollars each season to be fighters rather than scorers or defenders. Toronto Maple Leaf player Tie Domi has made a career out of fighting, amassing high amounts of penalty minutes, and suspensions for unfair conduct. In 2001, Domi elbowed the New Jersey Devils' player Scott Niedermayer during the playoffs causing him to suffer a concussion. Niedermayer said that Domi had threatened him during a previous game in the playoffs. The attack by Domi was unprovoked and, as Niedermayer was far back from the current play, it did nothing to help his team in the final seconds of the game. Domi received a suspension but Niedermayer suffered physical and mental trauma and was also not able to play in the rest of the playoffs due to his injuries. This type of violent behaviour has nothing to do with the game but it is typical of many tough players; hockey players who do not rely on this type of aggression are becoming a rare breed.

Hockey is not the only aggressive sport where the line between acceptable aggression and violence is blurred. In football a certain degree of aggressive behaviour is not only acceptable but also expected. Many of the best football players never make it past high school or college football leagues because they are injured in games. Football players must tackle each other and use the force of their bodies to stop their opponents. But football aggression turns to football violence when the intent is not to stop but to injure the other player. Injuries in football are commonplace, but intent cannot be the only way to decide whether players are using instrumental aggression or hostile aggression – and intent is a difficult thing for an official to determine. The opponent should not have to be carried off on a stretcher for us to decide whether the athlete was trying to harm the opponent or merely stop him.

Basketball has, to a lesser extent, a history of violent behaviour. In early 2002, Kenyon Martin of the New Jersey Nets was suspended for two games for trying to punch another player. Dennis Rodman has a history of being suspended for aggressive behaviour. Even figure skating has a violent chapter in its history. After figure skater Nancy Kerrigan was attacked during a skating practice in 1994, just weeks before the Olympics, it came to light that her attackers were not only friends of competing skater Tonya Harding but that Harding had given them information to make the attack successful. Harding was allowed to skate in the Olympics but placed eighth, while Nancy Kerrigan, despite her injury, took home the silver medal.

The following are some of the factors that could increase the likelihood of violence in a sporting event:

- the emotional intensity of the game;
- an increase in ticket sales;
- higher athlete salaries;
- athletes idolized for their participation in game violence;
- participating teams are at different levels or standings;
- incompetent or biased officials;
- strong fan attachment to a team;
- low scoring games;
- fans having unrealistically high expectations of a team; and
- a series of fouls or penalties are called early in the game.

In order for the outcomes to change, the approach has to change. Ethical conduct must be taught universally from a young age. Coaches and parents, making it easier for players to injure others, must not dehumanize the opposing team. Non-aggressive players

When Sports Fans Clash in the Stands
Is it all just part of the price of admission?

Most media reports of violence in sport focus on violent acts that take place between athletes on the playing surface. Sometimes this aggression takes place between supporters of opposing teams, and can spill outside the stadiums and into the streets, subways, and bars. Violent fans have also attacked coaches, players, and referees, and, in many instances, those attacked have retaliated. According to experts, this violence is often fuelled by the large quantities of alcohol that fans consume before and during the course of a game. But however it manifests itself, violence involving fans is an unfortunate, but very real, fact of sporting life.

Likely the worst example of fan violence in recent times occurred at the 1985 European Champions' Cup final match between two club teams, England's Liverpool and the Italian squad, Juventus of Turin. At the match venue, Heysel Stadium in Belgium, thirty-nine Italian fans were crushed to death by English supporters. As a result, the English teams were forbidden to play in the European competitions for six years.

What causes this kind of violence? In his 1993 book *Among the Thugs*, American writer Bill Buford wrote at length about how he spent a season travelling with English soccer fans, trying to determine why – and how – this violence starts and spreads. "It was obvious that the violence was a protest," writes Buford:

> It made sense that it would be: that football matches were providing an outlet for frustrations of a powerful nature. So many young people were out of work or had never been able to find any. The violence, it followed, was a rebellion of some kind – social rebellion, class rebellion, something.... I had read about the violence, and, to the extent that I thought about it, had assumed that it was an isolated thing or mysterious in the way that crowd violence is meant to be mysterious: unpredictable, spontaneous, the mob (excerpted at www.amazon.com).

Happily, the 2002 soccer World Cup, hosted jointly by Japan and Korea was, at least according to media reports, completely free of fan violence. Some

Dodgers tussle with Cubs' fans in the ninth inning at Wrigley Field in Chicago (AP PHOTO/*Sun-Times*-Tom Cruze).

commentators felt that this was because many of the traditionally violent fans from Europe did not – or could not – make the long trip to Asia. Others believed that it was part of an overall international crackdown on fan violence as a result of rampaging English fans who terrorized supporters of other nations in France at the previous World Cup in 1998.

There have been other well-publicized instances of violence involving fans and players recently as well. Just before the start of qualifying rounds for the 2002 World Cup, Nigerian soccer player Emmanuel Olisadebe switched nationalities and began representing Poland (some reports said that this switch was pushed through more quickly than normal by a decree by the Polish president) in international competition, becoming the first black player to play for the Eastern European nation. But when Olisadebe took to the field for games in the Polish league, he found that the reception was often less than welcoming. "I think they weren't used to seeing black people," Olisadebe told reporters of the online soccer magazine "Footballculture.net".

In one game in the city of Lodin, he recalls a particularly bad experience. "I took the ball to the corner flag and all of a sudden it was as if it was raining bananas. Around fifty or so [fans] from the other team were saying to me: 'Emmanuel, don't worry, they're hooligans, they're drunkards.' Afterwards the club sent me a letter of apology so I guess I've got to live with it. It doesn't bother me any more, but it's everywhere and if I can be involved in the fight against racism I would love to help." While Olisadebe was never physically attacked, it is hard not to interpret these actions as violent in a different way.

On January 8, 2002, a junior hockey player Bobby Chad Mitchell was, according to a report in the Associated Press (AP), charged with the felony assault of a fan in Kennewick, Washington, who kept beating a drum behind his team's bench. Mitchell, a forward with the Moose Jaw Warriors, was accused of swinging his stick at Jared Lembcke, a thirty-year-old spectator, after the Tri-City Americans defeated the Warriors 4-2 in a Western Hockey League game at the Tri-Cities Coliseum.

On May 16, 2000, a brawl broke out during a National League baseball game between the Los Angeles Dodgers and the Chicago Cubs. During the ninth inning, a fan reached over the wall at Chicago's Wrigley field close to the Dodgers' dugout and grabbed a player's hat. Amazingly, the players stormed into the stands to fight the fans.

In a truly unusual incident during the summer of 2002, several members of the Canadian Football League's Winnipeg Blue Bombers were assaulted by fans outside a nightclub in Winnipeg, including receiver Arland Bruce III and running back Troy Mills, who were severely injured and had to miss the following night's game. Several restaurant staff said that patrons had been taunting the players during the evening, and wanted to prove that they were "tougher" than the players by fighting them.

must be rewarded for their conduct and violent athletes must not be rewarded for their behaviour. Sportsmanship and fair play, rather than winning, must become the focus of sports in order for violence in sports to dissipate.

Spectator Violence

Spectator-versus-spectator violence is often the result of a few people that go to a sporting event specifically to start trouble. Spectator violence seems to rise when the sport is violent, such as at football or rugby games; when the spectators consume large amounts of alcohol, such as at baseball games; or when fan loyalty and team identification is extreme, such as with European football or soccer, and international cricket. Soccer spectator violence has been a large problem in England and in World Cup situations. Many British soccer hooligans have now been identified in an effort to reduce possible violence and are no longer allowed to attend World Cup games.

Soccer fans can often go to extremes. During the 2002 World Cup, a Korean man set himself on fire because he thought it would help the Korean team. The man's suicide note indicated that he thought in death he would become a spirit that could help the team on the field as an extra player. In Bangkok, a woman was killed by her husband for changing the television channel during a World Cup game. Both of these cases are extreme examples of team loyalty gone wrong.

Violence against Officials and Coaches

Officials and coaches are increasingly the victims of violence from sports fans and athletes. Nearly everyone who follows baseball, football, or hockey has seen coaches and athletes yelling, kicking, and threatening violence against an official who has made a call they did not agree with. Many people view this as a part of the game and as an entertaining moment for the television highlight reel. But many observers feel that coaches and officials should not be subject to this kind of aggression when they go to work.

Fans who are overly devoted to their sports team and are too serious about the outcome of a game are also quick to blame the coaching and officiating when their team is performing poorly. Too many fans forget that they are watching a game, something that should be fun. In September of 2002, Tom Gamboa, first-base coach for the Kansas City Royals, was attacked from behind by two spectators who had jumped onto the baseball field from the stands. Gamboa was preoccupied with a play in the game and did not see the attack coming. After hitting him from behind, the two attackers, a father and son, continued to deliver hits to the coach's body.

England's supporters clash with Italian police in the stands of Rome's Olympic Stadium during a Soccer World Cup qualifying match, October 1997 (AP PHOTO/Massimo Sambucetti).

Parents of young athletes are increasingly more aggressive with their children and the coaches and officials that their children play with. For this type of parent, the game is no longer about children having fun; they are only interested in pushing their children to excel at any cost and, in many cases, to fulfil the parents' frustrated dreams of becoming a professional athlete. Mothers and fathers can be seen yelling at their children to be more violent against their opponents, and becoming violent themselves when someone is aggressive against their children.

Parents attacking coaches and officials has become more common. Children who witness this hysterical violent behaviour imitate that behaviour. Stories in the media of young athletes ganging up on the coach of the opposite team and the officials are similar to the type of gang violence that is seen outside the sports world. In 2000, Thomas Junta's son was playing in a pickup game of hockey supervised by Michael Costin, whose son was also playing. Junta got into an argument with Costin, a man 120 pounds lighter. According to witnesses, Junta hit Costin in the head at least ten times and slammed his head into the mat in front

John Vanbiesbrouck, goalie, kicks at a plastic rat after a loss in the 1996 Stanley Cup final. Later, in 2002, as coach and general manager of the Soo Greyhounds, Vanbiesbrouck resigned and apologized for a racial slur against Trevor Daley, one of his own players (AP PHOTO/Hans Deryk).

of all the children. A main artery in Costin's neck ruptured, and he died the next day. Junta, who had a history of beating his wife in front of his children, was convicted of involuntary manslaughter and is serving a six- to ten-year sentence.

Because this type of violence has reached a critical point, many children's leagues are making parents, coaches, and officials sign agreements that they will remain calm at games. Several leagues are also initiating silent weekends. No talking or yelling is allowed at silent weekend games, and there is a zero-tolerance policy – any parent caught talking will be removed from the crowd.

Violence against Athletes

Tennis player Monica Seles was subject to one of the most violent attacks in recent history by a spectator. A mentally-ill fan of Steffi Graf, worried that Seles would pose a challenge to his favourite tennis player,

attacked Seles during a game in 1993. Nineteen-year-old Seles had gone to the sidelines to rest when a 5-inch steak knife was plunged between her shoulder blades by the attacker. Seles screamed, but no one initially knew what was wrong. Luckily, the knife missed both her spinal cord and her lungs, but the trauma of the event kept her from competing for more than two years. Her attacker received a suspended sentence of two years.

Colombian soccer player Andres Escobar paid the ultimate price for his sport at the hands of a crazed fan. In 1994, during a World Cup game between Colombia and the United States, Escobar tried to stop an American pass close to the Colombian net by sliding in front of the ball. But in doing so, Escobar accidentally pushed the ball into the Colombian goal – he had scored on his own team. The Americans won the game by one goal and the Colombian team was eliminated days later. Only a few days after the twenty-seven-year-old soccer player had returned home to Colombia, he was shot outside of a nightclub. His murderer shot him twelve times while apparently shouting the word "goal" repeatedly. Many people believe that his murder was connected to the country's drug traffickers, who lost money on bets due to losing the game.

Monica Seles and Andres Escobar are extreme examples but many other athletes are victims of violence at the hands of fans. Athletes also often suffer abuse from coaches. Many coaches believe that they have to be tough with their players in order to ensure that they play well. Verbal and physical abuse happen in a lot of locker rooms but are rarely talked about. Athletes that suffer verbal abuse in the form of temper tantrums or sudden bursts of rage often think that it is just part of sports, but it does not have to be. Good coaches and trainers encourage and nurture their athletes, and in return the athletes have good results.

Some organizations have taken steps to combat verbal abuse. In 2002, the International Cricket Council passed a regulation that will impose a ban for life on any international cricket player found guilty of verbal abuse. The council has clearly stated that abusive behaviour is unacceptable, including crude language and gestures. The Ontario Hockey League (OHL) had a recent incident of verbal abuse involving a coach that they also deemed unacceptable. John Vanbiesbrouck, coach of the Sault Ste. Marie Greyhounds and former NHL goaltender, directed several racial slurs against the African-Canadian captain of the team, Trevor Daley, in discussion with two other teammates. The OHL decided that this type of verbal abuse would not be tolerated and suspended Vanbiesbrouck indefinitely for his remarks. This is the kind of swift action that needs to be taken so that players and coaches know that verbal abuse is unacceptable.

CHEATING IN SPORTS

Cheating is an attempt to gain an unfair advantage in training or in competition by using methods or equipment prohibited by the rules of the sport. There are many different ways to cheat in sports, including the use of banned performance-enhancing substances, the use of illegal equipment, the attempt to bend the rules of the competition, the attempt to influence the judges or officials, and the attempt to influence the effort of your opponents.

This unsportsmanlike behaviour can be seen in every sport. Not all athletes partake in unethical activities, but the number of those who at least bend the rules is large. Many athletes are under pressure from their coaches or parents to use unfair means to win. Today, the importance of winning is much greater than the concept of fair play. In the win-at-all-costs mentality, winning or losing reflects on the athlete's country, city, community, and family, depending on the level of the sport. And there are financial incentives to winning for both professional and amateur athletes. Professional athletes can earn themselves a larger salary when a contract is up and can receive a number of commercial endorsements as a popular, high-scoring player. Amateur athletes who win gold medals at the Olympics have a chance of obtaining commercial endorsements when they turn professional. Many Olympic athletes announce their retirement from amateur sports almost immediately after winning a gold medal, as the opportunity to make money with their sport is presented for the first time.

Cheating, or bending the rules, has been taking place in baseball since the game was created. Pitchers are often the most flagrant abusers: they have been known to scratch the baseball with their fingernails, sandpaper, or an emery board; use petroleum jelly in their hair or glove to create a "spitball;" and throw the ball intentionally at the hitter. Other players cheat by corking their bats, creating a flat surface on their bats, using excessive pine tar for grip on the bat, sharpening the spikes on their shoes, intentionally stepping on an opponent, throwing the baseball at the base runner's head, intentionally losing a game, and using stealing signs. Many baseball players and coaches consider these unfair practices as cheating only if you get caught; with this attitude, there is no doubt as to why this unsportsmanlike behaviour continues.

Cheating athletes can be very creative in altering their equipment, bending the rules of the game, and trying to get away with cheating. In 1969, NHL goaltender Tony Esposito had a piece of mesh sewn between the legs of his uniform. The mesh blocked any puck that went between his legs from going into the goal. Unfortunately, the mesh rebounded shots backward, and one such puck nearly hit another player in the face. The mesh was banned outright. During the 1976 Olympics, German swimmers had nearly two litres of air pumped into their buttocks to improve buoyancy, giving the front crawl and backstroke swimmers an advantage over the other swimmers. At the 2000 Berlin Marathon, more than thirty runners decided to take the subway during the race to gain a lead on the other runners. Each runner was wearing a tracking device, however, and all of them were disqualified. During the 1950s, the coaches of the Chicago White Sox baseball team bought a submarine periscope so that they could see the signs the catcher was giving the pitcher.

Different sports bodies deal with cheaters in different ways, depending on the transgression. Some leagues ban players for cheating but more often a league is more lenient, giving the cheating player a suspension. Often the penalty depends on how serious the sports body considers the violation. If caught cheating in an event at the Olympics, medals for that event must be returned and any records are removed. The majority of sports and sporting events will not let a world record stand if the record holder has been found to be cheating.

NASCAR racing is one of the exceptions to the rule – it has a history of letting cheaters win. In 2000, Joe Nemechek used an illegal car in the Touchstone Energy 300 NASCAR Busch Series. His car was found to be too low in the rear, altering the aerodynamics of the car and giving him a clear advantage over the other drivers. Nemechek won the race, but officials in a post-race check discovered the illegal car. Nemechek was fined $20,000, but was allowed to keep the winnings, the title, and the trophy. His winnings totalled $38,125, far more than he was fined. In 1983, Richard Petty won a race with an oversized engine and unofficial tires; his victory was allowed to stand in the NASCAR record books. The problem with letting athletes who have gained an unfair advantage by cheating is that the people who are truly cheated are the ones who played fairly. These athletes are not given the chance to win.

Athletes who cheat in their sports are not anxious to be caught and, therefore, they, their coaches, and their doctors are constantly inventing new ways to avoid being detected. For example, unethical doctors and trainers are constantly coming up with new ways to conceal steroid use in their athletes. The technology of catching cheating athletes, particularly those that use banned substances, is always lagging behind the technology of covering up the cheating. Officials simply cannot devise a system to catch a certain kind of cheating if they are not yet aware that the cheating is taking place.

Vancouver Asahi Team Enters Baseball's Hall of Fame
A positive end to an unfortunate episode in Canadian sports history

The history of international sport is, unfortunately, filled with many examples of exclusionary practices towards various ethic groups. (See "'Restricted' and Segregated Sport" on page 297 for examples.) Canadian sport history has not been entirely immune from this phenomenon.

One interesting story that made the sports pages in the spring of 2003 highlighted both a significant – and tragic – intersection of sport and ethnicity, but also provided a happy ending to a six-decades-long saga.

Brains over Brawn

The story began in the 1920s, when the Canadian-born sons of Japanese immigrant parents began to have tremendous success in organized baseball in British Columbia. These *Nisei* (the Japanese term for second-generation immigrant offspring) organized powerful teams that came to dominate the competitive leagues in the Pacific Northwest. The strongest of these was the Asahi (or "morning sun") team that grew out of the baseball-mad "Little Tokyo" neighbourhood in Vancouver.

Japanese and non-Japanese fans alike began following the rapid progress of the Asahi, who soon established themselves as one of the city's best teams. They played a brand of baseball that sportswriters began calling "brain ball" because of their reliance on swift base-running and steals, superb fielding, and expert bunting as opposed to brute strength and power.

"Most of us couldn't bat for beans but we played with our heads," Jim Fukui, a pitcher on the squad recalled in a June 2003 *Toronto Star* article headlined "A new day of glory awaits famed Asahi baseball team." Another player, third baseman Kaye Kaminishi, was such an accomplished fielder that he earned the nickname "the vacuum cleaner."

This "brain ball" approach provided more than just entertainment – it also won games. In 1937, the Asahi team

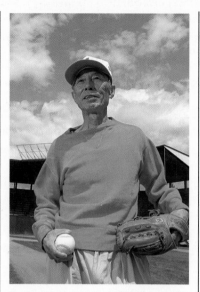

Former Vancouver Asahi third baseman Kaye Kaminishi, shown in 2003 near his home in Kamloops, B.C., played for Asahi from 1939-41 (PHOTO/Jeff Vinnick).

won the first of five consecutive Pacific Northwest League championships.

World War II Intervenes

But only a few months after earning their fifth title, things turned sour for the Asahi. In December 1941, Japanese planes bombed the American naval base at Pearl Harbor, a move that provoked the U.S. into joining the Allied effort in the Second World War.

With Canada already a member of the Allied Forces, the Canadian government responded by forcibly removing approximately 22,000 Japanese-Canadians from their homes on the British Columbia coast and transporting them to camps nearly 160 kilometres away, in the B.C. interior.

Despite the fact that many of these people were Canadian born and had been raised here – in fact, most had never even been to Japan – the government deemed them a wartime "threat," labelled them as "enemy aliens," and allowed them to take only a very limited number of personal belongings with them to the internment camps before

selling or destroying their land and remaining possessions.

By the end of the war, the imprisoned players were released but forced to move out of B.C. to settle in other parts of Canada. Luckily for Canadian baseball fans and sport historians, though, this was not the end of the Asahi's fame, but it took almost sixty years for them to make it back into the headlines.

Getting Their Due

In the spring of 2003, the Canadian Baseball Hall of Fame in St. Marys, Ontario, announced that the seventy-four-member Asahi team had been selected for induction, based on their stellar record and unfortunate past.

"In the end, it was one of the easiest calls our selection committee has had to make," Hall of Fame president Tom Valcke told the *Star*. "They have embraced Canada, despite the internment and the oppression, and I think it's only proper that we embrace them. I think we owe it to them."

Significantly, many of the ten Asahi players still living said that they bore little ill will towards Canada as a country for what they had to endure during the war, and still held fond memories of their favourite game.

"Baseball was really good to me," said eighty-one-year-old Kaminishi, after learning of his and his former teammates' induction. "It's just tremendous pride, no bitterness. That's all finished now."

For other players, the recognition goes a long way towards helping ease painful memories.

In 2003, the National Film Board of Canada brought this fascinating chapter of the nation's sporting history to the screen in a film called *Sleeping Tigers: The Asahi Baseball Story*. The film chronicles the exploits of the team and its demise during the Second World War.

RECRUITMENT VIOLATIONS

University sports are played at an amateur level, but in the United States, college sports can be big business for major schools. University football and basketball are watched by millions of people and are seen as precursors to the professional leagues. Players must maintain their amateur status if they want to play in the school system, but schools are anxious to recruit the best athletes. A good team ensures attention for the school and the team, and more dollars flowing in from game attendance. In the past, schools have been known to do more than simply provide scholarships to prospective recruits. Recruiting violations include expensive meals and hotel rooms; in-room service including movies, phone calls, and massages; money; and gifts. Money has also been paid to high-school coaches who may persuade a recruit to choose that school or speak negatively about another school to dissuade a student from choosing it. While this is not illegal, it is dishonest. In order for athletes to remain at amateur status in sports they must not be paid in any form or accept a promised payment; must not commit to any professional sports team, verbally or by contract; must not ask that their name be placed on a draft list; must not be paid for their athletic skills in any form, for example, in a commercial or demonstration; cannot play on a professional team; and must not have received salary, incentives, gratuity, educational expenses, monetary awards, or expense allowances for playing on an amateur team.

CORRUPTION OF OFFICIALS AND JUDGES

The corruption of judges and officials is always in question in sports. Unethical officials and judges have been a problem at the Olympic games since the modern games began. The majority of problems arise in sports in which medal results are based on subjective judging rather than time trials. With the countries represented at the Olympics divided down nationalist, political, and formerly Cold War lines, judges have been subject to bribes and favours from those trying to further an athlete's career. In the past, the International Olympic Committee (IOC) has tried to deny that such unethical behaviour exists, but as the media and the public become more aware of the judging process and the quality of events, the IOC has had to deal with suspect judges.

One of the worst offences in recent years was in the boxing ring. In 1988 at the Seoul Olympics, Korean judges and communist countries' judges conspired with each other to keep the American boxers from winning medals in boxing. Several good American boxers lost medals to less competent communist boxers, but the most blatant medal robbery was of Roy Jones Jr. Jones is considered to be one of the best middleweight boxers in history. During his gold-medal boxing match against Korean Park Si Hun, Jones landed eighty-six punches while Si Hun only threw thirty-two scoring blows. The judges announced that the Korean had won the match 3-2. Roy Jones Jr. was cheated out of his Olympic gold medal because, according to the judges, he came from the wrong country. More recently, Cuba, one of the few communist countries left in the world, stated that the refereeing of boxing is more corrupt than ever. Cuba's president, Fidel Castro, announced to the media that he believes several Cuban boxers were cheated out of medals at the 2000 Olympics because of corrupt judging. Castro believes that the judging of boxing has become controlled by the Mafia.

It is clear that the judging of certain sports need to be reformed. Some of the changes that have been suggested are not allowing judges to attend practices, not allowing judges to talk with athletes prior to events, choosing judging panels minutes before an event takes place, and barring judges from panels if athletes from their country are highly placed.

Olympic Bribery

When Pierre de Coubertin created the modern Olympics more than one hundred years ago, he had an idealist vision of the Games – that countries could compete ethically and with respect for one another. However, that ideal is not always the reality. While passionate nationalism is the appeal to the average viewer, it is also a problem. With the onset of the Cold War after the Second World War, it became a competition of capitalism versus communism; each event became a competition of political domination rather than athleticism. After mass televising of the Olympics began in 1960, commercial sponsorship entered the Games full force, and cities began to see the financial benefits of hosting the Olympics. With so much riding on the outcome and so much money to be made in the process, some of the members of the International Olympic Committee, who decide which city's bid is successful, began accepting money, trips, and gifts from cities that hoped to buy their votes. These dealings, though commonly known, came to light after Salt Lake City won the bid to host the 2002 Winter Olympics.

A local Salt Lake City television station reported that the Salt Lake City Organizing Committee, who had made the bid for the Olympics, had also paid for an IOC member's daughter to attend a university in the United States. After this revelation was made, a long list of bid violations became public. It was revealed that six relatives of IOC members had

World Champions David Pelletier and Jamie Salé at the end of their free skate to win the pairs competition at the Mastercard Skate Canada International, November 2001, in Saskatoon, Saskachewan (CP PHOTO/Adrian Wyld).

received these "scholarships," three people connected to the IOC had received free medical treatment, and the city had hired the son of an IOC member as an intern. The media also revealed the violations of other recent host cities. In Nagano, Japan, an average of $22,000 was spent on each of the visiting IOC members before Japan won the bid for the Olympics. In 1993 on the night before Australia won the bid to host the 2000 Olympics by two votes, the head of the Sydney Olympic Committee offered two IOC members $70,000 worth of incentives to vote for Australia. Tom Welch, president of the Salt Lake City Olympic Committee, and David Johnson, vice president of the committee, faced charges but maintained that they had done nothing different from any other city making a bid. The committee spent $1 million in scholarships, gifts, trips, medical expenses, and cash on IOC delegates and their families. Ten IOC members resigned or were expelled from the organization, and a series of bid process reforms were made.

Figure Skating Judging

Figure skating is one of the most popular sports in the Winter Olympics. The judging of these events is relatively subjective, and many maintain that there have been faults in judging procedures since the beginning of the Cold War in 1952. It became commonplace for judges to solicit votes from other countries' judges to predetermine the outcome of the events. Athletes from smaller countries were often the victims of this selling of votes, or block voting. In 1998 at the Olympic games in Nagano, Japan, Canadian judge Jean Senft revealed to the world that block voting was rampant in ice dancing. During the competition, she taped a phone conversation with another judge who was trying to get her to agree to place the Russian ice-dancing pair first. Senft refused and went public with her tape after the competition had ended. The Russian ice-dancing pair finished first despite falling during their performance, and the Canadian pair of Victor Kraatz and Shae-Lynn Bourne finished fourth, though many thought they deserved a medal.

Judging in Olympic figure skating reached a critical point at the 2002 games in Salt Lake City. Pairs figure skaters Jamie Salé and David Pelletier skated a flawless routine in the final event for pairs. The Russian pair of Elena Berezhnaya and Anton Sikharulidze, the other leading skaters, had made technical mistakes during their final performance. However, when the votes were tallied, it was five votes to four in favour of the Russian pair. Canadians Salé and Pelletier had come in second, winning the silver. Skating fans worldwide were dismayed with the decision, and the media dubbed the controversy "Skate Gate." The International Skating Union (ISU) said that it would investigate the judging of the event but would take its time in doing so.

The International Olympic Committee, unhappy with the bad press created by the judging, pushed the ISU to complete their investigation in a timely manner. The two committees decided to grant a second set of gold medals to the Canadian pair after French judge Marie-Reine Le Gougne admitted to being pressured into voting for the Russian pair, a claim that she later denied. With her vote nullified, the Russian and Canadian pairs were tied at four votes apiece. After a hearing by the ISU, Le Gougne and Didier Gailhaguet, the French federation chief who was accused of pressuring Le Gougne in her vote, were suspended for three years and banned from the next Winter Olympics. After Salé and Pelletier traded their silver medals for gold, they decided to leave amateur skating and become professional. During the entire "Skate Gate" affair, the Canadian skaters remained good sports, never disparaging the Russian skaters or accusing the judges of unfair voting.

DRUG USE IN SPORTS

Athletes have always tried to gain an advantage over other athletes – some are willing to use any means necessary to win. Unfortunately, that includes cheating and a large proportion of cheating in sports today is in the form of steroid use. The ease of obtaining steroids, and the quick results an athlete can achieve with them, makes steroids very seductive for athletes. However, the risks are high. Both an athlete's health and his or her career are on the line every time he or she uses a banned substance.

History of Drug Use in Sports

The first athletes charged with doping were swimmers in Europe in the 1860s. The first drugs used were stimulants to speed the athletes up, such as cocaine and heroin. Steroids were first developed by German Nazis in the 1930s, who tested them on dogs and then on concentration camp prisoners to keep them strong enough for work despite their lack of food. In the 1950s, Russian and European athletes began to find that steroids made them stronger, and they were soon beating world records in weightlifting and other strength-oriented sports. It was discovered that it was the testosterone in the steroids that improved the athletes' abilities. Doctors began to look for new forms of steroids to improve athletes' performance. The side effects of steroids were unknown until the late 1950s – with the development of anabolic steroids, the unpleasant side effects and health concerns were revealed.

However, athletes did not think that they could compete competitively without steroids. With the Cold War came the need to prove dominance over other countries, and steroid use in the athletic world grew rampant. In East Germany, athletic teenage girls were injected with steroids and other banned substances by sports officials. Essentially, these girls became walking drug experiments for the country, so that they could prove the superiority of the political system in those countries at the time.

Before this drug use, East German women had never won a medal in swimming; in the 1976 Olympics, after the excessive drug use began, the East German women's swimming team won eleven gold medals in thirteen events. After the demise of these regimes in the late 1980s and 1990s, records showing the extent of the drug abuse came to light. The drug plan's organizer served nearly two years in prison for endangering the lives of more than one hundred women, most of whom are currently suffering from major health problems. Today, many athletes still come under political pressure to use steroids regardless of the health and career risks attached to doping.

Drug Testing "Mistakes": Where Does the Responsibility Lie?

In competitive sport, many athletes knowingly ingest banned substances, hoping that they will avoid getting caught or that the "masking drugs" they have also taken will help them avoid detection. In other cases, however, athletes may unwittingly ingest certain substances that contain enough of a banned drug to cause them to be suspended from competition.

At the 1995 Pan Am Games, for example, Canadian rower Silken Laumann and her three teammates lost their gold medals after Laumann tested positive for a banned substance. Although Laumann was adamant that she had never knowingly taken a performance-enhancing drug, she was indeed guilty by the standards set forward by the Pan Am Games organizers. Her "crime"? An over-the-counter medicine she had been taking prior to competition contained enough of a banned substance to warrant her disqualification according to the doping rules of her sport.

More recently, triathlete Kelly Guest, who was expecting to represent Canada in the 2002 Commonwealth Games in Manchester, England, found himself instead denied a place on the national team after an international event in Edmonton just prior to the Games. Guest's urine sample contained traces of the steroid nandrolone, and, although there is every reason to believe his claim that he never knowingly took any form of performance-enhancing drug, there was no reversing his situation. In line with the policy set forward by the World Anti-Doping Agency (WADA) and the Canadian Centre for Ethics in Sport (CCES), "the use by an athlete of a substance or method banned by the International Olympic Committee, or prohibited by an International Sport Governing Body" as indicated by rigorous testing before and after a given event, leads to an automatic deletion of that athlete's performance from the records.

But, according to Paul Melia, the head of the CCES, the ultimate responsibility for how an athlete does on a urine test is up to him or her. "Athletes are ultimately responsible," he told CBC's sports reporter Linda Ward, "for anything that is found in their bodies."

The World Anti-Doping Agency and Drug Testing

The World Anti-Doping Agency, or WADA, is an independent, international, non-governmental organization that aims to eliminate doping in sports. Montreal-based WADA conducts unannounced drug tests during competition and out of competition to ensure that no banned substances are being used while athletes train; monitors the results of tests for major sports events, such as the Olympics; and has developed both the World Anti-Doping Code and the Athlete's Passport Program. The World Anti-Doping Code will

Ross Rebagliati celebrates his gold medal in the snowboard event at the 1998 Olympic Games in Nagano, Japan (CP PHOTO/COA).

ensure that athletes in every country have the same anti-doping standards and regulations; governments have to adopt the code by the 2006 Olympic Games. The Athlete's Passport Program is a way for athletes to demonstrate their commitment to keeping sports clean by signing on for the program. The passport provides the athlete with education and information about current rules and a list of banned substances. Each athlete who has signed on for the program will have their testing information stored in a secure database and will be able to communicate with WADA through the passport website. Keeping the testing current to detect new drugs and new methods to cover banned substances has been a problem since drug testing began. WADA funds research to improve the methods of testing and provides education about doping to coaches and athletes to help prevent athletes from starting to use banned substances.

Some athletes and organizations are against drug testing, especially unannounced testing, because they feel that their human rights are being infringed upon. Many athletes also believe that if a test is administered, then an athlete who fails the test deserves anonymity.

The National Hockey League Players Association is just one of the sports unions that are firmly against drug testing. The only substances banned by the NHL are the so-called "recreational drugs" for which any person could be arrested for using, possessing, and distributing. However, not all players covered by the union disagree with drug testing or with creating a list of banned substances. Many players fear getting into a fight with a player who has been taking steroids, and supplements that contain ephedrine or ephedra have been known to cause heart problems and death on more than one occasion. Baltimore pitcher Steve Belcher died due to heatstroke caused partly by his use of ephedra, an over-the-counter stimulant often used to aid in weight loss.

"Recreational" Drugs

"Recreational" drug use has been a problem in the sports world and in society for much longer than steroid use. Many athletes use so-called "recreational drugs," such as marijuana, cocaine, and heroin, as either a way to relax or in the mistaken belief that these drugs will boost their performance. These "recreational drugs" are just as harmful as sports-specific drugs, and they are illegal substances that can greatly harm an athlete's health and career. Marijuana can cause changes in personality and greatly impair short-term memory and perception. Cocaine was used by South American Aboriginals to increase endurance and efficiency for centuries; however, studies show that cocaine has no positive effect on running times. Cocaine can cause seizures, insomnia, paranoia, sexual dysfunction, delirium, anorexia, and heart failure, possibly resulting in death. Heroin also has no positive effects for the athlete and is one of the most addictive drugs available. A small amount of heroin is usually sufficient to addict the user.

In the 1998 Winter Olympics, Canadian snowboarder Ross Rebagliati was stripped of his gold medal because he tested positive for marijuana use. Many people questioned the decision of the IOC in disqualifying Rebagliati, who had the best performance in his sport, for using a drug that would not have helped his performance. The Court of Arbitration overturned the IOC's decision after the Canadian Olympic Association made an appeal, but opinion is still divided about whether social drug use should be allowed in the Olympics. If an athlete uses any illegal drug, performance enhancing or otherwise, should he or she be allowed to win an Olympic medal?

Though large amounts of caffeine, alcohol, and nicotine are not typically viewed as drugs, these agents still have an effect on the mind and body of the athlete. While caffeine has been shown to have some positive effects on athletes involved in endurance sports, it has no beneficial effect on the performance of athletes in sports that require short bursts of energy or high levels of coordination. Caffeine can cause headaches, nervousness, muscle pain, and can alter sleep patterns.

Smoking and drinking too much alcohol do not promote good health or physical fitness. Besides various cancers, smoking can cause lung disease, bronchitis, emphysema, weaken lung capacity, and can interfere with the healing of wounds and fractures. Nicotine is addictive, toxic, can cause multiple diseases, and can lead to poor health in general. An athlete who smokes will never perform at his or her optimum level.

Though fewer people regard alcohol intake as a problem for athletes, it is often used by athletes to ease stress and cope with anxiety. Frequent alcohol consumption can lead to addiction, poor athletic performance, heart conditions, and high blood pressure. When alcohol is combined with athletics, reaction time is decreased, coordination and balance are compromised, and vision can become impaired. Alcohol can also lower muscle glycogen. Alcohol does kill brain cells, and its extra calories are of little use to someone trying to maintain their fitness level.

TOBACCO AND ALCOHOL SPONSORSHIP

The fight between the tobacco industry and the Canadian government over the advertising of tobacco products has been long. Canada has been more vigilant in their quest to pass legislation restricting tobacco sales and advertising than most other countries. In the late 1800s, smoking became very popular, and the most sophisticated advertising at the time was produced for the cigarette industry. There was an immediate outbreak of anti-smoking groups, and in 1891, many Canadian jurisdictions passed laws prohibiting the sale of tobacco to anyone under the age of sixteen. However, these laws were rarely enforced. The Canadian government passed the *Tobacco Restraint Act* in 1908, making it illegal to sell cigarettes or chewing tobacco to minors, and for anyone under sixteen to use tobacco in a public place. In 1988, the *Tobacco Products Control Act* was passed, banning advertising on radio and television and in newspapers and magazines, and regulating the labelling of cigarette packaging.

Though tobacco companies had been using sporting events to promote their products for several years, with the ban on traditional advertising, cigarette company sponsorship of sports in Canada increased dramatically. Tobacco companies spent millions of dollars every year promoting sports across the country. Though events, teams, and leagues came to depend on cigarette dollars, tobacco advertising was reaching as many people as it had before and increasingly

reaching minors. With escalating numbers of teens and pre-teens smoking, knowledge of the dangers of second-hand smoke coming to light, and the growing number of people dying from lung and other cancers, the Canadian government passed Bill C-71, the *Tobacco Act*. This legislation greatly restricts sponsorship and promotion of sporting and cultural events by cigarette companies. The limitations placed on advertising ensure that sporting events do not promote smoking. Tobacco companies are not able to sponsor any youth-oriented event or activity or include their name as part of a sports facility. Canada is one of the few countries that have been able to pass this kind of legislation. The World Health Organization, a United Nations agency, has been attempting to pass this kind of legislation worldwide, but several governments are resistant.

Alcohol companies have not been treated in the same way as tobacco companies. In Canada, beer companies in particular sponsor a large number of sporting events and own several sports venues. Molson sponsors hockey, lacrosse, basketball, football, wrestling, and motorsport, and owns various sports venues across the country. Labatt Breweries is a large sponsor of hockey, including Hockey Night in Canada, as well as the Canadian Olympic team, baseball, and several different amateur sports and tournaments. Despite the dangers of excessive drinking, and the minors attending these events, there is no legislation to prevent alcohol companies from sponsoring sporting events and promoting their products at these events in youth-oriented lifestyle ads.

Although there is considerable evidence to suggest that smoking has an extremely damaging effect on the body and is completely incompatible with sports and exercise, there are still some who argue in favour of allowing tobacco companies to sponsor sporting events. Of course, the companies themselves, who stand to generate tremendous publicity, argue that, in a free economy, they should be allowed to sponsor high-profile events. But the manufacturers are not alone – they are joined by those who believe that without "tobacco dollars" these events would simply disappear.

In Canada, until recently, the du Maurier cigarette company, for example, sponsored the Canadian Open men's and women's tennis tournament for many years. Remarkably, advocates of this support argued that there were never any Canadians who turned to cigarettes after watching these tournaments and that other more powerful social forces actually determine whether a person smokes or not. Be that as it may, sponsorship of events that require tremendous physical fitness by cigarette and other companies whose products are physically harmful is hard to accept.

The American Steroid Scandal
Was Carl Lewis guilty too?

The Ben Johnson Olympic steroid case is a sports story that many Canadians have been hoping would simply go away. It has been almost two decades, after all, since Johnson's positive test at the 1988 Seoul Summer Games, and during that time, many great Canadian sports accomplishments have taken place, both inside and outside the Olympic arena. Nevertheless, when people around the world talk about Canadians in international sport, the Johnson story has a habit of coming up again and again. And, based on a major news story broken by *Sports Illustrated* magazine and a newspaper in California called the *Orange County Register*, it looks as though the steroid-fuelled events of 1988 are back in the media once again.

Both publications have alleged that nine-time Olympic gold medallist Carl Lewis and several other high-profile athletes failed their drug tests at the 1988 American Olympic Trials, the meet that qualified U.S. athletes to compete in Seoul. Lewis, as every Canadian sports fan will recall, is the sprinter who was given the gold medal in the 100-metre event after Johnson tested positive, and who was outspoken in his condemnation of Johnson as a cheater. If the allegations of the two U.S. publications are true, Lewis's hypocritical attitude would be especially hard for Canadians to take.

The multiple gold-medal winner was one of nineteen American medallists who were named in more than 30,000 pages of documents chronicling cases of drug cover-ups, released by Wade Exum, the former United States Olympic Committee (USOC) Director for Drug Control from 1991 to 2000. The reports claim that approximately one hundred positive drug results were recorded by top U.S. athletes from 1988 to 2000, as well as the fact that, in many instances, the athletes who tested positive were not prevented from competing by American officials. In addition to Lewis, two other 1988 winners were

Carl Lewis and Ben Johnson at the 1988 Olympic Games in Seoul, South Korea (CP PHOTO/ COA/Cromby McNeil).

implicated in Exum's report: the 200-metre winner Joe DeLoach, and the 400-metre hurdle champion Andre Phillips, both of whom allegedly tested positive at the Olympic trials in Indianapolis.

In his own defence, Lewis, now forty-one, told the *Register* that it was common at the time for the USOC to allow athletes who had failed the drug tests to compete while simply issuing them a warning. "There were hundreds of people getting off," said Lewis in a press conference. "Everyone was treated the same." Lewis's claims were disputed by the USOC.

Furthermore, Lewis maintained that he had only been taking (legal) herbal supplements to enhance his performance, but the report says that he tested positive three times for small amounts of banned stimulants – pseudoephedrine, ephedrine, and phenylpropanolamine – results that should, at the time, have led to his being banned for three months, and to his missing the 1988 Games. In fact, the USOC first disqualified him, then accepted his appeal, which was based on his assertion that he had

taken the stimulant inadvertently through an over-the-counter herbal remedy.

Interestingly, one of Lewis' contemporaries – and an athlete who has been active in anti-drug initiatives – told the *Register* that he supported Lewis. Roger Kingdom, another member of the U.S. team in Seoul and the winner of the 110-metre hurdles race, said that trying to victimize Lewis after the fact was a mistake. "If you're going to let it slide, then don't go back and make a mockery out of the people you let go," Kingdom said. "Blame all the people who let this stuff skirt to the point that it became a problem."

What impact does this case have on Canadian sport? Upon hearing the news of the Lewis case, many Canadians – including Dick Pound, the head of the World Anti-Doping Agency – were shocked. How, they wondered, could Lewis have been so vehement in his condemnation of Johnson when he himself had been a steroid user? If Johnson had to relinquish his medal in Seoul, why did Lewis not have to do the same, fifteen years later, since, by the rules in force at the time, he should not even have been competing at the 1988 Games?

More cynical Canadian sports fans interpreted the report a little differently, as yet another case of a Canadian athlete being victimized by international sporting law while an American competitor remains unpunished. Indeed, Morris Chrobotek, Johnson's former agent, called for an investigation into the possibility that Lewis would lose his medals.

"Of course [Lewis] is going to downplay what he did. Carl stood to gain millions and millions of dollars in endorsements," Chrobotek told the *Register*. "I want to know if anybody outside of the [United States Olympic Committee] knew about it. Carl doesn't want to face it because he doesn't want to go down with an asterisk by his name. He is no different than Ben."

SPORTS GAMBLING

When there is so much emphasis placed on winning in sports, and so much team loyalty, some level of sports gambling is perhaps inevitable. Many governments have made gambling illegal because the majority of the citizens in an area believe that gambling is immoral or can lead to other social problems, such as public drunkenness, prostitution, and violence. In Canada, betting on sporting events is legal but it is highly regulated. Sports fans in Ontario, for example, can bet on their favourite team with the government-sponsored PRO-LINE. Money from such government-run sports betting goes to fund public programs that help the needy. Though clearly gambling can be highly addictive, government-regulated gambling is considered acceptable for the average adult sports fan (although gambling is illegal for minors). Betting on horse racing and offshore wagering are also legal, as is betting on professional sports in designated areas such as Nevada.

Serious problems occur when sports gambling is illegally run by unscrupulous people or when athletes are involved in betting on their own sports. Since the 1919 incident of the Boston White Sox throwing the World Series for bribes to help bookies, the sports world has been wary of sports betting. Those players were banned from baseball for the rest of their lives, despite being some of the best players ever. "Shoeless" Joe Jackson, an outfielder for the team, is still not eligible for the Baseball Hall of Fame.

In fact, sports appeal to bettors because the outcomes of games are almost never predetermined. Athletes, however, can be prevailed upon to "fix" the outcome of a game. For example, a reportedly common practice in some sports is that of "point shaving." Since a common betting practice is to bet, not simply on who will win or lose a game, but on how many points the result will be decided (i.e., a betting "line" will hold that one team will win by eight points or more), players will be asked by gamblers to make sure that the "point spread" is met. Since players do not have to intentionally lose the game, but only ensure it is won by a predetermined number of points, it is extremely hard to prove that point shaving has taken place. There have been many instances of point-shaving scandals in American collegiate basketball, for instance, as gamblers have influenced young athletes with the promise of a share of their profits should their bets pay off.

Pete Rose is another baseball player who, despite his skill, is not eligible for the Baseball Hall of Fame. Rose, a former baseball player and manager of the Cincinnati Reds, had a gambling addiction. Over several years, he bet several times on Cincinnati baseball games. In 1989, Rose was banned for life from baseball. In 1990, he went to jail for five months because he had failed to report all of his earnings. Rose had the respect of the sports world and was often called Charlie Hustle because of his dedication to baseball – all lost to sports gambling.

WHERE DO WE GO FROM HERE?

This section on social and ethical problems concludes the Unit on social issues in sport and physical activity. We have covered a wide range of topics that, when combined with Unit 4, will provide you with a wide base from which to better understand the fields of sport and physical exercise and their impact on the larger worlds of politics, economics, social interaction, and communities.

All of the concepts and issues covered in Units 4 and 5 relate directly to the daily activities of ourselves, our friends, families, and fellow citizens. Whether you play a sport or engage in a physical activity, watch such events live or on television, read about them in a newspaper or a magazine, or discuss them with someone else, many of the topics we have covered will have relevance. In addition, you will be better equipped to offer suggestions to others who may be looking for information as to how sport and daily life interact.

Despite all the information available on health and physical activity, this field still remains one in which many unproven assumptions prevail. As better-informed consumers, you will be able to assess many of the questionable claims made by advertisers regarding the health benefits of certain products and services, and, perhaps more significantly, will be able to help friends and family exercise similar discernment. Those who wish to go into fields such as coaching will be able to assist their athletes in understanding the difference between what works in training, and which quick-fix approaches are unsuitable.

Final Thoughts

This section concludes the textbook. In it, you have covered an incredibly broad range of topics, from physiology to motor development to historical and social issues. Whatever your aspirations in terms of sport or exercise, it is likely that the topics covered in the preceding pages will be of help to you – not only from an academic standpoint, but from a real-life perspective as well.

We hope this textbook has stimulated your interest. If you go on to further study in any of the subject areas covered in this text, as we hope you will, this book will have provided you with a basis for any courses you decide to pursue in this area.

32

Careers and Websites

"I was able to go places I'd never imagined I'd be able to go, and I was able to last a long time doing what I really enjoyed doing. I can't imagine having done anything else."
— Veteran Canadian sports writer Trent Frayne on his fifty-year career, from a personal interview by Paul Challen in March 2003

Below is a guide to the many career choices that are available to those who are interested in specializing in one or more of the areas covered in this unit. On the following page are website links that you will find useful in connection with the many topics touched on in the unit.

CAREER OPPORTUNITIES

- **Commentator/Broadcaster**
  On television and radio, sports broadcasters and commentators provide play-by-play commentary, game analysis, and supply athlete and coach interviews. Often these announcers have a college or university degree in journalism or broadcasting, but in many notable instances, they are ex-athletes or coaches who bring a wealth of practical knowledge to the job.

- **Sports Licensing/Merchandising**
  People who work in the field of sports licensing and merchandising are responsible for promoting the logo of a team or athlete through its appearance on products such as shirts, mugs, pennants, stickers, and so forth. Often these projects involve obtaining the consent of the team or athlete (in exchange for a fee), and, in the case of professional athletes, the league in which they compete. They must also secure manufacturers to produce large quantities of the product.

- **Public Relations**
  In the context of sport and physical activity, public relations professionals work to promote events and athletes both to the public at large and to media outlets, which in turn provide coverage to a wide audience. In most cases, people who work in public relations have a thorough understanding of the inner workings of the media and are called upon to use writing and communications skills to craft press releases or articles.

- **Advertising/Endorsements**
  Often, commercial interests will solicit the assistance of athletes to promote certain products or ser-

vices. In this form of advertising, it is important that the athlete and the company be a good "match"; consequently, much of the work done in this field involves assessing an athlete's popularity among a target audience.

- **Doping Control Official**
  These professionals work in all aspects of drug-use detection and prevention in sport, from implementing policy on banned substances, to administering pre- and post-competition testing, to assessing which penalties will be levied on cheaters.

- **Professional Players Association Representative**
  Players who participate in sport in the various North American professional sports leagues are also members of the players' associations – often known as players' unions – of those leagues. These organizations act to represent the interest of athletes in areas such as contract disputes and renewals, health and injury benefits, and the development of drug-testing policies. As such, the associations require personnel, often with legal backgrounds, to assist with their efforts. The work involved can include legal research, the preparation of material to present at hearings, and working with the media to ensure that the associations' goals are understood by the public.

- **Community Centre Administrator/Staff**
  Because community centres are often at the heart of many of the sports and recreation activities offered in a defined geographical area, they require staff who work to ensure the delivery of these programs in a safe and efficient manner. These staff members can include coaches and/or instructors, program developers, publicists, and equipment and/or facilities managers.

- **Professional Sports Franchise Personnel**
  In many large urban areas, professional sports teams are one of the community's largest employers. Of course, these franchises require the services of those who are directly involved with the team's actual competitive performance (athletes, coaches,

trainers, and so forth), but these employees represent only a fraction of the franchise's staffing needs. Other roles that need to be filled are publicist/media relations, financial management, community outreach programs, facilities maintenance, crowd control, merchandise and food and beverage, and ticket sales and promotion.

Sports Ethics Policy Maker

In Canada and many other countries, the federal government has taken an active role in the creation of official national policy on the ethical aspects of sport. In order to create such policies, organizations such as the Canadian Centre for Ethical Sport require staff, often with a legal background, to work to formulate a strategy that can be applied to all citizens, and to make that strategy known to the population at large. This can also involve liaison with academics, sport administrators, coaches, and athletes to develop as realistic and as far-reaching a policy as is possible.

USEFUL WEB LINKS

The URLs for these websites were active at the time this book went to press. For an up-to-date listing check the supporting student workbook or the website for this textbook: www.thompsonbooks.com/hpe.

The World Anti-Doping Agency (WADA)
www.wada-ama.org
For those looking to learn more about how international sport organizations are working to fight the use of illegal performance-enhancing substances, the World Anti-Doping Agency site provides information on policy, testing procedures, enforcement practices, and banning practices around the world.

Canadian Centre for Ethics in Sport (CCES)
www.cces.ca
The CCES is dedicated to making information available to Canadians and those around the world on drug-free sport, non-violence, the fair-play philosophy, and safety. As such, it offers what is likely the most comprehensive "clearinghouse" of such information available on the web, including a regular poll that gauges public opinion on a wide range of issues relevant to ethical decisions and sport.

North American Society for the Sociology of Sport (NASSS)
www.nasss.org
A critical site for those looking to further their knowledge of sociological topics in sport, this is the official site of the North American Society for the Sociology of Sport. The NASSS site presents the latest research, information on professional conferences, and links to similar groups.

Health Canada Online
www.hc-sc.gc.ca
This government-sponsored site is responsible for helping the people of Canada maintain and improve their health. It maintains current content on all health issues facing Canadians.

YMCA
www.ymca.com
Although this site is the official site of the YMCA in the United States, it contains links to YMCA information around the world, a comprehensive history of the movement, and an enormous amount of information about the various programs the organization offers throughout the world. For those interested in travel, there is also a directory of YMCA accommodations worldwide.

Canadian School Sport Federation
www.schoolsport.ca
The Canadian School Sport Federation website provides detailed information about the organization of sport in all Canadian provinces except Quebec. It contains links to provincial school sport sites, as well as contact information for those responsible for the administration of the various provincial federations.

FIFA — Soccer's World Governing body
www.fifa.com
The official site of soccer's world governing body, this site offers everything a soccer enthusiast could want regarding World Cup play for both men and women, as well as all levels of international play. In addition, the site boasts a comprehensive archive of soccer history and the latest international rules governing the game that have been adopted (and in the case of many youth leagues, adapted) for all levels of play.

Various newspaper/magazine sites
www.globeandmail.com/sports (Globe and Mail)
www.torontostar.com/sports (Toronto Star)
www.nationalpost.com/sports (National Post)
www.cnnsi.com (Sports Illustrated magazine)
www.canoe.ca/slam (The Sun Newspapers)
Often, finding out more about current issues in sport and physical activity on the web is simply a matter of consulting the online sports section of major newspapers and magazines, and either browsing articles, or searching for key words on the sites' search engines. Above are some important English-language sources in Canada and the United States.

Samantha Bailey, of Mount Pearl, Newfoundland, makes a jump at the pole vault event at the Canada Summer Games in London, Ontario, August 2001 (CP PHOTO/Jonathan Hayward).

Glossary

Abduction. Abduction is movement away from the median plane. This movement occurs in the frontal (coronal) plane.

Abductor muscles. Muscles that move the limbs outward from the median plane.

Aboriginal Sports Circle. Canada's national voice for Aboriginal sport. Established in 1995 and funded by Sport Canada, the Circle promotes indigenous games and traditional approaches to amateur sport. Some pre-Columbian sports have been revived and fostered as a result of the Circle's work. The Circle pays to bring Aboriginal athletes together from across the country each year to participate in training in a high performance environment. It also sponsors the National Aboriginal Hockey Championships and the National Aboriginal High Performance Hockey Camp.

Acceleration. A change in velocity in a straight line.

Acclimatization. There has long been a debate as to whether athletes who have spent their lives at sea level can adjust, through training, to conditions at higher altitudes. This adjustment, over time, is known as acclimatization.

Actin. A cellular protein that contains two other proteins – troponin, which has a binding site for calcium, and tropomyosin, which is the "stringy looking" cord-like structure that covers the binding site on actin. Together, these two proteins behave like a swivel-locking mechanism – they will not allow the myosin head to attach until calcium is released by the sarcoplasmic reticulum.

Active recovery techniques. Moderate aerobic activity (i.e., a cooling down period of moderate aerobic exercise), undertaken to minimize the physiological effects of training, particularly lactic acid buildup.

ACTive. A program created by CAAWS in association with Sport Canada and Health Canada based on the Brighton Declaration on Women and Sport and the Windhoek Call for Action. ACTive is a coordinated effort between government and local organizations to promote physical activity for women and girls and provide opportunities for them to participate.

Adduction. Adduction is the opposite of abduction. It is movement towards the median plane.

Adductor muscles. Muscles that squeeze the limbs towards the median plane.

Adenosine triphosphate (ATP). Adenosine triphosphate (ATP) is the common energy molecule for all living things. In effect, ATP captures the chemical energy resulting from the breakdown of food and can be used, conveniently, to fuel the various cellular processes. (Fritz Albert Lipmann and Herman Kalckar discovered the importance of ATP in 1941.)

Advertising. The means by which commercial, government or non-profit organizations disseminate information about their products and services. This can include advertisements involving the print media, television, the Internet, billboards and radio, to name just a few. In the world of sports, advertisers often try to ally themselves with events or athletes since these provide maximum exposure for their messages.

Aerobic system. The aerobic process, which involves many enzymes and several complex sub-pathways, leads to the complete breakdown of glucose. Fats and protein also enter the cycle at this stage. The aerobic system takes place in the granular rod-shaped structures found external to the nucleus of cells (the mitochondria).

Afferent nerves. Sensory nerves (or afferent nerves) carry information from sensory receptors to the central nervous system.

Age-appropriate coaching strategies. A concept that maintains that different coaching practices are needed for athletes at varying stages of motor development.

Agonist muscle. The muscle primarily responsible for movement of a body part.

All-or-none principle. Motor units comply to a rule known as the all or none principle (or law). This principle stipulates that when a motor unit is stimulated to contract, it will do so to its fullest potential.

Alveoli (alveolar sacs). Grape-like structures, also known as alveolar sacs, found within the lungs. The alveolar sacs provide a large surface area for the diffusion of gases into and out of the blood.

Amateur athletes. Athletes who derive no direct financial or material rewards from their sporting efforts. The term derives from the Latin root meaning "to love"; that is, amateurs play sport primarily for the sheer love of their activity.

Amino acids. Protein in the body consists of at least twenty different amino acids, which are used by the body to form the various body tissues. Nine of these (called essential amino acids) cannot be synthesized by the body and must be consumed as food.

Anabolic steroids. The most highly publicized of performance-enhancing drugs, anabolic steroids are referred to interchangeably as androgens, androgenic steroids, or anabolic steroids. Anabolic steroids are synthetic derivatives of the male hormone testosterone.

Anaerobic system. There are two methods for resynthesizing ATP – anaerobic (without oxygen) and aerobic (with oxygen). The anaerobic system occurs relatively quickly in the cell fibre, utilizing chemicals and enzymes readily at hand for powerful but relatively short-lived physical actions.

Anaerobic threshold. The point at which lactate levels in the blood increase abruptly beyond resting values, also known as the blood lactate threshold. The anaerobic threshold varies from person to person, but if the threshold is reached at lower intensities of exercise, this suggests that the oxidative energy systems in the muscles are not working well or are being overtaxed.

Anatomical axes. For purposes of analyzing human position and movement, the human body is divided into anatomical axes – a series of imaginary lines (horizontal, vertical, antero-posterior). Axes are used to describe how rotation of the muscles and bones takes place.

Anatomical planes. For purposes of analyzing human position and movement, the human body is divided into three anatomical planes or sections. Anatomical planes are at right angles to one another – transverse, frontal, and sagittal.

Anatomical position. Diagrams of the anatomical position portray the body in an upright, standing position, face and feet pointing forward, with the arms at the side, and the forearms fully supinated (with palms facing forward). This anatomical position is accepted as an unambiguous starting point from which to begin to describe anatomical features and positions.

Anatomy. A branch of science that deals with the structural organization of living things – how they are "built" and what they consist of.

Angular acceleration. Angular acceleration, also called rotational acceleration, is a quantitative expression of the change in angular velocity that a spinning object undergoes per unit time.

Antagonist muscle. The muscle that counteracts the agonist, lengthening when the agonist muscle contracts.

Anxiety. Feelings of tension or nervousness that accompany preparation for, or participation in, an athletic event (or other kind of event).

Appendicular skeleton. The appendicular skeleton (126 bones) includes the movable limbs and the supporting structures (girdles). As such, the appendicular skeleton plays a key role in allowing us to move about.

Applied biomechanics. The adoption of biomechanical principles to "real-life" situations, such as sports or the workplace.

Arctic Winter Games. An event, held with the support of the governments of Canada, Yukon, and the State of Alaska, which seeks to promote sporting competition and cultural exchange among First Nations people in these areas. The first Arctic Winter Games were held in Yellowknife in 1968. Athletes from all over northern Canada and Alaska have traditionally competed in them; representatives from other countries started to attend in 1990.

Arousal. Often referred to as "being psyched up" or feeling "wired," arousal is the state in which an athlete feels ready – in mind and body – to do his or her very best in competition.

Artery. A vessel that carries blood away from the heart. In the systemic circulation, arteries carry oxygenated (red) blood from the left side of the heart towards body tissues. In the pulmonary circulation, arteries carry deoxygenated (blue) blood from the right side of the heart towards the lungs.

Arthroscopy. A surgical procedure in which a few small incisions are made so that small fibre optic camera devices can assess the damage. It is commonly used to diagnose and treat injuries.

Articulating cartilage. Cartilage located on both ends of long bone is referred to as articulating cartilage. It allows smooth movement (articulation) within joints while protecting the ends of bones.

Articulations. As the term implies, joints are the points of contact (or articulations) between two connected bones.

Artificial turf. Reputed to be less safe than natural grass in contact sports, these synthetic surfaces often offer less cushioning than grass, are harder to maintain and often consist of several pieces of playing surface joined together, which can cause players to trip over the raised seams between pieces. As a harder playing surface, artificial turf has been known to lead to impact-type injuries to the ligaments, joints, and tendons – including the foot injury known as "turf toe." Recent technological advances have addressed these hazards.

Asthma. A disease characterized by spasm of the smooth muscles that line the respiratory system, an oversecretion of mucous, and swelling of the cells lining the respiratory tract.

Atherosclerosis. Atherosclerosis is one of several types of *arteriosclerosis*, which is characterized by thickening and hardening of artery walls (the two terms are often used to mean the same thing). In the case of atherosclerosis, deposits or "plaque" of cholesterol collect on the interior walls of many of the body's major blood vessels.

Athlete Assistance Program. An initiative, similar to the practice of "carding," by which Sport Canada provides support to individual athletes to help meet living, training, and travel expenses.

Athlete's Passport Program. An initiative developed by the World Anti-Doping Agency as a way for athletes to demonstrate their commitment to keeping sports clean. Athletes who agree to obtain a passport receive education and information about current rules and a list of banned substances. Each athlete who has signed on for the program will have their testing information stored in a secure database and will be able to communicate with WADA through the passport website.

ATP-PC system. The ATP-PC system (also referred to as the phosphagen system), relies on the action of phosphocreatine, a compound that is normally stored in muscle and is readily accessible. Like ATP, phosphocreatine (PC) is a high-energy molecule where the phosphate can be broken off easily and can be used to convert ADP back to ATP. This small reservoir of creatine phosphate within the muscle can sustain the level of ATP required during the initial phase of short but intense activity.

Atrioventricular bundle. Specialized tissue within the ventricular septum, also called the bundle of His. The bundle branches pass the signal on to the Purkinje fibres, which in turn pass the electrical signal to the myocardium that forms the ventricles.

Atrioventricular node (AV node). The atrioventricular node passes the electrical signal from the atria into the ventricles. It also passes the signal along into another region of specialized tissue that runs down the ventricular septum, the tissue that separates the two ventricles. This specialized tissue within the ventricular septum is called the bundle of His (which is also sometimes called the atrioventricular bundle).

Autocratic coach. In general, this type of coach adopts a "do-as-I-say" approach. This type of coaching style can further be broken down into two subcategories – "telling" and "selling."

Automatic motor activity. Motor activity that involves very little thought, and results in movement that appears to be an almost unconscious reflex action. For example, a baseball batter who, in a split second, sees that an out-of-control pitch is heading right for his or her head, makes an involuntary move to duck out of the way.

Autonomic nervous system. The largely involuntary contraction of our cardiac muscles and the smooth muscles of our internal organs is regulated by the autonomic nervous system (ANS). This subsystem is comprised of two branches, which frequently act as opposing systems.

a-vO₂ diff. The difference between the amount of O_2 in the artery and vein reflects the amount of O_2 delivered to the muscle. This is termed the a-vO_2 difference (a-vO_2 diff).

Axial skeleton. The axial skeleton (80 bones) is comprised mainly of the vertebral column (the spine), much of the skull, and the rib cage.

Ball-and-socket (spheroidal) joints. In this type, the "ball" at one bone fits into the "socket" of another, allowing motion in three planes. The most familiar joints of this type are at the hip (the femur rests in the acetabulum cavity of the pelvis) and shoulder (the humerus rests in the glenoid cavity).

Basal metabolic rate (BMR). A measurement of the metabolic rate under rigorous (laboratory) conditions – 12-14 hours after the last meal, with the individual completely at rest (but not asleep) and a background temperature of 26-30°C.

Basic skill categories. The division of motor learning abilities into three basic categories: locomotor-moving skills, manipulative-handling skills, and stability balancing skills. Used by specialists in the study of human skills acquisition, these three categories are not necessarily independent of each other.

Beta oxidation. Before entering the energy supply chain, fatty acids need first to be converted to acetyl-CoA. This is achieved through a process known as beta oxidation.

Biceps tendinitis. An overuse injury that happens when adequate rest is not given to the biceps brachii muscle when it has been worked or overloaded. The symptoms include pain on the proximal end of the biceps.

Bioenergetic conversion. The food we take in is broken down into three energy nutrients in the course of digestion: (1) proteins, (2) fats, and (3) carbohydrates. It is through the bioenergetic conversion of these nutrients that our bodies are able to function and we are able to carry out physical activity.

Biomechanics. A field of study that takes the principles of physics and applies them to the workings of the body, specifically to how the body moves, how the muscles flex, how the joints interact, and how the skeleton is propelled by the muscular system.

Blood doping. As defined by the World Anti-Doping Agency, this practice involves the intravenous administration of blood, red blood cells, and related blood products to raise the blood's oxygen carrying capacity.

Blood lactate threshold. The point at which lactate levels in the blood increase beyond resting values is known as the blood lactate threshold.

Blood pH. A measure of how acidic or how basic the blood is. Generally, blood pH is maintained very close to a pH of 7.4.

Blood pressure. The force exerted by the blood against the walls of the arteries.

Body composition. A term often used in reference to a person's fat mass and lean body mass (non-fat). The total fat in the body is either essential fat or storage fat.

Body image. The ways in which one perceives one's physical appearance, or in which societal values as a whole determine how certain types of people are "supposed" to appear. At times, these values – and the expectations they place on a person – can be extremely harmful, for instance, in the case of young female athletes who attempt to achieve unreasonable body weights to conform with performance goals in their sport.

Body Mass Index (BMI). A measure widely and successfully used by researchers and medical practitioners to assess the extent to which individuals are balancing the energy equation (i.e., are underweight or overweight).

Bone remodelling. Bones cannot grow by cell division as other tissues do. Instead, they grow by a process known as "remodelling," which has two main phases: bone-resorbing cells called osteoclasts remove old bone by releasing acids and enzymes; following this, protein-secreting cells (the osteoblasts, mentioned in "ossification") deposit new tissue.

Borg Scale of Perceived Exertion. A method of determining one's level of exercise intensity. The scale starts at level 6 (no exertion at all) and finishes at level 20 (maximal exertion).

Bradycardia. A decrease in heart rate, bradycardia is one of the most classic and easily observed adaptations to the cardiovascular system that occurs with training.

Broadcasting rights. The result of an agreement between an organization that hosts an event, and the form of media – television, radio, or the Internet – that provides coverage of that event to a large audience not physically present at the event venue. In most sports, this usually involves the media outlet – i.e. the broadcaster – paying a sum of money to the organizer for the right to transmit images and sound to the audience.

Burnout and overtraining. The conditions in which many athletes find themselves after long periods of training and competition. In these conditions, the very act of training and competition can seem like an unendurable chore, injuries can occur, and performance, understandably, drops off.

Caffeine. An alkaloid, found in such foods as coffee, tea, and chocolate. The rate of its metabolism by the liver, its storage, and its clearance varies greatly depending on frequency of use.

Calisthenics. A series of vigorous exercises and stretches often done as a group, sometimes set to music, which became popular in schools during the Victorian period in Britain (although the term's origins are Greek). Although not as popular today, calisthenics are the basis for many of the exercises that are still done in classes, both in schools and in gyms, today.

Calorie. A calorie (lower case "c") is the amount of heat needed to raise the temperature of 1 gram of pure water by 1°C. When it comes to food and diet, however, what is commonly called a Calorie (capital "c") is, in fact, a kilocalorie – that is, a measure of the quantity of heat required to raise the temperature of 1 kilogram of pure water by 1°C. In Canada, the adoption of the metric system and SI units means that the energy content of foods is measured in joules (J) and kilojoules (kJ), although the term Calories is still widely used. One calorie is equal to 4.18 joules – 1 Calorie (or kilocalorie) equals 4,184 joules (4.184 kJ).

Canada Games. A multi-sport competition, first held in 1967, which alternates between winter and summer sports every two years. Young athletes represent their province in these events, in a wide variety of sports. Many top international- and national-level Canadian athletes made their first major sporting impact at this event.

Canada's Food Guide to Healthy Eating. Developed in the 1940s by the Canadian government, the guide provides recommendations for the number of servings people should eat each day from the main food groups.

Canadian Association for Health, Physical Education, Recreation and Dance (CAHPERD). The Canadian Association for Health,

Physical Education, Recreation and Dance is a "national, charitable, voluntary-sector organization whose primary concern is to influence the healthy development of children and youth by advocating for quality, school-based physical and health education." CAHPERD is active in developing numerous initiatives within schools and communities throughout Canada, and makes resource material available on the Internet and in print form. CAHPERD also works closely with various provincial organizations that are active in the promotion of physical activity and sport.

Canadian Association for the Advancement of Women in Sport. Founded in 1981, CAAWS is a non-profit organization to promote sports and physical activity for women across Canada. CAAWS works in communities across the country, in partnership with Sport Canada, to gain gender equality in sports. While working towards making women and girls active sports participants rather than just viewers, CAAWS also encourages females to break down all sports-related barriers including coaching and officiating.

Canadian Centre for Ethics in Sport (CCES). An organization, overseen by Sport Canada, which helps Canadians learn more about fair play and ethical conduct in sport. One of the group's main contributions has been the Canadian Strategy for Ethical Conduct in Sport, created to ensure that participation in sports at all levels and ages is safe; to prevent doping, violence, and harassment in sport; to create a place where sports disputes can be dealt with fairly; to encourage rewards for good sportsmanship; and to promote fair play to all sports participants. By 2012, all the stages of the implementation of the strategy are expected to be complete.

Canadian Football League (CFL). Currently the only fully professional football league in Canada, the CFL began as loosely organized group of amateur and collegiate teams, and did not convert to fully professional status until 1958, when it took on its current name. CFL teams compete for the league championship prize, the Grey Cup, named in honour of Governor General Earl Grey, who, in 1909, donated an annual trophy to the top team in Canadian football. Teams must include rosters comprised of a set number of Canadian and non-Canadian players, and, although the league has experimented with expansion into the U.S., all CFL teams are currently based in Canada.

Canadian Hockey Association (CHA). The current mandate of this Association, which held its first meeting on December 4, 1914, is to support amateur hockey in Canada. The CHA organizes provincial and regional playoffs and established Minor Hockey Week – a major promotional project held annually in January – making minor hockey even more popular.

Canadian Intramural Recreation Association. A national organization that works in partnership with the federal government as well as its provincial and territorial affiliates to encourage all children to participate in school sports. Volunteers are active on all levels – from working directly with students to training other volunteers and teachers in how to develop fun physical activity programs for all students, regardless of age, gender, size, skill, culture, or socioeconomic status.

Canadian Olympic Committee. A private, non-profit corporation, first recognized by the International Olympic Committee in 1907, which represents Canada in the international Olympic sports movement. It is also the largest private-sector funder of elite sports in Canada.

Canadian Paralympic Committee. A private non-profit charitable corporation that is the Canadian representative to the International Paralympic Committee, which organizes world Games for the disabled, parallel to the Olympic Games. Its foundations were laid in 1976 when the federal government first donated funds for an event called the Torontolympiad (later known as the 5th Paralympic Games). The World Paralympics, like the Olympic Games, are held every four years and attract disabled competitors from around the world.

Canadian Physical Activity, Fitness and Lifestyle Appraisal (CPAFLA). The Canadian Standardized Test of Fitness was originally developed in 1979 as a consistent approach to appraisal. It is now called The Canadian Physical Activity, Fitness and Lifestyle Appraisal (CPAFLA).

Canadian School Sport Federation. An umbrella group that operates in each Canadian province, which consists of volunteer coaches, students, and administrators dedicated to the promotion of sport in education. Aside from offering leadership and resources to sport educators, each federation organizes provincial championships, where school teams and individual athletes compete.

Canadian Sport Policy. A policy developed by the federal government in 2002, after two years of consultation with various members of the sport community. The result is a general consensus on the purpose of a Canadian sport policy and on how to manage and promote sport in such a vast and diverse country.

Canadian Sport Centres. Based in eight location across Canada, these centres serve to support elite athletes so that they can attain their highest potential in important international competitions.

Canadian Strategy for Ethical Conduct in Sport. Determined jointly by the Canadian Centre for Ethics in Sport and Sport Canada, this policy attempts to ensure that participation in sports at all levels and ages is safe; to prevent doping, violence, and harassment in sport; to create a place where sports disputes can be dealt with fairly; to encourage rewards for good sportsmanship; and to promote fair play to all sports participants. By 2012, all the stages of the implementation of the strategy will be complete.

Cancellous bone. Cancellous or spongy bone is filled with marrow in its matrix or small cavity-like spaces. Its appearance is similar to the structure of a bridge.

Capillaries. In the capillaries, oxygen, carbon dioxide, and nutrients are exchanged between the blood and cells.

Carbohydrates. The most abundant organic substances in nature, they are essential for human and animal life. They come to us almost entirely from foods that originate from plants, such as vegetables, fruits, and grain-based foods, such as bread and pasta.

Carbo-loading. Those who advocate the process of carbohydrate-loading (known among athletes as carbo-loading) believe that muscles with extra glycogen will perform better in long events such as marathon runs, cycling races, and swimming.

Cardiac cycle. The series of events that occurs through one heart beat. During this cycle there is both a phase of relaxation (diastole), where the heart is filling with blood, and a phase of contraction (systole), where the heart contracts and ejects the blood.

Cardiac muscles. Muscles that are, as the name suggests, found in only one place in the body – the heart. They are responsible for creating the action that pumps blood from the heart to the rest of the body and form the heart's thick wall. Cardiac muscles are involuntary muscles because they are not controlled consciously. Like skeletal muscle tissue, cardiac tissue is also striated.

Cardiac output. Cardiac output refers to the volume of blood that is pumped out of the heart in 1 minute, usually represented by the symbol Q and measured in litres per minute (L/min). Cardiac output can be calculated as the product of stroke volume and heart rate.

Cardiovascular disease. Any disease associated with the cardiovascular system.

Cardiovascular endurance. The ability of the lungs, heart, and blood vessels to deliver adequate amounts of oxygen to the cells to meet the demands of prolonged physical activity. The level of cardiovascular endurance, cardiovascular fitness, or aerobic capacity is determined by the maximal amount of oxygen (VO_2max) that the human body is able to utilize per minute of physical activity.

Carnitine. A substance believed to prevent the buildup of excess coenzymes in the mitochondria during abnormal metabolism caused by exercise. It is theorized that carnitine supplements could spare glycogen and reduce the production of lactate, thus delaying fatigue and increasing anaerobic power.

Cartilage. There are three main types of cartilage. Hyaline cartilage is the most widespread and is found at the ends of bones and free-moving joints; at the ends of the ribs; and in the nose, larynx, trachea, and bronchi. Fibrocartilage is the very strong tissue that is found mainly between the vertebrae of the spine. Elastic cartilage or "yellow cartilage" makes up the external ear, the auditory tube of the middle ear, and the epiglottis. Cartilage surface is covered by a membrane known as the perichondrium. Cartilage has no blood supply, and therefore, injuries to it take time to heal.

Cartilaginous joints. The type of joint (also known as fibrocartilaginous joints), in which the body of one bone connects to the body of another by means of cartilage, and slight movement is possible. The intervertebral discs of the spinal column (of which there are twenty-three) are of this type.

Cellular respiration. The process where the cells use O_2 to generate energy through the different metabolic pathways found in the mitochondria.

Central nervous system. The body's control system, divided into two parts: the brain and the spinal cord.

Centre of mass. The two terms mass and weight are not synonymous. On the moon, you would have the same mass as you do on Earth, but you would have less weight (due to the reduced gravity). Likewise, the term "centre of gravity," commonly used to describe the point at which the mass of a body seems to be focused, is a misnomer. The correct term is centre of mass since it is not really dependent on gravity.

Chaining. Since complex skills are made up of separate and distinct parts, this approach uses the metaphor of the links of a chain to break a skill down, and encourages athletes to join – or "chain" – these elements together.

Charitable activities. Most professional sports teams sponsor charitable activities either directly (e.g., having special game days for donations for a worthy cause or charitable organization) or indirectly (e.g., establishing their own charitable institution whose activities team players are expected to support in their off hours).

Cheating. An attempt to gain an unfair advantage in training or competition by using methods or equipment prohibited by the rules of the sport. There are many different ways to cheat in sports, including the use of banned performance-enhancing substances, the use of illegal equipment, the attempt to bend the rules of the competition, the attempt to influence the judges or officials, and the attempt to influence the efforts of your opponents.

Cholesterol. Chemically, cholesterol is a fatty lipid (and a steroid) that collects in the body's tissues. Large concentrations of cholesterol occur in the brain, spinal cord, and the liver. It is processed most often in the liver and secreted in a substance called bile. During this process, cholesterol can harden in the gall bladder to form often painful gallstones.

Chronic hypertrophy. Increase in muscle size resulting from long-term resistance training. It remains for days, months, or years, depending on the level of intensity and the frequency of workouts.

Chronic obstructive pulmonary disease (COPD). A general term that describes a family of diseases that lead to a dramatic reduction in airflow through the respiratory system.

Chronological age. Age measured in years, months, and days; that is, the "standard" use of the term.

Circumduction. Circumduction is a circular motion combining flexion, extension, abduction, and adduction.

Clap skate. An example of technological innovation, the clap skate allows the skater to raise the heel off of the ice, as the blade of the skate rotates on a hinge. The blade is in contact with the ice longer and delivers more power per stride.

Classes of levers. Physicists identify three classes of levers based on the location of the fulcrum in relation to the force. In a Class I lever (e.g., a teeter-totter), the fulcrum is located between the force and the resistance. In a Class II lever (e.g., a wheelbarrow), the resistance is between the force and the fulcrum. In a Class III lever (e.g., snow shoveling) the force is between the fulcrum and the resistance.

Closed skills. A skill that takes place in an environment that is predictable and permits participants to plan their movements in advance.

Coaching Association of Canada. A national organization that offers training and certification at all levels of competence and experience to coaches across the country. Through its National Coaching Certification Program (NCCP), the CAC provides courses in theory that enable coaches to become versed in the basics of coaching in all sports, up to the principles of working with top athletes at provincial, national, and international levels.

Coaching styles. There are as many different kinds of coaches as there are types of athletes. Certainly, anyone who has seen the coach-athlete dynamic in action will recognize a number of distinct coaching styles. One recent Australian survey of 500 sport coaches concluded that there are five distinct coaching styles, each with its own unique characteristics.

Cognitive development. The changes that take place in a person's ability to interpret and process information, as well as alterations in their emotional development, and the introduction and establishment of a person's self-concept or awareness of one's self.

Cold stress and heat stress. A person can withstand a drop in core body temperature of about 10°C, but a rise of only 5°C. Beyond these levels, conditions known as cold stress and heat stress can set in, and both have proven fatal in many cases directly related to sport situations.

Comminuted fracture. A comminuted fracture occurs when the broken ends of the bone have been shattered into many pieces, as might occur in the case of a major automobile accident.

Commission for Fair Play. An organization that addresses a number of ethical issues in sport, particularly those centred around violence, and seeks to promote Fair Play in schools and other educational outlets.

Commonwealth Games. A multi-sport competition, similar to the Olympics but restricted to nations from the so-called Commonwealth of nations – countries that were once part of the British Empire and are now voluntarily associated with each other and with the Queen, the head of the Commonwealth. The first Commonwealth Games were held in Hamilton, Canada, in 1930, and they are contested in countries throughout the Commonwealth every four years.

Community recreation centres. Common meeting areas where people from different social, economic, and cultural backgrounds can interact and support one another within a given community. Community sport programs support the belief that healthy individuals create a healthy society. Their services are therefore geared towards this end – they are meant to be inclusive, educational, and fun.

Compact bone. The thick part of the bone, responsible for the bone's structural integrity. It is thickest along the diaphysis, or shaft of the bone.

Complete proteins. Foods that contain all twenty amino acids are known as complete proteins, including animal products such as meat, eggs, cheese, and milk.

Complex carbohydrates. It is generally recommended that 55 to 60 percent of our daily calorie intake should come from carbohydrates, and that most – around 80 percent – should come from what are known as complex carbohydrates, such as cereals, fruits, vegetables, legumes, and pasta.

Components of human development. There are four basic areas of human development, and each of them plays a key role in the ways in which people progress to increasingly complicated levels of sport and physical activity – physical, motor skills, cognitive, and social.

Compound fracture. A compound fracture occurs when the bone breaks, as the result of a major blow, into separate pieces (sometimes referred to as a "transverse fracture" or a "complete fracture").

Computerized axial tomography. Also known as a CAT scan, computerized axial tomography is a technique that doctors use to obtain a relatively safe, quick, and painless diagnosis in various areas of the body, including the spine and brain.

Concentration. The ability to keep one's focus on the task at hand without being distracted from it by changes in the surrounding environment. Concentration is a key part of athletic success.

Concentric (shortening). This occurs when the muscle fibre shortens – for example, the biceps shorten when lifting an object.

Concurrent training. An attempt to train multiple energy systems by performing different types of training simultaneously. It is also known as cross-training.

Concussion. A common head injury caused by an accidental or intentional blow to the head.

Conductive zone. The area composed of all of the structures that convey air from the outside of the body through to the lungs. This zone includes the mouth and nose, pharynx, larynx, trachea, bronchi, bronchioles, and terminal bronchioles.

Conservation of energy. The concept that energy can never be created or destroyed, but can only be converted from one form to another.

Controlled motor activity. Controlled motor activity needs relatively more thought and time to perform in comparison to automatic motor activity. For example, a soccer player weaving in and out of traffic during a game is processing a lot of information rapidly, including his or her own speed and control of the ball, the challenges of opponents, and so on.

Cori cycle. The Cori cycle (named after Carl Ferdinand Cori, American biochemist, 1896-1984) is the name given to the process by which lactic acid is converted to pyruvate for future conversion to glucose and glycogen.

Coronary arteries. The system of vessels that supply blood to the heart. Blood is supplied to the heart through two main arteries, the right and left coronary arteries.

Coronary veins. As blood moves through the coronary venules, these coronary venules come together and form larger vessels called coronary veins. Eventually, all of the coronary veins come together to form the coronary sinus, which drains into the right atrium of the heart, completing the path of blood through the coronary circulation.

Corruption of judges and officials. Any attempt to induce a sport judge or official to change the result of a competition, or to favour a certain competitor or team. This corruption can take the form of financial inducements and the promise of other biased results being given to competitors in other sports or events.

Cortex. The exterior layer of bones, known as the cortex, is dense and smooth and of varying thickness, depending on the type of bone.

Crazy Canucks. The nickname given to the group of outstanding Canadian downhill skiers who excelled on the World Cup circuit during the 1970s and 1980s. Renowned for their daredevil styles and outgoing attitudes, the most prominent of this group were Ken Read, Dave Irwin, David Murray, and Steve Podborski. In 1975, Read was the first non-European to win a race in the World Cup circuit.

Creatine. This amino acid is readily present in normal skeletal muscle and facilitates the rapid production of ATP, providing an immediate source of energy during short periods of muscular exertion.

Crossed-extensor reflex. The reflex action by which one leg or arm automatically compensates for a reflex action in the opposing leg or arm.

Daily caloric need. The number of calories necessary to maintain one's current body weight.

Deceptive advertising. Companies that manufacture so-called "performance-enhancing" substances, such as dietary supplements or ergogenic aids, often resort to deceptive advertising tactics in order to convince consumers to purchase them. Unfortunately, many athletes fall prey to such tactics and fail to consider the underlying science or truth of claims made of a particular product.

Dehydration. A state that occurs when the body's water supply is lowered following exercise (sweating) or other reasons. Under physically active conditions, a constant replacement of fluids is required for the body to continue to operate at peak performance.

Democratic coach. A coach who encourages his or her athletes to be fully involved in the decisions being made about training and competition.

Deoxygenated blood. Blood that has returned from the body and is pumped by the right heart to the lungs (pulmonary circulation). It is dark red in colour.

Depression. The opposite action to elevation, depression, involves the pulling down to a more inferior position.

Developmental age. Age as expressed in one's ability to perform certain tasks.

Diaphragm. With stimulation from the brain, the diaphragm contracts and moves downward towards the abdominal cavity, creating more space in the chest cavity. With the contraction of the diaphragm, the air pressure within the chest and lungs is lower than the air pressure outside the body in the atmosphere. The lower air pressure in the chest causes air to rush into the lungs, resulting in an inspiration.

Diaphysis. The shaft and thickest part of the bone.

Diastolic blood pressure. The pressure observed in the arteries during the relaxation phase of the heart (i.e., 80 mmHg).

Dietary Reference Intakes (DRIs). Estimations of the amount of nutrients we need – not only to prevent nutrient deficiencies but also to lower the risk of chronic disease.

Diffusion. The movement of a gas, liquid, or solid from a region of high concentration to a region of low concentration through random movement. Diffusion can only occur if a difference in concentration exists, and such a difference is called a concentration gradient.

Diffusion pathway. The area through which gases move from the lungs into the blood and from the blood into the tissue, and back.

Dislocation. A bone is displaced from its original location. The most common form of dislocation occurs at the finger joints, usually involving damage to the joint capsule and the ligaments that hold the two bones together. A dislocation of the shoulder occurs when the humerus "pops out" of the glenoid fossa. This is usually a result of a hit or fall resulting in a tear to the glenohumeral ligament and joint capsule.

Doping. A practice defined by the World Anti-Doping Agency as "the use of an artifice, whether substance or method, potentially dangerous to athletes' health and/or capable of enhancing their performances."

Dorsiflexion. Dorsiflexion is movement of the ankle in the sagittal plane that decreases the angle between the foot and the lower leg.

Drop-in centre programs. Locations that are generally available to entire communities for the purpose of promoting sport and physical activity, and open to all members of that community, regardless of race, gender, language, and economic or social status. In contrast to more formally organized leagues or clubs, drop-in centres usually provide blocks of time and facilities that enable anyone to play a certain sport or game, i.e., pick-up basketball, floor hockey, and so on.

Drug masking. Over the last two decades, methods of avoiding drug-testing detection have expanded from the substitution of urine samples to include drug masking, whereby certain drugs are used to mask or reduce the presence of banned substances.

Drug policies. The five major North American pro sports leagues each have their own rules about drug use for their players. In each case, these policies have a direct relationship to the league's players through their collective labour organizations.

Drug testing. Urine tests taken at major sporting events for the purpose of detecting banned substances. Because new methods are continually being developed and current ones, improved, athletes who use banned substances in a competition run a high risk of detection. A successful drug testing program involves random, year-round, and unannounced testing.

Dubin Inquiry. Lead by Chief Justice Charles Dubin after the 1988 Summer Olympics, this investigation sought to ascertain just how widespread the use of illegal performance-enhancing drugs was in Canada.

Dynamic lung volumes. Lung volumes that are dependent, not only on volume, but also on the movement or flow of air.

Eccentric (lengthening). This occurs when a muscle lengthens – for example, the biceps lengthen as weight that has been lifted is placed back on the ground.

Ectomorphic type. Generally later to reach maturity, people with this body type develop a thinner body, characterized by narrow hips and longer legs and arms.

Edmonton Commercial Graduates Basketball Club. Better known as the "Grads," this all-women's basketball team is significant in the history of Canadian sports, not the least of which is the fact that, from 1915 to 1940, the Edmonton-based squad – which began as a team consisting of students and graduates of McDougall Commercial High School – won more than 500 games, and lost only 20, a record for any Canadian team in any sport. Historians who specialize in gender issues also often cite the team as an early pioneer in women's organized competitive sport.

Efferent nerves. Motor nerves (or efferent nerves) carry information from the central nervous system to the body's organs.

Ejection fraction (EF). The proportion of blood that is ejected from the left ventricle during a single heartbeat. The efficiency of stroke volume is measured through the calculation of ejection fraction.

Electrocardiogram. The electrical activity of the heart can be measured using an electrocardiogram (ECG). The ECG provides a graphical representation of the electrical sequence of events that occurs with each contraction of the heart.

Electron transport chain. During this, the final stage of aerobic respiration, large amounts of ATP are produced, with carbon dioxide and water as the only by-products.

Elevation. Elevation involves the raising up to a more superior position.

Ellipsoid joints. Similar to a ball-and-socket joints, ellipsoid joints allow movement in two planes. An example is found between the second metacarpal and the first phalanx of the second finger. The wrist is also an example of this type of joint.

Endomorphic type. People with this body type are generally characterized by more fatty tissue and thicker body parts.

Endomysium. A sheath of connective tissue that surrounds the muscle fibre. Beneath this lies a plasma membrane (the sarcolemma), which contains the muscle cell's cytoplasm (the sarcoplasm).

Endorsement. An agreement between a person – usually well known to a large public audience – and a commercial interest, by which that individual in some way promotes the product or service provided by the commercial interest, for example, a well-known athlete appearing on a television commercial in support of a beverage or piece of sports equipment. In most cases, this involves the individual being paid for their role.

Energy equation. A calculation of a person's energy and nutritional needs, specific to the individual. Children and teens need relatively more nutrients and energy because they are still growing. Physically active people will need more energy than those who are less active.

Epimysium. Connective tissue that holds together and envelopes the entire muscle.

Epiphyseal lines. Epiphyseal lines occur when epiphyseal plates have fused or have come together.

Epiphyseal plates. Epiphyseal plates, also known as growth plates, occur at various locations at the epiphyses of long bones.

Epiphysis. At the very ends of long bones is a region known as the epiphysis. This region can be easily spotted because its appearance is different than that of the diaphysis.

Equilibrium. Equilibrium can be thought of as kind of a "perfect" situation where more than one force acts on a body but, because the sum of forces is zero, no motion results.

Ergonomics. Those who study in a field known as ergonomics – sometimes called "human-factors engineering" or "biotechnology" – are interested in finding out how the relationship between humans and machines can be made as efficient as possible.

Erythropoietin (EPO). A natural protein hormone that is produced primarily in the kidneys. Synthetic erythropoietin has been shown to cause an increase in levels of hematocrit and hemoglobin, and this increases the oxygen-carrying capacity of red blood cells.

ESTEEM Team. Created from a small British Colombia program in 1993, the ESTEEM Team is now a national not-for-profit organization that seeks to motivate and inspire youth across the country to become active in sport. Professional athletes tour Canadian schools, speaking to students about the lessons they have learned and the challenges they have faced throughout their sport careers.

Eversion. Eversion occurs when the lateral border of the foot is raised such that the sole of the foot is turned outward.

Eversion sprains. Eversion sprains (when the sole of the foot is forced outward, away from the body) are rare because of the strength of the deltoid ligament. This ligament attaches the medial malleolus to three bones of the foot.

Excess post-exercise oxygen consumption (EPOC). The additional oxygen taken in during the recovery period in order to restore the balance is referred to as recovery oxygen uptake or excess post-exercise oxygen consumption.

Excitation-contraction coupling. Muscles work essentially by converting chemical energy (ATP) into mechanical energy. The process as a whole is often referred to as excitation-contraction coupling.

Exercise physiology. A branch of physiology, with the important distinction that exercise physiologists concentrate their research specifically on how the body responds and adapts to the stresses placed on it by exercise.

Exercise. Any activity that improves the body's basic functions, such as one's ability to take up and use oxygen, metabolic processes such as blood flow, muscular strength and endurance, or one's range of motion in the joints and muscles.

Exploitation. Any relationship in which one party engages in the majority of the effort without at the same time receiving a fair share of the results. In a sporting context, exploitation has the same connotation: any athlete who is performing an excessive amount of work (i.e., competing or training) without garnering an appropriate benefit (i.e., prize money, publicity, athletic advancement, and so on) can be said to be in an "exploitive" relationship.

Extension. Extension is straightening a joint to increase the angle. It occurs in the sagittal plane.

Extensor muscles. Muscles that extend the limbs and increase the angle between two limbs.

External respiration. The processes that occur within the lung involving the exchange of oxygen and carbon dioxide.

External rotation. External rotation of a limb moves its anterior surface laterally.

Factors affecting physical growth. Key factors affecting physical growth include glandular/hormonal activity, heredity, nutrition/diet, physical activity, and sociocultural factors.

Factors affecting skill acquisition. The wide range of variables that influence how well people learn skills. These include fatigue, nervousness, weather, distractions, and so on.

Fair play. A sports philosophy grounded in the belief that sport is a moral pursuit and emphasizes participation.

Fan loyalty. The extent to which a team supporter – i.e., a "fan" – will support that team. In the context of professional sport, fan loyalty can often be translated into increased revenue for the team, since loyalty will lead to the purchase of tickets as well as other sports-related merchandise.

FANTASTIC Lifestyle Checklist. A questionnaire that considers a variety of factors affecting health and well-being. The questionnaire includes health factors such as family and friends, physical activity, proper nutrition, and use of tobacco and other toxics.

Fartlek training. A training method developed in the 1940s by Swedish runners; the term literally means "speed play" and consists of continuous running at alternating speeds over varied terrain.

Fast-twitch muscle fibres. Paler in colour than slow-twitch fibres, these fibres have the ability to tense and relax quickly, and can generate large amounts of tension with relatively low endurance levels.

Fatigue. The onset of physical fatigue leads to a mental state where feelings of tiredness can cause a decrease in performance. Sport psychologists attempt to mitigate the influence of fatigue by helping athletes understand that, while inevitable, it can be overcome.

Fatty acids. Acids stored in the body as triglycerides. Through a process known as lipolysis, triglycerides are broken down and the resulting fatty acids become available as an energy source.

Feedback. The information a learner obtains regarding how he or she is progressing in learning to perform a skill. It can assist in performance improvement and lead to a steeper learning curve.

Female triad. A syndrome comprising disordered eating habits, amenorrhea, and osteoporosis. Many athletic women have a drive to excel that helps them to succeed in sports but also may lead them to achieve a weight goal that they believe to be realistic by any means necessary. In order to reach these levels, women develop eating disorders, which in turn leads to the other aspects of the triad.

Femininity. The particular ways in which women's behaviour, values, and appearances are perceived in a given society or group. Perceptions of femininity are important in the world of sports and physical activity because, through pursuing competitive and fitness goals during the last several decades, many women have successfully changed the way in which people "expect" them to look and act. In contrast to prevailing ideals of just a generation ago, concepts such as muscularity and the possession of a competitive drive have been included into many people's idea of what it means to be "feminine" through the accomplishments of successful female athletes.

Fibrous joints. Joints that are bound tightly together by connective tissue and allow no movement. These are the joints between the interlocking bones of the skull, known as sutures. After birth, all sutures joints become immobile.

Fitness objectives. Goals that may include an individual's desire to develop a more active lifestyle, recover from an injury, or improve athletic performance.

Fitness. Improvement in bodily functions, comprised of enhancements in two main areas: cardiovascular capacity, and muscular strength and endurance.

F.I.T.T. Principle. One of the key elements of training theory, which captures the four basic building blocks of any exercise plan: Frequency, Intensity, Type, and Time. These four dimensions apply to and need to be addressed when devising any fitness or training program.

Five-step method of skills teaching. A learning model that utilizes five basic building blocks in the teaching (and learning) of a skill, and has been found to be successful across a wide range of motor activities.

Flexibility. The ability of a joint to move freely through its full range of motion (ROM).

Flexion. Flexion is bending the joint to reduce the angle between two bones. It occurs in the sagittal plane. Flexion is motion in the anterior (forwards) direction at the joints of the neck, trunk, upper extremities, and hips. For the knee, ankle, foot, and toes, flexion occurs in the posterior (backwards) direction.

Flexor muscles. Muscles that withdraw the limbs and thereby decrease the angle between bones on two sides of a joint.

Force as a vector. The concept of force, as a push or a pull of a certain magnitude, in a particular direction.

For-profit sport. Any sporting activity organized and run for the express purpose of making a profit for team owners, athletes, sponsors, or others. Major-league sport in North America is an example of for-profit sport.

Frank-Starling Law. The ability of the heart to stretch and increase the force of contraction.

Full-body swimsuits. As an example of technological innovation in sport, these suits have been designed to reduce drag in the water. Made of super-stretch fabric with built-in edges similar to a shark's skin, the pattern of the suit causes the seams to emulate tendons and provide tension while its fabric panels stretch and return to their original shape, mimicking muscles.

Games of La Francophonie. A multi-sport competition, contested by nations of La Francophonie, the international community of peoples who speak French or use it to various degrees, either in their own country or internationally. Currently, the Games (known in French as Jeux de la Francophonie) include fifty-five participating states and governments; in Canada, participation consists of three teams: Canada, Canada-Quebec and Canada-New Brunswick.

Gas exchange. The exchange of gases both at the lung (where the blood becomes oxygenated and carbon dioxide is removed) and at the tissue (where oxygen is delivered for metabolism and carbon dioxide is removed).

Gender representation in leadership positions. The extent to which one gender – male or female – is included in a given activity or group. In sports, this term usually refers to the role that women play in prominent positions, such as coaches, officials, committee, league, or tournament members.

General Adaptation Syndrome. In the mid-1950s, stress researcher Hans Selye devised the theory of the General Adaptation Syndrome, also known simply as GAS, as the basis for the periodization theory of training.

Girls @ Play. A program developed by CAAWS and Nike Canada with a mandate of "getting more girls in the game" by "encourag[ing] girls and women to get off the bleachers and sidelines and onto the playing fields as participants and leaders."

Gliding (or plane or arthrodial) joints. This group of joints connects flat or slightly curved bone surfaces. Examples include joints in the foot between the tarsals and in the hand among the carpals. Movement does not occur about an axis (non-axial).

Glycemic index. The glycemic index indicates the rate of carbohydrate digestion and its effects on blood glucose levels. Foods such as sugar and honey have a high glycemic index. Whole-grained breads, rice, bran, and peas have a moderate glycemic index. Fruits, beans, and lentils have a low glycemic index.

Glycogen. Glucose is the usual form in which carbohydrates are assimilated by animals. It is stored within skeletal muscle and within the liver as glycogen.

Glycolysis. The name given to the body's second energy pathway. The ATP energy produced during this process will allow an athlete to engage in a high level of performance for about an additional 90 seconds.

Goal setting. The process by which an athlete identifies desired levels of performance in training or competition.

Golgi tendon organs. Named after the discoverer, Italian scientist Camillo Golgi, 1844-1926, GIOs are sensory receptors that terminate where tendons join to muscle fibre.

Grass Roots Canada Basketball. A Toronto-based group that uses the sport of basketball to attract and motivate youth, while keeping potentially high-risk youth away from crime.

Harris-Benedict Equation. This equation allows you to estimate your resting metabolic rate, with separate calculations for males and females.

Health-related fitness. The level of fitness that includes: body composition; muscle balance (strength, endurance, and flexibility, particularly of the postural muscles); cardiovascular functions; and metabolic components designed to improve health.

Heart rate. The number of times the heart contracts in a minute (beats per minute; beats/min), usually represented by the symbol HR.

Heart rate reserve. The Karvonen or heart rate reserve method (HRR) takes into account resting heart rate and is defined as the difference between maximal heart rate and resting heart rate (MHR – RHR).

Heat cramps. These occur when muscles spasm or tighten due to excessive loss of fluid and electrolytes through sweating. The symptoms include short painful muscle twitches, followed by total muscle cramp.

Heat exchange. In order to combat overheating, the body promotes a process called heat exchange, which can be accomplished by radiation (the emission of radiant heat from the body into the cooler environment); conduction (the transfer of heat through a liquid, solid, or gas – in the case of exercising in the heat, this can be accomplished by dousing oneself in cool water); convection (air movement around the skin); and evaporation (water – i.e., sweat – vaporization from the skin into the environment).

Heat exhaustion. A severe condition requiring medical attention, which is associated with a cumulative loss of water and a weakening of the body's ability to regulate its internal temperature. Symptoms include a high body temperature; pale, cool and clammy skin; light-headedness; and possibly loss of consciousness.

Heatstroke. A very serious condition when there is a complete failure of the body's heat-regulatory system, which should be treated as an absolute medical emergency. Symptoms include a very high body temperature, headache, confusion or behavioural change, and very possibly a loss of consciousness.

Hemoglobin. A specialized protein found in erythrocytes, each gram of hemoglobin in the blood has the capacity to bind 1.34 mL of O_2. The average concentration of hemoglobin is ~16 mg/100 mL of blood.

Henry's Law. The diffusion of a gas into a liquid is governed by Henry's Law, which states that the amount of gas that will dissolve and/or diffuse into a liquid is proportional to the partial pressure and the solubility of the gas.

Hinge (ginglymus) joints. Hinge joints have a convex portion of one bone fitting into a concave portion of another, and allow movement in one plane. The joints between the bones of the fingers (phalanges) and between the ulna ("inner" bone of the forearm) and the humerus are examples.

Hostile aggression. The deliberate intent to harm another player, fueled by anger and hostility, such as a baseball brawl or a hockey fight.

Human growth hormone (HGH). The body produces human growth hormone naturally through the pituitary gland, but athletes may seek to raise its level in their bodies by injecting synthetic preparations. Extra amounts are believed to increase muscle mass, strengthen bones, limit weight gain, and improve aerobic endurance.

Hyperbaric oxygen therapy. The process by which a person is placed inside a hyperbaric oxygen (HBO_2) chamber – a capsule filled with air that contains 95-100 percent oxygen at atmospheric pressures greater than those at sea level. This process may promote soft-tissue healing.

Hyperplasia. Muscles can also grow in size (and strength) by a process called hyperplasia or, literally, fibre splitting. The idea is that, once a fibre has reached its maximum hypertrophy, any further size and strength gains will come only through the formation of two "daughter cells" created by longitudinal fibre splitting.

Hypertension. Blood pressure is a commonly used indicator or measure of cardiovascular health. Persistently elevated blood pressure, also called hypertension (blood pressure consistently greater than 140/90 mmHg), is a major risk factor for cardiovascular disease.

Hypertrophy. The process of muscle growth in response to overload training. Hypertrophy in general means an increase in cell size.

Hypnosis. A state of intense concentration in which the mind directs the body to perform certain acts while blocking out all external stimuli except the ones that are essential to the completion of the ultimate goal.

Ideal performance state. The formal term for what many athletes refer to as "the zone" – they call it the ideal performance state.

Imagery and visualization. The process by which sport psychologists work with athletes to help them visualize or imagine themselves succeeding – almost like writing their own movie script, with them in the starring role – or to recall powerful images of past triumphs, all as ways of improving future performance.

Incomplete proteins. Vegetable proteins contain one or more amino acids in limited amounts and are called incomplete proteins. Care must be taken to choose foods that will provide the essential amino acids in sufficient amounts.

Insertion. The point where the muscle attaches to the bone that is moved most is known as the insertion.

Instrumental aggression. The result, during sporting competition, of one player being injured as a side effect of an aggressor's attempt to achieve something else; for example, a legal football tackle that nevertheless causes injury.

Internal respiration. Refers to the exchange of gases at the tissue level, where O_2 is delivered and CO_2 is removed.

Internal rotation. Internal rotation of a limb moves its anterior surface medially.

International Olympic Committee. A non-profit, non-governmental body of international members who represent the Olympic Movement in their respective countries but do not act as delegates for their country. Members are elected by means of a nominations committee and serve an eight-year renewable term. The members meet once a year, and their main responsibility is to govern the Winter and Summer Olympics.

Inter-Provincial Lottery Corporation. The federal government, under an agreement dated September 23, 1979, with the Inter-provincial Lottery Corporation, withdrew from the lottery field in exchange for payment of $24 million annually beginning in 1979. It agreed to allow private corporations to run lotteries, in exchange for a remittance of funds by these private lottery organizations.

Interval training. A popular form of training based on the idea that the body's energy systems can make both aerobic and anaerobic gains, not only by steady, uninterrupted exercise, but also by alternating periods of relatively intense exercise with periods of recovery within the same workout.

Inversion. Inversion occurs when the medial border of the foot is raised such that the sole of the foot is turned inward.

Inversion sprains. Inversion ankle sprains occur when the sole of the foot is turned inward – more commonly referred to as "rolling over on your ankle" or "twisting your ankle."

Isokinetic exercise. Exercise that involves using machines to control the speed of contractions within the range of muscle's motion and thereby seeks to combine the best features of both isometric and isotonic training.

Isometric exercise. Exercise in which the muscle fibres maintain a constant length throughout the entire contraction and there is no motion. These exercises are usually performed against an immovable surface or object (such as pressing one's arms against a wall).

Isotonic exercise. Exercise that involves a controlled shortening (concentric contraction) of the muscle. A classic example is weight training with dumbbells and barbells. As the weight is lifted throughout the range of motion, the muscle shortens.

Kinematics. The study of the space and time aspects of movement – that is, measuring how far and how fast things travel. Here, the emphasis is on the measurement and calculation of changes in space and time (displacement, velocity, and acceleration) rather than on explaining how and why objects move.

Kinesiology. The study of movement. The term comes from the Greek word *kinen* (to move) and *logos* (or, discourse). It is also defined as a combination of anatomy, the study of the body's structure, with physiology, the study of the body's functions.

Kinetics. The field of kinetics focuses on the forces that may be involved in a particular situation to make that movement happen in the first place.

Knee ligament tears. The most common knee ligament tears involve blows to the lateral side of the knee. When this happens, the severity of the blow determines the degree of the tear and the amount of tissue damage.

Krebs cycle. Also referred to as the citric acid cycle or the tricarboxylic acid cycle, in many ways the Krebs cycle can be considered as the beginning of the aerobic energy system. It occurs in mitochondria and is the common pathway to completely oxidize fuel molecules. Through a series of eight reactions, two ATP molecules are produced at this stage, along with new compounds capable of storing high-energy electrons.

Lactate threshold. It is possible to measure blood lactate repeatedly during incremental exercise. Eventually, a point is reached where blood lactate concentrations begin to rise. This point is referred to as the lactate threshold.

Lactic acid. The main product of glycolysis is pyruvate (pyruvic acid). Under aerobic conditions, pyruvate is the beginning of the third (aerobic) system that eventually leads to the complete breakdown of glucose. In the absence of adequate oxygen, the process is halted at the glycolysis stage. Pyruvic acid is converted to lactic acid and exhaustion or pain in the muscles begins to set in.

Léger "Beep Test." A test that uses an audiotape to control timed runs over a measured course. An audio tone communicates timing information for the test subjects.

Lifting shirt. For weightlifters, the shirt acts as a spring, aiding in control as the bar is lowered and also as the bar is pressed up. A too-tight shirt will lose its spring; a too-loose shirt is simply not

as effective. The use of these shirts has been banned in most international competitions.

Ligament. The tissue that attaches one or more bones together.

Linear (or translational) motion. Movement in a particular direction (and includes the diagonal result of more than one linear force acting on an object).

Low-fat food diets. Popular in the past twenty years or so, these diets have not been as successful as expected. The main reason is because low-fat foods often contain a high simple sugar content to make them appealing. The result is that people are not actually consuming less energy, which is what determines weight gain and loss.

Macronutrients. The human body's direct sources of energy. These are proteins, carbohydrates, and fats. These, in effect, supply the energy for daily life and for physical exercise and work.

Magnetic resonance imaging (MRI). A non-invasive exploratory process that uses a device called a nuclear magnetic resonance spectrometer. The spectrometer produces electronic cross-sectional images of the human cells, organs, and tissues that have been targeted for inspection.

Man in Motion World Tour. The name given to the 1985 around-the-world tour by wheelchair athlete Rick Hansen, in which he traversed four continents, thirty-four countries, and more than 40,000 kilometres to raise money for spinal cord injury research. Hansen concluded his tour in Canada, where thousands of people lined the route to support him, back to his home in Vancouver. The Man In Motion Tour ultimately raised $24 million for spinal cord injury research.

Marathon of Hope. The name given to the cross-country run embarked upon by cancer survivor Terry Fox, in 1980, in which he attempted to run across Canada. Although Fox had lost a leg to cancer three years previously, he began his run in St. John's, Newfoundland, and eventually received tremendous media attention due to the fact that he averaged a full marathon (42 km) per day through the Maritimes, Quebec, and Ontario. After 143 days, Fox was forced to end the run because the cancer had spread to his lungs, but the outpouring of public sentiment – and funds to support cancer research – was overwhelming. Fox passed away the following year, but the annual Terry Fox Run held in his honour has raised almost $300 million for cancer research.

Maximal heart rate. The heart rate at which the body is considered to be working at full cardiovascular capacity. In order to find maximal heart rate (MHR), subtract a person's age from 220. For example, an eighteen-year-old may have a MHR of $220 - 18 = 202$ bpm.

Maximal rate of oxygen consumption (VO$_2$max). The maximum volume (V) of oxygen (O$_2$) in millilitres that the human body can use in 1 minute, per kilogram of body weight, while breathing air at sea level.

Media. The collective term for all the means by which people gain access to information, including television, radio, the Internet, newspapers, magazines, and many others. The information received can be in the form of entertainment, news, educational messages, messages from commercial interests, or a combination of these three.

Media coverage of women's sports. Women's sports receive less than 10 percent of the total sports coverage of most networks and newspapers. With such a lack of media coverage of women's sports teams, leagues, and athletes, the media is sending the message that women's sports and athletic accomplishments are unimportant compared to men's sports.

Medullary cavity. The medullary cavity is found inside the shaft of the bone and is filled with red and yellow bone marrow.

Mesomorphic type. Often maturing early as children, people with this body type tend to develop stocky, heavily muscled, broader bodies.

Metabolic rate. A measurement of the energy that needs to be consumed in order to sustain essential bodily functions such as heartbeat, breathing, nervous activity, active transport, and secretion.

Metabolism. The highly complex process by which energy is supplied throughout the body and by which energy-rich material (fats and proteins as well as carbohydrates) are assimilated by the body for the purposes of energy renewal.

Micronutrients. Vitamins and minerals that act as co-agents in the bioenergetic process – they do not provide energy themselves but rather play an indispensable role in helping the process along.

Midnight Basketball League. A sports-based initiative, developed in the U.S. and popular in many urban centers, in which youth at risk of crime or social problems are encouraged to come for organized or informal games of supervised basketball between the "high-crime" hours of 10 p.m. and 2 a.m.

Mills Report. Officially called "The Mills Report: Sport in Canada," this document was published in December of 1998, and was the work of the members of Parliament on the Sub-Committee on the Study of Sport in Canada chaired by MP Dennis Mills. The report is the most comprehensive parliamentary review of the Canadian sports scene in thirty years, since the 1969 Task Force Report on Sport.

Minerals. Derived from the earth's waters and topsoil and absorbed by plants that we eat, the seven key minerals are calcium, phosphorous, magnesium, sodium, potassium, chloride, and sulfur. Trace minerals, of which we require less than 100 milligrams per day, include iron, manganese, and zinc.

Moment of force (torque). In comparison to linear motion, in rotational motion, the object in question spins around an axis; instead of force, there is what is known as the moment of force, or torque.

Moment of inertia. In rotational systems, the moment of inertia depends on the distribution of the mass in relation to the axis of rotation. In effect, the further the mass is from the axis, the greater the moment of inertia. The closer it is to the axis of rotation, the easier it is to rotate it or to stop it from rotating.

Morphology. Morphology is the study of structure or form – for example, the biological classification of plants. In the context of human growth and development, three main body types have identified in an attempt to classify people's appearance and physical structure: endomorphs, mesomorphs, and ectomorphs.

Motion analysis. The video camera with its slow-motion playback feature has provided a motion analysis tool for analyzing the minutest movements that affect performance. Recent improvements in the speed and graphics capabilities of computers have taken this even further – a computer can now analyze a video film of an athlete.

Motivation. In a sports setting, this refers to the direction and intensity of effort on the part of the athlete.

Motivational readiness. A measure of an individual's stage of psychological readiness for physical fitness training. The Canadian Society for Exercise Physiology has developed a Stages of Change Questionnaire that identifies five stages of motivational readiness stages. Once determined, strategies can be chosen that are effective for that specific stage.

Motor learning. The process by which a person develops, through a combination of physical and psychological factors, the ability to perform a task.

Motor unit. The motor neuron, its axon (pathway), and the fibres it stimulates are together referred to as the "motor unit."

Multi-Sport Service Organizations (MSOs). Somewhat underrecognized, but critically important in the complex Canadian sport system, various MSOs exist to provide support and services across the various sport organizations. These important organizations, funded mainly through Sport Canada, address the common needs of the different sport bodies and act in various ways to educate the general public and the sport community about issues and achievements.

Muscle atrophy. The process that occurs when a muscle is not exercised, and results in a shrinking of muscle size and strength. Atrophy can also occur as a result of malnutrition and disease.

Muscle spindles. Muscle spindles lie parallel to the main muscle fibre and send constant signals to the spinal cord regarding muscle stretch.

Muscle tissue. A collection of cells that shorten during contraction and, in doing so, create tension that results in movement of one kind or another.

Muscle twitch. Nerves transmit impulses in "waves" that ensure smooth movements. A single nervous impulse and the resulting contraction is called a muscle twitch. One neuron (called the "motor neuron") may be responsible for stimulating a number of muscle fibres.

Muscular Christianity. The popular idea, originating in nineteenth-century England, that physical activity was directly linked to moral righteousness. Muscular Christianity equated physical strength with spiritual fortitude, and its proponents believed that to engage in physical activity was to be a good Christian – or at least be on the path towards being one. This attitude was meant to inspire spiritual and patriotic fervour.

Muscular endurance. The ability of the muscle to perform repeated or sustained contractions over a period of time.

Muscular strength. The maximum tension or force a muscle can exert in a single contraction.

Myocardium. The muscle tissue that makes up the heart, similar in structure to the muscle tissue that is used to move the skeleton. Cardiac muscle cells are interconnected and allow the passage of electrical signals from cell to cell.

Myofibrils. Running along the muscle fibre's length are thread-like structures (myofibrils). Within these are finer "thick" and "thin" filaments (the cellular proteins myosin and actin).

Myoglobin. The protein that is the oxygen-storage unit that delivers oxygen to working muscles, thereby enabling energy-producing biochemical reactions to be sustained over a long period.

Myosin. A cellular protein comprised of a "head" and "tail," similar to the look of a golf club. The myosin head will have an attachment site for actin, and actin will have a binding site for the myosin head.

Myosin crossbridges. The explanation for the sliding of the filaments in muscle contraction is that a special set of conditions is created that causes the thick and thin filaments to interact at the molecular level. It is possible to detect small bridges on the thick filaments that extend to the thin filaments. These myosin crossbridges, as they are referred to, attach, rotate, detach, and reattach in rapid succession (in a ratchet-like fashion).

National Coaching Certification Program (NCCP). In Canada, the Coaching Association of Canada offers the National Coaching Certification Program (NCCP), a series of instructional courses for coaches. The NCCP instructs sport coaches in the basics of coaching and progresses all the way to advanced coaching theory and technique.

National Hockey League (NHL). The world's most prominent professional hockey league, containing thirty teams based across North America. The winning team in the NHL each season is awarded the Stanley Cup.

National Sport Organizations (NSOs). Federal bodies that provide administrative expertise and technical support for development of athletes and their participation in international competitions. These not-for-profit organizations service the various sports and are the principal means through which Sport Canada fosters sport, and especially elite sport, in Canada.

Neuromuscular junctions. The nerves that transmit the message directing the muscles to move come into contact with the muscles at points called neuromuscular junctions.

Neuromuscular system. The general term referring to the complex linkages between the muscular system (the various groups of muscles in the human body) and the nervous system (the system of nervous impulses originating in the brain and spinal cord).

Newton's Three Laws of Motion. In 1687, Sir Isaac Newton published his two-volume *Philosophiae Naturalis Principia Mathematica*, which laid out his famous three Laws of Motion: the Law of Inertia, the Law of Acceleration, and the Law of Reaction.

Not-for-profit sport. Sport contested mainly for reasons of enjoyment, personal fulfillment, and so on. A community jogging club is an example of not-for-profit sport.

Nutritional labelling. Most pre-packaged foods we purchase from the store carry nutritional labelling. However the information is often difficult to find, is inconsistent in its presentation, and is sometimes very hard to read. The Canadian government is currently in the process of introducing stricter regulations in this area.

Nutritional supplements. Products taken by athletes to enhance performance. These include vitamins, minerals, protein and amino acid supplements, so-called releasers of growth hormone, L-carnitine, creatine, caffeine, and various extracts from plant sources.

Obesity. A term used to describe the presence of excessive body fat in people. Contributing factors are many and include activity levels; diet; genetic factors; rates of metabolism; and environmental, social, and psychological factors. However, the two primary contributors to excessive weight gain are simply poor diet and inactivity.

Olympic Charter. The Olympic Charter, first penned by Baron Pierre de Coubertin, details the goals for the Olympic Movement, of which competitive sports are only a portion. The Charter emphasizes peace, tolerance, education, fair play, international understanding, and amateurism.

Olympic Games. The international multi-sport competition held every four years in different locations throughout the world. Originally, the Olympics was a creation of the ancient Greeks, with the first recorded one being held in 776 B.C., although the competition probably started long before then. In their modern form, the Olympics were instigated by the Frenchman Baron Pierre de Coubertin; the first modern Olympic Games were held in Athens in 1896. Today, both Winter and Summer Olympic Games are held at four-year intervals; the last Winter Games were contested in Salt Lake City, U.S., in 2000, and the last Summer Games were held in Sydney, Australia, in 2002.

Olympic Movement. The Olympic Movement is a general term referring to all activities and organizations associated with the holding of the Summer and Winter Olympic Games in countries around the world, and the history of these international sport competitions.

On The Move (OTM). A program developed by the Canadian Association for the Advancement of Women in Sport for implementation in communities across the country with the goal of making sports and physical activity available to females who might normally miss out on opportunities and the physical and psychological benefits of activity due to social barriers.

One repetition maximum (1RM). The maximal amount of weight an individual can lift for one repetition.

Onset of Blood Lactate Accumulation (OBLA). The point at which blood lactate levels begin to accumulate very rapidly (shortly after the lactate threshold is reached).

Open skills. An open skill is one that is performed in an unpredictable environment, which requires participants to adapt their movements to the changing nature of that environment.

Ophea (Ontario Physical and Health Education Association). Founded in 1921, Ophea is a leading authority on the health of children and youth. Ophea is a not-for-profit organization dedicated to supporting school communities through advocacy, quality programs and services, and partnership building. It provides quality programs, services, resources, training, and support to school communities to help enable children and youth to lead active healthy lives.

Opposition. Opposition occurs when the thumb comes into contact with one of the other fingers.

Origin. The point where the muscle attaches to the more stationary bone is known as the origin.

Osgood-Schlatter syndrome. This syndrome is a result of a condition known as osteochondritis, a disease of the ossification centres of the bones in young children. Specifically, Osgood-Schlatter syndrome affects the epiphyseal plate of the tibial tuberosity.

Ossification. The ossification of bone tissue takes two forms. Compact bone begins as cartilage. Bone-forming cells (osteoblasts) within the cartilage discharge a gelatin-like substance (osteoid) into which inorganic salts (minerals) are deposited to form the hardened material recognized as bone.

Osteoporosis. Osteoporosis (or porous bone) is a degenerative condition that involves low bone mass as well as a deterioration of the bone tissue. It leads to bone fragility and, therefore, an increased susceptibility to bone fractures, especially of the hip, spine, and wrist.

Oxygen consumption. The amount of oxygen taken up and consumed by the body for metabolic process, usually represented by the symbol VO_2.

Oxygen deficit. The amount of oxygen taken in during stressful exercise minus the amount that would otherwise have been required for steady-state aerobic exercise.

Oxygen transport. The process by which oxygen is carried within the blood, which is achieved in two ways: (1) a small amount of oxygen is actually dissolved within the plasma, or the fluid component of the blood, and (2) by binding to hemoglobin.

Oxygenated blood. Blood that has returned from the lungs and is pumped by the left heart to the rest of the body (systemic circulation). It is bright red in colour.

Pain-masking agents. A category of performance-enhancing drugs, known as narcotic analgesics, used by athletes, not to build up muscle or increase its ability to perform, but to allow them to ignore the tremendous pain that can result from injury.

Paralympics. In 1948, a man named Ludwig Guttmann organized a sports competition involving Second World War veterans with spinal cord injuries in Stoke Mandeville, England. In 1952, the number of competitors grew, and an international movement, now called the Paralympics, was underway.

Paraplegia. When there is a serious injury to the spinal cord, the nerves above the injury keep working, whereas those below the injury do not. If the injury prevents the use of the legs but not the arms, the injury is known as paraplegia.

Parasympathetic system. The part of the nervous system that helps to return the body to normal after it has been altered by the sympathetic system. For example, the sympathetic system increases the heart rate, while the parasympathetic system has the opposite effect.

Partial pressures. The system by which the concentration of specific gases involved in respiration is measured.

ParticipAction. An initiative, started by the Canadian federal government under the leadership of Prime Minister Pierre Trudeau, that encouraged Canadians to become more physically active, involving a series of television and radio commercials and promotions in other media. ParticipAction was created as a non-profit organization in 1971 at a time when it was estimated that only 5 percent of the population exercised enough to reap any health benefits.

Passive recovery techniques. Total rest, undertaken to minimize the negative physiological effects of training, particularly lactic acid buildup.

Patellofemoral syndrome (PFS). The major symptom of patellofemoral syndrome, or PFS, is the gradual onset of anterior knee pain or pain around the patella. PFS usually affects adolescents or young adults, and women are often affected more than men. Similar to Osgood-Schlatter syndrome, the pain is aggravated by sports such as running, volleyball, and basketball.

Performance-related fitness. The level of fitness necessary for higher levels of sport performance or optimal work performance. These include: motor skills, cardiovascular endurance, muscular power, strength and endurance, body composition, size, skill acquisition, and motivation.

Perimysium. A sheath of connective tissue that binds groups of muscle fibres together.

Periodization. The breakdown of an overall training plan into distinct training periods in an attempt to maximize performances at peak times, and to reduce the risk of injury and mental burnout.

Periosteum. The name given to the outer connective tissue that covers the entire length of the bone. Periosteum fibres and those of ligaments and tendons unite to connect bone to bone or muscle to bone.

Peripheral nervous system. Those parts of the nervous system that lie outside the central nervous system. This system can be thought of as a kind of massive road network (or computer network) carrying traffic (information) in and out of the central nervous system.

Personal protective equipment. Gear that protects players against injury and should be used whenever possible. This includes padding, bracing and taping, mouthguards, and headgear.

Phases of human movement. Those who study human movement – especially as it relates to sport and physical activity – have developed four distinct phases that most people go through from birth to adulthood: the reflexive, rudimentary, fundamental, and sport-related movement phases.

Phasic muscles. Muscles characterized by a higher percentage of Type IIA and Type IIB fibres. The biceps, for example – a key muscle for lifting and power in the arm – has a lower percentage of Type I fibres.

Physiology. The study of basic processes such as reproduction, growth, and metabolism as they occur within the various systems of the body.

Piaget's four stages of cognitive development. Based on his study of thousands of young children, psychologist Jean Piaget's four stages of cognitive development describe the ways in which cognitive development occurs in children. Piaget referred to these as the sensorimotor stage, the pre-operational stage, the concrete operational stage, and the formal operational stage.

P.I.E.R. principle. An acronym for pressure, ice, elevation, and restriction, a process commonly used to treat sport injuries.

Pivot (or trochoid) joints. This joint allows rotation in one plane (uni-axial) in which a rounded point of one bone fits into a groove of another. An example is the atlantoaxial articular joint between the first two vertebrae in the neck, which allows the rotation of the head.

Plantar flexion. Plantar flexion is movement of the ankle in the sagittal plane that increases the angle between the foot and the lower leg.

Platelets. Platelets are found in blood. They are not complete cells, but fragments of cells, and they are important in the regulation of blood clotting.

Player's agent. A person, often with a legal background, who represents athletes in all levels of business dealings, including contract negotiations, endorsement deals, entertainment appearances (i.e., movie/TV roles) and rights to use his or her image. Usually this process involves the agent charging a commission on all fees collected by the athlete.

Players' strikes. Work stoppages in professional sports that have been caused by players – via their agents or players unions – disputing clauses in their contracts, such as salary, pensions, or details regarding their status as "free agents" once a contract has expired, or by team owners who have disputed similar issues.

Plyometrics training. Also known as stretch-shortening exercises because of their ability to stretch and then shorten the muscles through exercise, plyometrics training is a form of resistance training that its advocates use for its potential to develop strength and power.

Polyunsaturated fats. Fats that come from plant sources and have higher concentrations of high-density lipoproteins (HDL).

Pott's Fracture. The most severe eversion injury is known as a Pott's Fracture, which is a break of the tip of the medial malleolus and a break of the fibula. This is a result of a force on the medial side of the ankle, causing the deltoid ligament to rip off the tip of the medial malleolus and a break of the fibula.

Principle of Diminishing Returns. An element of training theory based on the fact that a person's training gains will reflect that person's prior level of training.

Principle of Individual Differences. Also known as the Individuality Principle, this concept rests on the fact that every athlete has a different physical and psychological makeup, which means that every athlete will have different needs when it comes to training.

Principle of Overload. In order for physiological change to occur, the human body must be subjected to greater stresses than the ones to which it is accustomed. This is known as the Principle of Overload.

Principle of Progression. An element of training theory that holds that, in order for the overall – or absolute – effect of training to progress, an athlete must be subjected to greater and greater overloads, over time.

Principle of Reversibility. When a muscle or muscle group has undergone a period of training, and then has that training effect removed, the muscle(s) will, over a period of time, begin to lose the benefits the training brought to them in the first place.

Professional athletes. Athletes who derive direct financial or material rewards from their sporting efforts. This can be accomplished through player contracts, endorsement deals, the sale of merchandise and tickets, and many other ways.

Prohormones. A type of androgenic steroid. They either convert to testosterone or simulate it by forming derivatives similar to androgen.

Pronation. Pronation is the medial rotation the hand and forearm such that the palm faces backward from the anatomical position.

Proprioceptive neuromuscular facilitation (PNF). A form of exercise that involves intense isometric contractions – involving no movement of the bones connected by the muscle about to be stressed – followed by static stretching.

Proprioceptors. The part of the nervous system that provides sensory information about the state of muscle contraction, the position of body limbs, and body posture and balance.

Protein and amino acid supplements. Athletes who are concerned with increased muscle mass, strength, and endurance may use protein and amino acid supplements. Protein is an essential component of any balanced diet, but experts argue as to whether athletes should use protein supplements and/or individual amino acids supplements, or focus on increasing high-protein foods in their diets.

Protraction. Protraction is moving in an anterior (forward) direction.

Provincial Sport Organizations (PSOs). Sport organizations with provincial and territorial mandates, these volunteer-managed entities form an intermediary between community sport organizations and national sport organizations.

Psychological skills training. The interaction between sport and psychology in which sport psychologists and athletes use specific tools to improve athletic performance.

Pulmonary circulation. The main function of the right heart is to pump deoxygenated blood, which has just returned from the body, to the lungs (pulmonary circulation).

Q-angle. The Q-angle (quadriceps angle) is formed in the frontal plane by a line drawn from the centre of the patella to the anterior superior iliac spine, and another from the centre of the tibial tuberosity to the centre of the patella extending up the thigh. If the angle created by the intersection of these two lines above the patella is greater than twenty degrees, this puts the individual at greater risk of experiencing a knee injury.

Quadriplegia. When there is a serious injury to the spinal cord, the nerves above the injury keep working, whereas those below the injury do not. If the injury prevents movement of both arms and legs, the injury is quadriplegia.

Quality of life. An expression that refers to the overall benefits inherent in the life conditions of a person or group of people. Quality of life depends on many factors, including economic status, personal and political freedom, level of education, access to health care, and physical security. Sport can be a great contributor to our quality of life on an individual, family, community, or national level.

Radius of gyration. The average distance from the axis of rotation is known as the radius of gyration.

Reciprocal inhibition. In the case of a reflex action, such as the patellar reflex, the pulling on the tendon causes the muscle (quadriceps) to contract. It is now widely accepted that the opposing muscle group is also simultaneously inhibited as part of the reflex in a process known as reciprocal inhibition.

"Recreational" drug use. The use of chemical substances for non-performance-enhancing reasons such as relaxation or to achieve altered states of consciousness. In the sports world, athletes use "recreational drugs," such as marijuana, cocaine, and heroin, as either a way to relax or in the mistaken belief that these drugs will boost their performance. In most cases, the use of these drugs is banned – in the same way as steroids and other performance enhancers – by sport-governing bodies and leagues.

Recruiting violations. The attempt, within the context of university or college-level sports in Canada and the U.S., to induce a student athlete to attend one institution in favour of others. Violations include expensive meals and hotel rooms; in-room service including movies, phone calls, and massages; money; and gifts. Money has also been paid to high-school coaches who may persuade a recruit to choose that school or speak negatively about another school.

Red blood cells. The most abundant blood cells in the body, also known as erythrocytes. The erythrocytes are the specialized cells that transport oxygen, carbon dioxide, nutrients, and waste in the blood.

Reflex arc. The name given to the pathway (or circuit) along which the initial stimulus and the corresponding response message travel.

Reflex dilation of skin. The dilation of the blood cells in the skin, which forces blood to flow and transfers heat to the surface of the skin.

Relaxation. In sport, relaxation refers to the mind-body state in which an athlete is not inhibited by feelings of anxiety and nervousness, and is feeling "loose" and ready to do his or her best.

Renaissance man. An expression used to refer to a person who is equally good, at and interested, in multiple things, such as art, sport, science, and so forth. As the name suggests, this term originated as a reference to the ideal person during the Renaissance period of European history in the fifteenth and sixteenth centuries.

Repetition maximum (RM). The number of times a person can lift a given weight before failure.

Repetitive stress injury. Damage caused by repetitive movement to tendons, nerves, muscles, and other soft body tissues.

Resistance training. A form of training in which a weight or some other force or object provides resistance to the muscles, which in turn work to move the weight, thereby gaining strength in accordance with the principle of overload, which we examined above.

Respiratory control centres. The respiratory control centres are found within the brain stem. The areas of the brain stem that are important in the regulation of ventilation are the Medulla Oblongata and the Pons.

Respiratory exchange ratio. The ratio between the amount of carbon dioxide produced and the amount of oxygen consumed is used to calculate the respiratory exchange ratio, or RER. RER is indicative of which metabolic systems are being used within the working muscle.

Respiratory frequency. The number of breaths taken per minute usually represented by the symbol (f).

Respiratory zone. The area composed of the respiratory bronchioles, alveolar ducts, and the alveolar sacs. All of these structures are involved with the exchange of gases between inspired air and the blood.

Resting heart rate (RHR). The number of times the heart beats per minute during a resting state.

Resting metabolic rate (RMR). A measurement of the metabolic rate under less rigorous conditions.

Restricted pharmacological substances. Included on the International Olympic Committee's list of banned substances, these include alcohol, marijuana, local anaesthetics, corticosteroids, and beta blockers.

Retraction. Retraction is moving in a posterior (backward) direction.

Role models. Persons who occupy certain positions or "roles" in a society, and upon whom others (often young people) try to base – or "model" – certain aspects of their behaviour. Many modern athletes hold this position in today's society.

Role of the audience. Many athletes react positively to large crowds and the encouragement they can provide. Others seem to succeed better in settings where they are relatively isolated from spectators. Still others can become extremely discouraged or distracted by crowd noise. Sport psychologists work with athletes to help them to control their response to an audience and limit its impact on performance.

Rotational motion. Movement of a body about an axis. Unlike with linear motion, in rotational motion the force does not act through the centre of mass, but rather is "off-centre," and this results in rotation.

Rotator cuff tears. An injury to one or all four muscles that make up the rotator cuff: supraspinatus, infraspinatus, teres minor, and subscapularis. Supraspinatus, infraspinatus, and teres minor share a common tendinous insertion on the greater tubercle of the humerus.

Royal Commission on the Status of Women in Canada. The findings of a 1970 report that contained recommendations addressing the lack of equal opportunity for girls in school sports programs. In 1972, Fitness and Amateur Sport Canada commissioned research on defining and solving these problems; in 1974 the first National Conference on Women and Sport was held.

Saddle joints. Saddle joints allow movement in two planes (for example, flexion-extension and abduction-adduction), but do not allow for rotation as does a ball-and-socket joint. A key saddle joint is found at the carpo-metacarpal articulation of the thumb.

Sarcolemma. A plasma membrane that lies beneath the endomysium.

Sarcomeres. The repeating structural units of striated muscle containing myosin and actin.

Sarcoplasm. The muscle cell's cytoplasm, which is contained by the sarcolemma.

Saturated fats. Fats that come to us from animal sources and have higher concentrations of low-density lipoprotein (LDL).

Scholarships in sport. The practice by which an institution of higher learning subsidizes, in full or in part, the cost of a student's education in exchange for that student's participation in sport. Traditionally the domain of U.S. universities and colleges, the practice is becoming increasingly common in Canada.

Scientific models. Ways of conceiving a problem that reduce things to their essentials and establish a basis, not only for understanding how things work, but also for predicting how they will behave and, ultimately, for influencing them to behave in the ways we want.

Self-talk. The internal monologue that goes through one's mind, exhorting oneself to achieve success.

Separations. The process by which bones held together by fibrous ligaments, such as the acromioclavicular and sternoclavicular joints, tear and separate from each other.

Seven principles of biomechanics. The basic building blocks of the study of biomechanics, which can be grouped into four broad categories: (1) stability, (2) maximum effort, (3) linear motion, and (4) angular motion.

Shaping. The process by which learners are encouraged to develop, or "shape," a skill gradually.

Shin splints. A common overuse injury, with causes similar to stress fractures. Signs of a shin splints are pain on the medial or lateral side of the tibia, on its shaft, caused by the tearing of the interosseous membrane or the periosteum.

Shoulder separation. A tear of the acromioclavicular ligament, which holds together the acromioclavicular joint (also known as the AC joint, the union of the clavicle to the acromion).

Simple carbohydrates. Simple carbohydrates are also known as sugars and, as in the case of complex carbohydrates, exist in either a natural or refined form. Simple carbohydrates or natural sugars are found in fruit and vegetables. Simple carbohydrates or refined sugars are found in biscuits, brown and white cane sugar, cakes and pastries, and chocolate.

Simple fracture. A simple fracture occurs when there is no separation of the bone into parts, but a break or crack is detectable. This is also referred to as a "hairline fracture," "greenstick fracture," or an "incomplete fracture."

Sinoatrial node. A specialized region of tissue that is found in the right atrium, also known as the SA node. The SA node is also called the "pacemaker" of the heart.

Skeletal age. Age as indicated by the physical maturity of the skeleton; that is, the degree of ossification of bones, usually measured by an X-ray of the hand and wrist.

Skeletal muscles. Voluntary muscles that are attached to the bones (by tendons and other tissue) and are the most prevalent in the human body. They comprise 30-40 percent of human body weight. Skeletal muscle tissue is also referred to as "striated" (or striped) because of its appearance under a microscope as a series of long, alternating light and dark stripes.

Skeleton. The adult human skeleton is made up of 206 bones, accounting for about 14 percent of total body weight, although humans start life with more bones than that – about 300 bones at birth. Over time, several bones fuse as growth takes place (such as in the skull and lower part of the vertebral column).

Skill transferability. The concept that skills, when learned in the context of improving performance in one sport or activity, can often be applied, or transferred, to a different sport.

Sliding filament theory. A theory of muscle contraction that is accepted as a description of the process of muscular contraction. The discovery of sliding filaments dates back to the 1950s and accurately describes what happens during contraction.

Slow-twitch muscle fibres. Red or dark in colour, these muscle fibres generate and relax tension relatively slowly. The "trade-off," however, is that they are able to maintain a lower level of tension for long durations.

S.M.A.R.T. principle. One framework for establishing goals is known by the acronym S.M.A.R.T. This is the notion that goals should be: Specific, Measurable, Attainable, Realistic, and Timely.

Smooth muscles. Surrounding the body's internal organs, including the blood vessels, hair follicles, and the urinary, genital, and digestive tracts, are smooth muscles. This type of muscle tissue contracts more slowly than skeletal muscles, but can remain contracted for longer periods of time. Smooth muscles are also involuntary.

Socialization. Socialization is the complex process whereby an individual learns to interact cooperatively with others in society – in families, schools, sports, churches, clubs, and so on.

Somatic nervous system. Our awareness of the external environment – and the corresponding motor activity allowing us to cope with it – operates through the somatic nervous system.

Special Olympics. An organization that runs multi-sport competitions for persons with mental disabilities throughout the world. The worldwide Special Olympics attracts thousands of athletes, and each local branch in member countries is also active in organizing and sporting events at the community level.

Specificity Principle. Also known as the S.A.I.D. (Specific Adaptation to Imposed Demand) Principle, this concept holds that, in order for specific outcomes to occur, training exercises must be specific to those outcomes.

Sport Canada. The major granting agency for sports in Canada, operating under the auspices of the federal government. Sport Canada is active in funding international high-performance athletes by means of the "carding" system, which allots a certain amount of financial support based on an athlete's world ranking.

Sport Dispute Resolution Centre. Established by Bill C-54, the mission of this organization is to provide the sport community with a national alternative-dispute-resolution service for sports disputes, and expertise and assistance in that regard.

Sport equity. Sport equity exists whenever the same opportunities are afforded to one group of people as they are to another. In sports, these opportunities are usually considered to exist on the level of allowing people to take part in sport, such as the use of equipment, access to membership on a team or in a league, or the availability of top-notch coaching. They can also include equal access to publicity, government funding, or simply the ability to participate in a sports setting without harassment.

Sport franchises. A professional team, and all of its associated business interests, including licensing, concessions, broadcasting rights, equipment, as well as its stadium, players, coaches and the like.

Sport Leadership Program. Designed by the Coaching Association of Canada specifically for the community sport environment, this program provides support in such areas as liability, financial management, marketing, and volunteering screening practices.

Sport Participation Development Program. A Sport Canada program involved with spreading sports culture in younger age groups. This program is intended to provide financial support to National Sports Organizations in their efforts to increase participation levels, recruit new participants, and reduce dropout rates. Preference is given to projects that target children and youth, girls and young women, and underrepresented groups including Aboriginal people, people with disabilities, youth at risk, visible minorities, and economically disadvantaged individuals.

Sport psychology. Psychology is the scientific study of the thought processes and behaviour of humans in their interaction with the environment. In the sport context, it is the study of how people think, feel, and behave in sporting situations, and what mental processes motivate the way athletes behave in training and competition.

Sports gambling. The practice of betting on sports is legal in Canada but is highly regulated by the government. In addition to being potentially addictive, serious problems occur when sports gambling is illegally run by the unscrupulous or when athletes are involved in betting on their own sports.

Sports Select and PRO-LINE. Publicly available games in which Canadian bettors can place bets online on a limited selection of hockey, football, basketball, and baseball games. These are contests run by the government lottery boards and generate funds for the lottery commissions and thus indirectly for sports organizations.

Sports-as-entertainment industry. The broad term given to the many ways in which professional sports organizations attempt to attract consumers and make a profit. In many cases, the emphasis is on sport as a spectacle (i.e., as entertainment) and not on athletic competition for its own sake. This "industry" includes ticket sales, broadcasting rights, branded merchandise, endorsement contacts, and many more elements.

Stadium concessions. Areas at professional or amateur sports venues at which food and beverages are sold. An important source of revenue for stadium owners and clubs, the rights to establish such restaurants are sold for substantial sums. In order to recoup these costs, the price of foods and beverages for sale is typically much higher than is typical outside the sporting context.

Stages of human development. The division of human growth and development into four basic stages, each with is own fundamental aspects and characteristics and its own particular relationship to gender. These stages consist of: infancy/toddler; childhood; puberty/adolescence; and adulthood.

Stages of skill observation. The National Coaching Certification Program (NCCP) identifies two distinct stages of skills observation: a pre-observation stage and an observation stage.

Stages-of-learning model. One of the earliest and still widely embraced models of how people learn was developed in 1967 by two researchers named Paul Fitts and Michael Posner. Today, this is often referred to as the "classic" stages-of-learning model.

Standards of ethics and behaviour for coaches. Most leagues and sport associations have fairly well-defined standards governing coaches; in some instances, these are highly detailed statements to which all coaches must agree before working with athletes.

Static (isometric). This occurs when a muscle does not change in length – for example, when you try to lift an immovable object.

Static lung volumes. Lung volumes are determined by the actual structure of the lung and not determined or influenced by breathing or the flow of air.

Steady state. A condition of sub-maximal exercise in which oxygen uptake and heart rate level off, energy demands and energy production are evenly balanced, and the body maintains a steady level of exertion for a fairly extended period of time.

Strains, pulls, and tears. These terms describe injuries to all joint tissue types. Sprains are associated with ligaments and tendons while pulls and strains are associated with muscles.

Strategy. Strategy is an attempt to gain an advantage in competition through some form of advance planning.

Stress fracture. When muscles become too fatigued to absorb the shock placed on them – for example, through the continual pounding of long-distance running – the overstressed muscle transfers the impact to the bone. This causes the bone to develop a tiny crack, or stress fracture.

Stretch reflex. The simplest spinal reflex. Whereas most reflexes have several synapses in the reflex arc, the stretch reflex depends only on the single connection between primary afferent fibres and motor neurons of the same muscle.

Stretching. Most athletes follow a routine of stretching exercises to increase muscle flexibility. Flexibility is crucial for an athlete participating in a sport that involves muscles that are put through a wide range of motion; for example, diving or hurdling.

Stroke volume. The amount of blood, represented by the symbol SV, that is ejected from the left ventricle in a single beat, and is measured in millilitres (mL).

Supination. Supination is the lateral rotation of the hand and forearm such that the palm faces forward as in the anatomical position.

Sweating reflex. The reflex that activates the sweat glands and thereby sends excess fluid to the surface where it can evaporate.

Sympathetic system. The part of the nervous system that causes localized bodily adjustments to occur (e.g., sweating or cardiovascular changes), and prepares the body for emergencies.

Synovial joints. In this type of joint, the bony surfaces are separated by a lubricating fluid (the synovia) and by cartilage. They are also joined by ligaments, tough bands of elastic tissue that enclose the ends of articulating bones and form the capsule containing the synovial membrane. Typical synovial joints are the knee, the elbow, the shoulder, and the ankle.

Systemic circulation. The role of the left heart is to pump oxygenated blood, which has just returned from the lungs, to the rest of the body (systemic circulation).

Systolic blood pressure. The pressure observed in the arteries during the contraction phase (i.e., 120 mmHg).

Tactics. Tactics refers to specific adjustments made in the context of an ongoing event.

Target heart rate. The number of beats per minute (bpm) at which your heart should be beating during aerobic exercise in order to facilitate cardiorespiratory improvement.

Tendinitis. An inflammation of a tendon caused by irritation due to prolonged or abnormal use.

Tendons. Structures that attach muscle to bone, which are composed of large bundles of white, fibrous protein known as collagen. They possess a greater stretching range than ligaments.

Thermoregulation. The body's ability to regulate its core temperature – known as thermoregulation, or maintaining a thermal balance – is essential to our survival.

Thoracic pump. The second system that the body uses to assist in the return of blood in the veins to the heart is called the thoracic pump.

Tidal volume. The volume of air in each breath is also known as the tidal volume (V_T). At rest, a typical V_T is about 0.5 L/breath, while during exercise, V_T can increase up to 3 to 4 L/breath.

Title IX. A section of the landmark Educational Amendments of 1972, a piece of American legislation that prohibits gender discrimination of any kind in schools. It was particularly influential regarding athletic policies at all levels of educational institutions. Title IX allowed girls and women the same sports and physical education opportunities that men had taken for granted. This piece of legislation was very controversial when it was released; every year, many Canadian women are affected by Title IX because they compete for scholarships at U.S. universities and colleges.

Tonic muscles. Muscles that assist the body with maintaining posture or stability during activities such as standing, walking, and throwing. Tonic muscles are also characterized by a high percentage of Type I fibre; that is, slow-twitch fibres.

Trabeculae. The trabeculae consist of continuous units of bony fibres arranged in a strut-like system running throughout the cancellous tissue. The density of the trabeculae varies with the type of bone and the amount of stress it bears.

Training. A combination of exercises that serve to make the human body more efficient.

Transfats. Chemically, transfats are close in composition to saturated fats, and studies have found that they are equally harmful to people's health – they appear to increase concentrations of LDLs ("bad cholesterol") while reducing concentrations of HDLs ("good cholesterol").

Transient hypertrophy. Commonly called "the pump," transient hypertrophy is associated with an increase in fluid accumulation (edema) to a specific muscle or muscles during exercise.

Transverse tubulae system. A network of interconnecting rings, each of which surrounds a myofibril, and serves as a link between the outside of the muscle fibre and the actin and myosin deeper inside.

Troponin and tropomyosin. In the actin filament, there is one troponin and one tropomyosin molecule for every seven actin units. These troponin and tropomyosin proteins serve to "inhibit" or regulate the interaction of actin and myosin.

Type I or Slow-Oxidative (SO). These muscle fibres generate energy slowly, are fatigue-resistant, and primarily depend on the aerobic process.

Type IIA or Fast-Oxidative Glycolytic (FOG). These intermediate-type fibres allow for high-speed energy release as well as glycolytic capacity.

Type IIB or Fast-Glycolytic (FG). These fibres store large amounts of glycogen and sufficiently high levels of enzymes for quick contraction without requiring oxygen.

Underweight. The opposite condition to obesity. There is strong evidence that being underweight is linked to chronic conditions and a shortened lifespan.

Vascular system. The vascular system is formed by a network of vessels that transport blood throughout the body.

Vascularity. The amount of supplied blood a tissue has or requires. Ligaments and cartilage are said to be avascular – in other words, their nutritional needs are not met through blood.

Vein. A vessel that carries blood towards the heart. In the systemic circulation, veins carry deoxygenated (blue) blood towards the right side of the heart from body tissues. In the pulmonary circulation, veins carry oxygenated (red) blood towards the left side of the heart from the lungs.

Ventilation. The combination of inspiration and expiration together is known as ventilation (VE). More specifically, VE is the volume of air that is moved by the lungs in 1 minute.

Ventilatory threshold. A state in which ventilation increases much more rapidly than workload. It normally occurs at an exercise intensity that corresponds to 65-85 percent of VO_2max, depending on the individual's level of fitness.

Virtual reality technologies. Through the use of computers, virtual reality immerses viewers in "virtual worlds" even though their bodies are still in the real world. Virtual reality simulators are used to help athletes train without having to travel or risk injury.

Vitamins. Substances that assist the body in performing several important processes, and most come from the foods we ingest. They vary in chemical makeup, and include the vitamin groupings A, B, C, D, E, and K, as well as thiamine and riboflavin.

VO_2max (maximal rate of oxygen consumption). The maximum volume (V) of oxygen (O_2) in millilitres that the human body can use in 1 minute, per kilogram of body weight, while breathing air at sea level.

Water. Dietary experts recommend that a sufficient amount of water be consumed – up to 2 litres per day for adults – in order to assist the body with a wide range of functions, including aiding in digestion and carrying nutrients to (and eliminating waste products from) cells.

Weight management. The practice, common among athletes, of keeping one's weight within certain limits for successful training and competition.

Wheel of excellence. Canadian author Terry Orlick developed this concept that posits seven key elements of excellence: commitment, belief, full focus, positive images, mental readiness, distraction control and constructive evaluation. These combine to form a "wheel of excellence" that provides a working framework to guide the pursuit of excellence

White blood cells (leukocytes). White blood cells or leukocytes make up less than 1 percent of the blood and are an important part of the body's immune system.

Wicking properties. The ability of a fabric to draw moisture away from an athlete's skin. New innovation in sportswear design has much improved this property.

Withdrawal reflex. A reflex that involves the withdrawal of a body part from a painful stimulus (such as a sharp or hot object).

Women's Amateur Athletic Federation. The first national body where Canadian women could address issues in sports and gain the support they needed. Created in 1926 by athlete and journalist Alexandrine Gibb and several other sports pioneers, the WAAF was commonly called the Canadian Parliament of Women's Sport. WAAF encouraged women to participate in sporting events, especially in international competitions.

World Anti-Doping Agency. An independent, international, non-governmental organization that aims to eliminate doping in sports. The Montreal-based WADA conducts unannounced drug tests during competition and out of competition to ensure that no banned substances are being used while athletes train. It also monitors the results of tests for major sports events, such as the Olympics, and has developed both the World Anti-Doping Code and the Athlete's Passport Program.

World Anti-Doping Code. One major initiative of the World Anti-Doping Agency is the World Anti-Doping Code, which has been created to ensure that athletes in every country have the same anti-doping standards and regulations. Governments of athletes wishing to compete in Olympic Competition must adopt the code by the 2006 Winter Olympic Games.

Young Men's Christian Association (YMCA). Founded in England at the time of the Industrial Revolution, the YMCA has become a widespread organization with branches around the world. Created by a man named George Williams, YMCA branches are now active in promoting sport and physical activity, offering the physical space needed for several clubs and sport-based activities in their communities.

Zone Diet. A controversial diet that is high in proteins and low in carbohydrates introduced by author Barry Sears in his 1995 book.

Index

ossification and remodelling of, 29
Borg Scale of Perceived Exertion, 188-189
Boucher, Gaetan, 299
brachialis, 55
brachioradialis, 55
bradycardia, 119
brain, 95, 199, 249, 250, 251, 258, 268, 269
  main parts of, 95-96
  stem, 96
breathing
  mechanics of, 121-122
broadcasting rights, 359
bronchi, primary and secondary, 121
bronchioles, 121
bundle of His. *See* atrioventricular bundle
burnout and overtraining, 194, 195, 203
bursae (or bursas), 70
business of sport entertainment, 353-367

C

Cabbagetown Boxing Club and Youth Centre, 382
caffeine, 163, 166
calcium, 10, 29, 31, 37, 142, 143
  role in muscle contraction, 40, 42
calisthenics, 297
Calorie, 148, 152
Canada's Food Guide to Healthy Eating, 144-145
Canada Games, the, 307, 337, 341, 345
Canada-USSR "Summit Series," 307
Canadian achievements in sport, 307ff
Canadian Association for Health, Physical Education, Recreation and Dance (CAHPERD), 371, 376
Canadian Association for the Advancement of Women in Sport (CAAWS), 327, 332
  ACTive, 327
  Girls @ Play, 327
  On The Move, 327
Canadian Centre for Drug-Free Sport, 168
Canadian Centre for Ethics in Sport, 165, 168, 338, 340, 385, 401
Canadian Football League (CFL), evolution of, 305
Canadian Hockey Association (CHA), 375
Canadian Intramural Recreation Association, 371
Canadian Olympic Committee (COC), 333
Canadian Paralympic Committee (CPC), 342
Canadian Physical Activity, Fitness and Lifestyle Appraisal, The, 210
Canadian Professional Soccer League (CPSL), 305
Canadian School Sport Federation, 371
Canadian Sport Policy, 319, 330, 331
Canadian Sports Centres, 333
Canadian Strategy for Ethical Conduct in Sport, 385

Canadian Wheelchair Sport Association, 332
cancellous or spongy bone, 12
capillaries, 113, 115
carbohydrates, 81, 142, 156
  carbo-loading, 158
  counter, 146
  simple and complex, 142
carbon dioxide transport, 125
cardiac cycle, 113
cardiac muscle, 33, 111
cardiac output, 117-118
cardiorespiratory fitness, measuring, 188
cardiovascular and respiratory function integration of, 129
cardiovascular and respiratory systems, 109-133
cardiovascular system, 110
  disease, 119
  drift, 117
  dynamics of, 117
  effects of training, 119
  endurance of, 211
  exercise prescription model, 218
career opportunities
  occupations chart, viii-ix
  Unit 1: Anatomy and Physiology, 134
  Unit 2: Human Performance and Biomechanics, 240
  Unit 3: Motor Learning and Skills Development, 288
  Unit 4: Evolution of Physical Activity and Sport, 349
  Unit 5: Social Issues in Physical Activity and Sport, 402
carnitine, 162
cartilage, 12, 29-30, 69-70, 72-73
  damage to, 73
  elastic, 73
  fibrocartilage, 73
  hyaline, 70, 73
cartilaginous joints, 69
Catherwood, Ethel, 299
cellular respiration, 85, 121
central nervous system, 95
centre of mass, 227
cephalocaudal sequence, 251
cerebellum, 96
cerebrum, 95
chaining, as a way of teaching complex skills, 265
charities, 367
cheating, 166, 391, 395
Cherry, Don, 358
cholesterol, 145
chordae tendinae, 110
chronic obstructive pulmonary disease (COPD), 127
chronological age, 248
circulation, pulmonary and systemic, 110
circumduction, movement of, 4, 5
classes of levers. *See* lever systems
clavicle (collar bone), 13
coaching

advanced athletes, 283
age-appropriate strategies, 283
career opportunities, 287
coach-athlete relationship, 286
coaching the coaches, 284
ethical issues, 285
fair play amongst, 279
finding the right combination, 286
gender representation in, 339
questions to ask of a coach, 286
role of coach, 281
skills of, 282
strategy, tactics and planning, 284
styles, 277-279
Coaching Association of Canada (CAC), 128, 279, 284, 288-289, 332, 336, 373
coaching principles and practices, 277-287
coccyx (tailbone), 13
cognitive development, 253-254
Commission for Fair Play, 168
Commonwealth Games, 308
community
  concept of, 350
  programs, 373
  recreation centres, role of, 375
compact bone, 12
competitive versus non-competitive sport, 293
complete proteins, 141
complex carbohydrates, 142
computer technology in sport, 182
  computer simulations, use of, 184
computerized axial tomography (CAT scan), 104
concentration, as a factor in human performance, 270, 274
concrete operational stage, 253
concurrent training, 196
concussions, 107
  Eric and Brett Lindros, 106
  signs of, 107
conductive zone, 121
conservation of energy, 225
controlled and automatic motor activity, 258
coracobrachialis, 53
Cori Cycle, 88
coronary arteries, 113
coronary circulation, 113
corruption
  of judges and officials, 393
cortex, 12
corticosteroids, 169
Cowan, Ashley, 300
cranium and face bones, 13
Crazy Canucks, 309
creatine, 163
crossed-extensor reflex, 103
cruciate ligaments, 75
Cuba, sport system of, 362
culture, sport and, 293

D

daily caloric need, 148